KU-070-193

Holland

THE ROUGH GUIDE

There are more than one hundred Rough Guide titles
covering destinations from Amsterdam to Zimbabwe

Forthcoming titles include
Bangkok • Barbados
Japan • Jordan • Syria

Rough Guide Reference Series
Classical Music • European Football • The Internet • Jazz
Opera • Reggae • Rock Music • World Music

Rough Guide Phrasebooks
Czech • French • German • Greek • Hindi and Urdu • Hungarian • Indonesian
Italian • Japanese • Mandarin Chinese • Mexican Spanish • Polish
Portuguese • Russian • Spanish • Thai • Turkish • Vietnamese

Rough Guides on the Internet
http://www.roughguides.com

ROUGH GUIDE CREDITS

Text editors: Alison Cowan, Samantha Cook and Ann-Marie Shaw
Series editor: Mark Ellingham
Editorial: Martin Dunford, Jonathan Buckley, Jo Mead, Kate Berens, Amanda Tomlin, Paul Gray, Sarah Dallas, Chris Schüler, Helena Smith, Caroline Osborne, Kieran Falconer, Judith Bamber, Olivia Eccleshall, Orla Duane (UK); Andrew Rosenberg (US)
Online Editors: Alan Spicer (UK); Geronimo Madrid (US)

Production: Susanne Hillen, Andy Hilliard, Judy Pang, Link Hall, Nicola Williamson, Helen Ostick, James Morris
Cartography: Melissa Flack, Maxine Burke, Nichola Goodliffe
Picture research: Eleanor Hill
Finance: John Fisher, Celia Crowley, Neeta Mistry
Marketing & Publicity: Richard Trillo, Simon Carloss, Niki Smith (UK); Jean-Marie Kelly, SoRelle Braun (US)
Administration: Tania Hummel, Alexander Mark Rogers

ACKNOWLEDGEMENTS

Thanks on this edition to: Jules, Jane and Val in Amsterdam; Nick and Martayn in The Hague; Ros in Gouda; Jaap in Middelburg; Skanda in Friesland; Anouk and La Mouche in Maastricht; Trevor Hockey at the incomparable *Clifton Bookshop* in Bristol; Ann Carmody, Malijn Maat, Mariska Majoor and the PIC, Petra van Arum at the Amsterdam VVV and the Netherlands Board of Tourism (Els Wamsteeker in Amsterdam and Madeleine Tuinstra-Ralston in London). Thanks also to Elaine Pollard for proofreading; MicroMap (Romsey, Hants) for cartography.

Thanks are also due to all those who wrote with comments on previous editions, in particular: Carolyn Adolph and Andrew McIntosh, Marcus Blackhall, Maureen Buja, M. Buyjy, M. Chadwick, Laura Edwards, Peter Evans, Stephen Gardetto, Daniel Gooch, John Hemingway, David Hope, Phoebe McLeod, Marie O'Mahoney, Richard Pacey, Teresa Persighetti, Emma and Rob Scattergood, Barrie Smith, Georges Van Den Eshof, Paul Vermeulen, Neil and Ian Wright.

The authors

Martin Dunford and **Jack Holland** first met at the University of Kent at Canterbury. Following jobs as diverse as insurance collection, beer-barrel rolling and EFL teaching in Greece they co-founded the Rough Guides in the mid-1980s. After co-authoring several other titles, Martin is now editorial director of Rough Guides while Jack recently escaped from Berlin, where he lived for four years.

Phil Lee has worked as a freelance author with the Rough Guides for the last ten years. His other titles include Mallorca and Menorca; Canada; and the Pacific Northwest. He has also written extensively for British magazines and newspapers. He lives in Nottingham, where he was born and raised.

PUBLISHING INFORMATION

This first edition published May 1997 by Rough Guides Ltd, 1 Mercer St, London WC2H 9QJ.
Reprinted April 1998.
Distributed by the Penguin Group:
Penguin Books Ltd, 27 Wrights Lane, London W8 5TZ
Penguin Books USA Inc., 375 Hudson Street, New York 10014, USA
Penguin Books Australia Ltd, 487 Maroondah Highway, PO Box 257, Ringwood, Victoria 3134, Australia
Penguin Books Canada Ltd, 10 Alcorn Avenue, Toronto, Ontario, Canada M4V 1E4
Penguin Books (NZ) Ltd, 182–190 Wairau Road, Auckland 10, New Zealand
Typeset in Linotron Univers and Century Old Style to an original design by Andrew Oliver.
Printed in the UK by Clays Ltd, St Ives PLC.

Illustrations in Part One & Part Three by Edward Briant; illustrations on p.1 and p.317 by Henry Iles.
No part of this book may be reproduced in any form without permission from the publisher except for the quotation of brief passages in reviews.
© Martin Dunford, Jack Holland and Phil Lee 1997.
384pp, includes index
A catalogue record for this book is available from the British Library.
ISBN 1-85828-229-2

The publishers and authors have done their best to ensure the accuracy and currency of all the information in The Rough Guide to Holland; however, they can accept no responsibility for any loss, injury or inconvenience sustained by any traveller as a result of information or advice contained in the guide.

Holland

THE ROUGH GUIDE

written and researched by

Martin Dunford, Jack Holland and Phil Lee

with additional contributions by

Matthew Teller and Adam Vaitilingam

THE ROUGH GUIDES

THE ROUGH GUIDES

TRAVEL GUIDES • PHRASEBOOKS • MUSIC AND REFERENCE GUIDES

 We set out to do something different when the first Rough Guide was published in 1982. Mark Ellingham, just out of university, was travelling in Greece. He brought along the popular guides of the day, but found they were all lacking in some way. They were either strong on ruins and museums but went on for pages without mentioning a beach or taverna. Or they were so conscious of the need to save money that they lost sight of Greece's cultural and historical significance. Also, none of the books told him anything about Greece's contemporary life – its politics, its culture, its people, and how they lived.

So with no job in prospect, Mark decided to write his own guidebook, one which aimed to provide practical information that was second to none, detailing the best beaches and the hottest clubs and restaurants, while also giving hard-hitting accounts of every sight, both famous and obscure, and providing up-to-the-minute information on contemporary culture. It was a guide that encouraged independent travellers to find the best of Greece, and was a great success, getting shortlisted for the Thomas Cook travel guide award, and encouraging Mark, along with three friends, to expand the series.

The Rough Guide list grew rapidly and the letters flooded in, indicating a much broader readership than had been anticipated, but one which uniformly appreciated the Rough Guide mix of practical detail and humour, irreverence and enthusiasm. Things haven't changed. The same four friends who began the series are still the caretakers of the Rough Guide mission today: to provide the most reliable, up-to-date and entertaining information to independent-minded travellers of all ages, on all budgets.

We now publish 100 titles and have offices in London and New York. The travel guides are written and researched by a dedicated team of more than 100 authors, based in Britain, Europe, the USA and Australia. We have also created a unique series of phrasebooks to accompany the travel series, along with an acclaimed series of music guides, and a best-selling pocket guide to the Internet and World Wide Web. We also publish comprehensive travel information on our web site:

http://www.roughguides.com

HELP US UPDATE

We've gone to a lot of trouble to ensure that this edition of the Rough Guide to Holland is accurate and up-to-date. However, inevitably things change, and if you feel we've got it wrong or left something out, we'd like to know: any suggestions, comments or corrections would be much appreciated. We'll credit contributions and send a copy of the next edition – or any other Rough Guide if you prefer – for the best correspondence.

Please mark letters: "Rough Guide Holland Update" and send to:
Rough Guides, 1 Mercer St, London WC2H 9QJ, or
Rough Guides, 375 Hudson St, 9th floor, New York NY 10014.
Or send email to: mail@roughtravl.co.uk
Online updates about Rough Guides titles can be found on our website (see above for details)

CONTENTS

Introduction ix

● CHAPTER 3: SOUTH HOLLAND AND UTRECHT 155–200

● CHAPTER 4: THE NORTH AND THE FRISIAN ISLANDS 201–236

● CHAPTER 5: OVERIJSSEL, FLEVOLAND AND GELDERLAND 237–276

PART THREE CONTEXTS 317

LIST OF MAPS

MAP SYMBOLS

―――	Chapter division boundary	♦	Point of interest
―·―·―	International boundary	⏶	Campsite
― ― ― ―	Provincial boundary	△	Youth hostel
═════	Road	◉	Hotel
━━━━	Railway	✈	Airport
▬▬▬▬	River/canal	♣	Museum
― ―	Ferry route	■	Building
▓▓▓	Urban area	✝	Church
▨	Park	⊠	Post office

INTRODUCTION

Holland, or, to give the country its proper name, The Netherlands, is a country reclaimed in part from the waters of the North Sea, an artificially created land, around half of which lies at or below sea level. Land reclamation has been the dominant motif of its history, the result a country of resonant and unique images: flat, fertile landscapes punctuated by windmills and church spires; ornately gabled terraces flanking peaceful canals; huge, open skies; and mile upon mile of grassy dune, backing onto wide stretches of pristine, sandy beach.

A leading colonial power, its mercantile fleets once challenged the best in the world for supremacy, and its standard of living (for the majority at least) was second to none. These days Holland is one of the most developed countries in the world, small and urban, with the highest population density in Europe, its fifteen million or so inhabitants concentrated into an area about the size of the US state of Maine. It's an international, well-integrated place: many people speak English, at least in the heavily populated west of the country; communications and infrastructure are efficient; and its companies – Philips, Unilever, Shell – are at the forefront of the new, free-trading Europe. Politically, the Dutch government's policies are those of consensus – among Europe's (and the world's) most liberal, with relaxed laws regarding soft drugs, and forward-thinking attitudes on social issues – although there has been something of a backlash against these in recent years. The crime rate, too, though on the increase, is relatively low.

Where to go

If you say you're going to Holland, everyone will immediately assume you're going to Amsterdam. Indeed for such a small and accessible country, Holland is, apart from Amsterdam, relatively unknown territory. Some people may confess to a brief visit to Rotterdam or The Hague, but for most people Amsterdam *is* Holland – there's nothing remotely worth seeing outside the capital, so if you're not going there, why go at all?

It's an attitude exacerbated by the chauvinism of Amsterdammers themselves, many of whom rarely set foot outside the limits of their own city. It's true that in many ways the rest of Holland can seem terribly dull after the bright lights of the capital, but to write off the rest of the country would be to miss much, especially considering the size of the place and the efficiency of its transport systems, which make everywhere easily accessible.

Although throughout the guide we have used the name Holland to mean the whole country, in fact it refers only to two of The Netherlands' **twelve provinces – North** and **South Holland**, in the west of the country. These for the most part are unrelentingly flat territory, much of it reclaimed land that has since become home to a grouping of towns known collectively as the **Randstad** (literally "rim town"), a circular urban sprawl that holds the country's largest cities and the majority of its population. Travelling in this part of the country is easy, with trains and buses cheap and efficient and no language barrier for the English-speaking visitor; at times, you barely feel abroad at all. Amsterdam is rightly the main focus: no other city has its vitality and cosmopolitanism or, indeed, its features of interest. But the other Randstad towns are worth a visit, too: **Haarlem**, **Leiden** and **Delft** with their old canal-girded centres; the gritty port city of **Rotterdam**; the dignified architecture and stately air of **The Hague**, home of the government and the Dutch royal family; not to mention the **bulbfields** which spread all around – in spring, justifiably, the one thing that never fails to draw tourists out of Amsterdam.

Outside of the Randstad life moves more slowly, and although you're never far from civilization, travelling is marginally more time-consuming and the incidence of

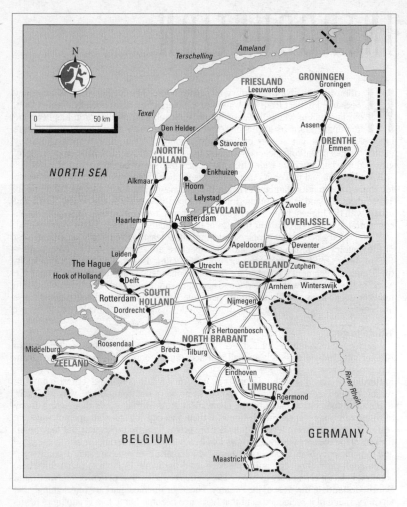

English-speakers more sporadic. The **islands** of the north, most of them off the coast of the province of **Friesland**, are prime resort territory for the Dutch, though they retain a rather untamed air, sparsely settled after the crowded Randstad cities. The rest of Friesland, too, can feel somewhat cut off, its inhabitants speaking a language, Frysk, not spoken – or understood – elsewhere in the country. Which isn't to say it's dull: Friesland's capital, **Leeuwarden**, is a likeable city, and neighbouring **Groningen** is one of the country's busiest cultural centres, given verve by its large resident student population. To the south, the provinces of **Overijssel** and **Gelderland**, at least in their eastern portions, herald Holland's first few bumps, the landscape undulating into boggy peat and wasteland around the towns of **Arnhem** and **Apeldoorn**, best experienced in the country's only national park, the **Hoge Veluwe**, and another lively college town, **Nijmegen**. Further south still lie the predominantly Catholic provinces of

Limburg, **North Brabant** and **Zeeland**. The latter is well named – literally "Sealand", made up of a series of low-lying islands connected by road and protected from the encroaching waters of the North Sea by one of Holland's most ambitious projects, the Delta Plan. Heading east, you reach **North Brabant**, gently rolling scrub and farmland which centres on the historic cities of **Breda** and **s'Hertogenbosch**, and, not least, the modern manufacturing hub of **Eindhoven**, home to the electronics giant Philips. Lastly, **Limburg** occupies the slim scythe of land that reaches down between the Belgian and German borders, perhaps the least Dutch of all Holland's provinces – its landscape, in the south at least, truly hilly, and with as cosmopolitan a capital, in **Maastricht**, as they come.

Climate and when to go

Holland enjoys a **temperate climate**, with fairly mild summers and cold winters. Generally speaking, temperatures rise the further south you go, with the south of the country perhaps a couple of degrees warmer than the north and east for much of the year. Rain is a possibility all year round. Above all, the climate is influenced by the ubiquitous proximity of water, and in winter city centre canals can make the streets alongside brutally cold – though the western, maritime side of the country is in general warmer than the eastern provinces, where the more severe climate of continental Europe begins to assert itself.

As regards **clothing**, you should take heavy coats, hats and gloves in winter, lighter clothes and warm sweaters for the evening in summer, with some kind of rain protection all year round.

AVERAGE DAILY TEMPERATURES (°C)											
Jan	Feb	Mar	April	May	June	July	Aug	Sept	Oct	Nov	Dec
2	2	5	8	12	15	17	17	15	11	6	3

GETTING THERE FROM BRITAIN

There are various ways of getting to Holland, but it basically comes down to deciding between a low-cost but time-consuming bus or train and ferry journey, and a swift but more expensive flight. Travelling by train through the Channel Tunnel is a fairly attractive alternative – it will take you directly from city centre to city centre but is little cheaper than a flight and considerably slower – around five and a half hours to Maastricht, six and a half to Amsterdam. Whichever method you opt for, you'll find a variety of competitive fares.

BY AIR

Flying to any of the **major airports** in Holland – Schiphol (for Amsterdam), Rotterdam, Eindhoven or Maastricht – saves a lot of time over the ferry or train connections: Schiphol, for example, is just 45 minutes' flying time from London. The large number of flights, particularly to Schiphol, has led to a mass of cheap tickets, and it's reasonably easy to find a return fare from London for £90–130. To find the best bargains, study the ads in the weekend travel sections of the quality newspapers, or, if you live in London, the back pages of *Time Out* or the *Evening Standard*. Alternatively, contact a **discount flight agent** (see box on p.41), who specialize in youth flights and, if you're under 26 (or a student under 32), can offer substantial savings; they also sell ordinary discounted tickets to non-students.

Approaching the **smaller airlines**, such as *British Midland*, *Air UK* and *Transavia*, can sometimes work out cheaper, but it's also worth trying the **national airlines** – *British Airways* and *KLM*. The best deal you'll get with a scheduled airline is an Apex (Advance Purchase Excursion) or Super Pex return ticket: these cost around £120 (a little more if you travel at the weekend) and usually have to be booked fourteen days in advance; you have to spend one Saturday night abroad, and can't make any changes to the flight. To gain more flexibility you'll need to buy a standard return, which is likely to prove more expensive.

For those wanting to reach Holland from central London with the minimum of hassle, *Air UK* run a regular service from **London City Airport** to both Schiphol and Rotterdam. Fares start at around £90 for midweek departures that include at least one Saturday night away, but special offers can bring

---

AIRLINES AND ROUTES

Air Excel (c/o *Air UK*) ☎0345/666777
London (Stansted) to Maastricht.

Air UK ☎0345/666777
London (City and Stansted), Aberdeen, Edinburgh, Glasgow, Humberside, Leeds/Bradford, Manchester, Newcastle, Norwich and Teesside to Schiphol. London (City) to Rotterdam.

British Airways ☎0345/222111
London (Gatwick and Heathrow), Birmingham and Manchester to Schiphol. London (Gatwick) to Rotterdam.

British Midland ☎0345/554554
London (Heathrow) and East Midlands to Schiphol.

KLM ☎0990/750900
London (Heathrow, Gatwick, City and Stansted), Aberdeen, Belfast, Birmingham, Bristol, Cardiff, Edinburgh, Glasgow, Guernsey, Humberside, Jersey, Leeds, Manchester, Newcastle, Norwich, Southampton and Teesside to Schiphol. London (Heathrow, City and Stansted) to Rotterdam. London (Heathrow) to Eindhoven.

Suckling Airways ☎01223/293393
Cambridge, Luton and Manchester to Schiphol.

Transavia ☎01293/538181
London (Gatwick) to Schiphol.

DISCOUNT FLIGHT AGENTS

Alpha Flights	☎0171/579 8444	**STA Travel**	
		London	☎0171/361 6161
APA Travel	☎0171/387 5337	Bristol	☎0117/929 4399
		Cambridge	☎01223/366966
Campus Travel		Manchester	☎0161/834 0668
London	☎0171/730 3402	Leeds	☎0113/244 9212
Birmingham	☎0121/414 1848	Oxford	☎01865/792800
Brighton	☎01273/570226	Plus other branches nationwide.	
Bristol	☎0117/929 2494		
Cambridge	☎01223/324283	**Trailfinders**	
Edinburgh	☎0131/668 3303	London	☎0171/937 5400
Manchester	☎0161/833 2046	Birmingham	☎0121/236 1234
Oxford	☎01865/242067	Bristol	☎0117/929 9000
Plus other branches on university campuses.		Glasgow	☎0141/353 2224
		Manchester	☎0161/839 6969
Council Travel	☎0171/287 3337		
		Travel Bug	☎0161/721 4000
Destination Group	☎0171/253 9000		
		Travel Cuts	☎0171/255 1944
Masterfare	☎0171/259 2000		
		Union Travel	☎0171/493 4343
Nouvelles Frontières	☎0171/629 7772		

return fares down as low as £59 – check with the airline and with flight agents. Check-in time at London City has been cut to a minimum (10min before departure) and tickets can be collected at the check-in desk. Shuttle buses for the airport leave every 20min from Liverpool Street station (Bus Stand A; £4; 30min) and every 15min from Canary Wharf station (North Colonnade; £2; 10min).

There are plenty of flights to Holland (again, particularly Amsterdam) direct from various **UK regional airports**, which can turn out to be very good value, particularly if you use the smaller operators (see box on p.3). As a broad guide, Apex fares work out at £130–185, depending on where you travel from. Carriers such as *Air UK* and *British Midland* have a wide network of domestic routes to connect with flights to Schiphol, and most discount flight agents can devise specific routings from almost any airport in the UK. It's also worth considering a **package deal** if you don't mind having your accommodation organized beforehand; these can be surprisingly good value (see p.8 for more details).

BY TRAIN

There are a couple of options if you want to travel to Holland by train. *International Rail* (formerly *British Rail International*) acts as an agent for the combined **boat-train services** of *South Eastern*

International and *Anglia International* between London and Holland; it also sells its own *InterRail* and *Euro Domino* ("Freedom") rail passes (see p.27). However, **Eurostar**'s passenger services through the **Channel Tunnel** (via Brussels) have cut boat-train travelling times in half, and, unless you're on the tightest of budgets, the good night's sleep you'll gain is worth the extra spent on a *Eurostar* ticket. Beware, though, that if you need a visa to visit France, you'll have to get one in order to use the *Eurostar* service.

EUROSTAR: THE CHANNEL TUNNEL ROUTE

Eurostar's rapid passenger service from **London Waterloo** through the Channel Tunnel can cut journey times to Holland down to a manageable 5hr 30min (6hr 30min for Amsterdam), but you have to change at Brussels Midi station (*Brussel–Zuid* in Dutch) for the last leg of your journey. Currently *Eurostar* are running seven trains daily from Monday to Saturday, with five on Sunday, though there are no overnight services. Travel is simple: you check in twenty minutes before departure, passports are checked on the train, and in Brussels you disembark without further formalities; the onward connection normally entails about half an hour's wait. If you're coming from the **south of England,** you don't necessarily have to go into

London, since many *Eurostar* trains stop at Ashford International station; Ashford has easy access from the motorway with parking space for 11,000 cars.

There is a range of **fares** on *Eurostar*, offering varying degrees of flexibility, although none is valid for more than three months. The standard adult return fare from London to any station in the Netherlands is £105, bookable fourteen days in advance with no date changes permitted; the "leisure return" fare of £135 must include either a Saturday or three other nights away, and does allow date changes; there is also a fully flexible £165 fare, plus business and first-class options. **Under-26s** pay a flat £77 return, but this fare has a number of restrictions. One-way tickets are available only to under-26s and cost £38.50. However, all these fares can be significantly reduced by *Eurostar*'s frequent **special offers** – call them for details, and also call *Trailfinders*, who offer a return on *Eurostar* from London to Brussels for a remarkable £59. *Eurostar* is planning to start a night-sleeper service direct from London to Amsterdam, though at the time of writing the service had not materialized.

Proposed services on *Eurostar* from **Scotland** and the **north of England** direct to Paris and Brussels (bypassing London) are planned to begin late in 1997. Until then, *Eurostar* are subsidizing two link-trains, one from **Glasgow** along the East Coast Line (via Edinburgh, Newcastle and York), the other from **Manchester** (via Birmingham), both of which arrive at London Waterloo to connect with onward services to Paris and Brussels. *Eurostar*'s **subsidies** on these two services mean that fares are drastically reduced: as an example, if you book a ticket through from Edinburgh to Amsterdam (currently £125 Apex return for the 14-hour journey), the Edinburgh–London leg costs just £20 return. Contact any travel agent, or *Eurostar* direct, for full details of these tickets and of any special promotions.

BOAT-TRAIN ROUTES

There are several routes used by the boat-trains to get to Holland. From **London Liverpool Street** there are two daily departures via **Harwich** to the **Hook of Holland** and on to **Rotterdam, the Hague & Amsterdam**; fares are £75 (£85 to Amsterdam) for an ordinary return valid for two months, £55 one-way. The much better value Apex one-month return fare costs £49, and has to be booked fourteen days in advance.

Alternatively, there are four daily departures from **London Victoria** to **Amsterdam** via

Ramsgate and **Oostende** in Belgium: two morning trains connect with both the ferry and the faster jetfoil, the afternoon service is via jetfoil only, and the overnight train uses the ferry. **Fares** are £75 for a two-month return, £49 one-way. Five-day excursion tickets cost £63. The jetfoil costs an extra £4.50 each way but knocks four hours off the journey time (13hr by ferry, 9hr by jetfoil).

Travelling at night on either route, you should add on the price of (obligatory) accommodation on the ferry – a minimum of £6 for a reclining seat, £9 upwards for a berth in a cabin. Tickets for either boat-train service can be bought from any large train station, many high street travel agents, or direct from *International Rail*. Bear in mind that all these tickets allow the option of stopping off en route as many times as you wish, and that you can travel out by one route and back by the other.

For those **under 26**, fares can be cut by way of *BIJ* youth tickets, which currently cost £64 return on the Harwich–Hook route, or £62 via Ramsgate–Oostende – though special Apex offers can undercut even these prices. *Campus Travel*'s *Eurotrain* tickets can be cheaper still, and check also for deals with *Wasteels*.

TRAIN PASSES

Though you're hardly likely to buy a **train pass** simply to get to Holland, it's worth knowing

---

TRAIN INFORMATION

Campus Travel
52 Grosvenor Gardens,
London SW1W 0AG ☎0171/730 3402
Main London office; their under-26 discounted *Eurotrain* tickets can only be bought in person.

Eurostar
☎0345/881881

Holland Rail
☎01962/773646, fax 773625

International Rail
Platform 2, Victoria Station, London
☎0171/834 2345

Wasteels
Platform 2, Victoria Station
☎0171/834 7066

BUS INFORMATION
Hoverspeed ☎01304/240241
National Express/Eurolines ☎0990/808080

that *InterRail* passes (see p.27) give discounts on certain ferry routes and on *Eurostar*'s service to Paris and Brussels; check for specific details. *Euro Domino* pass-holders (again, see p.27) are entitled to 50 percent reductions on the ferries between the UK and the Netherlands, as well as a 25 percent discount on the train journey across the UK to Harwich. There are a number of other passes that can be useful if you're including Holland on a wider trip around Europe. For students and those under 26, *Campus Travel* has a great variety of **Eurotrain Explorer passes**, some covering just one country, others a combination. Call them for details; they are also agents for *InterRail* and *Eurostar*, and sell *Euro Domino* passes. See p.27 for full details of the available options.

BY BUS

Travelling by long-distance **bus** can be one of the cheapest ways of reaching Holland. A major advantage is that you don't need to worry about looking after your bags: the storage compartment under the bus is locked in London and remains locked until arrival. Two companies operate between London and Amsterdam, giving a choice of Channel crossings and arrival points.

There are three Channel crossing options, all costing the same: from **Dover to Calais** by **hovercraft** (35min) or **ferry** (1hr 30min), or by ferry from **Ramsgate to Oostende** by ferry only (5hr 30min). Total journey times from London to Amsterdam clock in at approximately ten, eleven and twelve hours respectively. **Eurolines**, oper-

ated by *National Express*, uses only the ferries, with three daily departures year-round from London's Victoria Coach Station: one in the morning via Dover–Calais, one overnight via Dover–Calais, and a longer overnight routing via Ramsgate–Oostende (useful if you'd otherwise need to get a French visa). In July and August there's an additional, slightly faster daytime service via Dover–Calais. Prices are £36 one-way, £44 return (slightly reduced for under-26s), with an exceptionally good-value Apex-type seven day advance ticket at £27 return.

Eurolines act as agents for the other bus operator, **Hoverspeed**, which provides a relatively fast daytime service via the Dover–Calais hovercraft and an overnight service using the ferry. In July and August, *Hoverspeed*, too, put on an extra daytime bus. Their prices are identical.

Tickets for all services can be bought through travel agents or from the operators direct.

BY CAR: THE FERRIES AND CHANNEL TUNNEL

There are two ways to take a car or caravan to the Netherlands: by **ferry** to one of the coastal ports, or by **train** through the Channel Tunnel. In terms both of cost and convenience, though, the ferry is preferable by far.

The most direct ferry **crossings** into Holland from the southeast of England are from **Harwich to the Hook of Holland**, and from **Sheerness to Vlissingen**. If you're heading on to Amsterdam, it takes approximately one hour to drive from the Hook; from Vlissingen it's roughly two and a half hours. If you want to spend less time crossing the

FERRY ROUTES AND PRICES

	Operator	Frequency	Duration	Standard rtn	Foot Passenger
Harwich–Hook of Holland	*Stena*	2 daily	6–9hr	£228–312	£68
Hull–Rotterdam	*North Sea*	1 daily	14hr	£286	£80
Hull–Zeebrugge	*North Sea*	1 daily	15hr	£286	£80
Newcastle–IJmuiden	*Scandinavian*	3 weekly	16hr	£352	£79
Ramsgate–Oostende	*Sally*	6 daily	4hr	£128–221	£44
Sheerness–Vlissingen	*Eurolink*	2 daily	8–9hr	£75	£28

Fares and frequencies are for travel during the peak June–August period; "standard return" indicates an average price for two people plus a small car.

FERRY COMPANIES

Eurolink Ferries
Ferry Terminal, Sheerness Docks
Kent ME12 1RX ☎01795/581000

North Sea Ferries
King George Dock, Hedon Rd
Hull HU9 5QA ☎01482/377177

Sally Line
Argyle Centre, York St, Ramsgate
Kent CT11 9DS ☎01843/595566
and London ☎0181/858 1127

Scandinavian Seaways
Head Office – Scandinavia House
Harwich International Port, Harwich
Essex CO12 4QG ☎0191/293 6262

Stena Line
Charter House, Park St, Ashford
Kent TN24 8EX ☎01233/647047
24hr information ☎01304/240028

Le Shuttle
PO Box 300, Cheriton Park, Folkestone
Kent CT19 4QD ☎0990/353535

---

water, consider sailing instead from **Ramsgate to Oostende** in Belgium. From the northeast of England there are overnight services from **Hull to Zeebrugge** (Belgium) **and Rotterdam**. There is also an overnight ferry from **Newcastle-upon-Tyne** (North Shields), which docks in **IJmuiden** (pronounced "EYE-mao-dn") port, twenty minutes from Amsterdam city centre.

Numerous brochures detailing the various **fares** can be found in high-street travel agents; it's worth shopping around for the most competitive deals. Booking fourteen days or more ahead can often turn up extremely good fares, cheaper than the "standard return" prices quoted in our table; in any case, booking is strongly recommended for motorists (and essential at peak times). Foot passengers and cyclists can normally just turn up and board, although in the summer it's often advisable to reserve some kind of accommodation on the ferry, even if just a reclining seat. Bear in mind that some sort of accommodation is obligatory on all night sailings, and should be added on to the price of an ordinary ticket. Prices vary with the month, day and even hour that you're sailing, how long you're staying, the size of your car – and the ferry companies are always offering special fares to outdo their competitors. On most fares, operators don't insist that you cross over and back using the same port. If you're just going for a weekend break, check out the short-period excursion fares on offer – usually 53-hour or five-day returns – which can cut costs dramatically. All the operators have slightly different price deals for kids: you'll need to call around for the latest quotes.

Le Shuttle operate the car service through the **Channel Tunnel** (the equivalent of the *Eurostar* passenger train service). It's important to remember that all you're paying for is the 35-minute tunnel crossing and that the drive up from Calais to Holland could take the best part of a day. Trains run through the tunnel 24 hours a day; from 7am to midnight there are trains every 20 minutes or so, dropping to every 75 minutes at other times. All kinds of vehicle (including minibuses carrying up to 16 people) can use the service for the same price: £266 return at peak times of the day, £218 off-peak. There are no booking restrictions; indeed, you can just turn up, pay and board (though the process may take as long as 45 minutes). The **tunnel entrance** on the English side is near Folkestone, at junction 11a on the M20; on the French side, you emerge on the A16 motorway at junction 14, 4km south of Calais. *Le Shuttle* can also transport **bicycles** for £10 each way, but you need to book ahead.

HITCHING AND LIFT-SHARING

In much of northern Europe, **hitching** is a genuinely viable means of getting around – the locals are much more favourably inclined towards the whole practice than in Britain or America (as long as you don't look *too* outlandish on the roadside), and, although there are certain notorious blackspots for hitching (Oostende port is one of them), in general it's relatively easy to get lifts. As anywhere, though, hitching alone is inadvisable, and hitching after dark doubly so. Bear in mind also that since drivers have been made to account

TAKING YOUR BIKE

Most people who take their bikes to Holland go by **train**. In order to do this, you must take your bike with you to the station at least an hour before departure and register it with *International Rail*. It's then loaded onto the train for you and delivered at your destination station. However, there's no guarantee it will turn up when you do. In practice, bikes can arrive anything up to 48 hours later – and you should plan accordingly. Taking your bike on the **ferry** presents few problems. Bicycles are carried free by all the ferry operators listed above (except for a £5 charge on *Eurolink*'s night ferry between Sheerness and Vlissingen). Simply turn up with your bike and secure it in the designated area. Travelling by **plane** with your bike is equally straightforward, provided you let the airline know at least a week in advance. Contact them directly to make a cargo booking for your bike, then take your machine with you when you travel. At the airport you'll need to detach the wheels and fold down the handlebars. The bike will be included in your luggage allowance (usually 20kg); if the total exceeds that, you'll need to pay for the difference. Once you're in Holland, you can take your bike on Dutch trains for a smallish fee: ƒ10 one-way and ƒ17.50 return up to 80km; ƒ15 one-way over 80km and ƒ25 for a nationwide day ticket, which covers return journeys over 80km. However, you're not allowed to take your bike on Dutch trains during the weekday morning or evening rush hours; the only exception is if you're travelling in either direction on the Hook–Amsterdam boat train. For more on cycling, see p.29.

for unauthorized passengers, it's no longer possible to travel over on the ferry for free in a truck driver's cab.

However, the Channel Tunnel – and, more specifically, the fare structure on *Le Shuttle* – has significantly opened up the possibilities for reaching Europe for no money. All cars, vans and minibuses pay a flat fare to use the Folkestone–Calais shuttle train, regardless of the number of passengers they carry: if you can persuade someone to give you a lift through the formalities and onto the train, it'll cost them nothing (or nothing more than they were already going to pay), and it means you can be in France in half an hour, with as much money in your pocket as when you left England. If you're lucky, too, your lift might be moving on in the right direction; otherwise, use the half-hour crossing to find someone in your carriage who is driving north into Belgium, and try and cajole them into taking you along too. On the other hand, you could just as easily spend the day on the hard shoulder, watching all those fast, half-empty cars whizzing by without you.

If the uncertainties of hitching put you off, you might prefer to arrange a lift beforehand. *Freewheelers*, 25 Low Friar St, Newcastle-upon-Tyne, NE1 5UE (☎0191/222 0090), matches passengers and drivers for lifts across the UK and to Europe. Membership costs £10 for one year; £22 for three years.

INCLUSIVE HOLIDAYS

Don't dismiss the idea of going on a **package holiday**: most consist of no more than travel and accommodation (from two nights to two weeks or more) and can work out an easy way of cutting costs and hassle – especially if you live some distance from London, since many operators provide a range of good-value regional departures. In such a competitive market, too, many operators throw in free extras to entice customers – these can range from a glass of Dutch gin or a canal cruise up to a night's accommodation. Depending on the type of accommodation you opt for (anything from budget to five-star hotels are available with most companies), short breaks in Amsterdam start at around £130 per person for return bus or train travel (crossing the Channel via ferry or hovercraft) plus two nights' accommodation with breakfast in a one-star hotel. The same package with return flights from a London airport works out around £180 – a little more from regional airports – and travelling by *Eurostar* through the Channel Tunnel costs about the same as flying. Many operators can also do accommodation plus ferry tickets if you want to design your own self-drive package. There are even day trips to Amsterdam available through some companies, from around £110 per person from London. Before you book, check carefully exactly what your money buys you – although train travel from Schiphol Airport to Centraal Station is always included, few operators provide any means of transport on from the station to your hotel. Low and high season dates can also vary from operator to operator, and price differences between the two can be astonishing. Any good travel agent can advise further on the best deals available, or contact one of the operators listed in the box.

> **SELECTED TOUR OPERATORS**
> **Amsterdam Travel Service** ☎01992/456056
> **British Airways Holidays** ☎01293/723100
> **Cresta** ☎0161/927 7000
> **Crystal Holidays** ☎0181/390 9900
> **Eurobreak** ☎0181/780 7700
> **Time Off** ☎0345/336622 or 0171/235 8070
> **Travelscene** ☎0181/427 8800

GETTING THERE FROM IRELAND

Taking into account the time and inconvenience of crossing the UK and then the Channel, travelling by air is by far the simplest way to reach the Netherlands from Ireland. Unless you're on the tightest of budgets, the extra money spent on a flight is worth it for the savings in time and hassle.

BY AIR

Aer Lingus flies direct from Ireland to Amsterdam, with a daily flight from Dublin plus one from Cork on Saturday; there are connections to Dublin from Cork, Galway, Kerry, Shannon and Sligo. *KLM* also flies direct, with daily flights from Dublin and (in summer) from Cork. Ordinary scheduled Apex

fares in peak season work out at about IR£180 from Dublin, a little more from regional airports. *USIT* (see box on p.10) quotes peak-season **under-26** and student fares from Dublin of IR£145 return, IR£180 out of regional airports; these student tickets are mostly open for a year.

Other flight options involve **transfers** in the UK. These tickets almost always mean switching carriers from the Ireland–UK leg to the UK–Amsterdam leg. Flying with *Aer Lingus* to London Stansted, then with *Air UK* to Amsterdam works out around the same price as a direct *Aer Lingus* flight. Flying with various combinations of *Aer Lingus*, *British Midland*, *British Airways* or *KLM* via London Heathrow, Birmingham or Manchester costs around IR£210, IR£170 for under-26s. *USIT*, or any of the discount agents listed in the box, can advise you on the best deals.

BY TRAIN

The train journey between Dublin and Holland is a real endurance test. There are two daily depar-

> **AIRLINES, BUS, TRAIN AND FERRY COMPANIES**
> **Aer Lingus** ☎01/844 4777
> **KLM** ☎01/284 2740
> **Bus Éireann** Busaras, Store St, Dublin 1 ☎01/836 6111
> **Iarnród Éireann** Travel Centre, 35 Lower Abbey St, Dublin 1 ☎01/703 4095
> **Irish Ferries** 2–4 Merrion Row, Dublin 2 ☎01/661 0511

tures, both taking the best part of 24 hours. The favoured route is Dun Laoghaire to Holyhead on the ferry; then a train from Holyhead to London Euston (changing at Crewe). In London you must make your own way across the city to Liverpool Street station, then catch the train to Harwich and the ferry to the Hook of Holland, from where there are connecting trains to all parts of the country. The standard return fare quoted by *Iarnród Éireann* (formerly *Irish Rail*), which is valid for a month and includes all ferry costs, is a non-competitive IR£180.

There's a great variety of **InterRail passes** on offer, but bear in mind that to travel from Ireland you must buy a pass for two zones in order to cover travel across the UK. For under-26s resident in Ireland who buy the pass before they leave, an *InterRail* giving a month's unlimited travel throughout Zone A (UK) and Zone E (France, Belgium, Luxembourg and the Netherlands) costs IR£210; this also gives reductions on the ferries. Those **over 26** cannot use an *InterRail* pass in Belgium, France, Switzerland, Italy, Spain, Portugal or Morocco; this means that the only crossing from the UK that you can make is the Harwich–Hook ferry directly into Holland. A 15-day pass costs IR£200; a month-long pass IR£260. For travel around Holland, the *Euro Domino* pass is a better bet (see p.27 for details of the options available); note, too that *Euro Domino* pass-holders are entitled to 50 percent reductions on the ferries between Ireland and the UK, and between the UK and the Netherlands, as well as a 25 percent discount on the train journey across the UK to Harwich.

(see p.27 for details of the options available)

BY BUS

Despite the fact that the **bus journey** from Ireland to Holland can take about the same time as the train, prices are low enough for this option to appeal to those watching every punt. The only way to get there by bus is to go via London, where you pick up a *Eurolines* bus for Amsterdam (although you can buy through tickets in Ireland before you go) – see p.6 for details. *Bus Éireann* operate two daily services from Dublin to London, and they also act as agents for *Irish Ferries'* services; return prices can be as low as IR£44 for the twelve-hour trek. Add to this the cost of the London–Amsterdam leg (IR£39 return), and it becomes possible to reach Amsterdam within 24 hours for IR£83 return (or a rock-bottom IR£54 one-way). Fares do fluctuate, though, depending upon departure time, and on whether the Irish Sea crossing is via the fast Dublin–Holyhead route or the slower crossing from Dun Laoghaire, where you must get off the bus and board the ferry on foot. Check with *Bus Éireann* for exact details, and also for their connections and prices from other Irish cities. Bear in mind, though, that they do not take bookings over the phone: you must pay in person.

BY FERRY

There are no **ferries** direct from Ireland to the Netherlands or to Belgium. The nearest ferries get to Holland is the northwest of France, and, with the fare for a car plus two students on the

see p.6 for details

DISCOUNT TRAVEL AGENTS

Aran Travel		**Specialised Travel Services**	
Galway	☎091/62595	Dublin	☎01/873 1066
Discount Travel		**Student & Group Travel**	
Dublin	☎01/679 5888	Dublin	☎01/677 7834
Fahy Travel		**Travel Shop**	
Galway	☎091/563055	Belfast	☎01232/471717
Flight Finders International		**USIT**	
Dublin	☎01/676 8326	Belfast	☎01232/324073
Joe Walsh Tours		Cork	☎021/270900
Dublin	☎01/676 3053	Dublin	☎01/679 8833
Lee Travel		Galway	☎091/565177
Cork	☎021/277111	Limerick	☎061/415064
McCarthy Travel		Waterford	☎051/72601
Cork	☎021/270127		

Cork–Le Havre route currently at IR£464 in the peak season, this is a long way from being a competitive option.

INCLUSIVE HOLIDAYS

Package holidays – which can simply mean flights plus accommodation – are a feasible and sensible method of eliminating snags, and can easily cut costs as well. *USIT* (see box) do packages for a minimum of two nights, with prices ranging from IR£27 to IR£45 per person per night (sharing a double room), depending on the type of hotel you choose. Both *KLM* and *Aer Lingus* also offer several different "weekend break" packages to suit various budgets and styles; travel agents should have the relevant brochures, or you can call the airlines direct for information. Many trav-

el agents can also give deals on city breaks in Amsterdam (see box).

> **PACKAGE TOUR SPECIALISTS**
>
> **CIE Tours International**
> Dublin ☎01/703 1888
>
> **JWT Holidays**
> Dublin ☎01/671 8751 or 872 2555
>
> **Liffey Travel**
> Dublin ☎01/873 4900
>
> **Neenan Travel**
> Dublin ☎01/676 5181
>
> **Thomas Cook**
> Belfast ☎01232/240833
> Dublin ☎01/677 1721

GETTING THERE FROM FROM THE USA AND CANADA

Schiphol airport in Amsterdam is among the most popular and least expensive gateways to Europe from North America, and getting a convenient and good-value flight is rarely a problem. Virtually every region of the United States and Canada is well served by the major airlines, though only two scheduled carriers offer nonstop flights – KLM/Northwest Airlines and Delta. The rest fly via London and other European centres. Look out, too, for deals offered by the Dutch charter company Martinair, which offers mid-priced seats on nonstop flights from a number of cities in the USA and Canada.

SHOPPING FOR TICKETS

Barring special offers, the cheapest fare is usually an **Apex** ticket, although this will carry certain restrictions: you have to book – and pay – at least 21 days before departure, spend at least seven days abroad (maximum stay three months), and you tend to get penalized if you change your schedule. Some airlines also issue **Special Apex** tickets to people younger than 24, often extending the maximum stay to a year. Many airlines offer youth or student fares to **under-25s**; a passport or driver's licence is sufficient proof of age, though these tickets are subject to availability and can have eccentric

booking conditions. It's worth remembering that most cheap return fares will only give a percentage refund if you need to cancel or alter your journey, so make sure you check the restrictions carefully before buying.

You can normally cut costs further by going through a **specialist flight agent** – either a **consolidator**, who buys up blocks of tickets from the airlines and sells them at a discount, or a **discount agent**, who wheels and deals in tickets offloaded by the airlines, and often offers special student and youth fares and a range of other travel-related services, such as travel insurance, car rental and tours. Bear in mind, though, that the penalties for changing your plans can be stiff. Remember too that these companies make their money by dealing in bulk, so don't expect them to answer lots of questions. Some agents specialize in **charter flights**, which may be cheaper than any scheduled flight available, but again departure dates are fixed and withdrawal penalties are high (check the refund policy). If you travel a lot, **discount travel clubs** are another option – the annual membership fee may be worth it for benefits such as cut-price air tickets and car rental.

A further possibility is to see if you can arrange a **courier flight**, although the hit-and-miss nature of these makes them most suitable for the single traveller who travels light and has a very flexible schedule. In return for shepherding a package through customs and possibly giving up your baggage allowance, you can expect to get a heavily discounted ticket. See pp.13–14 or, for more options, consult *A Simple Guide to Courier Travel* (Pacific Data Sales Publishing).

Regardless of where you buy your ticket, the fare will depend on the **season**. Fares are highest in December, June, July and August, and fares during these months can cost between $100 and $300 more, depending on the airline. Flying on weekends can add $100 to the cost of a return ticket: prices quoted below assume midweek travel. In addition, any Apex fares quoted entail a maximum stay of thirty days, with tickets bought at least fourteen days in advance.

FLIGHTS FROM THE USA

KLM and Northwest Airlines, which operate a joint service from the United States and Canada to Amsterdam, offer the widest range of flights, with nonstop or direct services from eleven US cities and connections from dozens more via *Northwest*. Their Apex fares are usually identical to those offered by other carriers, so for convenience at least, *KLM/Northwest* is your best bet. It's also worth looking into deals offered by the Dutch charter carrier, **Martinair**, which flies nonstop from eight US cities — though note that many of them are served in summer only.

One-way fares are rarely good value, but if you're set on one, the best source is the seat consolidators that advertise in the back pages of the travel sections of the major Sunday newspapers – or see the box below.

Travelling from the **East Coast**, *KLM*'s nonstop flights out of New York JFK start at around $570 in low season, rising by around $150 in May and peaking at around $870 in July and August. Nonstop fares out of DC, Atlanta, Detroit, Chicago and Minneapolis cost $50–100 more; connecting flights from other major cities are usually thrown in for free. *Delta* has similar fares on its nonstop flights out of New York and Atlanta, as does *United* from Washington DC, and most carriers match these prices on their flights via London Heathrow. Especially during winter, many airlines have special offers that can reduce fares to well under $500 round-trip, and discount travel agents and consolidators can often find you fares as low as $350 (low season) or $650 (high season). *Martinair* operates twice-weekly **charter flights** out of Newark from May through September, costing $700–880, and a year-round service from Miami and Tampa (both 2 weekly) and Orlando (4 weekly).

As for the **West Coast**, *KLM/Northwest Airlines'* round-trip Apex fares on nonstop flights out of Los Angeles start at around $816 in low season, rising to $956 in May and $1100 in July and August. Consolidators can probably get you a seat for as little as $572 (low season) or $795 (high season). Fares from San Francisco or Seattle usually cost $50–100 more and most international carriers charge similar prices. Special offers sometimes bring the fares down to under $500, though these are usually only available during winter.

Martinair's round-trip charter fares out of Los Angeles (3 weekly), Oakland (2 weekly), Seattle (2 weekly) and Denver (weekly), start at around $670 for departures in April and May and climb to $830 in the summer peak season. On winter flights out of Denver, fares drop as low as $500.

ROUND-THE-WORLD TICKETS AND COURIER FLIGHTS

If you plan to visit Holland as part of a major world trip, then you might want to think about getting a **round-the-world** ticket that includes the city as one of its stops. A sample route from the West Coast, using a combination of airlines, might be San Francisco/Los Angeles/ Portland/Seattle–Taipei/Hong Kong–Bangkok– Cairo–Amsterdam–New York–Los Angeles, which costs $1297. From the East Coast, a ticket

DISCOUNT FLIGHT AGENTS, TRAVEL CLUBS & CONSOLIDATORS

Access International
New York ☎1-800/TAKE-OFF
Consolidator with good East Coast and central US deals.

Air Brokers International
San Francisco ☎1-800/883-3273
Consolidator selling round-the-world tickets.

Airkit
Los Angeles ☎213/957-9304
Consolidator with seats from San Francisco and LA.

Council Travel
New York ☎1-800/226-8624, e-mail cts@ciee.org
Agent specializing in student discounts; branches in 40 US cities.

Encore Short Notice
Lanham, MD ☎301/459-8020
East Coast travel club.

Flight Centre
Vancouver, BC ☎604/739-9539
Discount air fares from Canadian cities.

High Adventure Travel Inc.
San Francisco ☎1-800/428-8735
Round-the-world tickets.

Interworld
Miami ☎305/443-4929 or 1-800/468-3796
Southeastern US consolidator.

Last-Minute Travel Club
Boston ☎617/267-9800 or 1-800/LAST-MIN

Nouvelle Frontières
New York ☎212/779-0600
Montréal ☎514/288-9942
Main US and Canadian branches of the French discount travel outfit. Other branches in LA, San Francisco and Québec City.

Overseas Tours
Millbrae, CA ☎1-800/323-8777
Discount agent.

Pan Express Travel
Toronto ☎416/964-6888
Discount travel agent.

Rebel Tours
Valencia, CA ☎805/294-0900 or 1-800/227-3235
Good source of deals with Martinair.

STA Travel
New York ☎212/627-3111 or 1-800/777-0112
Other branches in the Los Angeles, San Francisco and Boston areas.
Worldwide discount firm specializing in student/youth fares.

TFI Tours
New York ☎212/736-1140 or 1-800/825-3834
The very best East Coast deals, especially if you only want to fly one-way.

Travac
St Louis ☎1-800/872-8800
Good central US consolidator.

Travel Cuts
Toronto ☎416/979-2406
Main office of the Canadian student travel organization. Many other offices nationwide.

Travelers Advantage
Nashville ☎1-800/548-1116
Reliable travel club.

Travel Avenue
Chicago ☎312/876-1116 or 1-800/333-3335
Discount travel agent.

Unitravel
St Louis ☎1-800/325-2222
Reliable consolidator.

covering New York–Hong Kong–Bangkok–Cairo–Amsterdam–New York costs $1384. See the box below for details of agents specializing in round-the-world tickets.

Round-trip **courier flights** to Amsterdam from major US cities are available for around $200–250,· with last-minute specials, booked within three days of departure, going for as little as $100. For more information about courier flights, contact *The Air Courier Association*, 191 University Blvd, Suite 300, Denver, CO 80206 (☎303/279-3600); *Discount Travel International*, 169 W 81st St, New York, NY 10024 (☎212/362-3636, fax 362-3236); or *Now Voyager*, 74 Varick St, Suite 307, New York, NY 10013 (☎212/431-1616, fax 334-5243).

FLIGHTS FROM CANADA

KLM/Northwest Airlines has the best range of routes from Canada, with nonstop flights from all the major airports, and fares approximately the same as they are from the USA. Round-trip tickets out of **Toronto** start at around CDN$668 in the low season, stepping up to CDN$888 in May and CDN$1048 in July and August. Fares from **Vancouver** start at around CDN$629, climbing to CDN$1158 and CDN$1368.

Canadian **charter** operations, such as *Air Transat* and *Fiesta West/Canada 3000* offer some of the best deals on spring through fall travel, with fares as low as CDN$569 round-trip from Halifax, CDN$539 from Toronto and CDN$738 from Vancouver and Calgary. Neither *Air Canada* nor *Canadian Airlines* serves Amsterdam, though *Martinair* flies twice-weekly nonstop out of Toronto (April–Oct): low-season fares start at CDN$599, rising to CDN$759 in high season.

Canadian departures for **round-the-world** tickets can usually be arranged for around CDN$150 more than the US fare (see above).

TRAVELLING VIA EUROPE

Even though many flights from North America to Holland are routed via London, because of the various special fares it's often cheaper to stay on the plane all the way to Amsterdam. In general you can't stop over and continue on a later flight, as US and Canadian airlines are not allowed to provide services between European cities.

However, if you want to combine a trip with visits to other European cities, **London** makes the best starting point, as onward flights are relatively inexpensive. Besides having the best range of good-value transatlantic flights (New York to London is the busiest and cheapest route), London also has excellent connections on to Amsterdam. **Paris**, too, is becoming a popular gateway to Europe. *United* and *American Airlines*, as well as *British Airways* and the British carrier *Virgin Atlantic*, all have frequent flights to London from various parts of the US, *BA* flying from Canada too; *Air France*, *United* and *American* fly daily to Paris. See "Getting There from Britain", p.3, for details on travel from Britain to Amsterdam and other Dutch cities.

RAIL PASSES

If you intend Holland to form just part of your European travels, or envisage using the European rail network extensively, then you should consider investing in a **Eurail train pass**. These are good for unlimited travel within 17 European countries, including Holland, and they should be purchased before you leave, as they cost ten percent more in Europe: you can get them from most travel agents in the USA and Canada or from *Rail Pass Express* (☎1-800/722-7151). The standard **Eurail** pass is valid for unlimited first-class travel for periods of 15 days ($498), 21 days ($648), 1 month ($798) or 2 months ($1098). For those under 26, the **Eurail Youthpass** allows second-class rail travel for 15 days ($398), 1 month ($578), 2 months ($768) or 3 months ($1398). There's also the **Eurail Flexipass**, which comes in three versions. One covers travel on any 5 days within a 2-month period and costs $348 for adults travelling first-class, $255 for under-26s travelling second-class; a second is valid for travel on any 10 days in 2 months ($560 and $398 respectively); the third version allows travel on 15 days within 2 months ($740 and $540).

For more **information** on European rail travel, call *Rail Europe*: ☎1-800/4EURAIL in the USA and ☎1-800/361-RAIL in Canada.

For more details on getting around Holland by train, and of the various passes available (remember that they usually cost more than if bought in advance), see p.27.

INCLUSIVE TOURS

There are any number of **packages and organized tours** from North America to Amsterdam and elsewhere in Holland. Prices vary, with some operators including the air fare, while others cover just accommodation, sightseeing, and activities such as cycling or hiking. In addition, many airlines offer fly-drive deals that include a week's hotel accommodation. As an example, *United Vacations* offers a six-night Amsterdam bed and breakfast package starting at $389, excluding airfare; a city sightseeing tour costs an extra $27 and day trips to Volendam, Marken and Edam (see p.3) are available for the same sort of price.

KLM/Northwest World Vacations do a two-night Amsterdam package from $114, including accommodation, breakfast and a diamond factory tour – sightseeing tours cost extra.

You'll find that most European tours include Amsterdam on their itineraries, too. Among the best of the Europe-wide operators are *Back Door Travel*, a specialist in independent budget travel, with the emphasis on simple accommodation and meeting local people.

SPECIALIST TOUR OPERATORS

Abercrombie & Kent
☎1-800/323-7308
Six-night river and canal cruising tours from Amsterdam to Bruges starting at $990. Airfare extra.

AESU Travel
☎1-800/363-7640
Tours, independent city stays, discount air fares. 31-day Classic Europe tour includes wind surfing, biking and canoeing in Holland, 2 days in Amsterdam and a stop in Brussels; $3100 including airfare.

Air Transat Holidays
☎604/688-3350
Canadian charter company offering discount fares from major Canadian cities, tours and fly-drive trips. Contact travel agents for brochures.

American Airlines Fly Away Vacations
☎1-800/433-7300
Package tours and fly-drive programmes. A 7-day, 6-night London and Amsterdam tour costs $919 including airfare, accommodation and sightseeing.

Back Door Travel
☎206/771-8303
Off-the-beaten path, small group travel with budget travel guru Rick Steves and his enthusiastic guides. 21-day "Best of Europe" Tour, including stops in Haarlem and Amsterdam, costs $2900. Call for a free newsletter.

British Airways Holidays
☎1-800/359-8722
Package tours and fly-drives. A 7-day, 6-night London and Amsterdam package including airfare costs from $919.

Canada 3000/FiestaWest
Discount charter flights, car rental, accommodation and package tours. Book through travel agents or by calling BCAA TeleCentre in Canada: ☎1-800/663-1956.

CBT Bicycle Tours
Affordable tours in Holland, Belgium and Luxembourg. 16-day Amsterdam to Luxembourg tour starts at $1570. Airfare extra. Available through travel agents.

Contiki Tours
☎1-800/CONTIKI
Budget tours to Europe. A 12-day tour of seven countries, including 2 days in Amsterdam, starts at $1299 including airfare from the USA.

Euro Bike Tours
☎1-800/321-6060
Upscale cycling tours and "bicycling and barging" tours in Holland, Belgium and Luxembourg starting at $1795. Airfare extra.

Saga International Holidays
☎1-800/952-9590
19-day Dutch waterways tours covering Amsterdam, North and South Holland and Belgium, starting at $1899 including airfare.

KLM/Northwest World Vacations
☎1-800/447-4747
Hotel and sightseeing packages and escorted tours. Two-night Amsterdam package from $114. Contact travel agents.

United Vacations
☎1-800/538-2929
Six nights in Amsterdam, starting at $389 including hotels and breakfast. Airfare extra. Contact travel agents.

GETTING THERE FROM AUSTRALIA & NEW ZEALAND

There is no shortage of flights to Holland from Australia and New Zealand, though all of them involve at least one stop. When buying a ticket, as well as the price, you might want to take into account the airline's route – whether, for example, you'd rather stop in Moscow or Bali. Some of the airlines allow free stopovers (see the box below).

Fares vary according to the time of year: for most airlines the **low season** runs from mid-

AIRLINES

Aeroflot
Sydney ☎02/9233 7911
No New Zealand office.
Twice-weekly flights to Amsterdam from Sydney via Bangkok and Moscow.

Air New Zealand
Sydney ☎02/9223 4666
Auckland ☎09/366 2803
Several flights a week to Amsterdam from major New Zealand cities via LA and London

Alitalia
Sydney ☎02/9247 1308
Auckland ☎09/379 4457
Three flights weekly to Amsterdam from Brisbane, Sydney, Melbourne and Auckland via Rome.

Britannia Airways
Sydney ☎02/9251 1299
No New Zealand office.
Several charter flights to Amsterdam per month during their charter season (Nov–March) from Cairns, Brisbane, Sydney, Melbourne, Adelaide, Perth and Auckland, via Singapore and Abu Dhabi.

British Airways
Sydney ☎02/9258 3300
Auckland ☎09/356 8690
Several flights weekly to Amsterdam from major Australian cities via Bangkok/Singapore and London, and from Auckland via LA and London.

Cathay Pacific
Sydney ☎02/9931 5500, local-call rate 13 1747
Auckland ☎09/379 0861
Several flights a week to Amsterdam from major Australian cities with a transfer or stopover in Hong Kong.

Garuda Indonesia
Sydney ☎02/9334 9944
Auckland ☎09/366 1855
Several flights weekly to Amsterdam from major Australian and New Zealand cities with a transfer or stopover in Bali/Jakarta.

KLM
Sydney ☎02/9231 6333, toll-free 1800/505 747
No New Zealand office.
Three flights weekly to Amsterdam from Sydney via Singapore.

Malaysia Airlines
Sydney, local-call rate ☎13 2627
Auckland ☎09/373 2741
Several flights weekly to Amsterdam from major Australian and New Zealand cities with a transfer or stopover in Kuala Lumpur.

Olympic Airways S.A.
Sydney ☎02/9251 2044
No New Zealand office.
Twice-weekly service to Amsterdam from Sydney, Melbourne and Auckland, with a transfer or stopover in Athens.

Qantas
Sydney ☎02/9957 0111
Auckland ☎09/357 8900
Several flights weekly to Amsterdam from Australian cities and Auckland via Singapore/Bangkok and London.

Singapore Airlines
Sydney, local-call rate ☎13 1011
Auckland ☎09/379 3209
Several flights weekly to Amsterdam from major Australian and New Zealand cities with a transfer or stopover in Singapore.

Thai Airways
Sydney ☎02/9844 0999, toll-free 1800/422 020
Auckland ☎09/377 3886
Several flights weekly to Amsterdam from eastern Australian cities and Auckland via Bangkok.

January to March, and October to November; **high season** fares apply from mid-May to the end of August and December to mid-January.

The cheapest option is to fly with *Britannia* during their charter season, which runs from November to March; a return ticket via Singapore and Abu Dhabi costs between A\$1200/NZ\$1420 and A\$1800/NZ\$2130, depending on the season. *Garuda* offers the next cheapest flights, stopping in Bali or Jakarta for around A\$1700/NZ\$1999 (high season) or A\$2100/NZ\$2450 (low season). For the same price *Aeroflot* fly twice a week from Sydney via Bangkok and Moscow. *Malaysia Airlines* (via Kuala Lumpur), *Olympic* (via Athens), *Alitalia* (via Rome), *Thai* (via Bangkok) and *Cathay Pacific* (via Hong Kong) have flights from all the major cities for around A\$1990/NZ\$2199 to A\$2490/NZ\$2899. Fares are the same with the Dutch national airline, *KLM*, on its flights from Sydney, via Singapore. For a little more – around A\$2399–2999/NZ\$2699–3399 – you can fly with *BA, Qantas, Air New Zealand* and *Singapore Airlines*: with these airlines you can

expect to get some good deals on European side trips, fly-drive/accommodation packages and free stopovers on route; check out, too, the offers provided by *Cathay Pacific, Alitalia* and *Thai Airways*. If you want to combine your trip with a stay in another European centre, probably your best bet is to get a cheap fare to London, which usually offers the best-value onward flights to Holland (see "Getting There from Britain", p.3).

As a general rule, **travel agents** can get you a better deal than buying direct from the airlines; they also have the latest information on limited special offers and can give advice on visa regulations. See the box on p.18 for the addresses of specialist agents.

ROUND-THE-WORLD TICKETS AND AIR PASSES

If your visit to Holland is just one stop on a worldwide trip, then you might want to buy a **round-the-world** ticket that includes Amsterdam as one of its stops. RTW tickets usually give six free

DISCOUNT TRAVEL AGENTS

Anywhere Travel
Sydney ☎02/9663 0411

Brisbane Discount Travel
Brisbane ☎07/3229 9211

Budget Travel
Auckland ☎09/366 0061, toll-free 1800/808 040
Other branches around the city.

Destinations Unlimited
Auckland ☎09/373 4033

Flight Centres
Australia: Sydney ☎02/9241 2422; Melbourne ☎03/9650 2899; plus other branches nationwide. New Zealand: Auckland ☎09/209 6171; Christchurch ☎03/379 7145; Wellington ☎04/472 8101; other branches countrywide.

Northern Gateway
Darwin ☎08/8941 1394

Passport Travel
Malvern ☎03/9824 7183

STA Travel
Australia: Sydney ☎02/9212 1255 or 1800/637 444; Melbourne ☎03/9654 7266; other offices in

state capitals and major universities. New Zealand: Auckland ☎09/309 0458; Wellington ☎04/385 0561; Christchurch ☎03/379 9098; other offices in Dunedin, Palmerston North, Hamilton and major universities.

Thomas Cook
Australia: Sydney ☎02/9248 6100; Melbourne ☎03/9650 2442; branches in other state capitals. New Zealand: Auckland ☎09/849 2071.

Topdeck Travel
Adelaide ☎08/8232 7222.

Tymtro Travel
Sydney ☎02/9223 2211.

YHA Travel Centres
Sydney ☎02/9261 1111
Melbourne ☎03/9670 9611
Adelaide ☎08/8231 5583
Brisbane ☎07/3236 1680
Perth ☎08/9227 5122
Darwin ☎08/8981 2560
Hobart ☎03/6234 9617

SPECIALIST OPERATORS

All the following can arrange sightseeing tours, car rental, and accommodation in Holland from $70 twin share.

Adventure World
Sydney ☎02/9956 7766, toll-free 1800/221 931; Brisbane ☎07/3229 0599; Perth ☎08/9221 2300; Auckland ☎09/524 5118.

CIT
Sydney ☎02/9267 1255; offices in Melbourne, Brisbane, Adelaide and Perth.
Also handles Eurail *passes.*

Creative Tours
Sydney ☎02/9386 2111

Eurolynx
Auckland ☎09/379 9716

European Travel Office
Melbourne ☎03/9329 8844; Sydney ☎02/9267 7727; Auckland ☎09/525 3074

KLM Vacations
Sydney ☎02/9264 8300 or 1800/505 074; Auckland ☎09/376 7029

stopovers, with limited backtracking and side trips, with additional stopovers charged at around $100 each. Fares start at A$2399/NZ$2699. *Cathay Pacific–UA*'s "Globetrotter" and *Air New Zealand–KLM–Northwest*'s "World Navigator" both take in Amsterdam. *Qantas–BA*'s "Global Explorer" is more restrictive, allowing six stopovers but no backtracking within the US. *Thai* and *Malaysia* also combine with other carriers to provide a variety of routes at similar prices. **Air passes** are available if your journey from Australia or New Zealand is made entirely on *British Airways, KLM* or *Alitalia–Qantas,* starting at A$100/NZ$115 per flight.

RAIL PASSES

If you're planning to travel around the Netherlands or the rest of Europe by **train**, then it's best to get hold of a rail pass before you go. **Eurail passes** (see p.14 for details on the full range) are available through most travel agents or from *CIT* (see box opposite), or from *Thomas Cook World Rail* (Australia ☎1800/422 747; New Zealand ☎09/263 7260). Once you get to the Netherlands, you can also buy a *Euro Domino* pass – see p.27.

RED TAPE AND VISAS

Citizens of Britain, Ireland, Australia, New Zealand, Canada and the USA need only a valid passport to stay for three months in Holland. On arrival, make sure you have **enough money to convince officials you can support yourself. Poorer-looking visitors are often checked and, if you come from outside the EU and can't flash a credit card or a few travellers' cheques or notes, you may not be allowed in.**

If you want to stay longer than three months, officially you need a *verblifsvergunning* or residence permit from the Aliens' police. Even for EU citizens, though, this is far from easy to obtain (impossible if you can't show means of support), and there is a lot of bureaucracy involved. In reality, if you hold a European Community passport, restrictions are fairly loose – they're rarely date-stamped when entering the country – though if you are definitely planning to stay and work it's probably best to get a stamp anyway.

Non-EU nationals should always have their documents in order, but the chance of gaining legal resident's status without pre-arranged work

DUTCH EMBASSIES AND CONSULATES ABROAD

Australia 19th Floor, 500 Oxford St, Bondi Junction, Canberra (☎02/9387 6644).

Canada 350 Albert St, Ottowa, Ontario (☎613/237-5030).

New Zealand Investment House, Tenth Floor, Balance and Featherstone streets, Wellington (☎04/473 8652).

UK 38 Hyde Park Gate, London SW7 5DP (☎0171/584 5040).

USA 4200 Linnean Ave NW, Washington DC 20008 (☎202/244-5300).

is extremely slim. To work legally, non-EU nationals need a work permit (*werkvergunning*), and these are even harder to get than a residence permit – every single EU citizen has preference in the job market over a non-EU citizen with the same skills. The only exception to this rule are Australians aged 18 to 25, who are eligible to apply for a year-long Working Holiday Visa.

CUSTOMS

With the advent of the Single European Market, EU nationals over the age of 17 can bring in and take out most things, as long as they've paid tax on them in an EU country and they are for personal consumption. However, there are still restrictions on the volume of tax- or **duty-free** goods you can take. In general, residents of EU countries travelling to other EU states are allowed a duty-free allowance of two hundred cigarettes or fifty cigars, one litre of spirits and five litres of wine; for non-EU residents the allowances are usually two hundred cigarettes, one litre of spirits and two litres of wine. If you're doing a lot of shopping, non-EU nationals who spend more than ƒ300 in one shop in one day and then export the goods within 3 months of purchase can reclaim the VAT (**sales tax**). Shops displaying the "Tax Free for Tourists" logo will help with the formalities.

British **customs officials** tend to assume that anyone youthful-looking coming directly from Holland is a potential dope fiend or pornographer – strip searches and unpleasantness are frequent, particularly at airports. If you are carrying prescribed drugs of any kind, it can be a good idea to have a copy of the prescription to flash at a suspicious customs officer.

FOREIGN EMBASSIES IN THE NETHERLANDS

Australia Carnegielaan 10–14, 2517 KH The Hague (☎070/310 8200).

Britain Embassy: Lange Voorhout 10, 2514 ED The Hague (☎070/364 5800).

Consulate-General: Koningslaan 44, 1075 AE Amsterdam (☎020/676 4343).

Canada Sophialaan 7, 2514 JP The Hague (☎070/361 4111).

Ireland Dr Kuyperstraat 9, 2514 BA The Hague (☎070/363 0993).

New Zealand Carnegielaan 10–14, 2517 KH The Hague (☎070/346 9324).

USA Embassy: Lange Voorhout 102, 2514 EJ The Hague (☎070/310 9209).

Consulate-General: Museumplein 19, 1071 DJ Amsterdam (☎020/664 5661).

INSURANCE AND HEALTH

As fellow members of the European Community, both the UK and Ireland have reciprocal health agreements with Holland.

In theory, this allows free medical advice and treatment on presentation of **certificate E111** – though in practice many doctors and pharmacists charge, and it's up to you to be reimbursed by the Department of Health once you're home: get receipts for all prescriptions and/or treatment. To get an E111, fill in a form at any post office, and you'll be issued with a certificate immediately: read the small print on the back to find out how to get reduced-price treatment (you'll probably have to explain things to the doctor who treats you). Without an E111 you won't be turned away from a doctor or hospital, but will almost certainly have to contribute towards treatment. **Australians** are able to receive treatment through a reciprocal arrangement with Medicare (check with your local office for details). For other **non-EU citizens travel insurance** is essential, and it's a wise additional protection for everyone, since policies can cover loss or theft of your cash and possessions as well as the cost of medicines, medical and dental treatment. Remember, though, that your policy may not cover all medical expenses, and that you'll need to keep **receipts** for any medicines you buy or treatment you pay for, to claim from your insurance company once you're home. Similarly, if you have anything **stolen**, report the theft to the police (see "Police and Trouble"), and keep a copy of your statement. It's also worth noting that bank and credit cards often have certain levels of medical or other insurance included, especially if you use them to pay for your trip – check the details before you arrange cover.

BRITISH AND IRISH COVER

Most travel agents and tour operators will offer you insurance when you book your flight or holiday, and some will insist you take it. These policies are usually reasonable value, though as ever you should check the small print. If you feel the cover is inadequate or you want to compare prices, any travel agent or bank should be able to help. Travel insurance schemes are also sold by various **specialist companies**. Two of the cheapest are *Endsleigh*, 97–107 Southampton Row, London WC1 (☎0171/436 4451) and *Columbus*, 17 Devonshire Square, London EU2 (☎0171/375 0011); premiums start at around £24 a month in Britain, IR£30 in Ireland, and are available from youth/student travel offices or direct from the companies themselves. Bear in mind that if you have a good "all risks" home insurance policy, it may well cover your possessions against loss or theft even when overseas, and many private medical schemes also cover you when abroad – make sure you know the procedure and helpline.

NORTH AMERICAN COVER

Before buying an insurance policy, check that you're not already covered. **Canadians** are usually covered for medical mishaps overseas by their provincial health plans. Holders of official **student/teacher/youth** cards are entitled to accident coverage and hospital in-patient benefits. **Students** will often find that their student health coverage extends during the vacations and for one term beyond the date of last enrolment. **Homeowners' or renters'** insurance often covers theft or loss of documents, money and valuables while overseas, although conditions and maximum amounts vary from company to company.

After checking the above possibilities, you might want to contact a specialist **travel insurance company**; your travel agent can usually recommend one or you could try *Access America* (☎1-800/284-8300), *Carefree Travel Insurance*

(☎1-800/645-2424), or *TravMed* (☎1-800/732-5309). Premiums vary so shop around. Policies are comprehensive but maximum payouts tend to be meagre. The best deals are usually to be had though student/youth travel agencies and start at around $65 for a two-week trip and $85 for three weeks to a month.

COVER IN AUSTRALIA AND NEW ZEALAND

Travel insurance is put together by the airlines and travel agent groups in conjunction with insurance companies. They are all comparable in premiums and coverage; you can expect to pay around A$190/NZ$220 for one month. Reputable **companies** include *Cover More*, 32 Walker St, N Sydney, NSW (☎02/9202 8000) and *Ready Plan*,

141–147 Walker St, Dandenong, Vic (☎1800/337 462) and 63 Albert St, Auckland (☎09/379 3208).

DRUGSTORES, PHARMACIES AND DOCTORS

If you get sick, minor ailments can be remedied at a **drugstore** (*drogist*), which sells toiletries, non-prescription drugs, tampons, condoms and the like; a **pharmacy** (*apotheek*), usually open Mon–Fri 9.30am–5.30pm (though some close on Monday morning), is where you go to get a prescription made up. Ask at the local tourist office if you want to **consult a doctor** or get a prescription: if you're in a large city, US and British embassies also keep a list of local English-speaking doctors.

INFORMATION AND MAPS

Before you leave home, there's a wealth of information on the country which you can pick up from branches of the Netherlands Board of Tourism (the NBT) detailed opposite.

The **NBT** has useful leaflets on the main tourist attractions, annual events and accommodation, and special interest leaflets on cycling and watersports. It also produces booklets detailing the country's campsites and hotels, as well as where to find private rooms, and publishes a reasonable map of the country.

Once in Holland, simply head for the nearest **VVV**. Just about every town (and even most

large villages) will have a VVV office, either in the centre of town or by the train station (sometimes both). In addition to handing out basic maps (often for free) and English info on the main sights, the VVV keeps lists of local accommodation options and, for a small fee, will book rooms for you. Most VVV offices also keep information on neighbouring towns, which can be a great help for forward planning. Hours vary, and are detailed – along with phone numbers – in the text.

NETHERLANDS BOARD OF TOURISM OFFICES

World Wide Web http://www.nbt.nl/holland

Canada 25 Adelaide St E, Suite 710, Toronto, Ontario M5C 1Y2 (☎416/363-1577, fax 363-1470).

UK and Ireland Write to PO Box 523, London SW1E 6NT for an information pack. For recorded info, call ☎0891/717777 (50p per minute).

USA 355 Lexington Ave, 21st Floor, New York, NY 10017 (☎212/370-7367, fax 370-9507).

225 N. Michigan Ave, Suite 326, Chicago, IL 60601 (☎312/819-0300, fax 819-1740).

There are no offices in Australia or New Zealand.

MAPS

For touring purposes, the best road **map** of Holland is the one published by *Kümmerly and Frey*. For more detailed **regional maps**, aside from the NBT's own plan, the Dutch motoring organization ANWB publishes an excellent 1:100,000 series that covers the whole country. Although our city maps should be adequate for most purposes, the best large-scale alternatives are the *Falk Plans*, most of which have gazetteers.

MAP OUTLETS IN BRITAIN AND IRELAND

Belfast
Waterstones, Queens Building, 8 Royal Ave, BT1 (☎01232/247355).

Dublin
Easons Bookshop, 40 O'Connell St, 1 (☎01/873 3811).
Figgis Bookshop, 56–58 Dawson St, 2 (☎01/677 4754).

Edinburgh
Thomas Nelson and Sons Ltd, 51 York Place, EH1 3JD (☎0131/557 3011).

Glasgow
John Smith and Sons, 57–61 St Vincent St (☎0141/221 7472).

London
Daunt Books, 83 Marylebone High St, W1 (☎0171/224 2295).
National Map Centre, 22–24 Caxton St, SW1 (☎0171/222 4945).
Stanfords, 12–14 Long Acre, WC2 (☎0171/836 1321).

Maps by **mail or phone order** are available from *Stanfords* (☎0171/836 1321).

MAP OUTLETS IN NORTH AMERICA

Chicago
Rand McNally, 444 N Michigan Ave, IL 60611 (☎312/321-1751).

Montréal
Ulysses Travel Bookshop, 4176 St-Denis (☎514/289-0993).

New York
The Complete Traveler Bookstore, 199 Madison Ave, NY 10016 (☎212/685-9007).
Rand McNally, 150 E 52nd St, NY 10022 (☎212/758-7488).
Traveler's Bookstore, 22 W 52nd St, NY 10019 (☎212/664-0995).

San Francisco
The Complete Traveler Bookstore, 3207 Filmore St, CA 92123 (☎415/923-1511).
Rand McNally, 595 Market St, CA 94105 (☎415/777-3131).

Seattle
Elliot Bay Book Company, 101 S Main St, WA 98104 (☎206/624-6600).

Toronto
Open Air Books and Maps, 25 Toronto St, M5R 2C1 (☎416/363-0719).

Vancouver
World Wide Books and Maps, 1247 Granville St (☎604/687-3320).

Note that *Rand McNally* has stores right across the US; phone ☎1-800/333-0136 (ext 2111) for the address of your nearest store, or for **direct mail** maps.

MAP OUTLETS IN AUSTRALIA AND NEW ZEALAND

Adelaide
The Map Shop, 16a Peel St, Adelaide, SA 5000 (☎08/231 2033).

Auckland
Specialty Maps, 58 Albert St (☎09/307 2217).

Melbourne
Bowyangs, 372 Little Bourke St, Melbourne, VIC 3000 (☎03/670 4383).

Perth
Perth Map Centre, 891 Hay St, Perth, WA 6000 (☎09/322 5733).

Sydney
Travel Bookshop, 20 Bridge St, Sydney, NSW 2000 (☎02/241 3554).

COSTS, MONEY AND BANKS

Though Holland is by a slim margin the least expensive country in the Benelux region, it could not be called cheap, and while prices won't be too alarming for British visitors, Americans will find that most things cost a little more than at home.

If you stay in one place, camp or sleep in youth hostels and eat out rarely, you can just about get by on around £20–25 ($32–40) a day; staying in modest hotels, travelling around the country, eating out most evenings, and doing some socializing, expect to spend at least £45 ($70) a day.

MONEY AND BANKS

Dutch **currency** is the guilder, written as "*f*", "fl" or "Dfl" (it was formerly known as the florin), and made up of 100 cents ("c"). It comes in **coins** worth 5c (irritatingly tiny), 10c, 25c, *f*1, *f*2.50, and *f*5; denominations of **bills** are *f*10, *f*25, *f*50, *f*100, and – rarely – *f*250 and *f*1000. At the time of writing the exchange rate was roughly *f*1.7 to one US dollar, just under *f*3 to one pound sterling.

WHAT TO TAKE

The best way of carrying the bulk of your money is in **travellers' cheques**, available from most high street banks (whether or not you have an account) for a usual fee of one percent of the amount ordered. For EU citizens, an alternative is the **Eurocheque** book and card – issued on request by most banks to account holders – which

can be used to get cash in the majority of European banks and bureaux de change or to pay for goods and services like a normal cheque. Bear in mind that you always need to have your passport with you as well as the Eurocheque card to obtain cash at Dutch banks.

CHANGING MONEY

As ever, **banks** are the best place to change travellers' cheques and cash. Their hours are Monday to Friday 9am to 4pm. In the larger cities, Amsterdam for example, some banks are also open Thursday 7 to 9pm and occasionally on Saturday mornings, though changing money at odd times is never a problem, as the nationwide network of *De Grenswisselkantoren* (*GWK*) exchange offices, usually at train stations, are open very late every day – sometimes (as in Amsterdam) even 24 hours. At these you can change money or travellers' cheques, obtain cash advances on all the major credit cards, even arrange travel insurance. You can also change money at most VVV offices, though the rate will be less favourable, as it will at numerous bureaux de change dotted about the larger cities. **Beware** of places such as *Chequepoint* that offer seemingly good rates but then charge very high commissions or, conversely, charge no commission but offer poor rates. Hotels, hostels, and campsites will also often change money: only use them when desperate though – they often give rip-off rates. Basically, when stuck, you're better off using *GWK*.

PLASTIC MONEY

Holland is a cash society; people prefer to pay and be paid with notes and coins. Quite a lot of smaller shops still refuse all other forms of payment (except for Eurocheques, which are widely accepted), although most larger shops, hotels and restaurants will accept at least one of the major **credit cards** – *Visa*, *Mastercard* (*Eurocard*), *American Express*, and *Diners Club* – for a purchase of around *f*50 or more. Subject to a roughly *f*200 minimum, you can also get a (pricy) cash advance on all cards from *GWK* offices and many banks.

COMMUNICATIONS: MAIL, PHONES AND THE MEDIA

Holland's mail and phone systems are easy to use and efficient, whether sending a postcard or calling abroad.

MAIL

Dutch **post offices** are plentiful and easy to use, usually open Monday to Friday 8.30am to 5pm and in cities also often on Saturday 8.30am to noon. Be sure to join the right queue if you only want stamps (*postzegelen*), as post offices handle numerous other services. The charges are ƒ1 for postcards anywhere in the world; ƒ1 for letters up to 20g within Europe, ƒ1.60 outside.

Post boxes are everywhere, but if you're sending something outside Holland, make sure you use the slot marked "Overige". If you're receiving mail rather than sending it, poste restante/general delivery is available at post offices countrywide; to collect items, you need your passport.; make sure they check under middle names and initials, as letters often get misfiled.

PHONES

The Dutch **phone system** is similarly straightforward. Most of the plentiful green-trim **telephone booths** have English instructions, which are normally displayed inside. Most take phonecards only; they're available from post offices, VVVs and train stations and cost ƒ5, ƒ10, or ƒ25. If you're using one of the much less widespread payphones, deposit the money

before making a call and a digital display tells you the amount of credit remaining. The slots take 25c, ƒ1, and ƒ2.50 coins; only wholly unused coins are returned. If you are calling home, in the larger cities it is sometimes easier to use a post office (except in Amsterdam where there's a separate place known as the "Telehouse"), where you can make your call from a booth and settle up afterward. They're open at least the same hours as post offices, sometimes later.

To make a direct call to the UK, dial the code in the box below, wait for the tone and then dial the number, omitting the initial 0. To make a direct call to the US, dial the code in the box below, wait for the tone and then dial the area code and number. To make a reverse charge or collect call, phone the operator (they all speak English). The **discount rate** for calls within Europe operates from 8pm to 8am; to the USA and Canada, it's cheaper to call between 7pm and 10am and (for the USA) at weekends; to Australia and New Zealand, between midnight and 7am. You can, obviously, also call from hotels, though expect this to be much more expensive than from anywhere else.

MEDIA

There's no problem finding **British newspapers**. They're widely available, on the same day of publication in the southern (Randstad) towns, the day after elsewhere, for around ƒ4. The only **American newspapers** available in Holland are the *International Herald Tribune*, which is published in Paris, and *USA Today*. Current issues of UK and US magazines can be found pretty much all over, and in Amsterdam you'll find *Time Out Amsterdam*, a monthly English-language listings guide to the capital. If you're having problems finding UK or US magazines, train station bookstalls are always a good bet, though most newsagents in the larger cities will stock at least a few overseas newspapers and magazines.

Of the **Dutch press**, the right-leaning *De Telegraaf* is one of the most widely read papers, as is the centre-right but less scandal-ridden *Algemeeen Dagsblad. De Volkskrant* is a centre-left daily and *NRC Handelsblad* is a relatively uncommitted paper supposedly favoured by the country's intellectuals.

British TV and radio stations can also be picked up in most parts of Holland. BBC Radio 4 is found on 198khz LW, Radio 5 Live on 693 and 909khz MW and the World Service on 648khz MW and short wave frequencies between 75m and 49m at intervals throughout the day and night. If you're staying somewhere with cable TV, it's possible to tune into BBC1 and BBC2 at most times during the day, and a flick through the stations might also turn up any number of cable and satellite options: Superchannel – an at times dreadfully amateurish mix of videos, soaps, and movies; MTV – 24-hour pop videos; CNN, which gives 24-hour news coverage; or Eurosport – up-to-the-minute footage of contests like the women's world curling championships or European Handball league. There are also the Dutch TV channels, which regularly run American and British programmes and films with Dutch subtitles. In most parts of the country, you've also got the programmes of the Belgian, French, and German networks to choose from, not to mention BBC1 and BBC2.

GETTING AROUND

Getting around is never a problem in Holland: it's a small country, and the longest journey you'll ever make – say from Amsterdam to Maastricht – takes under three hours by train or car. Public transport in and around towns and cities, too, is efficient and cheap, buses (and sometimes trams) running on an easy-to-understand ticketing system that covers the whole country. The two networks link up together neatly, and you'll find bus terminuses and train stations almost invariably next door to each other.

TRAINS

The best way of travelling around Holland is to take the **train**. The system, run by *Nederlandse Spoorwegen* or *NS* (*Netherlands Railways*), is one of the best in Europe: trains are fast, modern, frequent and, normally, very punctual; fares are relatively low, and the network of lines comprehensive. **Ordinary fares** are calculated by the kilometre, diminishing proportionately the further you travel. *NS* publishes a booklet detailing costs and distances, so it's easy enough to work out broadly how much a ticket will cost. As a rough guide, reckon on spending about ƒ13 to travel 50km or so; for a round-trip ticket simply double the price of one way; first-class fares cost about fifty percent on top. With any ticket, you're also free to stop off anywhere en route and continue your journey later that day. For a one-way ticket ask for an "enkele reis"; a return trip is a "retour".

Of a number of ways of saving money on these rates, the **dagretour**, or day return, is the most commonly used, valid for 24 hours and costing around ten percent less than two ordinary one-way tickets. If you're visiting some specific attraction on a day out from somewhere by train, consider also buying a **Rail Idee** ticket – a special

ticket which combines the price of admission to selected sights (say the Hoge Veluwe or the De Efteling theme park) with the price of a return ticket, usually saving a good deal. There are nearly 200 possible excursions in all; the booklet *Er Op Uit!*, (ƒ5.75) has full details of places to visit, though you'll need to read Dutch.

Netherlands Railways publishes mounds of **information** annually on the various services, passes, fares and suchlike – most of it in English. It also produces a condensed **timetable** detailing inter-city services (ƒ2) and a full timetable (*spoor-*

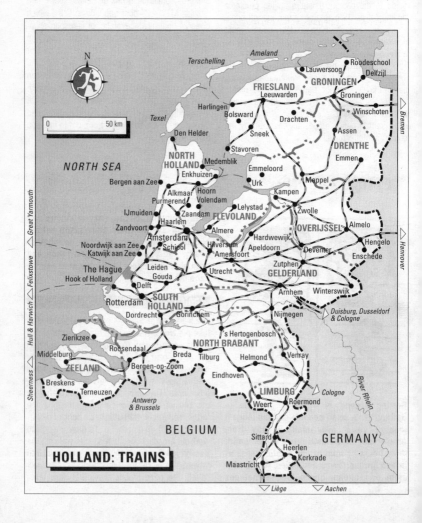

HOLLAND: TRAINS

boekje), available in advance either from the Netherlands Board of Tourism (see p.21 for addresses) or from any Dutch train station (ƒ9.75).

Finally, **train stations** are bright, well-equipped places, with information and facilities that – even in some of the smaller towns – include a coffee shop and restaurant, florist and newspaper/bookshop and often a GWK bureau de change. The food in the restaurants, incidentally, is usually good, filling and reasonably priced.

TRAIN PASSES

If you're travelling extensively by train, you should consider buying a **rail pass**, which can be bought at any train station. **Rover tickets** entitle the holder to unlimited travel anywhere in Holland at a cost of ƒ66 (second-class) for one day, and there are various deals and passes available in summer, as well as arrangements for **families and groups** of people travelling together.

There are also a number of passes that can be bought outside Holland, which can be useful if you're travelling through more than one country. For those **under 26** (and resident in Europe for six months) the **InterRail** pass works on a zonal basis: the Netherlands falls into Zone E (along with France, Belgium and Luxembourg). A pass to travel in this zone for 15 days currently costs £185, and can be bought in Britain from *International Rail*, larger train stations or student/youth travel agents. Those **over 26** are poorly served by *InterRail* passes, as the over-26 version costs £215 for fifteen days' travel, or £275 for a month, but is not valid for travel in France, Belgium, Switzerland, Italy, Spain, Portugal or Morocco. Stringing together combinations of *Euro Domino* passes (see below) is a better option.

A convenient alternative to *InterRail*, infinitely more convenient if you're over 26, is the **Euro Domino** pass (also called the "Freedom" pass), which is valid for unlimited travel within a single country, though you can buy several to run concurrently in different countries. There is no residence requirement for these tickets (very useful for non-EU visitors), and also no age restriction, and they are remarkably good value. *Euro Dominos* are valid for either three, five or ten days' travel within an overall period of one month: prices for Holland are, for under-26s, £29, £49 and £79 (IR£28, IR£42 and IR£73); for over-26s £39, £69 and £109 (IR£37, IR£59 and IR£105). The Netherlands is also unique in having a **Euro Domino Plus** pass, which covers travel on any form of public transport in the country (trains, buses, trams and the metro) for the same time periods. Prices are slightly higher, but can be extremely good value: under-26s pay £39, £59 or £99 (IRE36, IRE55 or IRE94); over-26s pay £49, £79 or £129 (IRE46, IRE72 or IRE125). Although you can't use an *InterRail* ticket for travel in the country in which you bought it, you *can* buy a *Euro Domino* ticket for Holland after you've arrived (you need to show your passport); this usually works out a little cheaper than buying in advance. **Bought in Holland**, over 26s pay ƒ90 (3 days), ƒ140 (5 days) or ƒ250 (10 days); for under 26s it's ƒ65/ƒ99/ƒ175. The extra card, giving additional free use of town and country buses and trams all over the country costs ƒ17 for three days, ƒ28 for five days, ƒ45 for ten days. An equivalent available to North Americans is the **Holland Rail** pass, which is valid for unlimited travel for either three, five or ten days within a period of one month. Prices are, for under-26s, $56, $79 and $130; for over-26s $68/88, $104/140 and $184/260, depending on whether you travel second- or first-class. You can also buy the pass once in Holland.

If you're planning to travel in Belgium and/or Luxembourg, consider too the **Benelux Tourrail Card**, valid for any five days within a specified seventeen on all three national rail networks as well as country buses in Luxembourg. It must be brought abroad and is available, in England, from *Holland Rail* for £80 (£54 if you're under 26), and in America from *Rail Europe* (see p.14), for $217 first-class, $155 second-class, and $104 for under-26s.

See also p.5, p.14 and p.18 for more information on train passes.

TREINTAXIS

Everywhere in Holland buses stop outside train stations, but if you don't wish to take a bus, *NS* has devised a **treintaxi** scheme, whereby for ƒ6 a head in many towns across the country, excluding Amsterdam, The Hague, Rotterdam and Utrecht, a taxi will take you from the train station to anywhere within the city limits, even if you're travelling alone – though drivers are supposed to wait ten minutes for other passengers. Vouchers for *treintaxis* should be purchased when you buy your train ticket, although you can sometimes get them at the other end if you show your ticket.

BUSES

Supplementing the extensive train network are **buses** – run by local companies but again ruthlessly efficient, spreading out to span the local surroundings from ranks of bus stops almost always located bang next to the train station. Ticketing is simple, organized on a system that covers the whole country. You need to buy just one kind of ticket wherever you are, a ***strippenkaart***. The country is divided into zones: the driver will cancel one strip on your *strippenkaart* for your journey plus one for each of the zones you travel through (on city trams and metro systems it's up to you to cancel it yourself: see the *Amsterdam* chapter). In the larger towns and cities you'll find you only need to use two zones for the centre. You can buy 2-, 3- or 8-strip *strippenkaarts* from bus drivers, or pick up the better-value 15-strip (*f*11) or 45-strip (*f*32.25) *strippenkaarts* in advance from train stations, tobacconists and local public transport offices. If you're in Holland during the summer months and are intending to travel around a lot by bus, it can be well worth investing in a *Zomerzwerfkaart*, which gives free access to all bus routes. It currently costs *f*16 per day for adults and *f*10 for under-12s and over-65s.

DRIVING AND HITCHING

Driving around Holland is pretty much what you would expect – painless and quick. The country has a uniformly good and comprehensive road network, most of the major towns are linked by some kind of motorway or dual carriageway, and things only get congested on the outskirts of the

major cities. **Rules of the road** are similar to other mainland European countries: you drive on the right; speed limits are 50kph in built-up areas, 80kph outside, 120kph on motorways – though some motorways have a speed limit of 100kph, indicated by small yellow signs on the side of the road. Drivers and front-seat passengers are required by law to wear seatbelts, and crackdowns on drunken driving are severe. There are no toll roads, and although petrol isn't particularly cheap, at around *f*2 per litre, the short distances mean this isn't much of a factor.

To drive in Holland, British and Irish drivers need their full home **driver's licence**. If you're driving your own car, check with your insurance company as to whether or not your policy covers you abroad: if not, you'll need a green insurance card, though you can obtain last-minute insurance cover at border exchange offices. North Americans and Australasians need an International Driver's Licence, obtainable from the *AAA* (USA), *RAC* (Australia) or *AA* (New Zealand) for a small charge. If you **break down**, the Dutch motoring organization, the ANWB – known as the *Wegenwacht* – offers reciprocal repair/breakdown services to members of most international motoring organizations, as long as they hold a Letter of International Assistance – available from your home organization. The ANWB's nationwide number is ☎06/0888, and there are special telephones by the side of the highway. If you're not a member of your home motoring organization, you can either pay for this service or, for a *f*150 fee, become a member of the ANWB (much the best option).

Car rental costs are comparable with the UK, although considerably higher than in the US:

CAR RENTAL COMPANIES			
IN AUSTRALIA and NEW ZEALAND		Eurodollar	☎0990/565656
Avis Australia ☎1800/225 533, New Zealand ☎09/579 5231		Europcar	☎0345/222525
		Hertz	☎0990/996699
Budget Australia ☎13 2848, New Zealand ☎09/375 2220		Holiday Autos	☎0990/300400
Hertz Australia ☎13 3039, New Zealand ☎09/309 0989		**IN NORTH AMERICA**	
		Avis	☎ 1-800/331-1084
IN THE UK		Budget	☎1-800/527-0700
Avis	☎0181/848 8733	Dollar	☎1-800/421-6868
Budget	☎0800/181181	Hertz	☎1-800/654-3001

prices for the smallest vehicle (inclusive of collision damage waiver and insurance) start at ƒ600 for a small car for a week or around ƒ60 a day plus 60c per kilometre. Of the international companies, *Hertz* tend to be the cheapest: you should make some savings by going to local operators. Bear in mind, too, that it's always cheaper to rent your car before you leave home and pick it up at the airport on arrival: a good agent for this in the UK is *Holiday Autos*.

Hitching is feasible throughout the country: the Dutch are usually well disposed towards giving lifts, and the dense population and road network means it's unusual to get stuck anywhere. Bear in mind, though, that highways are hard to avoid, and that it's only legal to hitch on approach roads or at the special places seen on the outskirts of some larger cities, known as *liftplaatsen*.

CYCLING

If you're not especially short of time, **cycling** is *the* way to see the country. Holland's largely flat landscape makes travelling by bike an almost effortless pursuit, and the short distances involved make it possible to see most of the country this way, using the nationwide system of well-marked cycle paths – which often divert away from the main roads into the countryside. The 1:100,000 ANWB maps show all the cycle paths and are perfectly adequate for touring. Ask also for the NBT booklet, *Cycling in Holland*, which details a number of suggested routes and has other advice for cyclists.

The NBT, in association with regional VVV offices, also organize **cycling package holidays** all over the country, which include bicycles, accommodation, maps and other information and are generally excellent value.

Most people, however, either **bring their own bike** or **rent one**. Bikes can be rented from all main train stations for ƒ8 a day or ƒ32 per week plus a ƒ50 deposit (ƒ200 in larger centres); if you have a valid train ticket, it costs just ƒ6 a day or ƒ24 per week with a *treinfiets* voucher. You'll also need some form of ID. The snag is that cycles must be returned to the station from which they were rented, making onward hops by rented bike impossible. Most bike shops rent bicycles out for around the same amount as train stations, though they may be more flexible on deposits – some accept a passport in lieu of cash; otherwise, again expect to leave ƒ50–200. Wherever you rent your bike from, in summer it is a good idea to reserve one in advance.

It is possible to take your **bike on trains**, but it isn't encouraged, and a ticket costs ƒ9–25 depending on the day and time of year. Be warned that space is limited and you're not allowed to load your bike on at all during the rush hour – between 6.30am and 9am and 4.30pm and 6pm. Bear in mind that you should never, ever, leave your bike **unlocked**, even for a few minutes. In the larger cities especially, used bikes are big business, the prey of thieves armed with bolt-cutters. Almost all train stations have somewhere you can store your bike for around ƒ2 a day.

ACCOMMODATION

Accommodation is not particularly cheap in Holland, though a wide network of official and unofficial youth hostels and generally well-equipped campsites can help to cut costs. Wherever you stay, you should book during the summer and over holiday periods like Easter, when places can run short.

HOTEL PRICE CODES

All the establishments we have listed in the *Guide* have been **graded** according to the following categories. They are above all a guide to price, and give no indication of the facilities you might expect to find other than the broad outlines given below. Note that, apart from grade ① which is calculated per person, the **prices** we give are for the cheapest double room – ie without private bath, etc – during high season. You will find many bottom-end hotels have a mixture of rooms, some with private facilities, some without; thus you may find that a good standard ③ category hotel has quite a number of ④ rooms as well.

① Up to ƒ40 per person. Hostel accommodation, either a private hostel or an official youth hostel, (part of the IYHF), where charges are in fact often slightly cheaper – up to ƒ25 a night. At most hostels this price will get you dormitory accommodation, shared facilities, and (sometimes) a frugal breakfast. Both official and private hostels will often have some level of private accommodation too – single-, double-, even triple-bedded rooms, which normally fall into the price range of the following category.

② ƒ60–100. Either private rooms arranged through the local tourist office, or the most basic form of hotel accommodation, not normally with any kind of private facilities beyond a washbasin in the room, and rarely recognized or rated by the tourist office. At this grade, given the choice between a hotel and a private room in someone's home, the latter will invariably be more appealing, if more restricting as regards your comings and goings.

③ ƒ100–150. Two-star hotel accommodation, where there will often be a choice of shared and private facilities. Probably the most common category we recommend, and definitely the best choice if you're not on too tight a budget and want to spend more than a night or two somewhere. At this price you may occasionally enjoy the use of a telephone and TV too, but don't count on it.

④ ƒ150–200. Two-star moving on occasion into three-star hotel accommodation, where facilities will always be private and you will invariably have the benefit of a TV, telephone, etc, though probably not room service.

⑤ ƒ200–250. Solid three-star hotels, probably bigger and better-equipped places than the previous category, and always with private facilities, telephone, and TV and room service in larger establishments, even if the rooms aren't likely to be hugely different in quality.

⑥ ƒ250–300. The bottom end of four-star hotels. Normally all rooms will have private facilities, telephone, TV and room service. There will usually be other facilities – laundry, etc – and there may even be bonuses like a gym or swimming pool. Once up to this sort of category, breakfast, oddly enough, is not always included in the price.

⑦ ƒ300–400. We've included this category in order to take in really decent four- and five-star hotels with excellent facilities, and to include really special places, which charge for their location, environment, or simply their service. They're definitely not places at which to spend every night of your trip, even if you could afford it, as there are almost always plenty of very desirable cheaper options. However, if you feel like pampering yourself, or it's a special occasion, they come highly recommended.

HOTELS AND PRIVATE ROOMS

All **hotels** in Holland are graded on a star system up to five stars. One-star and no-star hotels are rare, and prices for two-star establishments start at around ƒ75 for a double room without private bath or shower; count on paying at least ƒ100 if you want your own facilities. Three-star hotels cost upwards of about ƒ150; for four- and five-star places you'll pay ƒ250-plus, which won't always include breakfast. In cheaper places prices usually include a reasonable breakfast, though not always; be sure to check first as some hotels use this as a sneaky way of adding ƒ10 or so to your bill.

During the summer, in all parts of the country but especially in Amsterdam and the major tourist centres, it's a good idea to **reserve** a room in advance. You can do this most easily by calling the hotel direct – we've listed phone numbers throughout the *Guide*, and English is almost always spoken so there should be no language problem. You can also contact the *Netherlands Reservations Centre* (NRC), PO Box 404, 2260 AK Leidschendam (Mon–Fri 8am–8pm, Sat 8am–2pm; ☎070/317 5454, fax 320 2611), which can book hotel rooms, apartments, and cabins all over the country. Bookings are confirmed in writing and the service is free. In Holland itself, you can make advance bookings in person through VVV offices, usually for a fee of ƒ3.50 per person.

One way of cutting costs is, wherever possible, to use **private accommodation** – rooms in private homes that are let out to visitors on a bed and breakfast basis; they're sometimes known as pensions. Prices are usually quoted per person and are normally around ƒ30–35; breakfast is usually included, but if not will cost about ƒ5 on top. You have to go through the VVV to find private rooms: they will either give you a list to follow up independently or will insist they book the accommodation themselves and levy the appropriate booking fee. Bear in mind, also, that not all VVVs are able to offer private accommodation; generally you'll find it only in the larger towns and tourist centres.

HOSTELS, SLEEP-INS, STUDENT ROOMS

There are 37 official **youth hostels** in Holland, all affiliated to the IYHF (HI) and open to members for ƒ25 per person per night, including breakfast. Accommodation is usually in small dormitories, though some hostels have single- and double-bedded rooms. Meals are often available – about ƒ16 for a filling dinner – and in some hostels there are kitchens where you can cook your own food. It is possible for non-members to stay in official hostels, though they'll pay ƒ5 more; given the price of membership, it's worth joining even if you're only going to be doing a little hostelling. You should book in advance if possible during the summer, as some places get crammed. For a full list of Dutch hostels, contact the *Nederlandse Jeugdherberg Central* (*NJHC*), Prof. Tulpstraat 2, 1018 HA Amsterdam (☎020/622 2859, fax 639 0199).

In addition to official hostels, the larger cities – particularly Amsterdam – often have a number of **unofficial hostels** offering dormitory accommodation (and invariably double- and triple-bedded

YOUTH HOSTEL ASSOCIATIONS

American Youth Hostels (AYH), 733 15th St NW, PO Box 37613, Washington, DC 20005 (☎202/783-6161).

Australian Youth Hostels Association, Level 3, 10 Mallett St, Camperdown, Sydney (☎02/9565-1325).

Canadian Hostelling Association, Room 400, 205 Catherine St, Ottawa, Ontario K2P 1C3 (☎613/237-7884 or 1-800/663-5777).

England and Wales Youth Hostel Association (YHA), Trevelyan House, 8 St Stephen's Hill, St Alban's, Herts AL1

(☎01727/855215). London shop and information office: 14 Southampton St, London WC2 (☎0171/836 1036).

Ireland An Óige, 39 Mountjoy Square, Dublin 1 (☎01/830 4555).

New Zealand Youth Hostels Association, PO Box 436, Christchurch 1 (☎03/379 9970).

Northern Ireland Youth Hostel Association, 56 Bradbury Place, Belfast, BT7 (☎0232/324733).

Scottish Youth Hostel Association, 7 Glebe Crescent, Stirling, FK8 2JA (☎01786/451181).

rooms, too) at broadly similar prices, though inevitably standards are frequently not as high or as reliable as the official *IYHF* places (and some are extremely poor). We've detailed possibilities in the *Guide*. In some cities you may also come across something known as a **Sleep-in** – dormitory accommodation established and run by the local council, which is often cheaper than regular hostels and normally only open during the summer. Locations vary from year to year; again, we've tried to give some indication of locations in the *Guide*, but for the most current information contact the VVV. The same goes for **student accommodation**, which is sporadically open to travellers during the summer holidays in some university towns. We've detailed definite possibilities in the guide, but the VVV usually has up-to-date information.

CAMPSITES AND CABINS

Camping is a serious option in Holland: there are plenty of sites, most are very well equipped, and they represent a good saving on other forms of accommodation. Prices vary greatly, mainly depending on the number of facilities available, but you can generally expect to pay around *f*5 per person, plus another *f*5–10 for a tent, and another *f*5 or so if you have a car or motorcycle. Everywhere the VVV will have details of the nearest site, and we've given indications throughout the *Guide*. There's also a free NBT list of selected sites, and the ANWB publishes an annual list of Dutch campsites, available from bookstores in Holland. Alternatively, contact the camping association *Stichting Vrije Recreatie*, at Broekseweg 75–77, 4231 VD Meerskerk (☎0183/352 741, fax 351 234).

Some sites can also offer **cabins**, known as *trekkershutten* – spartanly furnished affairs that can house a maximum of four people for around *f*45 a night. Again, both the NBT and ANWB can provide a list of these, though you should normally book in advance – either by phoning the site direct or through the *Netherlands Reservations Centre* (address and phone number on p.31).

FOOD AND DRINK

Holland is – quite rightly – not renowned for its cuisine, but although much is unimaginative, it's rarely unpleasant, and if you're selective prices are rarely high enough to break the bank. There's a good supply of ethnic restaurants, especially Indonesian and Chinese; and even Dutch food holds one or two surprises. Drinking is easily affordable – indeed, downing a Dutch beer at one of the country's many good bars is one of the real pleasures of visiting Holland.

FOOD

Dutch food tends to be higher in protein content than in variety: steak, chicken and fish, along with filling soups and stews, are staple fare, usually served up in enormous quantities. It can, however, at its best, be excellent, some restaurants offering increasingly adventurous crossovers with French cuisine at good-value prices, especially *eetcafés* and bars.

BREAKFAST

In all but the very cheapest hostels or most expensive hotels **breakfast** (*ontbijt*) will be included in the price of the room. Though usually nothing fancy, it's always substantial: rolls, cheese, ham, hard-boiled eggs, jam and honey, or peanut butter are the principal ingredients. If you don't have a hotel breakfast, many bars and cafés serve rolls and sandwiches and some offer a set breakfast.

The **coffee** is normally good and strong, around ƒ2 a cup, served with a little tub of *koffiemelk* (evaporated milk); ordinary milk is rarely used. If you want coffee with warm milk, ask for a *koffie verkeerd*. Most bars also serve cappuccino and espresso, though many stop serving coffee altogether around 11pm. **Tea** generally comes with lemon if anything – if you want milk you have to ask for it. **Chocolate** (*chocomel*) is also popular, hot or cold: for a real treat drink it hot with a layer of fresh whipped cream (*slagroom*) on top. Some coffee shops also sell aniseed-flavoured warm milk or *anijsmelk*.

SNACKS, CAKES, CHEESES

For the rest of the day, eating cheaply and well, particularly on your feet, is no real problem, although those on the tightest of budgets may find themselves dependent on the dubious delights of **Dutch fast food**. This has its own peculiarities. Chips – *frites* or *patat* – are the most common standby (*vlaamse* or "Flemish" *frites* are the best), sprinkled with salt and smothered with huge gobs of mayonnaise (*fritesaus*) or, alternatively, curry, sate, goulash, or tomato sauce. If you just want salt, ask for "patat zonder"; fries with salt and mayonnaise are "patat met". Chips are complemented with *kroketten* – spiced minced meat covered with breadcrumbs and deep fried – or *fricandel*, a frankfurter-like sausage. All these are available over the counter at evil-smelling fast-food places (*Febo* is the most common chain), or, for a guilder or so, from heated glass compartments outside.

Tastier, and good both as a snack and a full lunch, are the **fish specialities** sold by street vendors: salted raw herring, smoked eel (*gerookte paling*), mackerel in a roll (*broodje makreel*), mussels, and various kinds of deep-fried fish. Look out, too, for "green" or *maatje* herring, eaten raw with onions in early summer. Tip your head back and dangle the fish into your mouth, Dutch-style. A nationwide chain of fish restaurants, *Noordzee*, serves up well-priced fish-based rolls and sandwiches as well as good-value fish lunches.

Another fast snack you'll see everywhere is **shoarma** – kebabs, basically, sold in numerous Middle Eastern restaurants and takeaways. A shoarma in pitta will set you back about ƒ6 on average. Other street foods include **pancakes**, sweet or spicy, also widely available at sit-down restaurants; **waffles**, doused with syrup; and **poffertjes**, shell-shaped dumplings served with masses of melted butter and powdered sugar – an extremely filling snack. Try also **oliebollen**, greasy doughnuts sometimes filled with fruit (often apple) or custard (a *berliner*) and traditionally served at New Year. Dutch **cakes and cookies** are always good, and filling, best eaten in a *banketbakkerij* with a small serving area; or buy a bag and eat them on the hoof. Apart from the ubiquitous *appelgebak* – wedges of apple and cinnamon tart – things to try include *spekulaas*, a cinnamon cookie with gingerbread texture; *stroopwafels*, butter wafers sandwiched together with runny syrup, and *amandelkoek*, cakes with a crisp cookie outside and melt-in-the-mouth almond paste inside. In Limburg you should also sample *Limburgse Vlaai* – a pie with various fruit fillings.

As for the kind of food you can expect to encounter in bars, there are **sandwiches and rolls** (*boterham* and *broodjes*) – often open, and varying from a slice of tired cheese on old bread to something so embellished it's almost a complete meal – as well as different kinds of more substantial fare. A sandwich made with French bread is known as a *stokbrood*. In the winter, *erwtensoep* (or *snert*) – thick pea soup with smoked sausage, served with a portion of smoked bacon on *pumpernickel* – is available in most bars, and at about ƒ6 a bowl makes a great buy for lunch. Or there's an *uitsmijter* (literally, "bouncer"): one, two, or three fried eggs on buttered bread, topped with a choice of ham, cheese, or roast beef – at about ƒ8, another good budget lunch.

Holland's **cheeses** have an unjustified reputation abroad for being bland. This is because they tend to export the lower quality products and keep the best for themselves. In fact, Dutch cheese can be delicious, although there isn't the variety you get in, say, France or Italy. Most are based on the same soft creamy Goudas, and differences in taste come with the varying stages of maturity – jong, belegen, or oud. Jong cheese has a mild flavour, belegen is much tastier, while oud can be pungent and strong, with a flaky texture not unlike parmesan. Among the other cheeses you'll find, best known is the round red Edam, made principally for export and not eaten much by the Dutch; Leidse, simply Gouda with cumin seeds; Leerdammer and Maasdammer, strong, creamy, and full of holes; and Dutch-made

DUTCH FOOD AND DRINK TERMS

Basics

Boter	Butter	*Nagerechten*	Desserts
Brood	Bread	*Peper*	Pepper
Broodje	Sandwich/roll	*Pindakaas*	Peanut butter
Dranken	Drinks	*Sla/salade*	Salad
Eieren	Eggs	*Smeerkaas*	Cheese spread
Groenten	Vegetables	*Stokbrood*	French bread
Gerst	Semolina: the type of grain used in Algerian *couscous*, popular in vegetarian restaurants	*Suiker*	Sugar
		Vis	Fish
		Vlees	Meat
		Voorgerechten	Appetizers, hors d'oeuvres
Honing	Honey	*Vruchten*	Fruit
Hoofdgerechten	Entrées	*Warm*	Hot
Kaas	Cheese	*Zout*	Salt
Koud	Cold		

Appetizers and snacks

Erwtensoep/snert	Thick pea soup with bacon or sausage	*Uitsmijter*	Ham or cheese with eggs on bread
Huzarensalade	Egg salad	*Koffietafel*	A light midday meal of cold meats, cheese, bread and perhaps soup
Patats/Frites	French fries		
Soep	Soup		

Meat and poultry

Biefstuk (hollandse)	Steak	*Kalfsvlees*	Veal
Eend	Duck	*Karbonade*	Chop
Fricandeau	Roast pork	*Kip*	Chicken
Fricandel	A frankfurter-like sausage	*Kroket*	Spiced meat in breadcrumbs
Gehakt	Ground meat	*Lamsvlees*	Lamb
Ham	Ham	*Lever*	Liver
Hutspot	Beef stew with vegetables	*Rookvlees*	Smoked beef
		Spek	Bacon
Kalkoen	Turkey	*Worst*	Sausages

Fish

Forel	Trout	*Kabeljauw*	Cod	*Schol*	Flounder
Garnalen	Shrimp	*Makreel*	Mackerel	*Schelvis*	Shellfish
Haring	Herring	*Mosselen*	Mussels	*Tong*	Sole
Haringsalade	Herring salad	*Paling*	Eel	*Zalm*	Salmon

terms

Doorbakken	Well done	*Gerookt*	Smoked
Gebakken	Fried/baked	*Gestoofd*	Stewed
Gebraden	Roasted	*Half doorbakken*	Medium
Gekookt	Boiled	*Hollandse saus*	Hollandaise (butter and egg sauce)
Gegrild	Grilled		
Geraspt	Grated		

Vegetables

Aardappelen	Potatoes	*Champignons*	Mushrooms	*Rijst*	Rice
Bloemkool	Cauliflower	*Erwten*	Peas	*Sla*	Salad, lettuce
Boerenkool	A kind of cabbage	*Knoflook*	Garlic	*Uien*	Onions
		Komkommer	Cucumber	*Wortelen*	Carrots
Bonen	Beans	*Prei*	Leek	*Zuurkool*	Sauerkraut

Indonesian, Chinese and Surinamese dishes and terms

Ajam	Chicken	*Nasi Rames*	*Rijsttafel* on a single plate
Bami	Fried noodles with meat/chicken and vegetables	*Pedis*	Hot and spicy
		Pisang	Banana
Daging	Beef	*Rijsttafel*	Collection of different spicy dishes served with plain rice
Gado gado	Vegetables in peanut sauce		
Goreng	Fried	*Sambal*	Hot, chilli-based sauce
Ikan	Fish	*Satesaus*	Peanut sauce to accompany meat broiled on skewers
Katjang	Peanut		
Kroepoek	Shrimp crackers	*Seroendeng*	Spicy fried, shredded coconut
Loempia	Egg rolls	*Tauge*	Bean shoots
Nasi	Rice		
Nasi Goreng	Fried rice with meat/chicken and vegetables		

Desserts

Appelgebak	Apple tart or cake	*Oliebollen*	Doughnuts
Drop	Dutch liquorice, available in *zoet* (sweet) or *zout* (salted) varieties – the latter an acquired taste	*Pannekoeken*	Pancakes
		Poffertjes	Small pancakes, fritters
		(Slag) room	(Whipped) cream
Gebak	Pastry	*Speculaas*	Spice- and honey-flavoured biscuit
Ijs	Ice cream	*Stroopwafels*	Waffles
Koekjes	Cookies	*Vla*	Custard

Fruit and nuts

Aardbei	Strawberry	*Druif*	Grape	*Peer*	Pear
Amandel	Almond	*Framboos*	Raspberry	*Perzik*	Peach
Appel	Apple	*Hazelnoot*	Hazelnut	*Pinda*	Peanut
Appelmoes	Apple purée	*Kers*	Cherry	*Pruim*	Plum/prune
Citroen	Lemon	*Kokosnoot*	Coconut		

Drinks

Anijsmelk	Aniseed-flavoured warm milk	*Met ijs*	With ice
Appelsap	Apple juice	*Met slagroom*	With whipped cream
Bessenjenever	Blackcurrant gin	*Pils*	Dutch beer
Chocomel	Chocolate milk	*Proost* !	Cheers!
Citroenjenever	Lemon gin	*Sinaasappelsap*	Orange juice
Droog	Dry	*Thee*	Tea
Frisdranken	Sodas	*Tomatensap*	Tomato juice
Jenever	Dutch gin	*Vieux*	Dutch brandy
Karnemelk	Buttermilk	*Vruchtensap*	Fruit juice
Koffie	Coffee	*Wijn*	Wine
Koffie verkeerd	Coffee with warm milk	*(wit/rood/rose)*	(white/red/rosé)
Kopstoot	Beer with a *jenever* chaser	*Zoet*	Sweet
Melk	Milk		

Emmentals and Gruyères. The best way to eat cheese here is the way the Dutch do it, in thin slices (cut with a cheese slice or kaasschaaf) rather than in large hunks.

SIT-DOWN EATING

The majority of **bars** serve food, everything from sandwiches to a full menu, in which case they may be known as an **eetcafé**. These type of places tend to be open all day, serving both lunch and dinner. Full-blown **restaurants**, on the other hand, tend to open in the evening only, usually from around 5.30pm or 6pm until around 11pm. Bear in mind that everywhere, especially in the smaller provincial towns, the Dutch tend to eat early, usually around 7.30pm or 8pm, and that after about 10pm you'll find many restaurant kitchens closed.

If you're on a budget, stick to **dagschotels** (dish of the day) wherever possible, for which you pay around ƒ12–15 for a meat or fish dish, heavily garnished with potatoes and other vegetables and salad; note, though, that it's often only served at lunchtime or between 6pm and 8pm. Otherwise, you can pay up to ƒ25 for a meat course in an average restaurant; fish is generally high quality but rarely cheap at ƒ25–30. The three-course **tourist menu**, which you'll see displayed at some mainstream restaurants, is – at ƒ25 or so – reasonable value, but the food is often dull. Surprisingly enough, **train station restaurants** are a good standby: every station has one serving full meals, in huge portions, for ƒ10–15. Consider also Holland's cheapest option for eating out, the university **mensa restaurants** in larger towns, where, with international student ID you can get a filling, if not especially exciting, meal for under ƒ12.

Eating vegetarian isn't a problem in Holland. Many *eetcafés* and restaurants have at least one meat-free menu item, and you'll find a few vegetarian restaurants in most towns, offering full-course set meals for ƒ10–15. Bear in mind that vegetarian restaurants often close early.

Of foreign cuisines, **Italian** food is ubiquitous: pizzas and pasta dishes start at a fairly uniform ƒ12 or so in all but the ritziest places. To eat **Spanish** and **Tex-Mex** costs a little more. **Surinam** restaurants are a good bet for eating on a budget: try *roti*, flat pancake-like bread served with a spicy curry, hardboiled egg, and vegetables. **Chinese** and **Indonesian** restaurants, too, are widespread (sometimes they're combined), and

are normally well worth checking out. You can eat à la carte – *Nasi Goreng* and *Bami Goreng* (rice or noodles with meat) are good basic dishes, though there are normally more exciting things on the menu, some very spicy and chicken or beef in peanut sauce (*sate*) is always available. Or try a *rijstaffel*: boiled rice and/or noodles served with a huge number of spicy side dishes and hot *sambal* sauce on the side. Eaten with the spoon in the right hand, fork in the left, and with dry white or rosé wine, or beer, this doesn't come cheap, but it's delicious and is normally more than enough for two; indeed that's the usual way to order it – reckon on paying around ƒ75 for two people.

DRINKING

Most **drinking** is done either in the cosy surroundings of a **brown café** (*bruin kroeg*) – so named because of the colour of the walls, often stained by years of tobacco smoke – or in more modern-looking **designer bars**, minimally furnished and usually catering for a younger crowd. Most bars open until around 1am during the week, 2am at weekends, though some don't bother to open until lunchtime, a few not until around 4pm. There is another drinking establishment that you may come across, though they're no longer all that common – *proeflokaalen* or **tasting houses**, originally the sampling houses of small distillers, now small, old-fashioned bars that only serve spirits and close around 8pm. Note that many cafés are a good source of budget **food**, when they're sometimes designated *eetcafés*. Most bars offer sandwiches and soup, or at least hard-boiled eggs from the bar.

BEER

Other than in tasting houses, the most commonly consumed beverage is **beer**. This is usually served in small measures (just under a British half-pint); ask for "een pils" – "may I have?" is "mag ik?", as in "mag ik een pils?". The Dutch like their beer with a foaming head, and requests to have it poured without a head meet with various responses, but it's worth trying. Prices are fairly standard: you don't pay much over the odds for sitting outside or drinking in a swanky bar or club; reckon on paying about ƒ2.75 a glass pretty much everywhere. Some bars, particularly those popular with the local English community, serve beer in larger measures, similar to the British pint, for which you can expect to pay ƒ6–8. Beer is much cheaper from a supermarket, most brands retailing at a little over *f*1 for a half-litre bottle (a little less than half a pint).

The most common names are *Heineken*, *Amstel*, *Oranjeboom* and *Grolsch*, all of which you can find more or less nationwide. Expect them to be stronger and more distinctive than the watery approximations brewed under licence outside Holland. In the southern provinces of North Brabant and Limburg you'll also find a number of locally brewed beers – *Bavaria* from Brabant, *De Ridder*, *Leeuw*, *Gulpen* and *Brand* (the latter the country's oldest brewer) from Limburg, all of which are worth trying. For something a little less strong, look out for *Donkenbier*, which is about half the strength of an ordinary pilsener beer.

You will also, of course, especially in the south of the country, see plenty of the better-known **Belgian brands**, like *Stella Artois* and the darker *De Koninck*, available on tap, and bottled beers like *Duvel*, *Chimay* and various brands of the cherry-flavoured *Kriek*. There are also a number of beers which are **seasonally available**: *Bokbier* (bock beer) is widespread in autumn; white beers (*witbieren*) like *Hoegaarden*, *Dentergems* and *Raaf* are available in summer, often served with a slice of a lemon – very refreshing.

WINE AND SPIRITS

Wine is reasonably priced – expect to pay around *f*6 or so for an average bottle of French white or red. As for **spirits**, the indigenous drink is **jenever**, or Dutch gin – not unlike British gin, but a bit weaker and oilier, made from molasses and flavoured with juniper berries: it's served in small glasses and is traditionally drunk straight, often knocked back in one gulp with much hearty back-slapping. There are a number of varieties: *Oud* (old) is smooth and mellow, *Jong* (young) packs more of a punch – though neither is extremely alcoholic. *Zeer oude* is very old jenever. The older jenevers are a little more expensive but are stronger and less oily. In a bar, ask for a *borreltje* (straight jenever) or a *bittertje* (with angostura); if you've a sweet tooth, try a *bessenjenever* – blackcurrant-flavoured gin; for a glass of beer with a jenever chaser, ask for a *kopstoot*. A glass of jenever in a bar will cost you around *f*3; in a supermarket bottles sell for around *f*15. Imported spirits are considerably more expensive.

Other drinks you'll see include numerous Dutch **liqueurs**, notably *advocaat* or eggnog, the sweet blue *curaçao* and luminous green *pisang ambon*, as well as an assortment of luridly coloured **fruit brandies** best left for experimentation at the end of an evening. There's also the Dutch-produced brandy, *Vieux*, which tastes as if it's made from prunes but is in fact grape-based, and various regional firewaters, such as *elske* from Maastricht – made from the leaves, berries and bark of alder bushes.

GALLERIES, MUSEUMS AND CHURCHES

Holland is strong on museums and galleries: most towns have at least a small collection of Dutch art worth looking at, as well as several other museums.

GALLERIES AND MUSEUMS

There are a number of **different kinds of museum** you'll come across time and again: a *Rijksmuseum* is a state-run museum, housing a national collection on a specific theme; a *Stedelijk* or *Gemeente* museum is run by the local town council and can vary from a small but quality collection of art to dusty arrays of local archeological finds; a *tentoonstelling* is a temporary exhibition, usually of contemporary art. **Hours** are fairly uniform across the country – generally Tuesday to Saturday 10am to 5pm, Sunday 1pm or 2pm to 5pm; entry prices for the more ordinary collections are usually around ƒ2–5, children half-price. Many museums offer at least some English information, even if it's just a returnable leaflet.

CHURCHES

Dutch **churches** are normally rather austere – stripped bare after the Reformation, their spartan, white-painted walls emphasizing the effect of their often soaring Gothic lines. Organs are often the only embellishment, with great, ornate cases that put out a terrific – and awesome – noise, and only in the Catholic south of the country does the occasional church still retain anything of the mystery of pre-Calvinist rituals. Hours for visitors vary, though northern churches do usually have set times when visits are possible – assuming, of course, that there's something inside worth seeing. Falling attendances, however, also mean that some churches have been pragmatically turned over to other purposes – exhibition halls, concert halls, even apartments. In the south, unless there's something of special interest, you may find visits confined to services.

MUSEUM DISCOUNTS

If you're planning to visit a fair number of museums in Holland – or even if you intend to visit just one museum three or four times – you'd be well advised to buy a **museumjaarkaart** ("museum year card"), which allows you free or reduced admission to more than 400 museums throughout the country for an entire year. They're sold at VVVs and at museums (you'll need a passport photo), and cost ƒ47.50 (ƒ15.50 for people under 24) – a bargain, considering you'll fork out a hefty ƒ25 to get into Amsterdam's Rijksmuseum or Van Gogh museum alone.

An alternative for people under 26 is the *Cultureel Jongeren Paspoort* or **CJP**, which gives reductions in museums and on theatre, cinema and concert tickets for ƒ20 – though bear in mind that the discounts vary wildly and in many cases are not that substantial. CJPs are valid across Holland and are available from the Uitburo in Amsterdam (see p.105). Note that student ID alone isn't enough to get you reduced admission at any of the country's museums. Finally, if you're travelling as a family, ask at the larger museums about discounted **family tickets**.

POLICE AND TROUBLE

There's little reason why you should ever come into contact with the police forces of Holland: this is an area of Europe that's relatively free of street crime. Even in Amsterdam and the larger cities you shouldn't have problems, though it's obviously advisable to be on your guard against petty theft: secure your things in a locker when staying in hostel accommodation, and never leave any valuables in a tent or car. If you're on a bike, make sure it is well locked up – bike theft and resale is one of the major industries in most cities.

As far as **personal safety** goes, it's normally possible to walk anywhere in the centres of the larger cities at any time of day, though women should obviously be wary of badly lit or empty streets; public transport, even late at night, isn't usually a problem.

If you are unlucky enough to have **something stolen**, report it immediately to the nearest police station. Get them to write a statement detailing what has been lost for your insurance claim when you get home, and remember to make a note of the report number – or, better still, ask for a copy of the statement itself. If you're detained by the police, you don't automatically have the right to a phone call, although in practice they'll probably phone your consulate for you. If your alleged offence is a minor matter, you can be held for up to six hours without questioning; if it is more serious, you can be detained for up to 24 hours.

If you find yourself in trouble, or simply need **assistance of a legal or social nature**, there are a couple of organizations in Holland that might be able to help. **JAC** gives free confidential help to young people, especially foreign nationals, on work, alien status, drugs and accommodation matters. There's also **MAIC**, which similarly specializes in legal advice, though not just for young people; and it will also help on other matters. Both organizations have offices in the larger cities; some of them are listed in the text.

Drugs are predictably visible in Holland, particularly Amsterdam. Many coffeeshops are sanctioned to sell cannabis, although the drugs policy is being tightened up in the face of pressure from France and Germany to bring it more into line with the rest of Europe. While busts for cannabis are rare, people over 18 are legally allowed to buy just five grammes (under one-fifth of an ounce) for personal use at any one time. Possession of amounts up to 28g (1oz) is ignored by the police although they are still technically entitled to confiscate any quantity they find. In practice, though, you'll probably never even see a policeman from one day to the next, and you'll certainly never be arrested for discreet personal use.

It's acceptable to smoke in some bars (it's usually pretty obvious which), but many are strongly against it so don't make any automatic assumptions. If in doubt, ask the barperson. "**Space cakes**" (cakes baked with hashish and sold by the slice), although widely available, count as hard drugs and are illegal; if you choose to indulge, spend a few days working your way up to them, since the effect can be exceptionally powerful and long-lasting. And a word of warning: since all kinds of cannabis are so widely available in coffeeshops, there's no need to buy any on the street – if you do, you're asking to be ripped off. Bear in mind, also, that a liberal attitude toward cannabis exists in Holland only in the capital and the large cities to the south that form the Randstad.

Needless to say, don't try to take cannabis products out of the country. Sniffer dogs regularly meet incoming flights and ferries, and customs officials around the world are well aware of the attractions of Holland's liberal drug policy.

BUSINESS HOURS AND PUBLIC HOLIDAYS

The Dutch weekend fades painlessly into the week with many shops staying closed on Monday morning, even in major cities.

Business hours are usually from 9am to 5.30 or 6pm; certain shops stay open later on Thursday and Friday evenings for *Koopavond* (shopping nights). *Avondwinkels* are nightshops found in major cities, notably Amsterdam, that usually open at 6pm and close at 1 or 2am. Things shut down a little earlier on Saturday, and only die-hard money makers open on a Sunday.

Most towns have a **market day**, usually midweek (and sometimes Saturday morning), and this is often the liveliest day to be in a town, particularly when the stalls fill the central square or *markt*; very occasionally you'll see elderly women wearing bona fide peasant costume. Though the tradition has died out in all but the smallest towns and villages, some shops close for the **half-day** on Wednesday or Thursday afternoon.

Though closed on Christmas Day, New Year's Day, the day after Christmas, and on Mondays, all

PUBLIC HOLIDAYS
New Year's Day
Good Friday (many shops open)
Easter Sunday and Monday
April 30 (Queen's Birthday, street parties and many shops open)
May 5 Liberation Day
Ascension Day (mid-May)
Whit (Pentecost) Sunday and Monday
December 5 (St Nicholas' day, shops close early).
Christmas Day
December 26

state-run museums adopt Sunday hours on the **public holidays** listed above, when most shops and banks are closed.

FESTIVALS AND ANNUAL EVENTS

Holland has few national annual events, and aside from the carnivals that are celebrated in the southern part of the country and a sprinkling of religious-oriented celebra-tions, most annual shindigs are arts- or music-based affairs, confined to a particular town or city. In addition there are also markets and folkloric events, rather bogusly sustained for tourists, which take place during summer only, the Alkmaar cheese market being one of the best-known examples.**

Most festivals, as you might expect, take place during the summer. Contact the local VVV for up-to-date details – and remember that wherever you might be staying, huge swathes of the country are no more than a short train ride away.

Of the country's **annual cultural events**, the *Holland Festival*, held in June in Amsterdam, Rotterdam and The Hague, is probably the most diverse, with theatre, opera and classical music, by mainly Dutch performers. The Hague's *North Sea Jazz Festival* in July probably has more prestige and attracts a host of big names. There's more jazz on offer in June with Apeldoorn's *Jazz in the Woods* binge; check out also the Europe-

FESTIVALS DIARY

January

Mid-Jan Leiden Jazz Week.

End Jan Rotterdam Film Festival.

February

Mid-Feb West Frisian Flora exhibition, Bovenkarspel.

Third week Carnivals in Breda, 'sHertogenbosch, Maastricht and in other southern towns.

March

Mid-March Amsterdam: Blues festival

End March–end May Keukenhof Gardens, Lisse: displays in the bulbfields and hothouses.

End March–end May Frans Roozen Nursery, Vogelenzang: displays in gardens and hothouses.

Sunday closest to March 15 Amsterdam: *Stille Ommegang* procession through the city streets to the St Nicolaaskerk (info on ☎023/524 5415).

April

April–Oct Amsterdam: city illuminations on bridges and buildings.

April–Oct Amsterdam: Tramline Museum, trams from Amsterdam South to Amstelveen and back.

April–Sept Alkmaar Cheese Market on Friday mornings.

Second week Nationaal Museumweekend: free entrance to all of the country's museums

Third weekend Groningen: avant-garde jazz festival.

Penultimate weekend Flower Parade from Noordwijk to Haarlem .

Last Sunday Rotterdam Marathon.

April 30 All Holland: *Koninginnedag* (Queen's Birthday), celebrated by street markets and fireworks.

May

May 5th Liberation Day: Bands, speeches and markets around the country

Second weekend Amersfort: jazz festival.

End May Breda: traditional jazz festival, with open-air concerts and street parades.

May 30 Scheveningen: "Flag Day" to mark the opening of the Dutch herring season.

June

June 1–30 Holland Festival in Amsterdam and, sometimes, the Hague and Rotterdam. Festival of modern theatre, music, dance and mime.

June to September Maastricht: European Summer Cultural Programme, with music, theatre, etc.

Early June Landgraaf: Pink Pop Festival.

Early June Bolsward: Frisian "eleven cities" cycle race, using bicycles instead of the traditional ice skates.

Early June Apeldoorn: "Jazz in the Woods" festival.

Mid-June Scheveningen: International Kite Festival.

Mid-June to mid-July Middleburg: International Festival of new avant-garde music.

End June–end Aug Schagen: West Frisian Folk Market, preceded by processions, etc, on Thursday mornings.

Last week in June Amsterdam: Festival van Verleiding, theatre productions and other events to celebrate Gay Pride Week.

July

Early July Drenthe Four-Day Cycle Event.

July 1–Sept 30 The Hague: International Rose Exhibition.

July–end Aug Hoorn: Traditional market, with folk dancing and old crafts, Wednesday mornings.

July–end Aug Purmerend: cheeese market, Thursday mornings.

Early July The Hague: North Sea Jazz Festival.

End July *Vierdaagse*, Nijmegen: Four-Day Walking Event.

August

Early Aug Sneek Week: international sailing event.

Mid-Aug Scheveningen: International Firework Festival, two displays each evening.

Mid-Aug Brabant Four-Day Cycle Event, starting in Tilburg.

continued overpage

FESTIVALS DIARY (CONTINUED)

September

Mid-Sept Aalsmeer: Flower parade to Amsterdam.

Last week Amsterdam city marathon

November

Mid-Nov Throughout the country: arrival of St Nicholas.

December

Dec 5 Pakjesavond. Though it tends to be a private affair, this is the day Dutch kids receive their Christmas presents. If you're here on that day and have Dutch friends, it's worth knowing that it's traditional to give a present together with a rude poem you have written caricaturing the recipient.

renowned *Pink Pop Festival*, held in Landgraaf, near Maastricht early the same month, which attracts top-level performers.

Outside summer, **other annual events** include, of course, viewing the **bulbfields** – at their best between March and May. There are a number of places you can visit in the bulbfield areas of North and South Holland, notably the dazzling Keukenhof Gardens and – for a taste of the industry in action – the Aalsmeer flower auc-tion. If you're visiting the country in February, a number of towns in Holland's southern provinces host pre-lenten **carnivals**, notably Maastricht; while an event to look out for also in February (though really any time when the weather is cold enough) is the **Elfstedentocht**, Friesland's uniquely exciting, and gruelling, canal skating race between the province's eleven towns – though it's only actually been held once in the last twenty years so don't plan your trip around it.

TRAVELLERS WITH DISABILITIES

Despite the country's social progressiveness in other ways, the Dutch provision for travellers with disabilities is a very mixed bag. *Netherlands Railways* offers a comprehensive service for disabled travellers, including a timetable in Braille, free escort service, and assistance at all stations (call ☎030/235 5555 for details), and most major museums, concert halls, theatres, churches and public buildings offer easy access to visitors in wheelchairs. However, apart from the rail service, it can be difficult to get around, as **public transport** systems tend to have no facilities for disabled passengers.

Before leaving home, it is worth contacting the nearest office of the NBT (see p.21) for their leaflet, which describes hotel and camping facilities throughout the country. In Holland itself, local **VVV** offices, themselves accessible, are usually the best bet for advice on places that have ramps and lifts, or where staff are trained to escort disabled visitors. If you're **flying** into Holland, the national carrier KLM has its own team of paramedics at Schiphol airport to help people with disabilities through the airport; all other airlines use the services of *International Help for the Disabled* (IHD), who can assist you in all stages of both arrival and departure. They can also be contacted directly on ☎020/316 1417, 24 hours a day. Last but not least, paper currency is marked in Braille to indicate its value to the visually impaired.

CONTACTS FOR TRAVELLERS WITH DISABILITIES

AUSTRALIA

ACROD (Australian Council for Rehabilitation of the Disabled), PO Box 60, Curtin ACT 2605 (☎06/682 4333); 55 Charles St, Ryde (☎02/9809 4488).

ENGLAND

Holiday Care Service, 2nd floor, Imperial Building, Victoria Rd, Horley, Surrey RH6 9HW (☎01293/774535). *Information on all aspects of travel.*

RADAR, 12 City Forum, 250 City Rd, London EC1V 8AS (☎0171/250 3222; Minicom ☎0171/250 4119). *Good source of advice on holidays and travel abroad.*

Tripscope, The Courtyard, Evelyn Rd, London W4 5JL (☎0181/994 9294). *National telephone information service offering free transport and travel advice.*

IRELAND

Disability Action Group, 2 Annadale Ave, Belfast BT7 3JH (☎01232/91011).

Irish Wheelchair Association, Blackheath Drive, Clontarf, Dublin 3 (☎01/833 8241).

NEW ZEALAND

Disabled Persons Assembly, PO Box 10, 138 The Terrace, Wellington (☎04/472 2626).

NORTH AMERICA

Directions Unlimited, 720 N Bedford Rd, Bedford Hills, NY 10507 (☎1-800/533-5343). *Tour operator specializing in custom tours for people with disabilities.*

Jewish Rehabilitation Hospital, 3205 Place Alton Goldbloom, Montréal, PQ H7V 1R2 (☎514/688-9550). *Guidebooks and travel information.*

Mobility International USA, PO Box 10767, Eugene, OR 97440 (Voice and TDD: ☎503/343-1284). *Information and referral services, access guides, tours and exchange programmes. Annual membership $20 (includes quarterly newsletter).*

Society for the Advancement of Travel for the Handicapped (SATH), 347 5th Ave, New York, NY 10016 (☎212/447-7284). *Non-profit travel-industry referral service that passes queries on to its members as appropriate; allow plenty of time for a response.*

Travel Information Service, Moss Rehabilitation Hospital, 1200 West Tabor Rd, Philadelphia, PA 19141 (☎215/456-9600). *Telephone information and referral service.*

Twin Peaks Press, Box 129, Vancouver, WA 98666; ☎206/694-2462 or 1-800/637-2256). *Publisher of the* Directory of Travel Agencies for the Disabled *($19.95), listing more than 370 agencies worldwide;* Travel for the Disabled *($19.95); and* Wheelchair Vagabond *($14.95), loaded with personal tips.*

DIRECTORY

ADDRESSES These are written, for example, as Haarlemmerstraat 15 III, meaning the third-floor (US – fourth-floor) apartment at no. 15 Haarlemmerstraat. The figures 1e or 2e before a street name are an abbreviation for *Eerste* and *Tweede* respectively – first and second streets of the same name. Dutch zip codes can be found in the directory kept at post offices; note that complete codes have a two-letter indicator as well.

AIRPORT TAX Not charged when leaving the Netherlands.

CLOGS You'll see these on sale in all the main tourist centres, usually brightly painted and not really designed for wearing. It's estimated that about three million clogs are still made annually in The Netherlands; interestingly, only about half are for the tourist market, the rest mainly being worn by industrial workers as foot protection. Only a few elderly farmers out in the sticks continue to wear clogs in the traditional way.

ELECTRIC CURRENT 220v AC – British equipment needs only a plug adaptor; American apparatus requires a transformer and will need new plugs or an adaptor.

EMERGENCIES Phone ☎06 11. In Amsterdam emergencies can be notified on: **Police** ☎622 2222; **Ambulance** ☎555 5555; **Fire** ☎621 2121; **rape/sexual assault** ☎612 7576.

FLOWERS It doesn't take long to notice the Dutch enthusiasm for flowers and plants of all kinds: windows are often festooned with blooms and greenery, and shops and markets sell sprays and bunches for next to nothing. Flowers are grown year-round, though obviously spring is the best time to come if this is your interest, when the bulbfields (and glasshouses) of North and South Holland are dense with colour – tulips, hyacinths, and narcissi are the main blooms. Later in the year there are rhododendrons and, in Friesland and Groningen, fields of yellow rapeseed; in summer roses appear, while the autumn sees late chrysanthemums. For more on Holland's flowers, pick up the NBT's *Flowers* booklet, and turn to p.161 for the best of the bulbfields.

GAY AND LESBIAN HOLLAND As you'd expect, it's in Holland's cities that gay life is most visible and enjoyable. Amsterdam is probably the best city in Europe in which to be gay – attitudes are tolerant, bars are excellent and plentiful, and support groups and facilities are unequalled. Elsewhere in Holland, while the scene isn't anywhere near as extensive, it's well organized: Rotterdam, The Hague, Nijmegen and Groningen each has an enjoyable nightlife. The native lesbian scene is smaller and more subdued than the gay one. Many politically active lesbians move within tight circles, and it takes time for foreign visitors to find out what's happening. All cities of any size have a branch of *COC*, the national organization for gay men and women, which can offer help, information and usually a coffee bar. The national HQ is at Rozenstraat 14, Amsterdam (Mon–Fri 9am–5pm; ☎020/626 3087).

ISIC CARDS Student ID is useful for mensas, but won't help you gain reduced admission to very much at all, and certainly not museums or mainstream tourist attractions.

LEFT LUGGAGE At all train stations. Where there is no actual office, there will always be lockers, charging either ƒ4 or ƒ6 – depending on size – for 24 hours.

MOSQUITOES These thrive in Holland's watery environment, biting their worst at campsites. An antihistamine cream such as *Phenergan* is the best antidote, although this can be difficult to find in Holland – in which case preventative sticks like *Autan* or *Citronella* are the best idea.

SHOPPING Two stores you'll see all over Holland are *Vroom & Dreesmann* and *HEMA* – department stores that are useful for stocking up on basic supplies such as toiletries, etc. Of the two, *HEMA* is the cheaper, a sort of Dutch *Woolworths* and many branches have a cheap restaurant. Most good bookstores stock at least a few English paperbacks, though at higher prices than in the UK and US; look out also for branches of *De Slegte*, a countrywide chain (with a couple of branches in Belgium) that sells secondhand and discounted books, a good proportion of which will be in English; we've listed addresses in the *Guide*. Among things to buy to take home, cheese (see p.33) is an obvious choice – it's better and there's more variety than at home. Flowers are also dirt cheap everywhere; buying bulbs is easiest by placing an order with a specialist company which will handle the packing and legal paperwork for you. You might also try *drop* or Dutch liquorice, which comes in myriad different varieties including salted, unsalted or with honey.

TIME One hour ahead of GMT; six hours ahead of Eastern Standard Time; nine hours ahead of Pacific Standard Time.

TIPPING Don't bother, since restaurants, hotels, taxis, etc, must include a fifteen percent service charge by law. Only if you're somewhere *really* flash is it considered proper to round up the bill to the nearest guilder. In public toilets, it's normal to leave about 25c.

TRAVEL AGENTS *NBBS* is the nationwide student/youth travel organization and the best source of *BIJ* tickets, discount flights and the like. They have branches in all the main Dutch cities – see our listings for addresses.

WAR CEMETERIES There was fierce fighting in parts of Holland during the last war, notably at Arnhem, where several thousand British and Polish servicemen are remembered at the Oosterbeek cemetery. There are other military cemeteries in the east and south of the country, not least at Margraten, where around eight thousand US soldiers are buried.

WINDMILLS The best place to see windmills is at Kinderdijk near Dordrecht; they're also still very much part of the landscape in the polderlands north of Amsterdam. Some, too, have been moved and reassembled out of harm's way in the open-air museums at Zaanse Schans (Zaandam) and the Netherlands Open-Air Museum just outside Arnhem.

WOMEN Amsterdam has the country's most impressive feminist infrastructure, and there's a good range of bars and discos, a few exclusively for women. Once outside the capital, however, you'll frequently be reminded just how parochial Holland is – attitudes and behaviour acceptable in Amsterdam will be frowned on elsewhere, especially in the Catholic south. Many towns in Holland have a *Vrouwenhuis* or women's centre, though these are diminishing; where still applicable, addresses are given in the *Guide*.

By and large, nowhere in Holland is unsafe for women travelling alone – the seedier areas of the big cities may feel threatening, but with common sense and circumspection you shouldn't have anything to worry about.

N

CHAPTER 4
**THE NORTH AND
THE FRISIAN ISLANDS**

CHAPTER 2
**NORTH
HOLLAND**

CHAPTER 1
AMSTERDAM

CHAPTER 5
**OVERIJSSEL, FLEVOLAND
AND GELDERLAND**

CHAPTER 3
**SOUTH HOLLAND
AND UTRECHT**

CHAPTER 6
**ZEELAND, NORTH BRABANT
AND LIMBURG**

GERMANY

BELGIUM

CHAPTER ONE

AMSTERDAM

A msterdam is a compact, instantly likeable capital. It's appealing to look at and pleasant to walk around, an intriguing mix of the parochial and the international; it also has a welcoming attitude towards visitors and a uniquely youthful orientation, shaped by the liberal counter-culture of the last three decades. It's hard not to be drawn in by the buzz of open-air summer events, by the intimacy of the clubs and bars, or by the Dutch facility with languages; just about everyone you meet in Amsterdam will be able to speak near-perfect English, on top of their own native Dutch and fluent German and French.

The city's layout is determined by a web of **canals** radiating out from a historical centre: these planned, seventeenth-century extensions to the medieval town make up a uniquely elegant urban environment, their tall, characteristically gabled houses reflected in still, green water. With its cobbled streets, tinkling bicycle bells and stately architecture, Amsterdam is acutely beautiful: the tranquillity of its tree-lined canals, each describing a ring around the city and hooped over with humpback bridges, is far removed from the hard lines, the traffic and the noise of many city centres.

The conventional sights are for the most part low-key – the **Anne Frank House** being a notable exception – but, with an active and continuing governmental policy of support for the arts, Amsterdam has developed a world-class group of museums and galleries. The **Van Gogh Museum** is, for many, reason enough to visit the city; add to it the **Rijksmuseum**, with its collections of medieval and seventeenth-century Dutch paintings, the contemporary and experimental **Stedelijk Museum**, and hundreds of smaller galleries, and the international quality of the art on display is evident.

But it's Amsterdam's **population and politics** that constitute its most enduring characteristics. Notorious during the 1960s and 1970s as the zenith – or nadir – of radical permissiveness, the city mellowed only marginally during the Eighties, and, despite the gentrification of the last ten years or so, retains a uniquely laid-back feel. However, Amsterdam is far from being a cosmopolitan place, particularly when compared to other European capitals such as London or Paris. Despite the huge numbers of immigrants coming into Amsterdam from former colonies in Surinam and Indonesia (among other places), almost all live and work in districts outside the centre, and are not much in evidence to the average tourist.

Amsterdam remains a uniquely casual, intimate place, with much to it that is both innovative and comfortably familiar. Indeed, Amsterdammers themselves make much of their city and its attractions being *gezellig*, a rather over-used Dutch word roughly corresponding to "cosy", "appealingly lived-in" and "warmly

If you intend spending some time in Amsterdam, or want to find out about it in greater detail, get hold of a copy of *The Rough Guide to Amsterdam*.

convivial" all at the same time. The city's unparalleled selection of *gezellig* drinking-places is a delight, whether you choose to visit a traditional, bare-floored **brown café** or one of the many designer bars and grand cafés. Amsterdam's unique approach to combating hard-drug abuse – embodied in the effective decriminalization of cannabis – has led to a proliferation of **coffeeshops**, which sell coffee only as a sideline to high-quality marijuana and hashish. Entertainment has a similarly innovative edge, exemplified by **multimedia complexes**, whose offerings are at the forefront of contemporary European film, dance, drama and music. There is any amount of affordable **live music** from all genres – although the Dutch have a particular soft spot for jazz – and Amsterdam has one of the world's leading classical **orchestras**, with generously subsidized ticket prices. The **club** scene is by contrast relatively subdued, even modest by the standards of other capital cities, and the emphasis is more on dancing than posing.

Gay men will discover that Amsterdam has Europe's most active and convivial nightlife network, although gay women might be more disappointed at the exclusivity of the supposed "Gay Capital of Europe".

Arrival, city transport and information

Amsterdam has one international airport, **Schiphol**. This is connected by train with Amsterdam's **Centraal Station** (often abbreviated to CS): a fast service leaves every fifteen minutes during the day, and every hour at night (1am–6am); the journey takes twenty minutes and costs *f*6 single (return tickets must be used the same day). The city has a number of suburban **train stations**, but all major domestic and international trains go through Amsterdam Centraal. Arriving here puts you at the hub of all bus and tram routes and just five minutes' walk from Dam Square. Long-distance **buses**, though, are less straightforward. The popular *Eurolines* services stop at **Amstel Station**, out to the southeast of the centre; from here take the metro to reach Centraal Station. *Hoverspeed* buses call first at **Stadionplein**, before terminating at **Leidseplein**, itself a major city centre square, and linked to Centraal Station by trams #1, #2 and #5.

The telephone code for Amsterdam is ☎020

City transport

By European capital-city standards Amsterdam is small, its public transport excellent and most of the things you might conceivably want to see can be found in the city's compact centre: **getting around** couldn't be easier.

The first place you visit should be the *GVB* public transport office in front of Centraal Station (Mon–Fri 7am–9pm, Sat & Sun 8am–9pm), where you can pick up a free transport map and an English guide to the **ticketing** system. All tram and bus stops have a detailed map of the entire network. For details of public transport throughout Holland, you can also call ☎06/9292 (Mon–Fri 7am–11pm, Sat & Sun 8am–11pm; 50c per min).

The most commonly used ticket is the **strippenkaart**. These are valid nationwide and work on a zonal basis whereby you cancel two strips for one zone (which covers most of the city centre), three strips for two and so on. Additional people can travel on the same *strippenkaart*, as long as the requisite number of strips is cancelled. Once validated, *strippenkaarts* can be used to transfer between all trams, buses and the metro within an hour. The most practical version has fifteen strips (currently ƒ11), and can be picked up all over the city at many postcard shops and tobacconists, *GVB* offices (Centraal Station; Prins Hendrikkade 108; Amstel Station), VVV offices, post offices and in all train stations at the ticket counters and from the yellow ticket machines (type in code "2222" and pay in coins only). There's also a 45-strip card available for ƒ32.25, which is economical if you intend to stay a while, or travel further afield. Otherwise you can buy two-, three- and eight-strip tickets on board the trams, but they work out considerably more expensive.

As a general rule, **trams** are boarded via the rear doors (push the button). Some trams have a conductor sitting in the back, in which case offer him/her your *strippenkaart* and ask for "one zone", or simply state your destination. On other trams, though, you're trusted to do it yourself; fold your *strippenkaart* over to expose only the last of the strips your journey requires, and feed it into the little yellow box near the tram doors. On **buses**, get on at the front and ask the driver to stamp your *strippenkaart*.

If you don't want to be bothered with the *strippenkaart* ritual, the easiest thing to do (although not very economical) is to buy a **dagkaart** or day ticket – valid for as many days as you need, up to a maximum of nine, on trams, buses and the metro: prices start at a steep ƒ8 for one day, going up to ƒ23.50 for four days, with each additional day after that charged at ƒ3.75.

Recently the city has been cracking down on fare evasion; if you're caught without a ticket, you're liable for a ƒ60 fine (plus the price of the ticket you should have bought), due on the spot.

Trams, buses and the metro
Apart from walking, **trams** offer the easiest transport alternative: the system is comprehensive and not at all expensive (city **buses** don't really go anywhere very useful). Amsterdam's **metro** starts at Centraal Station, but apart from a couple of stops in the eastern section of the centre, most of the stations are in the suburbs and are used mainly by commuters.

Trams, buses and the metro all run between approximately the same times (Mon–Fri 6am–12.15am, Sat 6.30am–12.15am, Sun 7.30am–12.15am). After midnight there are seven hourly **night bus** routes running, with those numbered between 73 and 76 serving the centre. Be warned, though, that for some reason there is a gap in the night bus service between 2 and 4am; the *GVB* has a leaflet detailing all the routes.

Taxis and cars
Taxis are plentiful but expensive, and are found in stands on main city squares, such as Stationsplein, Dam Square and Leidseplein, or by phoning the 24-hour radio-controlled central office on ☎677 7777; you can't hail them in the street. A fun alternative are the **water taxis** (daily 11am–10pm; ☎622 2181), which can be ordered to any place on a canal – if you can afford ƒ90 for 30min. Taxis aside, it's generally extremely unwise to travel **by car**: the whole of the city centre has a network of convoluted one-way systems that will, quite literally,

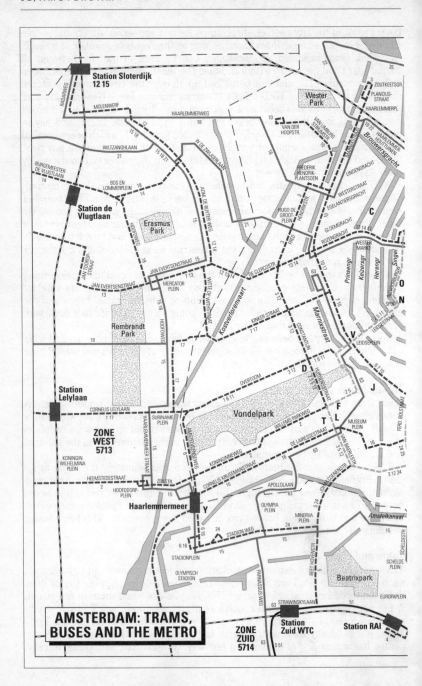

AMSTERDAM: TRAMS, BUSES AND THE METRO

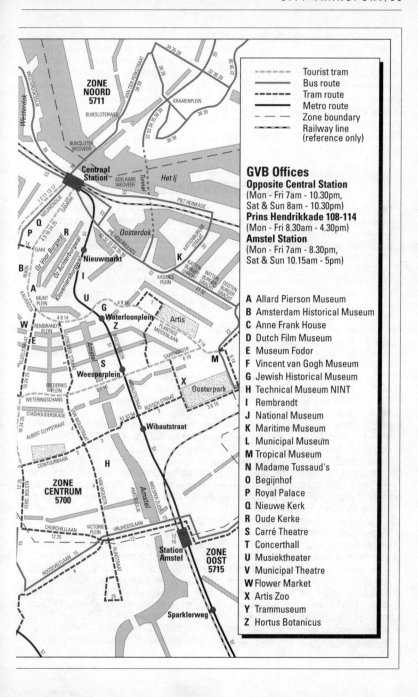

Tourist tram
Bus route
Tram route
Metro route
Zone boundary
Railway line
(reference only)

GVB Offices
Opposite Central Station
(Mon - Fri 7am - 10.30pm,
Sat & Sun 8am - 10.30pm)
Prins Hendrikkade 108-114
(Mon - Fri 8.30am - 4.30pm)
Amstel Station
(Mon - Fri 7am - 8.30pm,
Sat & Sun 10.15am - 5pm)

A Allard Pierson Museum
B Amsterdam Historical Museum
C Anne Frank House
D Dutch Film Museum
E Museum Fodor
F Vincent van Gogh Museum
G Jewish Historical Museum
H Technical Museum NINT
I Rembrandt
J National Museum
K Maritime Museum
L Municipal Museum
M Tropical Museum
N Madame Tussaud's
O Begijnhof
P Royal Palace
Q Nieuwe Kerk
R Oude Kerke
S Carré Theatre
T Concerthall
U Musiektheater
V Municipal Theatre
W Flower Market
X Artis Zoo
Y Trammuseum
Z Hortus Botanicus

send you round in circles, the official policy of the city government is to limit car-parking spaces – and there are zealous, fast-acting and merciless teams of traffic police roaming the city who will clamp or tow away your car. Paid parking applies Mon–Sat 9am–11pm and Sun noon–11pm (f4.25 per hr), although a number of hotels offer a special three-day **parking permit** for f60. Getting a **clamp** removed costs f130; if you've been **towed**, reclaiming a car from the pound adds at least another f350. The car pound is way out in the northeast of the city, at Cruquiuskade 25 (☎555 9800; open 24hrs; bus #22 or #28 from Centraal Station). For all enquiries concerning parking in Amsterdam, call ☎553 0300.

TAKING TO THE CANALS

One way of getting oriented is to take a **canal trip** on one of the ubiquitous glass-topped boats that jam the major canals during the summer season. While not exactly riveting, these trips are the best way to see the canal houses, and have a soporific charm if you're feeling lazy. Two of the better companies are *Amstel* (☎626 5636), which leave from Stadhouderskade, opposite the Heineken Brewery, and *P. Kooij* (☎623 3810), which leave from opposite Rokin 125; both have hour-long tours, with (atypically) a commentary that's just about bearable, for around f15.

An appealing alternative is to hang out on a **Smoke Boat Cruise** run by the American comedy company *Boom Chicago* (information ☎639 2707). Their open boat carries a maximum of 12 people and leaves at 3pm and 10.30pm daily from *Boom Chicago*'s theatre at Lijnbaansgracht 238, near Leidseplein, for a hash-hazed ninety-minute tour through the narrow canals of the Red Light District, which are inaccessible to the larger boats. A ticket costs f15 and includes a free drink, but note that priority is given to members of *Boom Chicago*'s audience on the evening boat.

For a more mainstream experience, the *GVB* offers a two-hour tour of the "nostalgic side of Amsterdam" by **ferry** (mid-April to mid-Oct Sun & holidays only at 11am, 12.45pm, 2.30pm and 4.15pm, from Pier 8 behind Centraal Station); tickets are a very reasonable f9, with a buffet on board.

The **canal bus** service combines a canal tour with genuine transportation: services run every twenty minutes along two circular lines beginning and ending on the Singelgracht opposite the Rijksmuseum; stopping points are Leidseplein, Keizersgracht (corner Raadhuisstraat), Prinsengracht (Westerkerk), Centraal Station and Waterlooplein. The whole journey takes about an hour, and a day ticket (10am–8pm) costs f19.50, and allows you to hop on and off all day; for f27.50, you get admission to the Rijksmuseum as well. They also run candlelight cruises after dark; more details on ☎623 9886.

Finally, more for fun than for serious transport are the **canal bikes**, pedalboats that take up to four people and can be rented by the hour (f12.50 each for the first and second person, f8 each for the third and fourth). Between July and September, they operate from 10am to 9.30pm daily (last pick-up 8.30pm) at four central locations – outside the American Hotel near Leidseplein, on the Singelgracht opposite the Rijksmuseum, the Prinsengracht outside the Westerkerk, and Keizersgracht near Leidsestraat. In the spring and autumn, hours are more limited (Mon–Thurs & Sun 10am–5pm, Fri & Sat 10am–8.30pm), while between November and March only the Rijksmuseum pick-up point is in use (daily 10am–5pm, barring ice). There is a deposit of f50, and a map is available for f3.50 showing five possible routes between the pick-up/drop-off points. For further information, phone ☎626 5574.

Bikes

Another possibility, and a practical one, is to go native and opt for a **bicycle**: the city's well-defined network of bicycle lanes (*fietspaden*) means that this can be a very safe and pleasurable way of getting around. You can **rent a bike** from the *Take-A-Bike* cycle store at Centraal Station (turn left when you come out of the station; about 75m), or from a number of bike-rental firms scattered around town (see "Listings", p.118) – rates start at around ƒ10 a day, plus a deposit or credit-card imprint as security. A word of warning, though: lock up your bike at *all times*. Bike **theft** is rife in Amsterdam, and it's common to see the dismembered parts of bicycles still chained to railings, victims of organized gangs armed with bolt cutters, or of junkies hoping a stolen bike will fetch the price of a fix. If you want to buy a bike from a legal outlet, a clapped-out boneshaker can be had for ƒ40 or so (and sold back when you leave).

Information

The place to head for information is the **VVV** (pronounced "fay-fay-fay"), the nationwide tourist organization. They have four branches: one inside Centraal Station (Mon–Sat 8am–7.30pm, Sun 9am–4.30pm); one immediately outside Centraal Station (daily 9am–5pm); another on Leidsestraat, on the corner with Leidseplein (Mon–Sat 9am–7pm, Sun 9am–5pm); and one at Stadionplein (Mon–Sat 9am–5pm). The main *VVV* telephone information line is ☎06/340 34066 (Mon–Fri 9am–5pm; 50c per min). Each office can sell you a map, book accommodation for a ƒ5 fee (plus a ƒ5 "deposit", which is deducted from the hotel bill), book theatre and concert tickets and provide informed answers to most other enquiries. An **alternative** to the *VVV* if the queues are too long is the *Dutch Tourist Information Office* on Damrak 35 (Mon–Sat 8.30am–10pm, Sun 9am–10pm; ☎638 2800). For information on **what's on**, see p.105.

Accommodation

Accommodation in Amsterdam is extremely difficult to find, and can be a major expense: even hostels are pricy for what you get, and hotels are among the most expensive in Europe. The city's compactness means that you're bound to end up somewhere **central**, but if you arrive without a reservation, you'll still need to search hard to find a decent place to stay. At peak periods throughout the year – July and August, Easter, Christmas – you should **book well ahead**; hotel rooms and even hostel beds can be swallowed up remarkably quickly, and if you leave finding a room to chance, you may well be disappointed (and/or out of pocket). The *VVV* will make advance bookings, and book rooms on the spot for a ƒ5 fee, or sell you a comprehensive leaflet on hotels in the city (ƒ4). Something to bear in mind when choosing a hotel is the fact that many of Amsterdam's buildings have narrow, very steep **staircases**, and not all hotels have installed lifts. If this is a consideration for you, check before you book.

Note that directions given below take Centraal Station (CS) as their starting point, and all hotels and hostels listed are marked on the map on pp.58–59.

Details of **campsites** are given on p.62.

ACCOMMODATION PRICE CODES

All the **hotels** and **hostels** detailed in this chapter have been graded according to the following price categories. Apart from ①, which is a per-person price for a hostel bed, all the codes are based on the rate for the cheapest double room during high season.

For more on accommodation, see p.30.

① Up to ƒ40 per person	④ ƒ150–200	⑦ ƒ300–400
② ƒ60–100	⑤ ƒ200–250	
③ ƒ100–150	⑥ ƒ250–300	

Hotels

Amsterdam's hotel prices start at around ƒ80 for a double, and although some form of **breakfast** – "Dutch" (bread and jam) or "English" (bacon and eggs) – is normally included at all but the cheapest and the most expensive hotels, some places can give the barest value for money. There are a huge number of what might be called comfortable **family hotels**, with basic, en suite double rooms hovering more or less around the ƒ175 mark: the ones listed here have something particular to recommend them over the rest – location, value for money, ambience. Don't be afraid to ask to see the room first, and to refuse it if you don't like it. Incidentally, it is illegal for a hotel to refuse entry to anyone on the grounds of sexual orientation.

The Old Centre

Centrum, map ref 5; Warmoesstraat 15 (☎624 3535, fax 420 1666); 3min walk from CS. Completely renovated and, considering the location, some rooms (high up and at the back) are very quiet and light. This friendly and accommodating hotel offers a choice of large and small rooms, with and without bath/shower. ②

Nes, map ref 19; Kloveniersburgwal 137 (☎624 4773, fax 620 9842); tram #4, #9, #16, #24, #25 to Muntplein. Extremely pleasant and quiet, with a lift; well-positioned away from noise but close to shops and nightlife. Wonderful views and helpful staff. ⑤

Nova, map ref 16; Nieuwezijds Voorburgwal 276 (☎623 0066, fax 627 2026, email <novahtl@pi.net>); tram #1, #2, #5, #11 to Spui. By far the best option in the city in this price bracket. Spotless rooms are all en suite with fridge and TV, staff are friendly, and there's a lift and secure access. Perfect, quiet location. ④

Rokin, map ref 17; Rokin 73 (☎626 7456, fax 625 6453); tram #4, #9, #16, #24, #25 to Dam or Spui. Something of a bargain considering the location. ③

St Nicolaas, map ref 3; Spuistraat 1a (☎626 1384, fax 623 0979); 3min walk from CS. Very pleasant, well-run little hotel housed in a former mattress factory (with a king-size lift to prove it). Scrupulously clean. ③

Winston, map ref 10; Warmoesstraat 123 (☎623 1380, fax 639 2308, email <winston@xs4all.nl>); 10min walk from CS. Completely refurbished, this is now an ultra-modern, very safe and affordable hotel, with light and airy rooms – ranging from singles to 8-person rooms – on 6 floors; some are en suite, and some share a communal balcony. Full disabled access, even extending to Braille in the lift. Highly recommended. ②

City centre west

De Bloeiende Ramenas, map ref 1; Haarlemmerdijk 61 (☎624 6030, fax 420 2261); 15min walk from CS. A cross between hostel and hotel, with comfortable rooms, friendly and welcoming management, and sensible prices. The only disadvantage is the location, to the north-west of the centre and away from any action. ②

Canal House, map ref 7; Keizersgracht 148 (☎622 5182, fax 624 1317); tram #13, #14, #17 to Westermarkt. A magnificently restored seventeenth-century building, centrally located on one of the principal canals, and run by an American family; friendly bar and cosy rooms. ⑥

Clemens, map ref 12; Raadhuisstraat 39 (☎626 9658, no fax); tram #13, #14, #17 to Westermarkt. One of the many options on this hotel strip in the Art Nouveau crescent of the Utrecht Building. Clean, neat and good value for money. As this is one of the city's busiest streets, ask for a room at the back. ③

Hegra, map ref 15; Herengracht 269 (☎623 7877, fax 623 8159); tram #1, #2, #5, #11 to Spui. Welcoming atmosphere and relatively inexpensive for the location, on a beautiful stretch of the canal. ③

Van Onna, map ref 9; Bloemgracht 102 (☎626 5801, no fax); tram #13, #14, #17 to Westermarkt. A quiet, comfortable little family-run place on a tranquil canal in the Jordaan district. ③

Wiechmann, map ref 14; Prinsengracht 328 (☎626 3321, fax 626 8962); tram #13, #14, #17 to Westermarkt. Family-run for 50 years, this canal-house restoration near to the Anne Frank House showcases dark wood beams and restrained style. Rooms are kept in perfect condition. ⑤

City centre south and east

De Admiraal, map ref 22; Herengracht 563 (☎626 2150, fax 623 4625); tram #4, #9, #14 to Rembrandtplein. Friendly hotel close to the nightlife, with wonderful canal views. ③

Adolesce, map ref 25; Nieuwe Keizersgracht 26 (☎626 3959, fax 627 4249); tram #9 or #14 to Waterlooplein. Nicely situated just off the Amstel, on a broad, quiet tree-lined canal, this place is neat and welcoming. ③

Asterisk, map ref 40; Den Texstraat 16 (☎624 1768, fax 638 2790); tram #16, #24, #25 to Weteringcircuit. Good-value budget hotel on the edge of the city centre, just across the canal from the Heineken Brewery. ③

Dikker & Thijs Fenice, map ref 23; Prinsengracht 444 (☎626 7721, fax 625 8986); tram #1, #2, #5, #11 to Prinsengracht. Small and stylish hotel on a beautiful stretch of water in the heart of the city. ⑤

Prinsenhof, map ref 28; Prinsengracht 810 (☎623 1772, fax 638 3368); tram #4 to Prinsengracht. One of the city's best-value options; go for the rooms at the back. ③

Quentin, map ref 27; Leidsekade 89 (☎626 2187, fax 622 0121); tram #1, #2, #5, #11 to Leidseplein. Very friendly, accommodating small hotel, often a stop-over for bands or artists performing at the *Melkweg*. Welcoming to all, and especially well-regarded among gay and lesbian visitors, but families with children might feel out of place. ③

Schiller Karena, map ref 21; Rembrandtplein 26 (☎623 1660, fax 624 0098); tram #4, #9, #14 to Rembrandtplein. Once something of an artists' hangout, and still home to one of the city's best-known and most atmospheric bars. Wonderful Art Deco furnishings in all the public areas. The drawback is its location on tacky Rembrandtplein. ③

Seven Bridges, map ref 24; Reguliersgracht 31 (☎623 1329); tram #4 to Prinsengracht. Perhaps the city's most charming hotel – and certainly one of the best-value ones – with a lovely and convenient canalside location, plus beautifully decorated spotless rooms. Small, though, and popular – often booked solid. ③

Museumplein and the Vondelpark

Abba, map ref 31; Overtoom 122 (☎618 3058, fax 685 3477); tram #1, #11 to 1e Constantijn Huygensstraat. Well-worn but clean rooms awaiting imminent renovation. Friendly, helpful staff. Busy street location, though. ②

Acro, map ref 39; Jan Luykenstraat 44 (☎662 0526, fax 675 0811); tram #2, #5 to Van Baerlestraat. Excellent, modern hotel, which has been completely refurbished with stylish rooms, a plush bar and self-service restaurant. ④

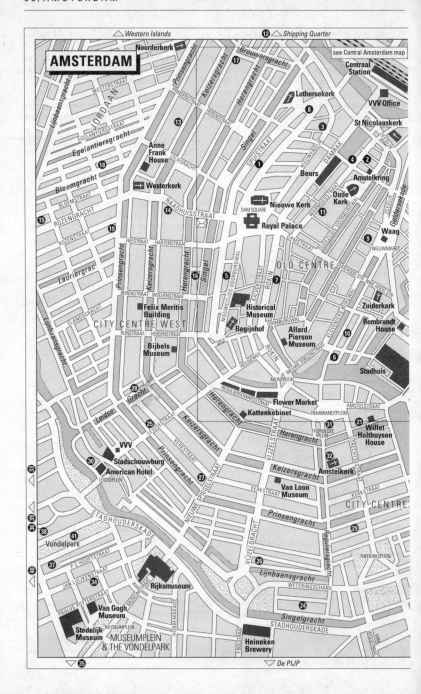

△ Western Islands   ⑫ △ Shipping Quarter

AMSTERDAM

Noorderkerk

see Central Amsterdam map

⑰   Brouwersgracht

Centraal
Station

Luthersekerk   ⑧

VVV Office

③   St Nicolaaskerk

⑬

Anne
Frank
House

Beurs   ④ ② ②

①   Amstelkring

Westerkerk

⑱

Nieuwe Kerk   Oude
Kerk

⑭   DAM SQUARE   ⑪

Royal Palace   Waag   ⑨

NIEUWMARKT

OLD CENTRE

⑮

⑲

⑯   ⑤   ⑦

Felix Meritis
Building

Zuiderkerk

CITY CENTRE WEST

Historical
Museum   Rembrandt
House

Begijnhof   Allard
Pierson
Museum   ⑩

Bijbels
Museum   ⑥

Stadhuis

MUNTPLEIN

㉘

Flower Market

㉕   Kattenkebinet   REMBRANDTPLEIN

③①   ㉑   Willet
Holthuysen
House

VVV   ㉜

Stadsschouwburg
American Hotel   ㉗   Amstelkerk

LEIDSEPLEIN   Van Loon
Museum   CITY CENTRE

㉚

㉝

㉙   ㉙

㊳   ㉖   ㉙

Vondelpark   ④①

㊲   FREDERIKSPLEIN

㊴

㉞   Rijksmuseum

Van Gogh
Museum   ㉔

Stedelijk
Museum   MUSEUMPLEIN
& THE VONDELPARK   Heineken
Brewery

▽ ㉟   ▽ De PIJP

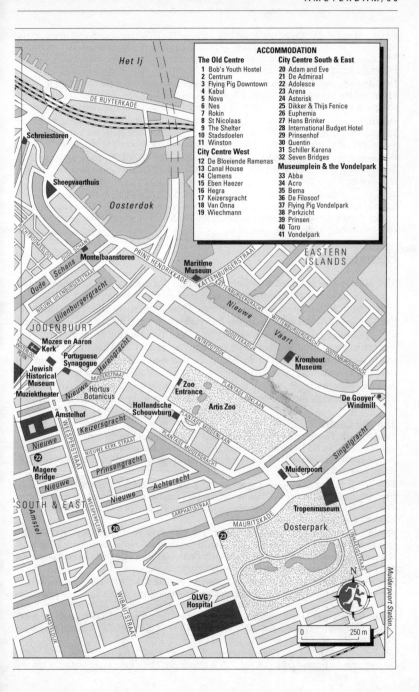

Het Ij

DE RUYTERKADE

ACCOMMODATION

The Old Centre
1 Bob's Youth Hostel
2 Centrum
3 Flying Pig Downtown
4 Kabul
5 Nova
6 Nes
7 Rokin
8 St Nicolaas
9 The Shelter
10 Stadsdoelen
11 Winston

City Centre West
12 De Bloeiende Ramenas
13 Canal House
14 Clemens
15 Eben Haezer
16 Hegra
17 Keizersgracht
18 Van Onna
19 Wiechmann

City Centre South & East
20 Adam and Eve
21 De Admiraal
22 Adolesce
23 Arena
24 Asterisk
25 Dikker & Thijs Fenice
26 Euphemia
27 Hans Brinker
28 International Budget Hotel
29 Prinsenhof
30 Quentin
31 Schiller Karena
32 Seven Bridges

Museumplein & the Vondelpark
33 Abba
34 Acro
35 Bema
36 De Filosoof
37 Flying Pig Vondelpark
38 Parkzicht
39 Prinsen
40 Toro
41 Vondelpark

Schreierstoren

Sheepvaarthuis

Oosterdok

Montelbaanstoren

PRINS HENDRIKKADE

Maritime Museum

KATTENBURGERSTRAAT

EASTERN ISLANDS

Oude Schans

NIEUWE UILENBURGERGRACHT

Uilenburgergracht

KATTENBURGERGRACHT

Nieuwe

WITTENBURGERGRACHT

Vaart

OOSTENBURGERGRACHT

JODENBUURT

Mozes en Aaron Kerk

ENTREPOTDOK

HOOGTEKADIJK

Kromhout Museum

Portuguese Synagogue

WATERLOO PLEIN

Herengracht

Jewish Historical Museum

MUIDERSTRAAT

Nieuwe

Muziektheater

Hortus Botanicus

PLANTAGE DOKLAAN

Zoo Entrance

Artis Zoo

'De Gooyer' Windmill

Amstelhof

Hollandsche Schouwburg

PLANTAGE KERKLAAN

Singelgracht

Keizersgracht

WEESPERSTRAAT

NIEUWE KERK STRAAT

PLANTAGE MIDDENLAAN

Nieuwe

Magere Bridge

Prinsengracht

PLANTAGE MUIDERGRACHT

Muiderpoort

Nieuwe

Achtgracht

Amstel

WEESPERPLEIN

Nieuwe

SARPHATISTRAAT

Tropenmuseum

SOUTH & EAST

MAURITSKADE

Oosterpark

WIBAUTSTRAAT

OLVG Hospital

N

Muiderpoort Station

AMSTELDIJK

0   250 m

Bema, map ref 41; Concertgebouwplein 19b (☎679 1396, fax 662 3688); tram #5 to Museumplein. Small but friendly place, kept very clean by the English-speaking manager. The rooms are not modern, but are full of character (high ceilings and pleasant decor). Handy for concerts and museums. ②

De Filosoof, map ref 32; Anna van den Vondelstraat 6 (☎683 3013, fax 685 3750); tram #1, #11 to Jan Pieter Heijestraat. Hospitable small hotel that for some reason names each of its rooms after a different philosopher, with suitably themed decor. Unique and characterful. ③

Parkzicht, map ref 34; Roemer Visscherstraat 33 (☎618 1954, fax 618 0897); tram #1, #11 to 1e Constantijn Huygensstraat. Quiet, unassuming little place on a pretty back street near the Vondelpark and museums, with an appealingly lived-in look – clean and charming. ③

Prinsen, map ref 33; Vondelstraat 38 (☎616 2323, fax 616 6112); tram #1, #11 to 1e Constantijn Huygensstraat. Affable, refurbished family-style hotel; quiet and with a large, secluded garden at the back. ③

Toro, map ref 38; Koningslaan 64 (☎673 7223, fax 675 0031); tram #2 to Emmastraat. Lovely hotel in two very comfortably furnished turn-of-the-century townhouses on a peaceful residential street out by the southern reaches of the Vondelpark. Boasts its own garden and terrace overlooking a lake in the park. ⑤

Hostels

The bottom line for most travellers is taking a **dormitory** bed in a hostel, and there are plenty to choose from; in fact you'll probably be accosted outside the train station with numerous offers of beds. Most hostels will either provide (relatively) clean bed **linen** or charge a few guilders for it. The cheapest deal you'll find is around ƒ20 per person per night; prices rise sharply at better-furnished and/or more central hostels to an average closer to ƒ30. Much more and you might as well be in a hotel room. Any place that won't allow you to check out the dorm before you pay is worth avoiding. If you want a little extra privacy, many hostels also offer triple, double and single **rooms** for less than you'd pay in a regular hotel, though the quality and size of rooms can leave a lot to be desired.

The Old Centre

Bob's Youth Hostel, map ref 8, Nieuwezijds Voorburgwal 92 (☎623 0063, no fax); 10min walk from CS. An old favourite of backpackers, this lively and smoky hostel has small, clean dorms. Breakfast is served in the coffeeshop on the ground floor (which also does cheap dinners); 3am curfew. ①

Flying Pig Downtown, map ref 4; Nieuwendijk 100 (☎420 6822, fax 624 9516); 5min walk from CS. Clean, large and well-run by ex-travellers familiar with the needs of backpackers. Free use of kitchen facilities, no curfew – and the hostel bar is open all night. Justifiably popular, and a very good deal. ①

Kabul, map ref 6; Warmoesstraat 38 (☎623 7158, fax 620 0869); 3min walk from CS. Huge, famous and bustling, with international clientele, multilingual staff, and rooms sleeping 1–16. Higher than usual prices, but it's immaculately clean, very safe, there's no lockout or curfew and there's a late bar next door. Doubles start at ƒ95. ①

The Shelter, map ref 11; Barndesteeg 21 (☎625 3230, fax 623 2282); metro Nieuwmarkt. A non-evangelical Christian youth hostel smack in the middle of the Red Light District: this is the cheapest bed in Amsterdam, with a sizeable breakfast included. Beds are in single-sex dorms, lockers cost ƒ1 and there's a midnight curfew (1am weekends). You might be handed a booklet on Jesus when you check in, but you'll get a quiet night's sleep and the sheets are clean. ①

Stadsdoelen, map ref 18; Kloveniersburgwal 97 (☎624 6832, fax 639 1035); walk, metro Nieuwmarkt, or trams #4, #9, #16, #24, #25 to Muntplein. The closest to the station of the two official hostels, with clean semi-private (partitioned beds) dorms. Sheets cost a steep *f*6.25 to rent. HI members have priority on bed-space in high season. If you stay here, you can take advantage of a range of discounts on activities in the city, including 10 percent off entry to the Van Gogh museum and 40 percent off a boat excursion; you can also book *Eurolines* bus tickets here. 2am curfew. ①

City centre west

De Bloeiende Ramenas, map ref 1; Haarlemmerdijk 61 (☎624 6030, fax 420 2261); 15min walk from CS. A cross between hostel and hotel, with comfortable rooms, friendly and welcoming management (and atmosphere), and sensible prices. Only disadvantage is the location, to the northwest of the centre and away from any action. ②

Eben Haezer, map ref 13; Bloemstraat 179 (☎624 4717, fax 627 6137); tram #13, #14, #17 to Marnixstraat. Another non-proselytizing Christian hostel, with some of the lowest prices in the city. Beds are in single-sex dorms, lockers cost *f*1 and there's a 1am curfew. Sited in a particularly beautiful part of the Jordaan, close to the Lijnbaansgracht canal. ①

Keizersgracht, map ref 2; Keizersgracht 15 (☎625 1364, fax 620 7347); 5min walk from CS. Terrific location on a major canal close to the station, with a good mixture of small dorms, single and doubles from *f*40 per person. Spotless rooms, although breakfast is extra. ①

City centre south and east

Adam and Eve, map ref 29; Sarphatistraat 105 (☎624 6206, fax 638 7200); metro Weesperplein. Good-quality, low-budget accommodation; outside the centre but not by too much, and well served by both the metro from Centraal Station and trams #6, #7 and #10 from Leidseplein. Mixed and single-sex dorms. ①

Arena, map ref 30; 's-Gravensandestraat 51 (☎694 7444, no fax); metro Weesperplein, then walk; or tram #6, #10 from Leidseplein to Korte 's-Gravensandestraat. A little way out of the centre to the east, in a renovated old convent on the edge of the Oosterpark, with probably the best-value cheap accommodation in the city. All sorts of dorms and rooms are available, although there is an inescapable (but returnable) *f*40 deposit. Women-only dorms at peak times. Other on-site facilities include an excellent and varied programme of live music, a centre providing tourist and cultural information (including bike rental), a great bar and restaurant and even parking facilities. Doubles start at *f*90. ①

Euphemia, map ref 36; Fokke Simonszstraat 1 (☎622 9045, fax 622 9045, email <euphjm@pi.net>); tram #16, #24, #25 to Weteringcircuit. Small dorms and large double rooms, with free showers and TVs. Likeable and laid-back, with very reasonable rates, which means it's usually full. ②

Hans Brinker, map ref 26; Kerkstraat 136 (☎622 0687, fax ☎638 2060); tram #1, #2, #5, #11 to Prinsengracht. Another well-established and raucously popular Amsterdam cheapie, though a little more upmarket than some, with dorm beds going for around *f*40. Good, basic and clean, and close to the Leidseplein buzz. ②

International Budget Hotel, map ref 20; Leidsegracht 76 (☎624 2784, no fax; email <euphjm@pi.net>); tram #1, #2, #5, #11 to Prinsengracht. An excellent budget option on a peaceful little canal in the heart of the city. Small, simple dorms and friendly young staff. ②

Museumplein and the Vondelpark

Flying Pig Vondelpark, map ref 37; Vossiusstraat 46 (☎400 4187, fax 400 4105); tram #1, #2, #5, #11 to Leidseplein. Immaculately clean and well-maintained by a staff of travellers, who well understand their backpacking guests. Free use of kitchen facilities, no curfew and good tourist information. Great value. ①

Vondelpark, map ref 35; Zandpad 5 (☎683 1744, fax 616 6591); tram #1, #2, #5, #11 to Leidseplein. For facilities, the better of the two HI hostels, with a bar, restaurant, TV lounge and kitchen; it's also well located on the edge of the city's major park. HI members have priority on bed-space in high season. Secure lockers and a lift. Curfew 2am. ①

Campsites

There are several campsites in and around Amsterdam, most of which are easily accessible by public transport or by car. The four listed below are recommended by the *VVV*, which divides them into the self-explanatory "**youth** campsites", and "**family** campsites", the latter being more suitable for those seeking some quiet, or if you're touring with a caravan or camper.

Youth campsites

Vliegenbos, Meeuwenlaan 138 (☎636 8855, fax 632 2723); bus #32 from CS. A relaxed and friendly site, just a 10min bus ride into Amsterdam North. Rates are *f*9.25 per person per night, plus *f*1 for a tent and *f*12.50 for a motorbike. Hot showers are included. Vliegenbos also has a few camping huts with bunk beds and basic cooking facilities for *f*63 per night for four people; phone ahead to check availability. Open April–Sept.

Zeeburg, Zuiderzeeweg 29 (☎694 4430, fax 694 6238); train from CS (or tram #10 from Leidseplein) to Muiderpoort Station, then bus #37. Slightly better equipped than the *Vliegenbos*, but more difficult to get to. Rates are *f*6.50 per person, plus *f*3.50 for a tent, *f*3.50 for a motorbike, *f*1.50 for a hot shower; huts are also available. Open March–Dec.

Family campsites

Amsterdamse Bos, Kleine Noorddijk 1, Aalsmeer (☎641 6868, fax 640 2378); yellow *NZH* bus #171 from CS. Many facilities, but a long way out to the south. Rates are *f*8.25 per person (*f*4.25 for under 12s), hot showers included, plus *f*5.25 for a tent (*f*4.25 for a motorbike or car, camper or caravan). Huts are available. Open April–Oct.

Gaasper Camping, Loosdrechtdreef 7 (☎696 7326, fax 696 9369); metro Gaasperplas. Amsterdam's newest campsite, in Amsterdam Zuidoost (South-East), easily reachable from Centraal Station by metro – and very close to the wonderful Gaasperplas park. Rates are *f*6 (*f*3.50 for under 12s), plus *f*7 per tent, *f*5.50 for a car, *f*8 for a caravan. Hot showers *f*1.50. Open March–Dec.

The city

Amsterdam is an easy city to find your way around. Centraal Station, where you're likely to arrive, lies on the northern edge of the city centre, its back to the River IJ: from the station, the city fans south in a web of concentric canals, surrounded by expanding suburbs. The **centre** of the city – along with the main canals, the area in which you'll spend most of your time – is the old medieval town, to the immediate south of Centraal Station; this revolves around the main streets of Damrak and Rokin, which lead into and out of Dam Square at the city's core. This area is Amsterdam's commercial heart, and has the best of its bustling street life: it is home to shops, many bars and restaurants and, not least, the infamous **Red Light District**. The Old Centre is bordered by the first of the major **canals**, the Singel, followed closely by the Herengracht, Keizersgracht and Prinsengracht; all four are collectively referred to as the *Grachtengordel* ("Girdle of Canals". These canals are part of a major seventeenth-century urban expansion and, with the radial streets of Raadhuisstraat, Leidsestraat, Vijzelstraat and Weesperstraat, create Amsterdam's distinctive web shape.

Beyond the *Grachtengordel*, the **Jordaan** district to the west grew up as a slum and immigrant quarter and remains the traditional heart of working-class Amsterdam, though these days the area has a more gentrified flavour. On the

In the city account that follows, major **museums** are mentioned in passing, but – to do them justice – Amsterdam's fine array of galleries and museums are covered separately, starting on p.87.

other side of town, the **Jodenbuurt** was once home to the city's Jewish community. Since the construction of the City Hall complex here, as well as the digging of the city's metro underneath the area, this is probably the district of Amsterdam that exhibits the most visible postwar changes.

Just beyond the meandering Singelgracht canal to the south, close to the pretty **Vondelpark**, lies **Museumplein**, around which are clustered Amsterdam's three major museums – the Rijksmuseum, the Van Gogh Museum and the Stedelijk – as well as the Concertgebouw concert hall.

Stationsplein, Damrak and the Red Light District

This is where you'll almost certainly arrive – the city's busiest and most vigorous district by far, lacking the gracious uniformity of much of the rest of the city centre, but making up for it in excitement. Here Stationsplein, international buskers' meeting-point and home of the *VVV* tourist office, rubs shoulders with the strategic tourist trap of Damrak and the studied (though real enough) sleaze of the Red Light District – not surprisingly one of Amsterdam's biggest tourist attractions.

Stationsplein and along Damrak

The neo-Gothic **Centraal Station** is an imposing prelude to the city. When it was built late in the last century, this was a controversial structure as it obscured the views of the port that brought Amsterdam its wealth. Since then, however, shipping has moved out to more spacious dock areas to the west, and the station is now one of Amsterdam's most resonant landmarks: stand here and all of Amsterdam, with its faintly Oriental skyline of spires and cupolas, lies before you.

Stationsplein, immediately outside, is a messy open space, but in the summer there's no livelier part of the city, as street performers compete for attention with the careering trams that converge dangerously from all sides. It's a promising place to arrive, and with that in mind the municipal authorities are cleaning up the area's image, notably in the southeastern corner, where there's a luxury hotel and new development slowly creeping down the once-notorious Zeedijk.

Close by here, the dome of the **St Nicolaaskerk** catches the eye. Despite a dilapidated exterior, it is the city's foremost Catholic church, having replaced the clandestine Amstelkring (see p.93) in 1887. Nicolaas is the patron saint of sailors, which explains the church's proximity to the harbour. If you manage to co-ordinate your visit with the limited opening hours (Easter to mid-Oct Mon 1.30–4pm; Tues–Sat 11am–4pm; closed to visitors in winter), in the lavishly gloomy interior, perched on the high altar, you'll find the crown of Austro-Hungarian Emperor Maximilian – very much a symbol of the city and one you'll see again and again (on top of the Westerkerk and on much of the city's official literature).

Above all, though, Stationsplein acts as a filter for Amsterdam's newcomers, and from here **Damrak**, an unenticing avenue lined by tacky, over-priced restaurants and the bobbing canal boats of Amsterdam's considerable tourist industry, storms south into the heart of the city. Just past the boats is the old Stock Exchange, or

Beurs (known as the "Beurs van Berlage"), designed at the turn of the century by the leading light of the Dutch modern movement, H P Berlage, and now used as a concert hall. With its various styles from Romanesque to neo-Renaissance interwoven with a minimum of ornamentation, it is something of a seminal work. Slip inside the entrance on Beursplein and look into the main hall, where exposed ironwork and shallow-arched arcades combine to give a real sense of space.

During the prewar years, the **De Bijenkorf** (literally "beehive") department store building, facing the Beurs and extending as far as Dam Square, was a successful Jewish concern – so much so that during the Nazi occupation the authorities, fearing possible altercations with the Jewish staff, forbade German soldiers from shopping on the ground floor.

Around the Red Light District

Had you turned left off Damrak before the Beurs, you would have found yourself in the **RED LIGHT DISTRICT**, bordered by the oldest street in the city, Warmoesstraat, and stretching across the two canals which marked the edge of medieval Amsterdam, Oudezijds Voorburgwal and Oudezijds Achterburgwal.

The **prostitution** here is world-renowned, and is sadly, but perhaps inevitably, one of the real sights of the city, and one of its most distinctive draws; the two canals with their narrow connecting passages are on most evenings of the year thronged with people keen to discover just how shocking it all is. Groups of men line the streets hawking peep shows and "live sex", while lingerie-clad women sit bored in red-lit shop windows. The nasty edge to the district is, oddly enough, sharper during the daytime, when the pimps hang out in shifty gangs and drug addicts wait anxiously, assessing the chances of scoring their next hit.

Narrow **Warmoesstraat** itself is seedy and uninviting; a little way along, the precincts of the **Oude Kerk** (Mon–Sat 11am–5pm, Sun 1–5pm; *f*5; tower mid-

---

COMMERCIAL SEX IN AMSTERDAM

Since the 1960s, Amsterdam's liberal approach to social policy has resulted in the city gaining worldwide notoriety as a major international centre for both **drugs** (see p.104) and the commercial **sex** industry. However, the tackiness of the Red Light District is the surface scum hiding a serious attempt to address the reality of sex-for-sale, and to allow it to take its place as one aspect of a normal, ordered society. In the eyes of Dutch law, prostitutes are seen as victims; prostituting oneself is legal here, but organizing it isn't – the last attempt to legalize brothel-keeping foundered in 1993, but a significant lobby remains in favour, led by the prostitutes' trade union, *De Rode Draad* ("The Red Thread") and backed by Cabinet support. There is much dynamism in the industry: prostitutes are now liable for income tax on their earnings, there are moves to set up health insurance and pension schemes for prostitutes, and recently a code of self-regulation has been established by the more reputable operators, to discourage clients from going to exploitative businesses.

One of the most endearing aspects of the Dutch approach is the lack of prudery, exemplified by the **Prostitution Information Centre** (PIC), at Enge Kerksteeg 3 (between Warmoesstraat and the Oude Kerk; Tues–Sat noon–9pm; ☎420 7328). This legally recognized charitable foundation was set up to provide prostitutes, clients and visitors with clear, cool-headed information about prostitution, and has done much to subvert the old exploitative dominance of underworld pimps and expose the living and working conditions of women who choose to be prostitutes.

DRUGS IN AMSTERDAM

Amsterdam's liberal attitude extends to **soft drugs**, and the city's reputation among dope-smokers worldwide as a place, uniquely and legally, to buy and smoke hashish and marijuana, is legendary. Technically, all drugs are illegal in Amsterdam; however, since 1976, the possession of small amounts of cannabis (up to 28g/1oz) has been ignored by the police, a situation which has led to the rise of "smoking" coffeeshops (see p.103), selling bags of dope much as bars sell glasses of beer.

With the move towards European integration, the Netherlands has recently come under increasing pressure to bring their drug policy into line with the rest of Europe, but the Dutch are still largely sticking to their guns, citing a lack of evidence linking the use of "recreational" drugs with **hard drugs**. In fact the country's figures for hard-drug addiction are among the lowest in Europe, and the city government has adopted a characteristically enlightened approach, instituting needle exchanges and free methadone supplies – policies intended to promote the health of addicts and social well-being, rather than unquestioning enforcement of the law.

June to Sept Wed–Sat 2–4pm; *f*3) offer a reverential peace after the excesses of the Red Light District – though even here many of the houses have the familiar *Kamer te Huur* ("Room for Rent") sign and window seat. There's been a church on this site since the late thirteenth century, even before the Dam was built, but most of the present building dates from the fourteenth century. Having been stripped bare during the Reformation and recently very thoroughly restored, the Oude Kerk is nowadays a survivor rather than an architectural masterpiece. Its handful of interesting features include – apart from a few faded vault paintings – some beautifully carved misericords in the choir, and the memorial tablet of Rembrandt's wife, Saskia van Uylenburg, who is buried here.

Very nearby, at the junction of Oudezijds Voorburgwal and Lange Niezel, is the clandestine **Amstelkring**, once the principal Catholic place of worship in the city and now one of the city's best and least demanding small museums (see p.93).

There's little else to stop for in wandering through the Red Light District, although the **Hash Marihuana Hemp Museum**, at Oudezijds Achterburgwal 148 is still going strong between intermittent battles with the police; displays of various types of dope and numerous ways to smoke it jostle for space with pamphlets on the medicinal properties of cannabis and a Bible made of hemp.

Zeedijk, a small alley running behind Oudezijds Achterburgwal, was once the centre of Amsterdam's thriving heroin-dealing trade; since a mid-Eighties clean-up, it is displaying signs of regeneration, with bars, coffeeshops and restaurants springing up among the still-ramshackle buildings.

Zeedijk opens out on to **Nieuwmarkt** and the bottom end of **Geldersekade**, which together form the hub of Amsterdam's tiny Chinese quarter. Nieuwmarkt has always been one of Amsterdam's most important markets, first for fish, later for the cloth traders from the adjacent Jewish quarter; however, during World War II, the whole area was cordoned off with barbed wire and turned into a holding pen for the city's Jews awaiting deportation. The old exuberance never returned, and these days the market has all but vanished: there is a small market for organic food on Saturdays and one for antiques on Sundays, with a few stalls selling fish, fruit and vegetables during the week.

The main focus of the square, the turreted **Waag** or old **Sint Antoniespoort**, has played a variety of roles over the years. Originally part of the fortifications that encircled Amsterdam, it later became the civic weighing house, and for more than two centuries housed the Surgeons' Guild; in a specially designed theatre, constructed in the octagonal tower in 1691, the guild held lectures on anatomy and public dissections – the young Rembrandt's *Anatomy Lesson of Dr Tulp* was based on the activities here. The building was recently bought by the Society for Old and New Media, and renovated from top to bottom; in addition to a café and restaurant (with a "Digital Reading Table"), the old anatomy theatre upstairs now plays host to changing exhibitions, lectures and readings.

Along Kloveniersburgwal

Kloveniersburgwal, which leads south from Nieuwmarkt, was the outer of the three eastern canals of sixteenth-century Amsterdam. A long, dead-straight waterway with dignified facades, it boasts, on the left at no. 29, one of the city's most impressive canal houses. Built for the Trip family in 1662, and large enough to house the Rijksmuseum collection for most of the nineteenth century, the **Trippenhuis** is a huge, overblown mansion, its Corinthian pilasters and grand frieze providing a suitable reflection of the owners' importance.

Further up the canal, on the corner of Oude Hoogstraat, the red-brick former headquarters of the **Dutch East India Company** is a monumental building, completed in 1605, shortly after the founding of the company. It was from here that the Dutch organized and regulated the trading interests in the Far East, which made the country so opulent in the seventeenth century. Expeditions established links with India, Sri Lanka, the islands of the Indonesian archipelago, and later with China and Japan, and used the Dutch Republic's fleet of vessels to rob the Portuguese and Spanish of trade – and the islanders of spices, textiles and exotic woods. Dutch expansionism wasn't purely mercantile: not only had the East India Company been given a trading monopoly in all the lands east of the Cape of Good Hope, but also unlimited military, judicial and political powers in the countries which it administered. Behind the satisfied smiles of the comfortable burghers of the Golden Age was a nightmare of slavery and exploitation.

For all that, the building itself is of little interest, occupied these days by offices. You'll do better to continue on toward the southern end of Kloveniersburgwal, and the **Oudemanhuispoort** passage, which was once part of an almshouse for elderly men, but is now filled with second-hand bookstalls and a group of buildings serving Amsterdam University. It comes out on Oudezijds Achterburgwal, from where you look across to the pretty **Huis op de Drie Grachten** ("House on the Three Canals"), on the corner of Grimburgwal. A little way down Oudezijds Voorburgwal on the right, through an ornate gateway, is the **Agnietenkapel** (Mon–Fri 9am–5pm; ƒ2.50), also owned by the university and containing exhibitions on academic life through the ages.

At the corner a passage cuts through to **Nes**, a long, narrow street leading to the Dam, once home to the philosopher Spinoza and now filled with theatres; or you can make your way back down the canal past the commercial art dealership **Galerie Mokum**, named after the old Jewish nickname for the city (which has now passed into general use). From here it's just a few yards out to the trams and traffic of Rokin. Also nearby, at Oude Turfmarkt 127, is the **Allard Pierson Museum**, a small but rewarding archeological collection (see p.92) – or you could simply sink into one of the terrace seats of '*t Gasthuys* café, at Grimburgwal 7 (see p.101), a popular student haunt and excellent for either a quick drink or a full lunch.

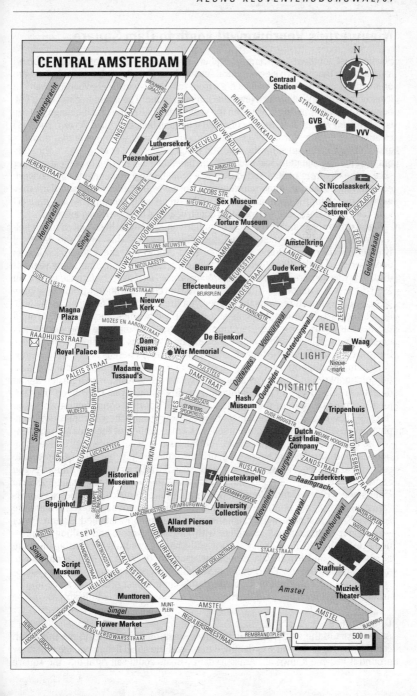

CENTRAL AMSTERDAM

Nieuwezijds Voorburgwal south to Dam Square

Starting just southwest of Centraal Station, Nieuwezijds Voorburgwal cuts a broad swathe down the western side of central Amsterdam. The city's outer boundaries were once ringed by a defensive wall, and it's from this that Nieuwezijds Voorburgwal ("In front of the Town Wall on the New Side") gets its name. The street begins with a bottleneck of trams swinging down from the station, and one of the first buildings you see is the *Holiday Inn*, built on the site of an old tenement building called **Wyers**. The 1985 clearance of squatters from Wyers ranks among the most infamous of that decade's anti-squatting campaigns, having involved much protest and some violence throughout the city. The squatters had occupied the building in an attempt to prevent another slice of the city from being handed over to a profit-hungry multinational and converted from residential use. Although widely supported by the people of Amsterdam, they were no match for the economic muscle of the American hotel company, and it wasn't long before the riot police were sent in; construction of the hotel soon followed.

The **Luthersekerk**, directly west from here on Kattengat, hasn't fared much better. With its copper-green dome, the church gives this area the label of **Koepelkwartier** or "Dome Neighbourhood"; however, the church itself was deconsecrated in the 1930s because of falling attendances, and, after many years of disuse, it was acquired by the nearby *Renaissance Hotel* as a conference centre. In 1993 there was a major fire which gutted the church; restoration work is now complete, but the church remains the property of the hotel and is not open to the public. To the east, **Spuistraat** begins at a fork in Nieuwezijds Voorburgwal. Around the St Dominicus Kerk and the Oude Nieuwstraat, a small red-light district sits uneasily in the alleyways between the canal and the trams. Little here is for show – these are the red lights the tourists miss – and business here is serious and seamy.

Heading south, you can't miss the glassy new complex of building at the junction of Nieuwezijds Voorburgwal and the Nieuwezijds Kolk, which forged ahead despite the discovery of archeological remains (thought to have been the thirteenth-century **castle** of the "Lords of Aemstel") during construction works on the site. The razing of old buildings to make way for this new complex, and simply the presence of the structure itself, has erased much of the area's character.

The trees that fringe Nieuwezijds Voorburgwal conceal some impressive canal houses, and specialized shops and private galleries try hard to preserve the refinement the street must have had before canal traffic gave way to trams. As you approach the Dam, the side-alleys (including the wonderfully named Zwarte Handsteeg, "Black Hand Alley") have a medieval eccentricity, and all seediness vanishes as designer boutiques appear in the old workshops clustered around the Nieuwe Kerk. Just across the road, the huge building now labelled **Magna Plaza** – an indoor shopping mall, complete with *Virgin Megastore* and fashion chains – used to be the old Post Office, and it still manages to hold its own against the Nieuwe Kerk and Royal Palace opposite. Built in 1899, its whimsical embellishments continue the town's tradition of sticking towers on things – here, as everywhere, purely for the hell of it. Amsterdam's central post office has since moved around the corner from here, to the corner of Singel and Raadhuisstraat.

Dam Square

At the heart of the city, **Dam Square** gave Amsterdam its name: in the thirteenth century the River Amstel was dammed here, and the small fishing village that grew around it became known as "Amstelredam". Boats could sail right into the square down the Damrak and unload their imported grain in the middle of the rapidly grow-ing town; later, the building of Amsterdam's principal church, the Nieuwe Kerk, along with the Royal Palace, formally marked Dam Square as Amsterdam's centre.

Though robbed a little of its dignity by the trams that scuttle across it, the square is still the hub of the city, with all the main streets zeroing in on a mael-strom of buskers, artists and ice-cream vans. On the far side there's a **War Memorial**, an unsightly stone tusk filled with soil from each of the Netherlands' provinces and Indonesia, which serves as a gathering place for the square's milling tourists who seem to be wondering if, among the musicians and drug pushers, they've really found the heart of liberated Amsterdam.

The main feature of the square, though, is the **Royal Palace** (Sept–May Tues–Thur 1–4pm, June–Aug daily 12.30–5pm; *f*5), which seems neither Dutch nor palatial – understandably so since it was originally built from imported stone as the city's town hall. At the time of its construction in the mid-seventeenth century, it was the largest town hall in Europe, supported by 13,659 wooden piles driven into the Dam's sandy soil. Inside, the **Citizen's Hall** proclaims the pride and confidence of the Golden Age, with the enthroned personification of Amsterdam looking down on the world and heavens laid out at her feet, the whole sumptuously inlaid in brass and marble. A good-natured and witty symbolism pervades the building: cocks fight above the entrance to the **Court of Petty Affairs**, while Apollo, god of the sun and the arts, brings harmony to the disputes. On a more sober note, death sentences were pronounced at the **High Court of Justice** at the front of the building, and the condemned were immediately executed on a scaffold outside.

The building received its royal associations in 1808 when Napoleon's brother Louis commandeered it as the one building fit for a king. Lonely and isolated, Louis briefly ruled from here, until forced to acquiesce to Napoleon's autocratic demands. On his abdication in 1810 he left behind a sizeable amount of Empire furniture, most of which is exhibited in the rooms he converted.

Vying for importance with the Palace is the **Nieuwe Kerk** (opening hours and admission prices vary), which, despite its name, is a fifteenth-century structure rebuilt several times after fires. Though impressive from the outside, the Nieuwe Kerk has long since lost out in rivalries with the Oude Kerk and the Royal Palace (it was forbidden a tower in case it outshone the new town hall), and is now used only for exhibitions, organ concerts and state occasions; Queen Beatrix was crowned here in 1980. The interior is neat and orderly, its sheer Gothic lines only slightly weighed down by seventeenth-century fixtures such as the massive pul-pit and organ case. Of the catalogue of household names from Dutch history rep-resented in the church, Admiral de Ruyter, seventeenth-century Holland's most valiant naval hero, lies in an opulent tomb in the choir, and the poet Vondel, a sort of Dutch Shakespeare, is commemorated by a small urn near the entrance.

South to the Flower Market

Three main streets head south from Dam Square. Broad Nieuwezijds Voorburgwal continues its march south to Spui (pronounced to rhyme with "cow"), its sidestreets littered with antique dealers and stamp shops – and some of Amsterdam's oldest and most exclusive restaurants. Damrak turns into the broad sweep of **Rokin**, which follows the old course of the River Amstel. Lined with grandiose nineteenth-century mansions – Sotheby's is here, and, further down, the *Maison de la Bonneterie* clothes store, with its elaborate *fin de siècle* interior – this stretch gives trams their sole chance to accelerate in the city; cross with care. Running parallel with Rokin, **Kalverstraat** has been a commercial centre since it hosted a calf market in medieval times; now it has declined into a standard European shopping mall, an uninspired strip of monotonous clothes shops differentiated only by the varying strains of disco music they pump out. About halfway down the street, a lopsided and frivolous gateway forms an unexpected entrance to the former municipal orphanage that's now the **Amsterdam Historical Museum** (see p.93). Directly outside the museum, the glassed-in **Civic Guard Gallery** draws passers-by with free glimpses of the huge company portraits commissioned by Amsterdam worthies from the 1540s through to the lighter affairs of the seventeenth century.

Connected to the Historical Museum is one of the gems of Amsterdam, neither obvious nor marked. Perhaps those who run the **Begijnhof** want it this way: enclosed on three sides, this small court of buildings is an enclave of tranquillity which is typically Dutch and totally removed from the surrounding streets. Most of the houses are seventeenth-century, but one, no. 34, dates from 1475 – the oldest house in Amsterdam, and built before the city forbade the construction of houses in wood, an essential precaution against fire.

These kinds of *hofjes* (little courtyards) are found all over the Low Countries. Built by rich individuals or city councils for the poor and elderly, the houses usually face inwards around a small court, their backs to the outside world. This sense of retreat suited the women who, without taking full vows, led a religious life in the *hofjes*, which often had their own chapel. The order here was known as *Begijnen*, and such was its standing in the city community that it was allowed to quietly continue its tradition of worship even after Catholicism was suppressed in 1587. Mass was inconspicuously celebrated in the concealed **Catholic Church**, a dark Italianate building with a breath-holding silence that seems odd after the natural peace outside. There's none of this sense of mystery about the **English Reformed Church** which takes up one side of the Begijnhof. Plain and unadorned, it was handed over to Amsterdam's English community when the Begijns were deprived of their main place of worship and, like the *hofje* itself, it's almost too charming, a model of prim simplicity. Inside are several old English memorial plaques, and pulpit panels designed by the young Piet Mondrian.

Spui and around

Back out in the noise and the trams, Spuistraat and Nieuwezijds Voorburgwal culminate in the newly repaved **Spui**, a chic corner of town with a mixture of bookshops, fashionable restaurants and packed bars and cafés centring on a small, rather cloying statue of a young boy – known as **'t Lieverdje** ("Little Darling") – which was a gift to the city from a large cigarette company in 1960.

In the mid-Sixties, Spui was the scene of a series of demonstrations organized by the Provos, an anarchist group devoted to *ludiek* ("pranks"); though they numbered only a few dozen people, the group had an impact on the city that lasted decades. In 1964, when the alternative subculture was at its most militant, the Provos branded 't Lieverdje an emblem of rampant capitalism – and the addicted smokers who would become its prey – and turned up every Saturday evening for *ludiek* with the Spui's assembled drinkers. When the police arrived to break up these small "happenings", they did little to endear themselves to the public, and much to gain sympathy for the Provos (see box opposite).

From Spui, you can rejoin the hubbub of Kalverstraat, which comes to an ignoble end in a stretch of ice-cream parlours and fast-food outlets before reaching

THE PROVOS AND THE KABOUTERS

Amsterdam's reputation as a wacky, offbeat city rests largely on its experiences in the 1960s, when social and political discontent began to coalesce into opposition to the city council's redevelopment plans. In contrast to similar movements in Paris and London, in Amsterdam the protests developed a uniquely playful aspect, and, possibly as a consequence, garnered substantial public support. In the early 1960s, one of the popular groupings that emerged, led by Roel van Duyn and called the **Provos** (a name derived from "provocation"), took to holding small "happenings" around the 't Lieverdje statue; for the most part, the reception they got was positive and enthusiastic. In 1965, when the police moved in to forcibly disperse a Provo gathering, serious unrest ensued. Rioting broke out again a few months later, at the wedding of Princess (now Queen) Beatrix; while the procession was passing through the city, rioters clashed with police amid smoke-bombs and tear-gas.

In 1966, the Provos won over two percent of the vote in municipal elections, and gained a seat on the city council. The ideas the Provos brought to city politics – the **White Plans** – are perhaps their most substantial legacy. Under the most famous of these, cars were to be banned from the centre of Amsterdam, and 20,000 white bicycles were to be distributed for people to use free of charge, before leaving them at their journey's end for someone else to use. Despite a couple of trials, the plan was never implemented, although it has recently been resurrected for a pilot project.

By 1967, the Provos' plans for the rejuvenation of Amsterdam had become wildly idealistic and unmanageable, and the grouping disintegrated. Van Duyn then founded the **Kabouters**, so-called after a helpful gnome who features in Dutch folklore. The group's manifesto described their form of socialism as "not of the clenched fist, but of the intertwined fingers, the erect penis, the escaping butterfly ..." Despite a degree of success on the margins of Amsterdam politics during the Seventies, the Kabouters finally came to grief in 1981; Van Duyn, though, continued his involvement in local politics, and today holds the single Green Party seat on the city council.

Muntplein. The tower here, called the **Munttoren**, was originally a mint and part of the old city walls; it was topped with a spire by Hendrik de Keyser in 1620 and is possibly the most famous of the towers dotting the city, a landmark perfectly designed for postcards when framed by the flowers of the nearby floating **Bloemenmarkt** (flower market; Mon–Sat 9am–6pm), which extends along the southern bank of the Singel west as far as Koningsplein. Although it's nearly always packed with visitors, and has much clogs-and-Delft tat, the flower market has many genuine bargains, including bulbs for export. Once at Koningsplein, the main Leidsestraat artery leads south to your left; ahead of you, the Singel canal curls away, while to your right, the cramped Heiligeweg leads back into the shopping heart of things.

The Grachtengordel

The central part of Amsterdam was originally encircled by the Singel, which was part of Amsterdam's original protective moat but is now just the first of the five **canals** that reach right around the city centre in a *grachtengordel* ("girdle of canals"), constructed in a period of seventeenth-century urban expansion. The three main waterways, Herengracht, Keizersgracht and Prinsengracht, were set aside for the residences and offices of the richer and more influential Amsterdam merchants, while the radial canals were left for more modest artisans' homes. Even the richest burgher had to conform to a set of stylistic rules when building his house, and taxes were levied according to the width of the properties. This produced the loose conformity you can see today: tall, narrow residences, with individualism restricted to heavy decorative gables and sometimes a gablestone to denote name and occupation.

Of the three main canals, **Herengracht** ("Gentlemen's Canal") was the first to be dug, and the burghers who held economic sway over Amsterdam soon lined it with big, ostentatious houses. The naming of the canals reflects very clearly the pecking order in the city at that time: the businessmen's Herengracht was closest in, followed by the **Keizersgracht**, or "Emperor's Canal" (after Holy Roman Emperor Maximilian I) and, further out still, the **Prinsengracht**, or "Princes' Canal" (after the princes of the House of Orange). These last two ended up with noticeably smaller houses – though both still hold some of the most sought-after properties in the city. Herengracht, though, remains the city's grandest stretch of water, especially the "Golden Curve" between Leidsestraat and Vijzelstraat (see p.78), but you may find the less pretentious houses and warehouses of Prinsengracht more appealing.

It's hard to single out particular points to head for along the three main canals. A lot of the canal houses have been turned into offices or hotels, although many are still lived in, and there's little of specific interest apart from the odd museum. Rather, the appeal lies in wandering along, admiring the gables and taking in the tree-lined canals' calm, so unusual in the centre of a modern European capital. For shops, bars, restaurants and the like, you're better off diving into the streets that connect the canals.

From Brouwersgracht to Leliegracht

In the northwest of the centre, running west to east along the top edge of all three main canals is **Brouwersgracht**, one of the most picturesque waterways in the city. In the seventeenth century, Brouwersgracht lay at the edge of Amsterdam's great harbour; it was where ships just returned from the Far East unloaded their booty of silks and spices. It was also one of the major arteries linking the open sea with the city centre, and was lined with storage depots, warehouses and breweries, which capitalized on the shipments of fresh water that had to be barged into the city along this canal; given the prevailing methods of sanitation, beer was then a far healthier drink than water. Today, the harbour bustle has moved elsewhere, and the warehouses have been converted into apartments, their functional architecture contrasting with the decorative facades that grace the major canals. Brouwersgracht has become a quiet, residential canal, full of trees and birdsong, with spectacular views down the lengths of the Heren-, Keizers- and Prinsengrachten.

From here, to pick any of the three main canals to head down is to miss the other two; this area, west of the centre, is one of the city's most untouched neighbourhoods – and one of its loveliest. The Prinsengracht, where it meets the Brouwersgracht, has a gentle beauty quite unlike its grander rivals, with tumble-down houseboats moored along its banks and small, closely packed houses. One of the most pleasant of the city's *hofjes*, or little courtyards, is here – the Van Brienen Hofje, at Prinsengracht 89–133 (although it's currently closed for renovation). The cross-street connecting the main canals here – **Prinsenstraat**, running into **Herenstraat** – is one of the most appealing little streets in Amsterdam, filled with flower shops, relaxed cafés, greengroceries and secondhand clothes shops.

Further south, the **Leliegracht** is one of the tiny radial canals cutting across the Grachtengordel, and is home to a number of bookshops and canalside bars. There are few examples of Art Nouveau and Art Deco architecture to be seen in Amsterdam, but one of the finest is the tall, strikingly elegant building at the junction of Keizersgracht and Leliegracht. The main building was designed by G van Arkel in 1905, and was added to in the late Sixties; it is now Greenpeace International's world headquarters.

The Anne Frank House and the Westermarkt
In 1957, the Anne Frank Foundation set up the **Anne Frank House** (see p.93) at Prinsengracht 263, in the house in which the young diarist used to listen to the Westertoren bells before they were taken away to be melted down for the Nazi war effort.

ANNE FRANK

Since World War II, Anne Frank has come to stand both as a symbol of the Holocaust and as an inspiration to all prisoners of conscience. Her **diary** – one teenager's record of life in hiding from the Nazis – was a source of inspiration for Nelson Mandela in prison in South Africa, and is still on many school syllabuses around the world today.

The story of Anne Frank, her family and friends is widely known. Anne's father, Otto, was a well-to-do Jewish businessman who ran a successful spice-trading business and lived in the southern part of the city. By 1942 the **Nazi occupation** was taking its toll: all Jews had been forced to wear a yellow star, and were not allowed to use public transport, go to the theatre or cinema or stray into certain areas of the city; roundups, too, were becoming increasingly common. As conditions became more difficult, Otto Frank decided to move into their warehouse on the Prinsengracht, the back half of which was unused at the time. The Franks went into hiding in July 1942, along with a Jewish business partner and his family, the Van Daans, shielded from the eyes of the outside world by a bookcase that doubled as a door. As far as everyone else was concerned, they had fled to Switzerland.

So began the two-year occupation of the *achterhuis*, or back **annexe**. In her diary Anne Frank describes the day-to-day lives of the inhabitants of the annexe: the quarrels, frequent occurrences in such a claustrophobic environment; celebrations of birthdays, or of some good news from the Allied Front; and her own, slightly unreal, growing up (much of which, it's been claimed, was subsequently deleted by her father). By 1944, an Allied victory was in sight, and it seemed as if the fugitives would soon be able to emerge. It wasn't to be. One day in the summer of 1944 the Franks were betrayed by a Dutch collaborator; the Gestapo arrived and forced Mr Kraler to open up the bookcase, whereupon the occupants of the annexe were all arrested and transported to Westerbork – the transit camp in the north of the country where all Dutch Jews were processed before being moved to Belsen or Auschwitz. Of the eight who had sought refuge in the annexe, ultimately Otto Frank was the sole survivor; Anne and her sister died of typhus within a short time of each other in Belsen, just one week before the German surrender.

Anne Frank's diary was among the few things left behind in the annexe. It was retrieved by one of the people who had helped the Franks and handed to Anne's father on his return from Auschwitz; he later decided to publish it. Since its appearance in 1947, it has been constantly in print, has been translated into 54 languages – and sold thirteen million copies worldwide.

Just down the Prinsengracht is **Westermarkt**, in the shadow of the Westerkerk. The seventeenth-century French philosopher René Descartes lived at here, at no. 6, for a short time, happy that the business-oriented character of the city left him able to work and think without being disturbed. As he wrote at the time, "Everybody except me is in business and so absorbed by profit-making I could spend my entire life here without being noticed by a soul".

However, it's the **Westerkerk** (Mon–Fri 10am–4pm, Sat 10am–1pm; tower April–Sept Mon–Sat 10am–4pm, ƒ3) that dominates the area, its 85-metre tower – Amsterdam's finest – soaring graciously above the gables of Prinsengracht. On its top perches the crown of Kaiser Maximilian, a constantly recurring symbol of the city. The church was designed by Hendrik de Keyser (architect also of the Zuiderkerk and Noorderkerk) as part of the seventeenth-century enlargement of the city, and completed in 1631. But while this is probably Amsterdam's most visually appealing church from the outside, there's little within of special note.

Rembrandt, who was living nearby when he died, is commemorated by a small memorial in the north aisle. His pauper's grave can no longer be precisely located; indeed, there's a possibility that he's not here at all, since many of the bodies were moved to a cemetery when underground heating was installed. The memorial is, however, close to where Rembrandt's son Titus is buried. Rembrandt worshipped his son – as is evidenced by numerous portraits – and the boy's death dealt a final crushing blow to the ageing and embittered artist, contibuting to his own death just over a year later. During renovation of the church in 1990 and 1991, bones were unearthed which could have been those of Titus and even of Rembrandt himself – a discovery that briefly excited the church authorities about tourist potential. The only thing that would confirm the bones' identity is a chemical analysis of their lead content: in the skeleton of an artist such as Rembrandt, this should prove unusually high, as lead was a major ingredient of paint at that time. The required analysis has, however, been stymied by lack of funds, and the bones still languish at the University of Groningen.

Just outside the church, on the Prinsengracht side, you can find a small, simple statue of Anne Frank by the Dutch sculptor Mari Andriessen – a careful and evocative site, recalling the long years Anne Frank spent in the *achterhuis* just a few steps away up the canal (see box on p.73).

Behind the church, on the corner of Keizersgracht and Westermarkt, are the pink granite triangles of the **Homo-Monument**, the world's first memorial to persecuted gays and lesbians. A resonant design by Karin Daan subverts the image of the pink triangle, which all homosexuals were forced to sew onto their clothing during the Nazi occupation. The sculpture serves to commemorate not only those homosexuals who died in Nazi concentration camps, but also known homosexuals who fought with the Allies and whose names were omitted from other remembrance monuments. The Homo-monument provides a continuing focus for the gay community in general, and is the site of ceremonies and wreath-laying throughout the year.

Raadhuisstraat to Leidsestraat

Below the Raadhuisstraat, the main canals retain their appeal for wandering, but it is the small **cross-streets** between them that hold the best possibilities for exploration: this is quintessential Amsterdam, filled with little nooks and crannies to explore, with shops selling everything from carpets to handmade chocolates, toothbrushes to beeswax candles.

On Keizersgracht, one mansion you'll notice in your wanderings is the **Felix Meritis Building**, at no. 324, near the corner with Berenstraat. A heavy neoclassical monolith built in the late eighteenth century to house the artistic and scientific activities of the society of the same name, the building used to be the headquarters of the Dutch Communist Party. The council now lease it to the *Felix Meritis Foundation*, a centre for experimental and avant-garde arts. One of the most imposing facades along **Herengracht** is the **Bijbels Museum**, at no. 366, an ecumenical musuem of the world's religions (see p.94).

Leidsegracht is another of the peaceful radial canals that cut across the Grachtengordel. It is mostly residential, with houses ranging from ramshackle old cottages to luxurious *nouveau riche* townhouses. Its tranquillity, though, is often shattered by flat-topped tourist boats, which use the Leidsegracht as a shortcut, sounding their horns and revving their engines to make the tight turn into Prinsengracht.

Just south of here, all three main canals are crossed by one of Amsterdam's principal shopping streets, **Leidsestraat** – a long, slender passage of airline offices, moderately upmarket designer fashion- and shoe-shops and uninspired restaurants. On summer afternoons, Leidsestraat can be choked full of promenading window-shoppers, who make way only for the trams that crash dangerously through the melee. On the corner with Keizersgracht, the designer department store *Metz & Co.*, with its corner dome by Gerrit Rietveld, boasts a top-floor restaurant and tearoom with one of the best views of the city.

Leidseplein to Vijzelstraat

At its southwestern end Leidsestraat broadens into **Leidseplein**, hub of Amsterdam's nightlife, but by day a rather cluttered and disorderly open space littered with rubbish from the surrounding burger joints. The amount of tram, bike, car and pedestrian traffic constantly forging across the cobbles gives the place a closed-in and frenetic hum of purpose. As for entertainment, there's probably a greater concentration of bars, restaurants and clubs here than anywhere else in the city, and the streets strike out from the square in a bright jumble of jutting signs and neon lights. Around the corner, in a converted dairy, lurks the famous *Melkweg* arts venue (see p.107), and just nearby is the *Boom Chicago* café-theatre (see p.110). However, the main reason to come here is for the people-watching. On summer nights especially, the square can ignite with an almost carnival-like vibrancy: drinkers spill out of cafés to ogle the antics of sword-swallowers and fire-eaters, while the restaurants eagerly play along, placing their tables outside so you can eat without missing the fun. On a good night Leidseplein is Amsterdam at its carefree, exuberant best.

Dominating the square, the **Stadsschouwburg** is one of the city's prime performance spaces, while to the side, and architecturally much more impressive, is the fairy-castle **American Hotel**. Even if you're not thirsty, it's worth a peek inside to feast your eyes on the leaded stained glass, shallow brick arches, chandeliers and carefully coordinated furnishings – as fine an example of the complete stylistic vision of Art Nouveau as you'll find. To the southwest, across the Singelgracht bridge and over the main Stadhouderskade road, the refined mansions of Vondelstraat and the beauty of Amsterdam's main park, the Vondelpark (see p.85) are mere minutes away.

Heading southeast from Leidseplein, **Weteringschans** makes for a less pleasant walk than the narrow **Lijnbaansgracht** ("Tightrope-walk Canal"), which runs parallel and reaches right around the modern city centre. At the first bridge, the Rijksmuseum (see p.88) is an imposing presence across the canal to the right; to the left, the tiny Spiegelgracht hosts an appealing mixture of bookshops and corner cafés, and leads into Nieuwe Spiegelstraat, the focus of the **Spiegelkwartier**, where Amsterdam's antiques traders congregate. There are around fifty dealers here, packed into a relatively small area – though bargains are a rare commodity.

Kerkstraat, a narrow street which, by contrast, features an eclectic mix of magic-mushroom shops, gay bars and art galleries, crosses Nieuwe Spiegelstraat. A right turn along Kerkstraat will bring you to the junction with Vijzelstraat, which becomes the filled-in **Vijzelgracht**. The southern end of Vijzelgracht culminates in the **Weteringcircuit** roundabout and, on its southern side, two low-key memorials to the horrors of World War II. To the southwest a small gravelled area surrounds a sculpture of a wounded man, holding a bugle: it was here, on March 12, 1945, that 35 people were shot by the Nazis in the last few weeks of the occupation. Across the road, on the southeastern side, is another memorial, this time to H M van Randwijk, a prominent figure in the Dutch resistance. In restrained style, the wording on the monument translates as:

> *When to the will of tyrants,*
> *A nation's head is bowed,*
> *It loses more than life and goods –*
> *Its very light goes out.*

In a wholly different vein, the **Heineken Brewery** looming on the other side of the canal (open to over 18s only; tours Mon–Fri 9.30 & 11am, June–Sept also 1 & 2.30pm, July–Aug also Sat noon & 2pm; *f*2) is one of the city's best-known attractions. *Heineken* decided to close down the original brewery in 1986 and move their operations to more efficient regional centres, but it's still interesting to explore the old plant. However, the main draw is that afterwards you are given snacks and **free beer** – the atmosphere is highly convivial, as you'd imagine when there are two hundred people downing as much free beer as they can drink. Whether you have just one, or drink yourself into a stupor, it's a diverting way to get a lunchtime aperitif.

Frederiksplein and along the Amstel

To the east of the Weteringcircuit is Reguliersgracht, the most easterly of the three surviving radial canals cutting across the *grachtengordel*, and perhaps the prettiest of all, with elegant greenery decorating its banks and distinctively steep bridges spanning the water.

Sandwiched in between Kerkstraat and Prinsengracht, the small open space of the **Amstelveld** is an oasis of village-like calm that few visitors happen upon. The **Amstelkerk**, a seventeenth-century white wooden church with a nineteenth-century Gothic interior overlooks the square, and a Monday **flower market** here adds a splash of colour. At right angles to Kerkstraat, **Utrechtsestraat**, with trams rattling by, is probably Amsterdam's most up-and-coming strip and contains most of the area's commercial activity – including many pleasant mid- to upper-bracket restaurants, seasoned with a lively mix of bars and bookshops.

Utrechtsestraat ends in the concrete wasteland of **Frederiksplein** – a huge, soulless square, presided over by the massive glass box of the Nederlandse Bank. Leading off Frederiksplein, **Sarphatistraat** crosses the wide and windy reaches of the **Amstel River**, whose eastern side is stacked with chunky buildings such as the **Carré Theatre**, built as a circus in the early 1900s, but now more often used as a performance space for music and drama. Walking north up the western bank of the river, you pass by the **Amstelsluizen**, or Amstel Locks, and then the **Magere Brug** ("Skinny Bridge"), which is (inexplicably) the focus of much attention in the tourist brochures, and hence the most famous of the city's swinging bridges. More worthy of a serious look is the **Amstelhof**, just north of the over-hyped bridge. A large and forbidding former *hofje*, this was one of a number of charitable institutions built east of the Amstel following the extension of the major canals toward the new harbour and shipbuilding quarter. The area was deeply unfashionable, takers for the new land were few, and the city had little option but to offer it to charities at bargain prices.

The three great *grachten* nearby don't contain houses quite as grand as those to the west, but there are a couple of exceptions that can be visited. The first is the elaborately decorated **Willet-Holthuysen Museum**, at Herengracht 605 (see p.96), recently refurbished and with a fine collection of period objets d'art; the second is the **Van Loon Museum** at Keizersgracht 672 (see p.96), which is less grand, and is perhaps the finest accessible canal house interior in Amsterdam, with a pleasantly down-at-heel interior of peeling stucco and shabby paintwork.

Rembrandtplein and around

The area cornered by Herengracht's eastern reaches is dominated by **Rembrandtplein**, a dishevelled patch of greenery fringed with cafés and their terraces. This claims to be one of the centres of city nightlife, though the square's crowded restaurants are firmly tourist-targeted; expect to pay inflated prices. Rembrandt's pigeon-spattered statue stands in the middle, wisely turning his back on the square's worst excesses, which include live (but deadly) outdoor music. Of the cafés, only the bar of the **Schiller Hotel** at number 26 stands out, with an original Art Deco interior reminiscent of a great ocean liner.

The streets leading north from Rembrandtplein to the Amstel River are more exciting, containing many of the city's mainstream **gay bars** – accessible to all, and less costly than their upstart neighbours. **Amstelstraat** is the main thoroughfare east, crossing the river at the **Blauwbrug** ("Blue Bridge") and affording views across the Stadhuis complex (see p.81); the Waterlooplein flea market is just over the bridge. Heading west, the supremely tacky **Reguliersbreestraat** links Rembrandtplein to Muntplein; tucked in among slot-machine arcades and sex shops, though, is the **Tuschinski**, the city's most famous cinema, with an interior that's a wonderful example of the Art Deco excesses of the 1920s. Expressionist paintings, coloured marbles and Moroccan carpets add to a general air of sultry decadence. Obviously you can enjoy all of this if you're here to catch a film (the Tuschinski shows all the most popular general releases); if you're not, guided tours are laid on during July and August (Sun & Mon, 10.30am; ƒ5).

Reguliersdwarsstraat also begins at Rembrandtplein, leading west to Koningsplein; the cobbled square to the south, **Thorbeckeplein,** scores points for having a lesser concentration of clog- and card-shops but is hardly a fitting memorial for Rudolf Thorbecke, a politician whose liberal reforms of the late nineteenth century furthered the city tradition of open-minded tolerance, and whose statue stands besieged by topless bars and fast-food joints. **Reguliersgracht** flows south from here, and on a clear day it's possible to align a beautiful view of seven canal bridges – a unique feat even in this city of 1281 of them.

The Golden Curve

From Thorbeckeplein, Herengracht leads west in an elegant sweep to Leidsestraat; the section from Vijzelstraat onwards is perhaps its most touted but least memorable stretch, known as the **"Golden Curve"**, where the double-fronted merchant residences of the sixteenth and seventeenth centuries – principally numbers 441–513 and 426–480 – try to outdo each other in size, if not in beauty. Most of the houses here date from the eighteenth century, with double stairways (the door underneath was the servants' entrance). The two-columned portal at Herengracht 502 betrays the mayor's official residence; and there are a couple of neat facades at number 539 and numbers 504–510, the second of which carries carved figures of dolphins on its crest. A little further west, **Herengracht 380** is an exact copy of a Loire château – solidly built of stone, with a main gable embellished with reclining figures, and a bay window with cherubs, mythical characters, and an abundance of acanthus leaves. But otherwise the houses in this part of town are mainly corporate offices, and markedly less fascinating than the tourist authorities claim. One exception, for its contents at least, is the **Kattenkabinet** ("Cats Cabinet") at Herengracht 468 (Tues–Sun 1–5pm; ƒ7.50). This enormous collection of art and artefacts relating to cats is housed in a seventeenth-century canal house with some original decor and paintings by Jacob de Wit; moggiephiles will be uncontrollable.

From the Kattenkabinet it's a few steps to Koningsplein, and the rattle and clatter of the Leidsestraat trams heading down to Leidseplein and up into the Old Centre.

The Jordaan and the Western Islands

Lying to the west of the city centre, bordered by Prinsengracht on one side and Lijnbaansgracht on the other, **The Jordaan** (pronounced *"yor-dahn"*) is a likeable and easily explored area of narrow canals, narrower streets and simple, architecturally varied houses. Long home to Amsterdam's working classes, it has seen a twentieth-century transformation into one of the city's most attractive and sought-after residential neighbourhoods. To the north used to be the docks area, known as the **Western Islands**, dredged out of the River IJ to increase warehouse space; the bustle of commerce has long since departed, though, and today it is an atmospheric area, cherished by artists.

The Jordaan

THE JORDAAN's name is said to come from the French word *jardin* ("garden"), stemming from the language of the area's earliest settlers, French Protestant Huguenots. At that time, the Jordaan was largely open country, and today many of the surviving streets and canals are named after flowers and plants. In contrast to the splendour of the three main *grachten*, the Jordaan became Amsterdam's slum quarter, home of artisans, tradespeople, and Jewish and Huguenot refugees from all over Europe fleeing religious persecution. Later, as the city expanded beyond its original frontiers, the Jordaan became the inner-city enclave of Amsterdam's growing industrial working class.

The last thirty years have seen increasing gentrification; these days, despite lingering traces of its former toughness, the Jordaan has become home to young, "alternative", monied Amsterdammers, although there's a core population of residents who retain long-standing roots in the district. As you wander through the long, narrow streets, you're just as likely to come across crowded pubs full of beery locals enjoying a knees-up as you are to encounter bohemian pop-art cafes serving espresso to arty types.

There are few specific sights to see in the Jordaan; however, it's a wonderful neighbourhood for an extended wander, along the way peeking into some of the district's **hofjes** – seventeenth-century almshouses for the city's elderly and needy population. There are *hofjes* all over the city (most famously the Begijnhof – see p.70), but there's a concentration in the Jordaan, and it's worth looking in on a courtyard or two. Many of them have real charm, but bear in mind that most are still lived in, so be discreet.

In its southern stretches, the Jordaan is relatively unremarkable. A good place to begin your meanderings is **Rozengracht** ("Canal of Roses"), which had the misfortune to be filled in and turned into a main traffic-route in and out of the city centre; it is now a non-descript main road. The house where Rembrandt spent the last ten years of his life, no. 184, has long since disappeared, and today only a plaque marks the spot ("Here Stood Rembrandt's House, 1410–1669"). Heading north, the area around the **Bloemgracht** ("Flower Canal"), particularly the maze of cross-streets that weave around it, exemplifies the new-found charm of the Jordaan. Tiny streets filled with cafes, bars and curious little shops generate a warm, easy community atmosphere; murals and slogans adorn the walls – even the bikes get a special paint job. Remnants of its history remain, though: the houses at nos. 87–91 each have striking gablestones, depicting a *Steeman* ("city-dweller"), *Landman* ("farmer") and *Seeman* ("sailor") living side-by-side. The Bloemgracht, along with the **Lauriergracht** ("Bay Tree Canal") to the south and the **Egelantiersgracht** ("Rose-Hip Canal") to the north, are especially pretty, small-scale leafy canals lined with houseboats.

Picking a path through the alleys, one of the Jordaan's hidden hofjes is tucked away on Egelantiersgracht, between nos. 107 and 114: the **St Andrieshofje** is a small, quiet courtyard surrounded by houses, its entrance-way lined with Delft tiles. Not far away, at Egelantiersgracht 12, *Cafe 't Smalle* is one of Amsterdam's oldest cafés, opened in 1786 as a *proeflokaal*, or tasting-house, for an adjacent distillery. The **Claes Claeszoon Hofje**, a haven of peace, has its entrance nearby on 1e Egelantiersdwarsstraat.

Westerstraat, to the north, is the main street of the district, with a diverse selection of local-oriented shops and a general Monday market of clothes, textiles and general bric-a-brac. The two nearby streets of **2e Anjeliersdwarsstraat** and **2e Tuindwarsstraat** hold the bulk of the Jordaan's ever-increasing trendy stores, and some of its liveliest bars and cafés for restorative sipping. Westerstraat runs east to join Prinsengracht at Hendrik de Keyser's **Noorderkerk**. This church, finished in 1623, was the architect's last creation, and probably his least successful. It's hard to believe that this uncompromisingly dour, squat building shares the same architect as the elegant and fanciful Westerkerk nearby. The square outside the church, the **Noordermarkt**, is desolate and empty most of the week, but is home to two of Amsterdam's best open-air markets: a junk market on Monday mornings, and the popular Saturday **Boerenmarkt** ("farmers' market"). If browsing gives you an appetite, tackle a huge wedge of some of the city's finest apple-cake at *Lunchcafé Winkel* on the edge of the market at the corner with Westerstraat.

On the opposite bank of the Prinsengracht, the **Van Brienen Hofje**, at Prinsengracht 89–133, is the grandest *hofje* in the city, built in 1804, according to the entrance tablet, "for the relief and shelter of those in need", although it's currently undergoing renovation. A little way down the canal at Prinsengracht 157–171, **Zon's Hofje** is smaller, with a leafier, more gentle beauty.

To the north of the Noorderkerk, **Lindengracht** and **Palmgracht** are two more of the Jordaan's seven filled-in waterways; at Palmgracht 26–38, you can see the buildings of the **Raep Hofje**, funded by the Raep family and sporting a carved *raep* (turnip) above the entrance.

North to the Western Islands

Just to the north of the Jordaan is a small area loosely known as the **SHIPPING QUARTER**, which centres on the long arteries of **Haarlemmerstraat** and **Haarlemmerdijk**. In the seventeenth century this district was at the cutting edge of Amsterdam's trade: the warehouses along Brouwersgracht were crowded with bounty brought back from the high seas, and **West Indies House**, on Haarlemmerstraat at Herenmarkt, was the headquarters of the Dutch West Indies Company. Today it's a good area for cheap restaurants and off-beat shops: the warehouses have been largely taken over and converted into spacious apartments, while the courtyard of West Indies House contains an overblown statue of Peter Stuyvesant, governor of New Amsterdam (later renamed New York).

Haarlemmerdijk used to be a bustling main street – until the trams were re-routed after the war; the street now feels somewhat bypassed and faded. At its western end, the **Haarlemmerpoort** is an oversized and dramatic former gate-way to the city. Beyond this you can either walk on to the **Westerpark**, one of the city's smaller and more enticing parks, or duck under the train tracks to the **WESTERN ISLANDS** district, where ships were once unloaded into more rows of gaunt warehouses. The district – comprising **Prinseneiland**, **Bickerseiland** and **Realeneiland** – has a rough-and-ready grittiness to it, and its residents are proud of their affinity with boats and water. While wandering through the cob-bled lanes, you'll come across thriving small boatyards and dozens of house-boats. Gentrification is relentless, though, and many of the long-forgotten ware-houses have been transformed into modern studios, eagerly sought-after by artists and musicians.

The Jodenbuurt and the Eastern Islands

Although there's hardly any visible evidence today, from the sixteenth century onward Amsterdam was the home of Jews escaping persecution throughout Europe. Under the terms of the Union of Utrecht, Jews enjoyed a tolerance and freedom unknown elsewhere, and they arrived in the city to practise diamond processing, sugar refining and tobacco production – effectively the only trades open to them since the city's guilds excluded Jews from following traditional crafts. This largely impoverished Jewish community lived in one of the city's least desirable areas, the marshland around what is now Waterlooplein. In time, Jews began to occupy houses nearby, in St Antoniesbreestraat and, later, to the south on the canals of Nieuwe Herengracht, Nieuwe Keizersgracht and Nieuwe Prinsengracht: the whole area became known as the **JODENBUURT**, or "Jewish quarter", of Amsterdam.

By the early years of this century, Jewish life was commercially and culturally an integral part of the city, the growing demand for diamonds making Jewish expertise invaluable and bringing wealth to the community for the first time. In the 1930s the community's numbers swelled with Jews who had fled persecution in Germany. But in May 1940 the Nazis invaded, sealing off the area to create a ghetto: taking advantage of Amsterdam's network of waterways to restrict movement in and out of the Jewish quarter, they raised many of the area's swing bridges. Jews were not allowed to use public transport or own a telephone, and were placed under a curfew. Round-ups and deportations continued until the last days of the war: out of a total of 120,000 Jews in the city, 115,000 were murdered in concentration camps.

After the war the Jodenbuurt lay deserted: those who used to live here were dead or deported, and their few possessions were quickly looted. As the need for wood and raw materials grew during postwar shortages, many houses were slowly dismantled and finally destroyed in the 1970s with the completion of the metro that runs beneath Waterlooplein. Today few people refer to the Jodenbuurt by that name, and many Amsterdammers are unaware of its history.

St Antoniesbreestraat and Jodenbreestraat

Nieuwmarkt lies at the edge of what was the Jodenhoek, and **St Antoniesbreestraat** leads to its heart, an uncomfortably modernized street whose original old houses were demolished to make way for the anticipated surge in traffic that the proposed Eighties redevelopment of Nieuwmarkt would bring – although public protest ultimately defeated the planners. Only the **De Pinto House** at no. 69 survives, easily spotted by its creamy Italianate facade. Nearby, the decorative landmark of Hendrik de Keyser's **Zuiderkerk** (Mon–Fri noon–5pm, Thurs noon–8pm; free; tower mid-June to Sept Wed–Sat 2–4pm; ƒ3) was the first church built in Amsterdam specifically for Protestant worship; today it has been deconsecrated and is now used as a Municipal Information Centre for Housing. As you leave the churchyard into St Antoniesbreestraat, the ghoulish skull motif above the entrance-way is the only sign left that this used to be the Zuiderkerk's cemetery.

St Antoniesbreestraat runs into **Jodenbreestraat**, at one time the Jodenhoek's principal market and centre of Jewish activity. After the shipbuilding industry moved further east, this area, made up of the small islands of Uilenburg and Marken, became the site of the worst living conditions in the city: it wasn't until 1911 that the area was declared a health hazard and redeveloped. After having been modernized and widened in the 1970s – losing much of its character in the process – Jodenbreestraat was redeveloped again in 1996, and it is now as narrow as it was in the 1930s; however it is only when you reach the **Rembrandt House** at no. 6 (see p.95) that you find any continuity with the past.

Waterlooplein and around

Jodenbreestraat runs parallel to its sibling development, the Muziektheater and **Stadhuis** on **Waterlooplein**, whose building occasioned the biggest public dispute the city had seen since the Nieuwmarkt was dug up in the 1970s to make way for the metro. The Waterlooplein, originally a marshy, insanitary area known as the Vlooyenburg, was the first neighbourhood to be settled by the Jews. By the latter part of the nineteenth century the slums had become so bad that the canals crossing the area were filled in and the shanty houses in the area were razed; the street markets then shifted here from St Antoniesbreestraat and Jodenbreestraat. The Waterlooplein quickly became the largest and liveliest market in the city, and a link between the Jewish community on the eastern side of the Amstel and the predominantly Gentile one to the west. During World War II the area became infamous again, this time as a site for Nazi round-ups; in the 1950s it regained some of its vibrancy with the establishment of the city's **flea market** here.

In the late 1970s, when the council announced the building of a massive new complex to accommodate the city hall and an opera house that would all but fill Waterlooplein, opposition was widespread. People believed that the area, which had been open space for centuries, should, if anything, be turned into a residential area – or at the very least, a popular performance space – anything but an elitist opera house. Attempts to prevent the building failed, and the **Muziektheater** opened in 1986, but it has since successfully established itself with visitors and performers alike. One of the story's abiding ironies is that the title of the protest campaign, "Stopera", has passed into common usage to describe the finished complex. If you'd like to explore backstage and get an idea of the workings of the Muziektheater, join a guided tour (Wed & Sat 3pm; *f*8.50; reserve on ☎551 8054).

Just behind the Muziektheater, on the corner of Mr Visserplein, is the **Mozes en Aaron Kerk**, originally a small (clandestine) Catholic church that was rebuilt in rather glum neoclassical style in the mid-nineteenth century. The area around Mr Visserplein, today a busy and dangerous junction for traffic speeding toward the IJ tunnel, contains the most tangible mementoes of the Jewish community. The brown and bulky **Portuguese Synagogue** (daily except Sat 10am–3pm; closed Yom Kippur; *f*2.50) was completed in 1675 by Sephardic Jews who had moved to Amsterdam from Spain and Portugal to escape the Inquisition, and who prospered here in the seventeenth and eighteenth centuries. When it was completed the Portuguese Synagogue was the largest in the world; today, its Sephardic community has dwindled to just 600, all of whom live outside the city centre.

Across from the Portuguese Synagogue, the **Jewish Historical Museum** (daily 11am–5pm, closed Yom Kippur; *f*7) is cleverly housed in a complex of High German synagogues dating from the late seventeenth century. For years after the war the buildings lay in ruins, until the museum's collection was transferred here from the Waag (on the Nieuwmarkt) in 1987. A full account of the museum is given on p.94.

Between the museum and the Portuguese Synagogue is the small triangle of **J D Meijerplein**. It was here that, in February 1941, around four hundred young Jewish men were rounded up, arrested, loaded on trucks, and taken to their eventual execution at Mauthausen concentration camp in reprisal for the killing of a Nazi sympathizer during a street fight between members of the Jewish resistance and the Dutch Nazi party. The arrests sparked off the "February Strike", a general strike led by Amsterdam's transport workers and dockers and organized by the outlawed Communist party in protest against the deportations and treatment of the Jews. Although broken by mass arrests after only two days, it was a demonstration of solidarity with the Jews that was unique in occupied Europe and unusual in the Netherlands, where the majority of people had done little to prevent or protest against the actions of the occupying German army. The strike is still commemorated annually by a wreath-laying ceremony here on February 25.

Along Plantage Middenlaan

Leaving Mr Visserplein via Muiderstraat, with the prim **Hortus Botanicus** (botanical gardens) to the right (see p.94), you come to yet another sad relic of the war at Plantage Middenlaan 24. The **Hollandsche Schouwburg**, a predominantly Jewish theatre before 1940, became the main assembly point for Dutch Jews prior to their deportation to the concentration camps. Inside, there was no daylight and families were jammed together for days in conditions that foreshadowed those in the camps. The house across the street, now a teacher-training college, was used as a day nursery; some – possibly hundreds – managed to escape through here, and a plaque outside extols the memory of those "who saved the children". Inside, on the second floor of the adjacent building, there's a small but impressive **exhibition** (daily 11am–4pm; *f*7) on World War II and the Holocaust, aimed specifically at children.

Further along Plantage Middenlaan, on the left-hand side, is the **Artis Zoo** (daily 9am–5pm; *f*19, children *f*12.50), one of the city's top attractions, and well worth a visit with kids in tow. To arrive in style, take the *Artis Express* canal boat (daily, every 30min 10am–5pm; return *f*12.50, children *f*8) from Centraal Station. At the end of Plantage Middenlaan stands the sturdy **Muiderpoort** (pronounced "*mao-der-port*"), one of the surviving gates into the city; over the canal lies the multicultural Oost ("East") district, with the Tropenmuseum (see p.95) and the pretty Oosterpark just steps away.

The docks and the Eastern Islands

The broad boulevard that fronts the grey waters of what became the Oosterdok is **Prins Hendrikkade**, running all the way from the Western Islands (see p.78) through Stationsplein and on into the Eastern Islands. In the seventeenth century merchant vessels packed the harbour, carrying the goods that created the city's enormous wealth: today Prins Hendrikkade is a major artery for cars flowing north via the IJ tunnel, and the only ships docked here belong to the police or navy. But the road is lined with buildings that point to its nautical past.

The first of these, the squat **Schreierstoren**, at the northern tip of Geldersekade, was traditionally the place where, in the Middle Ages, tearful women saw their husbands off to sea (the name could be translated as "weepers' tower") – though this is probably more romantic invention than fact. A sixteenth-century inlaid stone records the emotional leave-takings, while another much more recent tablet recalls the departure of Henry Hudson from here in 1609 – the fateful voyage on which he stumbled across a river that he modestly named after himself, and an island the locals called Manhattan. A little further east, the **Scheepvaarthuis** ("Shipping Building") at Prins Hendrikkade 108 is covered inside and out with bas reliefs and other decoration relating to the city's maritime history; it's also embellished with slender turrets and expressionistic masonry characteristic of the Amsterdam school of architecture that flourished early this century. Further east again, the wide **Oude Schans** canal was once the main entrance to the old shipbuilding quarter, and the **Montelbaanstoren** tower that stands about halfway down was built in 1512 to protect the merchant fleet. A century later, when the city felt more secure and could afford such luxuries, it was topped with a decorative spire by Hendrik de Keyser, the architect who did much to create Amsterdam's prickly skyline.

The chief pillar of Amsterdam's wealth in the sixteenth century was the **Dutch East India Company**, and the twin warehouses where the company began its operations still stand at Prins Hendrikkade 176 – but a better picture of the might of Dutch naval power can be found in the **Maritime Museum** on Kattenburgerplein (see p.95), housed in a fortress-like former arsenal of the seventeenth century.

As ill-gotten gains from the colonies poured in, the old dock area to the southeast around Uilenburg was no longer able to cope. To create additional dockland and warehouse space, the Dutch East India Company financed a major reclamation of the marshland to the east of the existing waterfront, forming the three **EASTERN ISLANDS** – **Kattenburg, Wittenburg,** and **Oostenburg,** cut through by wide canals. The company's shipbuilding industry was transplanted here – and, with the addition of houses, bars and even a church (see below), the Eastern Islands became the home of a large community working in the shipfitting and dockyard industries. The nineteenth century brought the construction of iron ships, and, on a wharf at Hoogte Kadijk 147, an old shipyard has been given a new lease of life as the **Kromhout Museum** (see p.94); the museum still patches up ancient boats and lays on a slide show that's a useful introduction to the area's history.

In time, the shipyards of the Eastern Islands declined, the working-class neighbourhood shrank, and today there's little to see. The **Oosterkerk**, across the water from the Kromhout, now functions as a social and exhibition centre, part of an attempt to restore some of the area's identity. South of the Kromhout, it's worth wandering through to the **Entrepotdok**, a line of old warehouses, each bearing the name of a destination above its door. Reinvented as hi-tech offices and apartments, but infiltrated by weird gurglings from the Artis Zoo across the way, it seems an odd sort of end for the Eastern Islands' rich maritime tradition.

Keep going down Oostenburgergracht and you'll reach "**De Gooyer**", a windmill that dates from 1814. Once mills were all over Amsterdam, pumping water and grinding grain; today this old corn mill is one of the few that remains, now converted into a brewery called *'t IJ*, though its sails still turn on the first Saturday of the month – wind permitting.

Museumplein and the Vondelpark

During the nineteenth century, unable to hold its mushrooming population within the limits of its canals, Amsterdam began to expand, spreading into the neighbourhoods beyond the Singelgracht which now make up the district known as the **Old South** – a large and disparate area that includes the leafy residential quarters immediately south of Leidseplein as well as the working-class enclaves further east. Most people visit this part of Amsterdam for its grand museums – the **Rijksmuseum** (see p.88), **Van Gogh Museum** (see p.91) and **Stedelijk Museum** (see p.92) – the trio imposingly grouped around the grassy wedge of **Museumplein**, which extends south from Stadhouderskade to Van

BEHIND THE SCENES AT MUSEUMPLEIN

In late 1996, work began on ambitious plans for the **redevelopment** of Museumplein. Both the Van Gogh and the Stedelijk museums are to have new wings added; the oval Van Gogh extension will be three-quarters buried below ground level. In addition, the southern half of Museumplein will conceal an underground car park, and a subterranean parking area for tour buses will be built near the Rijksmuseum. Nothing seems to have been overlooked: the complex will include an underground supermarket, a playground for children and a large shallow pond (which will no doubt become a public ice-skating rink in winter); the plans even take account of the popularity of the old skateboarding ramps in the area, which are to stay. Once all the dust has settled (probably sometime in 1998), the whole area is to be relandscaped – to maintain Museumplein's equally valuable function as an open space in the city.

Baerlestraat. Museumplein is a rather bare and windswept open space which nevertheless hosts a variety of outdoor activities, from visiting circuses to political demonstrations.

On Van Baerlestraat, at the bottom end of Museumplein, is the **Concertgebouw** ("Concert Hall"), completed in 1888 and renowned for its marvellous acoustics, is home of the famed – and much recorded – resident orchestra (see p.109 for details of concerts).

The Vondelpark

Five minutes' walk west of Museumplein, the **Vondelpark** is the city's most enticing park. Named after the seventeenth-century poet Joost van der Vondel, and funded by local residents, it was beautifully landscaped in the latter part of the last century in the English style, with a bandstand and an emphasis on nature rather than formal gardens. Today it's a forum for drama and other performance arts in the summer, and at weekends young Amsterdam flocks here to meet friends, laze by the lake or listen to music – in June, July and August bands give **free concerts**. If you wander far enough into the interior, you might chance upon the cows, sheep and even llamas who call the park home, while criss-crossing the whole is a network of dreamy canals spanned by tiny, elaborate bridges. Perhaps the highlight of a visit, though, is the extravagant and well-tended **rose garden**, where dozens of varieties perfume the air.

The area around the Vondelpark is one of Amsterdam's better-heeled residential districts, with designer shops and delicatessens along chic **P C Hooftstraat** and **Van Baerlestraat**, and some of the city's fancier hotels (and plenty of its cheaper ones, too) on their connecting streets.

The outer districts

Amsterdam is a small city and its residential outer neighbourhoods can be easily reached from the city centre. Of them, the **South** holds most interest, with the raucous "De Pijp" quarter and the 1930s architecture of the New South more than justifying the tram ride. As for the other districts, you'll find a good deal less reason for making the effort. The **West** is nothing special, aside from the occasional park and one lively immigrant quarter; nor is the **East**, although a multi-cultural influence lends a welcome diversity, and the Tropenmuseum is worth a jaunt. Amsterdam **North**, across the IJ, is entirely residential – peaceful for cycling through on the way to open country beyond, but the highlight of a visit is likely to be the short (free) ferry ride from behind Centraal Station.

De Pijp

The **Old South**, which also includes the area around the major museums and the Concertgebouw (see p.109) isn't all culture, and by no means is it all wealthy either. Walking east from Museumplein, across Hobbemakade, you enter the busy heart of the Old South, and the district known as "**De Pijp**" (The Pipe). The name was derived from the characteristically narrow, terraced streets running between long, sombre canyons of brick tenements; the apartments in each building were said to resemble pipe-drawers, since each had a tiny frontage onto the street but extended back a long way into the building. Today, the population is densely packed, with large contingents from Surinam, Morocco, Turkey and Indonesia – a rich mix that helps make de Pijp one of the city's liveliest and closest-knit communities. **Ferdinand Bolstraat**, running north–south, is the main street, but the long, slim east–west thoroughfare of **Albert Cuypstraat** is its heart, and the daily general **market** (which stretches for more than a kilometre between Ferdinand Bolstraat and Van Woustraat) is the largest in the city.

The New South

Aside from the small but pretty **Sarphatipark**, a few blocks south of the Albert Cuyp, there's little else to detain you in the Old South, and you'd be better off either walking or catching a tram (#4, #5 or #24) down into the **NEW SOUTH** – a real contrast to its neighbour and the first properly planned extension to the city since the concentric canals of the seventeenth century. The Dutch architect H P Berlage was responsible for the overall plan, but he died before it was started, and the design was largely carried out in the 1930s by two prominent architects of the Amsterdam school, Michael de Klerk and Piet Kramer. Cutbacks in the city's subsidy led them to tone down the more imaginative aspects of the scheme, and most of the buildings are markedly more sober than previous Amsterdam school works (such as the Scheepvarthuis on Prins Hendrikkade). But otherwise they followed Berlage faithfully, sticking to his plan of wide boulevards and crooked side streets, and adding the odd splash of individuality to corners, windows and balconies.

Nowadays the New South is one of Amsterdam's most sought-after addresses. **Apollolaan**, **Stadionweg** and, a little way east, **Churchill-laan** are home to luxury hotels and some of the city's most sumptuous properties, huge idiosyncratic mansions set well back from the street behind trees and generous gardens. **Beethovenstraat**, the main street of the New South, is a fashionable shopping boulevard, with high-priced mainstream stores catering for the wealthy residents.

The area achieved a fleeting notoriety in 1969, when John Lennon and Yoko Ono staged their week-long **Bed-In** for peace in the **Amsterdam Hilton** on Apollolaan. The press came from all over; fans crowded outside, hanging on the couple's anti-war proclamations, and the episode heralded John and Yoko's campaign for worldwide peace. At the far end of Beethovenstraat, the dense trees and shrubs of the **Beatrixpark** flank the antiseptic surroundings of the adjacent **RAI exhibition centre**, a complex of trade and conference centres built to attract more businesspeople (and their expense accounts) to Amsterdam; a visit to the excellent **Resistance Museum** at Lekstraat 63 (see p.95) might be more rewarding. The **Olympic Stadium**, built for the 1928 games, is a useful landmark although construction of the new "Amsterdam ArenA" stadium in Duivendrecht to the southeast has cast a shadow over its future. A few hundred metres to the north is the Haarlemmermeer Station, now operating only as the terminus of the **Museum Tramline**, on which old trams brought from as far away as Vienna and Prague run to and from the Amsterdamse Bos further south – a more appealing, though time-consuming, option than taking the bus.

The **Amsterdamse Bos** ("Amsterdam Forest") is the overly grand title of the city's largest open space, an 800-hectare woodland park planted during the 1930s in a mammoth project intended to harness the energies of the city's unemployed. The Bosbaan, a kilometre-long dead-straight canal in the north of the park, is used for boating and swimming; there are children's playgrounds and spaces for various sports; or you can simply walk or jog your way around any of fourteen planned trails. If it's out of season or you're not into old trams (see above), you can catch one of the yellow *NZH* buses (#170, #171 or #172) which run into

Amstelveen from Centraal Station; they leave from just outside the *Victoria Hotel*. Once there, the best way to get around is to rent a bicycle (March–Oct); it's also possible to rent canoes, canal bikes and motorboats. The **Bosmuseum**, near the southern end of the Bosbaan at Koenenkade 56 (daily 10am–5pm), has maps and basic information on the park's facilities.

The West

Of all Amsterdam's outer central districts, Amsterdam **WEST** is probably the least appealing – primarily a residential area with only a couple of nondescript parks as possible destinations. The **Old West**, beyond the Singelgracht and above the Vondelpark, has a busy Turkish and North African immigrant-based streetlife worth checking out if you find yourself in the vicinity: trams #7 and #17 run down **Kinkerstraat**, which is a good place to bargain-hunt if you're not after anything fancy, and there's also the vigorous **ten Katestraat market**, about halfway down Kinkerstraat on the right. Outside of this zone, in the New West districts of Bos en Lommer, De Baarsjes and Overtoomse Veld, there's little other than the large but run-of-the-mill **Rembrandtpark** to draw you out this far.

The East

A cupolated box topped with a crudely carved pediment, the sturdy **Muiderpoort** marks the boundary between Amsterdam's centre and the beginning of Amsterdam **EAST**. Across the canal on Mauritskade, the gabled and turreted **Royal Tropen Institute** has a marble-and-stucco entrance hall which you can peek into, though the only part open to visitors is the excellent **Tropenmuseum** around the corner (see p.95).

Behind the Tropen Institute, the **Oosterpark** is a peaceful oblong of green, and a gentle introduction to the area, which extends south and east. This is a solidly working-class district for the most part, particularly on the far side of Linnaeusstraat, and there's a high immigrant presence here; the street names, such as Javastraat, Balistraat, Borneostraat, are also reminiscent of Holland's colonial past. The housing is relatively poor, though there's ambitious urban renewal going on, and many of the ageing terraced houses have been torn down to make way for new and better-equipped public housing. As in the Old South, there's an underlying drug problem in the area, but while you're unlikely to need to come out here, it's by no means a forbidding district. Trams #6 and #10 run to bustling **Javaplein**, the heart of the district. Two specific attractions (apart from the Zeeburg campsite – see p.62), are the **Dapperstraat market** – a kind of Eastern equivalent of Albert Cuypstraat – and, at the end of the line for tram #14, the **Flevopark**, dull in itself but giving access to the IJsselmeer and patches of Dutch countryside right out of Ruisdael.

Amsterdam's museums

Slogging around museums isn't everyone's idea of fun, and you may find more than enough visual stimulation in Amsterdam's mansions and canals. But the city has a superb concentration of art galleries, of which three – the Rijksmuseum, the Van Gogh and the Stedelijk – are world-class. Add to this the famed Anne Frank House, and over thirty small musuems, and you begin to get some idea of what you're up against.

MUSEUM ADMISSION

If you intend to visit more than three or four museums – either in Amsterdam alone or if you're travelling elsewhere in Holland – you'd be well advised to buy a **museumjaarkaart** ("museum year card"), which allows you free or reduced admission to more than 400 museums throughout the country for an entire year (see p.38 in *Basics* for full details).

Anyone under 26 is also eligible for a **Cultureel Jongeren Passport** or CJP, which for f20 gets you reductions on entry to some museums, theatres, concerts and *filmhuizen* in the city; they're available from the **Amsterdam Uitburo** (AUB), in one corner of the Stadsschouwburg theatre on Leidseplein (Mon–Sat 9am–6pm, Thurs until 9pm; ☎621 1211).

Opening times, particularly of state-run museums, tend to follow a pattern: closed on Monday, open from 10am to 5pm Tuesday to Saturday and from 1 to 5pm on Sunday and public holidays – although the Monday closure is becoming less prevalent. Almost all the museums offer at least basic **information** in English or a written English guide.

If you like to take your museums the easy way, the **Museumboot** runs a regular boat service (daily 10am–5pm; every 30min, 45min in winter; day-ticket f22) between seven jetties located at or near eighteen of the city's major museums – including the Anne Frank House, the Amsterdam Historical Museum, Rijksmuseum, Van Gogh and Stedelijk Museums, Rembrandt House, Jewish Historical Museum and the Maritime Museum. However, since the larger museums can take some hours to explore (using up valuable hours on your day-ticket), the Museumboot is perhaps best used for spending a day cruising between the smaller museums. The office and main boarding point is in front of Centraal Station, but you can also buy tickets from the jetty opposite the Rijksmuseum; for more details, call ☎625 6464.

The Rijksmuseum

Stadhouderskade 42 (☎673 2121); South Wing entrance at Hobbemastraat 19 (☎573 2911). Tram #2, #5 (stop Hobbemastraat); tram #6, #7, #10 (stop Spiegelgracht). Daily 10am–5pm; f12.50, over 65s f7.50, under 18s, CJP f5. Wheelchair access. For more on Dutch art and artists, see Contexts, p.327.

The **Rijksmuseum** is the one museum you shouldn't leave Amsterdam without visiting. Its **seventeenth-century Dutch paintings** constitute far and away the best collection to be found anywhere, with twenty or so Rembrandts alone, as well as copious arrays of works by Steen, Hals, Vermeer and many other Dutch artists of the era – all engagingly displayed with the layperson in mind. There are, too, representative displays of all other pre-twentieth-century periods of Dutch and Flemish painting, along with rare treasures in the **medieval art** and **Asiatic** sections. To do justice to the place demands repeated visits; if time is limited, it's best to be content with the core paintings and a few selective forays into other sections. For ease of navigation, the museum shop stocks the comprehensive *Treasures of the Rijksmuseum* (f25), or pick up a free floor plan.

Paintings of the fifteenth to seventeenth centuries

From the museum shop, the eastern wing runs chronologically through the Rijksmuseum's collection of Low Countries paintings. After works from the early **Netherlandish period** begin the classic paintings of the **Dutch Golden Age**: portraits by Hals and Rembrandt, landscapes by Jan van Goyen and Jacob van Ruisdael, the riotous scenes of Jan Steen and the peaceful interiors of Vermeer and Pieter de Hooch. First, though, are some early-seventeenth-century works, including **Frans Hals'** expansive *Isaac Massa and His Wife* and more sensational paintings such as **Dirck van Baburen's** *Prometheus in Chains* – a work from the Utrecht School, which used Caravaggio's paintings as its model.

Beyond this are the works of **Rembrandt** and some of his better-known pupils. Perhaps the most striking is the *Portrait of Maria Trip*, but look, too, at Ferdinand Bol's *Portrait of Elizabeth Bas*, Govert Flinck's *Rembrandt as a Shepherd* – interesting if only for its subject – and the *Portrait of Abraham Potter* by **Carel Fabritius**, this last a restrained, skilful work painted by one of Rembrandt's most talented (and shortest-lived) students.

The next rooms take you into the latter half of the seventeenth century and include the carousing peasant paintings of **Jan Steen**. Steen's *Morning Toilet* is full of associations, referring either to pleasures just had or about to be taken, while his *Feast of St Nicholas*, with its squabbling children, makes the festival a celebration of pure greed – much like the drunken gluttony of the *Merry Family* nearby – and the out-of-control ugliness of *After the Drinking Bout* leaves no room for doubt about what Steen thought of all this ribaldry.

It's in the last few rooms, though, that the Dutch interior really comes into its own, with a gentle moralizing that grows ever more subtle. **Vermeer's** *The Letter* reveals a tension between servant and mistress – the lute on the woman's lap was a well-known sexual symbol of the time – and the symbolism in the use of a map behind the *Young Woman Reading a Letter* hints at the far-flung places her loved one is writing from. The paintings of **Pieter de Hooch** are less symbolic, more exercises in lighting, but they're as good a visual guide to the everyday life and habits of the seventeenth-century Dutch bourgeoisie as you'll find.

Mingling with these interior scenes are more paintings by **Hals** and **Rembrandt** – later works, for the most part, from the painters' mature periods. Hals weighs in with a handful of portraits, including the boisterous *Merry Toper*, while Rembrandt – here at his most private and expressive best – is represented by a portrait of his first wife *Saskia*, a couple of his mother and a touching depiction of his cowled son, *Titus*.

A small room off to the side of the last one offers an introduction to the **Gallery of Honour** and one of the Rijksmuseum's great treasures – Rembrandt's *The Night Watch*, the most famous and most valuable of all the artist's pictures, restored after being slashed in 1975 and recently cleaned. The painting is a so-called Civil Guard portrait, named after the bands of militia that grouped together in the sixteenth century to defend the home front during the wars with the Spanish. They later grew into social clubs for local dignitaries – most of whom would commission a group portrait as a mark of prestige. This one, of the Guards of the Kloveniersdoelen in Amsterdam, was erroneously tagged *The Night Watch* in the nineteenth century – a result both of the romanticism of the age and the fact that for years the painting was covered in soot. Though not as subtle as much of the artist's later work, it's an adept piece, full of movement and carefully arranged –

these paintings were collections of individual portraits as much as group pictures, and part of the problem in creating one was to include each individual face while simultaneously producing a coherent group scene. The sponsors paid for a prominent position in the painting, and the artist also had to reflect this.

Elsewhere, the Gallery of Honour houses the large-scale works from the museum's collection of Dutch paintings. Some of these are notable only for their size – the selection of naval battles particularly – but a number do stand out. Two of Rembrandt's better-known pupils crop up here: **Nicholas Maes**, with one of his typically intimate scenes in *Dreaming*, and **Ferdinand Bol**, both in his *Regents of the Nieuwezijds Workhouse* and the elegantly composed *Venus and Adonis*. The dashing *Self-portrait* is his too, a rich and successful character leaning on a sleeping cupid. By way of contrast, Rembrandt himself follows with a late *Self-portrait*, caught in mid-shrug as the Apostle Paul, a self-aware and defeated old man. Opposite, *The Staalmeesters* is an example of one of his later commissions, and, as do so many of Rembrandt's later works, it demonstrates his ability to capture a staggering range of subtle expressions. Nearby is *The Jewish Bride*, one of his last pictures, finished in 1665.

The South Wing – later Dutch painting

In 1996, the **South Wing** of the Rijksmuseum re-opened after three years of renovation and restoration work. Reached through a passageway from the main building, or via a separate entrance at Hobbemastraat 19, round the back of the main building, the South Wing has the same opening hours and ticket as the main museum.

The collection of **eighteenth- and nineteenth-century Dutch paintings** picks up chronologically where the Gallery of Honour left off. It begins with the work of **Cornelis Troost**, whose eighteenth-century comic scenes earned him the dubiously deserved title of the "Dutch Hogarth". More enduring are the later pictures, notably the pastels of Pierre-Paul Prud'hon and **Jan Ekels'** *The Writer* – small and simple, their lighting and attention to detail imitative of Vermeer.

After this, rooms follow each other in haphazard fashion, with sundry landscapes and portraiture from the lesser nineteenth-century artists. **Jongkind** is the best of the bunch, his murky *River Landscape in France* typical of the Impressionism that was developing in the nineteenth century. The chief proponents of Dutch Impressionism originated from or worked in The Hague, and the handy label of the **Hague School** covers a variety of styles and painters who shared a clarity and sensitivity in their depiction of the Dutch landscape. Of the major Hague School painters, the Rijksmuseum is strongest on the work of the **Maris Brothers** and **Jan Weissenbruch**, whose land- and seascapes, such as *View near the Geestbrug*, hark back to the compositional techniques of van Ruisdael.

While members of the Hague School were creating gentle landscapes, a younger generation of Impressionist painters working in Amsterdam – the **Amsterdam School** – were using a darker palette to capture city scenes. By far the most important picture from this turn-of-the-century group is **G H Breitner's** *Singelbrug near Paleisstraat in Amsterdam*, a random moment in the street recorded and framed with photographic dispassion.

Other collections

The collection of **Medieval and Renaissance applied art** is perhaps the most impressive of the remaining sections, filled with jewellery, religious art, woodcarvings and statuary from the Low Countries and northern Europe. There's a massive collection of **fine art** from later centuries, including galleries stuffed from floor to ceiling with **delftware**, furniture, ceramics and textiles from the sixteenth century on: it's mostly dull stuff, with only the **dolls' houses** providing diversion.

The **Dutch history section** focuses on the naval might that brought Holland its wealth, with fearsome **model ships** and galleries filled with relics of Holland's naval and colonial past. Holland's colonial connection with the East means that Asian art can be found in most of the museum's collections, but the **Asian col-lection** proper, housed in the South Wing, holds its most prized treasures – chiefly graceful paintings, ceramics and lacquerwork, and jewellery.

Rijksmuseum Vincent van Gogh

Paulus Potterstraat 7 (☎570 5200). Tram #2, #3, #5, #12 (stop Van Baerlestraat); tram #16 (stop Museumplein). Daily 10am–5pm; ƒ12.50, over 65s ƒ7.50, under 18s ƒ5. Wheelchair access.

Vincent van Gogh is arguably the most popular, most reproduced and most talked-about of all modern artists, so it's not surprising that the **Rijksmuseum Vincent Van Gogh**, comprising the extensive collection of the artist's art-dealer brother Theo, is Amsterdam's top tourist attraction. Housed in an angular build-ing designed by the aged Gerritt Rietveld and opened to the public in 1973, it's a gentle and unassuming introduction to the man and his art – and one which, due both to the quality of the collection and to the building, succeeds superbly.

The first works go back to the artist's **early years** in southern Holland, where he was born: these are dark and sombre for the most part, like the haunting, flick-ering light of *The Potato Eaters* – one of Van Gogh's best-known paintings. Across the hall, the sobriety of these early works is easily transposed onto the Parisian urban landscape, particularly in his *View of Paris*: but before long, under the sway of fellow painters and, after the bleak countryside of North Brabant and the sheer colour of the city itself, his approach began to change. This is most noticeable in the views of Montmartre windmills, a couple of self-portraits and the pictures from Asnières just outside Paris.

In February 1888, Van Gogh moved to **Arles**, inviting Gauguin to join him a lit-tle while later. With the change of scenery came a heightened interest in colour and the predominance of yellow as a recurring motif: it's represented most vivid-ly in *The Yellow House*. A canvas from the artist's *Sunflowers* series is justly one of his most lauded works, intensely, almost obsessively rendered in the deepest oranges, golds and ochres he could find.

In works completed at the asylum in **St Remy**, where Van Gogh committed himself after snipping off part of his ear and offering it to a local prostitute, nature assumed a more abstract form – trees bent into cruel, sinister shapes, skies coloured purple and yellow, as in the *Garden of St Paul's Hospital*. Van Gogh is at his most expressionistic here, the paint applied thickly, often with a palette knife, especially in the final, tortured paintings done at **Auvers**, including *Undergrowth*, *The Reaper* or *Wheatfield with Crows*, in which the fields swirl and writhe under black, moving skies. It was only a few weeks after completing this last painting that Van Gogh shot and fatally wounded himself.

On the second floor, the museum shows a revolving selection from its vast stock of Van Gogh's **drawings**, notebooks and letters. The top floor is used as a **tempo-rary exhibition space**, usually showing works loaned from other galleries that illustrate the artistic influences on Van Gogh, or his influence on other artists.

Stedelijk Museum of Modern Art

Paulus Potterstraat 13 (☎573 2737). Tram #2, #3, #5, #12 (stop Van Baerlestraat); tram #16 (stop Museumplein). April–Oct daily 11am–7pm, Nov–March daily 11am–5pm; f8, under 17s & CJP f4, under 7s free. Wheelchair access.

Amsterdam's number-one venue for modern art, the **Stedelijk** is still at the cutting edge; its permanent collection is unrivalled and its temporary exhibitions, based both on its own acquisitions and on loaned pieces, and often extending to photography or video art, are often of world renown.

Of the museum's **permanent collection**, there's always a good (rotating) scattering on the **first floor**. Briefly, and broadly, this starts off with drawings by Picasso, Matisse and their contemporaries, and moves on to paintings by major Impressionists (Manet, Monet, Bonnard) and Post-Impressionists (Ensor, Van Gogh, Cézanne). Further on, Mondrian holds sway, from his early, muddy-coloured abstractions to the cool, boldly coloured rectangular blocks for which he's most famous. Similarly, Kasimir Malevich is well represented, his dense attempts at Cubism leading to the dynamism and bold, primary tones of his "Suprematist" paintings – slices, blocks and bolts of colour that shift around. You may also find a good stock of Marc Chagall's paintings (the museum owns a wide selection), and a number of pictures by American Abstract Expressionists Mark Rothko, Ellsworth Kelly and Barnett Newman, in addition to the odd work by Lichtenstein or Warhol. Jean Dubuffet, too, with his swipes at the art establishment, may well have a profile, and you might catch Matisse's large cut-out, *The Parakeet and the Mermaid*.

Two additional large-scale attractions are on the ground floor – Karel Appel's *Bar* in the foyer, installed for the opening of the Stedelijk in the 1950s, and the same artist's wild daubings in the museum's restaurant. Look out, too, for Ed Kienholz's model of his local bar in Los Angeles, the *Beanery* (1965), housed in the basement of the museum.

Other museums

Touring the big museums of Amsterdam is one of the pleasures of the city, but you should remember that besides the big three, there are a large number of specialist galleries, some displaying bizarre oddities, that more than compete in interest.

Allard Pierson Museum

Oude Turfmarkt 127; (☎525 2556). Tram #4, #9, #14, #16, #24, #25 (stop Spui). Tues–Fri 10am–5pm; Sat–Sun & holidays 1–5pm. f6; over-65s, CJP, students f4.50; under-15s f3; under-12s free. Wheelchair access.

The city's premier archeological display, a small and excellent museum, which manages to overcome the fatigue normally induced by archeological collections by arranging its high-quality exhibits in intimate galleries that encourage you to explore. Simple background information personalizes what might otherwise be meaningless objects. The museum's highlights include a life-size model of a Greek chariot, a remarkably well-preserved collection of Coptic clothes and artefacts from the sixth century, good Greek pottery and jewellery, and fine gold and precious stones from all periods.

Amstelkring Museum

Oudezijds Voorburgwal 40 (☎624 6604). Walking distance from Centraal Station. Mon–Sat 10am–5pm, Sun 1–5pm; f7.50, under19s, over 65s & CJP f5, under 5s free. No wheelchair access.

In the seventeenth century, Catholics had to confine their worship to the privacy of their own homes – an arrangement which led to the growth of so-called clandestine Catholic churches throughout the city. Known as "Our Dear Lord in the Attic", this is the only one left; it occupies the loft of a wealthy merchant's house, together with those of two smaller houses behind it. The **church** is delightful and the **house** itself has been left untouched, its original furnishings (reminiscent of interiors by Vermeer or de Hooch) making the Amstelkring a tranquil and still relatively undisturbed escape from the excesses of the nearby Red Light District. One of the city's best and least demanding small museums.

Amsterdam Historical Museum

Kalverstraat 92 or Nieuwezijds Voorburgwal 357 (☎523 1822). Tram #1, #2, #4, #5, #9, #11, #14, #16, #24, #25 (stop Spui). Mon–Fri 10am–5pm, Sat–Sun 11am–5pm, guided tours Wed 2 & 3pm; f8, under 17s f4. Limited wheelchair access.

Housed in the restored seventeenth-century buildings of the Civic Orphanage, Amsterdam's Historical Museum attempts to survey the city's development with artefacts, paintings and documents from the thirteenth century onward. Much is centred around the "Golden Age" of the seventeenth century: a large group of paintings portrays the city in its heyday, and the good art collection shows how the wealthy bourgeoisie decorated their homes. Sadly, most of the rest of the museum is poorly labelled and lacks continuity. Still, it's worth seeing for the nineteenth-century paintings and photos and, more notably, the play-it-yourself **carillon** and the **Regents' Chamber**, unchanged since the Regents dispensed civic charity there three hundred years ago. Immediately outside the museum, the glassed-in **Civic Guard Gallery** draws passers-by with free glimpses of the large company portraits – there's a selection from the earliest of the 1540s to the lighter affairs of the seventeenth century.

Anne Frank House

Prinsengracht 263 (☎556 7100). Tram #13, #14, #17 (stop Westermarkt). June–Aug Mon–Sat 9am–7pm & Sun 10am–7pm, Sept–May Mon–Sat 9am–5pm & Sun 10am–5pm, closed Yom Kippur; f10, under 17s, over 65s & CJP f5, under 10s free, no museumcards. No wheelchair access.

This is one of the most deservedly popular tourist attractions in town; bearing this in mind, the best time to visit is early morning before the crowds arrive.

The rooms the Franks lived in for two years are left much the same as they were during the war, even down to Anne's movie star pin-ups in her bedroom and the marks on the wall recording the children's heights. A number of other rooms provide background on the war and occupation, including a video biography of Anne, while others detail the gruesome atrocities of Nazism – and the continuing threat presented by fascism and anti-semitism across Europe. Anne Frank was only one of 100,000 Dutch Jews who died during that time, but this, her final home, provides one of the most enduring testaments to the horrors of Nazism (see p.73 for more on Anne's life).

Bijbels Museum
Herengracht 366 (☎624 7949). Tram #1, #2, #5, #11 (stop Spui). Mon–Sat 10am–5pm, Sun 1–5pm; f5, over-65s, CJP f3.50, under-16s f2.50. Limited wheelchair access.

A multi-faith exposition which occupies a four-gabled, seventeenth-century stone house frilled with tendrils, carved fruit and scrollwork.

CoBrA Museum of Modern Art
Sandbergplein 1, Amstelveen (☎547 5050). Tram #5 (end-stop, then walk); bus #170, #171, #172. Tues–Sun 11am–5pm; f5, over 65s & CJP f3.50, under 16s f2.50. Wheelchair access.

Brand-new museum way out in the southern suburbs, dedicated to the CoBrA modern art movement of the 1950s and 1960s. CoBrA was founded by a group of Danish, Belgian and Dutch artists (thus Copenhagen, Brussels, Amsterdam), who took their inspiration from folk art, primitivism, and drawings by children and the mentally ill, embarking on wild spontaneous experimentation in both form and medium. The collection of work here is excellent, and well worth the trek.

Hortus Botanicus
Plantage Middenlaan 2a (☎625 8411). Tram #7 (stop Plantage Parklaan), tram #9, #14 (stop Mr Visserplein). April–Oct Mon–Fri 9am–5pm & Sat–Sun 11am–5pm, Nov–March Sat & Sun 9am–4pm; f7.50, under 14s f4.50, under 5s free; no museumcards. Wheelchair access.

Pocket-sized botanical gardens whose six thousand plant species make for a wonderfully relaxing break from the rest of central Amsterdam. Worth wandering in for the sticky pleasures of the hothouses, its terrapins and for the world's oldest pot plant. Stop off for coffee and cakes in the orangery.

Jewish Historical Museum
J D Meijerplein (☎626 9945). Tram #9, #14; metro (stop Waterlooplein). Daily 11am–5pm, closed Yom Kippur; f7, under 16s, over 65s & students f3.50, under 10s free. Wheelchair access.

Housed in a former Ashkenazi synagogue complex in the old Jewish quarter of Amsterdam, the award-winning Jewish Historical Museum is one of the most modern and impressive in western Europe. Four synagogues, built during the seventeenth and eighteenth centuries, have been restored and linked together as a centre for the study of the history of the Jewish community that's designed to be of interest to all. In addition to photos and mementoes from the holocaust, the award-winning museum gives an introduction to Jewish beliefs and life. As a sideline, the museum also has on permanent display a sequence of endearing and lively autobiographical paintings by Charlotte Salomon, who perished in the Auschwitz concentration camp at the age of 26; she paints a fascinating and highly articulate picture of her life in art, and this exhibition is well worth making time for.

Kromhout Shipyard Museum
Hoogte Kadijk 147 (☎627 6777). Bus #22, #28. Mon–Fri 10am–4pm; f2.50, over 65s f1.75, under 15s f1.50, no museumcards. Limited wheelchair access.

The Kromhout shipyard was one of the few survivors of shipbuilding's decline in the nineteenth century. It struggled along producing engines and iron ships until it closed in 1969 and was saved from demolition by being turned into this combination of industrial monument, operating shipyard and museum. Money is still tight, but the enthusiastic staff and good explanatory background material make this an up-and-coming place, and a useful adjunct to the Maritime Museum nearby.

Maritime Museum (Scheepvaartsmuseum)

Kattenburgerplein 1 (☎523 2222). Bus #22, #28. Tues–Sat 10am–5pm, Sun noon–5pm, June–Sept also Mon 10am–5pm; f12.50, under 12s f8, under 6s free. Wheelchair access.

A well-presented display of the country's seafaring past in an endless collection of maps, navigational equipment and weapons, though most impressive are the large and intricate **models** of sailing ships and men-of-war that date from the same period as the original vessels. Outside there's a replica of an eighteenth-century Dutch East India Company trading ship.

Rembrandt House

Jodenbreestraat 4–6 (☎638 4668). Tram #9, #14 (stop Mr Visserplein); metro Waterlooplein. Mon–Sat 10am–5pm & Sun 1–5pm; f7.50, over 65s f6, under 15s & CJP f5, under 9s free. Limited wheelchair access.

Rembrandt bought this house at the height of his fame and popularity, living here for over twenty years and spending a fortune on furnishings – an expense that contributed to his bankruptcy. The house itself is mostly a reconstruction and has no artefacts from Rembrandt's life on exhibit, but the main attraction is the enormous variety of the artist's etchings here. The biblical illustrations are the focus of most attention, though the studies of tramps and vagabonds are more accessible; an informative accompanying exhibit explains Rembrandt's engraving techniques.

Resistance Museum (Verzetsmuseum)

Lekstraat 63 (☎644 9797). Tram #4, #12, #25 (stop Victorieplein). Tues–Fri 10am–5pm & Sat–Sun 1–5pm; f5, under 15s, over 65s & CJP f2.50, under 8s free. Limited wheelchair access.

Strikingly installed in a former synagogue down in the New South, the Resistance Museum charts the rise of the resistance movement, from the Nazi invasion of the Netherlands in May 1940 to the country's liberation in 1945. The museum has a fascinating collection of contemporary material – photos, underground newsletters, anti-Jewish propaganda and deportation orders. The English guide to the exhibition is essential.

Tropenmuseum

Linnaeusstraat 2 (☎568 8215). Tram #9, #10, #14 (stop Mauritskade). Mon & Wed–Fri 10am–5pm, Tues 10am–9.30pm, Sat–Sun noon–5pm; f10, under 18s, over 65s, students & CJP f5, museumcard f2.50, under 5s free. Wheelchair access.

As part of the old Colonial Institute (now the less controversially titled Tropical Institute), this museum used to display only artefacts from the Dutch colonies. Since the 1950s, however, when Indonesia was granted independence, it has collected applied arts from all over, and its holdings now cover the world. Most of the collection is on permanent display, and is imaginatively presented. All of this makes for an impressively unstuffy exposition of the contemporary life and problems of the developing world – both the urban realm, covering the ever-expanding slum dwellings of cities such as Bombay, and rural areas, examining such issues as the wholesale destruction of the world's tropical rainforests. Highlights include creative and engaging displays devoted to music-making and puppetry, videos on traditional story-telling and reconstructions, right down to sounds and smells, of typical streets in India, China or Africa – really all well worth seeing. Also look in on the bookshop, which has a good selection of books on Third World subjects.

Van Loon Museum

Keizersgracht 672 (☎624 5255). Tram #16, #24, #25 (stop Keizersgracht). Mon 10am–5pm & Sun 1–5pm; f7.50, over 65s f5, under 12s free, no museumcards. No wheelchair access.

Less grand and more likeable than the nearby Willet-Holthuysen, this place, built in 1672, has a pleasantly down-at-heel interior of peeling stucco and shabby paint-work. The house's first tenant was the artist Ferdinand Bol; fortunately he didn't suffer the fate of many subsequent owners who seem to have been cursed with a series of bankruptcies and scandals for over two hundred years. The Van Loon family bought the house in 1884, bringing with them a collection of family portraits and homely bits and pieces that span the period from 1580 to 1949.

Willet-Holthuysen Museum

Herengracht 605 (☎523 1870). Tram #4, #9, #14 (stop Rembrandtplein). Mon–Fri 10am–5pm, Sat–Sun 11am–5pm; f5, under 16s f2.50. No wheelchair access.

Splendidly decorated in Rococo style, this is more museum than home, containing Abraham Willet's collection of glass and ceramics. But, save for the basement, a well-equipped replica of a seventeenth-century kitchen, it's very much look-don't-touch territory. Out back there's an immaculate eighteenth-century garden, which is worth the price of admission alone.

Eating

Amsterdam may not be Europe's culinary capital – Dutch cuisine is firmly rooted in the meat, potato and cabbage school of cooking – but as a recompense, the country's colonial adventures ensure that there's a wide range of non-Dutch **restaurants**. Amsterdam is acclaimed for the best Indonesian food outside Indonesia, at hard-to-beat prices, an always worthwhile choice is *rijsttafel*, a selection of six or eight different dishes and hot sauces. Other cuisines are also well-represented; aside from French-, Spanish- and Italian-influenced establishments, there are fine Chinese and Thai restaurants, a growing number of Moroccan and Middle Eastern places, and many devoted to the Indian subcontinent. Amsterdam also excels in the quantity and variety of its *eetcafés* and **bars** (see p.101), which serve increasingly adventurous food, quite cheaply, in a relaxed and unpretentious setting.

Unless otherwise stated, all the places listed below serve food daily from 5 or 6pm until 10 or 11pm. Some will stay open later for customers who are already installed, and times may vary depending on the time of year and how busy things are.

BUDGET EATING

At all the following, you can get a decent meal for less than ƒ13:

Bloemberg, Van Baerlestraat, more or less opposite the Concertgebouw. An award-winning seafood and herring stall – perhaps the best in the city. If you want your herring the Dutch way, tilt back your head and dangle the fish by the tail into your mouth.

Maoz Falafel, Reguliersbreestraat 45. The best street-food in the city – mashed chickpea balls deep-fried and served in Middle Eastern bread, with as much salad as you can eat, for the grand sum of ƒ5. Mon–Thurs & Sun 11am–2am, Fri & Sat 11am–3am.

Mr Hot Potato, Leidsestraat 44. The only place in town for baked potatoes – nothing fancy, but cheap (average ƒ5). Daily 10am–8pm.

Mensa Agora, Roeterstraat 11. Self-service student cafeteria, with all that that entails. Mon–Fri noon–2pm & 5–7pm.

Mensa Atrium, Oudezijds Achterburgwal 237. Central self-service cafeteria attached to the University of Amsterdam (but open to all); full meals for under ƒ10, though the quality leaves a little to be desired. Mon–Fri noon–2pm & 5–7pm.

La Place, part of *Vroom & Dreesman* department store, Kalverstraat 201. Self-service buffet-style restaurant, where it's possible to fill up for under ƒ10. Daily 10am–9pm.

Toko Sari, Kerkstraat 161. Fabulous Indonesian take-away. Tues–Sat 11am– 6pm.

In the main listings, also check out Dutch restaurants *Het Beeren* and *Keuken van 1870;* International restaurants *Bojo, Duende, New King* and *Rimini*; or the vegetarian *Silo*.

Dutch cuisine

Het Beeren, Koningsstraat 15. Huge portions of the simplest Dutch fare – cabbage, mashed potato and steaming stew – at budget prices. Daily 5.30–9.30pm.

De Blauwe Hollander, Leidsekruisstraat 28. Bargain Dutch food in generous quantities – a boon in an otherwise touristy, unappealing part of town. Expect to share a table.

Claes Claesz, Egelantiersstraat 24 (☎625 5306). Exceptionally friendly Jordaan restaurant that attracts a good mixed crowd and serves excellent Dutch food, at moderate prices. Live music most nights. Often has (pricey) special menus to celebrate specific occasions – carnival, Easter, the Queen's Birthday, and so on – call to check first. Closed Mon.

De Eettuin, 2e Tuindwarsstraat 10. Hefty and inexpensive portions of Dutch food, supplemented by a serve-yourself salad bar. Non-meat eaters can content themselves with the large, if dull, vegetarian plate, or the delicious fish casserole.

Haesje Claes, Spuistraat 275 (☎624 9998). Dutch cuisine at its best. Extremely popular – go early or call to reserve. Daily noon–10pm.

Hollands Glorie, Kerkstraat 220. Accessible, welcoming place with a good selection of inexpensive Dutch dishes and attentive service.

Keuken van 1870, Spuistraat 4. Former soup kitchen in the heart of the city, still serving Dutch meat-and-potato staples in a no-frills atmosphere. Mon–Fri 12.30–8pm, Sat & Sun 4–9pm.

Koevoet, Lindenstraat 17. A traditional Jordaan *eetcafé* serving unpretentious food at bargain prices. Closed Mon.

PANCAKES

In the tradition of simple cooking, **pancakes** are a Dutch speciality – ideal for fillers and light meals. Although there are plenty of drop-in places dotted around town, the three listed below are recommended.

Bredero, Oudezijds Voorburgwal 244. On the edge of the Red Light District, this offers one of the city's best pancake deals. Daily noon–7pm.

The Pancake Bakery, Prinsengracht 191. This beautiful old house serves a selection of filled pancakes, many of them a meal in themselves; prices start at *f*10. Daily noon–9.30pm.

Pannekoekhuis Upstairs, Grimburgwal 2. Minuscule place in a tumbledown house opposite the university buildings, with sweet and savoury pancakes at low prices. Also offers a student discount. Wed–Fri noon–7pm, Sat & Sun noon– 6pm.

Moeder's Pot, Vinkenstraat 119 (☎626 3557). Cheap Dutch food; recommended for the impecunious. Mon–Sat 5–9.30pm.

Witteveen, Ceintuurbaan 256 (☎662 4368). Held in high regard by locals, this is a thoroughly Dutch, highly atmospheric place for Amsterdam cooking – at a price.

International cuisine

Akbar, Korte Leidsedwarsstraat 33 (☎624 2211). Fabulous South Indian food, also especially strong on tandoori, with a fine choice and plenty of vegetarian options. Friendly service and moderate prices. Daily 5–11.30pm.

An, Weteringschans 199 (☎627 0607). Excellent and moderately priced Japanese cooking in a small, family-run place with an open kitchen. Closed Mon & Tues.

Aphrodite, Lange Leidsedwarsstraat 91. Refined Greek cooking in a street where you certainly wouldn't expect it. Fair prices too. Daily 5pm–midnight.

Beyrouth, Kinkerstraat 18. Small, inexpensive Lebanese place in the Old West; lacking in atmosphere, but with highly acclaimed food. Closed Tues.

Bojo, Lange Leidsedwarsstraat 51; with a branch round the corner at Leidsekruisstraat 12. Possibly the best-value – though certainly not the best – Indonesian place in town; expect to wait for a table. Service can be haphazard. Mon–Wed 4pm–2am, Thurs & Sun noon–2am, Fri & Sat noon–2am.

Bonjour, Keizersgracht 770 (☎626 6040). Classy, predictably expensive French cuisine in a romantic setting. Closed Mon & Tues.

Burger's Patio, 2e Tuindwarsstraat 12. Well-priced, young and convivial Italian restaurant. Despite the name, not a burger in sight.

Caramba, Lindengracht 342 (☎627 1188). Steamy, mid-priced Mexican restaurant in the heart of the Jordaan. The margaritas are almost on a par with those at *Rose's* (see below).

Casa di David, Singel 426 (☎624 5093). Solid-value dark wood Italian restaurant with a long-standing reputation. Pizzas from wood-fired ovens, fresh hand-made pasta, and more substantial fare. Try for one of the tables by the window. Highly recommended.

Christophe, Leliegracht 46 (☎625 0807). Classic Michelin-starred restaurant on a quiet and beautiful canal, drawing inspiration from the olive-oil-and-basil flavours of southern France and the chef's early years in North Africa. Reservations essential. Mon–Sat 6.30–10.30pm.

Dionysos, Overtoom 176 (☎689 4441). Fine Greek restaurant a little to the south of Leidseplein, with the distinct advantage of serving till late – but phone ahead if you're going to turn up after midnight. Daily 5pm–1am.

Duende, Lindengracht 62. Wonderful little tapas bar up in the Jordaan, with good, cheap tapas. Mon–Thurs 4pm–1am, Fri 4pm–2am, Sat 2pm–2am, Sun 2pm–1am.

1e Klas Grand Café Restaurant, Platform 2b, Centraal Station (☎625 0131). An unlikely setting, but good-value gourmet French cuisine from a well-balanced menu in the deeply atmospheric, restored late nineteenth-century restaurant.

Girassol, Weesperzijde 135 (☎692 3471). Close to Amstel Station, this inexpensive, family-run Portuguese restaurant is a fair hike out from the centre, but easily merits the journey.

Hamilcar, Overtoom 306. Fine Tunisian and North African place renowned for its couscous, which is usually prepared by the owner-chef. Closed Mon & Tues.

Hemelse Modder, Oude Waal 9 (☎624 3203). Tasty meat, fish and vegetarian food in French–Italian style at reasonable prices in an informal atmosphere; a very popular place. Closed Mon.

Hoi Tin, Zeedijk 122. One of the best places to try in Amsterdam's rather dodgy Chinatown, this is a perpetually busy place with an enormous menu (in English too) and some vegetarian dishes. Daily noon–midnight.

Iguazu, Prinsengracht 703 (☎420 3910). For carnivores only; a superb, reasonably priced Argentinian–Brazilian restaurant, with perhaps the best fillet steak in town. Daily noon–midnight.

Intermezzo, Herenstraat 28 (☎626 0167). Good French–Dutch cooking at above-average prices, but worth every penny. Closed Sun.

Lana Thai, Warmoesstraat 10 (☎624 2179). Among the best Thai restaurants in town, overlooking the water of Damrak. Quality food, chic surroundings but high prices. Closed Tues.

Lokanta Ceren, Albert Cuypstraat 40 (☎673 3524). Authentic, inexpensive and well-frequented local Turkish place, with *meze* to suit all tastes and fine kebab dishes. Let the *raki* flow. Daily 2pm–1am.

Mamma Mia, 2e Leliedwarsstraat 13. Good selection of pizzas, served in a pleasant, family atmosphere.

New King, Zeedijk 115. Extraordinary range of cheap Chinese dishes – don't count on quality, but your wallet will approve; wash it all down with free jasmine tea. Daily noon–midnight.

Puri Mas, Lange Leidsedwarsstraat 37 (☎627 7627). Exceptionally good value for money, on a street better known for rip-offs. Friendly and informed service preludes spectacular Indonesian *rijsttafels*, both meat and vegetarian. Recommended.

Rimini, Lange Leidsedwarsstraat 75. Surprisingly cheap pizza and pasta, mostly well-prepared. Daily 4–11.30pm.

Rose's Cantina, Reguliersdwarsstraat 38. In the heart of trendy Amsterdam, this qualifies as possibly the city's most crowded restaurant. No bookings, and you'll almost certanly have to wait, but it's no great hardship to sit at the bar nursing a cocktail and watching the would-be cool bunch. The margaritas are lethal.

Shiva, Reguliersdwarsstraat 72 (☎624 8713). The city's outstanding Indian restaurant and far from expensive, with a wide selection of dishes, all expertly prepared. Vegetarians are well catered for. Highly recommended.

Sluizer, Utrechtsestraat 43 (☎622 6376). Moderately priced French-influenced food, in one of Amsterdam's most atmospheric restaurants; check out the fish restaurant next door, too – see below. Daily noon–3pm & 5pm–midnight.

Tempo Doeloe, Utrechtsestraat 75 (☎625 6718). Reliable, reasonably priced Indonesian place close to Rembrandtplein. Be guided by the waiter when choosing – some of the dishes are very hot indeed. Daily 6–11.30pm.

Tom Yam, Staalstraat 22 (☎622 9533). Expensive, but high-quality Thai restaurant in the middle of town; also has take-away branches around town.

Warung Swietie, 1e Sweelinckstraat 1. Cheap and cheerful Surinamese–Javanese *eetcafé*. Daily 11am–9pm.

Fish

Albatros, Westerstraat 264 (☎627 9932). Family-run restaurant serving mouth-wateringly imaginative fish dishes. A place to splash out and linger over a meal. Closed Wed.

Lucius, Spuistraat 247 (☎624 1831). Pricey, but one of the best fish restaurants in town, with wonderful smoked salmon and a vast array of fish and seafood, delicately prepared. Very popular, so book ahead. Closed Sun.

Sluizer, Utrechtsestraat 45. Next door to its meat-based partner (which shares the same name – see above), serving simply prepared, good-quality fish at reasonable prices.

Vegetarian and natural food

Bolhoed, Prinsengracht 60. Something of an Amsterdam institution. Familiar vegan and vegetarian options from the daily changing menu, with organic beer to drink. More expensive than you might imagine. Daily noon–10pm.

Golden Temple, Utrechtsestraat 126. Laid-back place with a little more soul than the average Amsterdam veggie joint. Well-prepared food and pleasant, attentive service. Daily 5–9.30pm.

Shizen, Kerkstraat 148 (☎622 8627). Superbly prepared, affordable Japanese vegetarian and vegan macrobiotic dishes, with fish options. Closed Mon.

Silo, Westerdoksdijk 51 (the last door on the right, at the far end of the building). Housed in a huge old grain silo, this is one of the last remaining community squats in Amsterdam, home to 40-odd people and going through something of a rejuvenation as eviction looms. Fantastic food served in a stone-flagged restaurant hung with candelabras and overlooking the river. Sun, Tues & Wed are vegan, Thurs & Fri are merely vegetarian; limited quantities of food, so come at 6pm, order and relax; food is then served around 7 or 8pm.

Sisters, Nes 102. A popular vegetarian restaurant serving delicious, balanced meals, as well as plenty of snacks. Excellent value. Daily 5–9.30pm.

De Vliegende Schotel ("Flying Saucer"), Nieuwe Leliestraat 162. Perhaps the best of the city's cheap and wholesome vegetarian restaurants, serving delicious food in large portions. Lots of space, a peaceful ambience and a good noticeboard.

De Vrolijke Abrikoos, Weteringschans 76 (☎624 4672). All ingredients, produce and processes are organic or environmentally friendly in this mid-priced restaurant that serves fish and meat as well as vegetarian dishes. Daily except Tues 5.30–9.30pm.

De Waaghals, Frans Halsstraat 29. Inexpensive and well-prepared organic dishes are served in this co-operative-run restaurant near the Albert Cuyp. Tues–Sun 5–9.30pm.

Drinking

Amsterdam is well known for its drinking, and with good reason: the selection of **bars** is one of the real pleasures of the city. You can also use bars as a source for **budget eating**: many (often designated *eetcafés*) offer a complete menu, and most will fix you a sandwich or bowl of soup; at the very least you can always snack on hardboiled eggs from the counter for a guilder or so each.

And then, the whole universe of "coffeshops" awaits discovery, where smoking rather than drinking is the order of the day. Finally, the most sedate drinking venues are the tearooms scattered across the city.

Bars

There are, in essence, two kinds of Amsterdam bar. The traditional, old-style bar is the **brown café** – a *bruin café* or *bruine kroeg*; these are cosy places so named because of the dingy colour of their nicotine-stained walls. As a backlash, slick, self-consciously modern **designer bars** (lately dubbed "grand cafés") have sprung up, striving to be as un-brown as possible and catering largely to a young crowd. Bars, of any kind, open either around 10am or around 5pm; all stay open until around 1am during the week, 2am at weekends (sometimes until 3am). Reckon on paying roughly *f*2.50 for a small beer ("*pils*").

The Old Centre

De Buurvrouw, St Pieterspoortsteeg 29. Dark, noisy bar with a wildly eclectic crowd.

Cul de Sac, Oudezijds Achterburgwal 99. Down a long alley in what used to be a seventeenth-century spice warehouse, this is a handy retreat from the Red Light District. Small, quiet and friendly.

Dantzig, Zwanenburgwal 15. Easy-going grand café, right on the water behind the Waterlooplein, with comfortable chairs, friendly service and a low-key, chic atmosphere. Food served at lunchtime and in the evenings.

De Drie Fleschjes, Gravenstraat 16. Tasting house for spirits and liqueurs, which would originally have been made on the premises. No beer, and no seats either; its clients tend to be well heeled or well soused (often both). Closes 8pm.

Droesem, Nes 41. On a thin, theatre-packed alley behind the Dam, this is a highly recommended wine-bar, with your selection arriving in a carafe filled from a barrel, along with a high-quality choice of cheeses and other titbits to help it on its way.

Durty Nelly's, Warmoesstraat 115. Irish pub in the heart of the Red Light action. With a clean and well-run hostel above, this is one of the better expat Brit/Irish meeting-places, packed for the weekend footy by satellite.

De Engelbewaarder, Kloveniersburgwal 59. Once the meeting place of Amsterdam's bookish types, this is still known as a literary café. Relaxed and informal, it has live jazz on Sunday afternoons.

Flying Dutchman, Martelaarsgracht 13. Principal watering hole of Amsterdam's British expatriate community. Usually packed with stoned regulars crowding in to use the pool table or dartboards, or simply to cash in on the reasonably priced pints.

't Gasthuis, Grimburgwal 7. Convivial brown café packed during termtime with students from the university across the canal. Features include good food and summer seating outside by the water.

De Hoogte, Nieuwe Hoogstraat 2a. Small alternative bar on the edge of the Red Light District. Good music, engaging atmosphere, and cheapish beers.

Hoppe, Spui 18. One of Amsterdam's longest-established and best-known bars, and one of its most likeable, frequented by the city's dark-suited office crowd on their wayward way home. Summer is especially good, when throngs of drinkers spill out on to the street.

De Jaren, Nieuwe Doelenstraat 20. One of the grandest of the grand cafés: overlooking the Amstel next to the university, with three floors and two terraces, this place oozes elegance. All kinds of English reading material, too – this is one of the best places to nurse the Sunday paper. Also serves reasonably priced food and has a great salad bar. Daily from 10am.

Lokaal 't Loosje, Nieuwmarkt 32. Quiet old-style local brown café that's been here for 200 years – and looks its age. Wonderful for late breakfasts and pensive afternoons.

De Pilsener Club, Begijnensteeg 4. More like someone's front room than a bar – indeed, all drinks mysteriously appear from a back room. Photographs on the wall record generations of sociable drinking.

Scheltema, Nieuwezijds Voorburgwal 242. A journalists' bar, now only frequented by more senior newshounds and their occasionally famous interviewees, since all the newspapers moved their headquarters out to the suburbs. Faded turn-of-the-century feel, with a reading table and meals.

Tara, Rokin 89. Excellent Irish bar with regular live music. The location does it down, but it's worth taking the time to find.

Vrankrijk, Spuistraat 216. The best and most central of Amsterdam's few remaining squat bars. Cheap drinks, hardcore noise, and almost as many dogs-on-strings as people. Buzz to enter – from 10pm onwards.

City centre west

De Beiaard, Herengracht 90. Light and airy Fifties-style bar for beer aficionados. A wide selection of bottled and draught beers selected with true dedication by the owner, who delights in filling you in on the relative merits of each.

Hegeraad, Noordermarkt 34. Old-fashioned, lovingly maintained brown café with a fiercely loyal clientele.

Kalkhoven, Prinsengracht 283. One of the city's most characteristic brown cafés; nothing special, but warm and welcoming.

Koophandel, Bloemgracht 49. Empty before midnight, this is the after-hours bar you dream about, in an old warehouse on one of Amsterdam's most picturesque canals. Open until at least 3am, often later.

Het Molenpad, Prinsengracht 653. One of the most appealing brown cafés in the city – long, dark and dusty; also serves remarkably good food. Fills up with a young, professional crowd after 6pm.

Nol, Westerstraat 109. Probably the epitome of the jolly Jordaan singing bar, a luridly lit dive, popular with Jordaan gangsters and ordinary Amsterdammers alike. Opens and closes late, especially on weekends, when the back-slapping joviality and drunken sing-alongs contrive to keep you here until closing time.

De Prins, Prinsengracht 124. Boisterous student bar, with a wide range of drinks and a well-priced menu. A great place to drink in a nice part of town.

Saarein, Elandsstraat 119. Women only. Though some of the former glory of this café is gone, still a peaceful, relaxed place to take it easy. Also a useful starting point for contacts and information.

't Smackzeyl, Brouwersgracht 101, corner of Prinsengracht. Uninhibited drinking hole on the fringes of the Jordaan. One of the few brown cafés to have Guinness on tap; also a light, inexpensive menu.

't Smalle, Egelantiersgracht 12. Candle-lit and comfortable, with a barge out front for relaxed summer afternoons. One of the highlights of the city.

Soundgarden, Marnixstraat 164. Alternative grunge bar, packed with people and noise, with a canalside terrace for respite.

De Tuin, 2e Tuindwarsstraat 13. The Jordaan has some marvellously unpretentious bars, and this is one of the best: agreeably unkempt and always filled with locals.

De Twee Zwaantjes, Prinsengracht 114. Tiny Jordaan bar whose live accordion music and raucous singing you'll either love or hate. Fun, in an oompah-pah sort of way.

City centre south and east

Café Americain, American Hotel, Leidseplein 28. The terrace bar here has been a gathering place for media people for years. A place to be seen, with correspondingly high prices, but it's worth coming here at least once for the decor – Art Nouveau frills coordinated right down to the doorknobs. Good fast lunches, too.

De Druif, Rapenburgerplein 83. One of the city's most beguiling bars, and one that hardly anyone knows about, out to the northeast. Something of a village-pub feel.

De Duivel, Reguliersdwarsstraat 87, opposite the *Free I* coffeeshop. Tucked away on a street of bars and coffeeshops, this is the only hip-hop café in Amsterdam, with continuous beats.

't IJ, in the De Gooyer windmill, Funenkade 7. Situated in an early nineteenth-century windmill to the east of the centre, where the extremely potent beers (called *Natte, Zatte* and *Struis*) are brewed on the premises. A fun place to drink yourself silly. Wed–Sun 3–8pm.

Café Krull, Sarphatipark 2. On the corner of 1e van der Helststraat, and a few metres from the Albert Cuyp, this is an atmospheric place on a lively corner, serving all-day drinks, snacks and jazz from 11am.

Het Land van Walem, Keizersgracht 449. One of Amsterdam's nouveau-chic cafés: cool, light, and vehemently un-brown. Clientele are stylish in taste and dress, while the food is a kind of hybrid French–Dutch; there's also a wide selection of newspapers and magazines, including some in English. Usually packed.

Mulligan's, Amstel 100. By far the best Irish pub in the city, with an authentic atmosphere, superb Gaelic music and good service.

O'Donnells, Ferdinand Bolstraat 5. The best Guinness in town, in a pleasant Irish pub just behind the Heineken brewery. Seemingly limitless interior worms its way back into the building.

Café Schiller, Rembrandtplein 26. Art Deco bar of the upstairs hotel, authentic in both feel and decor. Although it's suffered something of a decline of late, it still offers a genteel escape from the tackiness of Rembrandtplein.

Café Vertigo, Vondelpark 3. Attached to the Film Museum, this is a wonderful place to while away a sunny afternoon (or to shelter from the rain) with a spacious interior and a large terrace overlooking the park.

Coffeeshops and tearooms

In Amsterdam, there is a crucial difference between coffeeshops and tearooms. To foreign ears, a **coffeeshop** brings to mind a quiet daytime place serving coffee and cakes. Far from it. Somewhere calling itself a "coffeeshop" is advertising just one thing: cannabis. You might also be able to get coffee and cake, but the main activity in a coffeeshop is smoking. There are almost as many different kinds of coffeeshop as there are bar: some are neon-lit, with loud music and day-glo decor, but there are plenty of others that are quiet, comfortable places to take it easy. The ones we list are a selection of the more characterful ones in the city. Most open around 11am and close around midnight.

Amsterdam's **tearooms** – calling themselves this to steer clear of druggy "coffeeshop" connotations – correspond roughly to the normal concept of a café: places that are generally open all day, might serve alcohol but definitely aren't bars, don't allow dope-smoking, but which have good coffee, sandwiches, light snacks and cakes. Along with *eetcafés* – which are listed with the bars – tearooms make good places to stop off for lunch, or to spend down time reading or writing without distractions.

Coffeeshops

The Bulldog, Oudezijds Voorburgwal 90 and 132 and 218; Singel 12; Leidseplein 15; Korte Leidsedwarsstraat 49. The biggest and most famous of the coffeeshop chains. The main Leidseplein branch (the "Palace"), housed in a former police station, has a large cocktail bar, coffeeshop, juice bar and souvenir shop, all with separate entrances. It's big and brash, not at all the place for a quiet smoke, though the dope is reliably good.

Global Chillage, Kerkstraat 51. Celebrated slice of Amsterdam dope culture, always comfortably filled with tie-dyed stone-heads propped up against the walls, so chilled they're horizontal.

Grasshopper, Oudebrugsteeg 16; Nieuwezijds Voorburgwal 57; Utrechtsestraat 21. One of the city's more welcoming chain of coffeeshops, though at times overwhelmed by tourists. The Utrechtsestraat branch is quietest.

Greenhouse, Tolstraat 4; Waterlooplein 345. Consistently sweeps the boards at the annual Cannabis Cup, with medals for their dope as well as "Best Coffeeshop". Tolstraat is way down south (tram #4), but worth the trek: if you're only buying once, buy here.

Homegrown Fantasy, Nieuwezijds Voorburgwal 87a. Attached to the Dutch Passion seed company, this has the widest selection of marijuana in Amsterdam, most of it local.

Kadinsky, Rosmarijnsteeg 9. Strictly accurate deals weighed out against a background of jazz dance. Chocolate chip cookies to die for.

Lucky Mothers, Keizersgracht 665. Perhaps the best general coffeeshop in the city – in an old canal house on a quiet stretch of the Keizersgracht near Rembrandtplein, with a welcoming atmosphere, good dope and a wonderful little terrace. Highly recommended.

Paradox, 1e Bloemdwarsstraat 2. For a change from the standard coffeeshop diet of cheeseburgers, *Paradox* satisfies the munchies with outstanding natural food, including spectacular fresh fruit concoctions. Live music on Sunday afternoons, when English becomes the *lingua franca*. Closes 7pm.

Siberië, Brouwersgracht 11. This very relaxed and friendly place has managed to avoid the over-commercialization of the larger chains; worth a visit whether you want to smoke or not.

Tearooms

Backstage, Utrechtsedwarsstraat 67. Run by the former cabaret stars, the Christmas Twins (Greg and Gary), this off-beat place also sells knitwear and African jewellery.

J G Beune, Haarlemmerdijk 156. Age-old chocolatier with a tea room attached.

Dialoog, Prinsengracht 261a. A few doors down from the Anne Frank House, one long room filled with paintings, restrained classical music, and downstairs, a gallery of Latin American art. A good choice of sandwiches and salads, too.

Café Esprit, Spui 10a. Swish modern café, with great sandwiches, rolls and superb salads.

COFFEESHOPS FOR BEGINNERS

The first thing to remember about Amsterdam's coffeeshops is that **locals** use them too; the second thing is that locals only use those outside the Red Light District. Practically all the coffeeshops you'll encounter in the centre are worth avoiding – for their decor, their deals, their clientele, or all three. A little effort will turn up plenty of more congenial, high-quality outlets for buying and enjoying cannabis without the tack.

When you first walk into a coffeeshop, how you buy the stuff isn't immediately apparent: it's actually illegal to advertise cannabis in any way. Ask to see the **menu**, which is normally kept behind the counter: this will list all the different hashes and grasses on offer, with – if it's a reputable place – exactly how many grammes you get for your money. Most of the stuff is sold either per gramme, or in bags for ƒ10 or ƒ25 (obviously the more powerful it is, the less you'll get); the in-house dealer should be able to answer your queries.

Gary's Muffins, Prinsengracht 454; Reguliersdwarsstraat 53; Marnixstraat 121. The best, and most authentic, New York bagels in town, with American-style cups of coffee (and half-price refills) and fresh-baked muffins. The Reguliersdwarsstraat branch stays open until 3am.

Greenwood's, Singel 103. Small, English-style tea shop in the basement of a canal house. Pies and sandwiches, pots of tea – and a decent breakfast.

Lindsay's Teashop, Kalverstraat 185. An attempt to recreate a little piece of England in the unlikely location of the basement of the American Book Center. The food, though, is fine: real English cream teas, with homemade pies and trifles.

Lunchcafé Winkel, Noordermarkt 43. A popular café on the corner with Westerstraat; something of a rendezvous on Saturday mornings, with the farmers' market in full flow, and some of the most delicious apple-cake in the city going like, well, like hot apple-cake.

Metz, Keizersgracht 455. Wonderful café on the top floor of the Metz department store, giving panoramic views over the canals of Amsterdam. Pricey, but then if you're shopping in Metz, you're not supposed to care.

Café Panini, Vijzelgracht 3. Tearoom-cum-restaurant that features good sandwiches and, in the evening, pasta dishes.

Puccini, Staalstraat 21. Lovely cake- and chocolate-shop and café, with wonderful handmade cakes, pastries and good coffee. Close to Waterlooplein.

Studio 2, Singel 504. Pleasantly situated, airy tearoom with a delicious selection of rolls and sandwiches; recommended.

Errol Trumpie, Leidsestraat 46. The place for pastries and chocolates, with a small tearoom at the back. Try the *koffie complet de patisserie* – a pot of coffee and plate of heavy calorific pastries.

Villa Zeezicht, Torensteeg 3. Small, centrally located place, serving excellent rolls and sandwiches; also some of the best apple-cake in the city, fresh-baked every 10 minutes or so.

Entertainment and nightlife

Although Amsterdam is not generally seen as a major cultural centre, the quality of music, theatre and film on offer is high – largely due to a continuing active government subsidy of the arts. Performance spaces tend to be small, and the city is not a regular stop on the circuits of major companies. Rather, it's a gathering spot for fringe events, and buzzes with places laying on a wide – and often inventive – range of affordable entertainment. Good venues to start are the major multimedia centres, which offer a taste of everything (see box on p.107).

Information and tickets

For information about **what's on**, a good place to start is the **Amsterdam Uitburo**, or AUB, the cultural office of the city council, which is housed in one corner of the Stadsschouwburg theatre on Leidseplein (Mon–Sat 9am–6pm, Thurs until 9pm; ☎621 1211). You can get advice here on anything remotely cultural, as well as tickets and copies of **listings magazines**. *Time Out Amsterdam* is now only available on the Internet – at <http://www.timeout.nl>, with its entertainment pages updated weekly. Otherwise, non-Dutch speakers will have to settle for the *VVV*'s bland and rather deadly *What's On In Amsterdam* (*f*3.50). The "Week Agenda", available from all cinemas, gives details of all **films** showing in the city, and lists most of the **live music** events as well. For a run-down of alternative events, seek out *Queer Fish*, available at the *Hair Police* (Kerkstraat 113) and other outlets for *f*2.

Tickets for most performances can be bought at the Uitburo (for a *f*2 fee) and VVV offices, or reserved by phone through the AUB *Uitlijn* (☎621 1211; *f*5 fee) or again, the VVV. Tickets to all live music events can be bought at the Nieuwe Muziekhandel shop at Leidsestraat 50 (☎627 1400; *f*3 fee) from three weeks ahead of time. You can also book seats at the major venues, from within Holland or abroad, through the *National Bookings Centre* (from overseas dial the international access code, followed by ☎31 70/320 2500; in Holland dial ☎070/320 2500; no booking fee). The **Cultureel Jongeren Passport** or **CJP** gets you reductions on entry to some theatres, concerts and *filmhuizen*.

Rock music

Amsterdam has become something of a testing ground for current **rock** bands. The three major city venues – the *Paradiso*, the *Melkweg* and the *Arena* (see box opposite) – supply a constantly changing seven-days-a-week programme of music to suit all tastes (and budgets); this is supplemented by the city's clubs, bars and multimedia centres, all of which sporadically host performances by live bands. As far as **prices** go, ordinary gigs cost *f*10–25, although some places charge a membership ("*lidmaatschap*") fee on top. Where no price is listed below, entrance is usually free.

Cruise Inn, Zeeburgerdijk 271 (☎692 7188). Off the beaten track, way out in the east, but with great music from the Fifties and Sixties. Saturday is R&B night.

De Buurvrouw, Pieterspoortsteeg 29 (☎625 9654). Eclectic bar featuring loud, local bands.

Korsakoff, Lijnbaansgracht 161 (☎625 7854). Late-night performances by some of the better-known local grunge bands in a lively setting with cheap drinks and a post-punk clientele.

Last Waterhole, Oudezijds Armsteeg 12 (☎624 4814). In the depths of the Red Light District, this is the favoured spot for Amsterdam's biker set; however, the Dutch variety lack bark as well as bite, and all are welcome at the pool tables and in the jam sessions onstage.

Maloe Melo, Lijnbaansgracht 163 (☎420 0232). Dark, low-ceilinged bar, with a small backroom featuring local bluesy acts. Next door to the Korsakoff.

Meander Café, Voetboogstraat 5 (☎625 8430). Live soul, funk and blues music daily.

OCCII, Amstelveenseweg 134 (☎671 7778). Cosy former squat bar at the far end of the Vondelpark, featuring live alternative music.

Twin Pigs, Nieuwendijk 100 (☎624 8573). A bar just yards from Centraal Station, with free rock and blues acts blasting a semi-stoned crowd.

Folk and world music

The Dutch **folk music** tradition is virtually extinct. But there is a still a small and thriving scene in Amsterdam, due mainly to a handful of American and British expatriates and a few sympathetic cafés. There are a couple of good outlets for **ethnic** and **world music** as well, and in early summer the *World Roots Festival* and the *Drum Rhythm Festival* showcase world-class acts; the exact dates vary – check with the VVV or major venues for details. The Dutch colonial connection with Surinam means there is a sizeable **Latin American** community in Amsterdam, and, although some Andean buskers on the Leidseplein may verge on the yawn-inducing, there is much authentic salsa and Latin to be discovered.

Akhnaton, Nieuwezijds Kolk 25 (☎624 3396). A "Centre for World Culture", specializing in African and Latin American music and dance parties.

■ MULTIMEDIA CENTRES

Three major venues in Amsterdam offer a vast range of entertainment, covering all bases. If you're unsure where to start your foray into night-time Amsterdam, check out the following.

Arena, 's-Gravensandestraat 51 (☎694 7444). A multimedia centre featuring live music, cultural events, a bar, coffeeshop and restaurant – and one of the cheapest hostels in the city (see p.61). Awkwardly located to the east of the centre (trams #6 and #10), the Arena's intimate hall tends to feature underground bands. Entrance ƒ8–15, with a start-time around 9.30pm. Also hosts popular dance parties on Fridays and Saturdays; ƒ5.

Melkweg ("Milky Way"), Lijnbaansgracht 234a (☎624 1777 after 1pm). Probably Amsterdam's most famous entertainment venue, and these days one of the city's prime arts centres, with a young, hip clientele, and touring foreign theatre companies often stage their only Amsterdam performance here. It used to be a dairy (hence the name), and now has two separate halls for live music, with a broad range of bands tending towards African music and lesser-knowns. Late on Friday and Saturday nights, excellent, off-beat disco sessions go on well into the small hours. Other features include a fine monthly film programme, a coffeeshop selling dope and space cake, and a bar and restaurant (Marnixstraat entrance). Concerts start between 9 and 11pm, and admission ranges from ƒ10–30, plus compulsory membership (ƒ4 for 1 month, ƒ6 for 3 months, free to CJP). After the bands have finished, the Melkweg plays host to some of the most enjoyable theme nights around, with everything from African dance parties to experimental jazz-trance. The whole centre is closed on Mondays.

Paradiso, Weteringschans 6–8 (☎623 7348). A converted church near the Leidseplein with bags of atmosphere. Bands range from the up-and-coming to the Rolling Stones, and it also occasionally hosts classical concerts, as well as debates, multimedia happenings and one-off dance events. Entrance ƒ12–30, plus ƒ4 membership. The bands usually get started around 9pm. On Fridays, the Paradiso turns into the unmissable VIP ("Vrijdag In Paradiso") Club, from midnight onwards.

Canecao, Lange Leidsedwarsstraat 68 (☎638 0611). A wonderful little place filled with the sounds of samba and salsa.

Mulligans, Amstel 100 (☎622 1330). Irish bar head and shoulders above the rest for atmosphere and authenticity, featuring Gaelic musicians and storytellers most nights.

Soeterijn, Linnaeusstraat 2 (☎568 8500). Part of the Tropenmuseum, this theatre specializes in the drama, dance, film and music of the developing world. A great place for ethnic music.

Jazz

For **jazz** fans, Amsterdam can be a treat. Since the Forties and Fifties, when many Black American jazz musicians began to relocate to Europe to escape discrimination back home, the city has had a soft spot for jazz. These days, Amsterdam boasts an excellent range of jazz outlets, from tiny bars staging everything from Dixieland to avant-garde, to the *Bimhuis*, which plays host to both international names and homegrown talent. Saxophonists Hans Dulfer, Willem Breuker and Theo Loevendie and percussionist Martin van Duynhoven are among the Dutch artists worth going out of your way for.

Café Alto, Korte Leidsedwarsstraat 115 (☎626 3249). Legendary little bar just off Leidseplein. Quality modern jazz every night from 10pm until 3am (though often much later). Big on atmosphere, though slightly cramped. Free entrance, and you don't have to buy a (pricey) beer to hang out and watch the band.

Bamboo Bar, Lange Leidsedwarsstraat 66 (☎624 3993). Legend has it that Chet Baker used to live upstairs and jam onstage to pay his rent. These days the Bamboo is an unpretentious, friendly bar with blues and jazz, plus occasional salsa nights. Also free entry, but they're rather more insistent that you buy a drink. 9pm onwards.

Bimhuis, Oude Schans 73–77 (☎623 1361). The city's premier jazz venue for almost 25 years, with an excellent auditorium and ultra-modern bar. Concerts Thurs–Sat (tickets available on day of performance only), free sessions Mon–Wed & Sun from 4pm in the bar.

Bourbon Street, Leidsekruisstraat 6 (☎623 3440). Friendly bar with a relaxed atmosphere and quality jazz nightly until 3am.

Casablanca, Zeedijk 26 (☎625 5685). Renovated, and a shadow of its former deeply hip self, though still with live jazz every night.

De Engelbewaarder, Kloveniersburgwal 59 (☎625 3772). Excellent live jazz sessions on Sun afternoons and evenings.

Du Lac, Haarlemmerstraat 118 (☎624 4265). Rather trendified bar with jazz sessions on Sunday.

Joseph Lam Jazz Club, Van Diemenstraat 242 (☎622 8086). Venture into the western harbour district for this trad and Dixieland centre. Fri & Sat only from 9pm.

Morlang, Keizersgracht 451 (☎625 2681). Super-trendy café with live music here and there. Soul, jazz and classical.

Winston Kingdom, Warmoesstraat 123 (☎625 3912). Theatre-café attached to the renovated Winston Hotel, with spoken word and jazz-poetry evenings attracting some acts from the US.

Classical music, opera and dance

Amsterdam is assured of a high ranking in the classical music stakes, thanks to its two resident orchestras. The *Royal Concertgebouw Orchestra* remains one of the most dynamic in the world, and occupies one of the finest **concert halls** to boot – and the whole experience is made accessible to a wide audience through an enlightened ticket-pricing policy. The *Netherlands Philharmonic*, based at the Beurs van Berlage concert hall, has a wide symphonic repertoire in addition to performing with the *Netherlands Opera* at the Muziektheater. As far as smaller ensembles go, Dutch musicians pioneered the use of period instruments, and the *Amsterdam Baroque Orchestra* and *Orchestra of the 18th Century* are two internationally renowned exponents. A number of Amsterdam's **churches** (and former churches) also play host to chamber and baroque concerts – the ones listed below have regular programmes of music, but others, including the huge Nieuwe Kerk on Dam Square, the Westerkerk, the Noorderkerk, the Mozes en Aaronkerk on Waterlooplein and the tiny Amstelkerk on Kerkstraat have one-off concerts, often for very reasonable prices.

The most prestigious outlet for **opera** is the *Muziektheater* (otherwise known as the *Stopera*) on Waterlooplein, which is home to the *Netherlands Opera* as well as the *National Ballet*. Visiting companies sometimes perform here, but more often at the *Carré* theatre and the *Stadsschouwburg* – the latter also stages **dance**.

The grandest **festival** by far is the annual **Holland Festival** every June, which attracts the best of local mainstream and fringe performances in all areas of the arts, as well as an exciting international line-up. Towards the end of August, there is a wonderfully atmospheric open-air **piano recital** held on a floating stage outside the Pulitzer Hotel on the Prinsengracht.

Beurs van Berlage, Damrak 213 (☎627 0466). The splendid interior of the former stock exchange has been put to use as a venue for theatre and music. The resident *Netherlands Philharmonic* and *Netherlands Chamber Orchestras* perform in the huge but comfortable Yakult Zaal and the AGA Zaal, the latter a very strange, glassed-in room-within-a-room.

Carré Theatre, Amstel 115–125 (☎622 5225). A stunning 100-year-old structure (originally built as a circus) that now hosts all kinds of top international acts: anything from Russian folk dance to "La Cage aux Folles", with reputable touring orchestras and opera companies squeezed in between.

Concertgebouw, Concertgebouwplein 2–6 (☎671 8345). After a facelift, the Concertgebouw is now looking – and sounding – better than ever. The acoustics of the Grote Zaal (Large Hall) are unparalleled, and a concert here is a wonderful experience. The smaller Kleine Zaal is used more for chamber concerts, often by the resident Borodin Quartet. Both halls have a star-studded international programme, plus swing/jazz nights from time to time. However, prices are on the whole very reasonable, rarely over ƒ35, and occasionally, for Sunday morning events, ƒ20 – though you can pay ƒ200 or more for the superstars. There are free Wed lunchtime concerts Sept–May (doors open 12.15pm, arrive early), and from July–August a heavily subsidized series of Summer Concerts.

Engelse Kerk, Begijnhof 48 (☎624 9665). Of the churches, this has the biggest programme – three to four performances a week, lunchtime, afternoon and evening, with an emphasis on using period instruments.

IJsbreker, Weesperzijde 23 (☎668 1805). Large, varied programme of international modern, chamber and experimental music, as well as obscure, avant-garde local performers. Occasional concerts held in the Planetarium of the Artis Zoo. Out of the town centre by the Amstel, with a delightful terrace on the water.

Muziektheater, Waterlooplein (☎625 5455). The *Netherlands Opera*, which is resident here, provides the fullest, and most reasonably priced, programme of opera in Amsterdam. Inevitably, tickets go very quickly. Free lunchtime concerts Sept–May.

Oude Kerk, Oudekerksplein 23 (☎625 8284). Organ and carillon recitals, as well as occasional choral events. In summer, the Oude Kerk, in conjunction with the Amstelkring Museum, organizes a series of "walking" concert evenings, with three separate concerts taking place at different venues, with time for coffee and a stroll between each.

Stadsschouwburg, Leidseplein 26 (☎624 2311). Somewhat overshadowed these days by the Muziektheater, but still staging significant opera and dance (it's a favourite of the Netherlands Dance Theatre), as well as visiting English-language theatre companies.

Waalse Kerk, Oudezijds Achterburgwal 157 (info from the Old Music Society; ☎030/236 2236). Weekend afternoon and evening concerts of early music and chamber music.

Theatre

Surprisingly for a city that functions so much in English, there is next to no **English-language drama** to be seen in Amsterdam. The *Stalhouderij*, which performs in a broom-cupboard of a theatre in the Jordaan, is the only company working in English, although the Theater de Bochel, converted from a bath-house, often hosts visiting English-language productions, as do the Melkweg (see p.107) and the Stadsschouwburg (see above). Apart from these, a handful of part-time companies put on two or three English productions during the summer.

As for English-language **comedy** and **cabaret**, Amsterdam is experiencing something of a revival, spearheaded by the resident and extremely successful

Boom Chicago company; during the summer in particular small venues also often hold mini-seasons of stand-up comedy and cabaret evenings.

De Balie, Kleine Gartmanplantsoen 10 (☎623 2904). A multimedia centre for culture and the arts, located off the Leidseplein, which often plays host to drama, debates, international symposia and the like, sometimes in conjunction with the *Paradiso* down the road.

Badhuis-Theater de Bochel, Andreas Bonnstraat 28 (☎668 5102). A former bath-house out near the Oosterpark, this is now a forum for visiting productions and guest directors.

Boom Chicago, Lijnbaansgracht 238 (☎639 2707). Something of a phenomenon in Amsterdam in recent years, this rapid-fire improv comedy troupe perform nightly to rave reviews. With inexpensive food, the cheapest beer in town and a Smoke Boat Cruise following the show at 10.30pm, the comedy needn't excel – but it does. Currently running from May–Oct, but due to move to a permanent location by 1998.

Comedy Café, Max Euweplein 29 (☎620 9164). Small cabaret theatre with bar that has been known to host English-language cabaret and stand-up comedy.

Stalhouderij, 1e Bloemdwarsstraat 4 (☎626 2282). Amsterdam's only non-subsidized English language theatre company, mounting new productions every 6 weeks or so in one of the city's smallest, most intimate theatre spaces. Contemporary and modern works, Shakespeare, readings, classes and workshops.

Film

Most of Amsterdam's commercial **cinemas** are huge, multiplexes showing a selection of general releases; pick up a copy of the "Week Agenda" from any cinema for details of all films showing in the city. Aside from places showing the latest blockbusters, there is a scattering of filmhouses (*filmhuizen*) showing **revival and art films** and occasional retrospectives; multimedia centres also have changing film and video programmes. All foreign movies playing in Amsterdam are shown in their **original language** and subtitled in Dutch – which is fine for British or American fare, but a little frustrating if you're in the mood for Tarkovsky or Pasolini. Films are very rarely dubbed into Dutch: if they are, *Nederlands Gesproken* will be printed next to the title in the listings.

Tickets can cost more than ƒ15 for an evening screening Fri–Sun, though it's not hard to find a ticket for ƒ11 during the week. Prices for the *filmhuizen* are a little less, and can drop as low as ƒ6 off-peak; for a paltry ƒ2.50 you can get in to see last year's blockbusters at the *Riksbioscoop* at Reguliersbreestraat 31 (☎624 3639).

Alfa, Hirschpassage, Leidseplein (☎627 8806). Interesting, occasionally inspired, movies on the edge of the mainstream.

Cavia, Van Hallstraat 52 (☎681 1419). Incongruously sited above a martial arts centre, this is one of the best small *filmhuizen*, with an eclectic and non-commercial programme of international movies. Tram #10.

Cinecenter, Lijnbaansgracht 236 (☎623 6615). Opposite the Melkweg, showing quality independent commercial films.

Desmet, Plantage Middenlaan 4a (☎627 3434). Often used by directors and actors to promote independent films. Retrospectives change every month. Gay movies Sat midnight and Sun noon. Tram #7, #9, #14.

Filmmuseum, Vondelpark 3 (☎589 1400). Subsidized by the government since the 1940s, with literally tens of thousands of prints, and showing all kinds of movies from all over the world. On summer weekend evenings there are free open-air screenings on the terrace. Also cheap matinees.

Kriterion, Roetersstraat 170 (☎623 1708). Stylish duplex close to Weesperplein metro. Arthouse and quality commercial films, late-night cult favourites, and a friendly bar. Tram #6, #7, #10.

The Movies, Haarlemmerdijk 161 (☎624 5790). Beautiful Art Deco cinema, a charming setting for independent movies. Worth a visit for the bar and restaurant alone, fully restored to their original sumptuousness. Late shows at the weekend. Tram #3.

Rialto, Ceintuurbaan 338 (☎675 3994). Mainly retrospectives or series with a theme, often with classics dotted in between. On the corner of the Sarphatipark. Tram #24 and #25 from the centre of town.

Tuschinski, Reguliersbreestraat 26 (☎626 2633). Stunning interior, and a programme dependent on the latest blockbuster.

Clubs and discos

Clubbing in Amsterdam is not the posing, style-conscious business it is in many other capital cities: most Amsterdam clubs – even hip ones – are neither wildly expensive nor difficult to get into. As for the **music** to expect, Amsterdam is not exactly at the cutting edge of experimentation: house is definitely the thing. Hip-hop has its devotees, as does modern and retro funk, jazz and underground trance and triphop, but a random dip into a club will probably turn up mellow, undemanding house beats.

Most clubs have very reasonable **entry prices**, but a singularly Amsterdam feature of clubbing is tipping the bouncer: if you want to get back into the same place next week (or any other time), ƒ5 across his palm will do very nicely thank you. Club toilets also cost money (25c or 50c), but the drinks prices are not excessively inflated. **Dress codes** tend to be minimal or non-existent – exceptions are noted below. Although most places **open** around 10pm or 11pm, there's not much point turning up anywhere before midnight; unless stated otherwise, they all carry on until 4am Sunday to Thursday, 5am Friday and Saturday. As far as **drugs** go, smoking joints is generally fine – though if you can't see or smell the stuff, ask the barman if it's OK. Should you need reminding, ecstasy, acid and speed are all completely illegal, and you can expect less than favourable treatment from the bouncers (and the long arm of the law) if they spot you with anything.

For **news** and flyers about clubs, upcoming parties and raves, drop in to places like *Clubwear House*, at Herengracht 265 (☎622 8766), and the *Hair Police* and *Conscious Dreams*, next door to each other at Kerkstraat 115/117.

Amnesia, Oudezijds Voorburgwal 3 (☎638 1461). Below the *Royal Kabul* hotel, and therefore attracting a mainly young, tourist clientele. Tends towards the hardcore. Thurs–Sun only; admission ƒ10–15 (free if you're staying in the hotel).

Club 114, Herengracht 114 (☎622 7685). One of the longest-established club locations in Amsterdam, recently reborn and playing all kinds of non-housey music, from hip-hop to R&B, with heavy trance nights. Prices vary. Open nightly.

Dansen bij Jansen, Handboogstraat 11 (☎620 1779). Founded by – and for – students, and very popular. Open nightly; admission ƒ4, though officially you need student ID to get in.

Escape, Rembrandtplein 11 (☎622 3542). Recently converted from an unexcitingly tacky disco, this is now home to Amsterdam's hottest Saturday night: "Chemistry", every so often featuring Holland's top DJ, Dimitri. A vast hangar, with room for 2000 people (although you may well still have to queue). Admission ƒ20 or more. Closed Sun.

iT, Amstelstraat 24 (☎625 0111). Large disco with a superb sound system. Has popular and glamorous gay nights (see box below), but Thursday and Sunday are mixed gay/straight and attract a dressed-up, uninhibited crowd. Admission ƒ17.50.

Mazzo, Rozengracht 114 (☎626 7500). Now back at its original location, one of the city's hippest and most laid-back discos, with a choice of music to appeal to all tastes. Perhaps the easiest-going bouncers in town. Open nightly; admission around ƒ10.

RoXY, Singel 465 (☎620 0354). Housed in an old cinema, this has one of the city's best sound systems. Wednesday at the RoXY is the most popular gay night in the city (see box below) – if you can get in. The door policy is very strict at weekends; better try on Thursday night, when DJ Dimitri is in residence. Admission ƒ7.50–12.50.

GAY AND LESBIAN NIGHTLIFE

Amsterdam has four recognized **gay areas**: the most famous and lively centres are on Kerkstraat and Reguliersdwarsstraat, although the latter has a more outgoing, international scene. The streets just north of Rembrandtplein are a camp focus, while Warmoesstraat, in the heart of the Red Light District, is cruisy and mainly leather- and denim-oriented. Many bars and clubs have "darkrooms", which are legally obliged to provide safe-sex information and condoms. Although there is a sizeable lesbian community in Amsterdam, there is just one women-only café – the *Saarein*, at Elandsstraat 119 – and one or two lesbian-only clubs that are constantly changing venue. Most bars are lesbian-friendly, though, and many clubs have mixed nights.

Among the best-known **gay bars** for men are *Café April*, *Havana* and *Downtown*, near each other on Reguliersdwarsstraat. *Argos*, at Warmoesstraat 95, the *Eagle* at Warmoesstraat 90 and *De Spijker* at Kerkstraat 4 are three of the most famous leather bars in the city. Mankind, Weteringstraat 60, is a relatively quiet, non-scene bar on a quiet stretch of the Lijnbaansgracht canal. For details of gay clubs in the city, see below.

If you want more information, get hold of a copy of the widely available **Gay Tourist Map** of Amsterdam, which has information, addresses and locations, or drop into the COC national gay and lesbian organization (see below). The English-speaking Gay and Lesbian Switchboard is on ☎623 6565 (daily 10am–10pm).

GAY CLUBS

COC, Rozenstraat 14 (☎626 3087). Very popular women-only disco and café, a favourite with the city's young lesbians. Friday night is mixed, when the music is pumping. ƒ5.

Cockring, Warmoesstraat 96 (☎623 9604). Currently Amsterdam's most popular – very cruisey – gay men's disco. Light show and bars on two levels. Get there early at the weekend to avoid queueing. Nightly; free.

Exit, Reguliersdwarsstraat 42 (☎625 8788). One of the city's most popular gay clubs, reached through the April café. Current sounds play nightly to an upbeat, cruisey crowd. Predominantly male, though women are admitted. Free.

Havana, Reguliersdwarsstraat 17 (☎620 6788). Small dancefloor above a bar slap in the middle of a buzzing gay district. Very popular with a mixed crowd (gay, yuppie, arty); mostly men, but women are admitted. Sun–Thurs 11pm–1am, Fri & Sat 11pm–2am; free.

iT, Amstelstraat 24 (☎625 0111). Saturday night here really is IT, as the city's most glamorous transvestites come out to play and the place gets packed out; men only. Thursday night is free if you're gay, and Sunday is a popular gay/straight night.

RoXY, Singel 465 (☎620 0354). Wednesday night is "hard", strictly gay only, and very popular with both men and women.

Silo, Westerdoksdijk 51 (☎420 5905). Although not really a club, this huge old place – one of the last surviving community squats – often has all-night dance parties at the weekend. Admission to these events can be high (*f*15 or more, plus "membership"), but they go on well past dawn, and give a taste of the dying Amsterdam underground.

Soul Kitchen, Amstelstraat 32a (☎620 2333). Relaxed club that's refreshingly oriented towards Sixties and Seventies soul and funk rather than the usual housey stuff. Fri & Sat only; admission around *f*10.

West Pacific, Westergasfabriek, Haarlemmerweg 8–10 (☎597 4458). After playing host to many an acid rave in the late Eighties, this converted gas factory is now *the* up-and-coming location in the city. An on-site café – with an open-hearth fireplace and an ambience to match – attracts a cutting-edge crowd of young Amsterdammers, who stay late to party.

Shopping

Where Amsterdam scores in the shopping stakes is in some excellent, unusual **speciality shops** (designer clocks, beads, clogs and condoms, to name just a few), a handful of great **street-markets** and its shopping convenience – the city centre concentrates most of what's interesting within its tight borders. The consumer revolution is noticeably absent from Amsterdam's cobbled alleys, and the majority of shops are still individual businesses rather than chains.

Shopping in Amsterdam can be divided roughly by area. Broadly, the **Nieuwendijk/Kalverstraat** strip running through Dam Square is where you'll find mostly dull, high-street fashion and mainstream department stores. **Magna Plaza**, just behind the Royal Palace, is a marvellous, striped castle of a building which has been transformed into a covered mall on five floors, complete with *Virgin Megastore*, espresso bars and teenagers joy-riding on the escalators. **Koningsplein** and **Leidsestraat** used to be ritzy areas, but these days much of the refined quality has migrated south, leaving postcard shops and uninspired restaurants, but a surprisingly good selection of affordable designer shoe- and clothes-shops. The **Jordaan** is where many local artists live and ply their wares; you can find individual items of genuine interest here, as well as more specialized, adventurous clothes shops and some affordable antiques. Less affordable antiques – the cream of Amsterdam's renowned trade – can be found in the Spiegelkwartier, centred on **Nieuwe Spiegelstraat**, while to the south, **P C Hooftstraat**, **Van Baerlestraat** and, further south still, **Beethovenstraat** play host to designer couturiers, upmarket ceramics stores, confectioners and delicatessens. When exploring, bear in mind that the most interesting and individual shops are scattered along the small radial streets which connect the main canals.

As for **opening hours**, most shops take Monday morning off, while Tuesday to Friday hours are generally 9am to 6pm; Thursday, though, is late-opening night, with most places staying open until 9pm. Saturday hours are generally slightly different, normally 8.30 or 9am to 5 or 5.30pm, and all except the larger places on main streets are closed all day Sunday. Larger shops accept **payment** by credit cards, and most will accept Eurocheques (but not travellers' cheques).

Books, magazines and card shops

Though prices are higher than at home, virtually all Amsterdam bookshops stock at least a small selection of **English-language books**, and in the city centre it's possible to pick up most English **newspapers** the day they come out, as well as the *International Herald Tribune*. English-language **magazines**, too, are available from newsstands and bookshops. The Friday open-air Boekenmarkt (see "Markets ", p.116) is also worth a look – and if you're after art books, don't forget the shops attached to the main musuems, especially the Stedelijk.

A la Carte, Utrechtsestraat 110. Large and friendly travel bookshop.

American Book Center, Kalverstraat 185. Vast stock, all in English, with lots of US imported magazines and books. 10 percent discount for students.

Art Book, Van Baerlestraat 126. The city's best source of high-gloss art books.

Art Unlimited, Keizersgracht 510. Enormous card and poster shop, with excellent stock. All kinds of images; good for communiqués home that don't involve windmills.

Athenaeum, Spui 14. Excellent all-round bookshop, with an adventurous stock. Also the best source of international newspapers and magazines.

The Book Exchange, Kloveniersburgwal 58. Rambling old secondhand shop with a crusty proprietor. Huge, dark and dusty.

The English Bookshop, Lauriergracht 71. A small but quirky collection of titles.

Fort van Sjakoo, Jodenbreestraat 24. Anarchist bookshop, stocking a wide selection of radical political publications.

Jacob van Wijngaarden, Overtoom 97. The city's best travel bookshop with knowledgeable staff and a huge selection of books and maps.

De Kloof, Kloveniersburgwal 44. Enormous higgledy-piggledy used bookshop on four floors; great for a rummage.

Lambiek, Kerkstraat 78. The city's largest international comic bookshop and gallery.

Paper Moon, Singel 419. Well-stocked card shop.

Pied-à-Terre, Singel 393. Hiking maps for Holland and beyond, most in English.

Psychedelic Bookstore, Lijnbaansgracht 90. Just what it says.

Scheltema Holkema Vermeulen, Koningsplein 20. Amsterdam's biggest and best bookshop, with 6 floors of absolutely everything. Open late and Sundays.

Vrolijk, Paleisstraat 135. Self-billed as "the largest gay and lesbian bookstore on the continent".

W H Smith, Kalverstraat 152. Branch of the UK high-street chain, with 4 floors of books and magazines. A predictable selection, but prices are sometimes lower than in other bookshops.

Xantippe, Prinsengracht 290. Wide range of books and resources by, for and about women.

Cheap and secondhand clothes

Amsterdam has a fair array of one-off, individually run places, youth-oriented and/or secondhand clothing shops dotted around in the **Jordaan**, plus a handful on **Oude/Nieuwe Hoogstraat**, and along the narrow streets that connect the major canals west of the city centre. The **Waterlooplein** flea market (see p.116) also makes a marvellous hunting ground.

Daffodil, Jacob Obrechtstraat 41. Designer labels only in this smart secondhand shop down by the Vondelpark.

Laura Dols, Wolvenstraat 7. Vintage clothing and lots of hats.

Jojo, Huidenstraat 23; also Runstraat 9. Good secondhand clothes from all eras. Particularly good for trench coats and Fifties jackets.

Kelere Kelder, Prinsengracht 285. Goldmine for used alternative clothing. Fri–Sun 1–6pm.

Lady Day, Hartenstraat 9. Good-quality secondhand fashion at reasonable prices.

Second Best, Wolvenstraat 18. Classy cast-offs.

Zipper, Huidenstraat 7; also Nieuwe Hoogstraat 10. Used clothes selected for style and quality – strong on jeans and flares. Prices start high, but everything is in good condition.

Department stores

Amsterdam's department stores can be rather dull. Venture inside only if you have an unfulfilled urge to shop till you drop; otherwise, save them for specifics.

De Bijenkorf, Dam 1. Dominating the northern corner of Dam Square, this is the city's top shop, a huge bustling place (the name means "beehive") that has an indisputably wide range and little snobbishness. Highlights include cosmetics and childrenswear.

HEMA, Nieuwendijk 174; also Reguliersbreestraat 10. A kind of upmarket Dutch Woolworth's: good for stocking up on toiletries and other essentials, and occasional designer delights – it's owned by *De Bijenkorf*, and you can sometimes find the same items at knockdown prices. Surprises include wine and salami in the back of the shop.

Metz & Co., Keizersgracht 455. By far the city's swishest shop, with the accent on Liberty prints (it used to be owned by Liberty's of London), stylish ceramics and designer furniture of the kind exhibited in modern art museums. Or you could settle for a cup of coffee in the top-floor restaurant, which affords great views over the canals.

Vroom & Dreesmann, Kalverstraat 203 (entrance also from Rokin). The main Amsterdam branch of the middle-ground nationwide chain, just near Muntplein. Still pretty unadventurous, but take comfort from the fact that their restaurant is quite outstanding (for a department store), and fresh bread is baked on the premises as well. Also, the listening stands in the CD section on the top floor are the best place for a free Mozart recital with a canal view.

Food, drink and supermarkets

If you're after provisions, from the mundane to pure luxury, you're in luck. Amsterdam has a fascinating selection of specialist gourmet shops, in addition to the usual supermarkets.

Albert Heijn, Koningsplein 4, Nieuwmarkt 18, Waterlooplein 131, Vijzelstraat 117. Central branches of the nationwide supermarket chain.

De Bierkoning, Paleisstraat 125. The "Beer King" is aptly named. 850 different beers – and the correct glasses to drink them from.

Bon Bon Jeanette, Centraal Station. Spectacular organic, hand-made, additive-free, preservative-free, low-sugar chocolates.

Bonbon Atelier Lawenda, 1e Anjeliersdwarsstraat 17. Dreamily wonderful chocolates.

Chabrol, Haarlemmerstraat 7. A fine selection of wines, and staff who know their stuff.

Dirk van den Broek, Heinekenplein 25. Supermarket that beats *Albert Heijn* hands down. Cheaper across the board; bigger too.

Drinkland, Spuistraat 116. Largest off-licence (*slijterij*) in the centre of the city.

Eichholtz, Leidsestraat 48. The only place you'll find Oreo cookies and Heinz beans.

La Tienda, 1e Sweelinckstraat 21. Musty old Spanish deli, with chorizos and cheeses galore.

Levelt, Prinsengracht 180. A specialist tea and coffee company has occupied this shop for over 150 years, and much of the original decor remains. Sound advice and friendly service.

Mediterrané, Haarlemmerdijk 184. Justifiably famous for the best croissants in town.

De Natuurwinkel, Weteringschans 133. Main branch of a supermarket chain selling only organic food. Better-tasting fruit and vegetables than anywhere else – and superb bread.

Olivaria, Hazenstraat 2a. Olive oil, and nothing but. Incredible range of oils, all from small- and medium-sized concerns around the world.

Paul Année, Runstraat 25. The best wholegrain and sourdough breads in town.

Taste of Ireland, Herengracht 228. Irish sausages, draught Guinness and freshly baked soda bread.

Wegewijs, Rozengracht 32. Majestic selection of cheeses and expert advice, with sampling possibilities.

Markets

In general, Amsterdam's markets are more diverting than its shops. There's a fine central **flea market** on Waterlooplein, vibrant **street markets** such as the Albert Cuypmarkt, emphasizing food and cheap clothing, and smaller **weekly markets** devoted to everything from stamps to flowers.

Albert Cuypmarkt, Albert Cuypstraat, between F Bolstraat and Van Woustraat. The city's main general goods and food market – Amsterdammers in their natural habitat. Mon–Sat 9am–5pm.

Amstelveld, Prinsengracht, near Utrechtsestraat. Flowers and plants, but much less of a scrum than the Bloemenmarkt. Friendly advice on what to buy, and the location is a beautiful little spot to enjoy the canal. Mon 10am–3pm.

Bloemenmarkt, Singel, between Koningsplein and Muntplein. Flowers, plants, and bulbs for export (with health certificate). Mon–Sat 9am–5pm; some stalls open Sundays as well.

Boekenmarkt, Spui. Wonderful rambling collection of secondhand books, with many a priceless gem lurking in the unsorted boxes. Fri 10am–3pm.

Boerenmarkt, Noordermarkt, next to Noorderkerk. Organic farmers' market, selling amazing fresh breads, exotic fungi, fresh herbs and hand-made mustards. Sat 9am–5pm.

Dapperstraat, south of Mauritskade. Covers roughly the same territory as the Albert Cuyp, but with not a tourist in sight. Bags of atmosphere, exotic snacks to be munched, and generally better prices. Mon–Sat 9am–5pm.

Kunstmarkt, Spui and Thorbeckeplein. Low-key but high-quality art markets in two locations; neither takes place during the winter. Sun 10am–3pm.

Lindengracht, south of Brouwersgracht. Rowdy, raucous general household supplies market, a complete switch from the jollity of the neighbouring Boerenmarkt. Sat 8am–4pm.

De Looier, Elandsgracht 109. Indoor antiques market, with dealers selling everything from 1950s radios to 16th-century Delftware. Sun–Thurs 11am–5pm, Sat 9am–5pm.

Nieuwmarkt. One of the last remnants of the Nieuwmarkt's ancient market history, and a rival to the more popular and better-stocked Boerenmarkt, with organic produce, breads, cheeses and arts and crafts. Sat 9am–5pm.

Nieuwmarkt. A low-key antiques market, with books, furniture and objets d'art dotted in amongst the tat. Sun 9am–5pm from May–Sept only.

Noordermarkt. Junk-lover's goldmine. Full of all kinds of bargains, tucked away beneath piles of useless rubbish. Get there early. Mon 7.30am–1pm.

Rommelmarkt, Looiersgracht 38. Basically a vast, permanent indoor flea market and jumble sale, awash with things left unsold at the city's other street-markets. Sun–Thurs 11am–5pm.

Stamp and coin market, N Z Voorburgwal, south of Dam Square. For collectors of stamps, coins and related memorabilia, organized by the specialist shops crowded in the nearby alleys. Wed & Sat 11am–4pm.

Waterlooplein, behind the Stadhuis. A real Amsterdam institution, and the city's best flea market by far. Sprawling and chaotic, it's the final resting place of many pairs of yellow corduroy flares; however, there are some wearable clothes to be found, and some wonderful antique/junk stalls to root through. Secondhand vinyl too. Mon–Sat 9am–5pm.

Westermarkt, Westerstraat, from Noorderkerk onwards. Another general goods market, very popular with the Jordaan locals. Mon–Sat 9am–5pm.

Miscellaneous shops

Perhaps more than any other city in Europe, Amsterdam is a great source of odd little shops devoted to one particular product or interest. What follows is a selection of favourites.

Compendium, Hartenstraat 14. The place to go if you're into games. All kinds from tin soldiers to computer games, mainly for adults.

Condomerie Het Gulden Vlies, Warmoesstraat 141. Condoms of every shape, size and flavour imaginable. All in the best possible taste.

Donald E Jongejans, Noorderkerkstraat 18. Hundreds of spectacle frames, none of them new, some of them very ancient; supplied the specs for Bertolucci's *The Last Emperor*.

P G C Hajenius, Rokin 92. Old, established tobacconist selling cigars, tobacco, smoking accessories and every make of cigarette you can think of.

Harrie van Gennip, Govert Flinckstraat 402. A huge collection of old and antique stoves from all parts of Europe, lovingly restored and all in working order.

The Head Shop, Kloveniersburgwal 39. Every dope-smoking accessory you could possibly want, along with assorted marijuana memorabilia.

Jacob Hooij, Kloveniersburgwal 10. In business at this address since 1778, this homeopathic chemist has any amount of herbs and natural cosmetics, as well as a huge stock of *drop* (Dutch liquorice).

Joe's Vliegerwinkel, Nieuwe Hoogstraat 19. Kites, frisbees, boomerangs, diabolos, yoyos, juggling balls and clubs.

't Klompenhuisje, Nieuwe Hoogstraat 9a. Amsterdam's best and brightest array of clogs.

Nieuws Innoventions, Prinsengracht 297. Specialists in modern designer items for the home – projector clocks, remote-control lamps, etc. Also round dice, chocolate body-paint and shark laundry pegs.

1001 Kralen, Rozengracht 54. "Kralen" means beads, and 1001 seems a conservative estimate for this place, which sells nothing but.

Pakhuis Amerika, Prinsengracht 541. Secondhand Americana – a US mailbox on a pole, crates for Coke bottles, a real American trashcan, et al.

't Winkeltje, Prinsengracht 228. A jumble of cheap glassware and crockery, old apothecaries' jars and flasks.

Listings

Addresses These are written, for example, as "Kerkstr. 79 II", which means the second-floor apartment at number 79, Kerkstraat. The ground floor is indicated by **hs** after the number; the basement is **sous**. Many streets share the same name, and to differentiate between them, the figures **1e** or **2e** are placed in front: these are abbreviations for *Eerste* ("first") and *Tweede* ("second") – first and second streets of the same name. There are plenty of **3e** (*Derde*, "third") and **4e** (*Vierde*, "fourth") streets too. To confuse matters further, sidestreets often take the name of the main street they run off, with the addition of the word *dwars*, meaning "crossing": hence Palmdwarsstraat is a side-street off Palmstraat. **T/O** indicates that the address is a boat: hence "Prinsengracht T/O 26" would indicate a boat to be found opposite the building numbered 26 on Prinsengracht. Dutch **post codes** – made up of four figures and two letters – can be found in the directory kept at post offices. The main canals begin their **numbering** from the top left at Brouwersgracht, and increase as they progress counterclockwise; by the time they reach the Amstel, house-numbers on Herengracht are in the 600s, Keizersgracht in the 800s and Prinsengracht in the 1100s.

Airlines *Aer Lingus*, Heiligeweg 14 (☎623 8620); *Air France*, Schiphol Airport (☎446 8800); *Air UK*, Schiphol Airport (☎601 0633); *British Airways*, Schiphol Airport (☎601 5413); *British Midland*, Strawinskylaan 721 (☎662 2211); *KLM*, G Metsustraat 2–6 (☎474 7747); *Martinair*, Schiphol Airport (☎601 1222); *Northwest Airlines*, Weteringschans 85c (☎627 7141); *Sabena*, Weteringschans 26 (☎626 2966); *Transavia*, Schiphol Airport (☎604 6555).

Babysitters *Oppascentrale Kriterion*, Roetersstraat 170 (☎624 5848, lines open 5–7pm only), is a long-established agency with a high reputation, using vetted students. 24-hr service: *f*7–10/hr, plus *f*5 administration charge and a weekend supplement; minimum charge *f*20.

Banks and bureaux de change The best rates are usually those at banks: hours are Mon–Fri 9am–4pm, with a few also open Thurs until 9pm or Sat morning; all are closed on public holidays. At other times you'll need to go to one of the many bureaux de change scattered around town: first choice is *GWK* in Centraal Station and at Schiphol Airport (both 24hr) and Leidseplein (daily 8am–11pm). *Change Express* at Damrak 86 and Leidsestraat 106 (both daily 8am–midnight), *Thomas Cook* at Dam Square and Leidseplein (both daily 9am–6pm), and *American Express* at Damrak 66 (Mon–Fri 9am–5pm, Sat 9am–noon) are other options. Beware of all other exchange places, some of which have deliberately misleading names like *GKW*; their rates are usually appalling. And steer well clear of *Chequepoint*, which charges an outrageous 9.8 percent commission on many simple transactions.

BBC World Service On 648kHz medium wave 24hrs a day. BBC Radio 4 is very clear on 198kHz long wave.

Bike and moped rental *Bike City*, at Bloemgracht 70 (☎626 3721) is one of the best, otherwise try *Damstraat Rent-a-Bike* just off Damstraat (☎625 5029) or *Macbike* at Houtkopersburgwal 16 (☎620 0985). For moped rental, try *Moped Rental Service* at Marnixstraat 208 (☎422 0266).

Bike tours *Yellow Bike*, Nieuwezijds Kolk 29 (April–Oct only, 9.30am & 1pm; 3hr; *f*29, including loan of bike; reservations advised, ☎620 6940), organizes three-hour guided bike tours around the city, taking in all the major sights (and a few minor ones). They also do a full-day bike tour of the countryside to the north of Amsterdam.

Car rental All the major firms are represented in Amsterdam, although the best deals are often with local operators, whose prices start at around *f*50–70 a day plus around 40c per kilometre over 100km – although for long journeys out of the city, the major firms' unlimited mileage rates can prove cheaper. Major firms include *Avis*, Nassaukade 380 (☎683 6061); *Budget*, Overtoom 121 (☎612 6066); *Eurodollar*, Overtoom 184 (☎616 2466); *Europcar*, Overtoom 51 (☎683 2123); *Hertz*, Overtoom 333 (☎612 2441). Local firms worth checking out are *Adams*, Nassaukade 344 (☎685 0111); *Bakker*, Hoofdweg 133 (☎612 4047); *Diks*, van Ostadestraat 278 (☎662 3366); *Ouke Baas*, van Ostadestraat 362 (☎679 4842).

Consulates *UK*, Koningslaan 44 (☎676 4343); *USA*, Museumplein 19 (☎664 5661).

Emergencies Dial ☎112. The services also have their own individual 24-hr alarm numbers: police ☎622 2222, ambulance ☎555 5555, fire ☎621 2121. Rape/sexual assault emergency line ☎612 7576 (Mon–Fri 10.30am–11.30pm, Sat & Sun 3.30pm–11.30pm). The most central hospital with a 24-hr casualty department is the *Onze Lieve Vrouwe Gasthuis*, or OLVG, just to the east of the centre at Eerste Oosterparkstraat 179 (☎599 9111; tram #3, #6, #10 or metro Wibautstraat). If you need a doctor or a late-night pharmacy, call the Central Medical Service on ☎06/350 32042. For urgent dental treatment, call the Dentist Administration Bureau on ☎06/821 2230.

Laundries *The Clean Brothers* is the best, at Kerkstraat 56 (daily 7am–9pm), with a sizeable load currently *f*8, and service washes, dry cleaning, ironing etc; branches at Jacob van Lennepkade 179 and Westerstraat 26.

Left luggage Centraal Station has self-service **lockers** (24hr, *f*4–6; maximum period 72hr); also a staffed **left luggage** office (24hr; *f*10 per item; maximum period 10 days, after which *f*50 per item per week).

Lost property For items lost on the trams, buses or metro, contact *GVB* Head Office, Prins Hendrikkade 108 (☎551 4911). For property lost on a train go to the *Gevonden Voorwerpen* office at Centraal Station (☎557 8544). If you lose something in the street or a park, try the police lost property at Stephensonstraat 18 (Mon–Fri noon–3.30pm; ☎559 3005). Schiphol Airport's lost and found number is ☎601 2325.

Nuclear alert On the first Monday of every month, at exactly noon, sinister wailing klaxons start up all over as the city's nuclear early-warning system is tested. You've been warned.

Parking *De Bijenkorf*, on Beursplein; *Byzantium*, near Leidseplein; *Centraal*, on Prins Hendrikkade near Centraal Station; *Europarking*, Marnixstraat 250; *De Kolk*, Nieuwezijds Kolk; *Kroon & Zn*, Waterlooplein; *Parking Prinsengracht*, Prinsengracht 540–542. Prices vary wildly. Main 24-hr filling stations are at Gooiseweg 10, Sarphatistraat 225, Marnixstraat 250 and Spaarndammerdijk 218.

Police Headquarters are at Elandsgracht 117 (☎559 9111); other central stations include Warmoesstraat 44, NZ Voorburgwal 104, Singel 455, Kloveniersburgwal T/O 26, Lijnbaansgracht 219 and Prinsengracht 1109.

Post office Main office at Singel 250, on the corner with Raadhuisstraat (Mon–Wed & Fri 9am–6pm, Thurs 9am–8pm, Sat 10am–1.30pm; ☎556 3311); post restante mail can be picked up, with ID, down the stairs to the left. The only late-opening (until 9pm) post office is at Oosterdokskade 5 (near Centraal Station); other central offices include St Antoniebreestraat 16, Keizersgracht 757, Kerkstraat 167, inside the Stadhuis on Waterlooplein, and Bloemgracht 300.

Religious services Christian in English – Sun 12.15pm, at *St John & St Ursula* (Catholic), Begijnhof 30 (☎622 1918); Sun 10.30am, at the *Anglican Church*, Groenburgwal 42 (☎624 8877); also Sun 10.30am, at *English Reformed Church*, Begijnhof 48 (☎624 9665). **Jewish** Liberal – Jacob Soetendorpstraat 8 (☎642 3562); Orthodox – Van der Boechorststraat 26 (☎646 0046). **Muslim** THAIBA Islamic Cultural Centre, Kraaiennest 125 (☎698 2526).

Telephones Most public phones in the street now take phonecards only – these can be bought at post offices and VVV offices in denominations of *f*5, *f*10 and *f*25, and can be used nationwide. Although the display starts out in Dutch with *"neem hoorn op"* ("pick up the receiver"), if you press the button marked "English Francais Deutsch", it will switch between languages. You can dial direct to anywhere in the world from these phones. The international operator is on ☎06/0410; international directory enquiries are on ☎06/8418. Off-peak tariffs apply 8pm–8am and all weekend.

Telephone helplines and services AIDS helpline (☎06/022 2220, Mon–Fri 2–10pm); Samaritans/Lifeline/Crisis Helpline (☎675 7575); Legal Advice Centre (☎626 4477), also free legal advice from student lawyers (☎548 2611); public transport information (☎06/9292); telegrams (☎06/0409); wake-up service (☎06/9655).

Tours The *GVB* runs a 90min hop-on, hop-off tram tour (Sun & holidays June–Sept, every 30min noon–4pm from the Victoria Hotel near Centraal Station; *f*10). For **bus** tours, operators like *Lindbergh* (the cheapest – Damrak 26, ☎622 2766), *Keytours* (Dam 19, ☎623 5051) and *Holland International* (Damrak 90, ☎625 3035) offer 3-hr tours with stop-offs and live commentary; prices start at around *f*30, often include a visit to a diamond factory and sometimes also include combinations of either a canal cruise or entry to the Rijksmuseum in the ticket (for a higher price). See also "Bike tours" on the opposite page.

Travel agents *NBBS* is the nationwide student/youth travel organization and the best source of discount flights and train tickets for anyone; branches at Rokin 38 and Utrechtsestraat 48; booking line ☎620 5071. Also worth checking out are: *Eurolines*, Rokin 10 (☎627 5151); *Budget Air*, Rokin 34 (☎627 1251); and *Nouvelles Frontières*, Van Baerlestraat 3 (☎664 4131).

Women's contacts Amsterdam has an impressive feminist infrastructure: there are support groups, health centres and businesses run by and for women. A good starting point to find out what's going on in the city is the *Vrouwenhuis*, Nieuwe Herengracht 95 (☎625 2066; phone info Mon–Fri 11am–4pm), an organizing centre for women's activities and cultural events. *Xantippe*, Prinsengracht 290 (☎623 5854), is a women's bookshop with a wide selection of feminist titles in English. See also the box on gay and lesbian nightlife on p.112.

travel details

Trains

Amsterdam CS to: Alkmaar (approx every 15min; 30min); Amersfoort (every 30min; 35min); Apeldoorn (every 30min; 1hr); Arnhem (every 30min; 1hr 10min); Den Bosch (every 30min; 1hr); Den Helder (every 30min; 1hr 10min); Dordrecht (every 30min; 1hr 30min); Eindhoven (every 30min; 1hr 30min); Enkhuizen (every 30min; 55min); Groningen (every 30min; 2hr 20min); Haarlem (every 10min; 15min); The Hague/*Den Haag* (approx every 15min; 47min); Hoorn (every 30min; 40min); Leeuwarden (hourly; 2hr 25min); Leiden (approx every 15min; 33min); Maastricht (hourly; 2hr 30min); Middelburg (hourly; 2hr 35min); Nijmegen (every 30min; 1hr 30min); Roosendaal (every 30min; 1hr 45min); Rotterdam (every 30min; 1hr 10min); Schiphol Airport (every 15min; 20min); Utrecht (every 30min; 30min); Vlissingen (hourly; 2hr 45min); Zwolle (hourly; 1hr 20min).

Buses

Amsterdam CS to: Landsmeer (#91; every 30min; 25min).

Amsterdam Marnixstraat to: Zandvoort (#80; every 30min; 30min).

Amsterdam St Nicolaskerke to: Broek-in-Waterland (#110, #111; every 30min; 15min); Edam (#110; every 30min; 40min); Marken (#111; every 30min; 30min); Monnickendam (#111; every 30min; 20min); Volendam (#110; every 30min; 30min).

Amsterdam Weesperplein and Amstel Station to: Muiden (#136; every 30min; 40min); Naarden (#136; every 30min; 55min).

International trains

Amsterdam CS to: Antwerp (hourly; 2hr 15min); Basel (6 daily; 8hr); Berlin (3 daily; 8hr); Bruges (hourly; 3hr 45min); Brussels (hourly; 3hr); Hamburg (4 daily; 3hr 15min); Innsbruck (4 daily; 13hr); Köln (12 daily; 2hr 45min); Lille (hourly; 4hr 20min); London (6 daily; 10–12hr); Marseille (1 daily; 15hr); Milan (1 daily; 15hr); Munich (4 daily; 8hr); Nürnberg (5 daily; 7hr 30min); Paris (5 daily; 6hr); Strasbourg (3 daily; 8hr); Vienna (3 daily; 13hr); Zürich (6 daily; 9hr).

CHAPTER TWO

NORTH HOLLAND

The province of **North Holland** is one of the country's most explored regions. Though not as densely populated as its sister province to the south, it's still a populous area, and holds some of Holland's prime tourist attractions. The landscape is typically Dutch, the countryside north of Amsterdam for the most part a familiar polder scene of flat fields, cut by trenches and canals, stretching far into the distance, the vast horizons broken only by the odd farmhouse or windmill. Lining most of the western coast are rugged areas of dune and long, broad sandy beaches, while on the other side the coast of the IJsselmeer, formerly the Zuider Zee (see box on p.146), is home to old ports turned yachting communities, which sport the vestiges of a glorious past in picturesquely preserved town centres.

The majority of North Holland is easily visited by means of day-trips from Amsterdam. But to do this would just skim the surface of the region. The urban highlight is undoubtedly **Haarlem**, an easy day-trip from Amsterdam but definitely worth treating as an overnight stop. It also gives access to some wild stretches of dune and beach, and one of the country's largest coastal resorts in **Zandvoort**. To the north, **Alkmaar** is also usually visited as a brief excursion from Amsterdam, primarily to see its rather bogus ceremonial Friday cheese market, but is worth a longer sojourn if you're keen to experience small-town provincial Holland. In the eastern part of the province, the villages nearest Amsterdam – **Marken**, **Volendam** and **Edam** – are kitsch places full of tourists in search of clogs and windmills during summer, but with considerable charm if you can escape the crowds (or visit off-season). Further north, **Hoorn** and **Enkhuizen** are of more interest, formerly major Zuider Zee ports, now pretty towns with yacht-filled harbours that again make either a good day-trip from Amsterdam, or pleasant stops if you're travelling up to Friesland by car and are in no hurry. In the far north of the province, the island of **Texel** is the most accessible and busiest of the Wadden Sea islands. It's very crowded during summer, but don't be

---

ACCOMMODATION PRICE CODES

All the **hotels** and **hostels** detailed in this chapter have been graded according to the following price categories. Apart from ①, which is a per-person price for a hostel bed, all the codes are based on the rate for the cheapest double room during high season.

For more on accommodation, see p.30.

① Up to ƒ40 per person	④ ƒ150–200	⑦ ƒ300–400
② ƒ60–100	⑤ ƒ200–250	
③ ƒ100–150	⑥ ƒ250–300	

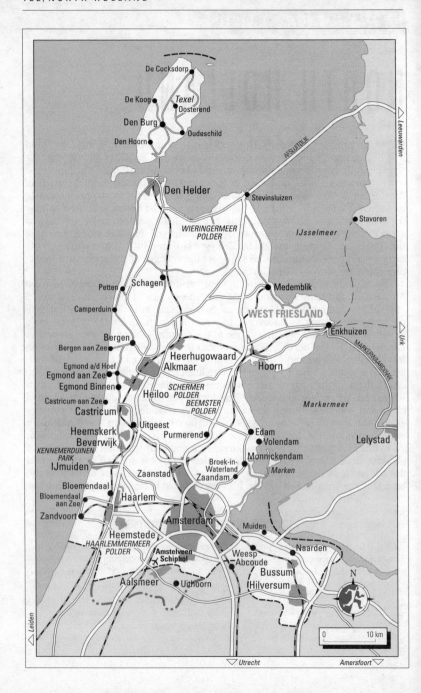

put off by the numbers: with a bit of walking you can find places well off the beaten tourist track – and far away from the hustle of Amsterdam.

Transport in North Holland is by a mixture of train to the main centres and then bus. For moving on, there's a fast road link along the top of the twenty-kilometre-long dike between Enkhuizen and Lelystad, on the reclaimed Flevoland polders. It was completed in 1976, the first stage of a plan to reclaim the enclosed area in the so-called **Markerwaard** scheme. This met considerable opposition when proposed and has now been indefinitely postponed (you'll still see posters and graffiti against the plan in places like Hoorn and Enkhuizen), but the road it spawned is still a useful way of getting to the east of the country without passing through Amsterdam. Similarly, the Afsluitdijk runs from the tip of the province across to Friesland, providing a quick and easy road-link to the towns of Leeuwarden and Groningen.

Het Gooi

Most of the province of North Holland is located, logically enough, north of Amsterdam. But the borders of the province also dip down beneath the capital, taking in Schiphol and parts of the bulb-growing areas around Aalsmeer (covered in *South Holland and Utrecht*; see p.161) and a suburban agglomeration which sprawls east toward Amersfoort. This is known as **Het Gooi**, an area which was mostly devoted to sheep-farming until 1874, when the Amsterdam–Amersfoort railway was built and the wealthy burghers of Amsterdam began to build mansions among the region's lakes, woods and heather. It remains a popular escape for weekending Amsterdammers, though the area is hardly essential viewing. If, however, you have time on your hands in Amsterdam and have seen all the more obvious sights, a couple of low-key towns might attract your attention – not to mention some modern architectural highlights further east.

Muiden

The first town you reach, **MUIDEN** (pronounced "*mao-dn*") is squashed around the Vecht, a river usually crammed with pleasure boats and dinghies sailing out to the IJmeer and beyond to the IJsselmeer. It's the most famous sailing harbour in the Gooi area, not least because the royal yacht, *De Groene Draek*, is often moored here. As well as the harbour, there are a couple of beaches on the IJmeer – Muiderberg and Muiderzand – and, although most of the sightseeing is done by weekend admirals eyeing up each other's boats, an extra spark of interest is provided by the **Muiderslot** at Herengracht 1 (April–Oct Mon–Fri 10am–4pm, Sat & Sun 1–4pm; Nov–March Sat & Sun 1–3pm; guided tours only – call ahead to arrange one in English; ☎0294/261 325; ƒ7.50). In the thirteenth century this was the home of Count Floris V, a sort of aristocratic Robin Hood who favoured the common people at the nobles' expense. They replied by kidnapping the count, imprisoning him in his own castle and stabbing him to death. Destroyed and rebuilt in the fourteenth century, Muiderslot's interior is these days a recreation of the period of a slightly more recent occupant, the poet Pieter Hooft. He was chatelain here from 1609 to 1647, a sinecure that allowed him to entertain a group of artistic and literary friends who became known as the Muiden Circle, and included Grotius,

Vondel, Huygens and other Amsterdam intellectuals. The obligatory tours centre on this clique, in a restoration that is both believable and likeable – two things period rooms generally aren't.

From the jetty outside the Muiderslot, boats leave regularly for the fortress island of **Pampus** (April–Oct Tues–Sun 10am–5pm; f17.50, including entry to the fortress), a few kilometres out to sea. It was built at the end of the nineteenth century as part of Amsterdam's defence system, but has now fallen into ruin.

Practicalities

The only way to reach Muiden is by *Midnet* **bus** #136, which leaves Amsterdam (Weesperplein and Amstel Station) every 30min for Hilversum, via Muiden (40min), Muiderberg (45min) and Naarden (55min). Be warned, though, that once you break free of the Amsterdam suburbs, signs telling you where you are are few and far between and you can easily sail past Muiden and Muiderberg without noticing – ask the driver to drop you off in the right place.

In Muiden, the bus drops you off on the edge of the small village; there are signposts to the Muiderslot castle and the **VVV** (Kazernestraat 10, April–Sept Mon–Fri 10am–5pm, Sat 10am–2pm; ☎0294/261 389). If you fancy pottering around in **boats**, the *Muiden Jachtverhuur Station* (MYCS), at Naarderstraat 10 (☎0294/261 413) rents out sailboats. As far as eating and drinking goes, though, there are a couple of obvious places in the village but you'd do far better to carry on to Naarden, where there's a better choice.

Naarden

Look at a postcard of **NAARDEN**, about 10km east of Muiden, and it seems as if the town was formed by a giant pastry-cutter: the double rings of ramparts and moats, unique in Europe, were engineered between 1675 and 1685 to defend Naarden and the eastern approach to Amsterdam. They were still used in the 1920s, and one of the fortified spurs is now the wonderfully explorable **Vestingmuseum** (Fortification Museum) at Westvalstraat 6 whose claustrophobic underground passages demonstrate how the garrison defended the town for 250 years. (April–Oct Tues–Fri 10.30am–5pm, Sat & Sun noon–5pm; June–Aug also Mon 10.30am–5pm; Nov–March Sun noon–4pm only; phone for details of extended opening times over the Christmas holiday period, ☎035/694 5459; f7.50, under 16s f5). For f4, you can also take a boat-trip around the fortress.

The rest of Naarden's tiny centre is peaceful and attractive. The small, low houses mostly date from after 1572 when the Spanish sacked the town and massacred the inhabitants, an act designed to warn other settlements in the area against insurrection. Fortunately they spared the late Gothic **Grote Kerk** (June to mid-Sept daily 2–4pm) and its superb vault paintings. Based on drawings by Dürer, these twenty wooden panels were painted between 1510 and 1518 and show an Old Testament story on the south side, paralleled by one from the New Testament on the north. To study the paintings without breaking your neck, borrow a mirror at the entrance. The church is also noted for its wonderful acoustics: every year there are several acclaimed performances of Bach's *St Matthew Passion* in the Grote Kerk in the days leading up to Easter – details from the VVV (see "Practicalities" below). A haul up the 235 steps of the Grote Kerk's highly visible square **tower** (tours May–Aug Wed–Sat 1, 2, 3 & 4pm, Sept Wed–Sat 2 &

3pm; ƒ3) gives the best view of the fortress island, and, less attractively, of Hilversum's TV tower. The elaborately step-gabled building opposite the church is the **Stadhuis**, built in 1601 and still in use today; if the door's open, you're free to wander round inside.

Naarden is best known, though, for the relatively low-key **Comenius Museum** at Kloosterstraat 33 (April–Oct Tues–Sat 10am–5pm, Sun noon–5pm; Nov–March Tues–Sun 2–5pm; ƒ2.50). Jan Amos Komenski, known as Comenius, was a seventeenth-century philosopher, cartographer and educational reformer. Born in Moravia (today part of the Czech Republic), he spent much of his life travelling across Europe as a religious exile before finally settling in Amsterdam in 1656 – much of his writing was far too radical for the time to be published anywhere else. After his death in 1670, though, for some unexplained reason he was buried 25km away in Naarden. Comenius is well known in the Czech and Slovak republics as a ground-breaking theorist on teaching and education – his 1658 book *Orbis Sensualium Pictus*, or "The Visible World in Pictures", was the first-ever picture-book for children and Bratislava, the capital of Slovakia, dedicated its Comenius University to his memory; even today, fully half the visitors to Naarden's Comenius Museum are Czech and Slovak tourists. The museum itself is interesting enough (with good English labelling), if a little rarefied; despite good exhibits relating Comenius' work to better-known philosophers of the time (such as Descartes), if you don't share the glow of national pride you might find it all a little overblown. Just next door, and with access through the museum, is Comenius' **Mausoleum**, the last remnant of a medieval convent on the site dating from 1438. In the 1930s the Dutch authorities refused the Czechoslovak government's request for the repatriation of the philosopher's remains, and instead sold the building (and the land it stood on) to them for the symbolic price of one guilder; the mausoleum remains today a tiny slice of Czech territory in Holland.

Practicalities

Naarden is on the same *Midnet* #136 **bus** route as Muiden (see above), with the journey taking 55 minutes. The bus drops you off within sight of the Grote Kerk's tower; the village is tiny enough – and packed with signposts on every corner – that you'll have no trouble finding any of the museums or the **VVV**, about ten minutes' walk away at Adriaan Dortsmanplein 1b (May–Sept Mon–Fri 9.15am–5pm, Sat 10am–4pm, Sun noon–4pm; Oct–April Mon–Fri 10.30am–2pm, Sat 10am–2pm, although outside these times you can also get information from the post office next door; ☎035/694 2836).

From the bus-stop, follow Cattenhagestraat to the main shopping street of Marktstraat and you'll find plenty of places to eat and drink; a nice little spot for a **beer** and a bite – *Café Demmers* at Marktstraat 52 – is right opposite the fancier tearoom *Salon de Thé Sans Doute*. Next to the Grote Kerk on the south side is the dark-wood *Café Petit Restaurant De Doelen* at Marktstraat 7, perfect for an inexpensive **meal**, and round the other side of the church is the more upmarket *Gooische Brasserie*, with a tiny terrace overlooking the tower. For some variety, check out the Chinese–Indonesian *Good Dates* at Cattenhagestraat 34 – and if you fancy a real splurge, the restaurant *Het Arsenaal*, set in the town's old weapons-store dating from 1688 (well-signposted), offers an à la carte menu of French–Dutch cuisine for around ƒ70 a head. Every Saturday, there's a small **market** outside the VVV between 8am and 2pm.

Hilversum

The main town of Het Gooi is **HILVERSUM**, a nineteenth-century commuter suburb for wealthy Amsterdammers, who created a well-heeled smugness that survives to this day. Their villas have been flashily converted into studios for Dutch broadcasting companies, and behind the neatly trimmed hedges and lace curtains live some of the country's more comfortably off.

One of the villas, the former studio of a radio broadcasting company, has been converted into the **Omroepmuseum**, at Oude Amersfoortseweg 121–131 (Tues–Fri 10am–5pm, Sat & Sun noon–5pm; $f5$), which has displays and videos on Dutch broadcasting history; take bus #1. The **Het Goois Museum**, Kerkbrink 6 (Tues–Sun 1.30–4.30pm; $f2.50$) details the history of the Gooi, the area around Hilversum. However, the main sight is the town's **Raadhuis** at Dudopark 1. Dating from 1931, the building is the work of the Frank Lloyd Wright-influenced architect W M Dudok, and is a deceptively simple progression of straw-coloured blocks rising to a clock tower, with long, slender bricks giving a strong horizontal emphasis to the buildings. The interior (open office hours; free) is worth seeing: essentially a series of lines and boxes, its marble walls are margined with black like a monochrome Mondrian painting, all coolly and immaculately proportioned. Dudok also designed the interior decorations, and though some have been altered, his style confidently prevails, right down to the ashtrays and lights.

Practicalities

Trains leave Amsterdam twice an hour for Hilversum, and take about 30min to get there. *Midnet* **bus** #136 also runs to Hilversum every half hour from Amsterdam (Weesperplein and Amstel Station), but its meandering journey takes about two hours; bus #137 is a slightly faster option.

W M Dudok was Hilversum's principal architect, and both the Goois Museum and the **VVV**, opposite the station at Schapenkamp 25 (mid-May to mid-Sept Mon–Fri 9am–5.30pm, Sat 10am–4pm; mid-Sept to mid-May Mon–Fri 9am–5pm, Sat 10am–3pm; ☎035/621 1651), sell a guide ($f2$) to the many other buildings he designed in the town. The VVV can also help with **rooms**, though with Amsterdam so close, and connections on to more interesting towns so easy, there's little reason to stay. The nearest **campsite** is *De Woensberg* (☎035/538 2481; March–Oct) at Woensbergweg 5, in the nearby village of Blaricum – take bus #136 or #137 to the Huizerhoogt stop. As usual, you can **rent bikes** most conveniently at Hilversum's train station; alternatively try *Firma Kok*, Koninginneweg 76–78 (closed Sun & Mon; ☎035/624 5724 – turn right out of the station and walk 200m), *Hunting*, Neuweg 48 (closed Sun; ☎035/621 4572) or *Bonhof*, Eikbosserweg 126 (closed Sun; ☎035/621 4851).

For **eating and drinking**, inexpensive options include *Café Cartouche* at Stationsstraat 22 and the self-styled brown café *De Vergaederingh* at Emmastraat 2, close to the station. *De Jonge Haan*, at 's-Gravelandseweg 62, has large enough portions of all kinds of fish and seafood to satisfy most appetites.

Around Hilversum: exploring Het Gooi

Hilversum makes a good base for seeing the best of **Het Gooi** (which you can easily do in a day), and the VVV (see above) sells an excellent walking and cycling map of the area, *"Wandel- en fietskaart Gooi en Vechtstreek"* ($f9.50$), which, although not in English, details good walking routes in addition to the well-signposted *ANWB* "Gooiroute" – a thirty-kilometre-long cycling route that leads across the heather to Laren, then via Blaricum to Huizen on the shore of the Gooimeer, and back via the woods to Hilversum. To get to the route from Hilversum train station, cross the rail line and continue along this road until just after you've crossed a roundabout, where you'll find the first "Gooiroute" signpost at a small road to the right. If you don't fancy the idea of biking, bus #136 (every 30min between Amsterdam and Hilversum) is almost like a guided tour, taking the most circuitous route possible through every town and village along the way.

The most attractive village in Het Gooi proper is **LAREN**, halfway between Hilversum and the Gooimeer, if only because of its excellent **Singer Museum** of modern art at Oude Drift 1 (Tues–Sat 11am–5pm, Sun noon–5pm; *f*7.50; bus #136 stops outside). A sheep-farming community for centuries, Laren became fashionable with artists in the 1870s, notably those of the Impressionist Hague School, and the surrounding landscape, as well as the village's farmers and weavers, and even the interiors of their farmhouses, all appear in their paintings. In later years Expressionist and Modernist painters also came to the Laren area, and their works were gathered together by the Singers, an American couple who moved from Pittsburgh to Laren in 1901. The museum, which is based on their collection, opened in 1956 and, as well as paintings by Laren artists, contains works from France and America. As for the rest of the town, its shady streets and diminutive houses centre around the main square of Brink, which has several pleasant bars and an outdoor pancake restaurant. On one side of Brink the **St Jans Basiliek**, built in 1925, is the starting-point of the St Jans procession, one of the many festivals celebrated in Laren.

If you want to sail or windsurf, head for the small town of **HUIZEN**, situated on the Gooimeer and known for its favourable windsurfing conditions. It has three modern yacht harbours and two beaches – **Zomerkade**, reputedly the most beautiful beach on the IJsselmeer, and **Stichtsebrug**, a little further out, which is better for windsurfing. Boards and sailing boats can be rented from *EHZ* at Kooizand 70 (April–Sept only; ☎035/525 5055). For more information on the area, call in to the **VVV** in the town hall at Graaf Wichman 10 (Mon–Fri 8.30am–5pm; ☎035/528 1227).

Haarlem and around

Though only fifteen minutes from Amsterdam by train, **HAARLEM** has a quite different pace and feel from the capital. An easily absorbed city of around 150,000 people that sees itself as a notch above its neighbours, you'd be mad to miss Haarlem if you've any time at all to spare. The Frans Hals Museum, in the almshouse where the artist spent his last – and for some his most brilliant – years, is worth an afternoon in itself; there are numerous beaches within easy reach, as well as some of the best of the bulbfields (see *South Holland and Utrecht*, p.161). In short, if you're tired of the crowds and grime of Amsterdam, Haarlem makes a good alternative base for exploring North Holland, or even the capital itself.

The Haarlem area telephone code is ☎023

Arrival, information and accommodation

The **train station**, connected to Amsterdam and to Leiden by four trains an hour and to Alkmaar by two an hour, is located on the north side of the city, about ten minutes' walk from the centre; **buses** stop right outside.

The **VVV**, attached to the station (April–Sept Mon–Sat 9am–5.30pm; Oct–March Mon–Fri 9am–5.30pm, Sat 9am–4pm; ☎06/320 24043, f1 per min), has maps (f1) and can book **private rooms** for a f7 fee, though you'll find more choice in Zandvoort, about twenty minutes away by bus #81 (every 30min from the train station) or bus #80 (every 30min from Tempelierstraat). The same goes for **hotels**, although Haarlem has a few reasonably priced and central places worth considering, like the *Carillon* at Grote Markt 27 (☎531 0591, fax 531 4909; ③), in a comfortable old building with steep stairs, and the more modern *Amadeus* at Grote Markt 10 (☎532 4530, fax 532 2328; ③). About fifteen minutes' walk from the centre (or bus #7 from the station, or train one stop to Overveen) is the *Fehres* at Zijlweg 299 (☎527 7368, no fax; ②), giving good access to Haarlem, the Kennemerduinen National Park and the sea. There's also a **youth hostel** at Jan Gijzenpad 3 (March–Oct only; ☎537 3793; ①); bus #2 or #6 runs frequently from the station – a ten-minute journey. **Campers** could try the campsites among the dunes out at Bloemendaal-aan-Zee – either *De Lakens* at Zeeweg 60 (☎525 1902; April–Oct) or *Bloemendaal* at Zeeweg 72 (☎526 3453; April–Sept). Bus #81 from the train station will take you to all of them, though they're all open between April and October only. Haarlem's own site, *De Liede* at Lieoever 68 (☎533 2360), is open all year – to get there take bus #80 from Tempelierstraat.

The town

For a long time the residence of the counts of Holland, Haarlem was sacked by the Spanish under Frederick of Toledo in 1572. There are reminders of this all over the town, since, after a seven-month siege, the revenge exacted by the inconvenienced Frederick was terrible: very nearly the entire population was massacred, including all the Protestant clergy. Recaptured in 1577 by William the Silent, Haarlem went on to enjoy its greatest prosperity in the seventeenth century, becoming a centre for the arts and home to a flourishing school of painters.

Nowadays, the place retains an air of quiet affluence, with all the picturesque qualities of Amsterdam but little of the sleaze. The core of the city is **Grote Markt**, an open space flanked by a concentration of Gothic and Renaissance architecture, most notably the gabled and balconied **Stadhuis**, at one end. This dates from the fourteenth century, though it has been much rebuilt over the years, the last time in 1630 – a date recorded on the facade. Inside, the main hall is normally left open for visitors during office hours; it's decorated with a few fifteenth-century paintings. At the other end of Grote Markt there's a statue of one **Laurens Coster**, who, Haarlemmers insist, is the true inventor of printing. Legend tells of him cutting a letter "A" from the bark of a tree and dropping it into the sand by accident. Plausible enough, but most authorities seem to agree that Gutenburg was the more likely source of the printed word.

Coster stands in the shadow of the **Grote Kerk of St Bavo** (March–Oct Mon–Sat 8am–4pm; Nov–Feb Mon–Sat 8am–3pm; f2), where he is believed to be buried. If you've been to the Rijksmuseum in Amsterdam, the church may seem familiar, at least from the outside, since it was the principal focus of the seven-

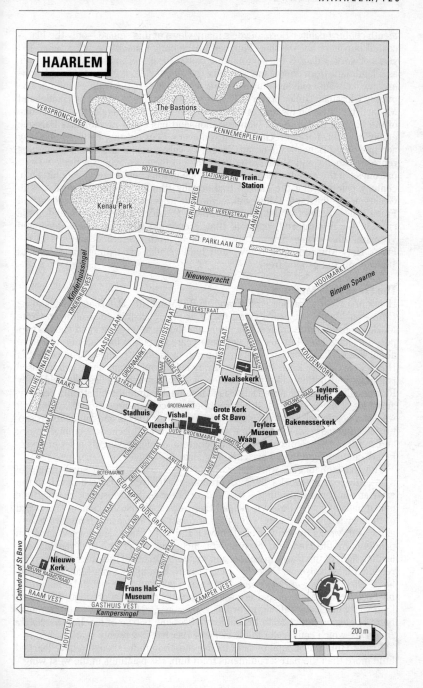

teenth-century painter Berckheyde's many views of this square – only the black-coated burghers are missing. Finished in the early sixteenth century, after 150 years of work, it dwarfs the surrounding clutter of streets and houses, and serves as a landmark from almost anywhere in the city. Inside, it is breathtakingly cavernous, its beauty enhanced by the stark, white power of the Gothic vaulting. The mighty Christian Müller organ of 1738 is said to have been played by Handel and Mozart (the latter on his tour of the country in 1766, at the age of ten) and is one of the biggest in the world, with five thousand pipes and razzamatazz Baroque embellishment. (Organ recitals are given every Tues evening between mid-May and mid-Sept.) Beneath the organ, Xaverij's lovely group of draped marble figures represent Poetry and Music, offering thanks to the town, which is depicted as a patroness of the arts, for its generosity, while in the choir there's a late fifteenth-century painting that the church traditionally (though dubiously) attributes to Geertgen tot Sint Jans, along with memorials to painters Pieter Saenredam and Frans Hals – both of whom are buried here. Outside, at the western end of the church, the **Vishal** and, opposite that, Lieven de Key's profusely decorated **Vleeshal** (the former fish and meat markets) both operate as annexes to the Frans Hals Museum (see below) and hold regular art exhibitions (Mon–Sat 10am–5pm, Sun 1–5pm; free).

The Frans Hals Museum

Haarlem's chief attraction, the **Frans Hals Museum** at Groot Heiligland 62 (Mon–Sat 11am–5pm, Sun 1–5pm; ƒ6.50), is just a five-minute stroll from Grote Markt, housed in the Oudemannenhuis almshouse where the aged Hals is supposed to have lived out his last destitute years on public funds. Little is known about Frans Hals. Born in Antwerp, the son of Flemish refugees who settled in Haarlem in the late 1580s, his extant *oeuvre* is relatively small: some two hundred paintings and nothing like the number of sketches and studies left behind by Rembrandt – partly because Hals wasn't fashionable until the nineteenth century, and a lot of his work was lost before it became collectable. His outstanding gift was as a portraitist, showing a sympathy with his subjects and an ability to capture fleeting expression that some say even Rembrandt lacked. Seemingly quick and careless flashes of colour form a coherent whole, leaving us a set of seventeenth-century figures that are curiously alive.

The museum begins with the work of other artists: first a small group of **sixteenth-century works**, the most prominent a triptych by Gerard David, and an early anti-imperialist painting – *West Indian Scene* by Jan Mostaert, in which the naked natives try fruitlessly to defend themselves against the cannon and sword of their invaders. Van Scorel's *Baptism of Christ* and *Knights of Jerusalem* follow, along with works by van Goyen, Brouwer and van Ostade, and a good group of paintings by the **Haarlem mannerists**, including works by Carel van Mander, leading light of the Haarlem School and mentor of many of the other painters represented here. Cornelis Cornelisz van Haarlem best follows van Mander's guidelines: *The Marriage of Peleus and Thetis* was a popular subject at the time, probably because it was interpreted as a warning against discord, appropriate during the long war with Spain – though Cornelisz gives as much attention to the arrangement of elegant nudes as to his subject. The same is true of his *Massacre of the Innocents*, which could refer to the siege of Haarlem just twenty years earlier.

Frans Hals was a pupil of van Mander too, though he seems to have learned little more than the barest rudiments from him. His paintings in the west wing –

a set of "Civic Guard" portraits of the companies initially formed to defend the country from the Spanish, but which later became simply social clubs – established his reputation as a portraitist and earned him a regular income. There was a special skill involved in painting these: for the first time Hals made the group portrait a unified whole instead of a static collection of individual portraits; his figures are carefully arranged, but so cleverly as not to appear contrived. For a time, Hals himself was a member of the Company of Saint George, and in the *Officers of the Militia Company of Saint George* he appears in the top left-hand corner – one of his few self-portraits.

After this, there are numerous scenes of Haarlem by Berckheyde and Saenredam, among others; landscapes by the Ruisdaels and Berchem; and some group portraits by Veerspronck and the elderly Frans Hals. Hals' later paintings are darker, more contemplative works, closer to Rembrandt in their lighting. The *Governors of the Saint Elizabeth Gasthuis*, painted in 1641, is a good example, as are the portraits of the *Regents* and *Regentesses of the Oudemannenhuis* itself – perhaps the museum's finest treasures. These were commissioned when Hals was in his eighties, a poor man despite a successful painting career, hounded for money by the town's tradesmen and by the mothers of his illegitimate children, and dependent on the charity of people like those depicted here. Their cold, hard faces stare out of the gloom, the women reproachful, the men only slightly more affable. The character just right of centre in the *Regents* painting has been labelled (and indeed looks) completely drunk, although it is inconceivable that Hals would have depicted him in this condition; it's more likely that he was suffering from some kind of facial paralysis, and his jauntily cocked hat was simply a popular fashion of the time. There are those who claim Hals had lost his touch by the time he painted these pictures, yet the sinister, almost ghostly power of these paintings, facing each other across the room, suggests quite the opposite. Van Gogh's remark that "Frans Hals had no fewer than 27 blacks" suddenly makes perfect sense.

Other galleries hold lesser works by lesser artists. There's a new wing, which houses temporary exhibitions, usually of modern and contemporary artists, and a permanent collection of paintings by Israëls, Appel and Jan Sluyters (though lamentably few of the last). More interesting is the Oudemannenhuis itself, a fairly typical *hofje* whose style of low buildings and peaceful courtyards you'll see repeated with slight variations all over town – and indeed the country. Classical concerts are held here throughout the year except from June to August, usually taking place in the afternoon on the third Sunday of each month. For detailed information, call ☎531 9180.

The hofjes … and Haarlem's other sights

As for the rest of town, Haarlem has a greater number of **hofjes** than most Dutch cities – proof of the town's prosperity in the seventeenth century. The VVV can give information on where to find them; most are still inhabited, so you're confined to looking around the courtyard, but the women who sit outside seem used to the occasional visitor and won't throw you out.

Second in the pecking order of Haarlem sights, the **Teylers Museum**, at Spaarne 16 (Tues–Sat 10am–5pm, Sun 1–5pm; *f*7), is Holland's oldest museum, founded in 1778 by wealthy local philanthropist Pieter Teyler van der Hulst. This should appeal to scientific and artistic tastes alike, containing everything from fossils, bones and crystals, to weird, H G Wells-type technology (including an enormous eighteenth-century electrostatic generator) and sketches and line drawings by Michelangelo, Raphael, Rembrandt and Claude, among others. The drawings are covered to protect them from the light, but don't be afraid to pull back the curtains and peek. Look in, too, on the rooms beyond, filled with work by eighteenth- and nineteenth-century Dutch painters, principally Breitner, Israëls, Weissenbruch and, not least, Wijbrand Hendriks, who was the keeper of the art collection here.

Teyler also bestowed his charity on the **Teylers Hofje**, a little way east around the bend of the Spaarne at Koudenhorn 64, a solid, late-eighteenth-century building that is more monumental in style than the town's other *hofjes*. Nearby, the elegant tower of the **Bakenesserkerk** forms the other main protrusion on the Haarlem skyline, a late-fifteenth-century church which is usually kept closed. Two other sights that may help structure your wanderings are on the opposite side of town. Van Campen's **Nieuwe Kerk** was built – rather unsuccessfully – onto Lieven de Key's bulbed, typically Dutch tower in 1649, though the interior is symmetrical with a soberness that is quite chilling after the soaring heights of the Grote Kerk. Just beyond, and much less self-effacing, the Roman Catholic **Cathedral of St Bavo** (April–Oct Mon–Sat 10am–noon & 2–4.30pm) is one of the largest ecclesiastical structures in Holland. Designed by Joseph Cuijpers and built between 1895 and 1906, it is broad and spacious inside, with cupolas and turrets crowding around an apse reminiscent of Byzantine churches or mosques, and the whole surmounted by a distinctive copper dome.

Eating and drinking

For **lunches and snacks**, try *Café Mephisto*, Grote Markt 29, which is open all day and serves Dutch food for ƒ15–25, snacks for much less. *Café 1900*, Barteljorisstraat 10, is also a good place for lunch, a trendy locals' hangout serving drinks and light meals in an impressive turn-of-the-century interior (it also has live music on Sundays); or sample the excellent patisserie in the *H Ferd Kuipers* tearoom at Barteljorisstraat 22. In the evening, there's *Alfonso's* Mexican restaurant) just behind the Grote Kerk at Oude Groenmarkt 8, which dishes up Tex-Mex **meals** for ƒ20 and up. The *Piccolo* restaurant, Riviervischmarkt 1, serves pasta and decent pizzas from ƒ13; while there's Indonesian food at *De Lachende Javaen*, on Frankestraat, where *rijsttafels* start at ƒ32 per person. *Pamukkale* is a lively Turkish restaurant at Gedempte Oudegracht 29, with music at the weekends.

Once you've eaten, *Ze Crack*, at the junction of Lange Veerstraat and Kleine Houtstraat, is a dim, smoky **bar** with good music and lots of English people drinking beer by the pint. On the same street, closer to Grote Markt at Lange Veerstraat 9, *'t Ouwe Proef* is more typically Dutch, a *proeflokaal* that also sells beer – at its liveliest in the early evening.

Around Haarlem

You'll find most of interest **west** of Haarlem. Take bus #80 from Tempelierstraat which goes via Bloemendaal-aan-Zee to Zandvoort, or bus #81 from the train station direct to Zandvoort; both run every half-hour. The moneyed Haarlem outskirts quickly give way to the thick woodland and rugged dune landscape of the **Kennemerduinen National Park**, which stretches down to the sea. Hardy types keen to leave the city behind for the day can take the train from Amsterdam or Haarlem to Bloemendaal, then walk 12km through the scrubby dunes to the ocean (there's a map outside the station); allow about three hours for the walk.

Bus #80, though, runs alongside the park and hits the coast at **Bloemendaal-Aan-Zee**, which is the rather grandiose name for a group of beachside shacks that house a thriving ice-cream trade. A little further south, **ZANDVOORT** is a major Dutch seaside resort, an agglomeration of modern and faceless apartment complexes rising out of the dunes. As resorts go it's pretty standard – packed and oppressive in summer, depressingly dead in winter. The best reason to visit is the championship motor racing circuit, which provides background noise to everyone's sunbathing. If you come for the beach, and manage to fight your way through the crush to the water, watch out – the sea here is murky and ominously close to the smoky chimneys of **IJMUIDEN** to the north. This is a sprawling, depressing town, with a modern centre spread along the wide North Sea Canal; the part around the enormous sea locks and fishing harbour is of most interest, but the detour isn't really worth making.

A few kilometres **north** of Haarlem, **SPAARNDAM** is known for its statue commemorating the boy who saved the country from disaster by sticking his finger in a hole in the dike. This tale seems to have had little basis in reality and few Dutch people even know it, but it had a sufficient ring of truth for a little-known American writer to weave a story around it, and so create a legend. The monument to the heroic little chap was unveiled in 1950 – more, it seems, as a tribute to the opportunistic Dutch tourist industry than anything else.

Continuing north, the train line cuts up through unrelenting suburbia to **BEVERWIJK**, not much of a place in itself but very much worth a visit if you're staying in either Haarlem or Alkmaar (or even Amsterdam) for its weekend indoor **market** (Sat 8am–4.30pm, Sun 8am–5.30pm; *f*4). This is basically a Turkish/Middle Eastern bazaar, rather incongruously situated on the outskirts of town in a number of large warehouses on an industrial estate. People come from all over the surrounding area at weekends to buy cheap hi-fi and clothes, leatherwear, Turkish garb and *rai* cassettes from a huge number of stalls. There are places, too, selling spices, olives, Turkish delight and dried fruits, as well as some excellent – and authentic – places to eat, serving up shawarma and thin, crispy Turkish pizzas, spread with minced meat, at tables on which huge pots of chilli and yoghurt are arranged. The market is a fifteen-minute walk from the train station – turn right out of the station, first right under the motorway and first left onto Parallelweg; follow this for 500m or so and turn right onto Buitenlanden. Alternatively jump on a bus bearing the legend "Zwartemarkt", which trundles regularly between the station and the market.

North of Amsterdam

The polders immediately north of Amsterdam and the small towns and villages that line the IJsselmeer are almost enforcedly quaint. The area is a favourite for day-trippers from Amsterdam, who arrive here by way of numerous bus excursions from the capital, and parts at least can be packed to the gills during the summer. The meadows and canals of Waterland, immediately north of Amsterdam have a certain charm, especially if you're touring by bicycle, but don't expect anything too pristine if you're heading up to the tourist towns that line the banks of the IJsselmeer.

Zaandam, Zaanse Schans and Purmerend

Most of the trains heading north from Amsterdam pass through the build-up of settlements that spreads north from the banks of the IJ and is collectively known as **ZAANSTAD**. Looking out of the train window, there seems no real reason to get off, and you won't be missing all that much if you don't. But some people take an hour or so to visit the central core of Zaanstad, known as **ZAANDAM**, a small, largely modern town that was a popular tourist hangout in the nineteenth century, when it was known as "La Chine d'Hollande" for the faintly Oriental appearance of its windmills, canals, masts and row upon row of brightly painted houses. Claude Monet spent some time here in the 1870s, and, despite being suspected of spying and under constant police surveillance, immortalized the place in a series of paintings.

Follow the main street of Gedempte Gracht from the train station for five minutes, passing the **VVV** at no. 76 (☎075/616 2221; Mon–Fri 9am–5.30pm, Sat 9am–4pm), turn right down Damstraat, right again and left down Krimp, and you can see something of this former look, the **harbour** spiked with masts beyond a grouping of wooden houses. Zaandam's main claim to fame is at Krimp 23, the **Czaar Petershuisje** (Tues–Fri 10am–1pm and 2–5pm, Sat & Sun 1–5pm; ƒ2.50), a house in which the Russian Tsar Peter the Great stayed when he came to study shipbuilding here. In those days Zaandam was an important centre for shipbuilding, and the tsar made four visits to the town, the first in 1697 when he arrived incognito and stayed in the simple home of one Gerrit Kist, who had formerly served with him. A tottering wooden structure enclosed within a brick shelter, the house is little more than two rooms, decorated with a handful of portraits of the benign-looking emperor and the graffiti of tourists that goes back to the mid-nineteenth century. Among the few things to see is the cupboard bed in which Peter is supposed to have slept, together with the calling cards and pennants of various visiting Russian delegations; around the outside of the house is a display on the shipbuilding industry in Zaandam. As Napoleon is supposed to have remarked on visiting the house, "Nothing is too small for great men".

Most visitors to Zaanstad are, however, here to see the re-created Dutch village of **ZAANSE SCHANS** (you can walk around at any time, but the mills and exhibitions are open March–Oct Tues–Sun 10am–5pm, Nov–Feb Sat & Sun 10am–5pm; admission ƒ1.50–3.50 apiece). The village is made up of houses, windmills and workshops assembled from all over the country, and is an energetic, but ultimately rather fake attempt to reproduce a Dutch village as it would have looked at the end of the seventeenth century. It's a pretty enough place, but gets crammed in summer, and is frankly not worth the bother for its clogmaking displays and pseudo artisans' premises. However, it does represent the closest chance to Amsterdam to see **windmills**, some of them working mills grinding mustard and producing oil. Among other specific attractions are a clock museum and period rooms, and you can also take boat trips on the Zaan River nearby (March–Oct every hour Tues–Sun 10am–5pm; ƒ8). To get to Zaanse Schans from Zaandam, take bus #88; to get there from Amsterdam, either take bus #92 or #94 (journey time 1hr), or take a train to Koog Zaandijk station, then walk about eight minutes – ask at Amsterdam Centraal Station for the all-in *Rail Idee* ticket, which includes the train, a boat cruise, entrance to the museums and refreshments at Zaanse Schans.

Further up the tracks from Zaandam, **PURMEREND** has a once-weekly summer cheese market on Thursday at 11am – a slightly less crowded affair than its counterpart at Alkmaar. That aside, though, there's not much reason to stop in what is essentially a rather dull suburb of Amsterdam these days.

Waterland

Directly north of Amsterdam, just through the city's northern suburbs, **Waterland** is an endless expanse of green peat meadows peppered with pretty villages. Despite its proximity to the city, very few tourists come to visit, making it an ideal – and straightforward – escape from the capital, especially if you opt to see all, or part, by bike.

A thousand years ago this land was a vast, high fen area with numerous little streams flowing through it and it's only this century that it actually became habitable, due to a combination of drought and the digging of drainage canals by the first settlers – a process which in fact lowered the water level and made it extremely flood prone (although the last major one was way back in 1916). Regular floods have created lakes such as the Kinselmeer, though others were drained, leaving enormous green craters in the flat landscape. The Waterland villagers coped matter-of-factly with their flood-prone habitat, and around 1300, when the water level became too high to farm crops, they switched to cattle-breeding and developed a lucrative sideline in commerce and shipping. Between the fourteenth and seventeenth centuries this area was – although it seems inconceivable now – one of the most prosperous parts of Holland, and rich traders built large wooden mansions painted as brightly as possible to show off their wealth. As Amsterdam's power increased, however, the area fell into poverty, only really reviving in the 1950s when wealthy Amsterdammers began to move into the area.

Landsmeer – and nature reserves

Though **LANDSMEER** is Waterland's largest village, it's a dull, mostly modern place, and there's little point in visiting unless it's to see its museum, or to visit the Ilperveld nature reserve or Het Twiske, a recreational area just to the north. The **Waterland Museum**, or, as it is officially known, the *Stichting Museum Grietje Trump*, at Zuideinde 69 (Sun only 2–5pm; ☎020/631 3455; *f*3.50), is housed in an original, garishly painted Waterland farmhouse, and filled with a century's worth of everyday paraphernalia. The aged proprietor (with the help of her English-speaking son) will tell you about her own childhood in the area.

A couple of kilometres north of Landsmeer, the **Het Twiske** nature reserve, two parts land, one part water, makes a fine place to go **canoeing**. You can rent bikes, canoes, boats and watersports equipment from *Jachthaven De Roemer* (☎075/684 4890), five minutes' walk south of Het Twiske, at Noorderlaaik 2 in the village of Oostzaan – canoes cost around *f*50–60 daily. For further information on the area, call in to the **Visitors' Centre** next door to the canoe-rental place at Noorderlaaik 1 (Easter–May & Sept–Oct Mon–Fri 8am–5pm, Sat & Sun 10am–6pm; June–Aug Mon–Fri 10am–9pm, Sat & Sun 10am–7pm; ☎075/684 4338).

Just to the east of Het Twiske, the nature reserve of **Ilperveld** is a unique landscape of meadows, marshes and water inhabited by large colonies of birds. It's accessible only by water from Landsmeer, but there are occasional organized excursions (call ☎0251/659 750 for details).

Broek-in-Waterland and Zuiderwoude

BROEK-IN-WATERLAND – at least the part northeast of the highway which bisects the village – is a likeable and surprisingly lively place, full of seventeenth- and eighteenth-century wooden mansions, painted in the so-called *Broeker* grey. It's a nice place to while away an hour or so, though there's not a lot to see or do. The village centres around a lake, **Het Havenrak**, from which a canal flows into town. On the lake by the canal is a seventeenth-century **church** (May–Sept Mon–Sat 10am–5pm; free) with a beautiful stained-glass window in its north aisle, showing the church being destroyed by the Spanish in 1573 and its rebuilding the following century. Otherwise, if you want targets for your wanderings, you could try the oldest house in Broek close by, supposedly painted the same bright pink it was in the fifteenth century; or head for the more conventionally touristy cheese farm, **De Domme Dirk**, at Roomeinde 17 (Mon–Sat 9am–12.30pm & 1.30–5pm; ☎020/403 1454). If you're after a bit of Dutch kitsch, there's also a **clog work-shop** at Havenrak 21 (daily 8am–6pm; ☎020/403 1432) or, if you're really desperate, it's possible to tour the whole area by horse-and-trap (May–Sept only; from ƒ45 per person per hour; information on ☎020/403 3107).

Three kilometres east of Broek is **ZUIDERWOUDE**, a tiny place consisting of little more than a single street and one café. It's more rustic than Broek, made up of farm buildings, rather than mansions, in which the house, stable and haystock stand in a single row – the last tarred black, the others painted dark green.

Monnickendam

A few kilometres north of Broek, just outside the boundaries of Waterland prop- er, **MONNICKENDAM** lies just to the right of the main road, nestling up to the edge of the IJsselmeer. Like the towns of West Friesland (Hoorn and Enkhuizen; see p.141–5), it was once one of the most important ports of the old Zuider Zee, but since the construction of the Afsluitdijk it has found a new niche as a water- sports centre for enthusiasts from the Dutch capital. Unless you're travelling by car and have time on your hands, there's no particular reason to join the yachties and windsurfers, although something of the fishy and nautical atmosphere of the place does survive (Monnickendam is known for its smoked fish, especially eels), and the centre is charmingly well preserved – and gets less tourist traffic than nearby Marken and Volendam (see p.138 for more on these).

Really the pleasantest way to spend time here is by idling away hours down by the harbour. On the way, the **Speeltoren**, the tower of the town hall, with its sixteenth-century carillon, is probably the most prominent thing to see, and hous- es a small **museum** of local bits and bobs (Noordeinde 4; June–Aug Mon & Sun 1–4pm, Tues–Sat 10am–4pm; free), while the undeniably picturesque nearby **Waag** is now home to a **restaurant** at which you can sample some smoked spe- cialities. The picturesque late-Gothic **Grote Kerk** (June–Aug Mon & Sun 2–4pm, Tues–Sat 10am–4pm; free) is worth poking your nose in for its beautifully deco- rative sixteenth-century wooden choir screen, as well as its tower.

Getting to – and around – Waterland

To reach **Landsmeer** by **bus** (journey time 25min), take #91 which runs every half-hour from Amsterdam Centraal Station, though the stop isn't easy to find –turn left out of the station and cross the bridge; for **Broek** (journey time 20min), buses #110, #111, #114 and #116 run every fifteen minutes from Amsterdam CS (opposite St Nicolaaskerk). Bus #111 is the best option to drop you in the centre of **Monnickendam**; the others bypass the village.

The VVV at Gedempte Gracht 76 in Zaandam (Mon–Fri 9am–5.30pm, Sat 9am–4pm; ☎075/616 2221) has **information** on Waterland, as does the VVV office in the Grote Kerk tower at Zarken 2 in Monnickendam (July & Aug Mon–Sat 10am–6pm, Sun 2–5pm; Sept–May Mon–Fri 9.30am–12.30pm & 1.30–5pm, Sat 9.30am–5pm; ☎0299/651 998) and the *Rekreatieschap Waterland* at De Erven 2 in Broek-in-Waterland (Mon–Fri 9am–5pm, but call to make sure someone is there; ☎020/403 3606).

Though there are buses around the region, to get the best out of the area you either need to **walk**, or switch to a bike or canoe. **Bikes** can be rented in Amsterdam; also at *Wim*, Laan 44 in Broek (closed Tues & Sun; ☎020/403 1462); at *Jachthaven De Roemer*, Noorderlaaik 2 in Oostzaan (closed Sun; ☎075/684 4890); and at two places in Monnickendam – *Ber Koning* (Noordeinde 12; closed Sun; ☎0299/651 267) and *Van Driel* (Corn. Dirksznlaan 109; closed Sun; ☎0299/653 264). If you're cycling, it's worth buying a good cycling map from any of the VVVs, or, more cheaply, getting hold of their Waterland **cycling route** leaflet, available in English and including a map and text on the route, which runs for 38km, and can at a pinch be done in a day. It starts in Amsterdam, skirts the drained Broekermeer, passes through Broek, continues to Zuiderwoude and then runs up to the coast of the IJsselmeer. From here it follows the coast south past the Kinselmeer and back to Amsterdam. There's also a possible diversion through the less interesting west of Waterland – worth considering if you want to visit the nature reserve of Ilperveld. **Canoe** rental is also available from several places: *Waterland*, Van Disweg 4 in Broek (☎020/403 3209); *De Paashaas*, Molengouw 40 in Broek (☎020/403 1492); *Rap Kanoverhuur* at Bloemendaal 2a in Monnickendam (☎0299/652 773); and *Jachthaven De Roemer*, Noorderlaaik 2 in Oostzaan (☎075/684 4890). Reckon on paying around *f*50 daily for a single-seater canoe, *f*60 daily for a two-seater.

Waterland accommodation and eating

Waterland is easily visited from Amsterdam, but if you want to stay in the area, **Broek** is your best option. There's one **hotel**, the *Garni De Bedstede*, located in two houses at Laan 22–28 and 36–38 (☎ & fax 020/403 1509; ②); the rooms in 36–38 are slightly more comfortable – and slightly more expensive. In between these two houses, there's also a pension, simply called *No.32* (☎020/403 1784, no fax; ②), with one large dormitory that sleeps up to ten people. If you don't mind staying in the new part of town, there's also *Pension Familie Mentink,* Keerngouw 4–6 (☎020/403 1678, no fax; ③). About 7km from Broek there's the relatively luxurious *Camping Uitdam*, at Zeedijk 2 on the Markenmeer shore 1km north of the village of Uitdam (☎020/403 1433; April–Oct). In **Monnickendam**, there's only one hotel, the nicely situated *Lakeland*, Jachthaven 1 (☎0299/653 751, fax 654 587; ③). There are no hotels, pensions or private rooms in **Landsmeer**, but there is a **campsite**, *Camping Het Rietveen*, at Noordeinde 122a (☎020/482 1468; April–Oct).

Broek-in-Waterland is not a great place to **eat or drink**, and your best bet is probably the pancake house, *De Witte Swaen*, Dorpstraat 11–13, near Het Havenrak, which serves pancakes from *f*9 and pizza-like contructions from *f*15, as well as more substantial dishes. Other than that, there's one overpriced restaurant and several brown cafés, but none are remarkable. **Monnickendam**, though, has a much better choice, including '*t Marker Veerhuis*, an inexpensive brasserie at Brugstraat 6, and, among several good options on Noordeinde, the distinctly upmarket *Posthoorn*, at no. 41, which serves French-Dutch cuisine. There are several restaurants in **Landsmeer**, including a cheap pizzeria, *Casa di Angelo* on Zuideinde, with pizza from *f*13.

Marken, Volendam and Edam

The majority of visitors heading out of Amsterdam make for the settlements on the banks of the IJsselmeer – which is as good a reason as any to avoid these places during the high season of June to September, when they can be positively swamped with tourists. If you visit at other times, you're likely to get a much more genuine impression of these long-lived communities which were founded on fishing but have now been forced into clog-selling to survive (see box on p.146 for the background to their demise).

Once an island in the Zuider Zee, **MARKEN** was, until its road connection to the mainland in 1957, largely a closed community, supported by a small fishing industry. At one time its biggest problem was the genetic defects caused by close and constant intermarrying; now it's how to contain the tourists, whose numbers increase yearly. Marken's distinctiveness has in many ways been its downfall; its character – or what remains of it – has been artificially preserved: the harbour is still brightly painted in the local colours, and local costumes and clogs are worn to impress. Recently a row of eel-smoking houses have been converted into the **Marken Museum**, Kerkbuurt 44 (April–Oct Mon–Sat 10am–5pm, Sun 1–4pm), devoted to the history of the former island and its fishing industry. Although visitors now supply the income lost when the Zuider Zee was closed off, it turns out to have been a dubious remedy.

Marken is accessible direct from Amsterdam by way of **bus** #111 from opposite the St Nicolaaskerk (near Centraal Station); it runs every half-hour and drops you off in the middle of the tiny village of Marken (30min), with the harbour and the sea in view. There's no VVV in Marken, but the Monnickendam office (see p.136) can oblige with **information** and maps for Marken.

Volendam

A larger village than Marken, **VOLENDAM** is, like its neighbour, worth visiting to salvage what scraps of local culture remain and to mull over the uniquely flat and silvery IJsselmeer. At one time, Volendam was something of an artists' retreat – Picasso and Renoir both stayed for a while at the *Hotel Spaander* on the harbourfront (still a wonderfully atmospheric place – see below), and the bar of the hotel is crammed with paintings and drawings. Although the harbour today mostly shelters ferries rather than fishing boats, it's still relatively easy to shut out the tawdry knick-knack stores running the length of the main street and find a quiet spot. One street back from the harbour you'll find the narrow Meerzijde; follow this to the nineteenth-century church at its western end and lose yourself in the maze of tiny alleys round the churchyard; one curiosity to look for is a plaque at the corner of Berend Demmerstraat and Josefstraat marking how high the floodwaters of 1916 rose in the village.

The Volendam Museum, at Zeestraat 37 (daily 10am–5pm; *f*3.50), however, is an eminently missable addition to the village, the highlight being a local character's collection of eleven million cigar-bands.

From Marken, a summertime **ferry** takes twenty minutes to reach Volendam (March–Oct daily 10am–5pm, every 30min; *f*4.50). If you don't fancy this, or if you're visiting in the off-season, you'll have to get **bus** #111 back to the Bernardbrug on the outskirts of Monnickendam in order to pick up half-hourly bus #110 that plys between Amsterdam (again, from opposite St Nicolaaskerk) and Volendam. The bus drops you on Zeestraat, within 50m of the **VVV** at Zeestraat 37 (April–Sept daily 10am–5pm; Oct–March Mon–Sat 10am–3pm; ☎0299/363 747), where you can buy a leaflet describing a walk through the old section of the village, away from the touristed strip (*f*1.50). To explore further afield, you can rent a **bike** from *Koning*, at Edammerweg 26 (☎0299/363 597) or *Bien*, at Plutostraat 40b (☎0299/364 029); and the VVV has plenty of cycling maps for sale.

Volendam's few **hotels** are all along the harbourfront within five minutes of each other (and everything else). *Hotel Spaander*, at Haven 15 (☎0299/363 595, fax 369 615; ③) is the best and most atmospheric by far, and is worth stopping off to have a drink in even if you don't stay. Needless to say, **fish** is the dish-of-the-day here, and you can easily and inexpensively snack your way along the waterfront fish stands. Otherwise, it's probably better to spurn the other places to stay here in favour of more pleasing accommodation just down the road in Edam.

Edam

Further on down the #110 bus route, just 3km from Volendam, you might expect **EDAM** to be a nightmare, especially considering its reputation for the rubbery red balls of cheese that the Dutch produce for export. In fact, it's a relief after the mob-rule of Volendam, a pretty little place with something of the charm that its neighbours have long since lost – although during the summer melee, you'd be well advised to suspend any illusions of authenticity. The main draw is the absolutely enormous **Grote Kerk** (April–Oct daily 2–4.30pm) on the edge of fields to the north of the village, with some spectacular stained-glass windows and a vaulted ceiling constructed in wood in an attempt to limit subsidence due to the massive weight of the building. Following lightning strikes on the church tower in 1602 and 1699, both of which led to extensive town fires, the spire was purposely shortened and looks almost comically stubby; the elegant tower you see from every point in the village belongs instead to the even older **Speeltoren** (1561), 100m to the south. Edam's nominal centre is the tiny square of Damplein, dominated by a hump-backed bridge over the Keizersgracht canal and the village's grandest building, the eighteenth-century **Stadhuis**, with a superabundance of luxuriant stucco work inside. The step-gabled brick house just next to Grote Kerkstraat on Damplein is Edam's oldest, dating from 1530, and houses the **Captain's House Museum** (April–Oct Mon–Sat 10am–4pm, Sun 2–4pm; *f*10), famous for its floating cellar, allegedly built by a retired sea-captain who could not bear the thought of sleeping on dry land. Left on Spui and right on Prinsenstraat will bring you to Kaasmarkt and the sixteenth-century **Kaaswaag**, or cheese weighing-house (April–Oct daily 10am–5pm; free); it's here that, between 1778 and 1922, Edam sold its cheese, although today there only remains a heavily touristed and utterly fake **cheese market** every Wednesday morning in July and August (10am–12.30pm). Edam's pleasures lie elsewhere, and a short wander through its cobbled lanes and rustic canals will deliver you from the crush. Aim for the impossibly skinny Kwakelbrug, due south of the Speeltoren tower, and follow Schepenmakersdijk west, on the other side of the water from quaint summer-house follies constructed in the gardens of former mayors' residences on the banks of the canal.

Practicalities

Bus #110 drops you off at the nominal **bus station** in Edam, a collection of battered shelters to the southwest of the village. Cross the distinctive swing-bridge, turn right and follow Lingerzijde as it kinks left and right around the base of the Speeltoren tower, and you'll arrive in Damplein, home of the VVV (April–Sept Mon–Sat 10am–5pm, Oct–March Mon–Sat 10am–12.30pm; ☎0299/371 727), who can supply you with all sorts of information about Edam and the surrounding areas, including a booklet describing a walking tour of Edam (*f*3.50). They can also sell you, for *f*1 each, lists of **hotels** and private homes offering **rooms**; the latter start from around *f*30 per person. There are only two hotels in Edam itself – the over-luxurious *Fortuna* at Spuistraat 7 (☎0299/371 671, fax 371 469; ③) and the much more appealing *Damhotel*, opposite the VVV at Keizersgracht 1 (☎0299/371 766, fax 374 031; ③). There is a **campsite** near Edam at Zeevangszeedijk 7 (☎0299/371 994); to walk there, follow the long canal east from Damplein for about twenty minutes.

Eating and drinking opportunities in Edam are surprisingly limited for such a popular village: the hotels listed above are probably your best bet for either a **beer** or a full **meal**, although the *Hof van Holland* and the *Café Suisse*, both next to the bus station, are possible alternatives. You can rent **bikes** from *Ronald Schot*, very close to the Speeltoren at Kleine Kerkstraat 9 (☎0299/372 155) or *Tweewielers* at Schepenmakersdijk 6 (☎0299/371 922). *Stichting VN4*, at Nieuwe Haven 23 (☎0299/372 166) can organize **boat tours** of Edam on request.

West Friesland

A little way north of Edam, the IJsselmeer shore curves east to form the jutting claw of land that makes up an area known as **West Friesland**, whose two main towns – Hoorn and Enkhuizen – can be visited either as day-trips from Amsterdam (both are connected by twice-hourly trains) or, more interestingly, as overnight stops on the way across the Afsluitdijk into Friesland proper. West Friesland is these days not actually a part of Friesland at all, but was one of the three Frisian districts recognized by Charlemagne and at one time boasted its own regional council, whose authority extended as far away as Alkmaar and Purmerend. The area clings jealously to its supposedly separate identity from the rest of North Holland, though it's hardly very different – the same flat polder landscapes, punctured by farmhouses and the odd windmill, that you see throughout the rest of the province. However, as long as the Markerwaard isn't reclaimed, Hoorn and Enkhuizen are the best and most appealing examples of old Zuider Zee ports you'll find.

Hoorn

HOORN, the ancient capital of West Friesland, "rises from the sea like an enchanted city of the east, with its spires and its harbour tower beautifully unreal". So
wrote the English travel writer E V Lucas in 1905, and the town is still very much
a place you should either arrive at or leave by sea – though you probably won't
get the chance to do either. During the seventeenth century this was one of the
richest of the Dutch ports, referred to by the poet Vondel as the trumpet and capital of the Zuider Zee, handling the important Baltic trade and that of the Dutch
colonies. The Dutch East India Company had one of its centres of operation here,
Tasman went off to "discover" Tasmania and New Zealand, and in 1616 William
Schouten sailed out to navigate a passage around South America, calling its tip
"Cape Hoorn" after his native town. The harbour silted up in the eighteenth century, however, stemming trade and gradually turning Hoorn into one of the so-
called "dead cities" of the Zuider Zee – a process completed with the creation of
the IJsselmeer (see box on p.146).

The town

Not surprisingly, Hoorn's former glories are hard to detect in what is today a
quiet provincial backwater: the harbour is a yacht marina, and the elegant
streets and houses, almost entirely surrounded by water, give only the faintest
of echoes of the town's balmy seventeenth-century prosperity. The centre is
Rode Steen, literally "red stone", an unassuming square that used to hold the
town scaffold and now focuses on the swashbuckling statue of **J P Coen**,
founder of the Dutch East Indies Empire and one of the bright lights of the seventeenth century. Coen was a headstrong and determined leader of the Dutch
imperial effort, under whom the Far East colonies were consolidated and rivals,
like the English, were kept at bay. His settling of places like Moluccas and
Batavia was something of a personal crusade, and his austere, almost puritani-
cal way of life was in sharp contrast to the wild and unprincipled behaviour of
many of his compatriots on the islands.

On one side of Rode Steen stands the early-seventeenth-century **Waag**,
designed by Hendrik de Keyser and now a smart restaurant. On the other side,
and dominating the square, the **Westfries Museum** (Mon–Fri 11am–5pm, Sat &
Sun 2–5pm; *f*5) is Hoorn's most prominent sight, housed in the elaborately
gabled former West Friesland government building, and decorated with the coats
of arms of the house of Orange-Nassau, West Friesland and the seven major
towns of the region. Inside, the museum convincingly re-creates the interiors of
the time when Hoorn's power was at its height. Along with any number of
unascribed portraits, furniture and ceramics, the walls of the council chamber
(room 7) are covered with militia portraits by Jan Rotius, who portrays himself in
the painting by the window – he's the figure by the flag on the left – and employs
some crafty effects in the other canvases. Walk past the figure in the far right of
the central painting and watch his foot change position from left to right as you
pass. On the second floor, in room 16, there's a painting of 1632 by Jan van Goyen
(*Landscape with a Peasant Cart*) and a wooden fireplace carved with tiny scenes
showing a whaling expedition – Hoorn was once a whaling port of some importance. Other items of interest include a view of Hoorn painted in 1622, a room containing portraits of various East India Company dignitaries, including one of the

severe Coen, while on the top floor are mock-ups of trades and shops of the time, even a prison cell.

Close to the harbour at Bierkade 4, is the **Museum of the Twentieth Century** (Tues–Sun 10am–5pm; *f*4.50), housed in two former cheese warehouses. Its permanent displays of daily life during this century, though not exactly gripping, are supplemented by changing exhibits with titles such as "Travel Posters – A Nostalgic Journey" and "100 Years of Blokker" (*Blokker* is the Dutch equivalent of *Woolworth's*). A scale model of Hoorn in 1650, and an audio-visual display describing the role of the town in the Dutch Golden Age, are more diverting, but cost an extra *f*2.50 (a combined ticket for museum and model is *f*6 – but both are free with a museum card (see p.38).

There's not all that much of special interest in the rest of Hoorn, but it's a good place to drift around aimlessly, and the old **harbour** and the canals which lead down to it (follow G Havensteeg from Rode Steen) are very pretty, the waterfront lined with gabled houses looking out to the stolid **Hoofdtoren**, a defensive gateway from 1532. On the other side of Rode Steen, on Kerkstraat, the **Boterhal**, formerly the St Jans Gasthuis, exhibits works by Hoorn artists (Sun & Tues–Sat 2–5pm; free; closed one week in every six; ☎0229/217 249). It's a delightful building with a so-called trap-gable, tapering to a single window and built at an angle to the main body of the house. Opposite, the Grote Kerk is a nineteenth-century church since converted into apartments.

Practicalities

If you're coming from **Amsterdam**, the easiest way to reach Hoorn is by the half-hourly trains (journey time 40min); from **Edam**, take bus #114 from the bus station, also half-hourly (and taking 30min). Both leave you at the train station in Hoorn, on the northern edge of town about ten minutes' walk from the centre; the **VVV** isn't immediately obvious – follow Veemarkt, the road leading more or less away from you, and you'll find the office almost at the end on the left, at Veemarkt 4 (Mon 1–6pm, Tues, Wed & Fri 9.30am–6pm, Thurs 9.30am–6pm & 7–9pm, Sat 9.30am–5pm; ☎06/340 31055, 50c per min). There's a **youth hostel** about 2km out from the centre at Schellinkhouterdijk 1a (☎0229/214 256) – take bus #132, #137 or #147 from the train station and get off at the home for stray animals. Otherwise the cheapest **hotels** are the small, family run *De Posthoorn*, close to the VVV at Breed 27 (☎0229/214 057, fax 270 167; ②), which has a pleasant terrace in summer; *De Magneet*, close to the harbour at Kleine Oost 5 (☎0229/215 021, fax 237 044; ③), with attached café-restaurant, and the modern *Bastion* at Lepelaar 1 (☎0229/249 844, fax 249 540; ③), which has free parking.

Sweet Dreams, at Kerkstraat 1, is a good cheap place for **lunch**, and couldn't be more central, with omelettes and Mexican dishes – and it's open until midnight (closed Sun). *Het Witte Paard*, by the Grote Kerk at Lange Kerkstraat 27, serves Dutch food and vegetarian dishes daily until 11pm. *De Eethoorn*, at Kerkplein 7, is an appealingly inexpensive *eetcafé*, open daily from 5pm amidst a number of reasonable **drinking** places. Other options include *Isola Bella*, Grote Oost 65 (closed Mon), five minutes from Rode Steen, which has pizza and pasta, and the upmarket *Weeg*, on Rode Steen, for French specialities (closed Tues); there's also a number of bars and restaurants grouped around the harbour.

Between May and October, Hoorn is the starting point of **steam train services** (information ☎0229/214 862) to Medemblik (see p.145), which can make a wonderful day out, especially if you're travelling with kids. Trains run daily (except Mon outside July & Aug) at 11.05am; in July and August the service is increased to up to 4 trains daily, all leaving between 11am and 2.20pm. The journey time is one hour, and tickets cost ƒ12.75 for adults, and ƒ9.50 for under 11s. From Medemblik, a ferry runs to Enkhuizen (March–June & Sept–Oct Tues–Sun 12.30pm, July–Aug also 4.30pm; 1hr 30min). Rather than buying separate tickets, though, you should buy a combination round-trip ticket in Hoorn, which gets you to Medemblik by steam train, Enkhuizen by ferry and back to Hoorn by a normal train; these cost ƒ25 for adults, ƒ18 for under 11s. Outside the summer season, if you want to get from Hoorn to Medemblik, catch half-hourly express bus #139, which takes about thirty minutes.

Enkhuizen

Another "dead city", though much smaller than Hoorn, **ENKHUIZEN**, twenty minutes further east by train, was also an important port during the seventeenth century, with the largest herring fleet in the country. However, it too declined at the end of the seventeenth century, and the town now offers much the same sort of attractions as Hoorn, retaining its broad, mast-spattered harbours and peaceful canals. It also has a genuinely major attraction in the Zuider Zee Museum, which brings busloads of tourists here to experience what is a very deliberate attempt to capture the lifestyle that existed here when the town was still a flourishing port – and which was destroyed once and for all with the building of the Afsluitdijk. Enkhuizen is also a good place to visit for its summer ferry connections to Stavoren and Urk across the IJsselmeer.

The town . . . and the Zuider Zee Museum

A few hundred metres from the two main harbours, **Westerstraat** is Enkhuizen's main spine, a busy pedestrianized street that is home to most of the town's shops and restaurants. At one end, the **Westerkerk** is an early fifteenth-century Gothic church with an odd wooden belfry, added in 1519. A right turn from here leads into a residential part of town, very pretty, with its canals crossed by white-painted footbridges. The other end of Westerstraat is marginally more monumental, zeroing in on the mid-sixteenth-century **Waag** on Kaasmarkt, which houses the **Stedelijk Waagmuseum**, a small local museum with the usual local artefacts (currently closed for renovation; call the VVV to check). Nearby is the solid, classically styled mid-seventeenth-century **Stadhuis** – behind which the dangerously leaning **Gevangenis** was once the town prison. This is closed to the public, but a peek through its barred windows gives some idea of the bleakness of conditions for the average prisoner three hundred years ago, most of the main furnishings still being in place.

Close by here, along the waterfront at Wierdijk 18, the indoor section of the Zuider Zee Museum, the **Binnenmuseum** (closed until May 1998; call ☎0228/310 122 for details, or contact the VVV; admission with Buitenmuseum, see below), has a collection of fishing vessels and equipment, and Zuider Zee arts and crafts, recently spruced up and displayed in bright, new surroundings. Exhibits include regional costumes and painted furniture from Hindeloopen (see *The North and the Frisian Islands*, p.219), an ice-cutting boat from Urk, once charged with the responsibility of keeping the shipping lanes open between the island and the port of Kampen, displays of sail- and rope-making implements – and much else besides.

Most people, however, give the Binnenmuseum a miss and instead make straight for the **Buitenmuseum** on the far side of the harbour (April–Oct daily 10am–5pm; ƒ15, under 12s ƒ10); the admission fee, which you pay either at the VVV office or at the free museum car park at the end of the Lelystad road, covers the compulsory boat ride to the museum and entry to both the Binnenmuseum and the Buitenmuseum). Here, buildings have actually been transported from 39 different locations to form a period portrayal of the vanished way of life around the Zuider Zee in a re-creation of various towns and villages. Once there, you can choose to tour the museum on one of the free hourly guided tours, or – rather nicer – simply wander around taking it all in at your own pace.

Close by the boat wharf there's a series of lime kilns, conspicuous by their tall chimneys, from which a path takes you through the best of the museum's many intriguing corners, beginning with a row of cottages from Monnickendam, near to which there's an information centre. A number of streets lined with cottages lead off from here, in a mock-up of a typical Zuider Zee fishing village, with examples of buildings from Urk among other places, their modest, precisely furnished interiors open to visitors and sometimes peopled by characters in traditional dress, hamming it up for the tourists. Further on, a number of buildings sit along and around a central canal. There's a post office from Den Oever; a grocery from Harderwijk; an old laundry, thick with the smell of washing; a chemist and a bakery from Hoorn, the latter selling pastries and chocolate; while a cottage from Hindeloopen doubles up as a restaurant. It all sounds rather kitsch, and in a way it is: there are regular demonstrations of the old ways and crafts; goats and sheep roam the stretches of meadow, and the exhibition is mounted in such an earnest way as to almost beg criticism. But the attention to detail is very impressive, and the whole thing is never overdone, with the result that many parts of the museum are genuinely picturesque. Even if you see nothing else in Enkhuizen (and many people don't), you really shouldn't miss it.

If you've time to kill, there are a couple of other low-key attractions in the town. Firstly, the **Flessenscheepjesmuseum**, a small museum devoted to ships-in-bottles (Zuiderspui 1; July & Aug daily 10am–9pm, June & Sept daily 10am–8pm, Oct–May daily 10am–6pm; ƒ5, under 12s ƒ3.50), set in a wonderful tiny old house near the Drommedaris tower. The exhibits are surprisingly interesting, ranging from a tiny scent bottle to a 30-litre wine flagon – and are well-presented and labelled. A little way out of town to the north, right next to the Enkhuizer Zand campsite is **Sprookjeswonderland** (Kooizandweg 9; April–Oct daily 10am–5.30pm; ƒ8), a tacky little model village full of gnomes and fairy-tale characters that kids'll probably love; there's also a children's farm and a mini-train.

Practicalities

Trains to Enkhuizen – the end of the line – stop right on the corner of the Buiten Haven harbour; on one side of the station are the ferry wharves, on the other is the bus station. There's a **VVV** office just outside the train station, at Tussen Twee Havens 1 (July & Aug Mon–Sat 9am–6pm & Sun 9am–5pm, April–June & Sept–Oct daily 9am–5pm, Nov–March Mon–Fri 9am–5pm & Sat 9am–2pm; ☎0228/313 164); in the summer (April–Oct) they open from 8.15am to sell tickets for the ferries (see below). From here, follow the edge of the small harbour round, turn left on Spoorstraat, and follow the street over the bridge (this is the larger Oude Haven) and on about 100m into the town to cross the main shopping street of Westerstraat.

If you're staying, the least expensive option is the wonderful circular dormitory in the Drommedaris Tower (open year-round, from 2pm; ☎0228/312 076; ①), a student house on Paktuinen in the outer harbour, and possibly the cheapest place in Holland – currently *f*12.50 for a bed. If you prefer to sleep in privacy, the cheapest **hotel** is the pleasingly down-to-earth *Het Wapen* at Breedstraat 59 (☎0228/313 434, fax 320 020; ②), conveniently close to the Zuider Zee museums and the harbours. Another inexpensive option, in the middle of town and boasting a pleasant internal courtyard, is *Villa Oud Enkhuizen*, at Westerstraat 217 (☎0228/314 266, fax 318 171; ③). There are two summer-only **campsites** handily located on the northern side of town: closest is the *Enkhuizer Zand* on the far side of the Zuider Zee Museum at Kooizandweg 4 (☎0228/317 289; April–Sept); to get to the *De Vest* (☎0228/321 221; April–Sept), follow Vijzelstraat north off Westerstraat, continue down Noorderweg, and turn left by the old town ramparts.

Restaurants in Enkhuizen tend to be expensive, although there are a few notable exceptions. *Desimir*, at Spoorstraat 12 serves Balkan-style food relatively cheaply; *Markerwaard*, at Dijk 62, is a good Dutch restaurant, and you can find reasonable pizza and pasta at *Marco Polo*, Melkmarkt 4. The *Het Wapen* hotel (see above) has a nice enough restaurant, though *Die Port van Cleve*, Dijk 74, is considerably more upmarket. The *Café Drommedaris*, in the Drommedaris tower, serves well-priced food for lunch and dinner.

During summer you can travel from Enkhuizen **by ferry** to the peaceful village of Medemblik (see below), and to Stavoren and Urk (see p.221 and p.252, respectively), on the other side of the IJsselmeer. Ferries leave from behind the train station, and you can buy tickets from the VVV (see above). Ferries to Stavoren run roughly three times daily and to Medemblik twice daily; Urk boats run only in July and August (Mon–Sat 3 daily). Prices range from *f*16–20 return, with an extra *f*9.50 return for a bike.

Medemblik, the Wieringermeer Polder . . . and into Friesland

Just a few kilometres along the coast from Enkhuizen, **MEDEMBLIK** is one of the most ancient towns in Holland, a seat of pagan kings until the seventh century, though there's not a great deal to entice you there nowadays, unless you're madly into yachts. The only sign visible today of Medemblik's ancient beginnings is the **Kasteel Radboud**, named after, but not really connected with, the most famous of the town's kings, a much-restored thirteenth-century fortress that sits by the harbour at Oudevaartsgat 8 (May–Sept Mon–Sat 10am–5pm & Sun 2–5pm, Oct–April Sun only 2–5pm; *f*3). Not much of what's left these days is original, indeed most of it is the result of a nineteenth-century restoration project under the supervision of P J H Cuijpers, but you are allowed in to take a look at a handful of exhibits relating to the fort's former inhabitants and a small exhibition covering the history of the building. The old train station, where the summer steam train draws in (see pp.142–3), houses the **VVV** (July & Aug daily 10am–5pm, April–June & Sept–Oct Mon–Sat 10am–5pm, Nov–March Mon–Sat 10am–noon & 2–4pm; ☎0227/542 852), while at Oosterdijk 4 there's the **Stoommachine Museum** (April–June and Sept–Nov Wed–Sat 10am–5pm & Sun noon–5pm, July–Sept Mon–Sat 10am–5pm & Sun noon–5pm; *f*5), an assembly of thirty ancient steam engines in a former pumping station. Otherwise most people come

THE CLOSING OF THE ZUIDER ZEE

The province of North Holland, surrounded on three sides by water, is intimately linked with the sea; the history of the towns and villages along the coast north of Amsterdam is one of early fishing communities that briefly found wealth and glory through maritime trade in the Golden Age and then declined, along with Holland's naval power. However, the single most important event this century to shape the economic and physical environment for the people of North Holland – and which finally put paid to the longstanding fisheries of the region – was the construction of the Afsluitdijk in 1932, and the consequent closing of the Zuider Zee.

Before this date, what is now the freshwater IJsselmeer was the saltwater Zuider Zee (Southern Sea), open to the Noord Zee (North Sea) beyond. The Zuider Zee harbours at Hoorn and Enkhuizen were central to the shipment of goods to and from the East and West Indies during the Dutch Golden Age, while small villages such as Volendam and Marken on the western coast of the Zuider Zee, and Stavoren and Urk on the eastern shore, depended upon fishing the waters of the Zuider Zee for their survival. However, the entire area had always been susceptible to flooding, and over-ambitious plans to seal off the Zuider Zee (thus stopping the floods) and let the land dry out (thus expanding the area of cultivable land) had been put forward as early as 1667 – at the height of the Golden Age, when anything must have seemed possible. It wasn't until 1891, though, that the technological advances of the Industrial Revolution made feasible Cornelis Lely's scheme to build a retaining dike. However, such complex and far-reaching plans had to be put to the vote, and still nothing had been done by the time devastating floods hit the entire region in 1916. Naturally, the floods gave extra impetus to Lely's plans. Work began in 1920 amidst some uncertainty and consternation among both fisherfolk and engineers as to the repercussions of shutting off the entire sea; the fisherfolk were concerned by the threat to their livelihood, while the engineers worried about a possible rise in sea-level around the Wadden Islands just to the north. A small 2.5-km test dike was built connecting the island of Wieringen to the mainland; after four trouble-free years, and despite intense lobbying from the fishing villages, work began in earnest on the Afsluitdijk itself.

On May 28, 1932, at 1.02pm, the last gap in the dike was filled, and the Zuider Zee ceased to exist. The feared rise in sea-level beyond the dike never happened. A roadway was built across the top of the Afsluitdijk, which today sees well over 30,000 journeys per week. The Northeast Polder, a huge area of reclaimed land in the east of the IJsselmeer, was drained and prepared for agriculture in the few years immediately following construction of the dike; the polders of Flevoland (whose main city was named Lelystad after the originator of the Afsluitdijk plans followed in the 1950s and 1960s.

However, the old coastal communities had lost their access to the open sea and although many tried to continue fishing, the death knell had sounded. Some villages adapted their methods to catch the freshwater species which were colonizing the Markermeer and IJsselmeer; others sent their fleets north to fish above the Afsluitdijk and transport the catch back to the village for sale at auction. These were desperate measures, though, and in 1970 a new law banned trawling in the IJsselmeer, effectively bringing the Zuider Zee's traditional way of life to an end. Today, villages such as Volendam and Urk are shadows of their former selves, forced to rely on tourist kitsch to survive; the old harbours at Hoorn and Enkhuizen are now filled with the masts of expensive pleasure yachts. For these communities, the security and wealth the Afsluitdijk has undoubtedly brought to North Holland and the whole country, rings rather hollow.

to Medemblik to sail: the harbour is busy throughout summer with the masts of visiting and resident yachtspeople.

North of Medemblik, the **Wieringermeer Polder** was the first of the Zuider Zee polders, created in the 1920s when the former island of Wieringen was connected to the mainland and the area behind it reclaimed. During the occupation, and only three weeks before their surrender, the Nazis flooded the area, boasting they could return Holland to the sea if they wished. After the war it was drained again, leaving a barren, treeless terrain that had to be totally replanted. Almost forty years later, it's virtually back to normal, a familiar polder landscape of flat, geometric fields, highlighted by farmhouses and church spires, that most people only pass through on their way to Friesland by way of the Afsluitdijk highway.

The sluices on this side of the **Afsluitdijk** are known as the **Stevinsluizen**, after Henry Stevin, the seventeenth-century engineer who first had the idea of reclaiming the Zuider Zee. He was, of course, constrained here by the lack of technology available, but his vision lived on, to be realized by Cornelis Lely in 1932. At the North Holland end, there's a statue of Lely by the modern Dutch sculptor Mari Andriessen, though the engineer died before the dike was completed. Further along, at the point where the barrier was finally closed, there's an observation point on which an inscription reads: "A nation that lives is building for its future".

Alkmaar and around

An hour from Amsterdam by train, **ALKMAAR** is typical of smalltown Holland, its pretty, partially canalized centre surrounded by water and offering a low-key, undemanding provincialism, which makes a pleasant change after the rigours of the big city. It's also a good base for exploring the nearby dunes and beaches, or even the towns of West Friesland.

Alkmaar is probably best known for its **cheese market**, an ancient affair which these days ranks as one of the most extravagant tourist spectacles in Holland. Cheese has been sold on the main square here since the 1300s, and although no serious buying goes on here now, it's an institution that continues to draw crowds – though nowadays they're primarily tourists. If you do want to see it (it's held every Friday morning, mid-April to mid-Sept), be sure to get there early, as by the official 10am opening time, the crowds are already thick. The ceremony starts with the buyers sniffing, crumbling and finally tasting each cheese, followed by heated bartering. Once a deal has been concluded, the cheeses – golden discs of Gouda mainly, laid out in rows and piles on the square – are borne away on ornamental carriers by four groups of porters for weighing. Payment, tradition has it, takes place in the cafés around the square.

The town

Even if you've only come for the cheese market, it's a good idea to see something of the rest of the town before you leave. On the main square, the **Waag** was originally a chapel dedicated to the Holy Spirit, but was converted, and given its magnificent east gable, shortly after the town's famous victory against the Spanish in 1573, when its citizens withstood a long siege by Frederick of Toledo – a victory which marked the beginning of the end for the Spaniards. Nowadays the Waag houses the VVV (see p.149) and the **Kaasmuseum**

(April–Oct Mon–Thurs & Sat 10am–4pm, Fri 9am–4pm; *f*3), which has displays on the history of cheese, cheese-making equipment and suchlike. Across the other side of the square, the **Biermuseum de Boom**, Houttil 1 (April–Oct Tues–Sat 10am–4pm, Sun 1–4pm; Nov–March Tues–Sun 1–4pm; *f*3), is housed in the building of the old De Boom brewery, and has displays tracing the brewing process from the malting to bottling stage, aided by authentic props from this and other breweries the world over. There's lots of technical equipment, enlivened by mannikins and empty bottles from once innumerable Dutch brewers – though few, curiously, from De Boom itself. It's an engaging little museum, lovingly put together by enthusiasts; it also has a top-floor shop in which you can buy a huge range of beers and associated merchandise, as well as a downstairs bar serving some eighty varieties of Dutch beer.

The **Stedelijk Museum** (Tues–Fri 10am–5pm, Sat & Sun 1–5pm; *f*3) 200m west of the Waag in Doelenstraat displays pictures and plans of the siege of 1573, along with a *Holy Family* by Honthorst and portraits by Maerten van Heemskerk and Caesar van Everdingen, the latter a local and very minor seventeenth-century figure who worked in the Mannerist style of the Haarlem painters. Five minutes south along Doelenstraat you'll spot the **St Laurenskerk**, a Gothic church of the later fifteenth century – worth looking into for its huge organ, commissioned at the suggestion of Constantijn Huygens by Maria Tesselschade, local resident and friend of the Golden Age elite. The case was designed by Jacob van Campen and painted by Caesar van Everdingen. In the apse is the tomb of Count Floris V, penultimate in the line of medieval counts of North Holland, who did much to establish the independence of the towns hereabouts but was murdered by nobles in 1296. Alkmaar's main shopping street, **Langestraat**, leads east from here; partway along is the street's only notable building – the **Stadhuis**, a florid affair, half of which (the eastern side and tower) dates from the early sixteenth century.

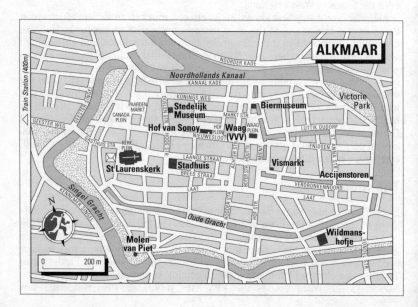

Practicalities

Alkmaar's **train station** is about fifteen minutes' walk west of the centre of town; from outside the station, turn right, then left at the traffic lights, and follow the road for ten minutes or so, across the water, and it'll bring you to the St Laurenskerk. The **VVV** is another five minutes away, housed in the Waag on Waagplein (Mon–Wed 9am–5.30pm, Thurs, Fri & Sat 9am–6pm; ☎072/511 4284), and has plenty of **private rooms** to rent, from about *f*28 per person. Failing that, *De Nachtegaal* is the cheapest and most central **hotel**, opposite the town hall at Langestraat 100 (☎072/511 2894, no fax; ②), with basic double rooms; otherwise, try *Henry's*, at Houttil 34 (☎072/511 3283, no fax; ②), who have some family rooms as well. The brand new *Motel Stad en Land* is a slightly more expensive option still in the centre, at Stationsweg 92 (☎072/512 3911, fax 511 8440; ③) . If you're **camping**, try *Camping Alkmaar* (☎072/511 6924; May–Sept), ten minutes' bus ride northwest of the town centre at Bergenweg 201; take #168 or #169 from the train station.

There are quite a few good places to **eat**. *Jelle's Eethuisje*, between Laat and Oude Gracht at Ridderstraat 24, is good for light lunches and economical suppers. *Ikan Mas*, one of several restaurants in the old part of town at Fnidsen 101–103, is a decent Indonesian that does a reasonable *rijsttafel*, while *Rose's Cantina*, two doors down, serves Tex-Mex dishes. *Eetcafé Vestibule*, at Ritsevoort 12, has cheap, filling meals, and *'t Gulden Vlies*, at Koorstraat 30, is a recommended grand café. *Porto Fino*, close to the Waag at Mient 5, is a small and simple Italian.

Drinking, too, is well catered for. There are two groups of bars: one on Waagplein itself, the other on the nearby canal of Verdronkenoord, by the old Vismarkt. Of the former, *De Kaasbeurs*, at Houttil 30, is a busy place with a young clientele; *Café Corridor*, virtually next door, is a lively hangout that plays loud music late into the night and has a small dancefloor at the back. *Proeflokaal 't Apothekertje*, a few doors down, is an old-style, quieter kind of bar altogether, open until 2am. On Verdronkenoord, *De Pilaren* is also noisy, though catering for a slightly older crowd; *Café Stapper*, next door, is a good refuge if the music gets too much. Tucked away in the alleys of the old part of town, at Hekelstraat 19, the *Odeon* bar is dark and dingy, with a pool table in the back.

If you just want to have a quick look around Alkmaar after the cheese market, in summer you can take a **boat trip** around the town (information ☎072/511 7750), departing from Mient, near the Waag. They run every twenty minutes from 9.30am on cheese-market days (Fridays from mid-April to mid-Sept), and every hour 11am–6pm the rest of the week from May to Oct (but there's no Sun service April, Sept & Oct); the trip lasts about 45 minutes and costs *f*6.

Around Alkmaar – and points north

The seashore close to Alkmaar is the area's best feature and, if the weather is warm, it's a good place to cool off after the crush of the cheese market. Bus #168 leaves Alkmaar station every fifteen minutes for the ten-minute ride to **BERGEN**, a cheerful village that has been something of a retreat for artists since the Expressionist Bergen School of the early twentieth century worked here. There are a number of galleries around the village, including the **KCB** gallery, next door to the VVV, at Plein 7 (Tues–Sat 11am–5pm, Sun 2–5pm; *f*2.50), which holds regular exhibitions of work by contemporary Bergen artists, and there's a small collection of older work in the **Sterkenhuis Museum** on Oude Prinsweg (May–Sept

Tues–Sat 10am–noon & 3–5pm, July & Aug also 7–9pm; *f*3), which also contains documentation on the defeat of the Duke of York here in 1799, along with period rooms and old costumes.

There's a permanent exhibition of Bergen School paintings on display at the **Smithuizen Museum**, Stationsweg 83 (Jan–Oct Fri–Sun 2–6pm, Nov & Dec Fri & Sat only 2–6pm; free), in **HEILOO**, just ten minutes south of Alkmaar by train. Heiloo is also important for bulbs, and has a summer exhibition of flowers and plants in its **Hortus Bulborum**. What's more, there's a **museum** devoted to bulb cultivation south of the town in **LIMMEN** at Dusseldorpweg 64, with exhibits on two centuries of bulb-growing in Holland (mid-April to mid-Sept Mon & Tues 9am–noon & 2–5pm, Fri 9am–noon; free). Half-hourly bus #176 runs from Alkmaar station through Heiloo (the bus-stop on Stationsweg) and on to Limmen.

From Alkmaar and Bergen, bus #168 goes once an hour though to **BERGEN-AAN-ZEE**, a bleak place in itself but with access to some strikingly untouched dunes and beach. It also has an **aquarium** at Van der Wijckplein 16 (daily April–Oct 10am–6pm, Nov–March 11am–5pm; *f*7.50, under 12s *f*5), crammed full of marine life, and useful if the weather turns or you have kids in tow. About 3km south, **EGMOND-AAN-ZEE** (accessible on hourly bus #165 from both Alkmaar and Bergen-aan-Zee, although it's an easy walk from the latter) is a little larger but not much more attractive, though it does have huge expanses of sand. A short way inland across the dunes, in **EGMOND-AAN-DE-HOEF**, you can see the remains of the castle of the counts of North Holland, destroyed in 1574. Egmond is also an entry point to the **Noordhollands Duinreservaat**, an area of woods and dunes that stretches south for more than 15km beyond Castricum and holds a couple of campsites and any number of cycle paths, not to mention a superb beach.

The coast north of Bergen, from **CAMPERDUIN** to **PETTEN**, has no dunes, and the sea is kept at bay by means of a 4.5-kilometre-long **dike** – something you can learn more about at the **de dijk te kijk** ("the dike on show") exhibition at Strandweg 4 just outside Petten (and signposted from the village); here you can find old maps, photos, and drawings illustrating the building of the defence (April, May & Oct Sat & Sun 2–5pm, June–Sept daily 10am–5pm; free).

SCHAGEN, inland from Petten, draws visitors for its summer market, held every Thursday in July and August, when the small town centre is entirely taken over by stands. Twenty minutes further north by train, **DEN HELDER** is a town of around sixty thousand, though it was little more than a fishing village until 1811, when Napoleon, capitalizing on its strategic position at the very tip of North Holland, fortified it as a naval base. It's still the principal home of the Dutch navy, and at weekends during June, national fleet days are held here – a chance, should you desire it, to check out a huge proportion of the Dutch navy (for details, contact the Den Helder VVV on ☎0223/625 544). Otherwise there's little interest to the place: its centre is an uninspiring muddle of modern architecture prefacing a seedier old quarter down near the harbour. The only real reason to come here is to take one of the plentiful ferries across the water to the island of Texel. If this is your plan, take *NZH* bus #3 direct from the train station to the harbour and miss out the town altogether; if you want to walk to the ferry through the town centre, follow Spoorstraat from the station and turn left at the end (about 20min). If you find you have some time to wait for the ferry, Den Helder's **Marine Museum**, part of which incorporates a visitable submarine, is close to the docks at Hoofdgracht 3 (Tues–Fri 10am–5pm, Sat & Sun 1–4.30pm; June–Aug also Mon 1–5pm; *f*7.50, under 15s *f*4).

Texel

The largest of the islands of the Wadden Sea – and the easiest to get to – **TEXEL** (pronounced "tessel") is a lush, green thumb of land, speckled with small towns and lined on its western side by large areas of dune and extensive beaches. Much of it has actually been reclaimed from the sea, and, until the draining of its main polder on the northeastern side of the island during the nineteenth century, it was shaped quite differently, the dunes providing a backbone to a much less even expanse of farmland. It's an incredibly diverse and pretty island – something borne out by the crowds that congregate here during the summer months. When the weather's hot, Texel is far from empty.

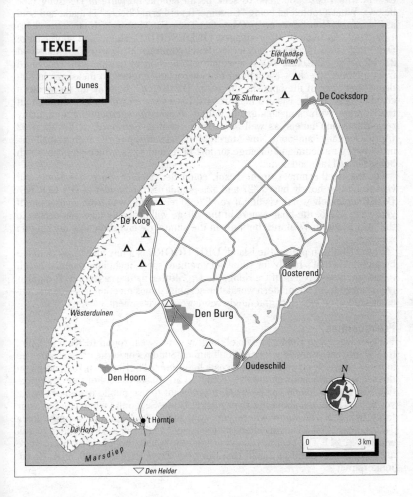

Ferries from the mainland (see "Practicalities" below) drop you in the middle of nowhere, near a tiny hamlet called **'t Horntje**, but buses connect with ferry arrivals to take you to **DEN BURG**, the main town – no more than a large village really, but home to the island's VVV office (details below). As for sights, there's not much to see in Den Burg beyond a small **museum** of local history (Kogerstraat 1; April–Oct Mon–Fri 10am–12.30pm and 1.30–3.30pm; ƒ3.50), but it makes a decent base for seeing the rest of Texel.

The VVV has booklets detailing good cycling routes, as well as the best places to view the island's many **bird colonies**, protected in sanctuaries right across Texel (the island is one of the most important breeding grounds in Europe). Though you can see them well enough from a distance, you may want to get closer – in which case you need to seek permission at *Ecomare* in De Koog (see below). What's touted as being "Genuine Texel Farm-Cheese" is made and sold at *Wezenspijk*, Hoornderweg 27 (May–Oct Tues–Sat 9.30am–12.15pm, Tues & Fri 1.30–6pm). As regards other villages, **OUDESCHILD**, about 3km southeast of Den Burg, is worth a quick look for its **Beachcombers Museum** (Barentszstraat 21; Mon–Sat 9am–5pm; ƒ5), a fascinating collection of marine junk recovered from offshore wrecks – everything from aeroplane engines to messages in bottles. Otherwise, in the opposite direction, **DE KOOG**, halfway up the western coast of Texel, is the island's main resort. It's a very crowded place throughout the summer, with campsites galore dotted all over the surrounding area, many restaurants and hotels, as well as a nature centre, **Ecomare**, at Ruyslaan 92 (April–Oct daily 9am–5pm, Nov–March Mon–Sat 9am–5pm; ƒ6), with a small natural history museum and a refuge for lost birds and seals, which you can watch being fed at 11am and 3pm.

On the northernmost tip of Texel, connected to Den Burg, De Koog and Oudeschild by hourly buses #27 and #29 (45min) is the hamlet of **DE COCKS-DORP**, definitely worth visiting if you like to feel a long way from civilization. If you want, one of the boat-owners in the village will probably take you across to the next island of **Vlieland**, but only in the summer – and then only during fine weather.

In the southern part of the island, **DEN HOORN** is a tiny village surrounded by bulbfields that's handy for some very remote spots, including a nudist beach to the southwest. North of De Koog, the **De Slufter** nature reserve feels similarly distanced from the modern world, the scrubby dunes meeting massive stretches of sand in an almost frighteningly windswept environment.

Practicalities

Ferries leave Den Helder for Texel roughly hourly year-round (6.30am–9.30pm, though the early-morning ferries don't run on Sundays or in the off-season). The journey takes twenty minutes, and costs between ƒ8.25–10 return, depending on the season; a bike adds another ƒ5–6, and a car ƒ40.50–48.50. For more information call ☎0222/369 600 or 06/9292. If you want to use public **transport** while you're on Texel, ask about the ƒ6 day-ticket (June–Sept only) when you buy your ferry ticket. If you know where you want to go, you can also arrange for a *Telekomtaxi* to take you anywhere on the island; again ask in Den Helder, or call ☎0222/322 211. The best way to get around the island, though, is by **bike**: there are a couple of **rental** outfits in Den Burg – *F. Zegel*, Parkstraat 16, or *A. Kievit*, Jonkerstraat 2.

The island's **VVV** is in Den Burg at Emmalaan 66 (Mon–Fri 9am–6pm, Sat 9am–5pm; July & Aug also Sun 4–7pm; ☎0222/314 741), where you can book **private accommodation** throughout the island. The cheapest **hotel** in Den Burg is *'t Koogerend*, Kogerstraat 94 (☎0222/313 301, fax 0222/315 902; ④); it's a friendly place, but you're paying over the odds for the location. There are also two **youth hostels** on either side of Den Burg on the roads to De Koog and Oudeschild – one called *Panorama* at Schansweg 7 (☎0222/315 441), the other, *De Eyercoogh*, at Pontweg 106 (☎0222/312 907). Both are open April to October only, and can be reached by bus #28 from the ferry jetty; for the *Panorama*, you can also get bus #29 from the same stop.

If you're **camping**, you're spoilt for choice. In and around Den Burg are four sites: best are the small, well-run *De Koorn Aar* at Grensweg 388 (☎0222/312 931; April–Oct), which has easy bus connections all over the island, and *'t Woutershok* at Rozendijk 38 (☎0222/313 080; April–Oct), which is run by Nivon, a nationwide organization devoted to culture, nature and recreation (info on ☎020/626 9661). Other sites dotted across the island include, in De Koog, *Kogerstrand*, Badweg 33 (☎0222/317 208; April–Sept), scattered among the dunes two minutes from the beach, and *Euroase Texel*, Bosrandweg 395 (☎0222/317 290; April–Oct), which also has bungalows on the beach. In De Cocksdorp, *De Krim*, Roggeslootweg 6 (☎0222/316 666; all year) is quite upmarket, with luxury bungalows and a pool. Finally, in Den Hoorn, *Loodsmansduin*, Rommelpot 19 (☎0222/319 203; April–Oct), is a large, isolated site with plenty of space for caravans

One of the best of a small range of places to **eat and drink** in Den Burg is *De Worsteltent* at Smitsweg 6; and in De Koog, you'll be spoilt for choice. If you make it as far as De Cocksdorp, you can refresh yourself with a drink, a pancake or a full meal at *Vliezicht* restaurant on the beach.

travel details

Trains

Alkmaar to: Haarlem (every 30min; 25min); Hoorn (every 30min; 25min).

Amsterdam CS to: Alkmaar (every 30min; 30min); Castricum (every 30min; 30min); Den Helder (every 30min; 1hr); Enkhuizen (every 30min; 55min); Haarlem (every 15min; 15min); Hilversum (hourly; 30min); Hoorn (every 30min; 35min); Purmerend (every 30min; 25min); Schagen (every 30min; 55min); Zaandam (every 15min; 10min).

Haarlem to: Alkmaar (every 30min; 25min); Hoorn (every 30min; 25min); Zandvoort (every 30min; 10min).

Hilversum to: Amersfoort (every 30min; 15min); Utrecht (every 20min; 20min).

Hoorn to: Medemblik (March–Oct 1–4 daily except Mon; 1hr).

Buses

Alkmaar to: Bergen (every 15min; 15min); Harlingen (hourly; 1hr 45min); Leeuwarden (hourly; 2hr 15min).

Amsterdam to: Broek-in-Waterland (every 15min; 20min); Edam (every 30min; 40min); Landsmeer (every 30min; 15min); Marken (every 30min; 30min); Muiden (every 30min; 40min); Naarden (every 30min; 55min); Volendam (every 30min; 30min); Zaandam (every 30min; 40min); Zaanse Schans (every 20min; 1hr).

Bergen to: Bergen-aan-Zee (hourly; 10min).

Broek-in-Waterland to: Monnickendam (every 30min; 10min).

Edam to: Hoorn (every 30min; 25min).

Enkhuizen to: Lelystad (every 2hr; 45min).

Haarlem to: Bloemendaal (every 30min; 15min); Zandvoort (every 15min; 20min).

Hoorn to: Medemblik (every 30min; 30–40min).

Marken to: Monnickendam (every 30min; 15min).

Monnickendam to: Volendam (hourly; 20min).

Muiden to: Hilversum (every 30min; 1hr 15min); Naarden (every 30min; 15min).

Ferries

Den Helder to: Texel (hourly; 20min).

Enkhuizen to: Medemblik (March–Oct 1–2 daily except Mon; 1hr 30min); Stavoren (May–Sept 3 daily; 1hr 25min); Urk (July & Aug Mon–Sat 3 daily; 1hr 30min).

Marken to: Volendam (March–Oct daily every 30min; 20min).

CHAPTER THREE

SOUTH HOLLAND AND UTRECHT

S outh Holland is the most densely populated province of the Netherlands, with a string of towns and cities that make up most of the **Randstad** or rim-town. Careful urban planning has succeeded in stopping this from becoming an amorphous conurbation, however, and each town has a pronounced identity – from the refined tranquillity of **The Hague** to the seedy lowlife of **Rotterdam**'s docklands. All the towns are able to offer good museums and galleries, some outstanding, like The Hague's **Mauritshuis**, Leiden's **Van Oudheden museum** and Rotterdam's **Boymans-van Beuningen**. Since it too now forms part of the Randstad, **Utrecht** is included here, again a city rich in galleries.

Historically, South Holland is part of what was once simply **Holland**, the richest and most influential province in the country. Throughout the Golden Age Holland was far and away the most dominant province in the political, social and cultural life of the Republic, overshadowing its neighbours whose economies suffered as a result of Holland's success. There are constant reminders of this pre-eminence in the buildings of this region: elaborate town halls proclaim civic importance and even the usually sombre Calvinist churches allow themselves little excesses – the later windows of Gouda's Janskerk a case in point. Many of the great painters either came from or worked here, too – Rembrandt, Vermeer, Jan Steen – a tradition that continued into the nineteenth century with the paintings of the Hague School. Outside of the coastal strip of cities, the countryside around the ancient port of **Dordrecht** is of most interest, featuring the windmills of the Kinderdijk, the Biesbosch reed forest and, around **Gouda**, the rural charms of the tidy town of **Oudewater**.

ACCOMMODATION PRICE CODES

All the **hotels** and **hostels** detailed in this chapter have been graded according to the following price categories. Apart from ①, which is a per-person price for a hostel bed, all the codes are based on the rate for the cheapest double room during high season.

For more on accommodation, see p.30.

① Up to ƒ40 per person	④ ƒ150–200	⑦ ƒ300–400
② ƒ60–100	⑤ ƒ200–250	
③ ƒ100–150	⑥ ƒ250–300	

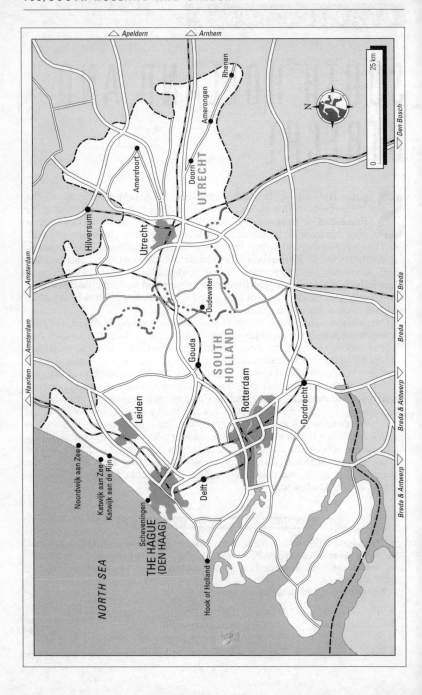

Uniformly flat, the countryside in this area is brightened only by the rainbow flashes of bulbfields. Travelling around is never a problem: none of South Holland's towns are more than 20km apart, and they're linked by a fast and efficient rail network.

Leiden and around

The home of Holland's most prestigious university, **LEIDEN** has an academic air. Like Haarlem to the north, you get the feeling it regards itself as separate from, and independent of, Amsterdam – which is fair enough. There's enough here to justify at least a day-trip, and the town's energy, derived largely from its students, strongly counters the myth that there's nothing worth experiencing outside the capital. Leiden's museums, too, are varied and comprehensive enough to merit a visit in themselves, though be selective. The town's real charm lies in the peace and prettiness of its gabled streets and canals.

The university was a gift from William the Silent, a reward for Leiden's enduring (like Haarlem and Alkmaar) a year-long siege by the Spanish. The town emerged victorious on October 3, 1574, when William cut through the dykes around the city and sailed in with his fleet for a dramatic eleventh-hour rescue. This event is still commemorated with an annual fair, fireworks and the consumption of two traditional dishes: herring and white bread, which the fleet were supposed to have brought with them, and *hutspot*, or vegetable and potato stew, a cauldron of which was apparently found simmering in the abandoned Spanish camp.

Arrival, information and accommodation

Leiden's ultra-modern **train station** is next to the **bus station** on the northwest edge of town, about ten minutes' walk from the centre. The **VVV** is opposite at Stationsplein 210 (Mon–Fri 9am–5.30pm, Sat 9am–4pm; ☎514 6846); it has useful maps and brochures detailing walking tours of the town, and can advise on **accommodation** or make room bookings in private homes. Other than that, Leiden is fairly short on hotel space for a town of its size, and there are no special bargains. *The Rose* (☎514 6630, fax 514 5127; ②) is attractive and well located at Beestenmarkt 14; to get there, follow Stationsweg from the train station until you reach the first square, where it's on your left. An alternative is *De Ceder* (☎517 5903, fax 515 7098; ②) at Rijnsburgerweg 80; turn left outside the station and left again under the train tracks. Closer to the centre is the pleasant *Nieuw Minerva* (☎512 6358, fax 514 2674; ③), at Boommarkt 23. There is a **youth hostel** at Lange Scheistraat 9, on a small alley behind the Lakenhal museum. Otherwise, reasonably priced accommodation is more plentiful in the nearby seaside resorts of Katwijk and Noordwijk. Of the two, Katwijk is the nicer option, with several hotels and pensions along its seafront Boulevard; try *Perk*, at no. 60 (☎401 2369; ②), or *Het Anker*, at no. 129 (☎401 3890, fax 407 3907; ②). If you're **camping**, the closest large site is the *Koningshof* in Rijnsburg, north of Leiden; take bus #40. Otherwise, Noordwijk and Katwijk have several campsites, open from April to October.

The Leiden area telephone code is ☎071

The town

Leiden's most appealing quarter is that bordered by Witte Singel and Breestraat, focusing on Rapenburg, a peaceful area of narrow pedestrian streets and canals. At Rapenburg 28 is perhaps the city's best-known attraction, the **Rijksmuseum Van Oudheden** (Tues–Sat 10am–5pm, Sun noon–5pm; *f*5), Holland's principal archeological museum, with a huge collection. You can see one of its major exhibits, the *Temple of Taffeh*, for free. Situated in a courtyard in front of the museum entrance, this was a gift from the Egyptian government in gratitude for the Dutch part in the 1960s UNESCO excavations in Abyssinia (Ethiopia), which succeeded in uncovering submerged Nubian monuments. Dating back to the first century AD, the temple was adapted in the fourth century to the worship of Isis, eventually being sanctified as a Christian church 400 years later. The Egyptians placed very firm conditions on their legacy: no one should have to pay to see it, and the temperature and humidity must be carefully regulated, with the lights overhead simulating the passage – and shadow – of the sun.

Inside the museum proper, the first exhibit is the remains of a temple to Nehellania – a goddess of sailors – which was uncovered in Zeeland. Next come classical Greek and Roman sculptures, leading chronologically through Hellenistic works to busts, statues, and friezes of Imperial Rome. The best collection, though, is the Egyptian one, beginning with wall reliefs, statues and sarcophagi from tombs and temples, and continuing in the rooms immediately above with a set of mummies and sarcophagi as complete as you're likely to see outside Egypt. The *Three Figures of Maya*, to name just one exhibit, are exceptionally well preserved. The third floor is specifically Dutch: an archeological history of the country, from prehistoric, Roman and medieval times, which is, perhaps inevitably, less interesting than the rest of the museum.

Further along Rapenburg, at no. 73, the original home of the **university** still stands, part of which is open as a **museum** (Wed–Fri 1–5pm; free) which details its history. Through the courtyard, the **Hortus Botanicus** gardens (Mon–Fri 9am–5pm, Sun 10am–5pm; April–Sept also Sat 9am–5pm; *f*5) are a lovely spot, lushly planted and subtly landscaped across to the Witte Singel canal. Planted in 1587, they are supposedly among the oldest botanical gardens in Europe, a mixture of carefully tended beds of shrubs and hothouses full of tropical foliage. Leave by the exit off to the left, across the canal, where a red door hides a reconstruction of the original garden, the **Clusiustuin** (same hours), named after the botanist who first brought tulips to Holland.

Cross Rapenburg from the university museum, and you're in the network of narrow streets constituting the medieval town, converging on a central square and the **Pieterskerk** (daily 1.30–4pm; free), the town's main church. This is deconsecrated now, used occasionally for a Saturday antique market, and it has an empty warehouse-like feel. But among the fixtures that remain are a simple and beautiful Renaissance rood screen in the choir, and a host of memorials to the sundry notables buried here, among them **John Robinson**, leader of the Pilgrim Fathers.

Robinson lived in a house on the site of what is now the **Jan Pesijn Hofje** on Kloksteeg, right by the church. A curate in England at the turn of the seventeenth century, he was suspended from preaching in 1604, later fleeing with his congregation to pursue his Puritan form of worship in the more amenable atmosphere of Calvinist Holland. Settling in Leiden, Robinson acted as pastor to growing numbers, but still found himself at odds with the establishment. In 1620, a hundred of his followers ("The

Pilgrim Fathers") sailed via Plymouth for the freedom and abundance of America, though Robinson died before he could join them; he's buried in the church.

If you want to find out more, stroll down to the **Leiden Pilgrim Collection** at Vliet 45 (Mon–Fri 9.30am–4.30pm; free), part of the city archives and a mine of information on Robinson's group during their stay in Leiden. Otherwise, continue east onto **Breestraat**, which marks the edge of Leiden's commercial centre, flanked by the long, ornate Renaissance front of the late sixteenth-century **Stadhuis**, the only part of the building to survive a fire in 1929. Behind, the rivers which cut Leiden into islands converge at the busiest point in town, the site of a vigorous Wednesday and Saturday general **market** which sprawls right over the sequence of bridges into the blandly pedestrian **Haarlemmerstraat** – the town's main shopping street.

The junction of the Oude and Nieuwe Rijn is marked by the mid-seventeenth-century **Waag**, a replacement for a previous Gothic structure, built to a design by Pieter Post and fronted with a naturalistic frieze by Rombout Verhulst. Across the water from here, on the island formed by the fork in the two sections of river, the **Burcht** (daily 10am–9pm; free) is the shell of a twelfth-century fort perched on an ancient mound; it's worth climbing up on the battlements for a panoramic view of Leiden's roofs and towers. The **Hooglandsekerk** nearby (April–Oct Tues–Sat 11am–4pm, Mon 1–3.30pm; free) is a light, lofty church with a central pillar that features an epitaph to the burgomaster at the time of the 1574 siege, Pieter van

der Werff, who became a hero during its final days. When the situation became so desperate that most people were all for giving up, the burgomaster, no doubt remembering the massacre of Haarlem, offered his own body to them as food. His invitation was rejected, but – the story goes – it succeeded in instilling new determination in the flagging citizens.

Across Oude Rijn from here is the **Museum Boerhaave** at Lange Agnietenstraat 10 (Tues–Sat 10am–5pm, Sun noon–5pm; *f*5), named after the seventeenth-century Leiden surgeon, which gives a brief but absorbing guide to scientific and medical developments over the last three centuries, with particular reference to Dutch achievements, including some gruesome surgical implements, pickled brains and suchlike. Five minutes' walk from here, Leiden's municipal museum, housed in the old **Lakenhal** (cloth-hall) at Oude Singel 28–32 (Tues–Sat 10am–5pm, Sun noon–5pm; *f*5), has a similarly engaging exhibition, with a picture gallery devoted to natives of the town as well as mixed rooms of furniture, tiles, glass and ceramics. It's also the only museum in Leiden to regularly exhibit modern Dutch art. Upstairs, the rooms look much as they would have when Leiden's cloth trade was at its height – though most have since been decorated with paintings or now house temporary exhibitions. Downstairs, there's a series of sixteenth-century paintings centring around Lucas van Leyden's *Last Judgment* triptych, plus canvases by Rembrandt, Jacob van Swanenburgh (first teacher of the young Rembrandt) and associated Leiden painters – among them Jan Lievens (with whom Rembrandt shared a studio), Gerrit Dou (who initiated the Leiden tradition of small, minutely finished pictures) and the van Mieris brothers. There's also a painting depicting the sixteenth-century siege that shows the heroic van der Werff in full flow.

Around the corner on Molenwerf, the **Molenmuseum de Valk**, 2e Binnenvestgracht 1 (Tues–Sat 10am–5pm, Sun 1–5pm; *f*5), is a restored grain mill, one of twenty that used to surround Leiden. The downstairs rooms are furnished in simple, period style; upstairs a slide show recounts the history of windmills in Holland, while displays detail their development and showcase their tools and grinding apparatus, all immaculately preserved. An absorbing way to spend an hour, and only five minutes' stroll from the station.

There's one other museum between here and the station, the **Rijksmuseum Voor Volkenkunde** at Steenstraat 1 (Tues–Fri 10am–5pm, Sat & Sun noon–5pm; *f*7), the national ethnological museum, which has complete sections on Indonesia and the Dutch colonies, along with reasonable ones on the South Pacific and Far East. However, it gives most other parts of the world a less than thorough showing and is not an essential stop by any means.

Eating and drinking

It's easy to **eat and drink** cheaply in Leiden. The streets around the Pieterskerkhof and the Hooglandsekerk both hold concentrations of bars and restaurants. For lunch, *M'n Broer*, by the Pieterskerkhof at Kloksteeg 7, has a reasonable Dutch menu, while *Barrera*, opposite the old university building on Rapenburg, is a cosy bar with a good range of sandwiches. In the evening, *De Brasserie*, Lange Mare 38, is popular, with Dutch food starting at *f*20; the French/Dutch bistro *Koetshuis de Burcht*, off Burgsteeg beside the Burcht, attracts a trendy crowd; the studenty *La Bota*, Herensteeg 9 by the Pieterskerkhof, has some of the best-value local food in town and an excellent array of beers; and *Cojico*, at Breestraat 33, is a lively Mexican place with main dishes for ƒ12–25. *Jazzcafe The Duke*, on the corner of Oude Singel and Nieuwe Beestenmarkt near the Lakenhal, has a friendly bar and live **jazz** several nights of the week; round the corner, next to the youth hostel, *Cafe Jazzmatazz* also has live music and is favoured by expats.

Because of the university Leiden is a good place to buy **books**. *Kooyker*, Breestraat 93, has a decent selection of books in English; there's also a branch of *De Slegte* at Breestraat 73. Consider also taking a **canal trip** around the city centre. These run from Beestenmarkt during summer and cost ƒ10 per person for a forty-minute tour.

Around Leiden: the bulbfields and the coast

Along with Haarlem to the north, Leiden is the best base for seeing something of the Dutch **bulbfields**, which have flourished here since the late sixteenth century, when one Carolus Clusius, a Dutch botanist, brought the first tulip bulb over from Asia Minor and watched it prosper on Holland's sandy soil. Although bulbs are grown in North Holland too, the centre of the Dutch bulb-growing industry is the area around Leiden and up toward Haarlem. The flowers are inevitably a major tourist pull, and one of Holland's most lucrative businesses, supporting some ten thousand growers in what is these days a billion-guilder industry. Obviously spring is the best time to see something of the blooms, when the view from the train – which cuts directly through the main growing areas – can be sufficient in itself, the fields divided into stark geometric blocks of pure colour. With your own transport you can take in the full beauty of the bulbfields by way of special routes marked by hexagonal signposts – local VVVs sell pamphlets listing the best vantage points.

A short train-ride away, the **coastal resorts** of Katwijk and Noordwijk, though hardly exciting, offer decent swimming and slightly cheaper accommodation than Leiden.

Lisse and the Keukenhof Gardens

Should you want to get closer to the flowers, **LISSE**, halfway between Leiden and Haarlem, is the place to look at the best of the Dutch flower industry, home to the **Keukenhof Gardens** (late-March to May daily 8am–7.30pm; ƒ16), the largest flower gardens in the world. The Keukenhof was set up in 1949, designed by a group of prominent bulb growers to convert people to the joys of growing flowers from bulbs in their own gardens. Literally the "kitchen garden", its site is the former estate of a fifteenth-century countess, who used to grow herbs and vegetables for her dining table here – hence the name. Some seven million flowers are on show for their full flowering period, complemented, in case of especially harsh winters, by 5000 square metres of greenhouses holding indoor displays. You could easily spend a whole day here, swooning among the sheer abundance of it all. There are three restaurants in the 28 hectares of grounds, and well-marked paths take you all the way through the gardens, which hold daffodils, narcissi and hyacinths in April, and tulips from mid-April until the end of May. Special express bus no. 54 (ƒ22, including admission to the gardens) runs to the Keukenhof from Leiden bus station twice an hour at ten and forty minutes past each hour, every day including Sunday. To get the best of it, come early before the tour buses pack the place.

THE BRITISH BULBERS: EXPLOITATION AND EXCESS

Behind the dazzling surface of the bulbfields lies the misery of exploitation. Each summer the bulbs need to be packed and labelled and the core of the workforce for this is around five hundred young British men, many of whom come back year after year to work sixteen-hour shifts for wages no Dutch person would look at. Many of the workers are migrant labourers who follow the various harvests throughout Europe, moving on south afterwards for oranges and, later, work in the vineyards. Others simply come for a good time: the beer is cheap in Holland, as are soft drugs, which are plentifully – and legally – available. The "bulbers", as they refer to themselves, line up for work at 7.30am and toil until the late evening packing and labelling tulip and hyacinth bulbs. The rest of the time they spend drinking in the English bars of Hillegom, Haarlem or Leiden, sleeping in makeshift camps outside the bulb warehouses. Not only are the terms and conditions of the job dire, it is also painful work. The dust from tulip bulbs rots the fingers of the packers, leading to a condition known as "bulb finger" – sometimes fingers become infected and swell up. Hyacinth bulbs are even worse: the dust from them lodges in the skin, causing itching and, again, infection. Bulbers are provided with coats and gloves to protect themselves, but the heat in the warehouses is intense, and most simply don't bother with them. There is a bulb-workers' union, the *Voedingsbond FNV*, but the British aren't members, and employers break every rule in the book each year when they take them on. Apart from the bulb barons, the Dutch see the British as a bizarre sub-culture during their time here, amazed at their capacities for an excessive intake of booze and dope; the Brits, for their part, are unconcerned, playing up to the role of "the crazy English".

Aalsmeer and more bulbs

You can see the industry in action in **AALSMEER**, 23km north of Leiden toward Amsterdam, whose flower auction, again the largest in the world, is held daily in a building approximately the size of 75 football fields (Mon–Fri 7.30–11am; *f*5). The dealing is fast and furious, and the turnover staggering. In an average year around *f*1.5 billion (about £500 million/US$800 million) worth of plants and flowers are traded here, many of which arrive in florist's shops throughout Europe on the same day. There are other places, too, with bulbs and flowers, though none as spectacular as the Keukenhof, nor as vibrant as the Aalsmeer auction. The **Frans Roozen nurseries** at Vogelenzangseweg 49 in **VOGELENZANG**, a little way south of Haarlem (late-March to June daily 8am–6pm; July–Sept Mon–Fri 9am–5pm; *f*2), have a show greenhouse displaying blooms. **RIJNSBURG**, just north of Leiden, has a flower parade in early August each year, from Rijnsburg to Leiden and Noordwijk, and there's a similar parade from Haarlem to Noordwijk (see below) in April, culminating with a display of the floats in the town.

The coast: Katwijk and Noordwijk

Like all of the towns in this part of Holland, Leiden has easy access to some fine beaches, though the coastal resorts themselves aren't much to write home about, and unless you're keen to swim, the only reason for visiting is for their larger – and cheaper – supply of accommodation and campsites. **KATWIJK-AAN-ZEE**, accessible by buses #31, #41 or express service #35 from the stop opposite the bus station, is the stock Dutch seaside town, less crowded than Zandvoort and without the pretensions of Scheveningen, but pretty dreary nonetheless – although it does preserve some of the features of an old coastal village in the lines of terraced housing that spread out around the seventeenth-century lighthouse. Its expanse of undeveloped sand dune, though, which stretches along the shore south toward The Hague, is an ideal area for secluded sunbathing. Otherwise its main attraction is the **Katwijk Sluices**, just north of the resort area, beside the main bus route. Completed in 1807, these are a series of gates that regulate the flow of the Oude Rijn as it approaches the sea: around high tide, the gates are closed; when they are opened, the pressure of the accumulated water brushes aside the sand deposited at the mouth of the river by the sea – a simple system that finally determined the course of the Oude Rijn, which for centuries had been continually diverted by the sand deposits, turning the surrounding fields into a giant swamp. The **VVV** (April–Aug Mon–Sat 9am–6pm, July–Aug also Sun 11am–3pm; Sept–March Mon–Fri 9am–5pm & Sat 9am–1pm; ☎407 5444), near the beach at Vuurbaakplein 11, is useful for finding accommodation when the town gets busy in summer. It also has information on the town's annual herring gutting competition.

NOORDWIJK-AAN-ZEE, some 3km up the coast and reachable by buses #40, #42 or express service #25 from the same stop, is of even less appeal, not much more than a string of grandiose hotel developments built across the undulating sand dunes behind the coast. However, it again offers some excellent stretches of beach. The one time when it's worth coming to see the town itself is the penulti-mate weekend in April, when a flower parade from Haarlem arrives and makes an illuminated tour of Noordwijk. The next morning the floats are displayed in the village.

The Hague and Scheveningen

With its urbane atmosphere, **THE HAGUE** is different from any other Dutch city. Since the sixteenth century it's been the political capital and the focus of national institutions, in a country built on civic independence and munificence. Frequently disregarded until the development of central government in the nineteenth cen-tury, The Hague's older buildings are a rather subdued and modest collection with little of Amsterdam's flamboyance. Most of the city's canal houses are demurely classical with a powerful sense of sedate prosperity. In 1859 English poet Matthew Arnold wrote: "I never saw a city where the well-to-do classes seemed to have given the whole place so much of their own air of wealth, finished cleanliness, and comfort; but I never saw one, either, in which my heart would so have sunk at the thought of living." Things haven't changed much: today's "well-to-do classes" – mostly diplomats in dark Mercedes and multinational executives – ensure that many of the city's hotels and restaurants are firmly in the expense account category, and the nightlife is similarly packaged. But, away from the mediocrity of wealth, The Hague does have cheaper and livelier bars and restau-rants – and even its share of restless adolescents hanging around the pizza joints.

The town may be rather drab, but it does have some excellent museums, prin-cipally the famed collection of old Dutch masters at the **Mauritshuis**, and more modern works of art at the **Gemeentemuseum**.

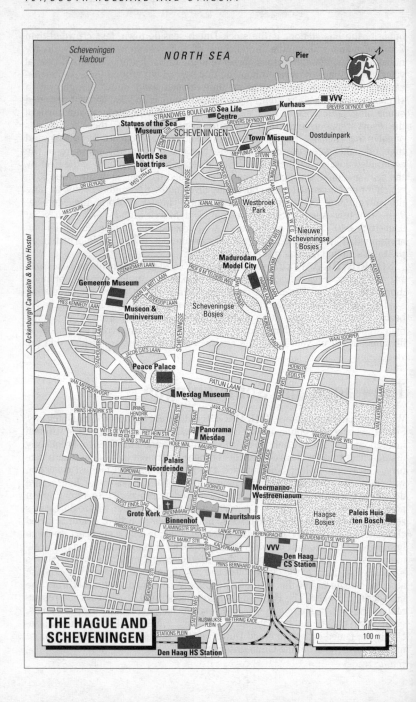

Scheveningen Harbour

NORTH SEA

Pier

△ Ockenburgh Campsite & Youth Hostel

VVV

STRANDWEG BOULEVARD
Sea Life Centre
GREVERS DEYNOOT WEG
Kurhaus

Statues of the Sea Museum
SCHEVENINGEN
Town Museum
Oostduinpark

North Sea boat trips

DR LELYKADE
WEG STRAAT
NEPTUNUS STR
STEVIN

WESTDUIN
STATEN LAAN
SCHEVENINGSE
KANAL WEG
Westbroek Park

Nieuwe Scheveningse Bosjes

EISENHOWER LAAN
Gemeente Museum
JOHAN DE WITT LAAN
DE GOEKOOP LAAN
PROF B M TELDERS WEG
Madurodam Model City

PRES KENNEDY LAAN
Museon & Omniversum
Scheveningse Bosjes

STADHOUDERS LAAN
JACOB CATS LAAN
WAALSDORPER

Peace Palace
PATIJN LAAN

VAN MEERDERVOORT
PRINS HENDRIK STR
PRINS HENDRIK PLEIN
Mesdag Museum
JAVA STRAAT

WITTE DE WITH STR
PIET HEIN STR
2E STRAAT
Panorama Mesdag

ELAND STRAAT
HOGE WAL
MAURITS

NORDWAL
Palais Noordeinde

WEST EINDE DAG
PRINSEGRACHT
Grote Kerk
GROENMARKT
Binnenhof
VLAMINGSTR SPUISTR
Mauritshuis
Haagse Bosjes
Paleis Huis ten Bosch

Meermanno-Westreenianum

GROTE MARKT STR
LANGE POTEN
KALVERMARKT
VVV
Den Haag CS Station

PRINS BERNHARD VIADUCT

BIEKHORST STR

THE HAGUE AND SCHEVENINGEN

STATIONS PLEIN
RIJSWIJKSE WETERING KADE
0   100 m

Den Haag HS Station

Arrival, information and accommodation

The Hague has two **train stations** – Den Haag HS (Hollands Spoor) and Den Haag CS (Centraal Station). Of the two, Den Haag CS is the more convenient, sited five minutes' walk east of the town centre and next door to a complex housing the **VVV** (Mon–Sat 9am–5.30pm, July–Aug also Sun 10am–5pm; ☎06/340 35051, 75c per min) and the bus and tram stations. Den Haag HS is 1km to the south, and frequent rail services connect the two. The Hague may be the country's third largest city, but almost everything worth seeing is within easy walking distance of Den Haag CS; if you intend to use the city's buses and trams, the VVV and counters at the train station sell the standard *strippenkaart* and a *dagkaart* – the best bet if you're only here for the day.

The Hague area telephone code, including Scheveningen, is ☎070

Accommodation

Hotels in The Hague are often expensive and, particularly at busy times, you might be better off basing yourself in Scheveningen, twenty minutes' ride away by tram (see p.173), where rooms are more plentiful and slightly cheaper. Otherwise, there's a cluster of reasonably priced, if rather down-at-heel, hotels just outside Den Haag HS Station, or you could pay a few guilders and let the VVV arrange a **private room** in one of the pensions spread out all over the city. The best **campsite** in the area is at Wijndaelerweg 25 (☎325 2364; March–Oct); take bus #4 from the station to Kijkduin and ask the driver to let you off at the stop nearest the site, about ten minutes' walk away.

Aristo, Stationsweg 164–166 (☎389 0847). Clean and tidy place near Den Haag HS station; some of the rooms are extremely cramped, so ask to see around. ②

Astoria, Stationsweg 139 (☎384 0401, fax 354 1653). A little smarter and more comfortable than its budget neighbours, with doubles from ƒ105. ③

Bristol, Stationsweg 130 (☎384 0073). Rather seedy feel but an option if the nearby places are full and, at ƒ45, the cheapest single rooms in town. ②

't Centrum, Veenkade 6 (☎346 3657, fax 310 6460). Small, friendly and cosy hotel by the canal west of the royal palace. ③

Ockenburgh, Monsterseweg 4 (☎397 0011, fax 397 2251). The official youth hostel, 10km to the west of the town centre just behind the beach at Kijkduin and attached to a budget hotel of the same name (③). Buses run from Den Haag CS station. ②

Paleis, Molenstraat 26 (☎362 2461, fax 361 4533). Good central location and the best value of The Hague's more upmarket hotels. Breakfast is an extra ƒ16 per person. ④

Parkhotel, Molenstraat 53 (☎362 4371, fax 361 4525). Luxury pad just below the Palais Noordeinde catering mostly to business travellers; double rooms from ƒ230. ⑥

The city centre

Right in the centre, and the oldest part of the city, the **Binnenhof** ("inner court") is the home of Holland's bicameral parliament. Count William II built a castle here in the thirteenth century, and the settlement that grew up around it became known as the "Count's Domain" – *'s Gravenhage*, literally "Count's Hedge" – which is still the city's official name. As the embodiment of central rather than municipal power, the Binnenhof had a chequered history – empty or occupied, feted or ignored – until the nineteenth century when The Hague shared political capital status with Brussels during the uneasy times of the United Kingdom of the Netherlands. Thereafter it became the seat of government, home to an effective legislature. The present rectangular complex is a rather mundane affair, a confusing mixture of shape and style that irritated nineteenth-century Dutch parliamentarians with its obvious lack of prestige, and their modern equivalents, members of the Tweedekamer, moved into a new extension in 1992.

The best view is from the front, where a small lake – the **Hof Vijver** (court pond) – mirrors the attractive symmetry of the front facade. Behind the lake, the Binnenhof is a major tourist attraction, but there's precious little to see except the **Ridderzaal** (Hall of the Knights), a slender-turreted structure used for state occasions. It's been a courtroom, market and stable, and so repeatedly replaced and renovated that little of the thirteenth-century original remains. An undramatic guided tour of the Ridderzaal and the chambers of parliament (often closed Mon & Tues) starts regularly from the information office at Binnenhof 8a (Mon–Sat 10am–4pm, last tour 3.45pm; ƒ5).

The Mauritshuis Collection

To the immediate east of the Binnenhof, the **Royal Picture Gallery Mauritshuis**, Korte Vijverberg 8 (Tues–Sat 10am–5pm, Sun 11am–5pm; ƒ10 paid as you leave the gallery), is located in a magnificent seventeenth-century mansion. Generally considered to be one of the best galleries in Europe, it's famous for its extensive range of Flemish and Dutch paintings from the fifteenth to the eighteenth centuries, based on the collection accumulated by Prince William V of Orange (1748–1806). All the major Dutch artists are represented, and it's well laid out, with multilingual cards in each room providing background notes on all the major canvases. At present the rooms are not numbered, and the policy of the museum is (rather awkwardly) to spread the works of many of the key artists through several rooms, rather than place them together. For further detailed information, there's a free brochure at the entrance, while the museum shop sells an excellent guidebook for ƒ25. Alternatively you can join one of the irregular and expensive conducted tours – prices depend on length; ask at reception for times. During major exhibitions, expect the paintings to be moved around or removed from show.

The entrance and museum shop are in the **basement** on the east side of the building, together with **Andy Warhol**'s *Queen Beatrix*, a twentieth-century aperitif to the collection above. Heading up the stairs to the **first floor**, walk back toward the old front doors and enter the room on the left, where **Hans Memling**'s *Portrait of a Man* is a typically observant work, right down to the scar on the nose. Close by, **Rogier van der Weyden**'s *The Lamentation of Christ* is a harrowing picture of death and sorrow, Christ's head hanging down toward the earth, surrounded by the faces of the mourners, each with a particular expression of anguish and pain. **Quentin Matsys** was the first major artist to work in Antwerp, where he was made a Master of the Guild in 1519. An influential figure, the focus of his work was the attempt to imbue his religious pictures with spiritual sensitivity, and his *Descent from the Cross* is a fine example – Christ's suffering face under the weight of the Cross contrasted with the grinning, taunting onlookers behind.

Proceeding in a counterclockwise direction, through a series of rooms on either side of the Italianate dining room, exhibits include two giant allegorical canvases by Jan Sanders van Hemessen; Lucas Cranach the Younger's spirited *Man with a Red Beard*; and two works by **Hans Holbein the Younger**, a striking *Portrait of Robert*

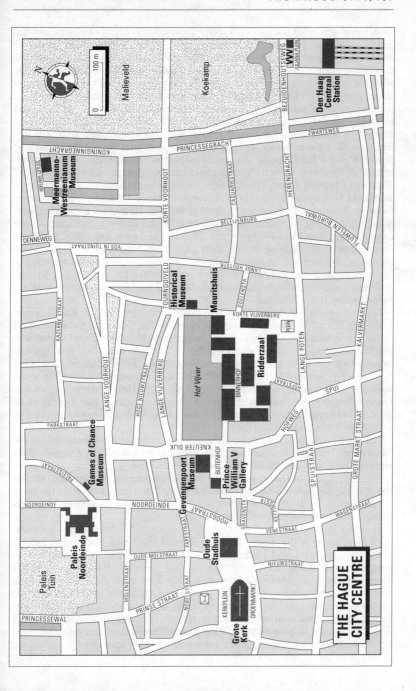

THE HAGUE CITY CENTRE

Den Haag Centraal Station

VVV

JUIIANAPLEIN

BEZUIDENHOUTSEWEG

ZWARTEWEG

Mahieveld

Koekamp

PRINCESSEGRACHT

HERENGRACHT

FLUWEELEN BURGWAL

KONINGINNEGRACHT

NIEUWE UITLEG

Meermanno-Westreenianum Museum

KORTE VOORHOUT

CASUARIESTRAAT

BELEIJENBURG

DENNEWEG

VOS IN TUINSTRAAT

LANGE HOUTSTR

KAZERNE STRAAT

TOURNOOIVELD

Historical Museum

Mauritshuis

DOELENSTR

KORTE VIJVERBERG

PLEIN

LANGE VOORHOUT

HOGE NIEUWSTRAAT

LANGE VIJVERBERG

Hof Vijver

Ridderzaal

BINNERHOF

LANGE POTEN

HOFSTRAAT

KALVERMARKT

PARKSTRAAT

Games of Chance Museum

KNEUTER DIJK

BUITENHOF

SPUI

HOFWEG

PALEISSTRAAT

Gevengenpoort Museum

Prince William V Gallery

GRAVENSTR

KETTI STR

SPUISTRAAT

GROTE MARKT STRAAT

NOORDEINDE

NOORDEINDE

HOOGSTRAAT

PAPESTRAAT

VENESTRAAT

WAGENSTRAAT

Paleis Noordeinde

OUDE MOLSTRAAT

Oude Stadhuis

NIEUWSTRAAT

Paleis Tuin

MOLENSTRAAT

NOBEL STRAAT

PRINSE STRAAT

KERKPLEIN

Grote Kerk

GROENMARKT

PRINCESSEWAL

N

100 m

0

Cheeseman, where all the materials – the fur collar, the falcon's feathers and the cape – seem to take on the appropriate texture, and his *Portrait of Jane Seymour*, one of several pictures commissioned by Henry VIII, who sent him abroad to paint matrimonial candidates. Holbein's vibrant technique was later to land him in hot water: an over-flattering portrait of Anne of Cleves swayed Henry into an unhappy marriage with his "Flanders' Mare" that was to last only six months.

Of a number of paintings by **Adriaen Brouwer**, *Quarrel at a Card Table* and *Inn with Drunken Peasants* are two of the better known, with thick, rough brush-strokes recording contemporary Flemish lowlife. Brouwer could approach this subject with some authority, as he spent most of his brief life in either tavern or prison. **Peter Paul Rubens**, the acclaimed painter and diplomat, was a contemporary of Brouwer, though the two could hardly be more dissimilar: Rubens' *Portrait of Isabella Brant*, his first wife, is a typically grand, rather statuesque work, not perhaps as intriguing as *Adam and Eve in Paradise*, a collaboration between Rubens, who painted the figures, and **Jan Brueghel the Elder**, who filled in the dreamlike animals and landscape behind. In the same room are two examples of the work of Rubens' chief assistant, **Anthony van Dyck**, a portrait specialist who found fame at the court of English King Charles I. His *Pieter Stevens of Antwerp* and *Quinton Simons of Antwerp* are good early examples of his tendency to flatter and ennoble that no doubt helped him into the job. Nearby, and again showing the influence of Rubens, is the robust *Adoration of the Shepherds* by Jacob Jordaens.

On the **second-floor** landing, the broad brush-strokes of **Frans Hals'** *Laughing Boy* are far removed from the restrained style he was forced to adopt in his more familiar paintings of the burghers of Haarlem. **Carel Fabritius**, pupil of Rembrandt and (possibly) teacher of Vermeer, was killed in a gunpowder explosion at Delft when he was only twenty-two. Few canvases survive but an exquisite exception is *The Goldfinch*, a curious, almost impressionistic work, with the bird reduced to a blur of colour. One of his Delft contemporaries was Gerard Houckgeest, who specialized in church interiors, like *The Tomb of William of Orange*, a minutely observed study of architectural lines lightened by expanses of white marble.

Off the second-floor landing, on the left at the front of the museum, is the Mauritshuis' most famous painting, **Jan Vermeer's** *View of Delft*, a superb townscape of 1658, with the fine lines of the city drawn beneath a cloudy sky, a patchwork of varying light and shade – though the dispassionate, photographic quality the painting has in reproduction is oddly lacking in the large canvas. In the same room, Gerard Ter Borch's *Lice Hunt* is in striking contrast to Vermeer's detachment, a vignette of seventeenth-century domestic life.

Heading in a counterclockwise direction, other highlights include the busy, stick-like figures of the *Winter Scene* by Hendrik Avercamp, the deaf and dumb artist from Kampen, and Paulus Potter's lifelike *Young Bull*, a massive canvas complete with dung and rather frightening testicles. Best known of the **Rembrandts** is the *Anatomy Lesson of Dr Tulp*, from 1632, the artist's first commission in Amsterdam. The peering pose of the "students" who lean over the corpse solved the problem of emphasis falling on the body rather than the subjects of the portrait, who were in fact members of the surgeons' guild. Hopefully Tulp's skills as an anatomist were better than his medical advice, which included the recommendation that his patients drink fifty cups of tea a day.

Dotted throughout the museum are no fewer than thirteen paintings by **Jan Steen**, including a wonderfully riotous picture carrying the legend "The way you hear it, is the way you sing it" – a parable on the young learning bad habits from the old – and a typically salacious *Girl Eating Oysters*.

The rest of the city centre

A few metres to the west of the Binnenhof, the **Gevangenpoort**, Buitenhof 33 (Prisoner's Gate Museum; Mon–Fri 10am–4pm, Sun 1–4pm; hourly tours only, last tour 4pm; *f*5), was originally part of the city fortifications. Used as a prison until the nineteenth century, it now contains an array of instruments of torture and punishment centred around its Chamber of Horrors. As well as the guillotine blades, racks and gallows, the old cells are in a good state of preservation – including the *ridderkamer* for the more privileged captive. Here Cornelius de Witt, Burgomaster of Dordrecht, was imprisoned before he and his brother Johan, another staunch Republican and leader of the States of Holland, were dragged out and murdered by an Orangist mob in 1672. The brothers were shot, beheaded and cut into pieces which were then auctioned to the crowd; Johan's tongue is preserved for a macabre posterity in the storerooms of the Gemeentemuseum. The Gevangenpoort is understandably popular; join the line about fifteen minutes before each hourly tour to guarantee a place.

Down the street at Buitenhof 35, the **Prince William V Gallery** (Tues–Sun 11am–4pm; *f*2.50, or free with Mauritshuis ticket) has paintings by Rembrandt, Jordaens and Paulus Potter among others, but it's more interesting as an example of an eighteenth-century gallery – or "cabinet" as they were known. The fashion then was to sandwich paintings together in a cramped patchwork from floor to ceiling: but though it's faithful to the period, this makes viewing difficult for eyes trained by spacious modern museums.

A five-minute walk away to the west, and easily the best of The Hague's old churches, St Jacobskerk or the **Grote Kerk** (July & Aug Mon 11am–4pm; free; otherwise closed to the public except during exhibitions, when it's usually open Mon–Fri 11am–4pm, Sun 1–5pm) is a hall church with an exhilarating sense of breadth and warmly decorated vaulting. The one thing you can't miss, as it's placed where the high altar should be, is the memorial to the unmemorable Admiral Opdam, who was blown up with his ship during the little-remembered naval battle of Lowestoft in 1665. Keep an eye open for the Renaissance pulpit: similar to the one in Delft's Oude Kerk, it has carved panels framing the apostles in false perspective. For the energetic, the church tower (open Wed at noon for groups of 8–10 people; ☎365 8665) provides blustery views over the town.

Back in the centre, **Lange Voorhout** is fringed by an impressive spread of diplomatic mansions and the *Hotel des Indes*, where the ballerina Anna Pavlova died in 1931 and where today you stand the best chance of being flattened by a chauffeur-driven limousine. Just to the east, the **Meermanno-Westreenianum Museum**, Prinsessegracht 30 (Mon–Sat 1–5pm; *f*3.50), has a small collection of remarkably well-preserved medieval illuminated manuscripts and Bibles; and nearby, the **Hague Historical Museum**, Korte Vijverberg 7 (Tues–Fri 11am–5pm, Sat & Sun noon–5pm; *f*7.50), mixes local history with temporary exhibitions on topical issues.

To the immediate west of Lange Voorhout, the sixteenth-century **Paleis Noordeinde** (no admission) is one of several royal buildings that lure tourists to this part of town. In 1980, Queen Juliana abdicated in favour of her daughter

Beatrix, who proceeded to return the royal residence from the province of Utrecht to The Hague. Despite the queen's attempts to demystify the monarchy, there's no deterring the enthusiasts who fill the expensive "Royal Tours" around the peripheries of the palace and Beatrix's other residence just outside town, the seventeenth-century **Huis ten Bosch** (literally "House in the Woods"; no admission). Across from the palace on Paleisstraat, the brand-new **Games of Chance Museum** (Mon–Fri 9am-4pm; free) is worth a glance for its small displays on the popular Dutch lotteries, dating back to 1496, though nothing is labelled in English yet.

Much of the rest of the centre is drab and dreary, an apparently unformulated mixture of the stately old and the brashly new (the giant *Babylon* shopping complex by the Centraal Station wins the ugliness award). During the war years the occupying German forces built a V2 launching site just outside the city: as a result it was almost as thoroughly bombed by the Allies as its neighbour Rotterdam had been by the Luftwaffe.

North of the city centre

Ten minutes' walk north of the centre along Noordeinde and accessible by trams #7 and #8, the **Panorama Mesdag**, Zeestraat 65b (Mon–Sat 10am–5pm, Sun noon–5pm; *f*6), was designed in the late nineteenth century by Hendrik Mesdag, banker turned painter and local citizen become Hague School luminary. His unremarkable seascapes are tinged with an unlikable bourgeois sentimentality, but there's no denying the achievement of his panorama, a depiction of Scheveningen as it would have appeared in 1881. Completed in four months with help from his wife and the young G H Breitner, the painting is so naturalistic that it takes a few moments for the skills of lighting and perspective to become apparent. Five minutes' walk from the Panorama at Laan van Meerdervoort 7f is the house Mesdag bought as a home and gallery. At the time it overlooked one of his favourite subjects, the dunes, the inspiration for much of his work, and today contains the **Mesdag Museum** (Tues–Sat 10am–5pm, Sun 1–5pm). His collection includes a number of Hague School paintings which, like his own work, take the seascapes of the nearby coast as their subject. There are also paintings by Corot, Rousseau, Delacroix and Millet, though none of them represents the artists' best achievements. Perhaps the most interesting exhibits are the florid and distinctive paintings of Antonio Mancini, whose oddly disquieting subjects are reminiscent of Klimt.

The Peace Palace

Round the corner from the Mesdag Museum, framing the Carnegieplein, the **Peace Palace** (occasionally closed to visitors during court sittings; otherwise Mon–Fri hourly guided tours at 10am, 11am, 2pm, 3pm, June–Sept also at 4pm; *f*5; check with the VVV for times of tours in English) is home to the Court of International Justice, and, for all the wrong reasons, is a monument to the futility of war. Toward the end of the nineteenth century, Tsar Nicholas II called an international conference for the peaceful reconciliation of national problems. The result was the First Hague Peace Conference of 1899 whose purpose was to "help find a lasting peace and, above all, a way of limiting the progressive development of existing arms". This in turn led to the formation of a Permanent Court of Arbitration housed obscurely in The Hague until the American industrialist Andrew Carnegie gave $1.5 million for a new building – the Peace Palace. These honorable aims came to nothing with the mass slaughter of World War I: just as the donations of tapestries, urns, marble and stained glass were arriving from all over the world, so Europe's military commanders were preparing their offensives. Backed by a massive law library, fifteen judges are still in action today, conducting trade matters in English and diplomatic affairs in French. Widely respected and generally considered neutral, their judgments are nevertheless not binding.

The Gemeentemuseum, Museon and Omniversum

North of the Peace Palace, the **Gemeentemuseum**, Stadhouderslaan 41 (Tues–Sun 11am–5pm; *f*8; bus #4 from Centraal Station), is arguably the best and certainly the most diverse of The Hague's many museums. Designed by H P Berlage in the 1930s, it's generally considered to be his masterpiece, although its layout can be confusing, and the labelling is erratic. However, the musical instruments are outstanding – especially the harpsichords and early pianos – and the Islamic ceramics are extraordinary. The manageable Delft collection is among the world's finest and, while the collection of modern art is frustrating, it does attempt to outline the development of Dutch painting through the Romantic, Hague and Expressionist schools to the De Stijl movement. **Mondrian**, most famous member of the De Stijl group, dominates this part of the gallery: the museum has the world's largest collection of his paintings, though much of it consists of (deservedly) unfamiliar early works painted before he evolved the abstraction of form into geometry and pure colour for which he's best known.

Adjoining the Gemeentemuseum is a modern building that houses the **Museon** (Tues–Fri 10am–5pm, Sat & Sun noon–5pm; *f*7), a sequence of non-specialist exhibitions of human activities related to the history of the earth. Self-consciously internationalist, it's aimed at school parties, as is the adjoining **Omniversum** or "Space Theatre" (shows on the hour, Tues–Wed 10am–5pm, Thurs–Sun 10am–9pm; *f*17.50). A planetarium in all but name, it possesses all the technical gadgetry you'd expect.

The Madurodam Miniature Town

Halfway between The Hague and Scheveningen, the **Madurodam Miniature Town** (April–Sept daily 9am–10pm; Oct–March daily 9am–5pm; *f*19.50), reachable on tram #1 or #9, is heavily plugged by the tourist authorities, though its origins are more interesting than the rather trite and expensive present, a copy of a Dutch town on a 1.5 scale. The original money was put up by one J M L Maduro, who wished to establish a memorial to his son who had distinguished himself during the German invasion of 1940 and died in Dachau concentration camp five years later. There's a memorial to him just by the entrance, and profits from the Miniature Town are used for general Dutch social and cultural activities. The replica town itself is popular with children and much as you'd expect; the attached **Sand World** (same hours), a recently added collection of sand sculptures, is rather more engaging.

Eating and drinking

There are plenty of cheap places to **eat** around the town centre. They include *Greve*, at Torenstraat 138, north of Grote Kerk, for snacks and sizeable Dutch meals; *Pinelli*, on the way to the Grote Kerk at DAG Groenmarkt 31, for great pizzas; *De Apendans* at Herenstraat 13, a popular, no-frills restaurant with a simple Dutch menu from *f*15; *Eethuis Nirwana*, Prinsestraat 65, an Indonesian café; and

Eethuis Neighbours, Papestraat 28, for large portions of local food. For something more interesting, head along Denneweg and Frederikstraat, just north of Lange Voorhout, on and around which are several good options. *De Dageraad*, Hooikade 4 (☎364 5666), is a popular vegetarian restaurant; *Pannekoekhuys Maliehuys* at Maliestraat 8–10 (☎346 2474), has pancakes and steaks; while *Plato*, at Frederikstraat 32, has an excellent French/Dutch menu.

There are loads of good **bars** scattered around town, too. In the busy Grote Markt, south of the Grote Kerk, *Zwarte Ruiter* and the cavernous *De Boterwaag* face each other across the square and boast a wide range of beers and a studenty clientele. Along Papestraat, *Cafe de Paap* at no. 32 has occasional live music while the *Old-Timer* at 23a is a more peaceful option. On Plein, just east of the Binnenhof, *Berger* at no. 18 and *Plein 19* attract a young professional crowd, while a few blocks north, on Denneweg, there are some mellow bars among the antique shops – try *De Pompernickel* at no. 27, *De Landeman* at no. 48, and *2005* opposite. A little south of town, *De Paas* occupies a lovely spot by the canal on Dunne Bierkade, just west of Wagenstraat.

The **North Sea Jazz Festival**, held every year in mid-July at the Nederlands Congresgebouw, Churchillplein 10, is The Hague's most prestigious event, attracting international media coverage and many of the world's most famous musicians. Details of performances are available from the VVV, which will also reserve accommodation, virtually impossible to find after the festival has begun. Various kinds of tickets can be purchased; a *dagkaart*, for example, valid for an entire day, costs ƒ80.

Listings

Bikes Can be rented from either of The Hague's train stations for ƒ8 a day (ƒ6 with a valid train ticket), plus a ƒ100 deposit.

Car rental *Achilles*, Prinses Marijkestraat 5 (☎381 1811); *Avis*, Theresiastraat 216 (☎385 0698); *Budget*, Mercuriusweg 9 (☎382 0609); *Europcar* (at the *Hotel Sofitel*), Koningin Julianaplein 35 (☎385 1708).

Chemists Night services listed in newspapers and at the VVV.

Dentist ☎397 4491.

Embassies *Australia*, Carnegielaan 12 (☎310 8200); *Canada*, Sophialaan 7 (☎361 4111); *Ireland*, Dr Kuyperstraat 9 (☎363 0993); *UK*, Lange Voorhout 10 (☎364 5800); *USA*, Lange Voorhout 102 (☎310 9209).

Gay scene There are several gay bars: try *Boko*, Nieuwe Schoolstraat 2, *Stairs*, Nieuwe Schoolstraat 11, or the gay/straight *de Landeman*, Denneweg 48.

Hospital Ambulances ☎06 11; general medical care day ☎345 5300, night ☎346 9669.

Information A free monthly magazine with details of concerts, theatre performances, special events and entertainments in The Hague and environs is available from the VVV.

Markets General: Herman Costerstraat (Mon, Wed, Fri & Sat 8am–5pm). Food: Markthof, Gedempte Gracht/Spui (Mon 11am–6pm, Tues–Sat 9am–6pm). Antiques, books and curios: Lange Voorhout (mid-May to Sept Thurs & Sun 10am–6pm); Plein (Oct to mid-May Thurs 10am–6pm).

Police Emergency ☎310 4911; tourist assistance service ☎310 3274.

Post office Nobelstraat; Prinsenstraat; Kerkplein (Mon–Fri 8.30am–6.30pm, Thurs also 6.30–8.30pm, Sat 9am–4pm).

Taxis *HTMC* ☎390 7722; *HCT* ☎364 2828.

Scheveningen

Situated on the coast about 4km from the centre of The Hague, the old fishing port of **SCHEVENINGEN*** has none of its neighbour's businesslike air, enjoying instead its status as Holland's top coastal resort, attracting more than nine million visitors a year to its beach, pier and casino. It's not a particularly attractive place, but it can make a good alternative base if you're keen to see something of The Hague, since, not surprisingly, hotels are cheaper and more plentiful. At certain times of year, too, it's worth a special visit – in mid-June for example, when the town hosts a massive international **kite festival** that takes over the beach and much of the town.

Scheveningen was a fashionable resort in the nineteenth century, but faded after the 1920s; it's currently being redeveloped as an all-year resort. The centre of town is called **Scheveningen Bad**, grouped around the massive **Kurhaus** hotel that's the most potent symbol of the town's bygone era. Sadly, it's the only reminder, the rest of the town centre is a rather tacky mix of shopping precinct, guesthouses and amusement arcades, both around the hotel and along the busy seafront. Inside, the *Kurhaus* has been refurbished and is worth a peek into its main central hall, which looks much as it would have done in the town's heyday, richly frescoed, with mermaids and semi-clad maidens cavorting high above the gathered diners. You can enjoy the atmosphere for the price of a cup of coffee, or attend one of the classical concerts occasionally held here.

The town **museum** at Neptunusstraat 92 (Tues–Sat 10am–5pm, April–Oct also Mon; ƒ3.50) recaptures some of the atmosphere of old Scheveningen, with figures in nineteenth-century costume, dioramas showing the cramped conditions on board the primitive fishing boats, and items such as nets and compasses from the boats themselves. Towards the beach, the brand-new **Statues on the Sea museum** (Beelden aan Zee), Harteveltstraat 1 (Tues–Sun 11am–5pm; ƒ6) has a thoughtfully arranged collection of modern sculpture, some of it outdoors on a patio overlooking the sea. Nearby at Strandweg 13, the children-friendly **Sea Life Centre** (Sept–June daily 10am–6pm, July–Aug daily 10am–9pm; ƒ14) has an aquarium with sharks and rays and exhibits on North Sea fish and crustaceans.

But most people come here for the **beach** – a marvellous strand, though very crowded in summer, and it's hard to be sure about the condition of the water. The **pier** isn't especially impressive either, its appendages packed with the rods of fishermen and various amusements, and you're better off strolling north to emptier beaches and dunes in the **Oostduinpark**. Otherwise, a kilometre or so in the opposite direction, Scheveningen's harbour and fishing port still flourish in the more workaday environs of **Scheveningen Haven**: the site of a large container depot and an early morning **fish auction**, by the more northerly of the two docks, at Visafslagweg 1 (Mon–Sat 7–10am) – though this is very much a technical, computerized affair. Boat trips on the **North Sea** (June–Sept daily at 4pm) start from Dr Lelykade, beside the southern dock – tram #8 from Den Haag HS – and fishing excursions can be arranged from the same place.

---

* One of the difficulties involved in getting to Scheveningen is pronouncing the name. During World War II, resistance groups tested suspected Nazi infiltrators by getting them to say "Scheveningen" – an impossible feat for Germans, apparently, and not much easier for English-speakers.

Practicalities

Trams #1, #7 and #9 run from Den Haag CS to Scheveningen, stopping by the *Kurhaus*; from Den Haag HS, take tram #8. Tram #1 also connects with Delft. If you're staying in Scheveningen, the **VVV**, at Gevers Deynootweg 1134 (Jan to mid-April & Oct–Dec Mon–Sat 9am–5.30pm, Sun 10am–5pm; mid-April to June & Sept Mon–Sat 10am–6.30pm, Sun 10am–5pm; July–Aug Mon–Sat 10am–8pm, Sun 10am–5pm; ☎06/3403 5051, 75c per min) can find you a room in a private home (reservations ☎363 5676). Failing that, there are plenty of **hotels**. Try *Bali*, Badhuisweg 1 (☎350 2434, fax 354 0363; ②); *Albion*, Gevers Deynootweg 118–120 (☎355 7987; ②); or one of the group on the seafront Zeekant, such as the comfortable *Aquarius*, nos. 107–110 (☎ & fax 354 3684; ②), and the *Strandhotel* at no. 111 (☎354 0193, fax 354 3558; ②). There are two **youth hostels**: the *Scheveningen*, at Gevers Deynootweg 2 (☎354 7003; ②), and *Marion*, at Havenkade 3a (☎354 3501; ②).

As for **eating**, there are a string of cheap if unexciting places along the seafront and, behind the *Kurhaus*, good Italian food at *La Galleria*, Gevers Deynootplein 120. In Scheveningen Haven there are some excellent waterside restaurants with guaranteed fresh fish: try the simple and inexpensive *Haven Restaurant* at Treilerdwarsweg 2 (☎354 5783) or, round the corner at Dr Lelykade 5, the more upmarket *Ducdalf* (☎355 7692). For evening **drinking**, try the *Kings' Arms*, a mock-English pub outside the *Kurhaus* on Gevers Deynootplein. Evening entertainment is limited but there's an eight-screen **cinema** (☎351 5738) behind the *Kurhaus*.

Delft

DELFT has considerable charm: gabled red-roofed houses stand beside tree-lined canals, and the pastel colours of the brickwork and bridges give the town a faded, placid tranquillity – one that from spring onwards is systematically destroyed by tourists. They arrive in their air-conditioned busloads and descend to congest the narrow streets, buy an overpriced piece of gift pottery and photograph the spire of the Nieuwe Kerk. And beneath all the tourists, the gift shops and the tearooms, old Delft itself gets increasingly difficult to find.

Why is Delft so popular? Apart from its prettiness, the obvious answer is **Delftware**, the clunky and monotonous blue-and-white ceramics to which the town gave its name in the seventeenth century. If you've already slogged through the vast collection in Amsterdam's Rijksmuseum it needs no introduction; and though production of the "real" Delftware is down to a trickle, cheap mass-produced copies have found a profitable niche in today's shops. For those interested, the **Huis Lambert van Meerten Museum** at Oude Delft 199 (Tues–Sat 10am–5pm, Sun 1–5pm; f3.50) has the town's best collection of Delft, and a splendid collection of tiles from around the world, while the *De Porceleyne Fles* factory at Rotterdamsweg 196 (Mon–Sat 9am–5pm, Sun 10am–5pm; f3.50) continues to produce Delftware and is open for visits.

Another reason for Delft's popularity is the **Vermeer** connection. The artist was born in the town and died here, too – leaving a wife, eleven children and a huge debt to the local baker. He had given the man two pictures as security, and his wife bankrupted herself trying to retrieve them. Only traces remain of the town as depicted in Vermeer's famous *View of Delft*, now in the

Mauritshuis in The Hague. You'll find them most easily on foot – it's not a difficult place to explore. The **Markt** is the best place to start, a central point of reference with the Renaissance Stadhuis at one end and the Nieuwe Kerk at the other. Lined with cafés, restaurants and teenagers blaring disco music on ghetto-blasters, it really gets going with the Thursday general market – not, therefore, the ideal day to visit.

The **Nieuwe Kerk** (March–Oct Mon–Sat 9am–6pm; Nov–Feb Mon–Sat 11am–4pm; *f*4, ticket allows access to Oude Kerk) is new only in comparison with the Oude Kerk, as there's been a church on this site since 1381. Most of the original structure, however, was destroyed in the great fire that swept over Delft in 1536, and the remainder in a powder magazine explosion a century later – a disaster, incidentally, which claimed the life of the artist Carel Fabritius, Rembrandt's greatest pupil and (debatably) the teacher of Vermeer. The most

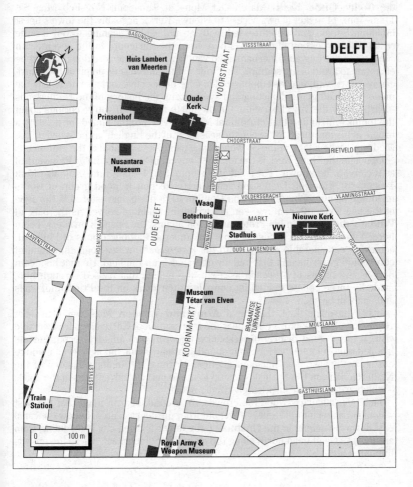

striking part of the restoration is in fact the most recent – the 100-metre spire (closes 30min before the church; *f*2.50), replaced in 1872 and from whose summit there's a great view of the town. Unless you're a Dutch monarchist, the church's interior is rather uninspiring: it contains the burial vaults of the Dutch royal family, the most recent addition being Queen Wilhelmina in 1962. Only the mausoleum of William the Silent grabs your attention, an odd hodgepodge of styles concocted by Hendrik de Keyser, architect also of the Stadhuis opposite.

South of the Stadhuis, signs direct you to the **Koornmarkt**, one of the town's most characteristic seventeenth-century streets. At no. 67 is the **Museum Tétar van Elven** (May to mid-Oct Tues–Sat 1–5pm; *f*3.50), slightly drab in appearance but an authentic restoration of the eighteenth-century patrician house that was the studio and home of Paul Tétar van Elven, a provincial and somewhat forgettable artist/collector. **Wynhaven**, another old canal, leads to Hippolytusbuurt and the Gothic **Oude Kerk** (March–Oct Mon–Sat 9am–6pm; Nov–Feb Mon–Sat 11am–4pm; *f*4, ticket allows access to Nieuwe Kerk), arguably the town's finest building. Simple and unbuttressed, with an unhealthily leaning tower, it's the result of a succession of churches here from the thirteenth to the seventeenth century; the strong and unornamented vaulting proves interiors don't have to be elaborate to avoid being sombre. The pride of the church is its pulpit of 1548, intricately carved with figures emphasized in false perspective, but also notable is the modern stained glass, depicting and symbolizing the history of the Netherlands – particularly the 1945 liberation – in the north transept. If you're curious about the tombs – including that of Admiral Maarten van Tromp, famed for hoisting a broom at his masthead to "sweep the seas clear of the English" as he sailed up the Medway – take a look at the *Striking Points* pamphlet available at the entrance.

Opposite the Oude Kerk is the former Convent of Saint Agatha or **Prinsenhof** as it came to be known (Tues–Sat 10am–5pm, Sun 1–5pm; June–Aug also Mon 1–5pm; *f*5). Housing Delft's municipal art collection (a good group of works including paintings by Aertsen and Honthorst), it has been restored in the style of the late sixteenth century – an era when the building served as the base of **William the Silent** in his Protestant revolt against the Spanish invaders. From here William planned sorties against the imperial Catholic troops of Phillip II, achieving considerable success with his *Watergeuzen* or sea-beggars, a kind of commando-guerrilla unit that initially operated from England. He met his death here at the hands of a French assassin: the bullets that passed through him, made by three pellets welded into one, left their mark on the Prinsenhof walls and can still be seen.

If you have the time, the **Royal Army and Weapon Museum** (Tues–Sat 10am–5pm, Sun 1–5pm; *f*4.50), near the train station at Korte Geer 1, is worth a visit. It has a good display of weaponry, uniforms and military accoutrements labelled only in Dutch – which may sound supremely dull, but isn't, even if you're not an enthusiast. The museum attempts to trace the military history of the Netherlands from the Spanish wars up to the imperialist adventures of the 1950s – which are shown in surprisingly candid detail.

Finally, particularly when the crowds are around, bear in mind that the best way to get a feel for old Delft is to get out from the centre a little. Follow the canal east down Oosteinde to the **Oostpoort**, the only surviving city gate, dating from around 1400, and head north along the main Rijn Schiekanaal, where the crowds thin out a little.

Practicalities

From the train station it's a short walk into town and the **VVV** at Markt 85 (April–Oct Mon–Fri 9am–6pm, Sat 9am–5pm, Sun 10am–3pm; Nov–March closes 5.30pm Mon–Fri; ☎015/212 6100). The cheapest **accommodation** is in the pensions around the station or the Markt; details from the VVV. The lowest-priced hotels are also around the Markt: *Les Compagnons* at no. 61 (☎015/214 0102; ②), *'t Raedthuys* at no. 38 (☎015/212 5115; ②) and *Monopole* at no. 48 (☎015/212 3059; ②). More upmarket and canal-side, there's *Leeuwenbrug*, Koornmarkt 16 (☎015/214 7741, fax 215 9759; ③), and the very comfortable *de Ark*, Koornmarkt 65 (☎015/215 7999; ④). There's a **campsite**, *De Delftse Hout*, Kortftlaan 5 (bus #60 from the station) which is open from April to October.

Most places to **eat** around the Markt are a little overpriced, although *Sunrise Pub*, at no. 66a is okay for a quick snack. *Grand Cafe Central*, Wijnhaven 4, is also popular for snacks and heavier meals, and the day menus at *'t Walletje*, just south of Markt at Burgwal 7, are usually good value. *La Fontanella*, Voldersgracht 8, has decent Italian food from around *f*15 while *V*, at Voorstraat 9, attracts a big student crowd to its large bar and restaurant. *Locus Publicus*, at Brabantse Turfmarkt 67, is another popular hangout, serving a staggering array of beers as well as snacks.

Rotterdam

ROTTERDAM lies at the heart of a maze of rivers and artificial waterways that form the seaward outlet of the rivers Rijn (Rhine) and Maas (Meuse). An important port as early as the fourteenth century, it was one of the major cities of the Dutch Republic, sharing its periods of fortune and decline, until the nineteenth century when it was caught unawares, for the city was ill-prepared for the industrial expansion of the Ruhr, the development of larger ships and the silting up of the Maas. Prosperity returned in a big way with the digging of an entirely new ship canal (the "Nieuwe Waterweg") between 1866 and 1872, and was only brought to a temporary halt during World War II when, without warning, the Germans bombed the city centre to pieces in 1940 and systematically destroyed the port in 1944.

The postwar period saw the rapid reconstruction of the docks and the town centre, and great efforts were made to keep Rotterdam ahead of its rivals. Consequently, when huge container ships and oil tankers made many port facilities obsolete, the Dutch were equal to the challenge and built an entirely new deep-sea port some 25km to the west of the old town. Completed in 1968, the **Europoort** juts out into the North Sea and can accommodate the largest of ships, contributing to Rotterdam's handling of 300 million tonnes of fuel, grain and materials needed or sold by western Europe each year.

Rapid postwar rebuilding transformed Rotterdam's town centre into a giant covered shopping area, a sterile and formless assembly of concrete and glass. This prospect of docks and shops probably sounds unalluring, but Rotterdam has its moments: in the **Boymans-Van Beuningen Museum** it has one of the best –

The telephone code for Rotterdam is ☎010

and most overlooked – galleries in the country, and between the central modernity and dockland sleaze is **Delfshaven**, an old area that survived the bombs. By way of contrast, there's **Oudehaven**. As its name suggests it's an old – in fact the city's oldest – harbour, and was also bombed during the war. However, it's been dazzlingly redeveloped, and is now home to a host of popular bars and cafés. There's not much else, but redevelopment hasn't obliterated Rotterdam's earthy character: the prostitution and dope peddling are for real, not for tourists; if you want to avoid the high spots of the low life, stick to the centre.

Arrival, information and accommodation

Rotterdam has a large and confusing centre edged by its main rail terminus, **Centraal Station**, that serves as the hub of a useful tram and metro system for the city and its suburbs – though it's a seamy, hostile place late at night. The **VVV** office, ten minutes' walk away at Coolsingel 67 (Mon–Thurs & Sat 9am–7pm, Fri 9am–9pm, Sun 10am–5pm; ☎06/340 34065, 50c per min), provides all the usual tourist information, plus a useful city brochure incorporating a street map for ƒ2.50, and free maps of the tram, bus and underground system, divided into zones for the calculation of fares (two sections of a *strippenkaart* or ƒ4 for a single trip in the central zone). It also sells theatre and concert tickets.

The VVV's **accommodation** booking service can be handy in summer, when cheaper hotels tend to fill up, but it won't book pensions for you. There are a clutch of reasonably priced hotels a kilometre or so to the southwest of the station, easily accessible by tram. These include the small *Roxane*, 's-Gravendijkwal 14 (☎436 6109, fax 436 2944; tram #1, #7 or #9; ②), and the larger and more comfortable *Wilgenhof*, Heemraadssingel 92–94 (☎476 2526, fax 477 2611; tram #1 or #7; ③). To the immediate north of Centraal Station, the *Bienvenue*, by the canal at Spoorsingel 24 (☎466 9394, fax 467 7475; ②), is excellent value, as is the *Holland*, nearby at Provenierssingel 7 (☎465 3100, fax 467 0280; tram #3, #5 or #9; ②). The *Breitner* is another good option, close to the Boymans Museum at Breitnerstraat 23 (☎436 0262, fax 436 4091; metro Dijkzigt or tram #4 or #5; ③). The **youth hostel** is 3km from the station at Rochussenstraat 107 (☎436 5763; tram #4 or #6, or metro Dijkzigt & bus #39); the nearest **campsite** is north of the station at Kanaalweg 84 (☎415 9772; bus #32). The **Sleep-In**, Mauritsweg 29b, a five-minute walk south of the station (☎412 1420), is open mid-June to mid-August for very cheap dormitory accommodation.

The city

From Centraal Station, Kruisplein leads south onto Westersingel/Mauritsweg, cutting this part of the city into two sections – to the west is the deteriorated housing of many of the city's migrant workers, and to the east is the **Lijnbaan**, Europe's first pedestrianized shopping precinct, completed in 1953. The Lijnbaan connects into a baffling series of apparently endless shopping areas hemmed in by Weena, Coolsingel, Westblaak and Mauritsweg. To the east of Coolsingel, just off Beursplein, the fifteenth-century **St Laurenskerk** (Grote Kerk; Tues–Sat 10am–4pm; Oct–May closed Thurs; free) has been the object of a clumsy renovation which has left it cold and soulless. Nearby, and marginally more exciting, is the redevelopment of the **Blaak** area with a new central library adjoining a remarkable series of cubist houses, replacing a part of the old city centre destroyed by the bombing.

The curious **Kijk-Kubus** (Cube House; March–Oct daily 11am–5pm; Nov–Feb Fri–Sun 11am–5pm; ƒ3.50) is at Overblaak 70, near Blaak train station, offering a rather disorientating tour of an upside-down house where you're likely to bang your head on a beam and feel dizzy if you peer out of the windows.

Heading west, the **Maritime Museum Prins Hendrik** (Tues–Sat 10am–5pm, Sun 11am–5pm; ƒ6) is situated in the old harbour area beside the Leuvehaven.

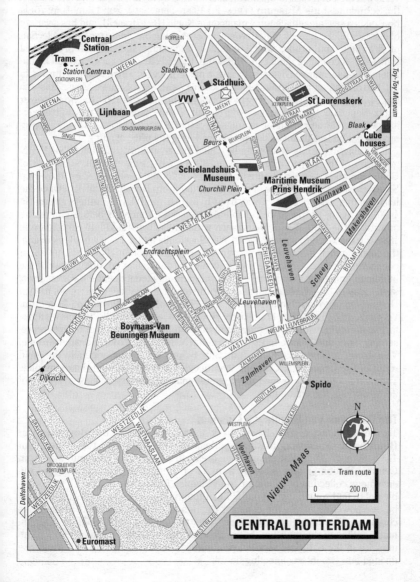

CENTRAL ROTTERDAM

Apart from an enterprising programme of temporary nautical exhibitions, the outside area has been spruced up for the museum's prime exhibit – an immaculately restored mid-nineteenth-century ironclad, the *Buffel*, complete with communal sinks shaped to match the angle of the bows, a couple of ships' figureheads and a string of luxurious officers' cabins.

Across the boulevard to the north, surrounded by highrise apartment buildings, the **Schielandshuis Museum** (Tues–Fri 10am–5pm, Sat & Sun 11am–5pm; *f*6) is housed in a seventeenth-century mansion at Korte Hoogstraat 31, and has a variety of displays on the history of Rotterdam, incorporating the *Atlas van Stolk* collection of drawings and prints, which includes fascinating sketches of pre-colonial Indonesia. A couple of minutes to the south, the old city docks are enclosed by the Boompjes, a former sea dyke that's now a major freeway, which leads southwest to the **Euromast**, on a rather lonely park corner beside the Nieuwe Maas. This was originally just a drab, grey observation platform thrown up in 1960; the **Spacetower** (April–Sept daily 10am–7pm; Oct–March daily 10am–5pm; *f*14.50) was added later, its revolving elevator rising on the outside of the 185-metre tower. The view is spectacular, but no less than you'd expect considering the price of entry.

If nothing in the city centre can be called exactly picturesque, **DELFSHAVEN** goes part of the way to make up for it. It's a good 45-minute walk southwest of Centraal Station – fifteen minutes by tram #4 or #6 (direction Schiedam, tram stop Spanjaardstraat), or a couple of minutes on foot from Delfshaven metro. Once the harbour that served Delft, it was from here that the Pilgrim Fathers set sail in 1620, changing to the more reliable *Mayflower* in Plymouth before continuing onward to the New World. Delfshaven was only incorporated into Rotterdam in 1886 and managed to survive World War II virtually intact. Long a neglected area, the town council has recently recognized its tourist potential and has set about conserving and restoring the whole locality as rapidly as possible. Most of the buildings lining the canals are eighteenth- and nineteenth-century warehouses, seen today as "desirable residences" by the upwardly mobile, who are set to turn Delfshaven into a chichi suburb. The **Dubbelde Palmboom Museum**, Voorhaven 12 (Tues–Sun 11am–5pm; *f*6), once a jenever distillery, is now an historical museum, with a wide-ranging, if unexceptional collection of objects representing work and leisure in the Maas delta. Nearby, the **Zakkendragershuisje**, Voorstraat 13 (Tues–Sat 10am–5pm, Sun 1–5pm; free), was originally the guild room of the Grain Sack Carriers, who decided the allocation of duties by dice. Today, it's a privately owned, fully operational tin foundry, selling a variety of items made in the old moulds.

The Boymans-Van Beuningen Museum

To the northeast of Delfshaven, back toward the centre, the **Boymans-Van Beuningen Museum**, Mathenesserlaan 18–20 (Tues–Sat 10am–5pm, Sun 11am–5pm; *f*7.50), is Rotterdam's one great attraction, a fifteen-minute walk from Centraal Station or accessible by tram #5 or Eendrachtsplein metro. Amid the enormous collection of paintings, from Flemish Masters to Pop Art, it's impossible not to find something to your liking, though the sheer size of the displays can be overpowering, while the constant rotation of exhibits can make guidebooks confusing. The information desk provides an updated and simplified diagrammatic outline of the museum, but in general terms pre-nineteenth-century paintings are in the old wing, modern paintings in the new wing and both wings are divided into two interconnecting floors.

The entrance to the new wing leads to the modern paintings, best known of which are the **Surrealists**. De rigueur for student bedrooms in the 1970s, it's difficult to appreciate Salvador Dali's *Spain* as anything more than the painting of the poster – not that Dali would have been bothered. Other works by René Magritte, Max Ernst and Giorgio de Chirico provide a representative sample of a movement whose images seem to have lost much of their power. Surrealism was never adopted by Dutch artists, though the Magic Realism of **Carel Willink** has its similarities in the precise, hallucinatory technique he uses to distance and perturb the viewer in *Self Portrait with a Pen*. **Charley Toorop**'s *Three Generations* is also realism with an aim to disconcert – the huge bust of her father, Jan, looms in the background and dominates the painting. Most of the rest of the new wing is devoted to a roughly chronological series of galleries exhibiting applied art and design, from the jewellery and household items of the Middle Ages, through Dutch silverware, tiles and glass, to the latest industrial design.

On the first floor, the **Van der Vorm Collection**, under renovation at the time of writing, has paintings from many of Europe's most famous artists, including Monet, Van Gogh, Picasso, Gauguin, Cézanne and Munch, alongside a series of small galleries containing most of the significant artists of the Barbizon and Hague schools, notably **J H Weissenbruch**'s *Strandgezicht*, a beautiful gradation of radiant tones.

Adjoining the Vorm Collection, and arranged in chronological order (from Room 1), are the museum's earlier paintings, beginning with an excellent **Flemish and Nederlandish religious art section**, whose sumptuous *Christ in the House of Martha and Mary* by Pieter Aertsen is outstanding. **Hieronymus Bosch**, famed for his nightmarish visions, is represented by four of his more mainstream works. Usually considered a macabre fantasist, Bosch was actually working to the limits of oral and religious tradition, where biblical themes were depicted as iconographical representations, laden with explicit symbols. In his *St Christopher*, the dragon, the hanged bear and the broken pitcher lurk in the background, representations of danger and uncertainty, whereas the Prodigal Son's attitude to the brothel behind him in *The Wanderer* is deliberately ambivalent. Bosch's technique never absorbed the influences of Renaissance Italy, and his figures in the *Marriage Feast at Cana* are static and unbelievable, uncomfortably

SPECIAL INTEREST MUSEUMS

Accessible by bus and tram from Centraal Station, Rotterdam has a number of special interest **museums**, including a collection of rare dolls and mechanical toys dating from 1700 to 1940 at the *Toy-Toy Museum*, east of the city centre at Groene Wetering 41 (Sun & Mon 11am–4pm; ƒ7.50; tram #3 or #7). The *National Museum of Schools*, south of the station at Nieuwe Markt 1a (Tues–Sat 10am–5pm, Sun 1–5pm; ƒ3.50; metro Blaak), has six fully furnished classrooms of various periods; the ethnological *Museum Voor Volkenkunde*, Willemskade 25, has displays on non-European cultures (Tues–Fri 10am–5pm, Sat & Sun 11am–5pm; ƒ7.50; metro Leuvehaven, tram #5); the Marine Corps museum, *Mariniersmuseum*, on Wynhaven (Tues–Sat 10am–5pm, Sun 11am–5pm; ƒ6; tram #1, #3 or #6), outlines the history of the brigade from its establishment in 1665; the *Trammuseum*, Nieuwe Binnenweg 362 (April–Nov Sat 11am–4pm; free; tram #4), has several interesting old trams; and there are shiny steam trains and engines at the *Steam Depot Museum*, Giessenweg 82 (Sat 10am–5pm; free; bus #38).

arranged around a distorted table. Other works in this section include paintings by **Jan van Scorel**, who was more willing to absorb Italianate styles as in his *Scholar in a Red Cap*; the Bruges artist **Hans Memling**, whose capacity for detail can be seen in his *Two Houses in a Landscape*; **Pieter Brueghel the Elder**'s mysterious, hazy *Tower of Babel*; and **Geertgen tot Sint Jans**' beautiful, delicate *Glorification of the Virgin*.

Further on, a small selection of **Dutch Genre** paintings reflects the tastes of the emergent seventeenth-century middle class. The idea was to depict real-life situations overlaid with a symbolic moral content. Jan Steen's *Extracting the Stone* or *The Physician's Visit* are good humorous examples, while Gerrit Dou's *The Quack*, ostensibly just a passing scene, is full of small cameos of deception – a boy catching a bird, the trapped hare – that refer back to the quack's sham cures.

Dotted across the museum are a number of **Rembrandts**, including two contrasting canvases: an analytic *Portrait of Alotta Adriaensdr*, her ageing illuminated but softened by her white ruff, and a gloomy, indistinct *Blind Tobias and his Wife* painted twenty years later. His intimate *Titus at his Desk* is also in marked contrast to the more formal portrait commissions common to his day. Most of the work of Rembrandt's pupil **Carel Fabritius** was destroyed when he was killed in a Delft gunpowder explosion in 1654; an exception is his *Self-Portrait*, reversing his master's usual technique by lighting the background and placing the subject in shadow.

Waterway excursions

One way of exploring the waterways you can see from the Euromast is on the **Spido cruises** that leave from beside the Willemsplein, to the south of Centraal Station (tram #5 or Leuvehaven metro).

Between April and September tours run every 45 minutes between 9.30am and 5pm, less frequently at other times of year, and take an hour and fifteen minutes; prices start at *f*14.50 per person. They head off past the wharfs, landings, docks and silos of this, the largest port in the world, though it's most impressive at night, when the illuminated ships and refineries gleam like Spielberg spaceships. In season, there are also longer, less frequent trips to Dordrecht, the windmills of Kinderdijk, the Europoort and the Delta Project (see below), from between *f*22.50 and *f*45 per person. Further details are available from the VVV, or the boat operators at Willemsplein (☎413 5400).

The Spido excursion to the series of colossal dams that make up the **Delta Project**, along the seaboard southwest of Rotterdam, only provides the briefest of glances, and it's better to visit by bus, though it'll take you a couple of hours: take the underground to Spijkenisse (30min) and catch bus #104 for Vlissingen (Mon–Sat hourly, Sun every 2hr), which travels along the road that crosses the top of the three dams that restrain the Haringvliet, Grevelingen and Oosterschelde estuaries. For more on the Delta Project and Delta Expo, see *Zeeland, North Brabant and Limburg*, pp.286–288.

Eating and drinking

The best bet for a cheap sit-down **meal** during the day is around the Lijnbaan shopping centre. Dozens of cafes, snack bars and fast-food outlets line the streets, with *dagschotels* generally around *f*12.50. For lunch or dinner, there are a couple of places serving Dutch food on Mauritsweg, between the station and the Boymans museum: *de Eend*, at no. 28, and the slightly better *Het Varken* at no. 43b. There's a decent cafe at the Boymans museum while *De Pijp*, Gaffelstraat 90 (☎436 6896), is a good international restaurant five minutes' walk north of the museum and often crowded in the evening. Oude and Nieuwe Binneweg are lined with cafés and bars – try *De Vijgeboon* at Oude Binneweg 146a and *Rotown* at Nieuwe Binneweg 19, both with affordable dinner menus of Dutch staples. There are seven international menus in the giant *Restaurant Engels* at Stationsplein 45, including Hungarian, Spanish and English food; mostly unexciting and a little overpriced but worth a look if you're nearby.

There are a couple of popular **drinking** places further east: *Cafe Cambrinus*, Blaak 4 beneath the cube houses, has an excellent beer selection and good food, while *Locus Publicus* also attracts a big drinking crowd at Oostzeedijk 364 (tram #3, stop Oostplein). For **music**, *Rotown* is a popular spot, with a live band most nights; the VVV has up-to-date information on local concerts and theatre.

Listings

Airport enquiries Rotterdam Airport, Heathrowbaan 4 (☎446 3455; bus #33).

Bureau de change At most banks (Mon–Fri 9am–4pm) or Centraal Station (Mon–Sat 7.30am–10pm, Sun 9am–10pm).

Car rental *Avis*, Rotterdam Airport (☎415 8842) and Kruisplein 21 (☎433 2233); *Hertz*, Schiekade 986 (☎404 6088); *Europcar*, Pompenburg 646 (☎411 4860).

Chemists 24-hr service details ☎411 0370.

Dental care ☎455 2155.

Football At *Feyenoord* stadium – bus #49 or Stadion train from Centraal Station. Game details from the VVV; most games are on Sundays.

Left Luggage Coin-operated lockers at the train station.

Markets General, including antiques, on Mariniersweg (Tues & Sat 9am–5pm). Stamps, coins and books on Grotekerkplein (Tues & Sat 9.30am–4pm).

Medical assistance ☎411 5504; ambulance ☎0611.

Police Police Station, Doelwater 5 (☎424 2911).

Post office Coolsingel 42 (Mon 11am–6pm, Tues–Thurs 9am–6pm, Fri 8.30am–8.30pm, Sat 9.30am–3pm); Delftseplein 31 (Mon–Fri 8.30am–6pm).

Taxis *Rotterdam taxi* ☎462 6060.

Train enquiries Domestic ☎06/9292; international ☎411 7100.

Gouda and Oudewater

A pretty little place some 25km northeast of Rotterdam, **GOUDA** is almost everything you'd expect of a Dutch country town: a ring of quiet canals that encircle ancient buildings and old docks. More surprisingly, its **Markt**, a ten-minute walk from the train station, is the largest in Holland – a reminder of the town's prominence as a centre of the medieval cloth trade, and later of its success in the manufacture of cheeses and clay pipes.

Gouda's main claim to fame is its **cheese market**, held in the Markt every Thursday morning from June to August. Traditionally, some one thousand local farmers brought their home-produced cheeses here to be weighed, tested and graded for moisture, smell and taste. These details were marked on the cheeses and formed the basis for negotiation between buyer and seller, the exact price set by an elaborate hand clapping system, which itself was based on trust and memory, for deals were never written down. Today, the cheese market is a shadow of its former self, a couple of locals in traditional dress standing outside the Waag, surrounded by modern open-air stands. The promised mixture of food and tradition is mercilessly milked by tour operators, who herd their victims into this rather dreary scene every week – but don't let this put you off a visit, since Gouda's charms are elsewhere.

There's a jazz festival in town in early September and, if you happen to be in the area in mid-December, it's worth phoning the Gouda VVV to find out exactly when the town will be holding its splendid candlelit pre-Christmas festival. All electric lights are extinguished on the main square, which is lit up instead by thousands of candles.

The town

Slap-bang in the middle of the Markt, the **Stadhuis** is an elegant Gothic building dating from 1450, its facade fringed by statues of counts and countesses of Burgundy above a tinkling carillon that plays every half-hour. Nearby, on the north side of the square, the **Waag** is a tidy seventeenth-century building, decorated with a detailed relief of cheese-weighing, now converted into a cheese museum (April–Oct Tues–Sat 10am-5pm & Sun noon–5pm; free). To the south, just off the Markt, **St Janskerk** (March–Oct Mon–Sat 9am–5pm; Nov–Feb Mon–Sat 10am–4pm; *f*3) was built in the sixteenth century and is famous for its magnificent **stained-glass windows**. As well as their intrinsic beauty, the windows show the way religious art changed as Holland moved from a society dominated by the Catholic Church to one dominated by a Calvinist Church. The biblical themes executed by Dirk and Wouter Crabeth between 1555 and 1571, when Holland was still Catholic, have an amazing clarity of detail and richness of colour. Their last work, *Judith Slaying Holofernes* (window no. 6), is perhaps the finest, the story unfolding in intricate perspective. By comparison, the post-Reformation windows, which date from 1572 to 1603, adopt an allegorical and heraldic style typical of a more secular art. *The Relief of Leiden* (window no. 25) shows William the Silent retaking the town from the Spanish, though Delft and its burgomasters take prominence – no doubt because they paid the bill for its construction. All the windows are numbered and a detailed guide is available at the entrance for *f*3.

By the side of the church, the flamboyant **Lazarus Gate** of 1609 was once part of the town's leper hospital, until it was moved to form the back entrance to the **Catharina Gasthuis**, a hospice till 1910. A likeable conglomeration of sixteenth-century rooms and halls, including an old isolation cell for the insane, the interior of the Gasthuis has been turned into the municipal **Stedelijk Museum** (Mon–Sat 10am–5pm, Sun noon–5pm; *f*4). The collection incorporates a fine sample of early religious art, notably a large triptych, *Life of Mary*, by Dirk Barendsz and a characteristically austere *Annunciation* by the Bruges artist Pieter Pourbus. Other highlights include a spacious hall, *Het Ruim*, that was once a sort of medieval hostel, but is now dominated by paintings of the Civic Guard, principally two group portraits by Ferdinand Bol; the intricate silver-gilt *Chalice and Eucharist Dish* was presented to the Guard in the early fifteenth century. Two later rooms have a modest selection of Hague and Barbizon School canvases, notably work by Anton

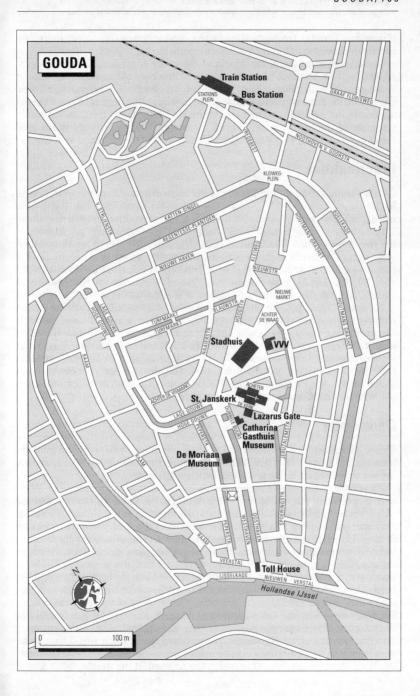

Mauve and Charles Daubigny. Downstairs, beside the isolation cell, there is a charming collection of torture instruments from the old city jail.

Gouda's other museum, **De Moriaan** (Mon–Sat 10am–5pm, Sun noon–5pm; ƒ3, or free with Stedelijk Museum ticket), is in a cosy old merchant's house at Westhaven 29, with a mixed bag of exhibits from clay pipes to ceramics and tiles. Westhaven itself is a winsome jumble of old buildings that head off toward the old toll house and a dilapidated mill beside the Hollandse IJssel river, on the southern edge of the town centre. There's a restored, fully operational **grain mill** (Mon–Sat 9am–5pm; ƒ1.50) five minutes' walk west of the Markt, at Vest 65.

Practicalities

Gouda's **train** and **bus stations** are to the immediate north of the town centre, ten minutes from the **VVV**, Markt 27 (Mon–Fri 9am–5pm, Sat 10am–4pm; ☎0182/513 666), which has a limited supply of private **rooms**, and will ring ahead to make a booking for a small cover charge. The most reasonably priced **hotel** is the *Het Blauwe Kruis*, Westhaven 4 (☎0182/512 677; ②). There are three other, more agreeable hotels in the centre, the reasonably priced *De Utrechtse Dom*, a couple of minutes' walk to the east of St Janskerk at Geuzenstraat 6 (☎0182/527 984; ②), the *De Keizerskroon*, to the west of Westhaven at Keizerstraat 11 (☎0182/528 096; ③), and the *Het Trefpunt* at Westhaven 46 (☎0182/512 879; ③).

For **food**, Gouda has literally dozens of cafés and snack bars catering for the hundreds of tourists who day-trip here throughout the season. *'t Groot Stedelijk*, Markt 44, has a variety of cheap dishes; there are pancakes at *'t Goudse Winkeltje*, Achter de Kerk 9a; pizzas at the *Rimini*, Markt 28; and decent Indonesian food at *Warung Srikandi*, Lange Groenendaal 108. In the evening, *Cafe Central*, Markt 26, is a reasonable place to eat and drink, while the most popular spot for beer and Dutch food is the excellent *Eetcafe Vidocq*, Koster Gijzensteeg 8, left out of the market past *Cafe Central* and first on the right.

Oudewater

Eleven kilometres east of Gouda and easily accessible by bike (rent one from the train station) or bus, **OUDEWATER** is a compact and delightful little town that holds a unique place in the history of Dutch witchcraft.

It's estimated that over a million people across Europe were burned or otherwise murdered in the widespread **witch-hunts** of the sixteenth century, and not only from fear and superstition: anonymous accusation to the authorities was an easy way of removing an enemy – or even a wife, at a time when there was no divorce. Underlying it all was a virulent misogyny and an accompanying desire to terrorize women into submission. There were three main methods for investigating accusations of witchcraft: in the first, **trial by fire**, the suspect had to walk barefoot over hot cinders or have a hot iron pressed into the back or hands. If the burns blistered, the accused was innocent as witches were supposed to burn less easily than others; naturally, the (variable) temperature of the iron was crucial. **Trial by water** was still more hazardous: dropped into water, if you floated you were a witch, if you sank you were innocent – and probably dead from drowning. The third method, **trial by weight**, presupposed that a witch would have to be unduly light to fly on a broomstick, so many towns – including Oudewater – used the Waag (town weigh-house) to weigh the accused. If the weight didn't accord with a notional figure derived from the height, the woman was burned. The last Dutch woman to be burnt as a witch was a certain Marrigje Ariens, a herbalist from Schoonhaven, whose medical efforts, not untypically, inspired mistrust and subsequent persecution. She died in 1597.

Oudewater's Waag gained its fame from the actions of Charles V (1516–52), who saw a woman accused of witchcraft in a nearby village. The weighmaster, who'd been bribed, stated that the woman weighed only a few pounds, but Charles was dubious and ordered the woman to be weighed again in Oudewater, where the officials proved unbribable, pronouncing a normal weight and acquitting her. The probity of Oudewater's weighmaster impressed Charles, and he granted the town the privilege of issuing certificates, valid throughout the empire, stating that "The accused's weight is in accordance with the natural proportions of the body". Once in possession of the certificate, one could never be brought to trial for witchcraft again. Not surprisingly, thousands of people came from all over Europe for this life-saving piece of paper, and to Oudewater's credit no one was ever condemned.

Oudewater's sixteenth-century Waag has survived, converted into the **Heksenwaag** (witches' weigh house; April–Oct Tues–Sat 10am–5pm, Sun noon–5pm; *f*2.50), a family-run affair, where you can be weighed on the original rope and wood balance. The owners dress up in national costume and issue a certificate in olde-worlde English that states nothing, but does so very prettily. There's not much else to see here, but it's a pleasant little place, whose traditional stepped gables spread out along the River Hollandse IJssel as it twists its way through town.

If you decide to **stay**, the **VVV**, Markt-Oostzyde 8 (April–Sept Tues–Sat 10.30am–4.30pm, Sun 1–4.30pm; Oct–March Tues 10am–noon, Thurs 1.30–3.30pm, Sat 11am–3pm; ☎0348/564 636), has details of several private rooms and a pension; there are no hotels. *Eethuis de Waeghols*, by the canal at Markt Westzuide 7, has good food and beer; *'t Bactertje*, opposite, does decent snacks.

Dordrecht and around

Some 15km southeast of Rotterdam, the ancient port of **DORDRECHT**, or "Dordt" as it's often called, is a very likeable town beside one of the busiest waterway junctions in the world, where tankers and containers from the north pass the waterborne traffic of the Maas and Rijn. Eclipsed by the expansion of Rotterdam and left relatively intact by World War II, Dordrecht has been spared the worst excesses of postwar development and preserves a confusion of ancient and dilapidated buildings that stop it from being just another tidy Dutch showpiece. Within easy reach is some of the province's prettiest countryside, including the windmills of the **Kinderdijk** and the **Biesbosch** nature reserve.

Granted a town charter in 1220, Dordrecht was the most important and powerful town in Holland until well into the sixteenth century. One of the first cities to declare against the Habsburgs in 1572, it was the obvious site for the first meeting of the Free Assembly of the Seven Provinces, and for a series of doctrinal conferences that tried to solve a whole range of theological differences among the various Protestant sects. After all, the Protestants may have hated the Catholics, but they also inherited the medieval church's desire for theological debate. In 1618, at the Synod of Dordt, the Remonstrants or Arminians had prolonged arguments with the Calvinists over the definition of predestination, though this must have seemed pretty important stuff compared to the Synod of 1574, when one of the main rulings had required the dismantling of church organs.

From the seventeenth century, Dordrecht lost ground to its great rivals to the north, slipping into comparative insignificance, its economy sustained by trade and shipbuilding.

Arrival, information and accommodation

Well connected by train to all the Randstad's major cities, Dordrecht's adjoining **train** and **bus** stations are a ten-minute walk from the town centre, straight down Stationsweg/Johan de Wittstraat and left at the end along Bagijnhof/Visstraat. A couple of minutes from the station, the **VVV**, Stationsweg 1 (Mon–Fri 9am–5.30pm, Sat 9.30am–1pm; May–Aug open Sat until 5.30pm; ☎078/613 1783), has a superb booklet describing a **walking tour** of the city, well worth the ƒ1.50 investment if you've got an hour or two to spare.

The VVV also has a list of **pensions** and **private rooms**, which it will reserve for a cover charge of ƒ3.50 per person. There are three central **hotels**: the *Klarenbeek*, near the VVV at Johan de Wittstraat 35 (☎078/614 4133, fax 614 0861; ③); the *Dordrecht*, by the river near the west end of Spuiboulevard at Achterhakkers 12 (☎078/613 6011, fax 613 7470; ④); and the excellent *Bellevue*, Boomstraat 37 (☎078/613 7900, fax 613 7921; ④), overlooking the Maas from the northern tip of the old town by the Groothoofdspoort. There are cheaper alternatives approximately 4km east of town along Baanhoekweg, the road that forms the northern perimeter of the Biesbosch (bus #5 from the station), in a complex that includes *De Hollandse Biesbosch* at no. 25 (☎078/621 2167, fax 621 2163; ②), a campsite of the same name (April–Oct) and a **youth hostel** (☎078/621 2167). The most agreeable **campsite**, *De Kleine Rug* (☎078/616 3555; April–Oct, advance bookings essential July & Aug), is about 1km south of Baanhoekweg on a sandspit at Loswalweg 1: take bus #3 to Stadspolder, walk fifteen minutes down to the end of Loswalweg and ask the people at *Camping 't Vissertje*, Loswalweg 3 (☎078/616 2751; April–Sept) to ring across for the boat to ferry you over.

The town

The old part of Dordrecht juts out into the Maas, divided by three concentric waterways that once protected it from attack. From the train station, the second canal is the heart of the town, flowing beside the **Voorstraat**, today's main shopping street. At the junction of Voorstraat and Visstraat, the Groenmarkt spans the canal with a heavy-handed **monument** to the de Witt brothers, Johan and Cornelius, prominent Dutch Republicans who paid for their principles when they were torn to pieces by an Orangist mob in The Hague in 1672. To the right, Voorstraat bends its way northeast, a chaotic mixture of the old, the new, the restored and the decayed, intersected by a series of tiny alleys that once served as the town's docks. Cutting off Voorstraat at Nieuwebrug, the **Wijnhaven** was used by the city's merchants to control the import and export of wine when they held the state monopoly from the fourteenth to the seventeenth centuries. To the right of the Nieuwebrug, just past the Augustijnekerk, a handful of buildings around the courtyard of **Het Hof** mark the remains of the Augustine monastery founded here in 1275. Largely rebuilt after a fire in 1512, the complex houses the

Statenzaal (Tues–Sat 1–5pm; ƒ3.50), where the free states held their first assembly in 1575; a little of the atmosphere of those heady times still lingers, with grand tapestries hanging on the walls and the coats of arms of the participating provinces proudly engraved on the windows.

At the end of Voorstraat, the **Groothoofdspoort** was once the main city gate and has a grand facade dating from 1618, pushed up against the *Hotel Bellevue*, with its fine views over the surrounding waterways. The town's innermost canal is just along the waterfront from here, divided into two harbours, home to the cruisers, barges and sailing boats that ply up and down the Maas. Fringed by stately buildings and criss-crossed by rickety footbridges, it's an attractive setting for the **Museum Simon van Gijn**, Nieuwe Haven 29 (Tues–Sat 10am–5pm, Sun 1–5pm; ƒ6), whose collection of local memorabilia and period rooms is of moderate interest, best of all the eighteenth-century Brussels tapestries and a fine Renaissance chimneypiece of 1550, transferred from the old guild house of the arquebusiers.

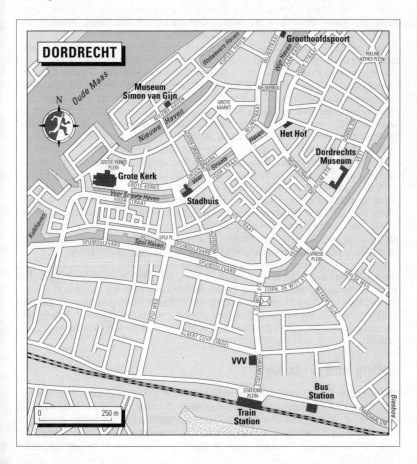

Near the southwest end of Nieuwe Haven, the **Grote Kerk** (April–Oct Tues–Sat 10.30am–4.30pm, Sun noon–4pm; Nov & Dec first & third Sat of the month 2–4pm; free) is visible from all over town, its fourteenth-century **tower** (April–Oct same times, except July & Aug also Mon noon–4pm; Nov–March Sat & Sun 1–4pm if the weather's fine; ƒ2) topped with incongruous seventeenth-century clocks. One of the largest churches in Holland, it was built to emphasize Dordrecht's wealth and importance, but it's heavy and dull, despite its attractive environs, and there's only an elaborately carved choir inside to hold your interest. Climb the tower for a great view over the town and its surrounding waters. From beside the church, Grotekerksbuurt leads to the stolid classicism of the **Stadhuis**, back on the Voorstraat.

The Dordrechts Museum

To the southeast of the town centre, the **Dordrechts Museum**, Museumstraat 40 (Tues–Sat 10am–5pm, Sun 1–5pm; ƒ7.50), is a ten-minute walk from the train station: turn right off Johan de Wittstraat on the far side of the first canal as you head into town, and follow the signs. Well presented and clearly labelled, the museum concentrates on the work of local artists, both in its permanent and temporary displays. Highlights of the permanent collection include a couple of finely drawn portraits by Jacob Cuyp, and a whole room devoted to the work of his son, Albert. Born in Dordrecht in 1620, **Albert Cuyp** was influenced by those of his contemporaries who had visited Italy, modulating his work with the soft, yellowish tones of the Mediterranean. Noted for his Italianate landscapes, seascapes and town scenes, his *Resting Riders in a Landscape* is representative of his work, in contrast to the muted tones of traditional Dutch landscape painting, as illustrated by Jan van Goyen's *View of Dordrecht*, the city's bustle restricted to the bottom section of the canvas, beneath a wide sky and flattened horizon.

A student of Rembrandt, **Nicolaes Maes** first specialized in informal domestic scenes, as in *The Eavesdropper*, turning his skills to portrait painting after his visit to Antwerp in 1670. A good example of his later work is his flattering picture of *Jacob de Witt the Elder*. More curiously, *De Dordtse Vierling* (the Dordt quadruplets) is an odd, unattributed seventeenth-century painting of a dead child and her three swaddled siblings, a simple, moving tribute to a lost daughter; and on the staircase nearby, the massive *Gezicht op Dordt* (View of Dordt) is a masterpiece of minutely observed naturalist detail by Adam Willaertz (1577–1644).

On the second floor, there's a selection of work by the later and lesser Ary Scheffer, who was born in Dordrecht in 1795, but lived in Paris from 1811. His much-reproduced *Mignon Pining for her Native Land* struck a chord in the sentimental hearts of the nineteenth century. Jozef Israels' *Midday Meal at the Inn* and G H Breitner's *Lauriergracht 1891* are among a small collection of Amsterdam and Hague School paintings, though the collage style of their Italian associate, Antonio Mancini, is of more immediate appeal.

Eating and drinking

Voorstraat is lined with good **restaurants**. *Costa d'Oro*, near the Grote Kerk at Voorstraat 444, has tasty Italian dishes from ƒ9. Nearby at no. 455, *'t Carillon* has cheap food all day, and there is another good Italian, *Piccolo Italia*, at no. 259. Near Visbrug, *Crimpet Salm*, at Visstraat 7, is a gorgeous old building that was once the fish merchants' guild house; it still serves fine seafood in the evening for around *f*25 and lunches from *f*10. *Pim's Poffertjes Pannekoekhuis* at Nieuwestraat 19 has hearty cheap pancakes and other dishes; the cavernous cafe-restaurant *de Pontonnier*, Grote Kerksplein 13, is another decent spot for typical Dutch food; *De Stroper*, at Wijnbrug 1, specializes in fish, with three-course menus from *f*29.50. For **drinking**, *'t Avontuur*, Voorstraat 193, is about the cheapest bar in town, with a reasonable selection of beers. Other good bars include the nearby *Cafe de Tijd* at Voorstraat 170, the lively *Taverne in de Klandermuelen* at Statenplein 86 and the *Centre Ville* on Visbrug. There's live music at the *Jazzpodium*, Grotekerkplein 1, usually on Wednesday, Friday and Saturday (☎078/614 0815), and occasionally at *de Klandermuelen*.

Around Dordrecht: the Biesbosch and the Kinderdijk

On November 18, 1421, South Holland's sea defences gave way and the "St Elizabeth Day flood" formed what is now the Hollands Diep sea channel and the **Biesbosch** (reed forest) – an expanse of river, creek, marsh and reed covering around fifteen square kilometres to the south and east of Dordrecht. It was a disaster of major proportions, destroying some seventy towns and villages, and early accounts put the death toll at over one hundred thousand. The catastrophe disrupted the whole of the region's economy, breaking up the links between South Holland and Flanders and accelerating the shift in commercial power to the north. Even those hamlets and villages that did survive took generations to recover, subject, as they were, to raids by the wretched refugees of the flood.

Inundated twice daily by the rising tide, the Biesbosch produced a particular **reed culture**, its inhabitants using the plant for every item of daily life, from houses to baskets and boats, selling excess cuttings at the local markets. It was a harsh and gruelling existence that lasted well into the nineteenth century, when the reeds were no longer of much use, replaced by machine-manufactured goods.

Today, the Biesbosch is a nature reserve whose delicate eco-system is threatened by the very scheme that aims to protect the province from further flooding. The Delta Project dams (see *Zeeland, North Brabant and Limburg*, pp.286–288) have controlled the rivers' flow and restricted the tides' strength, forcing the reeds to give ground to other forms of vegetation incompatible with the area's special mixture of bird and plant life. Large areas of reed have disappeared, and no one seems to know how to reconcile the nature reserve's needs with those of the seaboard cities.

The park divides into two main sections, north and south of the Nieuwe Merwede channel, which marks the provincial boundary between South Holland and North Brabant. The undeveloped heart of the nature reserve is the **Brabantse Biesbosch**, the chunk of land to the south, whereas tourist facilities have been carefully confined to the north, on a strip of territory to the immediate east of Dordrecht, along the park's perimeter. Here, the **Bezoekerscentrum De Hollandsche Biesbosch**, Baanhoekweg 53 (Tues–Sun 9am–5pm; April–Oct also Mon noon–5pm; free), accessible by bus #5 from Dordrecht train station, has displays on the flora and fauna of the region, a beaver observatory and an hourly audiovisual show (*f*4). **Boat trips** for the Brabantse Biesbosch leave from the jetty beside the Bezoekerscentrum (July & Aug daily; Sept & Oct only Wed & Sun). Prices vary according to the itinerary, but start at *f*22.50 for the day ("Dagtocht") and at *f*9.50 for a two-hour excursion ("Panoramatocht"); call ☎078/621 1311 for times. Some of the longer excursions visit the

Biesboschmuseum, on the southern shore of the Nieuwe Merwede at Spieringsluis 4 (Mon 1–5pm, Tues–Sat 10am–5pm, Sun noon–5pm; *f*2.50), where there are further details on the ecology of the Biesbosch and the origins of its distinctive reed culture. Further details of boat trips are available at the Dordrecht VVV and direct from both visitors' centres.

The other way of visiting the nature reserve is by **bike**, for rent at standard rates from Dordrecht train station and the VVV, which also sells detailed maps of the district and brochures on suggested cycle routes. The ride from town to the Biesbosch takes about half an hour, via the shuttle passenger boat service that runs from the dock by Kop van 't Land, 5km southeast of the town centre, to a point about 1km northeast of the Biesboschmuseum.

The Kinderdijk

Some 12km north of Dordrecht, the **Kinderdijk** (child's dyke) sits at the end of a long drainage channel which feeds into the River Lek, whose turbulent waters it keeps from flooding the polders around Alblasserdam. Sixteenth-century legend suggests it takes its name from the time when a cradle, complete with cat and kicking baby, was found at the precise spot where the dyke had just held during a particularly bad storm. A mixture of symbols – rebirth, innocence and survival – the story encapsulates the determination and optimism with which the Dutch fought the floods for hundreds of years, and is repeated in many different forms across the whole province.

Today, the Kinderdijk is famous for its picturesque, quintessentially Dutch **windmills**, all eighteen stringing alongside the main channel and its tributary beside the Molenkade for some 3km. Built around 1740 to drive water from the Alblasserwaard polders, the windmills are put into operation every Saturday afternoon in July and August, and one of them is open to visitors from April to September (Mon–Sat 9.30am–5.30pm; *f*3). If that hasn't satisfied your curiosity, there's also a **mill exhibition centre** at Molenstraat 236 (Tues–Sun 9.30am–5.30pm; *f*5).

Without a car, the easiest way to explore the district from Dordrecht is by **bike**; alternatively, take bus #252 to Alblassendan, then #154 (direction Utrecht) to the mills. If you decide to **stay**, the tiny village of Kinderdijk is to the immediate west of the dyke, on the banks of the Lek. There's just one **hotel**, *Kinderdijk*, West Kinderdijk 361 (☎078/691 2425, fax 691 5071; ②). Advance booking is essential from June to August.

Utrecht

"I groaned with the idea of living all winter in so shocking a place", wrote Boswell in 1763, and **UTRECHT** still promises little as you approach: surrounded by shopping centres and industrial developments, the town only begins to reveal itself in the old area around the Dom Kerk, roughly enclosed by the Oude and Nieuwe Grachts. These distinctive sunken canals date from the fourteenth century, and their brick cellars, used as warehouses when Utrecht was a river port, have been converted to chic cafés and restaurants. Though the liveliest places in town, they don't disguise Utrecht's provincialism: just half an hour from Amsterdam, all the brashness and vitality of the capital is absent, and it's for museums and churches rather than nightlife that the town is enjoyable.

The telephone code for Utrecht is ☎030

Founded by the Romans in the first century AD, the city of Utrecht became home to a wealthy and powerful medieval bishopric, which controlled the surrounding region under the auspices of the German emperors. In 1527 the bishop sold off his secular rights and shortly afterward the town council enthusiastically joined the revolt against Spain. Indeed, the **Union of Utrecht**, the agreement that formalized the opposition to the Habsburgs, was signed here in 1579. Some two hundred years later, the **Treaty of Utrecht** brought to an end some of Louis IV of France's grand imperial ambitions.

Arrival, city transport, information and accommodation

Train and bus stations both lead into the Hoog Catharijne shopping centre, on the edge of the city centre; the main **VVV** office is at Vredenburg 90 (Mon–Fri 9am–6pm, Sat 9am–4pm; ☎06/340 34085, 50c per min), a seven-minute walk away. Though the city is compact enough to explore on foot, touring the canals, either by boat or by cycling along towpaths, adds another dimension to a visit. **Bikes** can be rented from the train station, while **canal trips** depart hourly from Oude Gracht at the corner of Lange Viestraat and Potterstraat near the Viebrug (Oct–May daily 11am–5pm; June–Sept also Tues and Thurs 6–9pm; ƒ10; ☎272 01 11). If you're keen to visit Utrecht's museums, you might consider using the **Museumboot**, which leaves from the Viebrug (daily 11am, noon, 1pm, 2pm & 3pm; ƒ7 single, ƒ13 return), spanning Oude Gracht near the main post office, and chugs along to Gaardbrug (for the Speelklok tot Pierement Museum and Dom Tower), to the Centraal Museum, the Railway Museum and the Catharijne Convent Museum.

The VVV offers the usual help with **accommodation**. Among the cheaper hotels there's the tiny *Parkhotel*, near the Centraal Museum at Tolsteegsingel 34 (☎251 6712, fax 254 0401; ②), and the *Hotel Ouwi*, fifteen minutes' walk northeast from the centre at FC Donderstraat 12 (☎271 6303, fax 271 4619; ②). The luxurious *Hotel Smits* is the most central place to stay at Vredenburg 14 (☎233 1232, fax 232 8451; ⑤); the small and attractive *Malie*, east of the centre at Maliestraat 2 (☎231 6424, fax 234 0661; ④), is better value. The **youth hostel** at Rhijnauwenselaan 14, Bunnik (☎656 1277, fax 657 1065), linked to the train station by bus #40 or #41, is a little far out but beautifully sited in an old country manorhouse; the well-equipped **campsite**, *Camping de Berekuil*, northeast of the town centre at Arienslaan 5 (☎271 3870), can be reached by a #57 bus from the Centraal Station.

The town

The focal point of the centre is the **Dom Tower**, at over 110m the highest church tower in the country. It's one of the most beautiful, too, its soaring, unbuttressed lines rising to a delicate, octagonal lantern added in 1380. Hourly guided tours (April–Oct Mon–Fri 10am–5pm, Sat & Sun noon–5pm; Nov–March Sat 11am–5pm & Sun noon–5pm; last entry one hour before closing; ƒ4) take you unnervingly near to the top, from where you can see Rotterdam and Amsterdam

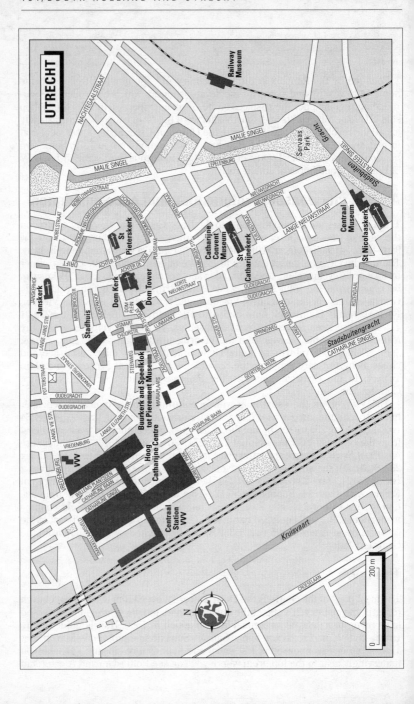

on a clear day. Only the eastern part of the great cathedral remains, the nave having collapsed (with what must have been an apocalyptic crash) during a storm in 1674. It's worth peering inside (May–Sept Mon–Fri 10am–5pm, Sat 10am–3.30pm, Sun 2–4pm; Oct–April Mon–Fri 11am–4pm, Sat & Sun same hours; free) to get a sense of the hangar-like space the building once had, and to wander through the **Kloostergang**, the fourteenth-century cloisters that link the cathedral to the chapterhouse. The Kloostertuin, or cloister gardens, are reckoned to be the best place in town to listen to the carillon concerts from the Dom Tower, which you can do from a pleasant tea-house. If bells are not your thing, you might be lucky enough to catch music played on more conventional instruments during the classical concerts that are regularly performed here.

Except for the Dom, Utrecht's churches aren't all that interesting: the oldest is the **St Pieterskerk** (Tues–Fri 11am–4.30pm, Sat 11am–3pm; free), a shabbily maintained building that's a mixture of Romanesque and Gothic styles with twelfth-century paintings and reliefs. Heading northwest from here to the bend in the Oude Gracht, between the ludicrously grandiose nineteenth-century **Stadhuis**, and the huge, brick Amsterdam School **post office**, is the oldest house in Utrecht, the fourteenth-century **Huis Oudaen**, with a café on the ground floor, the *Proeflokaal*, where you can sample beer brewed in the steam brewery in its basement.

Not far from the Stadhuis are a couple of unusual little museums, well worth checking out. The **Museum voor het Kruideniersbedrijf** at Hoogt 8 (Tues–Sat 12.30–4.30pm; free) is possibly the world's only museum devoted to groceries – not exactly a vital stop, but something at least to base a walk around. Close by, further down Oude Gracht, the **Buurkerk** was the home of one sister Bertken, who was so ashamed of being the illegitimate daughter of a cathedral priest that she hid away in a small cell here – for 57 years, until her death in 1514. It's now the peculiar location of the **Speelklok tot Pierement Museum** (Tues–Sat 10am–5pm, Sun 1–5pm; ƒ7.50), a collection of burping fairground organs and ingenious musical boxes worth an hour of anyone's time.

The city's other museums are a little way from the centre. The national collection of ecclesiastical art, the **Catharijne Convent Museum** (Tues–Fri 10am–5pm, Sat & Sun 11am–5pm; ƒ7), at Nieuwe Gracht 63, has a mass of paintings, manuscripts and church ornaments from the ninth century on, brilliantly exhibited in a complex built around the old convent. This excellent collection of paintings includes work by Geertgen tot Sint Jans, Rembrandt, Hals and, best of all, a luminously beautiful *Virgin and Child* by van Cleve. Part of the convent is the late Gothic **St Catharijnekerk**, whose radiant white interior is enhanced by floral decoration.

Keep walking down along Nieuwe Gracht and you reach Utrecht's other important museum, the **Centraal Museum**, at Agnietenstraat 1 (Tues–Sat 11am–5pm, Sun noon–5pm; ƒ6). Its claim to hold "25,000 curiosities" seems a bit exaggerated, but it does have a good collection of paintings by Utrecht artists of the sixteenth and seventeenth centuries. Van Scorel lived in Utrecht before and after he visited Rome, and he brought the influence of Italian humanism north. His paintings, like the vividly individual portraits of the *Jerusalem Brotherhood*, combine High Renaissance style with native Dutch observation. The central figure in white is van Scorel himself: he made a trip to Jerusalem around 1520, which accounts for his unusually accurate drawing of the city in *Christ's Entry into Jerusalem*. A group of painters influenced by another Italian, Caravaggio, became known as the Utrecht School. Such paintings as Honthorst's *The Procuress* adapt his chiaroscuro technique to genre subjects, and develop an erotic content that would itself influence later genre painters like Jan Steen and Gerrit Dou. Even more skilled and realistic is Terbrugghen's *The Calling of St Matthew*, a beautiful balance of gestures dramatizing the tax collector's summoning by Christ to become one of the apostles.

Gerrit Rietveld, the de Stijl designer, was most famous for his brightly coloured geometrical chairs, displayed in the applied art section. Part of the de Stijl philosophy (see *Contexts*) was that the approach could be used in any area of design, though Rietveld's angular furniture is probably better to look at than to sit on. There are more pieces of his furniture out of town, in the **Schröderhuis** at Prins Hendriklaan 50, accessible on bus #4 from the train station, which he designed and built in 1924 for one Truus Schröder and her three children (organized tours only Wed–Sat 11am–5pm;*f*9; call first on ☎236 2310). It's hailed as one of the most influential pieces of modern architecture in Europe, demonstrating the organic union of lines and rectangles that was the hallmark of the de Stijl movement. The ground floor is the most conventional part of the building, since its design had to meet the rigours of the building licence. However, Rietveld was able to let his imagination run riot on the top floor, the actual living space, designing an utterly flexible environment where only the outer walls are solid – indeed the entire top floor can be subdivided in any way you want by simply sliding the temporary walls.

Back in Utrecht, there are two final museums that might detain you. The **Spoorweg (Railway) Museum** (Tues–Sat 10am–5pm, Sun 1–5pm; *f*11) is at Maliebaanstation – bus #3 from the station – with trains, buses and trams sitting in Utrecht's out-of-use train station: not much information, but enthusiastic attendants. The **Moluks Historisch Museum**, Kruisstraat 313 (Tues–Sun 1–5pm; *f*4.50), has displays on the Moluccans and their integration into Dutch society and exhibitions of their art; bus #11 runs from the station.

Eating and drinking

There are masses of decent places to **eat** along Oude Gracht, both on the street and below, by the canal, including the cheap waterside pancake bakery *De Oude Muntkelder* at no. 112, the Italian *Le Connaisseur* at no. 59, the vegetarian *De Werfkring* at no. 123, and the pricier but popular *Tantes Bistro* at no. 61. North a little around the Janskerk, *Cafe Zeezicht* at Nobelstraat 2 serves reasonably priced breakfasts, lunches and dinners, to an accompaniment of live music on Tuesday nights. Also check out nearby *Grand Cafe Polman's Huis*, on the corner of Jansdam and Keistraat, if only for its turn-of-the-century interior. For breakfast or coffee try the media hang-out *Cafe Orloff*, by the junction of Oude Gracht and Wed, just south of the Dom.

There are several good **bars** on and around Oude Gracht. *Kafe Belgie* at Oude Gracht 196 has a lot of beers and loads of noise, while *De Witte Ballons* at Lijnmarkt 10–12 is friendly. Other noteworthy hostelries include *Winkel van Sinkel*, Oude Gracht 158, a large and often crowded bar fronted by a group of caryatids, and *Stadkasteel Oudaen*, Oude Gracht 99, with beer brewed on the premises and reasonable Dutch food. As for Utrecht's **gay scene**, try *De Wolkenkrabber* at Oude Gracht 47, and the mixed disco, *De Roze Wolk*, right underneath. For alternative movies, try one of Utrecht's many *filmhuizen*, such as *'t Hoogt* at Hoogt 4.

East of Utrecht

The Utrechtse Heuvelrug (Utrecht Ridge) stretches across the eastern edge of the province of Utrecht, a wooded region that attracts many local tourists for its gentle walking and cycling. **Amersfoort**, twenty minutes from Utrecht by train, is the main town in the area – an attractive and easy-going place with a handful of decent museums, and certainly worthy of a day-trip if you're staying in Utrecht. The countryside south of here is dotted with the remains of medieval castles, most of them subsequently converted into grand chateaux. The castles at **Doorn** and **Amerongen**, in particular, warrant a brief detour if you're heading east towards Arnhem, while the little town of **Rhenen**, prettily set beside the Rhine, pulls in tourists aplenty to view the fifteenth-century church of Saint Cunera.

Amersfoort

Near the border between the provinces of Utrecht and Gelderland, the town of **AMERSFOORT** was first fortified in the eleventh century and received its charter in 1259. Surprisingly, it managed to avoid the attentions of the rival armies during the Revolt of the Netherlands, and some of today's centre dates from the fifteenth century, lying at the heart of a series of twisting canals that once served to protect the town from assault and to speed the import and export of goods. The main square, the Hof, where the market is held on Friday and Saturday, is edged by the giant hulk of the **St Joriskerk** (June–Aug daily 9.30am–6.30pm; free), an unusual, predominantly Gothic edifice finished in 1534. The nave and aisles are of equal height, and only the south porch stops the exterior from resembling an aircraft hangar. Like most churches of the period, it was an enlargement of an earlier building, but here the original Romanesque tower was left inside the later fifteenth-century construction.

A few minutes' walk northeast along Langestraat, the **Kamperbinnenpoort** is a turreted thirteenth-century gate, extensively renovated in the 1930s. From here, north and south of Langestraat, Muurhuizen follows the line of the old city moat, and is named for its **"wallhouses"**, built into the city walls. At the northern end of Muurhuizen, the **Museum Fléhite**, Westsingel 50 (Tues–Fri 10am–5pm, Sat & Sun 2–5pm; *f*5), is located in a wallhouse, a fancifully gabled building of neo-Renaissance design. This is the town's main museum, but it's packed with a dreary assortment of items of strictly local interest. The museum also has a bizarre annexe across the road, the chapel and male ward of a medieval hospice, the **St Pieter's-en-Bloklands Gasthuis** (Tues–Fri 10–5pm, Sat & Sun 2–5pm; same ticket). Close by, spanning the canal, is the ridiculously picturesque **Koppelpoort**, a fifteenth-century town gate, which defended Amersfoort's northern approach by dropping down a wooden panel and sealing off the canal.

Back on Westsingel, 500m past the museum, all that remains of Amersfoort's other main church, the **Onze Lieve Vrouwekerk** (June–Aug daily 9.30am–4pm; free) also known as Langejan, is the fifteenth-century tower: the rest was accidentally blown up in 1797. The original building was paid for by pilgrims visiting the *Amersfoort Madonna*, a small wooden figure that had been thrown into the town canal by a young girl in 1444. Legend has it that the girl was on her way to enter one of Amersfoort's convents when she became ashamed of her simple figurine, so she decided to throw it away. In the manner of such things, a dream commanded her to retrieve the statuette, which subsequently demonstrated miraculous powers. Part morality play, part miracle, the story fulfilled all the necessary criteria to turn the figure into a revered object, and the town into a major centre of medieval pilgrimage. Otherwise, art lovers may troop into town to visit the **Mondrian House**, near the tower at Kortegracht 11 (Tues–Fri 10am–5pm, Sat & Sun 1–5pm; *f*5), birthplace of Piet Mondrian, with a small exhibition about his life and reproductions of many of his paintings, but the final call for secular pilgrims to the town should be the **Brewery de Drie Ringen**, Kleine Spui 18 (Thurs–Sat noon–6pm; free), in whose adjoining bar you can sample the local brew.

Practicalities

A good ten minutes' walk west of the town centre, Amersfoort **VVV** is near the **train station** at Stationsplein 9 (Oct–April Mon–Fri 9am–5.30pm, Sat 9am–1pm; May–Sept Mon–Fri 9am–6pm, Sat 9am–2pm; ☎033/463 5151); turn left out of the station and follow the road for 400m. It has a good supply of private **rooms** and **pensions**, and will call ahead to make a booking, though most of them are way out of the town centre. There are, however, several convenient and reasonably priced **hotels**, the cheapest being *De Tabaksplant* at Conickstraat 15 (☎033/472 9797; ②) – go out of the town centre through the Kamperbinnenpoort and take the first major left turn. The slightly larger *De Witte* is just to the southwest of the Onze Lieve Vrouwetoren at Utrechtseweg 2 (☎033/461 4142, fax 463 5821; ③), and the unimposing *Terminus* is near the station at Stationsstraat 42 (☎033/461 3025, fax 465 2627; ③). The closest **campsite**, *De Bokkeduinen*, is about 2km west of the station at Barchman Wuytierslaan 81 (☎033/461 9902; April–Oct), take bus #70 (direction Soest), from the train station.

For **food**, there are a number of snack-bars along the main shopping street, Langestraat, and outdoor cafes around Hof and Groenmarkt, including *Onder de Linde* at Groenmarkt 15. *Chez Hubert*, Krommestraat 7 (closed Mon), is a good bet for nibbles during the day and full meals at night. In the evening, *De Kluif* at Groenmarkt 4 (closed Mon) is one of the most popular spots in town for decent Dutch food; there's the Mexican restaurant *Gringo*, by the old Catholic church at 't Zand 18; and the excellent Italian *San Giorgio*, Krommestraat 44. There are some first-rate bars in town, among them the ever-buzzing *'t Nonnetje* on Groenmark, the ancient *Linden Grooten Slock* on the corner of Hof and Langestraat, and the atmospheric *Mariposa*, off Langestraat at Valkestraat 10, with the best beer selection in town and live music on Fridays.

Doorn

Just south of the A12 motorway between Utrecht and Arnhem, **DOORN**, reachable by bus #51 from Utrecht or #55 from Amersfoort, holds one of the more awkward skeletons in Holland's modern history cupboard. The **Kasteel Huis Doorn** (mid-March to Oct Tues–Sat 10am–4pm & Sun 1pm–5pm, guided tours only every 20min; *f*7.50), a medieval castle converted into a classical manorhouse in 1792, was home to Kaiser Wilhelm II from 1920 to 1941, following his flight from Germany at the end of World War 1. At a time when the British government, in particular, was mounting a "Hang the Kaiser" campaign, the Dutch, neutral during the war, allowed Wilhelm into their country; although he was supposedly under house arrest, you won't feel much sympathy for him when you see the comfortable rooms and extensive grounds of the manor. The guided tour takes in the usual trappings of a stately home – elegantly decorated rooms, furnished here in the style of the 1920s – and, among Wilhelm's personal souvenirs, an extraordinary collection of snuffboxes from the era of Frederick the Great of Prussia. There's a bust of the Kaiser in the gardens and it's hard not to feel, particularly when you see the House of Hohenzollern tea-cloths in the souvenir shop, that the whole place is rather too reverential.

There's not much else to Doorn, other than walking in the surrounding woods. There are a couple of **campsites** and a single reasonably priced **hotel** – the *Rodestein*, Sitiopark 10 (☎0343/412 409; ②). The **VVV** is near the castle at Dorpsstraat 4 (Mon–Fri 9.30am–5pm, Sat 9am–2pm; Oct–March closed for lunch Mon–Fri 12.30–1.30pm; ☎0343/412 015) and has details of a few local pensions.

Amerongen and Rhenen

Eight kilometres east of Doorn, the most interesting feature of **AMERONGEN** is its thirteenth-century **castle** (April–Oct Tues–Fri 10am–5pm, Sat & Sun 1–5pm; *f7*), the present structure largely dating from the 1680s, when it was rebuilt by Godard Van Reede after the French wars. A classic example of interconnected European aristocracy, Van Reede's son went to England with William of Orange in 1688, becoming Earl of Athlone after he helped defeat the Irish at the Battle of the Boyne in 1690. The castle stayed in the family's hands until 1879, when it was inherited by the German Count van Aldenburg – first host to Kaiser Wilhelm after he left Germany in November 1918 – and is now owned by the state. It's rather a stuffy place, awash with tedious family portraiture, but redeems itself with a handful of interesting features from the seventeenth-century restoration. The splendid painted ceilings in the state room and the hall include a cheerful white elephant (Van Reede belonged to the Danish Order of the Elephant, a sort of ambassadorial post), there are some Flemish tapestries scattered throughout the house, and the giant eighteenth-century backgammon set in the master bedroom contrasts nicely with the tiny furniture of earlier, physically smaller generations. The **VVV** office (same hours as the castle plus Oct–March Tues & Thurs 1.30–4pm; ☎0343/452 020) adjoins the entrance to the castle at Drostestraat 20 and can help with finding accommodation.

Eleven kilometres further on, **RHENEN**'s strategic position on the north bank of the Rhine made it one of the first places in the area to be settled, and the **Gemeentemuseum** (Tues–Fri noon–5pm, Sat 1–5pm, July & Aug also Sun 1–5pm; *f2.50*) in the town centre has a neat collection of historical finds, including Merovingian weapons, jewellery and pottery and a bronze burial urn, the largest found in Holland. The museum also holds a collection of gargoyles, statues of saints and other relics from the **Sint Cunerakerk**, a late Gothic church, with an attractive 84-metre tower (July to mid-Sept 2–3.30pm; free) that's the town's main attraction. According to legend, Saint Cunera, a fifth-century English princess on a pilgrimage to Rome, was attacked by the Huns and had to be rescued by Radboud, king of Rhenen, who brought her here to his castle. Cunera became hugely popular with the locals because of her work with the poor and the sick, but was murdered by Radboud's jealous queen; since then, her spirit has supposedly carried out dozens of miracles. The legend brought so many pilgrims to Rhenen that the town was able to afford the monumental tower, started in 1492 and completed 31 years later. There's little reason to **stay** over in Rhenen but, if you get stuck, the cheapest place in town is *Pension Rhenen*, Herenstraat 75 (☎0317/617 214; ②), and the **VVV** office is in a kiosk at Frederik van de Paltshof 46 (July–Aug Mon–Fri 9am–1pm & 1.30–5.30pm, Sat 9am–noon; Sept–June Mon–Fri 9am–5pm, Sat 10am–noon; ☎0317/612 333).

travel details

Trains

Amersfoort to: Amsterdam CS (every 15min; 35min); Utrecht (every 15min; 20min); Zwolle (every 30min; 35min).

Leiden to: Amsterdam CS (every 30min; 35min); The Hague CS (every 30min; 35min).

The Hague to: Amersfoort (every 20min; 1hr); Delft (every 15min; 12min); Dordrecht (every 30min; 40min); Gouda (every 20min; 20min); Rotterdam (every 15min; 25min); Utrecht (every 20min; 40min).

Rotterdam to: Dordrecht (every 10min; 20min); Gouda (every 20min; 20min); Utrecht (every 20min; 45min).

Utrecht to: Amersfoort (every 15min; 20min); Arnhem (every 15min; 30min); Leeuwarden (hourly; 2hr); Zwolle (2 an hour; 1hr).

International trains

Dordrecht to: Antwerp (hourly; 1hr); Brussels (hourly; 1hr 40min).

The Hague HS to: Antwerp (hourly; 1hr 35min); Brussels (hourly; 2hr 15min); Paris (4 daily; 5hr 10min).

Leiden to: Antwerp (hourly; 1hr 50min); Brussels (hourly; 2hr 30min).

Rotterdam CS to: Antwerp (hourly; 1hr 15min); Brussels (hourly; 1hr 55min); Paris (4 daily; 4hr 45min).

Buses

Amersfoort to: Doorn (hourly; 30min).

Gouda to: Oudewater (hourly; 20min).

The Hague to: Katwijk (every 30min; 25min).

Leiden to: Katwijk (every 10min; 25min); Noordwijk (every 30min; 40min).

Utrecht to: Doorn (hourly; 25min).

CHAPTER FOUR

THE NORTH AND THE FRISIAN ISLANDS

U ntil the opening of the Afsluitdijk in 1932, which bridged the mouth of the Zuider Zee, the **north** of Holland was a relatively remote area, a distinct region of small provincial towns that was far from the mainstream life of the Randstad, further south. Since the completion of the dyke, the gap between north and west Holland has narrowed, and fashion and custom seem almost identical. The main exception is linguistic: Friesland has its own language, more akin to Low German than Dutch, and its citizens are keen to use it.

Three provinces make up the north of the country – **Drenthe**, **Groningen** and **Friesland** – though for a long time the Frisians occupied the entire area. Charlemagne recognized three parts of Friesland: West Frisia, equivalent to today's West Friesland, across the IJsselmeer; Central Frisia (today's Friesland); and East Frisia – now Groningen province. At that time much of the region was prey to inundation by the sea, and houses and sometimes entire settlements would be built on artificial mounds or *terpen* (known as *wierden* in Groningen), which brought them high above the water level. It was a miserable sort of existence, and not surprisingly the Frisians soon got around to building dykes to keep the water out permanently. You can still see what's left of some of the mounds in Friesland, though in large settlements they're usually obscured.

During the Middle Ages the area that is now Friesland proper remained independent of the rest of Holland, asserting its separateness regularly until it was absorbed into the Hapsburg empire by Charles V in 1523. It's still something of a maverick among Dutch provinces, although the landscape is familiar enough – dead flat and very green, dotted with black-and-white cattle and long thatched farmhouses crowned with white gable finials or *uleburden*, in the form of a double-swan motif, which were originally meant to deter evil spirits. Of the towns, **Leeuwarden**, the provincial capital of Friesland, is pleasant, if sedate, with two outstanding museums, one of which has the largest collection of tiles in the world. However, many visitors prefer the west coast of the province, where a chain of small towns prospered during the sixteenth-century trading heyday of the Zuider Zee. Each coastal town has its own distinct charm and character, from the splendid merchant houses of **Harlingen**, to the painted furniture and antique neatness of **Hindeloopen** and the tile manufacturers of **Makkum**. Inland, southwest Friesland is a tangle of lake and canal that's been transformed into one of the busiest water sports areas in the country, centring on the town of **Sneek**.

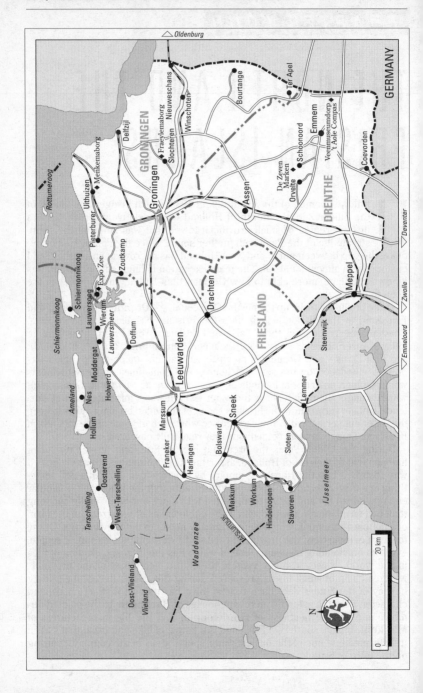

ACCOMMODATION PRICE CODES

All the **hotels** and **hostels** detailed in this chapter have been graded according to the following price categories. Apart from ①, which is a per-person price for a hostel bed, all the codes are based on the rate for the cheapest double room during high season.

For more on accommodation, see p.30.

① Up to ƒ40 per person	④ ƒ150–200	⑦ ƒ300–400
② ƒ60–100	⑤ ƒ200–250	
③ ƒ100–150	⑥ ƒ250–300	

East of Friesland, the province of Groningen, equivalent to Charlemagne's East Frisia, has comparatively few attractions. Its villages tend to be dull and suburban, and most tourists stick to the university town of **Groningen**, a lively, cosmopolitan place that makes up for its shortage of historic sights with its busy bars and restaurants and the best nightlife in the north. Off the north coast lie the **Frisian Islands**, a fragmented extension of the sandbank that runs the length of Holland's western coastline. There are five populated Dutch islands in all, four of which are in Friesland (Texel, the fifth, is officially part of the province of North Holland, and is covered in the chapter of the same name; see pp.151–153). The most westerly two, **Vlieland** and **Terschelling**, are accessible by boat from Harlingen; further east, **Ameland** is reachable by bus and ferry from Leeuwarden, **Schiermonnikoog** by bus and boat from Leeuwarden or Groningen. One of the few areas of the country you have to put any effort into reaching, the islands preserve a rare peace and constitute an important nature area, with thriving colonies of birds and a rich flora and fauna. They're also, inevitably, popular holiday destinations, although the tourists who arrive here each summer are easily absorbed into the miles of beach and wide expanses of dune. Plans to build dykes connecting the islands to the mainland and reclaim the shallows all around were met with such resistance from naturalists and islanders that they have now been abandoned, and there's a strong feeling among the people here that they should remain as distinct from the Dutch mainland as possible.

South of Groningen, **Drenthe** is the most sparsely populated and least visited of the Dutch provinces, and it's not hard to see why. Though the Hondsdrug, the range of low hills that spreads northeast of Emmen towards Groningen, bears traces of settlement dating back to around 2500 BC – the earliest sign of any civilization in Holland – for most of its history Drenthe was little more than peat bog and barren moor, of little military or economic significance.

During the nineteenth century, the face of much of the province was changed by the founding of innumerable peat colonies, whose labourers drained the land and dug the peat to expose the subsoil below. As a result of their work, parts of Drenthe are given over to prosperous farmland, with agriculture the dominant local industry. Drenthe's two main towns are of no special interest and have only a couple of attractions that could conceivably bring you this far off the beaten track: **Assen**, the capital, has the Drents Museum, which has a superb collection of prehistoric finds, and **Emmen** is the best place to see Drenthe's most original feature – its *hunebeds*, or megalithic tombs.

Leeuwarden and around

An old market town at the heart of an agricultural district, **LEEUWARDEN** was formed from the amalgamation of three *terpen* that originally stood on an expanse of water known as the Middelzee. Later it was the residence of the powerful Frisian Stadholders, who vied with those of Holland for control of the United Provinces. These days it's the neat and distinctly cosy capital of Friesland, with an air of provincial prosperity and a smug sense of independence. It lacks the concentrated historic charm of many other Dutch towns, but it has a number of grand buildings and two outstanding museums, not to mention an appealingly compact town centre that is almost entirely surrounded and dissected by water.

Arrival, information and accommodation

Leeuwarden's **train and bus stations** virtually adjoin each other, five minutes' walk south of the town centre. The **VVV** at the train station (Mon–Fri 9am–5.30pm, Sat 10am–2pm, June–Aug Sat until 6pm; ☎06/320 24 060; ƒ1 per min) publishes a leaflet in English detailing a brick-by-brick walking tour of the centre and has a short list of private **rooms** that covers the whole of Friesland, including the town itself. There are only two reasonably priced **hotels** in town: the *De Pauw*, near the train station at Stationsweg 10 (☎212 3651, fax 216 0793; ③), is convenient and comfortable enough; the *Hotel 't Anker*, on the north side of the centre at Eewal 69–75 (☎212 5216, fax 212 8293; ③), is a good and more central alternative, though it does sometimes get full – book in advance if you can. The *Bastion* is a reliable fallback if the others are full, though it's a good walk out of town at Legedyk 6 (☎289 0112, fax 289 0512; ④); the plushest option is *Oranje*, across from the train station at Stationsweg 4 (☎212 6241, fax 212 1441; ⑤). **Camping Kleine Wielen** (☎431 660; April–Sept) is about 6km out toward Dokkum, nicely sited by a lake; take bus #20, #23, #51 or #62 from the station.

The town

If you've swallowed all the tourist office myths about Friesland being a land of historic beauty, rural charm and the like, Leeuwarden is initially a bit of a disappointment, with the southern part of the town centre near the station an indeterminate, rather careless mixture of the old and new. Heading north, high-rise blocks and shopping centres line Wirdumerdijk into the centre of town at **Waagplein**, a long, narrowing open space cut by a canal and flanked by cafés and large department stores. The **Waag** itself dates from 1598, but it's been converted into a restaurant and bank. Walking west, **Nieuwestad** is Leeuwarden's main shopping street, from where Kleine Kerkstraat, a turn on the right, leads to the **Oldehoofster Kerkhof** – a large square-cum-car park near the old city walls. At the end of the square stands the precariously leaning **Oldehove**. Something of a symbol for the city, this is part of a cathedral started in 1529 but never finished because of subsidence, a lugubrious mass of disproportion that defies all laws of gravity and geometry. To the right stands a statue of the Frisian politician and trade unionist P.J. Troelstra, who looks on impassively, no doubt admonishing the city fathers for their choice of architects. Those brave enough can climb the tower for a couple of guilders (Tues–Sun noon–4pm).

A little further west is the **Prinsentium**, a small park that was once the pleasure garden of the ruling Nassaus and which is still a quiet place to wander by the river and admire, on the other side, the bronze and rather thoughtful Frisian cow, donated to the city by the Frisian Cattle Syndicate.

Along Grote Kerkstraat

Grote Kerkstraat leads east from the square, following the line of the track that connected two of Leeuwarden's original *terpen*, Oldehove and Nijehove. Close by, at Grote Kerkstraat 11, is **Het Princessehof** (Mon–Sat 10am–5pm, Sun 2–5pm; *f*5), a house from 1650 that was once the residence of the Stadholder William Friso. It's now a ceramics museum, with the largest collection of tiles in the world, though the layout is a little confusing and there are no English-language guide-

books available. If you're really interested in ceramics you could spend days here; if not, be selective, as the sheer quantity of material is overwhelming.

Of the many displays, two are outstanding. The first, through the ornamental arch at the reception desk and up the stairs to the third floor, is the collection of **Chinese, Japanese and Vietnamese ceramics**, which outlines the rise and fall of Far Eastern "china" production. In the sixteenth century Portuguese traders first began to bring back Chinese porcelain for sale in Europe. It proved tremendously popular, and by the seventeenth century the Dutch, among others, had begun to muscle in. Ships crammed with plates and dishes shuttled back and forth to the China coast, where European merchants bargained with local warlords for trade and territorial concessions or "hongs" – hence Hong Kong. The benefits of the trade were inevitably weighted in favour of Western interests, and the Chinese could only watch with dismay as the bottom fell out of the market when European factories began to reproduce their goods. The Dutch soon modified the original, highly stylized designs to more naturalistic patterns with a lighter, plainer effect, with the result that Chinese producers were forced to make desperate attempts to change their designs to fit Western tastes.

The earliest pieces on display in this section date from the sixteenth century, notably several large blue and white plates of naive delicacy, decorated with swirling borders and surrealistic dragons. Although Chinese producers began to work to European designs in the early eighteenth century, it was many years before the general deterioration in manufacture became apparent, and some of the most exquisite examples of Chinaware date from as late as the middle of the eighteenth century – not least those from the Dutch merchantman *Geldermalsen*, which sank in the waters of the South China Sea in 1752 and was salvaged in 1983. Some 150,000 items of cargo were retrieved, and there's a small sample here, including a magnificent dish of bright-blue entwined fish bordered by a design of flowers and stems – in stark contrast to the crude, sad-looking Chinese imitations of Western landscapes and coats of arms across the room.

On the second floor, to the left of the stairs, you'll find another room devoted to the development of **Chinese porcelain** from prehistory onward, with representative examples illustrating major trends. The finest work dates from the Ming Dynasty (1368–1644), with powerful open-mouthed dragons, billowing clouds, and sharply drawn plant tendrils. This room leads to the other section you shouldn't miss, a magnificent array of **Dutch tiles**, with good examples of all the classic designs – soldiers, flowers, ships, and so forth – framed by uncomplicated borders. Well documented and clearly laid out, the earliest tiles date from the late fifteenth century, the work of Italians based in Antwerp who used a colourful and expensive tin-glazing process. By the seventeenth century, tiles were no longer exclusive to the wealthy, and the demands of a mass market transformed the industry. Popular as a wall covering – the precursor of wallpaper – thousands of identical tiles were churned out by dozens of Dutch factories (there were seven in Friesland alone). The emphasis was on very simple designs, characteristically blue on white, the top end of the market distinguished by extra colours or the size of the design: the more tiles it took to make the "picture", the more expensive the tile.

The collection of **European ceramics and porcelain** slots awkwardly around the other exhibits: best are the Art Deco and Art Nouveau pieces on the second floor, and the modern work in the basement. More interesting, if you're not too exhausted, is the small collection of **Middle Eastern tiles** in the basement, including thirteenth-century pieces from Persia and a few flamboyant Iznik tiles from the sixteenth century.

East of the museum along Grote Kerkstraat, the mildly diverting **Frisian Literary Museum** (Mon–Fri 9am–12.30pm & 1.30–5pm), is housed in the building (no. 212) where Mata Hari, something of a local heroine, spent her early years. Her old home has become a repository for a whole range of Frisian documents and a handful of pamphlets in English on the Frisian language. A permanent display details P J Troelstra, the Frisian socialist politician and poet, who set up the Dutch Social Democratic party in 1890 and headed the Dutch labour movement until 1924.

At the far end of Grote Kerkstraat, the **Grote** or **Jacobijner Kerk** (June–Sept Tues–Fri 2–4pm), though restored in the last few years, remains an unremarkable Gothic construction. Another victim of subsidence, the whole place tilts slightly toward the newer south aisle, where you can see some fragmentary remnants of sixteenth-century frescoes. In front of the church a modernistic **monument** remembers Leeuwarden's wartime Jewish community, based on the classroom registers of 1942; it's an imaginative and harsh reminder of suffering and persecution. Three minutes' walk west of the church, the **Frisian Nature Museum** at Schoenmakersperk 2 (Tues–Sun 10am–5pm & Sun 1–5pm; *f*5) has exhibitions on the flora and fauna of Friesland.

The Fries Museum and around

South of here, on Turfmarkt, the **Fries Museum** (Mon–Sat 11am–6pm, Sun 1–5pm; *f*6.50) is one of Holland's best regional museums. Founded by a society that was established in the nineteenth century to develop interest in the language and history of Friesland, the museum traces the development of Frisian culture from prehistoric times up until the present day. It has recently expanded to incorporate the Frisian Resistance Museum, with its story of the local resistance to Nazi occupation, and an exhibition on local heroine Mata Hari. Note that at the time of writing the museum is being overhauled to accommodate its new acquisitions, so some of the exhibits detailed below may well have been shifted.

For now, the museum's extensive collection of silver is concentrated on the ground floor of the main building. Silversmithing was a flourishing Frisian industry throughout the seventeenth and eighteenth centuries, most of the work commissioned by the local gentry, who were influenced by the fashions of the Frisian Stadholder and his court. The earliest piece is an elegant drinking horn of 1397, and there are some particularly fine examples of chased silver in Baroque style, where each representation is framed by a fanciful border or transition. This distinctive "Kwabornament" design flourished in Friesland long after it had declined in the rest of Holland. Some of the more curious exhibits date from the mid-seventeenth century when it was fashionable to frame exotic objects in silver: a certain Lenert Danckert turned a coconut into a cup, while Minne Sikkes fitted silver handles to a porcelain bowl to create a brandy cup. Most of the later exhibits are ornate, French-style tableware.

Upstairs, on the first floor, there's a selection of early majolica, many examples of different sorts of porcelain and a mundane collection of seventeenth-century Frisian painting. Rather more interesting are the rooms devoted to the island of Ameland and the painted furniture of Hindeloopen – rich, gaudy and intense, patterned with tendrils and flowers on a red, green or white background. Most peculiar of all are examples of the bizarre headgear of eighteenth-century

Hindeloopen women – large cartwheel-shaped hats known as *Deutsche muts* and (the less specifically Frisian) *oorijzers*, gold or silver helmets that were an elaborate development of the hat clip or brooch. As well as an indication of social standing, a young girl's first *oorijzer* symbolized the transition to womanhood.

The top floor of the main building has a chronological exhibition tracing the early days of the Nazi invasion, through collaboration and resistance on to the Allied liberation. A variety of photographs, Nazi militaria, Allied propaganda and tragic personal stories illustrate the text, but the emphasis is very much on the local struggle rather than the general war effort.

Back by the ticket desk downstairs, a passage leads through to the museum's second building where an exhibition on **Mata Hari** is currently under preparation. A native of Leeuwarden, Mata Hari's name has become synonymous with the image of the "femme fatale". A renowned dancer, she was arrested in 1917 by the French on charges of espionage and subsequently shot, though what she actually did remains a matter of some debate. In retrospect it seems likely that she acted as a double agent, gathering information for the Allies while giving snippets to the Germans. Photographs, letters and other mementoes illustrate the rather pathetic story.

Near the Fries Museum stands one of the most striking buildings in Leeuwarden – the **Kanselarij**, a superb gabled Renaissance structure of 1571, which hosts art exhibitions in the summer. The original plan placed the gable and the corresponding double stairway in the centre of the facade, but they are in fact slightly to the right because the money ran out before the work was finished. Just south of the Fries Museum, at Turfmarkt 48, the weirdly wonderful 1930s **Utrecht Building** today contains a restoration workshop. A little way north of Turfmarkt is the Catholic church of **St Boniface**, a belated apology to an English missionary killed by the pagan Frisians in 754, along with 52 other Christians, at nearby Dokkum. It's a neo-Gothic building of 1894 designed by P.J.H. Cuypers, its ornamented spire imposing itself on what is otherwise a rather flat skyline. The spire was almost totally destroyed in a storm of 1976 and many people wanted to take the opportunity to pull the place down altogether – even to replace it with a supermarket. Fortunately the steeple was replaced at great expense and with such enormous ingenuity that its future seems secure, making it one of the few Cuypers churches left in Holland.

Eating and drinking

One of the most popular places to **eat** in Leeuwarden is *Eetcafé Spinoza* on Eewal, a youthful, reasonably priced restaurant with a range of vegetarian dishes. Groente Markt nearby (and Uniabuurt which runs off it) offer a reasonable choice of restaurants including *Antonio's Pizzeria* and the Dutch-French *Eetcafe de Linde*, with early evening *dagschotels* at ƒ14.75, and *Eetcafe Havana*. There is Mexican food at the *Yucatan* on St Jacobsstraat or, further east, the rather smart *Café He Teven*, at Druifsteeg 57. If you're splashing out, the *Oranje Hotel* has two excellent restaurants; expect to pay around ƒ45 for three courses at the bistro and the same for one course at the main restaurant. Next door, and much cheaper, *Onder de Luifel* has a long though not particularly thrilling menu.

For **drinking** in a quiet atmosphere, settle down in the delightful old furniture at the bar of the *Hotel De Pauw*, Stationsweg 10; boisterous types prefer the *Herberg De Stee*, next door. In the centre of town, the *Fire Palace*, at Nieuwestad

N.Z. 49, overlooking the canal, is a big bar that doubles as the town's main disco at weekends. There's a series of lively bars on Doelesteeg, most with loud music, and quieter drinking spots across the bridge on Nieuwesteeg, including *de Bottelier* and *de Twee Gezusters*.

Listings

Boat tours For information on guided boat trips to the Frisian lakes contact the VVV.

Books *Van der Velde*, Nieuwestad 90, has a good stock of English-language titles.

Car parking Behind the train station (*f*5 per day).

Car rental *Budget*, Valeriusstraat 2 (☎213 5626).

Cinemas Nieuwestad 42 and 85.

Emergencies ☎0611.

Left luggage Lockers (*f*4 per day) at the station (daily 6am–midnight).

Markets General market on Mon & Fri, Wilhelminaplein.

Pharmacy Details of nearest (emergency) pharmacy on ☎213 5295.

Police Holstmeerweg 1 (☎213 2423).

Post office Oldehoofsterkerkhof 4 (Mon–Fri 9am–6pm & Sat 10am–1.30pm).

Around Leeuwarden: Popta Slot

On the western outskirts of Leeuwarden, the tiny village of **MARSSUM** incorporates **Popta Slot** (guided tours only: April–May & Sept–Oct Mon–Fri 2.30pm; June Mon–Fri 11am, 2pm & 3pm; July & Aug Mon–Sat hourly 11am–5pm; *f*6). The trim, onion-domed eighteenth-century manor house sits prettily behind its ancient moat; inside, the period rooms are furnished in the style of the local gentry. Doctor Popta was an affluent lawyer and farmer who spent some of his excess wealth on the neighbouring **Popta Gasthuis**: neat almshouses cloistered behind an elaborate portal of 1712. Buses #71 and #91 leave Leeuwarden bus station for the ten-minute trip to Marssum approximately every thirty minutes during the week, every hour on Sunday.

West of Leeuwarden: Franeker, Harlingen and the islands

Seventeen kilometres west of Leeuwarden, **FRANEKER** was the cultural hub of northern Holland until Napoleon closed the university in 1810. Nowadays it's a quiet country town with a spruce old centre of somewhat over-restored old buildings. The train station is five minutes' walk to the southeast of town – follow Stationsweg round to the left and over the bridge, first left over the second bridge onto Zuiderkade and second right along Dijkstraat. Buses from Leeuwarden drop off passengers on Kleijenburg, at the northwest corner of the old town centre.

All the town's key sights are beside or near the main street, **Voorstraat**, a continuation of Dijkstraat, which runs from east to west to end in a park, **Sternse Slotland** – the site of the medieval castle. Near the park at Voorstraat 51, the VVV is housed in the **Waag** of 1657, which also serves as the entrance to the **Museum**

't Coopmanshus (Tues–Sat 10am–5pm; May–Sept also Sun 1–5pm; *f*2.75) next door, whose ground floor has bits and pieces relating to the university and its obscure alumni. In the old senate room, there is a pile of slim boxes carved to resemble books that contain dried samples of local flora and fauna, the gift of Louis Bonaparte.

Heading east along Voorstraat, past the stolid **Martenahuis** of 1498, the Raadhuisplein branches off to the left; opposite, above the Friesland Bank, is the **Kaatsmuseum** (May–Sept Tues–Sat 1–5pm; *f*2.50), devoted to the Frisian sport of Kaatsen or Dutch tennis. The nearby **Stadhuis** (Mon–Fri 9am–noon & 2–4pm; free), with its twin gables and octagonal tower, is rather more interesting. It's a magnificent mixture of Gothic and Renaissance styles built in 1591 and worth a peek upstairs for the leather-clad walls – all the rage until French notions of wallpaper took hold in the eighteenth century. Opposite, at Eise Eisingastraat 3, there's a curious, primitive eighteenth-century **Planetarium** (Tues–Sat 10am–12.30pm & 1.30–5pm; May–Aug Mon–Sat 10am–12.30pm & 1.30–5pm, Sun 1–5pm; *f*5) built by a local woolcomber, Eise Eisinga, in his own home and now the oldest working planetarium in the world. Born in 1744, Eisinga was something of a prodigy: he taught himself mathematics and astronomy, publishing a weighty arithmetic book at the age of only seventeen. In 1774, the unusual conjunction of Mercury, Venus, Mars and Jupiter under the sign of Aries prompted a local paper to predict the end of the world. There was panic in the countryside, and an appalled Eisinga decided on his life's work, the construction of a planetarium that would dispel superstition by explaining the workings of the cosmos. It took him seven years, almost as long as he had to enjoy it before his distaste for the autocratic Frisian Stadholder caused his imprisonment and exile. His return signalled a change of fortunes. In 1816 he was presented with the order of the Lion of the Netherlands, and, two years later, a royal visit persuaded King Willem I to buy the planetarium for the state, granting Eisinga a free tenancy and a generous annual stipend until his death in 1828.

The planetarium isn't of the familiar domed variety but was built as a false ceiling in the family's living room, a series of rotating dials and clocks indicating the movement of the planets and associated phenomena, from tides to star signs. The whole apparatus is regulated by a clock which is driven by a series of weights hung in a tiny alcove beside the cupboard-bed. Above the face of the main dials, the mechanisms – hundreds of hand-made nails driven into moving slats – are open for inspection. A detailed guidebook explains every aspect and every dial and there's an explanatory video, in English, shown on request.

Practicalities

Franeker's **VVV** is at Voorstraat 51 (Tues–Sat 9am–5pm; ☎0517/394 613), five minutes' walk northwest of the train station. Of the town's **hotels**, your first choice should be the friendly *De Stadsherberg*, on the continuation of Stationsweg at Oude Kaatsveld 8 (☎0517/392 686, fax 398 095; ③), or failing that *De Bogt Fen Gune*, on the left turn at the west end of Voorstraat, Vijverstraat 1 (☎0517/392 416, fax 0517/393 111; ③) or the more basic *De Bleek*, near the station at Stationsweg 1 (☎0517/392 124; ③).

The town **campsite** (April–Sept) is ten minutes' walk north of the train station at Burg J Dijkstraweg 3 – up Stationsweg, Oud Kaatsveld and Leeuwarderweg, then left. For **food**, try *La Terraz*, Zilverstraat 7 or *De Grillerije* at Groenmarkt 14, both good for a sandwich or croissant at lunchtime. *Amicitia*, Voorstraat 9, is a reasonably priced cafe; *Grillerije*, Zilverstraat 14, is nice in the evening. The hotel *De Bogt Fen Gune* has the oldest student **bar** in the country and it's still worth dropping in for a drink.

Harlingen

Just north of the Afsluitdijk, 30km west of Leeuwarden, **HARLINGEN** is more compelling than Franeker. An ancient and historic port that serves as the ferry terminus for the islands of Terschelling and Vlieland, Harlingen is something of a centre for traditional Dutch sailing barges, a number of which are usually moored in the harbour. A naval base from the seventeenth century, the town straddles the **Vliestroom** channel, once the easiest way for shipping to pass from the North Sea through the shallows that surround the Frisian islands and on into the Zuider Zee. Before trade moved west, this was Holland's lifeline, where cereals, fish and other foodstuffs were brought in from the Baltic to feed the expanding Dutch cities.

Harlingen has two **train stations**: one on the southern edge of town for trains from Leeuwarden, the other, Harlingen Haven, right next to the docks, handling trains connecting with boats to the islands. From Harlingen Haven the old town spreads east, sandwiched between the pretty Noorderhaven and more functional Zuiderhaven canals, a mass of sixteenth- to eighteenth-century houses that reflect the prosperity and importance of earlier times. However, Harlingen is too busy to be just another cosy tourist town: there's a fishing fleet, a small container depot, a shipbuilding yard and a resurgent ceramics industry. The heart of town is the **Voorstraat**, a long, tree-lined avenue that's home to an elegant eighteenth-century **Stadhuis**, the **VVV** and the **Hannemahuis Museum** at no. 56 (July to mid-Sept Tues–Sat 10am–5pm; mid-Sept to Nov 1 & April–June Mon–Fri 1.30–5pm; *f*2.50). Sited in an eighteenth-century merchant's house, the museum concentrates on the history of the town and includes some interesting displays on shipping and some lovely, locally produced tiles – for once in manageable quantities.

Harlingen was once a tile-making centre, and the industry flourished here until it was undermined by the rise of cheap wallpaper. The last of the old

---

REACHING THE ISLANDS

Ferries leave Harlingen for the crossings (about 1hr 45min) to the islands of Terschelling and Vlieland at least three times daily throughout the summer and twice daily during the winter. The return fares are currently *f*33.40 for either island, plus *f*16.70 for bikes. The ferries dock at West Terschelling and Oost-Vlieland, the islands' main settlements. From May to the end of September there's an additional ferry service connecting Terschelling and Vlieland (*f*7.50 one-way). There's also a fast **hydrofoil** service: from May to September it runs three times a day to Terschelling, twice daily to Vlieland and from September to May twice a day to Terschelling only. The hydrofoil costs an extra *f*10 each way, but at around only 45 minutes it's worth it if you're going for a day trip.

Visitors' cars are not allowed on Vlieland, but in any case the best way of exploring any of the Frisian islands is by **bike**. There are rental companies near the ferry terminals on both islands, charging a uniform rate of *f*8 per day, *f*32 per week, for a basic bike – although given the steep, stony hills, it's worth shelling out a few extra guilders for a machine with decent gears.

factories closed in 1933, but the demand for traditional crafts has led to something of a recovery, with the opening of new workshops in the Seventies. If you like the look of Dutch tiles, this is a good place to buy. The **Harlinger Aardewerk en Tegelfabriek** at Voorstraat 84 sells an outstanding range of contemporary and traditional styles, if you've got the money – Dutch handicrafts don't come cheap. Finally, the **Galerie de Vis** at Noordehaven 40 (Wed–Fri 1–5pm & Sat 11am–5pm) has occasional displays of local art and merits a brief detour.

Practicalities

No great bargains on the **accommodation** front in Harlingen. The *Heerenlogement* is on the eastern continuation of Voorstraat at Franekereind 23 (☎0517/415 846, fax 412 762; ④), while the slightly more expensive *Anna Casparii* (☎0517/412 065, fax 414 540; ④) is more central, on the canal at Noorderhaven 6. Third choice is the *Zeezicht*, by the harbour at Zuiderhaven 1 (☎0517/412 536; ⑤), which, despite its higher rates, isn't in such a nice location. For about half the price, the **VVV** at Voorstraat 34 (May–Aug Mon–Fri 9am–6pm, Sat 9am–12.30pm & 1.30–5pm; Sept–April Mon–Fri 9am–5pm, Sat 10am–3pm; ☎06/916 81625; ƒ1 per minute) has a stock of **rooms** and **pensions**, many of which you'll spot by walking down Noorderhaven. The nearest **campsite**, *De Zeehoeve* (April–Sept), is a twenty-minute walk along the sea dyke to the south of town at Westerzeedijk 45 – follow the signs from Voorstraat.

As you'd expect, Harlingen's speciality is fresh **fish**, and there are fish stands, fish restaurants and snack bars dotted around the centre of town. Best is *Veltman's* on the edge of the Noorderhaven at Rommelhaven 2, a combined snack bar and restaurant with a wide range of North Sea delicacies. Alternatives are the *de Gastronoom* next to the VVV, *de Noordepoort* at Noorderhaven 17, which has good-value daily specials, and the hotel restaurants. **Nightlife** is quiet but there are several decent **bars**, including *'t Skutsje*, on the corner of Frankereind and Heligeweg.

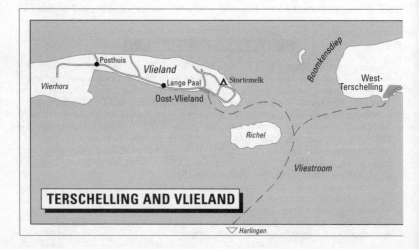

Terschelling

Of all the Frisian islands, **Terschelling** is the easiest to reach – which is both an attraction and a problem. If you just want a taste of the islands without making too much effort, this is the place to head for; but, if you're looking for tranquillity, Vlieland, Ameland or Schiermonnikoog are a better bet. A major tourist resort in its own right, the town of **WEST TERSCHELLING** is a rather unappealing sprawl of chalets, bungalows and holiday complexes that spreads out from what remains of the old village – a mediocre modernity that belies West Terschelling's past importance as a port and safe anchorage on the edge of the Vliestroom channel, the main shipping lane from the Zuider Zee.

Strategically positioned, West Terschelling boomed throughout the seventeenth century as a ship supply and repair centre, with its own fishing and whaling fleets, paying the price for its prominence when the British razed the town in 1666. The islanders were renowned sailors, much sought after by ships' captains who also needed them as pilots to guide vessels through the treacherous shallows and shifting sandbanks that lay off the Vliestroom. Despite the pilots, shipwrecks were common all along the island's northern and western shores – the VVV sells a sketch of the island marked with all the known disasters. The most famous victim was the *Lutine*, which sank while carrying gold and silver to British troops stationed here during the Napoleonic wars. The remains are still at the bottom of the sea, and only the ship's bell was recovered – now in Lloyd's of London, where it's still rung whenever a big ship goes down.

The best place to bone up on Terschelling's past is the excellent **Museum 't Behouden Huys**, near the ferry terminus at Commandeurstraat 30 (April 1–Oct 31 Mon–Fri 10am–5pm; June 15–Sept 30 also Sat 1–5pm; *f*5). Prime exhibits here include maps of the old coastline illustrating Terschelling's crucial position, various items from the whaling fleet, lots of sepia photos of bearded islanders and a shipwreck diving room. There's also a rather desultory tribute to the local explorer Willem Barents, who hit disaster when pack ice trapped his ship in the Arctic

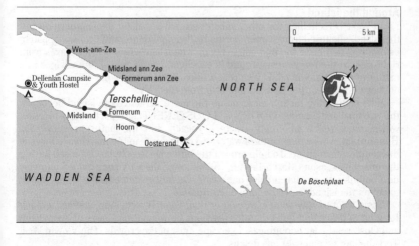

in 1595. Undaunted, he and his crew managed to survive the whole winter on the ice and sailed back in the spring. Barents mounted other, more successful expeditions into the Arctic regions, discovering Spitzbergen and naming the Barents Sea – all in the fruitless search for the northwest passage to China. He died in the Arctic in 1597. If you're extra keen on things aquatic, there's a tiny **Fishing Museum** at the back of a shop on Radhuisstraat (Mon–Sat 10am–noon & 2–5pm; *f*1.50) and, just east of town, the **Centre for Nature and Landscape**, Burg Reedekerstraat 11 (April–Oct Mon–Sat 9am–5pm, Nov–March Mon–Sat 2-6pm; *f*7.50), which contains a decent aquarium.

Throughout the summer West Terschelling is packed with tourists sampling the restaurants and bars that line the main streets, Torenstraat in particular, while others cycle off across the island to the beach at **WEST-AAN-ZEE** where there's a café, *Zilver Meeuw*, and as much empty beach as you're prepared to look for. On a more sombre note, the more northerly of the two cycling routes passes through an odd cemetery in a wood, with a small Commonwealth forces graveyard – as ever the inscriptions make sad reading, with few of the downed bomber crews aged more than 25.

West Terschelling practicalities

Accommodation is hard to come by in July and August when all the cheaper places tend to be booked up months in advance. At other times you have a wide choice – try *Pension Spitsbergen*, Burg Reedekerstraat 50 (☎0562/443 162; ③), or *Hotel Aletha*, Trompstraat 6 (☎0562/442 050), both not far from the ferry terminus. There's a **youth hostel** at Burgmeester Van Heusdenweg 39 (April–Sept; ☎0562/442 338), and several **campsites** east of town along the southern shore.

The **VVV** (Mon–Fri 9am–noon & 2–5.30pm, Sat 11am–noon & 4–5pm; ☎0562/443 000), near the ferry port, provides a full list of pensions and **rooms** and operates a booking service (*f*5). They also take bookings for the rest of the island, offer a variety of **walking tours**, and can give details of cycling routes.

Around the island

From West Terschelling the other villages stretch out along the southern part of the island, sheltered from winter storms by the sand dunes and occasional patches of forest that lie to the immediate north. The island's **bus** service leaves from right next to the ferry terminus and is excellent, connecting all the villages in a matter of minutes; you could also rent a **bike**, for about *f*8 a day from a number of shops down near the harbour and also from the VVV.

Quite simply, the further east you go the more attractive the island becomes: the two final settlements, **HOORN** and **OOSTEREND**, are particularly pleasant within easy reach of empty tracts of beach and the nature reserve **De Boschplaat**, where thousands of waterfowl congregate in the marshy shallows of the southeastern shore. To help protect the birds, De Boschplaat is closed during the breeding season (March 15–Aug 15), although the VVV runs guided tours for bird enthusiasts. Oosterend also has a **café**, *De Boschplaat*, one of the best places to eat on the island, and a handful of **campsites**.

If you want to **stay** somewhere other than West Terschelling, and are looking for a bit of peace and quiet, aim for pensions between the villages of Formerum and Oosterend – far enough east to escape most of the crowds. The VVV in West Terschelling (see above) has details.

Vlieland

The complex pattern of sandbank shallows that lies to the south of **Vlieland**, just west of Terschelling, helped to make the island one of the most isolated and neglected parts of nineteenth-century Holland. Of minor importance during the great days of the Zuider Zee trade, Vlieland lost one of its two villages to the sea in the eighteenth century, and there was never enough money to have it rebuilt. Tourism has brought wealth to the thousand or so islanders, but it's all very low key: development has been restrained and the island is popular for family holidays – cycling, windsurfing, beaches and country walks. The quietest of the Frisian islands, no cars are allowed, and the only settlement, **OOST-VLIELAND**, is little more than a restaurant-lined main street surrounded by second homes, chalets and bungalows. There's little to see in the village as such, although the plastic globe in the small square is a surprising tribute to Esperanto, and the Armenhuis behind it a particularly attractive seventeenth-century country dwelling. The town's museum, the **Tromps Huys** at Dorpsstraat 99 (Mon–Sat 10am–noon & 2–5pm), has a mundane collection of antiques and Vlieland bygones.

Practicalities

Accommodation is limited, and virtually impossible to find throughout the summer, although the **VVV** at Havenweg 10 (Mon–Fri 9am–5pm; Oct–April also Sat 11am–noon; May–Sept also Sat & Sun 11am–noon & 4–5pm; ☎0562/451 111) does its best with the few private **rooms**, and will help groups rent apartments and "dune houses". Cheapest of the hotels and pensions is the *Duin en Dal* on the main street at Dorpsstraat 163 (☎0562/451 684; ③); you'll find more for around the same price along the road, as well as the more comfortable *Badhotel Bruin*, Dorpstraat 88 (☎0562/451 301, fax 451 227; ④) and the smart *De Wadden*, Dorpstraat 61 (☎ & fax 0562/451 955; ⑤). The most convenient **campsite**, *De Stortemelk* (☎0562/451 225), is on the sand dunes behind the beach, about half an hour's walk or a ten-minute bike ride northeast of Oost-Vlieland, at Kampweg 1.

The best way of seeing the island is by bike, though there's also a limited **bus** service that travels along the southern shore from near the ferry terminus. For **excursions**, the VVV run birdwatching expeditions, and private operators organize day-trips to the northern tip of Texel (*f*15 return) by means of a tractor-like lorry, which crosses the great expanse of sand ("Vliehors") that forms Vlieland's western extremity to connect with a boat.

South of Leeuwarden: Sneek, the lakes, and the IJsselmeer ports

The Leeuwarden–Stavoren train line passes through a series of small Frisian towns with a speed that gainsays their earlier isolation. Until well into the nineteenth century, the lakes, canals and peat diggings south and east of Sneek made land communications difficult, and the only significant settlements were built close to the sea or on major waterways. Dependent on water-borne commerce, these communities declined with the collapse of the Zuider Zee trade, but, because of their insularity, some maintained particular artistic and cultural traditions – from the painted furniture and distinctive dialect of Hindeloopen to the style and design of many of Makkum's tiles. Passing through by train, the small settlements resemble what in fact they once were – islands in the shallow marshes. Nowadays, all the tiny old towns are popular holiday destinations, of which **Sneek**, the centre of a booming pleasure-boat industry, is by far the busiest.

Sneek

Twenty minutes by train from Leeuwarden, **SNEEK** (pronounced "snake") was an important shipbuilding centre as early as the fifteenth century, a prosperous maritime town protected by an extensive system of walls and moats. Clumsy post-war development has robbed the place of most of its charm – its centre has one of the most interminable shopping precincts in western Europe – but there are still some buildings of mild interest.

Sneek's **train** and **bus** stations are five minutes' walk from the old centre, directly east down Stationsstraat. This leads to the scruffy main square, **Martiniplein**, whose ponderous sixteenth-century **Martinikerk** (mid-June to Aug Mon–Sat 2.30–5pm, Tues–Fri also 7.30–9pm; free) is edged by an old wooden belfry. Around the corner at the end of Grote Kerkstraat, the **Stadhuis**, Marktstraat 15, is all extravagance, from the Rococo facade to the fanciful outside staircase; inside (July–Aug Mon–Fri 2–4pm) there's an indifferent display of ancient weapons in the former guardroom. Heading east along Marktstraat, veer right after the VVV and follow the signs to the nearby **Scheepvart Museum en Oudheidkamer**, Kleinzand 14 (Mon–Sat 10am–5pm, Sun noon–5pm; ƒ3.50), a well-displayed collection of maritime models, paintings, and related miscellany. There's also a room devoted to the Visser family, who made a fortune in the eighteenth century, transporting eels to hungry Londoners. A little further along, at Kleinzand 32, the **Weduwe Joustra** off-licence has an original nineteenth-century interior, worth glancing in for its old barrels and till, even if you decide not to indulge in a bottle of *Beerenburg*, a herb-flavoured gin that's a local speciality. Similarly worth a passing look is **De Tovebal**, an old sweetshop directly south of the Martiniplein at Oude Koemarkt 17. Turn right at the end of Koemarkt and you reach the grandiose **Waterpoort** – all that remains of the seventeenth-century town walls.

If you want to see more of the lakes, there are **boat trips** in July and August leaving from the Oosterkade, over the bridge by the east end of Kleinzand. Itineraries and prices vary and there's no fixed schedule of sailings: you can do anything from a quick whizz around the town's canals to venturing out into the open sea. Contact the VVV or the boat owners at the dock for up-to-date details.

Practicalities

Sneek gets exceptionally busy and accommodation is impossible to find during **Sneek Week**, the annual regatta held at the beginning of August, when the flat green expanses around town are thick with the white of slowly moving sails. At other times, if you want to stay in Sneek, the **VVV**, right in the centre of town near the Stadhuis at Marktstraat 18 (Mon–Fri 9am–5pm & Sat 9am–2pm; ☎0515/414 096), will arrange private **rooms** for a small fee. The town's cheapest **hotel** is the down-at-heel *Ozinga,* immediately south of the Waterpoort at Lemmerweg 8 (☎0515/412 216, fax 419 212; ③). The *Bonnema,* by the train station at

Stationsstraat 64 (☎0515/413 175, fax 425 455; ④), is more comfortable, while *De Wijnberg*, Marktstraat 23 (☎0515/412 421, fax 413 369; ④) is good value and central. The **youth hostel** (☎0515/412 132; mid-June to mid-Sept) is some 2km southeast of the town centre at Oude Oppenhuizerweg 20 – head east to the end of Kleinzand, turn right down Oppenhuizerweg, and it's the first major road on the left. The nearest **campsite** is *De Domp*, Domp 4 (☎0515/412 559; no buses), a couple of kilometres northeast of the centre on Sytsingawiersterleane, a right turn off the main road to Leeuwarden. *Camping De Potten*, Paviljoenweg (☎0515/415 205; April–Sept), lies some 5km east of town beside the pretty **Sneekemeer**, the nearest of the Frisian lakes, and a bus runs from the town in July and August. *De Potten* rents a good range of watersports equipment at reasonable prices and the VVV can give you a list of other rental options.

Sneek has a large number of **restaurants**, few of which have much character: Leeuwenburg, behind the VVV, is the best place to look for reasonably priced *dagschotels* – try *Van der Wal* – while *'t Stoofje*, Oude Koemarkt 11, has a variety of tasty pancakes. *Hinderlooper Kamer*, Oosterdijk 10, is a smart, cheerful bistro with reasonably priced Dutch food; *Klein Java*, Singel 65, offers Indonesian meals. The best **bars** are on Leeuwenburg too, including *Amicitia*, with a cinema next door providing distraction from the quiet night-life.

Bolsward

Some 10km west of Sneek, **BOLSWARD** (pronounced "Bozwut" in the local dialect) is the archetypal Frisian country town, with tractors on the roads and geese in the streets. Founded in the seventh century, this was a bustling and important textile centre in the Middle Ages, though its subsequent decline has left a small population of around ten thousand and only a handful of worthwhile sights. Your first stop should be the **Stadhuis**, at Jongemastraat 2 – a magnificent red-brick, stone-trimmed Renaissance edifice of 1613. The facade is topped by a lion holding a coat of arms over the head of a terrified – or surprised – Turk, and below a mass of twisting, curling carved stone frames a series of finely cut cameos, all balanced by an extravagant external staircase. Inside there's a small **museum** of local archeological/historical bits and pieces (April–Nov Mon–Fri 9am–noon & 2–4pm; slightly longer hours in summer). Ten minutes' walk away, the fifteenth-century **Martinikerk** at Groot Kerkhof (Mon–Fri 9am–noon & 1.30–5pm; *f*2.50) is Bolsward's other major sight, originally built on an earthen mound for protection from flooding. Some of the wood carving inside is quite superb: the choir with its rare misericords from 1470 and, particularly, the seventeenth-century pulpit, carved by two local men from a single oak tree. The panels depict the four seasons: the Frisian baptism dress above the young eagle symbolizes spring, while the carved ice skates (winter) on the other side are thought to be unique. The Reformation was a little less iconoclastic here than elsewhere, and the only visible damage is the odd smashed nose on some of the figures. The stone font dates from around 1000, while the stained-glass windows at the back depict occupation by the Nazis and subsequent liberation by the Canadians.

Practicalities

Buses #98 and #99 connect Sneek train station with Bolsward (Mon–Sat 3 hourly, Sun hourly; 15min), and, should you decide to **stay**, the **VVV**, Marktplein 1 (Mon

1.30–5.30pm, Tues–Fri 9am–12.30pm & 1.30–5.30pm, Sat 9.30am–1.30pm; ☎0515/572 727), has a handful of private **rooms**. There are two convenient **hotels**, the *Centraal*, Nieuwmarkt 10 (☎0515/572 589; ③), and, a little pricier, *De Wijnberg*, Marktplein 5 (☎0515/572 220, fax 572 665; ③), and a couple of **pensions** by the Martinikerk.

Workum

Ten minutes southwest of Sneek by train, **WORKUM**, a long, straggly town with an attractive main street, has the appearance of a comfortable city suburb, protected by several kilometres of sea defences. In fact, until the early eighteenth century it was a seaport, though nowadays indications of a more adventurous past are confined to the central square, 3km from the train station, with its seventeenth-century **Waag** at Merk 4, which contains a standard nautical-historical collection (March–Oct Tues–Fri 10am–5pm, Mon, Sat & Sun 1–5pm; ƒ2.50). Immediately behind, the **St Gertrudskerk** (Mon–Sat 11am–5pm; ƒ1.50), the largest medieval church in Friesland, contains a small collection of mostly eighteenth-century odds and ends. Far more absorbing, if you're into religious art, is the **Museum Kerkelijke Kunst** in the neo-Gothic St Werenfridus Kerk at Noard 175 (June to mid-Sept Mon–Sat 1.30–5pm; ƒ2.50). Just down the road at Noard 6, the likeable **Jopie Huisman Museum** (April–Oct Mon–Sat 10am–5pm; ƒ5) is devoted to paintings by a contemporary artist, most of which have an appealingly unpretentious focus on Frisian life.

If you want to **stay over**, the VVV (Tues–Sat 10am–5pm, Sun & Mon 1–5pm; ☎0515/541 300) across from the Merk at Noard 5, has a limited number of **private rooms**. Alternatively, head for the *Gulden Leeuw*, Merk 2 (☎0515/542 341, fax 543 127; ④) where facilities include a decent restaurant, or the *Hotel de Wijnberg*, next door at Merk 3 (☎0515/541 370; ④).

Makkum

From Workum train station a minibus service (#102, Mon–Sat every 2–3hr; 30min) heads south to Hindeloopen (see opposite) or north to the agreeable town of **MAKKUM** – in fact more easily accessible from Bolsward by bus #98 (Mon–Sat hourly, Sun afternoon every 2hr; 20min). Though saved from postcard prettiness by a working harbour, Makkum's popularity as a centre of traditional Dutch ceramics manufacture means it can be overwhelmed by summer tourists. The local product rivals the more famous Delftware in quality, varying from the bright and colourful to more delicate pieces. The VVV (Mon–Fri 10am–noon & 1–5pm; summer Mon–Sat 10am–5pm & Sun 1.30–5pm; ☎0515/231 422) is sited in the old Waag beneath the **Fries Aardewerkmuseum** (May–Sept Mon–Sat 10am–5pm, Sun 1.30–5pm; ƒ3), which features, predictably enough, representative samples of local work. If you haven't seen enough tiles here to satisfy your curiosity, there's plenty more, notably in the Tichelaar family **workshops** at Turfmarkt 65 (Mon–Fri 9am–5.30pm, Sat 10am–5pm; ƒ3), or you can visit their two shops for free, at Kerkstraat 9 and Plein 10. There are no bargains, though, and most of the modern tiles have either staid traditional motifs or ooze an unappealing domestic cosiness; the vases and larger plates are more exciting but also more expensive.

If you decide to **stay**, the VVV has a few **private rooms**; otherwise try *Hotel de Prins* at Kerkstraat 1 (☎0515/231 510; ③), or the more pleasantly located *De*

Waag, two minutes around the corner at Markt 13 (☎0515/231 447; ③). Both hotels contain basic, low-priced restaurants; or head for *De Maitak* on Markt, which does a good range of sandwiches, pizzas and light lunches.

Hindeloopen

Next stop down the rail line, the village of **HINDELOOPEN** juts into the IJsselmeer twenty minutes' walk west of the train station, its primness extreme even by Dutch standards. Until the seventeenth century Hindeloopen prospered as a Zuider Zee port, concentrating on trade with the Baltic and Amsterdam. A tightly knit community, the combination of rural isolation and trade created a specific culture, with a distinctive dialect – *Hylper*, Frisian with Scandinavian influences – a sumptuous costume and, most famous of all, an elaborate style of painted furniture. Adopting materials imported into Amsterdam by the East India Company, the women of Hindeloopen dressed in a florid combination of colours where dress was a means of personal identification: caps, casques and trinkets indicated marital status and age, and the quality of the print indicated social standing. Other Dutch villages adopted similar practices, but nowhere were the details of social position so precisely drawn. The development of dress turned out to be a corollary of prosperity, for the decline of Hindeloopen quite simply finished it off. Similarly, the furniture was an ornate mixture of Scandinavian and Oriental styles superimposed on traditional Dutch carpentry. Each item was covered from head to toe with painted tendrils and flowers on a red, green or white background, though again the town's decline resulted in the lapsing of the craft. Tourism has revived local furniture-making, and countless shops now line the main street selling modern versions, though even the smallest items aren't cheap, and the florid style is something of an acquired taste.

Tradition apart, Hindeloopen is a delightful little village pressed against the sea in a tidy jigsaw of old streets and canals, crossed by wooden footbridges; it's popular – and very busy – in summer with yachting types who keep their boats in the huge marina, and windsurfers who benefit from the shallow, sloping beach to the south of the town. There are no particular sights, but the **church** – a seventeenth-century structure with a medieval tower – has some Royal Air Force graves of airmen who came down in the Zuider Zee, while the small **Schaats Museum**, Kleine Wiede 1 (Mon–Sat 10am–6pm & Sun 1–5pm), displays some skating mementoes relating to the great Frisian ice-skating race, "De Friese Elfstedentocht" (see p.220), as well as plenty of painted Hindeloopen-ware in its out-front shop. You can see original examples of this in the small village museum, the **Hidde Nijland Museum**, next door to the church (March–Oct Mon–Sat 10am–5pm, Sun 1.30–5pm; *f*3.50), although there's a wider display at the Fries Museum in Leeuwarden.

Practicalities

Hindeloopen's popularity makes finding **accommodation** a problem during the summer, and the town's hotels – the *Skipshotel*, Oosterstrand 22 (☎0514/522 452, fax 521 680; ④), and the newer *De Stadsboerderij*, Nieuwe Weide 9 (☎0514/521 278; ④) – tend to fill up early. Book well in advance if you want to be sure of getting a room. The **VVV**, on the main street at no. 26 (summer Mon–Sat 10am–noon & 1–5pm; ☎0514/522 550) can organize the odd private **room**, and the only other

THE ELFSTEDENTOCHT

The **Elfstedentocht** is Friesland's biggest spectacle, a gruelling ice-skating marathon around Friesland that dates back to 1890, when one Pim Muller, a local sports journalist, skated his way around the eleven official towns of the province – simply to see whether it was possible. It was, and twenty years later the first official Elfstedentocht or "Eleven Towns Race" was born, contested by 22 skaters. Weather – and ice – permitting, it has taken place regularly ever since, nowadays a major ice-skating event, attracting skaters from all over the world.

The race is organized by the Eleven Towns Association, of which you have to be a member to take part. Perhaps not surprisingly, current interest means membership is restricted and very difficult to obtain, over-subscribed by around seventeen times at the last count. The route of the race, which measures about 200km in total, takes in all the main centres of Friesland, starting in Leeuwarden, at about 5am in the town's Friesland Hall, when the racers sprint, skates in hand, 1500m to the point where they start skating. The first stop after this is Sneek, taking in Hindeloopen and the other old Zuider Zee towns before finishing in Dokkum in the north of the province. The contestants must stop briefly at each town to have their card stamped. These days the event is broadcast live on TV across the country, and the route lined with spectators. Of the seventeen thousand or so who take part in the race, only around three hundred are serious skaters; the rest are there just to see if they can complete the course.

All the skaters need to have all-round fitness. They attempt to skate the whole route, but it's not always possible, and at times – crossing from one canal to another, for example, or avoiding a stretch of thin ice – they have to try something called *kluning*, a Frisian word which basically means walking on dry land in skates: not easy. Casualties are inevitably numerous. Of the ten thousand who took part in 1963, only seventy or so finished, the rest beaten by the fierce winds, extreme cold and snowdrifts along the way. On the last few occasions things have been gentler, around three-quarters of those who started out crossing the finishing line. But competitors still go down with frostbite, and many have to drop out because their sweat turns to ice and clogs up their eyes – a condition only a trip to hospital will put right.

alternative is the **campsite**, 1km or so to the south of town near the coast at Westerdijk 9. For **eating**, try the smart *De Gasterie*, just off the harbour at Kalverstraat 13, a lovely place to dine in the evening, or *De Brabander*, Nieuwe Wiede 7, which has main dishes on offer for under *f*20 and a wide array of excellent pancakes – good for both lunch and dinner. Failing that, the stands on the harbour serve fishy snacks during the day.

Sloten

Close to the southern coast of Friesland, the main problem with **SLOTEN** is getting there. Of the possible permutations, the easiest option is to take bus #42 (Mon–Fri every 30min Sat & Sun hourly; 35min) from Sneek train station to the bus change-over point on the motorway at Spannenburg, where connecting service #41 continues west to Sloten, and #44 runs on to Sloten and Bolsward. Double-check your destination with the driver as there are connecting buses with the same numbers heading east.

The smallest of Friesland's eleven towns, Sloten was ruined by the demise of the Zuider Zee trade, and, robbed of its importance, it became something of a museum-piece. Little more than a main street on either side of a central canal, Heerenval, it's really not worth going out of your way for, although it *is* undeniably charming, even if there are a lot of other people sharing its cobbled alleys, windmill, old locks and decorated gables. There's a small **museum** in the town hall on Heerenval (Tues–Fri 10am–noon & 2–5pm, Sat & Sun 2–5pm) but otherwise nothing at all to see. **Accommodation** is limited to a **campsite**, the *Lemsterpoort*, Jachthaven 3, and the **pension** *'t Brechje* at Voorstreek 110 (☎0514/531 298; ②), so call ahead to make sure of a vacancy. The **VVV**, at Heerenwal 57 (Tues, Wed, Fri & Sat 10am–noon & 2–4pm; ☎0514/531 583), rarely has rooms to rent. A couple of **restaurants** on the canal by the bridge do good light lunches and more expensive evening meals, and have nice outdoor seating.

Stavoren

At the end of the rail line, **STAVOREN** – also once a prosperous port – is now an ungainly combination of modern housing and old harbour, from where **ferries** make the crossing to Enkhuizen (see p.143) for connecting trains to Amsterdam (see *North Holland* for rough frequencies and prices). Named after the Frisian god Stavo, Stavoren is a popular boating centre and has a large marina adjoining a **campsite** that in turn is just behind a pleasant sandy beach, some ten minutes' walk south of the train station. The campsite is surrounded by a swampy strip of water, so come equipped with mosquito repellent. The best place to **stay** is the hotel *De Vrouwe van Stavoren,* Havenweg 1 (☎0514/681 202, fax 681 205; ③), attractively sited by the harbour and surprisingly good value. The **VVV** is on the harbour, two minutes' walk from the station (April–Oct Mon–Sat 9.30am–noon, 1–4.30pm & 5.45–6.15pm, Sun 9.45–10.15am, 1.45–2.15pm & 5.45–6.15pm; ☎0514/681 616) and has details of pensions and private rooms, but you'll probably want to move straight on.

North of Leeuwarden: Dokkum and the islands

Edged by the Lauwersmeer to the east and protected by interlocking sea-dykes to the north, the strip of Friesland between Leeuwarden and the Waddenzee is dotted with tiny agricultural villages that were once separated from each other by swamp and marsh. Sparsely inhabited, the area's first settlers were forced to confine themselves to whatever higher ground was available, the terpen which kept the treacherous waters at bay.

DOKKUM, the only significant settlement and one of Friesland's oldest towns, is half an hour by bus from Leeuwarden (#50 & 51; Mon–Fri 3 per hour, Sat & Sun hourly). The English missionary Saint Boniface and 52 of his companions were murdered here in 754 while trying to convert the pagan Frisians to Christianity. In part walled and moated, Dokkum has kept its shape as a fortified town, but it's best by the side of the Het Grootdiep canal, which cuts the town into two distinct sections. This was the commercial centre of the old town and is marked by a series of ancient gables, including the **Admiralty Building**

which serves as the town's mediocre **museum** (April–Sept Mon–Sat 10am–5pm; rest of year Mon–Sat 2–5pm; ƒ3). There's not much else: a couple of windmills, quiet walks along the old ramparts and all sorts of things named after St Boniface. Give it a couple of hours and move on. If you decide to stay, the **VVV** at Grote Breedstraat 1 (Mon 1–5pm, Tues–Fri 9am–6pm, Fri also 7–9pm, Sat 9am–5pm; ☎0519/293 800) has a supply of private **rooms**, while the cheapest hotel is the *Van der Meer*, Woudweg 1 (☎0519/292 380; ③). There's not much choice as far as **eating** goes: at lunchtime *De Waag*, at Waagstraat 11, serves a good variety of sandwiches and croissants; in the evening your best bet is *'t Raadhuis* on Nauwstraat, or try *Pizzeria Romana*, on Koornmarkt just off the main canal.

Wierum and Moddergat

Of all the tiny hamlets in north Friesland, two of the most interesting are Wierum and neighbouring Moddergat. **MODDERGAT**, the more easterly of the two, spreads out along the road behind the seawall 10km north of Dokkum, merging with the village of Paesens. At the western edge of the village, a memorial commemorates the 1893 tragedy when seventeen ships were sunk by a storm with the loss of 83 lives. Opposite, the **'t Fiskerhuske Museum**, Fiskerpad 4–8 (March–Oct Mon–Sat 10am–5pm; ƒ3) comprises three restored fishermen's cottages with displays on the history and culture of the village and details of the disaster: as such small museums go, it's pretty good. Huddled behind the sea-dyke 5km to the west, **WIERUM** has one main claim to fame, its twelfth-century church with a saddle-roof tower and (as in Moddergat) a golden ship on the weather vane. The dyke offers views across to the islands and holds a monument of twisted anchors to the local fishermen who died in the 1893 storm and the dozen or so claimed in the century since. The Wadloopcentrum here organizes guided walks across the mud flats: times vary with conditions and tides; further details from Dokkum VVV.

Readily accessible from Dokkum, Moddergat and Wierum are on the same bus route (#52; Mon–Sat 7 daily, Sun 2 daily). There are a couple of places to stay, the farmhouse pension *Meinsma*, at Meinsmaweg 5 in Moddergat (☎0519/589 396; ③), or the pension *Visser* in Wierum (☎0519/589 727; ③).

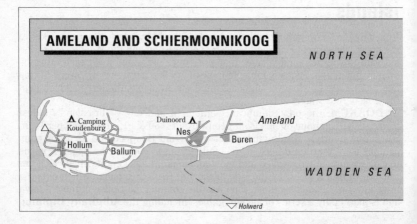

AMELAND AND SCHIERMONNIKOOG

NORTH SEA

▲ Camping Koudenburg Duinoord ▲ *Ameland*
Nes
Hollum Ballum Buren

WADDEN SEA

▽ Holwerd

Ameland

Easy to reach from the tiny port of Holwerd, a few kilometres from Wierum, the island of **Ameland** is one of the major tourist resorts of the north Dutch coast, with a population that swells from a mere three thousand to a staggering thirty-five thousand during summer weekends. Boats dock near the main village, **NES**, a tiny place that nestles among the fields behind the dyke. Once a centre of the Dutch whaling industry, Nes has its share of cafés, hotels and tourist shops, though quite a bit of the old village survives. High-rise development has been forbidden, and there's a focus instead on the seventeenth- and eighteenth-century captains' houses, known as *Commandeurshuizen*, which line several of the streets. Perhaps surprisingly, the crowds rarely seem to overwhelm the village, but rather to breathe life into it, which is just as well as there's not a lot to do other than wander the streets and linger in cafés. Even if you do hit peak season at Nes, it's fairly easy to escape the crowds on all but the busiest of days, and **bikes** can be rented at a number of shops in the village. If it's raining, you might consider the **Natuurcentrum** at Strandweg 38 (Mon–Fri 10am–noon & 1–5pm, Sat & Sun 1–5pm; ƒ6), an aquarium and natural history museum with no information in English.

Nes practicalities

Nes has a wide range of **accommodation**, but prices do rise dramatically in summer, when many places are full, peaking at high-season weekends. It's advisable to call ahead if you are visiting in July or August. For a small charge, the **VVV** (Mon–Fri 8.30am–12.30pm & 1.30–6.30pm, Sat 8.30am–4pm; ☎0519/542 020) will fix you up with a pension or private room anywhere on the island. Failing that, you could try the rather basic *Domingo* at De Worteltuin 3 (☎0519/542 371), the central *Hotel De Jong* at Reeweg 29 (☎0519/542 016; ③) or the cosier *Noordzee*, Strandweg 42 (☎0519/542 228, fax 542 380; ③). The best-appointed **campsite** is *Duinoord* (☎0519/542 070), by the beach about half a mile north of Nes at Jan van Eijckweg 4.

Around the island

Ameland is only 2km wide, but it's 25km long, and its entire northern shore is made up of a fine expanse of sand and dune laced by foot and cycle paths. The

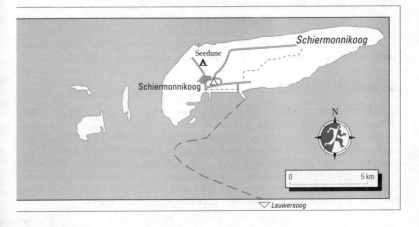

REACHING THE ISLANDS

It only takes 35 minutes by bus #66 to get from Leeuwarden to Holwerd, where you can catch the connecting ferry to **Ameland** (Mon–Fri 7.30am, 8.30am [July & Aug only], 9.30am, 11.30am, 1.30pm, 3.30pm [June–Aug only], 5.30pm & 7.30pm; Sat hourly 7.30am–3.30pm during the summer, otherwise 9.30am, 1.30pm, 5.30pm & 7.30pm; Sun 9.30am, 1.30pm, 4.30pm [June–Aug only], 5.30pm, 6.30pm [June–Sept only] & 7.30pm). The trip takes 45 minutes and costs *f*18.80 return. In the other direction, the boat leaves Ameland an hour earlier in each case.

For **Schiermonnikoog**, bus #51 runs from Dokkum (30min) and Leeuwarden (1hr 30min), and bus #63 from Groningen (1hr), for the port of Lauwersoog. Connecting boats take 45 minutes to make the crossing and cost *f*19.30 return (Mon–Sat 6.30am, 9.30am, 11.30am [July & Aug only], 1.30pm [not Sat Nov–Feb] & 5.30pm, Sun 9.30am, 11.30am [June–Aug only] 3.30pm [March–Dec only], 5.30pm & 7.30pm [July–Aug only]). The returning boat leaves from the island one hour later in each case. There are also combined trips direct from Groningen. Taking your bike over will cost extra. Only residents' cars are allowed on Schiermonnikoog.

---

east end of the island is the most deserted, and you can cycle by the side of the marshy shallows that once made up the whole southern shore before the construction of the sea-dyke. If you're heavily laden, a summer island **bus** service runs between the principal villages from three to nine times daily, connecting with ferries. There are a variety of **boat** excursions from Nes, including trips to the islands of Terschelling and Schiermonnikoog, and to the sandbanks to see sea lions – though sadly these have been decimated following a recent pollution-based viral epidemic. Details from the VVV or tour operators in Nes. Of the smaller villages that dot the island, the prettiest place to stay is **HOLLUM**, a sedate settlement of old houses and farm buildings west of Nes. If you're an aquatic addict or seriously bored there are a couple of small museums here: the **Sorgdragermuseum** at Herenweg 1 (Mon–Fri 10am–noon & 1–5pm, Sat & Sun 1.30–5pm; *f*3), an old *commandeurshuis*, and the **Reddingsmuseum Abraham Fock**, Oranjeweg 18 (same times), devoted to the local lifeboat teams and the horses that used to drag the boats to the sea.

The pension *de Welvaart* here, at Burenlaan 4 (☎0519/554 634; ③) is good value and convenient. Alternatives include the **campsite**, *Koudenburg* (☎0519/554 367), by the heath to the north at Oosterhemweg 2; and to the west, near the lighthouse and the tip of Ameland, there is a good **youth hostel** (☎0519/554 133; April–Sept), surrounded by sand dune and forest.

Schiermonnikoog

Until the Reformation, the island of **Schiermonnikoog** belonged to the monastery of Klaarkamp, on the mainland; its name means literally "island of the grey monks". Nothing remains of the monks, however, and these days Schiermonnikoog's only settlement is a prim and busy village bordering on long stretches of muddy beach and sand dune to the north and mud flat and farmland to the south. Schiermonnikoog is the smallest of the Frisian islands, and, once you're clear of the weekend homes that fringe the village, it's a wild, uncultivated place, criss-crossed by cycle paths, and, not surprisingly, a popular spot for day-trippers.

Boats from Lauwersoog dock at the island jetty, some 3km from the village; a connecting bus drops you off outside the VVV in the centre. It's even possible to walk to the island across the mud flats from Kloosterburen, a distance of about 8km, but this is not feasible without a guide; see p.229 for details.

Accommodation becomes difficult to find in season, when prices rise sharply, and it's essential to ring ahead. The **VVV** (Mon–Sat 9am–1pm & 2.30–6.30pm; ☎0519/531 233) will help by booking private rooms and pensions. The cheapest **hotel** on the island is the *Zonneweelde* (☎0519/531 133, fax 531 199; ③), in the heart of the village at Langestreek 94; the *Strandhotel Noderstraun* (☎0519/531 111, fax 531 857; ⑤), about twenty minutes' walk from the VVV and overlooking the beach at Badweg 32, is a more luxurious alternative; the large *Van der Werff*, Reeweg 2 (☎0519/531 203, fax 531 748; ④) is a third possibility. Schiermonnikoog's **campsite**, *Seedune* (☎0519/531 398), is to the north, in the woods just east of Badweg at Seeduneweg 1. The **youth hostel** at Knuppeldam 2 (☎0519/531 257) is on the east side of the village, fifteen minutes' walk from the VVV.

The *Strandhotel* has **windsurfing** equipment for rent; **bikes** are available from several small shops in the village, and the VVV sells good **maps**. For **food and drink** have a wander along Langestreek and Badweg to the north of the VVV.

Groningen and around

Nominally a fiefdom of the bishops of Utrecht from 1040 until 1536, the city of **GRONINGEN** was once an important centre of trade, in reality an autonomous merchant state ruled by a tightly defined oligarchy, whose power was exercised through the city council or *Raad*. In 1536 Charles V forced the town to submit to his authority, but Groningen was nevertheless still hesitant in its support of the Dutch rebellion against his successors. The dilemma for the city fathers was that, although they stood to gain economically from independence, the majority of the town's citizens were Catholic, deeply suspicious of their Protestant neighbours. In the end, the economic argument won the day, and the town became the capital of the Dutch province of Groningen in 1594.

Virtually destroyed during the Allied liberation in 1945, the city is not immediately attractive, with few obvious sights and an eclectic jumble of architectures. However, it does benefit from the presence of its large and prestigious university – one in eight of the town's population are students – which gives the place a cosmopolitan and vigorous feel quite unexpected in this part of the country, and keeps prices in its restaurants and bars surprisingly low. This, combined with a superb and innovative museum, a number of good budget places to stay, and a wide range of contemporary arts performances and exhibitions, especially during the academic year, makes Groningen the best urban target in the north Netherlands.

Arrival, information and accommodation

Groningen's **bus** and **train** stations are side by side on the south side of town. There is a small **VVV** office at the station (Mon–Sat 9.30am–5.30pm); the main branch is ten minutes' walk away at Ged Kattendiep 6 (Mon–Fri 9am–5.30pm, Sat

The Groningen area telephone code is ☎050

PEDAL POWER IN GRONINGEN

One of the best things about Groningen is the lack of traffic: almost all the centre is car free, the result of municipal decisions dating back to the mid-Seventies, when the city was suffering from some of the worst congestion in Europe. In a typically bold and sensible Dutch way, Groningen decided to get rid of a six-lane motorway intersection in its city centre, close most of its roads to cars and spend a fortune on cycle paths and bus lanes.

This paid off. Now 57 percent of Groningeners travel regularly by **bike**, the highest percentage in the country. Meanwhile city planners have realized how well they spent their money: the £20 million invested in cycle paths over recent years has brought industries and popularity to the city in a way the usual publicity campaigns would never have managed; and, for every car kept out of the city centre, it's reckoned that almost £200 a year is saved in environmental damage. Groningen is now one of the most popular cities in the Netherlands, and there are demands for even more stringent restrictions on cars.

9am–4pm; ☎06/320 230 50; ƒ1 per minute). Both offices offer a range of services, from tourist information (much of it in English) on the town and province to tickets for visiting bands, theatre groups and orchestras. They also have a short list of **private rooms** in both Groningen and the surrounding area, though hardly any are near the city centre.

Groningen has plenty of good, reasonably priced **accommodation**, though it's always wise to call ahead to reserve a room. Straight across the museum bridge from the train station, the third road on the right, Gemempte Zuiderdiep, is a good street to start looking, with the likeable old *Weeva* at no. 8 (☎312 9919, fax 312 7904; ④) and more basic *Tivoli* at no. 67 (☎312 5728; ③). Two blocks north, *Friesland*, Kleine Pelsterstraat 4 (☎312 1307; ③) is another simple choice, while ten minutes' walk east of Gemempte Zuiderdiep, at Damsterdiep 94, the *Groningen* (☎313 5435; ③) is friendly if a little spartan, and often a good alternative if the more central hotels are full. Most central of all, *De Doelen*, Grote Markt 36 (☎312 7041, fax 314 6112; ⑤) is as comfortable as you'd expect for the price. If money's tight, head for the *Simplon Jongerenhotel*, Boterdiep 73 (☎313 5221; ①), which boasts clean and well-kept dorms; from the Grote Markt follow Oude Ebbingestraat north over the canal, turn first right and then first left. If you're camping, catch bus #2 via Piezerweg from the main square for the ten-minute journey to **Camping Stadspark** (March–Oct).

The town

Groningen's effective centre is **Grote Markt**, a wide open space that was badly damaged by wartime bombing and has been reconstructed with little imagination. At its northeast corner is the tiered tower of the **Martinikerk** (June–Sept Tues–Sat noon–4pm; ƒ1), a beacon of architectural sanity in the surrounding shambles. Though the oldest parts of the church go back to 1180, most of it dates from the mid-fifteenth century, the nave being a Gothicized rebuilding undertaken to match the added choir. The vault paintings in the nave are beautifully restored, and in the old choir there are two series of frescoes on the walled-up niches of the clerestory. On the right, a series of eight depicts the story of Christmas, beginning with an *Annunciation* and ending with a portrayal of the young Christ in the temple. On the left, six frescoes complete the cycle with the story of Easter. Also in the choir is a maquette of the city centre as it looked before wartime destruction: fifteen years in the making, it's painstakingly accurate. Adjoining the church is the essentially seventeenth-century **Martinitoren** (April–Sept daily noon–4.30pm; ƒ2.50). If you've got the energy, it offers a view that is breathtaking in every sense of the word – fainthearts be warned. Behind the church is the lawn of the **Kerkhof**, an ancient piece of common land that's partly enclosed by the **Provinciehuis**, a rather grand neo-Renaissance building of 1915, seat of the provincial government.

On the opposite side of the Grote Markt, the classical **Stadhuis** dates from 1810, tucked in front of the mid-seventeenth-century **Goudkantoor** (Gold Office); look out for the shell motif above the windows, a characteristic Groningen decoration. From the southwest corner of the Grote Markt, the far

side of Vismarkt is framed by the **Korenbeurs** (Corn Exchange) of 1865. The statues on the facade represent, from left to right, Neptune, Mercurius (god of commerce) and Ceres (goddess of agriculture). Just behind, the **A-kerk** is a fifteenth-century church with a Baroque steeple, attractively restored in tones of yellow, orange and red. The church's full name is the *Onze Lieve Vrouwekerk der A*, the A being a small river which forms the moat encircling the town centre. Immediately to the west along A-Kerkhof N.Z., the **Noordelijk Scheepvaart Museum**, Brugstraat 24 (Tues–Sat 10am–5pm, Sun 1–5pm; *f*5), is one of the best-equipped and most comprehensive maritime museums in the country, tracing the history of north Holland shipping from the sixth to the twentieth centuries. Housed in a warren of steep stairs and timber-beamed rooms, each of the museum's twenty displays deals with a different aspect of shipping, including trade with the Indies, the development of peat canals and a series of reconstructed nautical workshops. The museum's particular appeal is its imaginative combination of models and original artefacts, which are themselves a mixture of the personal (seamen's chests; quadrants) and the public (ship figureheads; tile designs of ships). In the same building, the much smaller **Niemeyer Tabaksmuseum** (same times) is devoted to tobacco smoking from 1600 to the present day. Exhibits include a multitude of pipes and an outstanding collection of snuff paraphernalia in all sorts of materials, from crystal and ivory to porcelain and silver. The Niemeyer family built their fortune on the tobacco trade, and here you can see the origins of those familiar blue tobacco packets.

To the northwest of here, down a passage off Zwanestraat, the **Groningen University Museum** (Tues–Fri noon–4pm, Sat & Sun 1–4pm; *f*2) gives a taste of the university's history, with exhibits ranging from scientific equipment to photos of derby-hatted students clowning around at the turn of the century. Further north still, up Nieuwe Kijk in 't Jatstraat 104, the **Geraldus van de Leeuw ethnological museum** (Tues–Fri 10am–4pm, Sat & Sun 1–5pm) has collections from Asia, Africa, the Pacific and South America. Alternatively, just south of the Scheepvart Museum, the **Natuurmuseum** (Tues–Fri 10am–5pm, Sat & Sun 2-5pm; *f*4.50), at Praediniussingel 59, has a permanent exhibition (in Dutch) on the ice age, complete with woolly mammoths, and the usual exhibitions on wildlife, geology and land reclamation in the local area.

The town's main draw, though, is the excellent **Groninger Museum** (Tues–Sat 10am–5pm & Sun 1–5pm; *f*9), housed in Alessandro Mendini's spectacular pavilions directly across from the train station. The museum's four main sections take you through a melange of revolving exhibitions on archeology, arts and applied arts, but it is the design of the place almost as much as the contents that impresses. Enter beneath the yellow-gold tower; one floor down via the mosaic-clad staircase, the lower western pavilion holds "The Story of Groningen" – a chronological and well-labelled display on the **archeology and history** of Groningen province, from early terp culture to the local impact of World War II and beyond. Upstairs, and probably the museum's highlight, the **decorative arts** section is beautifully displayed in a circular glass case, with an extensive collection of local silver and Far Eastern ceramics, notably a two hundred-piece sample of porcelain rescued from the *Geldermalsen*, which sank in the South China Sea in 1572. Of the examples on display, several have been "resunk" in an aquarium on the museum's floor, still encrusted with accumulated detritus, but others have been cleaned and polished to reveal designs of delicate precision – fine drawings of flowers and stems, and bamboo huts where every stick is distinct.

On the other side of the complex, a series of rooms in the lower east pavilion holds the museum's temporary exhibitions and a fast-revolving selection of contemporary art spreading upstairs to the **visual arts** pavilion, whose deconstructivist design has rendered it the most controversial part of the museum. The collection here includes Rubens' energetic *Adoration of the Magi* among a small selection of seventeenth-century works, Isaac Israels' inviting *Hoedenwinkel* from a modest sample of Hague School paintings, and a number of later works by the Expressionists of the Groningen *De Ploeg* association, principally Jan Wiegers, whose *Portrait of Ludwig Kirchner* is typically earnest. An adventurous acquisition policy has also led the museum to dabble in some of the more unusual trends in modern art, like Carel Visser's 1983 collage *Voor Dali* and the bizarre *Can the Bumpsteers while I Park the Chariot* by Henk Tas. The paintings are regularly revolved, so don't pin your hopes on catching any particular item.

Contemporary art is also displayed at the **Visual Arts Centre** in the Osterpoort, Trompsingel 27 (Tues–Fri 10am–5pm, Sat & Sun 1–5pm) and there are two more specialist museums you might want to see. The **Printing Museum** at Rabenhauptstraat 65 southeast of the train station (Tues–Fri & Sun 1–5pm; *f*4), outlines the history of printing with everything from a nineteenth-century steam-driven printing press to wordprocessors and lastly, certainly most weirdly, the **Museum of Anatomy and Embryology**, east of the centre at Oostersingel 69 (Mon–Fri 9am–4.30pm), is even nastier than you might imagine.

WADLOPEN

Wadlopen, or mud-flat walking, is a popular and strenuous Dutch pastime, and the stretch of coast on the northern edge of the provinces of Friesland and Groningen is one of the best places to do it: twice daily, the receding tide uncovers vast expanses of mud flat beneath the Waddenzee. It is, however, a sport to be taken seriously, and far too dangerous to do without an experienced guide – the depth of the mud is too variable (you have to walk up to thigh-depth in places) and the tides inconsistent. In any case, channels of deep water are left even when the tide has receded, and you need to be aware of the whereabouts of these; the currents, too, can be perilous. The timing of the treks depends on weather and tidal conditions; most start at anything between 6am and 10am. It's important to be properly equipped, not least with adequate clothing. The weather can change rapidly up here, and group leaders request you take or wear walking shorts or a bathing suit, a sweater, a wind jacket, knee-high wool socks, high-top trainers and a complete change of clothes stored in a watertight pack. In recent years *wadlopen* has become extremely popular, and it's advisable to book at least a month in advance between May and August.

Prices of **organized excursions** are not bad, in the region of *f*30 a head, and include the cost of the return ferry crossing; the VVVs in Dokkum, Leeuwarden and Groningen can provide details, or you could contact one of the *wadlopen* organizations direct: *Dijkstras Wadlopencentrum*, Hoofdstraat 118, Pieterburen (☎0595/528 345), has the most multilingual guides; there's also *Stichting Wadlopcentrum Pieterburen*, Hoofdstraat 68, Pieterburen (☎0595/528 300).

Groningen's final sight is its **train station**: built in 1896 at enormous cost, it was one of the grandest of its day, decorated with the strong colours and symbolic designs of Art Nouveau tiles from the Rozenburg factory in The Hague. The grandeur of much of the building has disappeared under a welter of concrete, glass and plastic suspended ceilings, but the old first- and second-class waiting rooms have survived pretty much intact and were recently refurbished as restaurants. The epitome of high Gothic style, the oak-panelled walls are edged by extravagantly tiled chimney pieces, while a central pillar in each room supports a papier-mâché fluted ceiling. The third-class waiting room is now a travel agency, but a yellow, blue and white tiled diagram of the Dutch rail system still covers one wall.

Eating, drinking and nightlife

Groningen's nicest places to **eat and drink** are concentrated in three loose areas, each only a couple of minutes' walk from the next. Best of the three is centred on Poelestraat, where an array of open-air cafés pulls in mainly youthful punters. *Cafe d'Opera* at no. 15 has good Dutch food and *dagschotels* from *f*12.50; around the corner on Peperstraat, *'t Pakhuis,* down a small alley at no. 8 offers cheapish meals and a lively bar in an atmospheric building; *Andy Warhol*, roughly opposite *'t Pakhuis*, is a cool night café. South of Poelstraat the elegant *Schimmelpennink Huys*, Oosterstraat 53, has excellent and reasonably priced daily specials; there is the Mexican-American *Four Roses* at the junction of Oosterstraat and Gedempte Zuiderdiep; and Dutch food at *Cafe 't Katshuys*, Gedempte Zuiderdiep 33. Across the canal from Poelestraat, the tiny boisterous *Café Kachel* at Schuittendiep 62 is the best of the town's traditional Dutch **bars**, and there are several other decent places to drink nearby.

On the south side of the Grote Markt, the best of a flank of outdoor cafés are the cosy *De Witz* at no. 48, the civilized *De Drie Gezusters* at no. 29, with a great old interior, and the *Café Hooghoudt* in the old Lloyds Insurance building at no. 41; this last also contains a night café serving food until 4am at weekends. Northwest of the Grote Markt, around Zwanestraat, the *Ugly Duck* at no. 28 has fish and Dutch food, including a good-value tourist menu; just to the west, *Soest Dijk*, at Elleboog 6, is pricier and posher; while *Brussels Lof* at A-Kerkstraat 24, is a vegetarian restaurant with good fondues.

For **live music** try *De Vestibule*, Oosterstraat 24; *Vera*, in the basement below the *mensa*, at Oosterstraat 44; or *Troubadour*, Peperstraat 19. The jazz café *De Spieghel* at Peperstraat 11 has live performances (including some reasonably big names) nightly, and there is occasional jazz at *Cafe de Nimf*, Poelestraat 5, as well as a nightly piano bar at Hoogstraat 7. Most of the more important visiting bands play in the municipal concert hall, the *Stadsschouwburg*, Turfsingel 86, in the *Oosterpoort*, Trompsingel 27, just east of the train station. On Sundays in July and August, there are also concerts in the **Stadspark**, about 3km southwest of the town centre (bus #2 from the Grote Markt to Peizerweg on the northern edge of the park, but confirm with the driver as routes vary). Good **discos** include *Gdansk*, Poelestraat 53, and the *Palace*, Gelkingestraat 1, which occasionally host live bands. The **cinema** with the most varied programme is the *Filmhuis*, Poelestraat 30, though the *Simplon* at Boterdiep 73 shows some good alternative movies and also has live music. **Listings** of all events are contained in *Uitgaanskrant*, available free from the VVV.

Listings

Boat trips Summer trips along the old town moat around the town centre, ƒ7.50 for 75min. Times of sailings and bookings at the VVV.

Books A good range of English-language titles at *Scholtens* on Guldenstraat

Car rental *Budget*, Hereweg 36 (☎527 2877).

Emergencies ☎0611.

Laundry Self or service wash at *Handy Wash*, Schuitendiep 56

Left luggage At the train station (daily 8am–noon & 1–5.30pm); also coin-operated lockers in the ticket hall.

Markets General market, including fruit and vegetables, on the Grote Markt (Tues–Sat from 8am), with curios and miscellaneous antiques on Tues, Fri, and Sat.

Police Herebinnsingel 2 (☎513 1313).

Post office on Munnekeholm by the A-kerk (Mon–Fri 8.30am–6.30pm, Sat 10am–1pm) or at Stationsweg 10 (Mon–Fri 9am–5pm, Sat 9am–noon).

Around Groningen

A patchwork of industrial complexes and nondescript villages, the **province of Groningen** has few major attractions; unless you fancy a night in the country near the old monastery at Ter Apel, there's nowhere that really warrants a stay. The easiest trip is to the **botanical gardens** at **HAREN** (daily 9am–5pm; ƒ12.50) a few kilometres to the south via train or bus #51 or #53. There is a small Chinese garden and some extensive rose-gardens, although the real highlight is the tropical greenhouse complex, with a vast range of cacti and some wonderful old cycads, as well as the more familiar palms, bananas and ferns. For day-tripping from Groningen city, the most agreeable journey is to the village of **UITHUIZEN**, 25km to the north (hourly trains; 35min), where the moated manor house of **Menkemaborg** (April–Sept daily 10am–noon & 1–5pm; Oct–March Tues–Sun 10am–noon & 1–4pm; closed Jan; ƒ8) is a marked ten-minute walk from the station. Dating from the fifteenth century and surrounded by formal gardens in the English style, the house has a sturdy compact elegance and is one of the very few mansions, or *borgs*, of the old landowning families to have survived. The interior consists of a sequence of period rooms furnished in the style of the seventeenth century. Something of a specialist interest, the **Bevrijdingsmuseum**, Dingeweg 1–3 (April–Sept daily 10am–6pm; ƒ6) has an excellent collection dedicated to World War II military artefacts – uniforms, weapons and secret radios, etc.

The trip to Uithuizen can be combined with a guided walk across the coastal **mud flats** (*wadlopen* – see p.229) to the uninhabited sand-spit island of **Rottumeroog**. Excursions leave from outside Menkemaborg by bus to the coast, between three and four times monthly from June to September. It costs ƒ25 per person and booking is essential; contact Groningen VVV. Without a guide, it's too dangerous to go on the mud flats, but it is easy enough to walk along the enclosing dyke that runs behind the shoreline for the whole length of the province. There's precious little to see as such, but when the weather's clear, the browns, blues and greens of the surrounding land and sea are unusually beautiful. From

Uithuizen, it's a good hour's stroll north to the nearest point on the dyke, and you'll need a large-scale map for directions – available from Groningen VVV.

The Lauwersmeer

Some 35km northwest of Groningen, the **Lauwersmeer** is a broken and irregular lake that spreads across the provincial boundary into neighbouring Friesland. Once an arm of the sea, it was turned into a freshwater lake by the construction of the Lauwersoog dam, a controversial Sixties project that was vigorously opposed by local fishermen, who ended up having to move all their tackle to ports on the coast. Spared intensive industrial and agricultural development because of the efforts of conservationists, it's a quiet and peaceful region with a wonderful variety of sea-birds, and increasingly popular with anglers, windsurfers, sailors and cyclists.

The local villages are uniformly dull, however; the most convenient base is **ZOUTKAMP**, near the southeast corner of the lake on the River Reitdiep, accessible by bus from Groningen (#65; hourly; 1hr). The **VVV**, Dorpsplein 1 (June–Aug Mon–Fri 10am–noon & 1.30–4.30pm, Sat 1.30–4.30pm; Sept–May Mon–Fri 10am–noon & 1.30–4pm; ☎0595/401 957) has a limited supply of private **rooms**. These can also be reserved at Groningen VVV.

At the mouth of the lake, some 10km north of Zoutkamp, the desultory port of **LAUWERSOOG** is where **ferries** leave for the fifty-minute trip to the island of Schiermonnikoog (see p.224). It's also the home of **Expo Zee** (April–Sept Tues–Fri 10am–5pm, Sat & Sun 2–5pm; ƒ5), 500m south of the harbour, which gives background information on the Lauwersmeer, the Waddenzee and Dutch land reclamation in general. Bus #63 (5 daily; 1hr) connects Groningen with Lauwersoog and the ferries.

Fraeylemaborg and Bourtange

Some 20km east of Groningen on the northern edge of the small town of Slochteren, accessible by bus #78 from the town centre, the typically northern **Fraeylemaborg** (March–Dec Tues–Sun 10am–noon & 1–5pm; ƒ5) is a well-preserved, seventeenth-century moated mansion, set within extensive parkland. More interesting, some 60km southeast of Groningen, **BOURTANGE** is a superbly restored fortified village which lies close to the German frontier. Founded by William of Orange in 1580 to help protect the eastern approaches to Groningen, Bourtange fell into disrepair during the nineteenth century, only to be entirely refurbished as a tourist attraction in 1964. The design of the village is similar to that of Naarden, outside Amsterdam, and is best appreciated as you walk round the old bastions of the star-shaped fortress. Bus #71 runs from Groningen (Mon–Fri, hourly; 1hr) and drops you by the car-park, from where you enter the village through the VVV building and information centre (April–Oct Mon–Fri 10am–5pm, Sat & Sun 11am–5pm; Nov–March Mon–Fri 9am–noon; ☎0599/354 600). Entry to the village is free, but there is a charge of ƒ8 if you want to see the slide-show which gives a history of Bourtange and to visit the various exhibitions depicting traditional life in the village. There's a **campsite**, at Vlagtwedderstraat 88, and one **hotel**, *De Staakenborgh*, up the road at no. 33 (☎0599/354 216; July–Aug; ③).

Ter Apel

South from Bourtange, the **Museum Klooster** (Mon–Sat 10am–5pm, Sun 1–5pm, Nov–April closed Mon; ƒ5), in the small town of **Ter Apel** near the

German border, is the definite highlight in this part of the country, although it's difficult to reach without a car. This was the monastery of the Crutched Friars, built in 1465, and probably unique among rural monasteries in surviving the Reformation intact, after the enlightened local authorities allowed the monks to remain here during their lifetimes. The chapel, superbly restored, preserves a number of unusual features, including the tripartite sedilia, where the priest and his assistants sat during mass, and a splendid rood-screen that divides the chancel from the nave. Elsewhere, the east wing is a curious hybrid of Gothic and Rococo styles, the cloister has a small herb garden and the other rooms are normally given over to temporary exhibitions of religious art. The monastery is surrounded by extensive beech woods and magnificent old horse-chestnut trees; follow one of the marked walks or simply ramble at your leisure. Opposite, the *Hotel-Restaurant Boshchuis* (☎0599/581 208, fax 581 906; ③) is ideal for lunch or dinner or for spending a quiet night in the country.

Drenthe

Until the early nineteenth century, the sparsely populated province of **Drenthe** was little more than a flat expanse of empty peat bog, marsh and moor. Today its only conspicuous geographical feature is a ridge of low hills that runs northeast for some 50km from Emmen toward Groningen. This ridge, the **Hondsrug**, was high enough to attract prehistoric settlers whose **hunebeds** (megalithic tombs) have become Drenthe's main tourist attraction. There are few others. **Assen**, the provincial capital, is a dull place with a good museum, and **Emmen**, the other major town, can only be recommended as a convenient base for visiting some of the *hunebeds* and three neighbouring open-air folk culture museums.

Governed by the bishops of Utrecht from the eleventh century, Drenthe was incorporated into the Hapsburg empire in 1538. The region sided with the Protestants in the rebellion against Spain, but it had little economic or military muscle and its claim to provincial status was ignored until the days of the Batavian Republic. In the nineteenth century, work began in earnest to convert the province's peat bogs and moors into good farmland. *Veenkulunies* (peat colonies) were established over much of the south and east of Drenthe, where the initial purpose of the labourers was to dig drainage canals (*wiels*) and cut the peat for sale as fuel to the cities. Once cleared of the peat, the land could be used to grow crops, and today the region's farms are some of the most profitable in the country.

Assen and around

Some 16km south of Groningen, **ASSEN** is a possible first stop, though not at all a place that you'd wish to get stuck in. Its train and bus station are about five minutes' walk from the centre of town, moving straight ahead across the main road down Stationsstraat. On the eastern side of the central square, Brink is home to both parts of the **Drents Museum** (Tues–Sun 11am–5pm; July & Aug also Mon; ƒ5), which, spread over a pleasant group of old houses, is the only thing that makes a stop in town worthwhile. Of the buildings, the *Ontvangershuis*, Brink 1, holds no more than a predictable plod of period rooms, but on the second floor of Brink 5 there's an extraordinary assortment of prehistoric bodies, clothes and other artefacts that have been preserved for thousands of years in the surrounding peat bogs. The bodies are the material remains of those early settlers who built the *hunebeds*, and the museum has a modest display dealing with what is known of their customs and culture. There's also the much vaunted *Pesse Canoe*, the oldest water vessel ever found, dating from about 6800 BC and looking its age. Five kilometres west of the centre of Assen, straight down Torenlaan, the **Automuseum**, Rode Heklaan 3 (April–Oct daily except Sat 9am–6pm; ƒ12), has a wide selection of antique and vintage cars. To get there take a bus marked *Verkeerspark* from the train station.

Practicalities
Assen's **VVV** is in the town centre at Brink 42 (Mon–Fri 9am–5.30pm, Sat 10am–1pm; June–Aug Sat until 3pm; ☎0592/314 324). The cheapest place to **stay** is the *Christerus* (☎0592/313 517; ③), on the way in from the station at Stationsstraat 17. The *De Nieuwe Brink Hotel*, Brink 13, is a reasonable place to **eat**.

South of Assen: Westerburk Concentration Camp
If you have your own transport, you might want to visit the **Herinneringscentrum Kamp Westerburk** (April–Sept Mon–Fri 9.30am–5pm, Sat & Sun 1–5pm; ƒ5) a little south of town, on the road between the villages Amen and Hooghalen. It was here that Dutch Jews were gathered before being transported to the death camps in the east, and, although little remains of the camp itself, the documents and artefacts on display are deeply affecting.

Emmen and around

To all intents and purposes **EMMEN** is a new town, a twentieth-century amalgamation of strip villages that were originally peat colonies. The centre is a modernistic affair, mixing the remnants of the old with boulders, trees and shrubs and a selection of municipal statues that vary enormously in quality.

Emmen is well known for two things: its *hunebeds* and its zoo. The **Zoo** (daily 9am–5pm; ƒ17), right in the middle of town at Hoofdstraat 18, boasts an imitation African savanna, where the animals roam "free", a massive sea lion pool – the biggest in Europe – and a giant hippo house. Emmen is also the most convenient place to see *hunebeds*, of which the best is the clearly marked **Emmerdennen Hunebed**, in the woods 1km or so east of the station along Boslaan. This is a so-called passage-grave, with a relatively sophisticated entrance surrounded by a ring of standing stones. The other interesting *hunebed* within easy walking distance is the **Schimmer-Es**, a large enclosure containing two burial chambers and a standing stone; to get there follow Hoofdstraat north from the VVV, take a left down Noorderstraat, right along Noordeinde, left along Broekpad, and first right at Langgrafweg – a distance of about 2km. The **VVV** sells detailed maps of a circular car route along the minor roads to the north of town that covers all the principal remains.

Practicalities

Emmen **train** and **bus** stations adjoin each other, five minutes' walk north of the town centre: head straight down Stationsstraat into Boslaan and turn left down Hoofdstraat, the main drag. The VVV (Mon–Fri 9am–5.30pm & Sat 9am–4pm; ☎0591/613 000), in the central Raadhuisplein, can arrange **accommodation**. Their list includes pensions, private rooms and hotels. Cheapest pension is the *Centrum* at Sterrenkamp 9 (☎0591/614 158; ③), first left after the zoo, heading south; for the same price you could stay in the cheapest hotel, the *Bos en Zon* at Burg Tymesstraat 1 (☎0591/611 369; ③), which is immediately behind the train station. For **food**, try the first-floor café of the *Hotel Boerland*, Hoofdstraat 57.

Around Emmen

BORGER, some 20km northwest of Emmen, has the largest *hunebed* in the country, 25m long on the northeast edge of the village; an adjoining information centre (Mon–Fri 10am–5pm, Sat & Sun 1–5pm) explains how the dolmens got here. While you're in the area you can also visit the Pfeiffer **glass-blowing workshop** and showroom, just west of town at the junction of Rolderstraat and Nuisveen (Mon–Thurs 9am–noon & 12.30–4pm, Fri 9am–noon & 12.30–2.30pm; *f*2). Should you decide to stay, the VVV (May–Sept Mon–Sat 9.30–5pm, Oct–April 10am–noon & 2–4pm; ☎0599/234 855) has a list of private rooms, or you could try the *Hotel Nathalia*, Hoofdstraat 87 (☎0599/234 791; ③). Bus #59 runs to Borger on its way between Emmen and Groningen; #24 comes from Assen.

Approximately 11km east of Emmen, toward the German border, the **Veenmuseumdorp 't Aole Compas** (daily 9am–5pm; *f*12; bus #43 hourly from Emmen station; 30min) is a massive open-air museum-village that traces the history and development of the peat colonies of the moors of southern Groningen and eastern Drenthe. The colonies were established in the nineteenth century, when labour was imported to cut the thick layers of peat that lay all over the moors. Isolated in small communities, and under the thumb of the traders who sold their product and provided their foodstuffs, the colonists were harshly exploited and lived in abject poverty until well into the 1930s. Built around some old interlocking canals, the museum consists of a series of reconstructed villages that span the history of the colonies. It's inevitably a bit folksy, but very popular, with its own small-gauge railway, a canal barge, and working period bakeries, bars and shops. A thorough exploration takes the whole day.

Thirteen kilometres northwest of Emmen, **De Zeven Marken** (April–Oct daily 9am–6pm; *f*3; bus #21 from Emmen), on the northern edge of the village of **SCHOONOORD**, is another open-air museum concerned with life in Drenthe. Exhibits here concentrate on the end of the nineteenth century and cover a wide range of traditional community activities – from sheep farming to education and carpentry. Seven kilometres west, tiny **Orvelte** (May–Sept Mon–Fri 10am–5pm, Sat & Sun 11am–5pm; *f*8.50) is another village-museum, fully operational and inhabited this time, though certain buildings may be closed at any time. Owned by a trust which exercises strict control over construction and repair, Orvelte's buildings date from the seventeenth to the nineteenth centuries and include examples of a toll house, a dairy, a farmhouse and a number of craft workshops. Most are open to the public, but you'll need a car to get here.

travel details

Trains

Emmen to: Zwolle (every 30min; 70min).

Groningen to: Amsterdam (every 30min; 2hr 20min); Assen (every 30min; 20min); Leeuwarden (every 30min; 50min); Zwolle (every 30min; 70min).

Leeuwarden to: Amsterdam (every 30min; 2hr 25min); Franeker (every 30min; 15min); Groningen (every 30min; 50min); Harlingen (every 30min; 25min); Hindeloopen (hourly; 35min); Sneek (hourly; 20min); Stavoren (hourly; 50min); Zwolle (every 30min; 1hr).

Buses

Bolsward to: Makkum (hourly; 20min).

Groningen to: Emmen (hourly; 1hr 10min); Zoutkamp (hourly; 1hr).

Leeuwarden to: Alkmaar (hourly; 2hr 20min); Dokkum (every 30min–hourly; 30min); Franeker (hourly; 25min).

Sneek to: Bolsward (3 hourly; 15min).

Buses and connecting ferries

Groningen to: Lauwersoog (*GADO* bus #63: 5 daily; 1hr) for boats to Schiermonnikoog (2–6 daily; 50min).

Leeuwarden to: Holwerd (*FRAM* bus #66: 5–7 daily; 50min) for boats to Ameland (4–8 daily; 45min); Lauwersoog (*FRAM* bus #51: 4–7 daily; 90min) for boats to Schiermonnikoog (2–6 daily; 50min).

Ferries

Harlingen to: Terschelling (2–3 boats daily; 1hr 30min); Vlieland (2–3 daily; 1hr 30min).

Stavoren to: Enkhuizen (May–Sept 3 boats daily; 1hr 20min).

Terschelling to: Vlieland (2–3 boats weekly; 65min).

Vlieland to: Terschelling (2–3 boats weekly; 65min).

International trains

Groningen to: Oldenburg, Germany (2 or 3 daily; 2hr 10 min).

CHAPTER FIVE

OVERIJSSEL, FLEVOLAND AND GELDERLAND

With the eastern provinces of Holland, the flat polder landscapes of the north and west of the country begin to disappear, the countryside growing steadily more undulating as you head toward Germany. Coming from the north, **Overijssel** is the first province you reach, "the land beyond the IJssel", which forms the border with Gelderland to the south. Its more appealing western reaches are a typically Dutch area, in part cut by lakes and waterways around the picturesque water-village of **Giethoorn**, at the heart of a series of towns – **Kampen**, **Deventer**, **Zutphen** and the provincial capital of **Zwolle** – which enjoyed a period of immense prosperity during the heyday of the Zuider Zee trade, from the fourteenth to the sixteenth centuries. At the junction of trade routes from Germany in the east, Scandinavia to the north and South Holland in the west, their future seemed secure and all of them were keen to impress their rivals with the splendour of their municipal buildings. The bubble burst in the seventeenth century, when trade moved west and the great merchant cities of South Holland undercut their prices, but today all are well worth a visit for their ancient centres, splendid churches and extravagant defensive portals. Southeast of here, **Twente** is an industrial region of old textile towns that forms the eastern district of the province, near the German frontier. It's one of the least visited parts of the country and with good reason, only **Enschede**, the main town, providing a spark of interest with an excellent local museum.

The boundary separating Overijssel from the reclaimed lands of Holland's twelfth and newest province, **Flevoland**, runs along the old shoreline of the Zuider Zee. Divided into two halves, the drab **Northeast Polder** in the east and the later **Flevoland Polder** to the west, there's not really much to attract the visitor here, although the fishing village of **Urk** – an island until the land reclamation scheme got under way – is an unusual historical relic. The provincial capital is **Lelystad**, a pretty dire modern town redeemed by some fine museums and an impressive reconstruction of an early-seventeenth-century trading ship.

Gelderland, spreading east from the province of Utrecht to the German frontier, takes its name from the German town of Geldern, its capital until the late fourteenth century. As a province it's a bit of a mixture, varying from the fertile but dull agricultural land of the **Betuwe** (Good Land), which stretches west from Nijmegen as far as Gorinchem, to the more distinctive – and appealing – **Veluwe** (Bad Land), an expanse of heath, woodland and dune that sprawls down from the old Zuider Zee coastline to Arnhem. Infertile and sparsely populated, the Veluwe separated two of medieval Holland's most prosperous regions, the ports of the River IJssel and the cities of the Randstad and today it constitutes one of the most

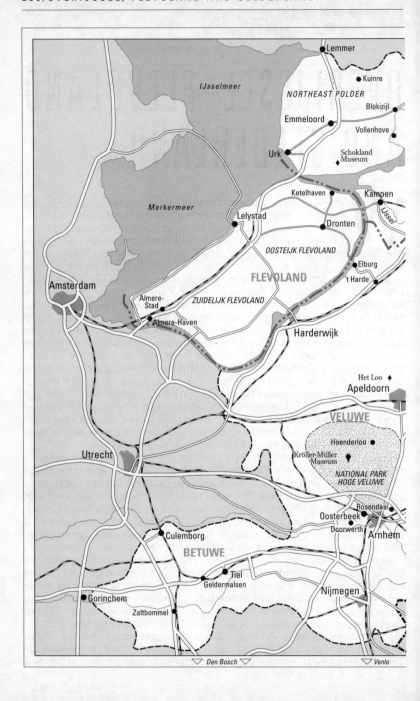

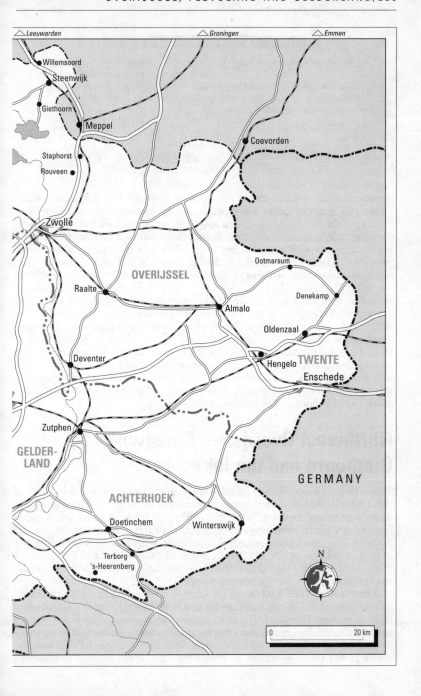

ACCOMMODATION PRICE CODES

All the **hotels** and **hostels** detailed in this chapter have been graded according to the following price categories. Apart from ①, which is a per-person price for a hostel bed, all the codes are based on the rate for the cheapest double room during high season.

For more on accommodation, see p.30.

① Up to ƒ40 per person	④ ƒ150–200	⑦ ƒ300–400
② ƒ60–100	⑤ ƒ200–250	
③ ƒ100–150	⑥ ƒ250–300	

---

popular holiday destinations in the country, strewn with campsites, second homes and bungalow parks. Some people use **Apeldoorn** as a base for the area, but it's a dreary town and if you want to visit the less developed southeastern sector, which has been set aside as the Hoge Veluwe National Park (and its Kröller-Müller Museum with a magnificent array of modern art, including one of the largest collections of Van Goghs in the world), you'd be better off basing yourself in Arnhem itself. **Arnhem** is most famous for its bridge, a key objective in the failed Operation Market Garden of 1944 – Field Marshal Montgomery's audacious attempt to shorten the war by dropping parachute battalions behind enemy lines to secure a string of advance positions across the rivers of southeast Gelderland – which left most of the city centre ruined. But it's a lively, agreeable place and a base for other attractions besides the Veluwe – the Netherlands Open-Air Museum, and, of course, the sites remembering the 1944 battle. The ancient town of **Nijmegen** too, 21km to the south, is a fashionable university city, with a quality contemporary music and arts scene, despite similarly extensive war damage, and makes a good, if brief, stop before heading south into the province of Limburg or east into Germany.

Northwest Overijssel: Steenwijk, Giethoorn and the lakes

Trains from Leeuwarden slip into the province of Overijssel near the village of **WILLEMSOORD**, in the northernmost corner of the province. The area was no more than empty moorland until the nineteenth century, when the so-called "Society of Charity" established a series of agricultural colonies here to cater for the poor. The Dutch bourgeoisie was as apprehensive of the unemployed pauper as its Victorian counterpart in Britain and the 1900 *Baedeker* noted approvingly that, "the houses are visited almost daily by the superintending officials and the strictest discipline is everywhere observed".

Trains stop at **STEENWIJK**, on the edge of the old moorlands, an unremarkable settlement that's only really useful as a base for exploring the surrounding lakes of western Overijssel. The town has seen more than its fair share of siege and assault, and, as a result, the towering mass of the Grote Kerk is an inconclusive mixture of styles that's suffered repeatedly from war damage. Otherwise, the centre is still roughly circular, following the lines of the original fortifications whose remains can be seen on the south side of town in a chain of steep, moated earth ramparts.

The town's **train** and **bus stations** are five minutes' walk north of the centre; head straight out of the station and follow the road around until you reach the ring road, cross over onto Doelenstraat, take a right at the T-junction and the Markt is in front of you. The VVV, Markt 60 (May–Aug Mon–Fri 9am–5.30pm, Sat 9am–4pm; Sept–April Tues–Fri 10am–5.30pm, Sat 10am–4pm; ☎0521/512 010), is the place to find out about bus services around the lakes; for up-to-date timetables, ask for the *DVM/NWH* bus book, which costs ƒ3.95. Steenwijk has one reasonably priced **hotel**, *De Gouden Engel*, at Tukseweg 1 (☎0521/512 436; ②), five minutes' walk northwest of the Markt – follow Kerkstraat around into Paardenmarkt and Tukseweg is dead ahead. The VVV also has details of a small number of private **rooms**.

Meppel, Staphorst and Rouveen

South of Steenwijk, the railway tracks from Leeuwarden and Groningen join at **MEPPEL**, a second possible base for travelling on to the lakes, though frankly it's a dull town and its **bus** and **train stations** are a good ten minutes' walk southeast of the centre. The town's VVV is at Kromme Elleboog 2 (Mon–Fri 9am–5.30pm, Sat 9am–noon; ☎0522/252 888). There's one hotel, the *De Poort van Drente*, at Parallelweg 25 (☎0522/251 080; ③), and a **youth hostel**, at Leonard Springerlaan 14 (☎0522/251 706); it's marked from the train station and takes about five minutes to reach on foot.

Beyond Meppel lie the elongated villages of **STAPHORST** and **ROUVEEN**, tiny squares of brightly shuttered and neatly thatched farmhouses that line some 10km of road in the shadow of the motorway. Despite significant industrial development in the last decade, both these communities still have strong and strict Calvinist traditions: the majority still observe the Sabbath and many continue to wear traditional costume as a matter of course – and do not wish to be photographed. That said, apart from the custom of painting their houses in vicious shades of green and sky blue, Staphorst and Rouveen are undistinguished.

Giethoorn and the lakes

Meppel and Steenwijk in the east and the old seaports of Vollenhove and Blokzijl in the west, rim an expanse of lake, pond, canal and river that's been formed by centuries of haphazard peat digging. Although it's a favourite holiday spot for

---

BUSES AROUND THE LAKES

From Steenwijk train station #70 to Giethoorn/Zwartsluis (Mon–Fri hourly, Sat 8 daily, Sun 4 daily; 15/30min); change at Zwartsluis for connecting #71 to Vollenhove (Mon–Fri every 30 min, Sat & Sun hourly; 20min); to Blokzijl #75 (Mon–Fri hourly, Sat 4 daily, Sun 3 daily; 15min).

From Meppel train station #73 to Zwartsluis (Mon–Fri 8 daily, Sat 5 daily, Sun 3 daily; 20min); change at Zwartsluis for Vollenhove, as above.

From Zwolle train station #70 or #71 to Zwartsluis & Vollenhove (Mon–Sat every 30 min, Sun every 2hr; 30/50min); #71 continues to Vollenhove; #70 continues to Giethoorn and Steenwijk.

watersports enthusiasts, public transport is limited and in any case you really miss the quiet charm of the region if you aren't travelling by **boat**. Fortunately these are available for rent at Giethoorn, in a variety of shapes and sizes, from canoes to motorboats and dinghies. Prices vary, but reckon on *f*80 per day for a motorboat down to *f*30 for a canoe. The other alternative is to come on a **boat trip** from Kampen (see pp.247–9). Itineraries vary, but once or twice weekly, from mid-July to mid-August, boats sail from Kampen to Vollenhove, Blokzijl and Giethoorn. Further details from Kampen VVV.

Giethoorn

The best-known and most picturesque lakeland village is **GIETHOORN**, which flanks a series of interlocking canals that lie some 200m east of the minor N334 road from Steenwijk to Zwolle – not to be confused with the modern village of the same name on the main road itself. Bus #70 from Steenwijk station travels right through modern Giethoorn before reaching the VVV beyond; make sure the driver lets you off at the old village.

Giethoorn's origins are rather odd. The marshy, infertile land here was given to an obscure sect of flagellants in the thirteenth century by the lord of Vollenhove. Isolated and poor, the colonists were dependent on local peat deposits for their livelihood, though their first digs only unearthed the horns of hundreds of goats who had been the victims of prehistoric flooding, leading to the settlement being named "Geytenhoren" (goats' horns). Nowadays Giethoorn's postcard-prettiness of thatched houses and narrow canals criss-crossed by arching footbridges draws tourists in their hundreds, Dutch and German weekenders swarming into the village throughout summer to jam the busy footpaths and clog the waterways in search of some sort of northern Venice. The high prices and water-borne hubbub are certainly similar, although sadly Giethoorn has little else to offer besides.

If you decide to stay, Giethoorn **VVV**, based in a houseboat on Beulakerweg roughly 2km further along the N334 (mid-May to mid-Sept Mon–Sat 9am–6pm & Sun 10am–5pm, mid-Sept to Oct & March to mid-May Mon–Sat 9am–5pm, Nov–Feb Mon–Fri 9.30am–5pm & Sat 10am–1pm; ☎0521/361 248), has a list of private **rooms** and **pensions** and will telephone ahead to make a booking; clarify the exact location beforehand, or you could end up walking for miles. Two of the more convenient **hotels** are *'t Centrum* (☎0521/361 225, fax 362 429; ②) and *De Pergola* (☎0521/361 321, fax 362 408; ②), both beside Giethoorn's central canal, at Ds Hylkemaweg 39 and 7. Other alternatives include *Hotel Giethoorn* (☎0521/361 216, fax 361 919; ③), conveniently located near the VVV, and the cheaper *De Jonge* (☎0521/361 360, fax 362 549; ②) back up the road at Beulakerweg 30. Accommodation is very tight between June and August. On the eastern edge of old Giethoorn, **Lake Bovenwijde** has no fewer than seven **campsites** on its western shore. The two nearest ones, at the end of the main canal, are the *Botel Giethoorn*, Binnenpad 47a (☎0521/361 332) and *De Kragge*, Binnenpad 113 (☎0521/361 319); both are open April to October.

For **eating**, most of the hotels have reasonable restaurants. Alternatively, you could try the *Achterhuis*, on the main canal at no. 43, or *Café Fanfare*, further east at Binnenpad 68, which has cheap daily dishes on its wide-ranging menu. **Nightlife** tends to be pretty quiet, although there are jazz and blues festivals over succeeding weekends in August. You're really here, though, for the waterways; most of the campsites and hotels rent **boats**, and the VVV can provide details of more than a dozen other operators. **Water taxis** leave from pretty much everywhere and cost about ƒ7 per hour for a trip round the village.

Zwartsluis
South of Giethoorn, bus #70 travels the length of the dyke across Lake Belterwijde before cutting down into **ZWARTSLUIS**, once the site of an important fortress at the junction of waterways from Zwolle and Meppel. There's nothing much to the place today, but a couple of minutes' walk east of the bus station, at the bottom of Dawarsstraat, off Handelskade, is a small Jewish **cemetery** with a touching memorial to those locals who died in the concentration camps.

Vollenhove
At the bus station on the edge of Zwartsluis passengers change for the journey west to **VOLLENHOVE**, one of the most agreeable little towns in northwest Overijssel. Once a maritime fortification guarding the approach to Zwolle, Vollenhove spreads out east from the Vollenhover Kanaal that marks the path of the old Zuider Zee coastline. Buses stop on Clarenberglaan, a five-minute walk away from the main square (straight up Doelenstraat), where the **Onze lieve Vrouwekerk** is a confusion of towers, spires and gables. The elegant, arcaded **Stadhuis** is attached to the church, and, across Kerkplein, the weathered stone gateposts outside the bank were originally part of the entrance to the **Latin School**. Around the corner from the church is the town's charming ancient **harbour**, a cramped, circular affair encased in steep grass banks.

Vollenhove **VVV** (July–Aug Mon–Sat 10am–noon & 1.30–5pm, May–June & Sept–Nov 10am–noon & 2–4.30pm; ☎0527/241 700) is beside the harbour, although it can't offer much help with accommodation. There's just the one **hotel**, the *Saantje*, Kerkplein 1 (☎0527/241 403; ②). Of the two local **campsites**, the nearest is at Noordwal 3 (☎0527/241 452) five minutes' walk southwest of the VVV along the canal. The **restaurant** *De Vollenhof*, Kerkplein 12, serves good fish dishes and has a three-course menu; more appealing – and more expensive – is the *Seidel* restaurant in the old Stadhuis at Kerkplein 3. If you can't afford a meal, pop in for a coffee: the decor is delightfully antique.

Blokzijl
Some 6km to the north, **BLOKZIJL** is more beguiling still, an orange-pantiled cobweb of narrow alleys and slim canals surrounding a trim little harbour. Formerly a seaport, Blokzijl has scores of restored seventeenth-century houses reflecting is mercantile past and one of the grandest has been converted into the *Hotel Kaatje Bijde Sluis*, Brouwerstraat 20 (☎0527/291 833; ⑤), overlooking the main canal. More basic accommodation is available through the **VVV**, Kerkstraat 12 (June–Sept Mon–Sat 9am–6pm, Sun 10am–noon & 1.30–4.30pm; ☎0527/291 414), but it's wise to book in advance in season. *Camping De Sas* is on the south edge of town at Zuiderkade 22 (April–Sept).

The town is stuffed with **restaurants**: the *Kaatje Bijde Sluis* hotel (see above) has the finest food for miles around, but it is expensive and its restaurant is closed on Monday and Tuesday. Cheaper choices for local food include the *Prins Mauritshuis*, Brouwerstraat 2.

Blokzijl is easily reached in summer by boat from Vollenhove and Zwartshuis, but is a little awkward to reach by bus from Vollenhove: take #71 or #171 heading west and change at **Marknesse** to #75 travelling east. Bus #75 (Mon–Fri hourly,

Sat 4 daily, Sun 3 daily) connects Blokzijl direct with Steenwijk – the easier approach – and drops you on the north edge of town, five minutes' walk from the harbour. Blokzijk also makes a good base for exploring the surrounding countryside, in particular the **National Park De Weerribben**, a chunk of protected canal and marshland starting about 3km to the northeast of the town. The VVV will suggest cycle routes through the Weerribben, linking up with any of many motorboat trips. The *Bezoekerscentrum*, at Hoogweg 27 (Tues–Fri 10am–5pm & Sat–Sun noon–5pm), on the north edge of the park, has information on the local flora and fauna.

Bikes can be rented in Blokzijl at *Het Keldertje*, Zuiderstraat 21 (☎0527/291 747), at ƒ10 per day. For the less energetic, **boat trips** leave Blokzijl for Vollenhove and Zwartshuis three times daily in July and August, charging ƒ15 per person. The VVV will have the latest details.

Zwolle

The first major rail junction as you come from the north, **ZWOLLE** is the small and compact capital of Overijssel. An ancient town, it achieved passing international fame when Thomas à Kempis settled here in 1399 and throughout the fifteenth century Zwolle prospered as one of the principal towns of the Hanseatic League, its burghers commissioning an extensive programme of public works designed to protect its citizens and impress their rivals. Within the city walls, German textiles were traded for Baltic fish and grain, or more exotic products from Amsterdam, like coffee, tea and tobacco. The boom lasted for some two hundred years, but by the middle of the seventeenth century the success of Amsterdam and the general movement of trade to the west had undermined its economy – a decline reflected in Zwolle's present-day status as a small market town of no particular significance.

Refortified in successive centuries, today's centre is still in the shape of a star fortress, nine roughly triangular earthen bulwarks encircling both the old town and its harbour, whose waters separate a northern sector off from the rest. Prettily moated and still partly walled, Zwolle is engaging, though the surrounding suburbs, by comparison, are an unattractive modern sprawl.

Arrival, information and accommodation

Well connected by train to many of Holland's major cities and by bus to most of Overijssel's tourist attractions, Zwolle's **train** and **bus** stations are some ten minutes' walk south of the centre, a little way from the moat down Stationsweg. If you're intending to travel around the lakes and Flevoland by bus, it's well worth buying timetables from the bus station kiosk (Mon–Fri 8am–6pm).The **VVV** is at Grote Kerkplein 14 (Mon–Fri 9am–5.30pm & Sat 9am–4pm; ☎038/421 3900) and can help with finding a **room**. There are no great bargains for accommodation. The dependable *Cityhotel*, Rode Torenplein 10 (☎038/421 8182, fax 422 0829; ③), is just northwest of the Grote Markt at the end of Melkmarkt, while the best bargain for those counting every penny is the no-frills *Sleep-In* at Rode Torenplein 4 (☎038/422 7484; ①), although this is run by volunteers and open only in July and August. A little out of town the *Postiljon Zwolle*, at Hertsenbergweg 1 (☎038/421 6031, fax 422 3069; ③) has rooms from *f*110 at weekends. The town's nearest **campsite**, *Camping Agnietenberg*, Haersterveerweg 22 (☎038/453 1530; April–Sept), is by the River Vecht on the northeastern outskirts of town and difficult to reach without a car; take the Meppel bus #40 from Zwolle station and ask for the campsite. You'll be let off on the east side of the bridge across the Vecht on the A28. Immediately east of the bus stop, Ordelseweg goes under the A28 and leads north to the campsite, a distance of about 2km.

The town

In the centre of the Grote Markt stands the recently restored **Grote Kerk**, dedicated to St Michael, patron saint of the town. If the exterior seems a little plain it's because it's been dogged by ill luck. Its bell tower used to be one of the highest in the country and was struck by lightning three times in 1548, 1606 and 1669. After the third time it was never rebuilt and eventually the bells were sold. Inside,

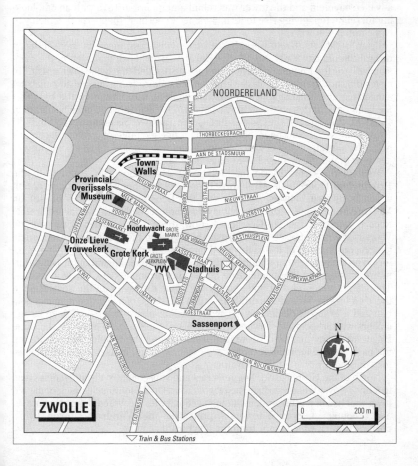

the church has the familiar austerity of Dutch Protestantism, with the choir a bare and dusty forgotten corner and the seats arranged on a central pulpit plan. The pulpit itself is an intricate piece of Renaissance carving by the German Adam Straes, where the grace of Christ is emphasized by the brutal ugliness of the faces of the sinners.

Attached to the church is the **Hoofdwacht** of 1614, an ornately gabled building which once served as a guardhouse. In front was the place of public execution, the remaining inscription "Vigilate et Orate" (Watch and Pray) a stern piece of advice to the crowds who gathered to witness these bloody spectacles. Appropriately, the building later housed the town's main police station.

A little way west, down an alley off the Grote Markt, the primly restored **Onze Lieve Vrouwekerk** (mid-May to mid-Sept Mon–Fri 1–4pm & Sat 11am–4pm; mid–Sept to mid-May Mon–Sat 1–3pm; tower *f*2) is a discordant mixture of styles dating from the fifteenth century. Once again, the church has been plagued with difficulties – the original building contractor ran off with an advance payment and the tower was rebuilt after a fire in 1815 with an odd-looking turret on top, giving rise to its nickname "Peperbus" (pepperpot), which you can climb if you wish.

From beside the Grote Kerk, Sassenstraat twists and turns its way southeast toward the old city walls. No. 33, the **Karel V Huis**, is all that's left of the mansion built for the Emperor Charles V in case he decided to pay the town a visit. He never did, but then all the major cities of his empire were obliged to construct similarly grand buildings for his possible convenience. Strangely, the bas-relief medallion of Charles on the gable is dated 1571, thirteen years after his death in 1558. At the end of the Sassenstraat, the massive **Sassenpoort** (Mon–Fri 10am–5pm & Sat–Sun noon–5pm; free) is a fine example of a fifteenth-century defensive portal, complete with boiling oil and water holes; it gives some idea of just how grand the medieval town must have been.

West of the Grote Markt, at Melkmarkt 41, is the main entrance to the **Provinciaal Overijssels Museum** (Tues–Sat 10am–5pm & Sun 1–5pm; *f*2.50), which is divided between two houses: the **Drostenhuis** (bailiff's house) on Melkmarkt, a grand sixteenth-century mansion topped with an uncomfortable Rococo pediment and the **Gouden Kroon**, through the garden at the side on Voorstraat. Pride of place in the Drostenhuis goes to the Blokzijl room, a meticulous reconstruction of a wealthy local family's seventeenth-century living quarters. The walnut, leather-upholstered chairs are a good illustration of Dutch furniture making and the mantelpiece holds some examples of Chinese ceramics. There's not much else of note, but of the items displayed on the second floor, there's a bizarre Vollenhove drinking cup in the shape of a bearded man in a doublet and a group of distinctive Art Nouveau Rozenburg vases – all deep strong colours with insects and flowers at the heart of the design – made by the same Hague company that tiled Groningen train station. The Gouden Kroon, around the back, is used for modest temporary exhibitions and houses a tiny natural history museum.

North of the Grote Markt, Roggenstraat and subsequently Vispoortenplas lead to a bridge over what was once the city harbour. On its south side much of the old town wall has been restored, including sections with a covered defensive parapet and a couple of fortified towers – principally the **Wijndragerstoren** (wine-porters' tower), which dates from the fourteenth century.

Eating and drinking

Zwolle is surprisingly short of interesting places to **eat**. Grote Kerkplein has the inexpensive *Bella Napoli*, offering pizzas from ƒ10, and *Eetcafe de Klein*, with cheap snacks available all day. The *Kota Radja*, Melkmarkt 50 (☎038/421 3534), has reasonable Chinese/Indonesian food; *La Cucuracha*, Sassenstraat 54 (☎038/421 8172), has a standard Mexican selection; while *Thor*, near the Wijndragerstoren, is a resturant-ship with Dutch food on deck starting at around ƒ20. Of Zwolle's **bars**, the *Grand Cafe het Wijnhuis* is the best bet on Grote Kerkplein, while *De Docter* at Voorstraat 3 and *Music Hall X-Ray* at Blijmarkt 15 have live music at the weekend.

Kampen

Just ten minutes from Zwolle by train, the small town of **KAMPEN** strings along the flat flood plain of the IJssel, a bold succession of towers and spires that, together with the other towns along the river, enjoyed a period of real prosperity in the fifteenth century as members of the Hanseatic League. Their success was short-lived, however and by the late sixteenth century they were in decline as trade moved west and Amsterdam mopped up what was left by undercutting their merchants. Indeed, the IJssel towns slipped into obscurity just as Amsterdam rose to the full height of its glory.

The town

Sidelined by history, Kampen nowadays is little more than four roughly parallel streets edging the river, dotted with the remnants of the town's heyday. A bridge from beside the station spans the IJssel, leading directly into the centre. Clearly visible to the right of the bridge is a leaning tower with a bizarre top that resembles a hollowed-out onion, part of the Stadhuis. Just across the street is a second tower, the seventeenth-century **Nieuwe Toren**, which becomes Kampen's main tourist attraction every summer on five consecutive Thursdays, beginning at the end of July, when the **Kampen cow** is pulled up to its top. Insult turned to civic celebration, the cow is a symbol of the stupidity of the inhabitants of Kampen, who are unlucky enough to be the butt of the Dutch equivalent of "Irish jokes". The legend is that when grass began to grow at the top of the tower, local farmers asked if they could graze their cattle up there, without considering how the animals could get up and down. To commemorate this daft request, an animal has been hoisted up the tower every year ever since, though thankfully it's recently been replaced by a stuffed model.

The **Stadhuis** itself (Mon–Thurs 11am–noon & 2–4pm, May–Sept also Sat 2–5pm; ƒ1.50) is divided into two parts, the **Oude** and **Nieuwe Raadhuis**: the former was built in 1543, the latter added during the eighteenth century. Of the two, it's the old building which has most of interest, namely the *Schepenzaal* or "Magistrates' Hall", a claustrophobic medieval affair with dark-stained walls capped by a superbly preserved barrel-vault roof and a magnificent stone chimneypiece – a grandiloquent, self-assured work carved by Colijn de Nole in tribute to Charles V in 1545, though the chimney's typically Renaissance representations of Justice, Prudence and Strength speak more of municipal pride than imperial glory. To the right, the magistrate's bench is the work of a more obscure local carpenter, a Master Frederik, who didn't get on with de Nole at all. Angry at not getting the more important job of the chimneypiece, his revenge can still be seen on the left-hand pillar, where a minute, malevolent satyr laughs maniacally at the chimney. For further details, pick up the glossy booklet on your way in – entry through the Nieuwe Raadhuis.

Near the Stadhuis, the **Stedelijk Museum**, Oudestraat 158 (Tues–Sat 11am–12.30pm & 1.30–5pm; free), is housed in an attractive fifteenth-century merchant's house and merits a brief stop as much for the building as for the collection of local bits and pieces contained within. In the other direction Oudestraat leads directly south to the **Bovenkerk** (mid-April to mid-Sept Mon & Tues 1–5pm, Wed–Fri 10am–5pm; mid-Sept to mid-April Mon–Fri 1–4pm; free), a lovely Gothic church with a light, spacious sandstone interior. Generally regarded as one of the most important Dutch medieval churches, its choir – with thirteen radiating chapels – was the work of Rotger of Cologne, a member of the Parler family of masons who worked on Cologne Cathedral. In the south transept an urn contains the heart of Admiral de Winter, a native of Kampen who fought to rid his country of what he considered to be the yoke of the House of Orange. A staunch Republican, he took part in the successful French invasion of 1795 that created the Batavian Republic; the rest of him lies in the Pantheon in Paris. **Concerts** are held in the church on Saturday afternoons in July and August at 3pm.

Beside the Bovenkerk is the earliest of Kampen's three surviving gates, the fourteenth-century **Koornmarktpoort**. The others, the **Cellebroederspoort** and the **Broederpoort**, are of a later, more ornamental design and lie on the west side of town along Ebbingestraat, reached from the Bovenkerk via Schoolstraat.

Practicalities

It takes ten minutes for the twice-hourly train from Zwolle to reach Kampen **station**, five minutes' walk from the town centre. Finding somewhere to **stay** can be difficult as the town has only three **hotels** and these are often full in high season. There's the *Van Dijk*, IJsselkade 30 (☎038/331 4925, fax 331 6508; ③) and the *De Stadsherberg*, IJsselkade 48 (☎038/331 2645; ③), both beside the river, and the slightly less salubrious *De Zon*, near the Nieuwe Toren at Torenstraat 9 (☎038/331 2398; ②). The nearest **campsite** is the *Seveningen* (☎038/331 4891; April–Sept) some 3km northeast of town at Frieseweg 7: heading out of Kampen, cross the bridge and turn left; follow the main road around until it crosses the Ganzendiep canal and the campsite is just beyond – watch out for signs. If you're in difficulties, the Kampen **VVV** is on the main street at Botermarkt 5 (Mon–Fri 9am–5pm, Sat 9am–4pm; ☎038/331 3500) and has a very short list of **private rooms**.

If you do manage to get fixed up, Kampen makes a good base for **day-trips** into Flevoland and the Northeast Polder. Throughout June, July and August **boat trips** leave Kampen to explore the surrounding waterways; there are two- or three-times weekly excursions to Urk, Giethoorn and Enkhuisen. Prices vary according to the itinerary, but the longest trips will only cost about *f*30; up-to-date schedules and bookings are available at the VVV. Alternatively, **bikes** can be rented, as ever, from the train station or from *Potkamp*, Oudestraat 152 (☎038/331 3495), for ƒ8 a day.

For **food**, there's rather stolid Dutch fare at the *De Stadsherberg* hotel, pancakes and snacks at *'t Trappetje*, Oudestraat 25, Chinese/Indonesian meals at *Kota Radja*, Oudestraat 119, or the fish and Dutch specialities of *D'Olde Vismark*, IJsselkade 45.

Elburg

Half an hour from Zwolle by bus, just across the provincial boundary in Gelderland, the tiny coastal town of **ELBURG** once looked out across the Zuider Zee, whose perimeter is now marked by the path of the Veluwemeer as it snakes its way between the mainland and the polders of Flevoland. These days it's one of the most popular day-trip destinations in this part of Holland, awash with visitors throughout the season, here to enjoy the town's seaside flavour and to tour the homeopathic gardens on the outskirts.

Elburg was a successful port with its own fishing fleet from as early as the thirteenth century. However, in 1392 the governor, a certain Arent thoe Boecop, moved the whole town a little inland as a precaution against flooding. Familiar with the latest developments in town planning, Boecop and his overlord, the Count of Zutphen, laid out the new town in the shape of a grid-iron, encircled by a protective wall and moat. Not all of Elburg's citizens were overly impressed – indeed the street by the museum is still called Ledigestede, literally "Empty Way" – but the basic design, with the notable addition of sixteenth-century ramparts and gun emplacements, survived the decline that set in when the harbour silted up and can still be observed today. Elburg's two main streets are Beekstraat, which forms the north–south axis and Jufferenstraat/Vischpoortstraat, which runs east–west; they intersect at right angles to form the main square, the Vischmarkt and all of Elburg's streets radiate from one or the other.

Buses from Zwolle drop visitors just outside the old town, a couple of minutes' walk from the **Gemeentemuseum**, Jufferenstraat 6 (Sept–May Mon 2–5pm, Tues–Fri 10am–noon & 2–5pm; June–Aug Mon–Fri 10am–5pm; ƒ2.75), housed in an old convent, with predictable period rooms and objects of local interest. Heading north across Jufferenstraat, the **St Nicolaaskerk** (Mon & Fri 2–5pm, Tues–Thurs 10–noon & 2–5pm; ƒ1.50) dominates the landscape, even without its spire, which was destroyed by lightning in 1693. West of the church, down Van Kinsbergenstraat, is the old **Stadhuis**, which once served as Boecop's home. At the end of Van Kinsbergenstraat, turn left into Beekstraat for the town's main square, the Vischmarkt, from where Vischpoortstraat leads straight to the best preserved of the medieval town gates, the **Vischpoort**, a much restored brick rampart tower dating from 1594. Inside there's a modest exhibition on the local fishing industry (mid-June to Aug Mon 2–4.30pm, Tues–Fri 9.30am–noon; ƒ2 or same ticket as Gemeetemuseum).

Outside the gate, the pattern of the sixteenth-century defensive works is clear to see – from interior town wall, to dry ditch, to earthen mound and moat. The interior of one of the subterranean artillery **Kazematten** (casements) is open from mid-June to August (Mon 2–4.30pm, Tues–Fri 9.30am–noon & 1–4.30pm, ƒ2.75). Cramped and poorly ventilated, it's easy to see why the Dutch called such emplacements *Moortkuijl*, literally "Pits of Murder". From the Kazematten it's about an hour's stroll right around the ramparts.

Ten minutes' walk northwest from the Vischpoort – turn right along Havenkade and take the second left – lie the **De Vier Jaargetijden** homeopathic gardens (April–Oct Mon–Fri 9.30am–4pm; June–Aug also Sat 10am–3.30pm; guided tours only – see below), six hectares of land that hold a comprehensive collection of homeopathic plants, the life's work of one Alfred Vogel. They form part of a successful business and are in fact Elburg's main tourist attraction. In the summer, free guided tours of two hours' duration begin at the visitors' centre (see below) once every two hours, on the hour, subject to demand and within opening times. It's easy to tag onto any of the groups visiting the gardens, but if you're keen to have the tour in English, call ahead (☎0525/687 373) to make arrangements. It's possible to negotiate a tour in English on the spot, but you may have to wait a couple of hours. The visitors' centre, or **Bezoekerscentrum**, at Industriestraat 15, has a variety of illustrative displays and a mock-up of an old chemist's. However, it's all in Dutch and the surrounding gardens are of far more interest.

Practicalities

Elburg is easily reached from **Zwolle bus station** by service #101 (Mon–Sat every 30min, Sun hourly; 35min). The nearest **train station** is 8km from town at **'T HARDE**, on the Zwolle–Amersfoort line, with trains in both directions every half-hour; however, bus #123 from 't Harde station to Elburg runs infrequently (Mon–Fri only 4 daily; 15min).

Elburg's **VVV** is around the corner from the Gemeentemuseum at Ledige Stede 31 (May–Aug Mon–Fri 9am–5.30pm & Sat 9am–5pm; Sept–April Mon 1.30–5pm, Tues–Fri 9am–12.30pm & 1.30–5pm, Sat 11am–4pm; ☎0525/681 520). It has a list of private **rooms** and will phone around to make a booking, but try to get a room in the old centre and come early in high season when accommodation often runs short. The one **hotel**, *Hotel Elburg*, Smedestraat 5 (☎0525/683 877; ③), has double rooms for *f*140 and is just off Beekstraat on the southwest side of the centre. The nearest **campsite** is the *Old Putten*, Zuiderzeestraatweg 65 (☎0525/681 938; May–Oct), some 500m east of the VVV; head out of the old town along Zwolseweg and Zuiderzeestraatweg is the first on the right.

Of Elburg's many **restaurants** it's difficult to find any of real note. However, *'t Olde Regthuys*, Beekstraat 33, serves a reasonable range of fish dishes underneath fishing nets and ship models; *da Pietro*, Vischpoortstraat 20, has good pizzas starting at *f*13, and *de Tapperij* at the Hotel Elburg has *dagschotels* for *f*15. If you're after a **drink**, the *Beekzicht*, Beekstraat 39 has a fantastic selection of beers.

For **boat trips**, there are hour-long excursions from Elburg around the Veluwemeer throughout the summer (*f*6 per person). There are also day-trips to Urk (July & Aug 3 weekly) and occasional sailings to Ketelmeer and Harderwijk, among other destinations, which cost around *f*18 per person. The VVV has the latest schedules and will make bookings on your behalf.

The **strip of coast** on both sides of the Veluwemeer around Elburg is popular with Dutch holidaymakers for its watersports, nature reserves and forests. The whole region is dotted with campsites and the best way to explore it all is by **bike**. Cycles are available for rent in Elburg at *Koops*, Beekstraat 1 (☎0525/684 461), for about *f*8 a day. The VVV has a comprehensive range of suggested cycle routes.

Flevoland

With the damming of the Zuider Zee and the creation of the IJsselmeer, the coastline north and west of Kampen and Elburg has been transformed, creating two
new polder areas, the **Oostelijk and Zuidelijk Flevoland polders**, which form
an island of reclaimed land in front of the old shoreline and make up the greater
part of Holland's twelfth and newest province – **FLEVOLAND**. To the north, the
reclaimed land mass of the **Northeast Polder** forms the rest of the new province,
the small towns that mark the line of the old coast – Vollenhove, Blokzijl and
Kuinre – cut off from open water and now marking the provincial boundary
between Flevoland and Overijssel.

The Northeast Polder

The **Northeast Polder** was the first major piece of land to be reclaimed as part
of the Zuider Zee reclamation scheme, which began in earnest with the Zuider
Zee Reclamation Act of 1918. The key to the project was the completion of the
Afsluitdijk between Den Oever in North Holland and Zurich in Friesland in
1932, which separated the open sea from the Zuider Zee and thereby created
the freshwater IJsselmeer lake. The draining of the polder was completed in
1936: drained and dried, it provided 119,000 acres of new agricultural pasture,
which the government handed out under an incentive scheme to prospective
settlers. The original aims of the project were predominantly agricultural and
(unlike later polders) little consideration was given to the needs of the settlers,
with the result that most of the Northeast Polder is unimaginably boring (the
only town of any size, **Emmeloord**, is like a vast housing development) and it's
no surprise that, even with the incentives, there were difficulties in attracting
settlers. Also, a number of design faults soon became apparent. Without trees
the land was subject to soil erosion and the lack of an encircling waterway
meant the surrounding mainland dried out and began to sink – problems that
have persisted until the present day.

The Schokland Museum

The Northeast Polder incorporates the former Zuider Zee islands of Urk and
Schokland, which in Roman times were actually connected as one island.
Schokland, however, was abandoned in the last century because of the threat of
flooding and only the church of 1834 has survived, converted into the **Schokland
Museum** (April–Sept daily 10am–5pm, Oct–March Tues–Sun 11am–5pm; *f*3.50),
with displays of all sorts of bits and pieces found during the draining of the
polders. From beside the museum, a circular foot- and cycle-path follows the old
shoreline of the island, a distance of about 10km. Bikes can sometimes be rented
by the hour from the museum; phone ahead (☎0527/251 396) to confirm. The
museum is a 400-metre walk south of the minor road between Ens and
Nagele/Urk – some 3km west of Ens. Buses drop you off on the stretch of road
nearest the museum, but it's an awkward journey without a car: take the bus from
Zwolle or Kampen station to Ens bus station (Mon–Fri every 30 min, Sun hourly),
from where you can either walk or take the connecting bus which passes
Schokland on its way to Urk (Mon–Fri 4 daily, none at weekends; 5min).

Urk

The only place really worth a visit in the Northeast Polder is **URK**, a trim harbour and fishing port that was a reluctant addition to the mainland. Centuries of hardship and isolation bred a tight-knit island fishing community here, with its own distinctive dialect and version of the national costume – aspects that have inevitably become diluted by connection to the mainland. However, the island's earlier independence does to some extent live on, rooted in a fishing industry which marks it out from the surrounding agricultural communities.

The damming of the Zuider Zee posed special problems for the islanders and it's hardly surprising that they opposed the IJsselmeer scheme from the beginning (see box on p.146). Some feared that when the Northeast Polder was drained they would simply be overwhelmed by a flood of new settlers, but their biggest concern was that their fishing fleet would lose direct access to the North Sea. After futile negotiations at national level, the islanders decided to take matters into their own hands: the larger ships of the fleet were sent north to fish from ports above the line of the Afsluitdijk, particularly Delfzijl and transport was organized to transfer the catch straight back for sale at the Urk fish auctions. In the meantime, other fishermen decided to continue to fish locally and adapt to the freshwater species of the IJsselmeer. These were not comfortable changes for the islanders and the whole situation deteriorated when the Dutch government passed new legislation banning trawling in the IJsselmeer in 1970. When the inspectors arrived in Urk to enforce the ban, years of resentment exploded in ugly scenes of dockside violence and the government moved fast to sweeten the pill by offering substantial subsidies to compensate those fishermen affected. This arrangement continues today and the focus of conflict has moved to the attempt to impose EU quotas on the catch of the deep-sea fleet.

There's nothing spectacular about Urk but its setting is attractive, its waterfront a pleasant mixture of the functional and the ornamental, and an appealing series of narrow lanes of tiny terraced houses indicate the extent of the old village. A surprising number of the islanders still wear traditional costume and further examples are on display in the **Museum Het Oude Raadhuis**, Wijk 2, no.2 (April–Oct Mon–Sat 11am–5pm; ƒ3.50).

The only convenient way of reaching Urk is by **bus** from Kampen and Zwolle (Mon–Sat every 30min, Sun 3 daily after 4pm; 60–80min): ask the driver to drop you off at the stop nearest the centre. From early May to mid-September, Monday to Saturday, **ferries** cross the IJsselmeer between Enkhuizen and Urk two or three times daily and the trip takes around ninety minutes: check with any VVV for times and prices.

Adjoining the museum, Urk **VVV**, Wijk 2, no. 2 (April–Oct Mon–Fri 10am–5pm, Sat 10am–1pm; ☎0527/684 040), will help arrange **accommodation**. There are several cheap **pensions** near the harbour: *De Kroon*, Wijk 7, no. 54 (☎0527/681 216; ②), *De Kaap*, Wijk 1, no. 5 (☎0527/681 509; ②) and the unnamed pension of *Mw. J. Bakker* at Wijk 3, no. 76 (☎0527/682 363; ②). The nearest **campsite** is *De Vormt*, Vormtweg 9 (☎0527/681 785; April–Sept), in the woods some 4km north of Urk along the coastal road. Finally, Urk is a great place to eat **fresh fish** – *De Kaap* (see above), does good lunch specials and all-you-can-eat deals in the evening and has fine views over the IJsselmeer from its window tables; there are also plenty of cheap snack bars along Radhuisstraat and the more expensive *De Zeebodem*, by the harbour at Wijk 1, no. 67.

The Flevoland polders

The Dutch learned from their mistakes on the Northeast Polder when, in the 1950s and 1960s, they drained the two polders that make up the western portion of the province of Flevoland, ringing the new land with a water channel to stop the surrounding land drying out and sinking. The government also tried hard to make these polders attractive – they're fringed by trees and watersports facilities – but it remains an uphill struggle and people have moved here reluctantly, only persuaded by large financial carrots and very cheap housing. **Lelystad**, along with the other new town of **Almere**, 25km to the west, is where most of them end up, and it is here, if anywhere, that you're likely to come, as a handful of attractions on its outer edge repay a short visit.

Lelystad and around

Home to some of Amsterdam's most poorly paid workers, **LELYSTAD** is a largely characterless expanse of glass and concrete surrounded by leafy suburbs. It takes its name from the pioneer engineer who had the original idea for the Zuider Zee scheme but, the epitome of 1960s and early 1970s urban design, the place is something of a disaster. Still, though you certainly won't want to stop here for long, **Batavia Werf** and the adjacent **museums** make it worthy of a look-in.

Just on the outskirts of Lelystad, the shipbuilding yard at **Batavia Werf**, Oostvaardersdijk 1–9 (July–Sept daily 10am–9pm; Oct–June daily 10am–5pm; ƒ15) pulls in over 300,000 visitors a year. The yard is a working centre for traditional shipbuilding, but its principal attraction is the 56-metre *Batavia*, a reconstruction of a merchant ship – one of the largest of its time – built in 1628 for the Dutch East India Company to bring home the exotic cargo of Holland's new colonies in Asia. Heavily armed and loaded with 341 crew and passengers, many of them soldiers employed by the company to protect against enemies and pirates, the original *Batavia* sank on its maiden voyage off the west coast of Australia. The reconstruction project began in 1985, but because of the traditional materials and methods used, it was not until April 1995 that the new *Batavia* received its official launch at the hands of Queen Beatrix.

There's no guided tour and you're free to clamber all over the ship at will. The hold, down below, has mountains of space for the anticipated freight of wine, coffee, wood and spices, while the orlopdeck above demonstrates the suffocatingly cramped living space of the soldiers, in stark contrast with the comfortably proportioned quarters of the captain and officers. Up on the gundeck, replicas of the *Batavia*'s 32 cannon were cast in moulds created to the design of the seventeenth-century originals. Throughout, it is the attention to detail that really catches the eye, particularly in the late-Renaissance style carving, from the bright-red Dutch lion figurehead to the golden heroes on the stern – William of Orange alongside Julius Civilis, leader of the Batavians in their revolt against the Romans in 69 AD.

Once you've finished on board, you can check out the latest work-in-progress, a reconstruction of the man-o-war *The Seven Provinces* – the seventeenth-century flagship of Admiral Michiel Adriaensz De Ruyter – due for completion in 2005.

While you're in the area there are a couple of good museums worth catching. The **Nieuw Land Poldermuseum**, opposite Batavia Werf at Oostvaardersdijk 1–13 (Mon–Fri 10am–5pm, Sat & Sun 11.30am–5pm; ƒ8.50), is the country's definitive museum on land reclamation. It gives the background on the Zuider Zee plan, with photos, models, films and slides and a worthwhile multimedia show. Most of the information is translated into English and you get a good idea of what's happened and what's scheduled to happen.

Five minutes' walk back up the main road, the **Nederlands Sport Museum**, Museumweg 10 (Mon–Fri 10am–5pm, Sat & Sun noon–5pm; $f7.50$), is also worth seeing. Photographs and exhibits cover every sport the Dutch have ever been involved in, and interactive displays let you test your skill at fencing and other events. The place is brand new and, while still finding its feet, already has ambitious plans for expansion.

Lelystad can be reached by **train** from Amsterdam CS (every 30min; 40min). A bus runs to Batavia Werf from the station once an hour during the summer, in the absence of which you'll have to pay $f6$ for the train-taxi or hike the 3km on foot. The town can also be reached direct from Kampen on **bus** #143 (Mon–Sat every 30min, Sun hourly; 55min). Coming by car, take the exit to Lelystad from the A6 and follow the signs to Batavia Werf. There is no reason at all to spend a night in Lelystad but, if you have to, the **VVV** is at Stationsplein 86 (☎0320/243 444) and can arrange **accommodation**.

Ketelhaven

The area's other attraction, the excellent **Museum of Maritime Archeology** (Mon–Fri 9am–5pm, Sat & Sun 10am–5pm; $f3.50$), is on the northeastern edge of the polder at tiny **KETELHAVEN**, although it is due to move to Lelystad in late 1997. It's a collection of all sorts of material retrieved as the land was drained and there is a detailed guide in English which you can normally borrow. Most of the exhibits come from the extraordinary number of ships that foundered in the treacherous shallows of the Zuider Zee. The centrepiece is the hull of a thirty-metre early-seventeenth-century merchant ship, while the contents of the *Lutina*, which went down with its two-man crew in a storm in 1888, are touching in their simplicity – a cargo of claypipes from Gouda, silver coins and some personal effects. Once again, though, you really need a car to get here: the nearest bus stop is some 6km away on the main Dronten–Kampen road. For the determined, take bus #143 from Kampen station and tell the driver where you're going. The bus stop is a couple of hundred metres east of Colijnweg, a right turn that takes you from the main road right into Ketelhaven.

Eastern Overijssel: Twente

Southeast of Zwolle, the flat landscape of western Holland is replaced by the lightly undulating, wooded countryside of **Twente**, an industrial region whose principal towns – **Almelo**, **Hengelo** and **Enschede** – were once dependent on the textile industry. Hit hard by cheap Far Eastern imports, they have been forced to diversify their industrial base with mixed success: the largest town, Enschede, still has a serious unemployment problem.

Enschede

If you visit anywhere in Twente it should really be **ENSCHEDE**, the region's main town. Laid waste by fire in 1862, it has a desultory modern centre that's been refashioned as a large shopping precinct, but it's a lively place, with regular festivals, exhibitions and the like and it has a museum with an excellent collection of Dutch art and some interesting 1930s architecture. All in all it's a worthwhile detour if you're heading east into Germany.

The town

Five minutes' walk south of the train station, **Langestraat** is Enschede's main street. At its northern end, **Markt** is the town's main square, home to the nineteenth-century **Grote Kerk** (July & Aug Sat 2–4pm) in the middle, with its Romanesque tower, and the **St Jacobuskerk** (July & Aug Tues 1–2.30pm & Sat 11am–12.30pm; outside these times, ask at the VVV for an appointment) just across the Markt, completed in 1933 on the site of a previous church that burned down in 1862. The severe rectangular shape of the St Jacobuskerk is punctured by angular copper-green roofs, huge circular windows and a series of Gothic arches. The church is built in a beautiful domed and cloistered neo-Byzantine style, with some good modern sculpture and stained glass. The **Stadhuis**, a couple of minutes away down Langestraat, was finished in the same year and is also something of an architectural landmark, its brown brick tower topped by four eye-catching blue and gold clocks. No expense was spared in its construction and the interior is richly decorated with mosaics and, again, stained glass.

Fifteen minutes' walk north of the centre at Lasondersingel 129 – over the railway tracks at the crossing beside the station, first right, second left and follow the road to the end – the **Rijksmuseum Twente** (Tues–Sun 11am–5pm; *f*5) is housed in a building of the same era, an Art Deco mansion of 1929, the gift to the nation of a family of mill owners, the Van Heeks, who used the profits they made from their workers to build up one of eastern Holland's finest art collections. The museum is being extensively renovated at the time of writing but normally contains three main sections: fifteenth- to nineteenth-century art, modern art, primarily Dutch with the emphasis on Expressionism, and applied art, based on exhibits from the region of Twente – prehistoric and medieval artefacts, tiles and porcelain, tapestries and a reconstructed farm.

It's the paintings, inevitably, that provide the most interest, especially the Dutch and Flemish sections. Among a fine sample of early religious art are seven brilliant blue and gold fragments from a French hand-illuminated missal; a primitive twelfth-century wood carving of *Christ on Palm Sunday*; a delightful cartoon strip of contemporary life entitled *De Zeven Werken van Barmhartigheid* (The Seven Acts of Charity); and an extraordinary pair of fifteenth-century altar doors by one Tilman van der Burch, where a deep carved relief of a pastoral scene resembles a modern pop-up book. Of later canvases, Hans Holbein's *Portrait of Richard Mabott* is typical of his work, the stark black of the subject's gown offset by the white cross on his chest and the face so finely observed it's possible to make out the line of his stubble. Pieter Brueghel the Younger's *Winter Landscape* is also fastidiously drawn, down to the last twig, and contrasts with the more loosey contoured bent figures and threatening clouds of his brother Jan's *Landscape*. Lucas Cranach's studies of a bloated *Frederick Grootmoedige* and the spectacularly ugly *Barbara van Saksen* must have done little for the self-confidence of their subjects. Jan Steen's *The Alchemist* is all scurrilous satire, from the skull on the chimneypiece, to the lizard suspended from the ceiling and the ogre's whispered advice and compares with the bulging breasts and flushed countenance of the woman in his *Flute Player*, where the promise of forthcoming sex is emphasized by the vague outline of tussling lovers on the wall in the background. The modern section, too, has a few highlights – Claude Monet's volatile *Falaises près de Pourville*; a characteristically unsettling canvas by Carel Willink, *The Actress Ank van der Moer*; and examples of the work of less well-known Dutch modernists like Theo Kuypers, Jan Roeland and Emo Verkerk.

From beside the Stadhuis, it's a ten-minute walk southwest to Enschede's **Museum Jannink** (Tues–Fri 10am–5pm, Sat & Sun 1–5pm; *f*1.50), at the junction of Haaksbergerstaat and Industriestraat (head straight down Van Loenshof, turn right at Boulevard 1945 and take the first left), housed in a former mill and devoted to portraying everyday life in Twente from the nineteenth century onward. The most intriguing displays are a series of representative living rooms and a bewildering variety of looms reflecting the development of the textile industry from its origins as a cottage industry to large-scale factory production.

A third museum, the **Natuurmuseum**, De Ruyterlaan 2 (Tues–Fri 10am–5pm, Sat & Sun 1–5pm; *f*3), is also worth a quick look: there's a vivarium on the second floor, some well-presented fossils on the first floor and a mineralogy section in the basement. To get there, turn right leaving the train station along Stationsplein and then down the first major road on the left – a five-minute walk.

Practicalities

The best place to **stay** in Enschede is the unpretentious *Hotel Chaplin*, right in the centre at Korte Haaksbergerstraat 2 (☎053/431 1787; ③). Alternatively, and somewhat more cheaply, both the *Parkhotel*, Hengelosestraat 200 (☎053/432 3855; ②) and the *Modern*, Parkweg 39 (☎053/432 3438; ②), are a short walk out of the city centre. The **VVV**, in the centre of town at Oude Markt 31 (Mon 10am–5.30pm, Tues–Fri 9am–5.30pm, Sat 9am–1pm; June–Aug also Sat 1–5pm; ☎053/432 3200), has details of a limited number of private **rooms**.

For **food**, stick to the Markt and the streets around. *Graffity*, Markt 6, and *Eetcafe Sam Sam* by the Grote Kerk, both have good daily specials, and popular bars nearby include *De Kater*, *De Geus* and *Poort Van Kleef*. There's also a friendly bar and a varied menu at the *Twente Schouwberg* around the corner from the St Jacobuskerk on Langestraat, the town's principal venue for plays, dance, films and occasional live music.

Around Enschede: Hengelo, Almelo, Oldenzaal, Ootmarsum and Denekamp

Some 10km northwest of Enschede, **HENGELO** has about eighty thousand inhabitants and is Twente's second town, a grim place whose old centre was destroyed during World War II. **ALMELO**, a further 17km northwest, is the region's third largest town, but this too has few attractions: the only buildings of any real interest are the centrally sited **Waag**, whose stepped gables date, surprisingly enough, from 1914 and, in a park east of the Marktplein, a stately seventeenth-century mansion, the **Huize Almelo** (no entry).

Things pick up a little north of Enschede with **OLDENZAAL**, the most agreeable of Twente's other settlements. Founded by the Franks, it was a medieval city of some importance and it was from here, too, that Overijssel's textile industry began its rapid nineteenth-century expansion, spurred on by the introduction of the power loom by Englishman Thomas Ainsworth. The town's principal sight, the **St Plechelmusbasiliek**, is right in the centre (June–Aug Tues 2–3pm, Wed 2–4pm, Thurs 2–3pm; free), an impressive, essentially Romanesque edifice dating from the thirteenth century. Named after Saint Plechelm, the Irish missionary who brought Christianity here, the interior (visits organized by the VVV – see below) is an exercise in simplicity – strong, sturdy pillars supporting a succession of low semicircular arches. Above, the bell tower is the largest in Europe with a carillon of no less than 46 bells.

Bus #60 leaves Enschede for the twenty-minute trip to Oldenzaal train station every thirty minutes from Monday to Saturday and once hourly on Sunday. The approach by **rail** is less convenient as passengers have to change at Hengelo, where it can be up to a thirty-minute wait for the right connection. Oldenzaal's **train station** is ten minutes' walk south of the centre – head down Stationsplein, turn right at the end onto Haerstraat, first left along Wilhelminastraat and it's dead ahead – where the **VVV**, Ganzenmarkt 3 (Mon–Fri 9am–5pm, Sat noon–4pm; ☎0541/514 023), has information on private **rooms**. There are several **hotels**: the cheapest is *de Zon*, Bentheimer-straat 1 (☎0541/512 413; ②), two minutes from Markt; alternatively, try *de Kroon*, Steenstraat 17 (☎0541/512 402; ③). For **eating**, Markt is lined with **bars** and **restaurants** that liven up dramatically on weekend evenings: the best bar is *de Engel* at Markt 14, which also serves food; *Las Carretas* at no. 21 has Mexican fare for around *f*20.

Oldenzaal is a good base for visiting the wooded countryside that stretches northeast from near the town to the German border. This is a popular holiday area, littered with campsites, summer cottages, and bungalow parks. The village of **OOTMARSUM** (bus #64 from the station hourly; 15min) is noted for its half-timbered houses and quaint Markt.

By comparison, **DENEKAMP** (bus #52 from the station; hourly; 30min) is rather drab, though the elegant classicism of the **Kasteel Singraven**, some 2km west of the centre, partly makes up for it. Details of guided tours around the castle (mid-April to Sept) are available from the Denekamp **VVV**, Kerkplein 2 (Mon–Fri 9am–12.30pm & 2–5pm, June–Aug also Sat 1–4pm; ☎0541/351 205). While you're up at the castle, look out for the **watermill** on the banks of the river, built in 1448 and still functioning.

Deventer and Zutphen

South of Zwolle, the River IJssel twists its way through flat, fertile farmland as it marks out the boundary between Overijssel and Gelderland. For two hundred years the towns of the lower IJssel, **Deventer** and **Zutphen**, shared with Zwolle and Kampen a period of tremendous prosperity as the junction of trade routes from Germany, the Baltic and Amsterdam. Although both towns suffered grievously during the wars with Spain, the underlying reasons for their subsequent decline were economic – they could do little to stop the movement of trade to the west and could not compete with the great cities of South Holland. By the eighteenth century, they had slipped into provincial insignificance.

Deventer

Twenty-five minutes by train from Zwolle, **DEVENTER** sits calmly on the banks of the IJssel, an intriguing and – in tourist terms – rather neglected place, whose origins can be traced to the missionary work of the eighth-century Saxon monk, Lebuinus. An influential centre of medieval learning, it was here in the late fourteenth century that Gerrit Groot founded the Brotherhood of Common Life, a semi-monastic collective that espoused tolerance and humanism within a philosophy known as *Moderne Devotie* (modern devotion). This progressive creed attracted some of the great minds of the time and Thomas à Kempis and Erasmus both studied here.

The town

Five minutes from the train station, the centre of town is **Brink**, an elongated marketplace that runs roughly north to south, dividing the old town in two. The **Waag** edges the southern end of the square, a late Gothic edifice that retains an ancient dignity despite something of a rickety appearance. Inside, the **Town Museum** (Tues–Sat 10am–5pm, Sun 2–5pm; ƒ5, or ƒ6 including the Toy Museum – see below) has a thin collection of portrait paintings and a few antique bicycles. More intriguing is the large pan that's nailed to the outside of the Waag's western wall. Apparently, the mintmaster's assistant was found making a tidy profit by debasing the town's coins, so he was put in the pan and boiled alive. The bullet holes weren't an attempt to prolong the agony, but the work of idle French soldiers taking, quite literally, "pot shots".

Behind the Waag, the **Speelgoed en Blikmuseum** (Toy and Tin Museum; Tues–Sat 10am–5pm, Sun 2–5pm; ƒ6, including Town Musuem) specializes in mechanical dolls. Walking west from here, Assenstraat's **window cuts** were completed in the early 1980s by a local artist, J Limburg. Precise and entertaining, each illustrates a particular proverb or belief: at no. 119 the hedgehog's inscription translates as "Thrift yields big revenues" and at no. 81, on a house called *Gevaarlijke Stoffen* (Dangerous Materials), the totem pole is surrounded by slogans including *E pericolose sporcare* (It is dangerous to pollute). Continuing to the west along Assenstraat and veering left down Grote Poot (Big Leg), the **Lebuinuskerk** (Mon–Sat 11am–5pm; free) is one of the most impressive Gothic buildings in eastern Holland and is an expression of Deventer's fifteenth-century wealth and self-confidence. Carefully symmetrical, the massive nave is supported by seven flying buttresses, trimmed by an ornate stone parapet. The interior has recently been restored and today the expanse of white stone is almost startling, high arched windows and slender pillars reaching up toward a distant timber roof. Below, the church has two magnificent Baroque organs, the delicate remnants of some medieval murals and an eleventh-century crypt with a simple vaulted roof supported by Romanesque, spiral columns.

Back outside, the rear of the Lebuinuskek is joined to the fourteenth-century **Mariakerk**. Services haven't been held here since 1591 and the town council considered demolishing it as early as 1600, but in the event it survived as the town's arsenal and now houses a smart restaurant. Back at Brink, east of the Waag, Rijkmanstraat takes you into the **Bergkwartier**, an area of fairly ancient housing that was tastefully refurbished during the 1960s, one of Holland's first urban renewal projects. Turning left onto Kerksteeg, there's a small piece of iron, the remnants of a ring, embedded in a hole on the right-hand wall. The 1570s were desperate times for the inhabitants of Deventer, fearful of marauding Spanish armies, and, in their efforts to reinforce the town's defences, iron rings were embedded in the walls of many of the streets so that chains could be hung across them. At the end of Kerksteeg, the **Bergkerk** is fronted by two tall towers dating from the thirteenth century, the differences in the colouring of the brick indicating the stages of construction. From the church, Roggestraat leads downhill to the east side of Brink; opposite is a tiny triangle edged by the **Penninckshuis**, whose florid Renaissance frontage is decorated with statuettes of six virtues. The inscription *Alst Godt behaget beter benyt als beclaget* is smug indeed – "If it pleases God it is better to be envied than to be pitied".

Practicalities

Deventer's **bus** and **train** stations are a five-minute walk north of the town centre – left out of the station and first right straight down Keizerstraat and onto the Brink. The **VVV**, Keizerstraat 22 (Mon–Fri 9am–5.30pm, Thurs also until 8.30pm, Sat 9am–4pm; ☎0570/613 100) is five minutes on foot from the station. For a place of this size, **accommodation** is thin on the ground: there's only one central **hotel**, the grimly modern *Royal*, Brink 94 (☎0570/611 880; ②) and one budget place, *Shita*, at Tjoenerstraat 25 (☎0570/626 085; ②), a twenty-minute walk from the centre, which charges extra for sheets and blankets. Bookings should be made at the VVV, who will also give you directions on how to get there. The other alternative is the **campsite**, *De Worp* (☎0570/613 601; May–Sept), west of the centre in the fields across the IJssel. A shuttle boat service crosses the river from the landing stage at the bottom of Vispoort and on the other side it's a five-minute walk down the first turn on the right, Langelaan.

Bars and **restaurants** line both sides of Brink: *In de Waagschaal*, no. 77, is a pleasant brown café and there is a varied French and Dutch menu at *La Balance*, no. 72; there are Dutch meals at *De Drie Nissen*, Grote Poot 19, good if pricy Portuguese fare at *Chez Antoinette*, Roggestraat 8, and cheap *dagschotels* at *d'Oude Wijze*, Grote Kerkhof 28. The local speciality is a sort of honey gingerbread, *Deventer koek* and the best place to try it is the antique cake shop, *Bussink*, at no. 84.

The VVV has a walking tour of the city for ƒ0.50 and details of **boat trips** up the IJssel leaving from the jetty near the Vispoort. A weekly programme throughout July and August includes excursions to Enkhuizen, Urk, Kampen, Zwolle and Zutphen, once or twice a week; prices vary according to the itinerary, but for the longer trips reckon on ƒ30 per person return.

Zutphen

A sleepy little town some 15km south of Deventer, over in Gelderland, **ZUTPHEN** was founded in the eleventh century as a fortified settlement at the junction of the Berkel and IJssel rivers. It took just one hundred years to become an important port and today's tranquillity belies an illustrious and sometimes torrid past. Attacked and sacked on numerous occasions, the massacre of its citizens by Spanish forces in 1572 became part of Protestant folklore, strengthening their resolve against Catholic cruelty and absolutism. It was also here that Sir Philip Sidney, the English poet, soldier and courtier, met his death while fighting with the Earl of Leicester's forces against the Spanish in 1586. Sir Philip personified the ideal of the Renaissance man and died as he had lived – in style: wounded in the thigh as a consequence of loaning his leg-armour to a friend, he had every reason to feel outraged by his poor luck. Instead, realizing he was about to die, he offered his cup of water to another wounded soldier, uttering the now commonplace phrase "thy need is greater than mine".

The town

A five-minute walk from the train station, the effective centre of Zutphen is the **Wijnhuis**, a confused building of pillars and platforms that was begun in the seventeenth century and now houses the VVV. All the old town's main streets radiate from here and although there aren't many specific sights, the place does have charm, a jangle of architectural styles within much of the medieval street plan.

Around the corner from the Wijnhuis, Lange Hofstraat cuts down to the **Grote Kerk** of St Walburga (presently under major restoration, but normally open early May to end-Sept Mon 2–4pm & Tues–Sat 11am–4pm; *f*2.50), an indifferent, though immense Gothic church. Inside, the most impressive features are an extravagant brass baptismal font and the remarkable medieval **Library**, sited in the sixteenth-century chapterhouse. Established in 1560, the library has a beautiful low-vaulted ceiling that twists around in a confusion of sharp-edged arches rising above the original wooden reading desks. It has all the feel of a medieval monastery, but it was in fact one of the first Dutch libraries to be built for the general public, a conscious effort by the Protestant authorities to dispel ignorance and superstition. The collection is wonderful, ranging from early illuminated manuscripts to later sixteenth-century works, a selection of which are still chained to the lecterns on which they were once read. There are also two manuscript volumes – one a beautiful sixteenth-century illuminated missal, the other an original manuscript attributed to Thomas à Kempis. Curiously, the tiles on one side of the floor are dotted with paw marks, which some contemporaries attributed to the work of the Devil.

Down the alleys east of the church entrance is the fifteenth-century **Drogenapstoren**, one of the old city gates. This is a fine example of a brick rampart tower, taking its name from the time when the town trumpeteer, Thomas Drogenap, lived here.

Heading back toward the Wijnhuis along the Zaadmarkt, you'll come to the **Museum Henriette Polak** at no. 88 (Tues–Fri 11am–5pm, Sat & Sun 1–5pm; *f*5) which has a modest collection of twentieth-century Dutch paintings, notably *Landschap* by Wim Oepts, a profusion of strong colours, roughly brushed, that manages a clear impression of a Dutch landscape. The **Stedelijk Museum** (same times, same ticket), on the other side of town toward the station at Rozengracht 3, is housed in the shell of a thirteenth-century Dominican monastery and has a fairly predictable selection of shards, armour and silver. In the old refectory on the second floor there's an altarpiece from around 1400, originally from the Grote Kerk. Finally, the **Graphics Museum**, near the Grote Kerk at Kerkhof 16 (Weds–Fri 1–4.30pm & Sat 11am–3pm; *f*3.50) merits a quick stop for its collection of printing presses and other paraphernalia relating to the industry.

Practicalities

Zutphen's **VVV**, in the Wijnhuis (Mon 10am–5.30pm, Tues–Fri 9am–5.30pm, Sat 9am–noon; ☎0575/519 355), has details of a couple of centrally situated **rooms**, though in July and August it's advisable to arrive early as they disappear fast. Of the **hotels**, the pension-like *Berkhotel* is the best value, straight down the Groenmarkt from the VVV at Marschpoortstraat 19 (☎0575/511 135; ②); alternatively, try the rather more comfortable *Hotel Inntel*, De Stoven 37 (☎0575/525 555, ④).

There are two good and reasonably priced **restaurants** in Zutphen: *Pizzeria da Enzo*, near the Drogenapstoren at Pelikaanstraat 1a and the *Berkhotel*'s vegetarian café *De Kloostertuin*, Marschpoortstraat 19 (closed Mon). For **bars**, try the lively *'t Winkeltje*, Groenmarkt 34, or the quieter *De Korenbeurs*, Zaadmarkt 84. There is occasional live music at *Musiekcafe de Overkat* on Broederen Kerkstraat.

Boat trips run north up the IJssel in July and August with occasional excursions to Deventer (sailing schedules from the VVV). Prices vary according to the route, but a day-trip will cost about *f*30.

Around Zutphen: the Achterhoek

Extending some 30km southeast from Zutphen to the German border, the **Achterhoek** (Back Corner) is aptly named, a dozy rural backwater whose towns and villages have little to hold your attention. The easy hills have, however, made it a popular spot for cyclists. Small enough to tour from Zutphen, there are no really noteworthy monuments, with the possible exception of the old frontier settlement of **'S-HEERENBERG**, whose tedious, modern centre edges the medieval Raadhuis, church and castle that once belonged to the counts Van de Bergh. Of the three, its castle, the Huis Bergh, that dominates, its impressive red-brick walls bedecked with shutters, rising abruptly above the moat. Its present appearance was acquired in 1912 when an Enschede industrialist, J H van Heek, bought the place and had it restored. Guided tours (March to mid-Dec; call ☎0314/661 281 for times; *f*8.50) whisk you round an interior littered with sundry late medieval paintings, statues, prayer books and other paraphernalia installed by Heek.

The quickest way to reach 's-Heerenberg is by train from **PRODEM** to **DOETINCHEM**, where you can pick up the bus from the train station for the twenty-minute trip (Mon–Fri every 30min, Sat & Sun hourly). In 's-Heerenberg the bus stops outside the **VVV** (Mon–Fri 9am–5pm, Sat 9am–2pm, July and August also Sun 11am–3.30pm; ☎0314/663 131), which has good suggestions for walking and cycling. If you need to **stay over**, try *The Mill*, Molenstraat 18 (☎0314/661 369; ②).

Through the Veluwe: Apeldoorn

Extending west of the River IJssel, the **Veluwe** (literally "Bad Land") of the province of Gelderland is an expanse of heath, woodland and dune edged by Apeldoorn and Amersfoort to the east and west and the Veluwemeer and Arnhem to the north and south. For centuries these infertile lands lay almost deserted, but today they make up Holland's busiest holiday centre, a profusion of campsites, bungalow parks and second homes that extends down to the Hoge Veluwe National Park, a protected zone in the southeast corner that is much the prettiest part and the best place to experience the area – though, unless you're camping, it's more sensibly seen from Arnhem.

Apeldoorn

The administrative capital of the Veluwe, **APELDOORN** was no more than a village at the turn of the century, but it's grown rapidly to become an extensive garden city, a rather characterless modern place that spreads languidly into the surrounding countryside. However, as one-time home of the Dutch royal family, Apeldoorn is a major tourist centre in its own right, popular with those Dutch senior citizens who like an atmosphere of comfortable, rather snobbish privilege. The only sign of life is the annual jazz festival, the **Jazztival**, usually held on the first Friday in June, with jazz musicians performing in the bars and clubs around town. Further details from the VVV.

The Paleis Het Loo

Apeldoorn is most famous for the **Paleis Het Loo** (Tues–Sun 10am–5pm; ƒ12.50), situated on the northern edge of town and reachable by half-hourly minibus #1 from the station. Designed in 1685 by Daniel Marot for William III and his Queen Mary, shortly before he acceded to the throne of England and Scotland, the palace was later the favourite residence of Queen Wilhelmina, who lived here until her death in 1962. No longer used by the Dutch royal family – they moved out in 1975 – it was opened as a national museum in the early 1980s, illustrating three hundred years of the history of the House of Orange-Nassau. Inside, seven years of repair work have restored an apparently endless sequence of bedrooms, ballrooms, living rooms and reception halls to their former glory, supplemented by displays of all things royal – from costumes and decorations in the West Wing, to documents, medals and gifts in the East Wing and dozens of royal portraits and miscellaneous memorabilia spread across the main body of the palace. You can view the rooms of William and Mary, including their colourful individual bedchambers, as well as the much later study of Queen Wilhelmina. It's an undeniably complete display, but, unless you've a special interest in the House of Orange, not especially diverting. Better are the formal **gardens** (both William and Mary were apparently keen gardeners), a series of precise and neatly bordered flowerbeds of geometric design that are accessible by long walkways ornamented in the Dutch Baroque style, with fountains, urns, statuettes and portals. The other part of the palace, the **Royal Stables** of 1906, has displays of some of the old cars and carriages of past monarchs, including a baby carriage that's rigged up against gas attack.

Other attractions

The town's second main draw is the **Apenheul** (daily April–June 9.30am–5pm, July–Aug 9.30am–6pm, Sept–Oct 10am–5pm; ƒ16, children ƒ10), just west of town via bus #2. The highlights of this monkey reserve are its gorillas – among the world's largest colonies of the creatures – living on wooded islands that isolate them from the visitors and from the dozen or so species of monkey that roam around the rest of the park. It's best to go early to catch the young gorillas fooling around and antagonising the elders; as the day warms up they all get a bit more slothful. The park is well designed, with a reasonable amount of freedom for most of the animals (at times it's not obvious who is watching who) and you'll see other wildlife including otters, deer and capybara. Finally, in July and August an old **steam train** is put back into service between Apeldoorn and Dieren (a 75-min ride) or you can do a three-legged half-day journey Apeldoorn–Dieren–Zutphen–Apeldoorn by steam train, boat and regular train. Details from the VVV.

Practicalities

The Apeldoorn **VVV** (Mon–Fri 9am–6pm, Sat 9am–5pm; closes at 5.30pm and 1pm respectively out of season; ☎06/916 81636) is at Stationstraat 72. They have maps of the town and the surrounding area and (if you need to stay) lists of **rooms** – in season it's advisable to ask them to ring ahead to confirm vacancies. The most reasonably priced **hotel** near the town centre is the *Abbekerk*, Canadalaan 26, a ten-minute walk north of the centre (☎055/522 2433, fax 521 1323; ③), with double rooms for ƒ102; head up Stationstraat and Canadalaan is the fourth left turn after the Marktplein. There's also a **youth hostel**, 4km to the west of town at Asselsestraat 330 (☎055/355 3118, fax 355 3811; April–Sept), reachable with bus #3 from beside the train station. The nearest **campsite**, *De Veldekster* (☎055/542 4711), is some 5km southwest of the centre, off Europaweg at Veldekster 25 (bus #110 from the train station).

Don't expect a lot of night-time excitement in Apeldoorn. The main hive of evening activity is the **Caterplein**, where Hoofdstraat meets Nieuwstraat. *Tipico*, an excellent Italian with food for all budgets, is nearby at Kapelstraat 11, while *Old Chap* next-door is a decent bar for a pre- or post-prandial drink. *Eetcafe 't Pakhuys*, Beekpark 9, has reasonable Dutch food and there are plenty of cheap shoarma joints nearby. Further south on Hoofdstraat, Radhuisplein has several good café-bars, including *Brasserie de Kabouter*; the *Blues Café* on Nieuwstraat has occasional live music.

An easy way to see the countryside around town is by **bike**. Details of suggested routes are available from the VVV and cycles can be rented at *Harleman*, Arnhemseweg 28. The VVV can also provide details of walking trails in the forests around the Palace Het Loo.

Arnhem and around

Around 20km south of Apeldoorn, on the far side of the heathy Hoge Veluwe National Park, **ARNHEM** was once a wealthy resort, a watering-hole to which the merchants of Amsterdam and Rotterdam would flock to idle away their fortunes. This century it's become better known as the place where thousands of British and Polish troops died in the failed Allied airborne operation of September 1944, codenamed Operation Market Garden. The operation gutted the greater part of the city and most of what you see today is a postwar reconstruction – inevitably not particularly enticing. However, Arnhem is a lively town that makes a good centre for seeing the numerous attractions scattered around its forested outskirts – the war museums and memorials, the Dutch open-air museum and the Hoge Veluwe Park itself, incorporating the Kröller-Müller Museum and its superb collection of modern art.

Arrival, information and accommodation

Arnhem is a major rail junction, well connected with both Dutch and German cities. The town's **train** and **bus stations**, a couple of minutes' walk from the centre, are next door to the **VVV**, Stationsplein 45 (Mon 11am–5.30pm, Tues–Fri 9am–5.30pm & Sat 10am–4pm; ☎06/320 24075; 75c per min), which has a good selection of Dutch maps, books on "Operation Market Garden", brochures and up-to-date cultural information.

Walking is the best way to **get around** Arnhem town centre, although to see any of the outlying attractions and for some of the accommodation, you'll need at some point to use a **bus**. Arnhem has a rather odd system of trams which describe a figure-of-eight pattern over town. This means there'll often be two buses at the station with the same number and different destinations, so it's important to get the direction as well as the number right.

Accommodation

The VVV operates an **accommodation-booking service** – useful in July and August when Arnhem's handful of reasonably priced **pensions** and **hotels** can fill up early. The cheapest rooms in town are at *Hotel Pension Parkzicht*, Apeldoornsestraat 16 (☎026/442 0698; ②) and the nearby and friendly *Hotel Rembrandt*, Paterstraat 1 (☎026/442 0153; ②). Both are a ten-minute walk east from the station: head round the northern edge of Willemsplein onto Jans Buiten Singel; Apeldoornsestraat is at the far end on the left and Paterstraat is just behind the Rembrandt theatre. If money's not too tight, there's the reassuringly comfortable *Hotel Haarhuis* opposite the train station at Stationsplein 1 (☎026/442 7441; ④) while, if you're on a budget, there's a **youth hostel** some 5km north of town at Diepenbrocklaan 27 (bus #3, direction Altaveer; ☎026/442 01 14). The nearest **campsite** is *Camping Warnsborn*, northwest of the centre at Bakenbergseweg 257 (bus #2 direction Schaarsbergen; ☎026/442 3469), although there are many others around the edge of the Hoge Veluwe Park, 5km further north, and one actually in the park itself – an ideal spot for a quiet night's camping.

If you have problems finding something, there's a good alternative outside the city proper, the *Pension Little Tower*, Vijverlaan 29 (☎026/463 5176; ②), in the leafy suburb of **VELP** (trains every 30min; 10min), bookable at Arnhem VVV. Untouched by the war, parts of Velp are still much as they were at the turn of the century – comfortable country mansions and landscaped streets and gardens. The *Little Tower* is right in the middle of Velp, ten minutes' walk from the train station: turn right along Stationsstraat, left at the main road, first right down Overbeeklaan and first left.

The town

Since the war, Arnhem has been something of a place of pilgrimage for English visitors, who flock here every summer to pay their respects to the soldiers who died, or to view the spots immortalized by the battle; only recently have the graves begun to seem distant reminders of an ancient conflict, as World War II veterans age and memories fade. Predictably, the postwar rebuilding has left Arnhem a patchy place with the usual agglomerations of concrete and glass, surrounded by formless empty spaces. Five minutes' walk southeast from the train station, the best part of what's left is the northwest part of town, around the **Korenmarkt**, a small square which escaped much of the destruction and has one or two good facades. The streets which lead off the Korenmarkt are pleasantly animated, full of restaurants and bars, while the **Filmhuis**, at Korenmarkt 42, has an excellent programme of international films and late-night showings.

Arnhem deteriorates as you walk southeast from the Korenmarkt and into the area most badly damaged by the fighting. Here you can find "The Bridge too Far", the **John Frostbrug**, named after the commander of the battalion that defended it for four days. It's just an ordinary modern bridge, but it remains the symbol and centre of people's remembrance of the battle, Dutch and British alike. Around its north end you can see the results of the devastation – wide boulevards intersect broad open spaces edged by haphazardly placed tower blocks and car parks.

Overlooking this rather desolate spot, at the end of the characterless **Markt**, is the church of **St Eusabius** (Tues–Fri 11am–5pm & Sat–Sun noon–5pm; ƒ3, ƒ8 for the tower), with the dainty fifteenth-century **Stadhuis** tucked in behind. The church is a fifteenth- to sixteenth-century structure surmounted by a valiantly attempted but rather obvious replacement tower and was extensively renovated for the fiftieth anniversary of Operation Market Garden in September 1994; you can now take a lift to the top for fine views around the surrounding area.

From outside the train station, it's a fifteen-minute walk west along Utrechtsestraat and then Utrechtseweg (or take bus #1 direction Oosterbeek) to

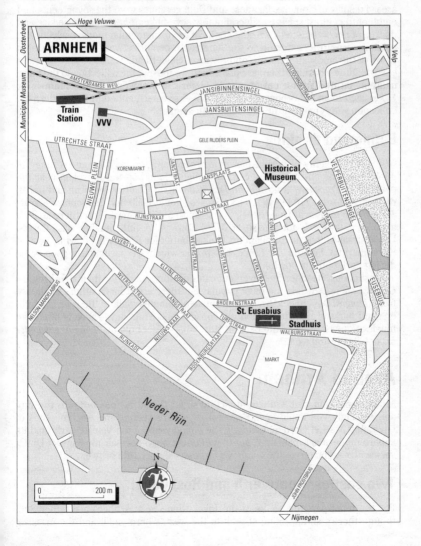

the **Municipal Museum** at no. 87 (Tues–Sat 10am–5pm & Sun 11am–5pm; *f*3.50), whose speciality is temporary exhibitions of modern Dutch art. The nucleus of the permanent collection is the work of the **Magic Realists**, particularly Carel Willink and Pyke Koch, whose *Vrouwen in de Straat* is a typically disconcerting canvas, the women's eyes looking out of the picture in a medley of contrasting emotions. The paintings of Renier Lucassen, for example *The Kiss* of 1976, establish the stylistic link between the Magic Realism of the 1930s and Dutch contemporary art, the familiar once again given a disturbing and alienating slant. The collection includes numerous archeological finds from the surrounding area; a display of Chinese, Japanese and Delft ceramics from the seventeenth and eighteenth centuries; Dutch silver, notably several *guild beakers*, whose size and degree of decoration indicated the status of the owner; and a modest selection of paintings from the sixteenth to the nineteenth centuries, with the emphasis on views of the landscape, villages and towns of Gelderland.

At the time of writing there are plans to move most of the collection to the more centrally located **Historical Museum** (Tues–Sat 10am–5pm & Sun 11am–5pm; *f*5) located in an old orphanage at Bovenbeekstraat 21, although the modern art collection will remain at the Municipal Museum.

Eating and drinking

Arnhem has plenty of decent places for reasonably priced food and a range of good bars. The cheapest food can normally be found on the Jansplein near the post office; *Trocadero* at no. 49 and *Donatellos* at no. 50 offer Mexican and Italian respectively from *f*10 per head. Carnivores should make for the popular *Eetcafe Mejuffrouw Janssen* at Duizelsteeg 7, just south of Korenmarkt, and there are half a dozen *dagschotels* for *f*17.50 at *Midi*, Pauw 4. A little further east *Ceylon*, Looierstraat 11, has an excellent Sri Lankan buffet for *f*25 per head, while back at Korenmarkt 1 *Pizzeria Da Leone*, has pizzas which are particularly good value during its 4–6pm "happy hour".

Most people head for the pavement cafes of Korenmarkt for their **drinking**; *Le Grand Café* is probably the most popular but there are a dozen others to choose from. *Dingos*, Boyenbeekstraat 28, a couple of minutes' walk to the east, is another good bar and has cheap food on Tuesday and Thursday. There is often live music at one or other of the bars on Korenmarkt; get hold of a copy of *Uit Loder* for details of what's on.

Around Arnhem

Most people who visit Arnhem in fact do so for the attractions **outside the city** and certainly you could spend several days here visiting the wartime sites of Operation Market Garden, taking in the countryside of the Veluwe park (and its superb modern art museum), not to mention a huge open-air museum of Dutch vernacular archicture – the country's largest – and a castle or two.

Two castles: Doorwerth and Rosendaal

For the most part the banks of the River Rhine near Arnhem are rather dull, though there's an appealing stretch to the west, where you'll find the massive,

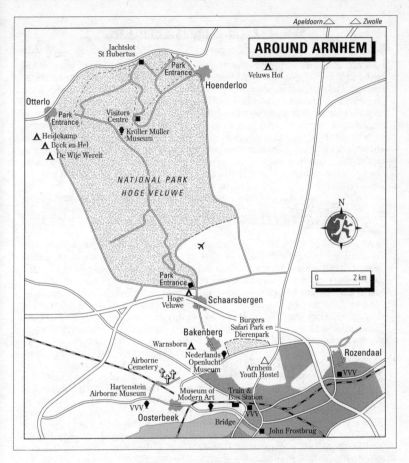

moated thirteenth-century **Kasteel Doorwerth** (April–Oct Tues–Fri 10am–5pm,
Sat & Sun 1–5pm; ƒ7.50), carefully reconstructed after war damage. To get there,
take bus #6 from the Municipal Museum and ask to be dropped at the stop nearest the Kasteel – from where it's a thirty-minute walk along the river. There's an
excellent and pricey **restaurant** there too, which for most people is more of an
attraction than the collection of stuffed carcasses and old weapons at the **Nature
Museum** (same times, ƒ5) which occupies the castle.

On the opposite side of Arnhem, lying on the edge of the suburbs of Velp,
there's another castle, the **Kasteel Rosendaal** (mid-April to Oct Tues–Sat
10am–5pm & Sun 1–5pm; ƒ7.50; bus #4 direction Velp Zuid) – an attractive mixture of medieval and eighteenth-century architecture, set in its own parkland. Not
far away, on the west side of Velp, the **Museum Bronbeek**, Velperweg 147
(Tues–Sun 9am–noon & 12.30–5pm; ƒ2.50; bus #1 direction Velp), occupies a
building gifted to ex-soldiers by William III in 1859. The collection has all sorts of
curious relics left over from the Dutch occupation of Surinam and Indonesia.

OPERATION MARKET GARDEN

By September 1944 most of France and much of Belgium had been liberated from Nazi occupation. Fearing that an orthodox campaign would take many months and cost many lives, Field Marshal Montgomery decided that a pencil thrust north through Holland and subsequently east into the Ruhr, around the back of the Siegfried line, offered a good chance of ending the war early. To speed the advance of his land armies, Montgomery needed to cross several major rivers and canals in a corridor of territory stretching from Eindhoven, a few kilometres north of the front, to Arnhem. The plan, **Operation Market Garden**, was to parachute three airborne armies behind enemy lines, each responsible for taking and holding particular bridgeheads until the main army could force their way north to join them. On Sunday September 17, the 1st British Airborne Division parachuted into the fields around Oosterbeek, their prime objective to seize the bridges over the Rhine at Arnhem. Meanwhile, the 101st American Airborne Division was dropped in the area of Veghel to secure the Wilhelmina and Zuid-Willemsvaart canals, and the 82nd was dropped around Grave and Nijmegen, for the crossings over the Maas and the Waal.

All went fairly well with the American landings and, by the night of September 20, sections of the main British army, 30 Corps, had reached the American bridgehead across the River Waal at Nijmegen. However, despite Polish reinforcements, the landings around Arnhem had run into problems. Allied Command had estimated that immediate opposition was unlikely to exceed a force of some three thousand men, but as luck would have it, the entire 2nd SS Panzer Corps was refitting near Arnhem just when the 1st Division landed. Taking the enemy by surprise, 2nd Parachute Battalion, under Lieutenant-Colonel John Frost, did manage to capture the north end of the road bridge across the Rhine, but it proved impossible either to reinforce them or capture the southern end. Surrounded, out-gunned and out-manned, the 2nd Battalion held their position from the 17th to the morning of the 21st, far longer than anybody could have anticipated, a story of extraordinary heroism. There were more heroics elsewhere, for the Polish and British battalions of the rest of the Division had concentrated around the bridgehead at Oosterbeek, which they held at tremendous cost under the command of General Urquhart. Elements of 30 Corps made desperate efforts to join up with them, but by the morning of the 25th it was clear that it was not going to be possible to provide reinforcements in sufficient numbers. Under cover of darkness, a dramatic withdrawal saved 2163 soldiers from an original force of 10,005.

World War II memorials: Oosterbeek

The area around Arnhem is scattered with the graveyards of thousands of soldiers who died during **Operation Market Garden**. If you're a devotee of battle grounds and battle plans, Arnhem VVV sells specialist books on the campaign and provides details of organized tours. Otherwise, the easiest way to get some idea of the conflict and its effect on this part of Holland is to visit **OOSTERBEEK**, once a small village and now a prosperous suburb of Arnhem (every 15min; 4min).

Following the signs from beside Oosterbeek train station, it's a five-minute walk east to the **Airborne Cemetery**, a neat, symmetrical tribute to nearly two thousand paratroopers, mostly British and Polish, whose bodies were brought here from the surrounding fields. It's a quiet, secluded spot; the personal inscriptions on the gravestones are especially poignant. Ten minutes' walk (or bus #1) south of the station down Stationsweg, the village proper has spruced lawns and walls dotted with details of the battle – who held out where and for how long – as the Allied forces were pinned back within a tighter and tighter perimeter.

The **Airborne Museum** (Mon–Sat 11am–5pm & Sun noon–5pm; ƒ5) is just to the west of the village centre along Utrechtseweg, reachable direct from Arnhem on bus #1, housed in the former *Hotel Hartenstein*, where the British forces were besieged by the Germans for a week before retreating across the river, their numbers depleted from 10,005 to 2163. With the use of an English commentary, photographs, dioramas and original military artefacts – from rifles and light artillery to uniforms and personal memorabilia – the museum gives an excellent outline of the battle and, to a lesser extent, aspects of World War II as it affected Holland as a whole. The Army Film and Photographic Unit landed with the British forces, and, perhaps more than anything else, it's their photographs that stick in the memory – grimly cheerful soldiers hauling in their parachutes, tense tired faces during the fighting, shattered Dutch villages.

The Nederlands Openluchtmuseum

Immediately north of Arnhem, the **Nederlands Openluchtmuseum** (April–Oct Mon–Fri 9am–5pm, Sat & Sun 10am–5pm; ƒ16, children ƒ10.50), reachable by bus #3, direction Alteveer (every 20min), or direct by special bus #13 (July & Aug only; every 20min), is a huge collection of Dutch buildings open to public view. One of the first of its type, the museum was founded in 1912 to try to "present a picture of the daily life of ordinary people in this country as it was in the past and has developed in the course of time". Over the years, original and representative buildings have been taken from all over the country and assembled here in a large chunk of the Veluwe forest. Where possible, buildings have been placed in groups that resemble the traditional villages of the different regions of Holland – from the farmsteads of Friesland to the farming communities of South Holland and the peat colonies of Drenthe. There are about 120 buildings in all, including examples of every type of Dutch windmill, most sorts of farmhouse, a variety of bridges and several working craftshops, demonstrating the traditional skills of papermaking, milling, baking, brewing and bleaching. Other parts of the museum incorporate one of the most extensive regional costume exhibitions in the country and a comparatively modest herb garden.

All in all, it's an imaginative attempt to recreate the rural Dutch way of life over the past two centuries. The museum's guidebook costs ƒ7.50 and explains everything with academic attention to detail, although it's by no means essential as most of the information is repeated on plaques outside each building.

The Hoge Veluwe National Park and Rijksmuseum Kröller-Müller

Spreading north from the Open-Air Museum is the **Hoge Veluwe National Park**, an area of sandy heath and thick woodland that was once the private estate of Anton and Helene Kröller-Müller. Born near Essen in 1869, Helene Müller came from a wealthy and influential family whose money was made in the blast-furnace business. She married Anton Kröller of Rotterdam, whose brother ran the Dutch side of their trading interests and the couple's fortunes were secured when the death of her father and his brother's poor health placed Anton at the head of the company at the age of 27. Apart from extending their business empire and supporting the Boers in South Africa, they had a passionate desire to leave a grand bequest to the nation, a mixture of nature and culture which would, she felt, "be an important lesson when showing the inherent refinement of a merchant's family living at the beginning of the century". She collected the art, he the land and in the 1930s ownership of both was transferred to the nation on the condition that a museum was built in the park. The museum opened in 1938 and Helene acted as manager until her death in 1939. Today, the park is one of Gelderland's most popular day-trip destinations, although it's large enough to absorb the crowds quite comfortably on all but the sunniest of summer weekends.

Around the park

The Hoge Veluwe Park has three entrances – one near the village of Otterlo on the northwest perimeter, another near Hoenderloo on the northeast edge and a third to the south at Rijzenburg, near the village of Schaarsbergen, only 10km from Arnhem. The **park** is open daily (April–Aug 8am–sunset, Sept–March 9am–sunset; ƒ8, including Rijksmuseum admission; cars ƒ8 extra), though in September and early October certain areas are off-limits during the rutting season.

There are a number of ways to get to the park by **bus**; easiest is to take the museum special from outside Arnhem train station (June–Sept daily except Mon, bus #12 direction Hoge Veluwe; hourly; ƒ7 return, plus ƒ8 park entrance: pay the driver) to the **Bezoekers Centrum** or visitors' centre (April–Oct daily 9.30am–5pm; Nov–March Sun 10am–4pm only), in the middle of the park, not far from the museum. The centre has information on the park and the **Museonder** (same hours; free), the world's first underground museum, with displays (including the living roots of a giant beech tree) on all things subterranean. The centre is also one of the places (along with the three entrances) where you can pick up one of the eight hundred white bicycles that are left out for everyone's use at no extra charge – definitely the best way of getting around once you're here. When the bus isn't running, you can either rent a bike at Arnhem train station or take bus #107 (direction Lelystad; hourly; 25min) to the entrance at Otterlo. From here it's a four-kilometre cycle ride east to the visitors' centre. Before you enter the park, there is a small **Tile Museum** (Mon–Fri 10am–noon & 2–5pm, Sun 2–4pm; ƒ3), in Otterlo village, ten minutes' walk from the entrance at Eikenzoom 12 (across from the VVV) and worth an hour of your time. If you are coming to the park from Apeldoorn take bus #110, direction Ede, which runs via the visitors' centre.

Once mobile you can cycle around as you wish, along clearly marked tracks and through stretches of dune and woodland where, particularly in the south of the park, it's possible to catch sight of some of the park's big game – principally red deer, roe and moufflon (Corsican sheep). By comparison, the park's wild boar keep to themselves. Apart from the Kröller-Müller Museum (see below), the only thing to see is the **Jachtslot St Hubertus** (guided tours only, every 30min May–Oct Mon–Fri 10–11.30am & 2–4.30pm; free), some 3km north of the visitors' centre, a hunting lodge and country home built for the Kröller-Müllers by the modernist Dutch architect, H P Berlage, in 1920. Dedicated to the patron saint of hunters, it's an impressive Art Deco monument, with lots of plays on the hunting theme. The floor plan – in the shape of branching antlers – is representative of the stag bearing a crucifix that appeared to Saint Hubert, the adopted patron of hunters, while he was hunting and each room of the sumptuous interior symbolizes an episode in the saint's life – all in all a somewhat unusual commission for a committed socialist who wrote so caustically about the *haute bourgeoisie*.

The Rijksmuseum Kröller-Müller

Most people who visit the Hoge Veluwe Park come for the **Rijksmuseum Kröller-Müller** (Tues–Sun 10am–5pm; admission included in park entrance fee – see previous page), made up of the private art collection of the Kröller-Müllers. It's one of the country's finest museums, a wide cross-section of modern European art from Impressionism to Cubism and beyond, housed in a low-slung building that was built for the collection in 1938 by the Belgian architect Van de Velde.

The bulk of the collection is in one long wing, starting with the most recent Dutch painters and working backward. There's a good set of paintings, in particular some revealing *Self-portraits* by Charley Toorop, one of the most skilled and sensitive of twentieth-century Dutch artists. Her father Jan also gets a good showing throughout the museum, from his pointillist studies to later, turn-of-the-century works more reminiscent of Aubrey Beardsley and the Art Nouveau movement. Piet Mondrian is well represented too, his 1909 *Beach near Domburg* a good example of his more stylized approach to landscape painting, a development from his earlier sombre-coloured scenes in the Dutch tradition. In 1909 he moved to Paris and his contact with Cubism transformed his work, as illustrated by his *Composition* of 1917 – simple flat rectangles of colour with the elimination of the object complete, the epitome of the De Stijl approach. Much admired by Mondrian and one of the most influential of the Cubists, Fernand Léger's *Soldiers Playing Cards* is typical of his bold, clear lines and tendency toward the monumental. One surprise is an early Picasso, *Portrait of a Woman*, from 1901, a classic post-Impressionist canvas very dissimilar from his more famous works.

The building as a whole gravitates toward the works of **Vincent Van Gogh**, with one of the most complete collections of his work in the world, housed in a large room around a central courtyard and placed in context by accompanying contemporary pictures. The museum owns no fewer than 278 examples of his work and doesn't have the space to show them all at any one time; consequently exhibits are rotated, with the exception of his most important paintings. Of earlier canvases, *The Potato Eaters* and *Head of a Peasant with a Pipe* are outstanding; rough, unsentimental paintings of labourers from around his parents' home in Brabant. From February 1886 till early 1888 Van Gogh lived in Paris, where he came into contact with the Impressionists whose work – and arguments – convinced him of the importance of colour. His penetrating *Self-portrait* is a superb example of his work of this period, the eyes fixed on the observer, the head and background a swirl of grainy colour and streaky brush-strokes. One of his most famous paintings, *Sunflowers*, dates from this period also, an extraordinary work of alternately thick and thin paintwork of dazzling, sharp detail and careful colour.

The move to Arles in 1888 spurred Van Gogh to a frenzy of activity, inspired by the colours and light of the Mediterranean. The joyful *Haystacks in Provence* and *Bridge at Arles*, with its rickety bridge and disturbed circles of water spreading from the washerwomen on the river bank, are from these months, one of the high points of his troubled life. It was short-lived. The novelty of the south wore off, Gauguin's visit was a disaster and Van Gogh's desperate sense of loneliness intensified. At the end of the year he had his first attack of madness – and committed his famous act of self-mutilation. In and out of mental hospital till his suicide in July of the following year, his *Prisoners Exercising* of 1890 is a powerful, sombre painting full of sadness and despair: heads bent, the prisoners walk around in a pointless circle as the walls around them seem to close in.

Finally, outside the museum, behind the main building, there's a **Sculpture Park** (April–Oct Tues–Sun 10am–4.30pm; free), one of the largest in Europe and spaciously laid out with works by Auguste Rodin, Alberto Giacometti, Jacob Epstein and Barbara Hepworth, all appearing at manageable intervals. Notable is Jean Debuffet's *Jardin d'email*, one of his larger and more elaborate jokes.

Nijmegen

One of the oldest towns in Holland, **NIJMEGEN**, some 20km south of Arnhem, was built on the site of the Roman frontier fortress of *Novio Magus*, from which it derives its name. Situated on the southern bank of the Waal, just to the west of its junction with the Rhine, the town's location has long been strategically important. The Romans used Nijmegen as a buffer against the unruly tribes to the east; Charlemagne, Holy Roman Emperor from 800 to 814, made the town one of the principal seats of his administration, building the Valkhof Palace, an enormous complex of chapels and secular buildings completed in the eighth century. Rebuilt in 1155 by another emperor, Frederick Barbarossa, the complex dominated Nijmegen right up until 1769, when the palace was demolished and the stonework sold; what was left suffered further demolition when the French occupied the town in 1796. More recently, in September 1944, the town's bridges were a key objective of Operation Market Garden (see p.268) and although they were captured by the Americans, the disaster at Arnhem put the town on the front line for the rest of the war. The results are clear to see: the old town was largely destroyed and has been replaced by a centre reconstructed to a new plan.

Arrival, information and accommodation

Nijmegen's **train** and **bus stations** are a good fifteen-minute trudge west of the town centre and the **VVV** at St Jorisstraat 72 (May to mid-Sept Mon–Fri 9am–5.30pm & Sat 10am–5pm; mid-Sept to April Mon–Fri 9am–5pm & Sat 10am–5pm; ☎06/911 22344, 75c per min). If you don't like the idea of a walk, take any bus into the centre.

Between June and August, there are a variety of **boat trips** on the Waal. Prices vary according to the itinerary, but excursions range from an hour's river tour to sailings all the way to Rotterdam.

Accommodation

Cheap **accommodation** is pretty thin on the ground in Nijmegen; it's easiest to let the VVV make a booking by phone. Alternatively, there are two **pensions** not far southeast of the train station – the *Catharina*, St Annastraat 64 (☎024/323 1251; ②) and *De Herbergierster*, Groesbeekseweg 134 (☎024/322 0922; ②). To reach them head east along one of the southern pair of roads from the station to the Keizer Karelplein; from here St Annastraat is the road heading southeast, with Groesbeekseweg the first turn on the left. The cheaper **hotels** are a little

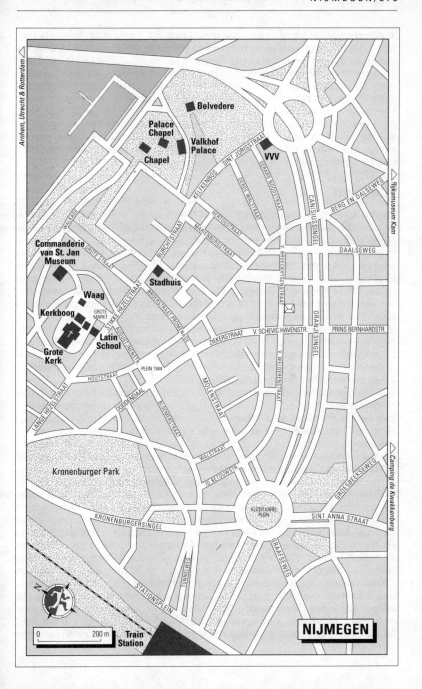

Arnhem, Utrecht & Rotterdam

Rijksmuseum Kam

Camping de Kwakkenberg

Belvedere

Palace
Chapel

Valkhof
Palace

Chapel

VVV

SINT JORISSTRAAT

KELFKENBOS

GERARD NOODSTRAAT

OUDE WALSTRAAT

HERTOGSTRAAT

MARIENBURGSTRAAT

BURCHTSTRAAT

BERG EN DALSEWEG

CANISIUSSINGEL

V. BROECKHYSENSTRAAT

DAALSEWEG

WALKADE

GROTE STRAAT

Commanderie
van St. Jan
Museum

Stadhuis

Waag

Kerkboog

GROTE
MARKT

STIKKE HEZELSTRAAT

AUGUSTIJNENSTR.

BROERSTRAAT PROMENADE

ZIEKERSTRAAT

V. SCHEVIC HAVENSTR.

ORANJESINGEL

PRINS BERNHARDSTR.

Latin
School

Grote
Kerk

HOUTSTRAAT

PLEIN 1944

V. WELDERENSTRAAT

LANGE HEZELSTRAAT

DOODENDAAL

BLOEMERSTRAAT

MOLENSTRAAT

WALSTRAAT

ID BEJOUWSTR.

Kronenburger Park

GROESBEEKSEWEG

KRONENBURGERSINGEL

KEIZER KAREL
PLEIN

SINT ANNA STRAAT

TUNNELWEG

GRAAFSEWEG

STATIONSPLEIN

0   200 m

Train
Station

NIJMEGEN

more expensive but tend to be more convenient: the *Apollo* is on the street running east off Keizer Karelplein, at Bisschop Hamerstraat 14 (☎024/322 3594, fax 323 3176; ③); and the rather seedy *Europa Hotel* (☎024/322 6645, fax 323 7058; ②) is between the train station and Grote Markt at Bloemerstraat 65. If you're stuck, the *Atlanta*, right in the centre at Grote Markt 38 (☎024/360 3000, fax 360 3210; ③), isn't as pricey as you might imagine, although it can be rather noisy. The nearest **campsite** is *De Kwakkenberg*, Luciaweg 10 (☎024/323 2443; April–Sept), a few kilometres south of town, reachable from the station by bus #5, direction Berg en Dal, every twenty minutes. Ask the driver to drop you off at your stop, which will be on the main road, Kwakkenbergweg; Luciaweg runs roughly parallel, a block to the south.

The town

The town centre is **Grote Markt**, a good fifteen-minute walk from the train station, or five minutes by any bus from immediately outside. Much of the Grote Markt survived the shelling and is surprisingly well preserved, in stark contrast to the modern shopping streets across the road. The **Waag**, with its traditional stepped gables and shuttered windows, stands beside a vaulted passage, the **Kerkboog**, which leads through to the peaceful precincts of the much-renovated Gothic **Grote Kerk of St Stephen**. The church is entered around the back to the left, past the attractively carved facade of the old **Latin School** and inside there's some fine Renaissance woodwork. The **tower**, with its vaguely oriental spire, offers a commanding vista over the surrounding countryside (early-June to early Sept Tues–Sun 12–6pm; *f*1). The view over the streets beside and behind the church isn't what it used to be – the huddle of medieval houses that sloped down to the Waal was almost totally destroyed during the war and has been replaced by a hopeful but rather sterile residential imitation.

A few metres away, down toward the river, the **Commanderie van St Jan** is more authentic looking, a reconstruction of a seventeenth-century building that now houses the **Municipal Museum** (Mon–Sat 10am–5pm, Sun 1–5pm; *f*2.50). Here you'll find a variety of exhibits with a local flavour, including innumerable paintings of Nijmegen and its environs – none particularly distinguished except for Jan van Goyen's *Valkhof Nijmegen*, which used to hang in the town hall. Painted in 1641, it's a large, sombre-toned picture – pastel variations on green and brown – where the Valkhof shimmers above the Waal, almost engulfed by sky and river.

Returning to the Grote Markt, Burchtstraat heads east roughly parallel to the river, past the dull reddish-brown brick of the **Stadhuis**, a square, rather severe edifice with an onion-domed tower, another reconstruction after extensive war damage. A couple of minutes away, in a park beside the east end of Burchtstraat, lie the scanty remains of the **Valkhof Palace** – a ruined fragment of the Romanesque choir of the twelfth-century palace chapel and, just to the west, a sixteen-sided chapel built around 1045, in a similar style to the palatinate church at Charlemagne's capital, Aachen. The smaller chapel (May–Oct Mon–Sat 1–5pm, Sun 2–5pm) is complete, though the atmosphere is somewhat marred by the crowds and piped choral music. These bits and pieces are connected by a footbridge to a **belvedere**, which was originally a seventeenth-century tower built into the city walls; today it's a restaurant and a lookout platform with excellent views over the river.

Nearby museums

Some fifteen minutes' walk southeast of the town centre, the **Provinciaal Museum G M Kam**, Museum Kamstraat 45 (Tues–Sat 10am–5pm, Sun 1–5pm; ƒ3), is the best of Nijmegen's many other museums. Devoted mainly to the history of Roman Nijmegen and founded by the eminent archeologist G.M. Kam, who died in 1922, the museum features his collection alongside other artefacts that have been added more recently; together they form a comprehensive picture of the first Roman settlements. To get there walk east along Burchtstraat and onto Kelfkensbos, which brings you to the island beside the VVV. Heading south off the island, down Mr Franckenstraat, you reach Mariaplein, where you turn left down Berg en Dalseweg; Museum Kamstraat is the third on the left.

More bizarre, southeast of Nijmegen on the road to Groesbeek, the **Biblical Open-Air Museum**, Profetenlaan 2 (*Heilig Land Stichting*; Easter–Oct daily 9am–5.30pm; ƒ11), is accessible by bus #84 (destination Groesbeek; every 30min, 15min), from beside the train station. Ask the driver to indicate your stop on Nijmeegsebaan, from where it's a five-minute walk northeast along Meerwijkselaan to the museum. Here you'll find a series of reconstructions of the ancient Holy Land, including a Galilean fishing village, a complete Palestinian hamlet, a town street lined with Egyptian, Greek, Roman and Jewish houses and, strangely enough, "Bedouin tents of goats' hair as inhabited by the patriarchs". An experience not on any account to be missed.

There's another unusual museum 2km east of here, along Meerwijkselaan – the **Afrika Museum** at Postweg 6, Berg en Dal (April–Oct Mon–Fri 10am–5pm & Sat–Sun 11am–5pm; Nov–March Tues–Fri 10am–5pm & Sat–Sun 1–5pm; ƒ7.50), where there's a purpose-built West African village, a small animal park and a museum full of totems, carved figurines and musical instruments. You can get here on bus #5, which runs every twenty minutes to Berg en Dal, though from the bus stop it's still a twenty-minute walk to the museum.

Eating, drinking and nightlife

As you'd expect in a student town, Nijmegen has a wide range of places to eat and drink at sensible prices. For **food**, Kelfkensbos is a good place to start: *'t Circus* at no. 21 has excellent Dutch fare, *La Palmera* at no. 25 is a reasonable Mexican while the Dutch-French food at *Les Entrees* (☎ 024/324 1627) at no. 30 is a notch up in price. *Roberto*, Smetiusstraat 7, has good Italian food, and there are several decent places around the Waag, including the popular *Café de Waag*, whose *dagschotels* run around ƒ17.50. For drinking, head down Grote Straat to the waterfront; *Kandinsky Café* at Walkade 65 is usually a lively spot or you could try *Le Figaro* at Walkade 47. If you don't want to be outdoors, *Café in de Blaauwe Hand* is a cosy little bar behind the Grote Kerk and, supposedly, the oldest bar in town.

Every inch a fashionable town, Nijmegen attracts some top-name rock **bands**, especially during the academic year. Most perform at the municipal concert hall, the *Stadsschouwburg*, at Van Schaeck Mathonsingel 2, close to the train station; for latest details see the VVV. For **films**, the *Filmcentrum*, Marienburg 59 (☎024/322 1612), has good international programmes and some late-night shows.

travel details

Trains

Apeldoorn to: Amersfoort (every 30min; 25min); Deventer (every 30min; 10min); Zutphen (every 30min; 15min).

Arnhem to: Amsterdam (every 30min; 1hr 10min); Cologne (14 daily; 1hr 50min); Nijmegen (every 30min; 20min); Roosendaal (every 30min; 1hr 45min).

Enschede to: Amsterdam (hourly; 2hrs); Zutphen (hourly; 55min).

Zutphen to: Arnhem (every 30min; 30min); Deventer (every 30min; 12 min).

Zwolle to: Amersfoort (every 15min; 35–50min); Amsterdam CS (every 30min; 1hr 15min); Arnhem (every 30min; 1hr); Deventer (every 30min; 25min); Emmen (2 hourly; 50min–1hr 10min); Groningen (2 hourly; 1hr 5min); Kampen (2 hourly; 10 min); Leeuwarden (every 30min; 55min); Meppel (every 30min; 15min); Nijmegen (2 hourly; 65–75min); Schiphol (every 30min; 1hr 40min); Steenwijk (2 hourly; 15min); Zutphen (2 hourly; 25–35min).

Buses

Enschede to: Oldenzaal (Mon–Sat every 30min, Sun hourly; 20min).

Kampen to: Lelystad (*VAD* bus #143 every 30min; 55min); Urk (2 hourly; 60min).

Lelystad to: Enkhuizen (*VAD* bus #150 every 30min; 35min).

Steenwijk to: Giethoorn (*NWH* bus #72 Mon–Sat hourly, Sun 5 daily; 15-30min).

Zwolle to: Elburg (*VAD* bus #101 Mon–Sat every 30min, Sun hourly; 35min); Kampen and Urk (*VAD* bus #141 hourly; 20 min and 1hr 20min respectively).

Ferries

Urk to: Enkhuizen (May, June & Sept 2 daily, July & Aug 3 daily; 1hr 30min).

CHAPTER SIX

ZEELAND, NORTH BRABANT AND LIMBURG

T hree widely disparate provinces make up the southern Netherlands: Zeeland, North Brabant and Limburg. **Zeeland** is a scattering of villages and towns whose wealth, survival and sometimes destruction have long depended on the vagaries of the sea. Secured only in 1986, when the dykes and sea walls of the Delta Project were finally completed, once and for all stopping the chance of flooding, at their best – for example in the small wool town of **Veere** or the regional market centre of **Middelburg** – they seem held in suspended animation from a richer past.

As you head across the arc of towns of **North Brabant** the landscape slowly fills out, rolling into a rougher countryside of farmland and forests, unlike the precise rectangles of neighbouring provinces. Though the change is subtle, there's a difference in the people here, too – less formal, less Dutch, and for the most part Catholic, a fact manifest in the magnificent churches of **Breda** and **'s Hertogenbosch**. But it's in solidly Catholic Limburg that a difference in character is really felt.

Continental rather than Dutch, **Limburg** has only been part of Holland since the 1830s, but way before then the presence of Charlemagne's court at Aachen deeply influenced the identity of the region. As Frankish emperor, Charlemagne had a profound effect on early medieval Europe, revitalizing Roman traditions and looking to the south for inspiration in art and architecture. Some of these great buildings remain, like **Maastricht**'s St Servaas, and most have a wealth of devotional art that comes as a welcome change after the north. What's more, the landscape steepens sharply and you're within sight of Holland's first and only hills.

ACCOMMODATION PRICE CODES

All the **hotels** and **hostels** detailed in this chapter have been graded according to the following price categories. Apart from ①, which is a per-person price for a hostel bed, all the codes are based on the rate for the cheapest double room during high season.

For more on accommodation, see p.30.

① Up to ƒ40 per person	④ ƒ150–200	⑦ ƒ300–400
② ƒ60–100	⑤ ƒ200–250	
③ ƒ100–150	⑥ ƒ250–300	

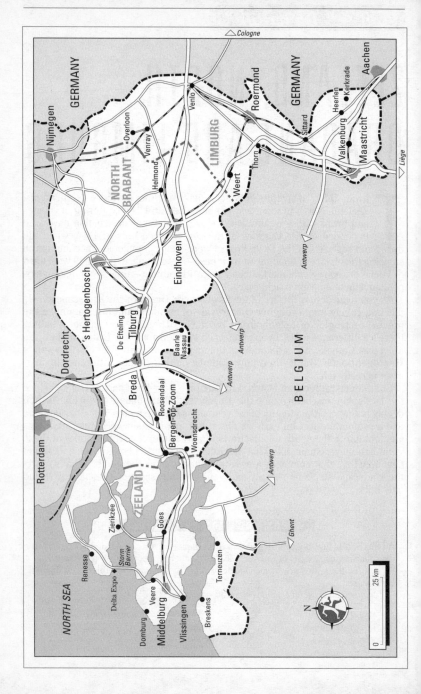

ZEELAND

Formed by the delta of three great rivers, the Rijn, the Schelde and the Maas, **Zeeland** comprises three main peninsulas, each consisting of a cluster of islands and semi-islands, linked by dykes, which as well as providing protection from flooding, also form the main lines of communication between each chunk of land. The northernmost landmass, Goeree-Overflakkee, is linked by two dams to Schouwen-Duiveland; the southern cluster is known as Noord and Zuid Beveland, with its western tip, traversed by a narrow canal, known as Walcheren.

Before the Delta Project (see p.286) secured the area, silting up and fear of the sea had prevented any large towns developing and Zeeland remains a condensed area of low dunes and nature reserves, popular with holidaymakers escaping the cramped conurbations nearby. Zeeland also has more sun than anywhere else in Holland: the winds blow the clouds away. Getting around isn't a problem, with bus services making up for the lack of north–south train connections, though undoubtedly the best way to see these islands is to **cycle**, using **Middelburg** as a base and radiating out to the surrounding smaller towns.

Vlissingen (Flushing)

VLISSINGEN is an important ferry terminus, linked to Sheerness in England by twice-daily ferries. The best thing to do on arrival at the bleak ferry port is leave; a bus takes you to the **train station**, from where there are hourly departures to Amsterdam and intermediate stations. There's also a **ferry service**, leaving from outside the train station, to **BRESKENS** on the southern side of the Westerschelde estuary (Mon–Sat 4.50am–11.50pm every 30min, Sun 6.50am–11.10pm hourly, every 30min in July & Aug), from where buses go on to Bruges.

Perhaps significantly, there are no buses from the ferry dock to the centre of town, although bus #56 plies between the train station and the centre. Here you'll find the unremarkable **St Jacobskerk** on Kleine Markt (July & Aug Mon–Sat 10am–noon; ƒ1), the improbably named **Cornelia Quackhofje**, an eighteenth-century almshouse for sailors just north of the Lange Zelke shopping precinct and a **Stedelijk Museum** at Bellamypark 19 (Mon–Fri 10am–5pm, Sat & Sun 1–5pm; ƒ2.50), whose collection includes a room devoted to local naval hero Michiel de Ruyter. Alternatively and rather more fun, you could head for **The Arsenal** on Arsenaalplein (April–Sept daily 10am–8pm; Oct–March Tues–Sun 10am–6pm; ƒ15, children under 12 ƒ10; ☎0118/415 400), a maritime theme park where you can go on a simulated sea voyage, climb an observation tower and walk on a mocked-up seabed among tanks of sharks.

The **VVV** at Nieuwendijk 15 (Sept–June Mon–Sat 9am–5pm; July & Aug Mon–Sat 9am–6pm, Sun 1–5pm; ☎0118/412 345) has a list of **pensions** including the nearby *Pension Queen of Holland*, Nieuwendijk 23–25 (☎0118/419 738, fax 418 362; ④) and *Pension El Porto*, Nieuwendijk 5 (☎0118/412 807; ③). *Hotel de Belgische Loodsensocieteit* is on the seafront at Boulevard de Ruyter 4 (☎0118/413 608, fax 410 427; ④), near the end of Nieuwendijk.

Middelburg

MIDDELBURG is the largest town in Zeeland and by any reckoning the most likeable. While not crammed with things to see, its streets preserve some snapshots of medieval Holland and a few museums and churches provide targets for your wanderings. Rimmed with the standard shopping precinct, its centre holds a large Thursday market, and, if you can only make it for a day, this is the best time to visit, with local women still wearing traditional costume – to picturesque effect. However Middelburg is best used as a base for exploring the surrounding area, with good regional bus connections and plentiful accommodation.

Arrival, information and accommodation

The **train station** is just a short walk from the centre of town as are the main bus stops, across the bridge on Loskade, opposite the *Hotel du Commerce*. Head up Segeersstraat and Lange Delft and you find yourself on the Markt, where the **VVV** office at Markt 65a (March–Oct Mon–Sat 9.30am–5pm, Sun noon–4pm; Nov–Feb Mon–Fri 9.30am–5pm, Sat 10am–3pm; ☎616 851) has details of summer events in the city and a list of **private rooms**. Most of Middelburg's **hotels and pensions** are just minutes away from the Markt: the *du Commerce*, Loskade 1 (☎636 051, fax 626 400; ④), just across the bridge from the train station, and the *Beau Rivage*, nearby at Loskade 19 (☎638 060, fax 629 673; ③), are the most convenient. More central is the *De Huifkar*, Markt 19 (☎612 998, fax 612 386; ④), though it only has six rooms. Pensions include *Bij de Abdij*, by the abbey at Bogardstraat 14 (☎613 032; ③) and *Cafe-Pension Dampoort*, east of the centre at Nederstraat 24 (☎629 068; ③). The nearest **campsite**, *Camping Middelburg*, Koninginnelaan 55 (☎625 395; April–Oct), is about 2km out of town. Head down Zandstraat and Langeviele Weg, south and east of the Koveniersdoelen, or take bus #57 (every 30min) from the station. Further flung is the nearest **youth hostel**, *Kasteel Westhove* (☎583 342; April–Oct), 10km away outside Domburg, bus #54 from the station.

The town

Middelburg owed its early growth to the comparative safety of its situation in the centre of Walcheren. The slight elevation gave the settlement protection from the sea and its position on a bend in the River Arne made it reasonably easy to defend. Though its abbey was founded in 1120, the town's isolation meant that it did not start to develop until the late Middle Ages, when, being at the western end of the Scheldt estuary, it began to get rich off the back of Antwerp, Bruges and Ghent. Conducting its own trade in wool and cloth, it became both the market and administrative centre of the region and some of the town's street names – Houtkaai (Timber Dock), Londense Kaai (London Dock), Korendijk (Grain Dyke) and Bierkaai (Beer Dock) – reveal how various its trade became. Most of Middelburg's most interesting buildings come from this period, though the town's **Stadhuis**, generally agreed to be Zeeland's

The telephone code for Middelburg is ☎0118

finest, is a wonderfully eclectic mix of architectural styles. The towering Gothic facade is especially magnificent, dating from the mid-fifteenth century and designed by the Keldermans family from Mechelen. Ranged in niches across the front are 25 statues of the counts and countesses of Holland, starting with Charles V and ending with queens Wilhelmina and Juliana placed above the **Vleeshal**, a former meat hall that now houses changing exhibitions of contemporary art which can be visited on conducted tours. Hour-long **tours** of the Stadhuis (March–Oct Mon–Sat 10am–5pm, Sun noon–5pm; check noticeboard outside for exact times; ƒ4) take in the mayor's office, council chambers and various reception rooms.

The Stadhuis' impressive pinnacled tower was added in 1520, but it's as well to remember that this, along with the Stadhuis itself and much of Middelburg's city centre, is only a reconstruction of the original. On May 17, 1940 the city was practically flattened by German bombing in the same series of raids that destroyed Rotterdam. In 1944, in an attempt to isolate German artillery in Vlissingen, Walcheren's sea defences were breached, which resulted in severe flood damage to Middelburg's already treacherous streets.

Restoration was a long and difficult process, but so successful that you can only occasionally tell that the city's buildings have been patched up. Middelburg's most distinctive tower, that of the **Abdijkerken (Abbey Churches)** on Onderdentoren, collapsed under German bombing, destroying the churches below. Today the abbey complex – really three churches in one – is pretty bare inside, considering that it's been around since the twelfth century. There's a reason for this: Middelburg was an early convert to Protestantism following the uprising against the Spanish, and in 1574 William the Silent's troops threw out the Premonstratensian monks and converted the abbey to secular use. The abbey's three churches (May–Oct Mon–Fri 10am–5pm; free) were adapted to Protestant worship and most of what can be seen inside dates from the seventeenth century.

The **Nieuwe Kerk** has an organ case of 1692 and the **Wandel Kerk**, the outrageously triumphalistic tomb of admirals Jan and Cornelis Evertsen, brothers killed fighting in a naval battle against the English in 1666. The **Koor Kerk**, on the eastern side of the tower, retains the oldest decoration, including a Nicolai organ of 1478. Best fun of all is to climb the 207 steps of the tower (April–Nov Mon–Sat 10am–5pm, Sun noon–5pm; ƒ3), known locally as *Lange Jan* (Long John). As long as the weather is clear, there's a tremendous view from its 91-metre summit across Middelburg and over Walcheren as far as the Zeelandbrug and the eastern Scheldt, giving a good idea of how vulnerable Zeeland is to the sea and estuaries. Finally, the history of the abbey is presented in the **Historama**, in the cloister at Abdijplein 9 (April–Oct Mon–Sat 11am–5pm, Sun noon–5pm, ƒ6).

At the rear of the abbey, housed in what were once the monks' dormitories, the **Zeeuws Museum** (Zeeland Museum; Mon–Sat 10am–5pm, Sun noon–5pm; ƒ6) holds a mixed bag of collections and finds from the Zeeland area. The museum has a tiny but choice collection of twentieth-century painting by Mesdag, Jan and Charley Toorop and other (local) artists. Downstairs, there's a well-documented assembly of Roman and medieval artefacts, including Nehallenia altar stones. Like those in Leiden's Van Oudheden Museum (see p.158), these seem to have been votive offerings, given by sailors in Roman times in thanks for safe passage across the English Channel. Little more is known about the goddess Nehallenia,

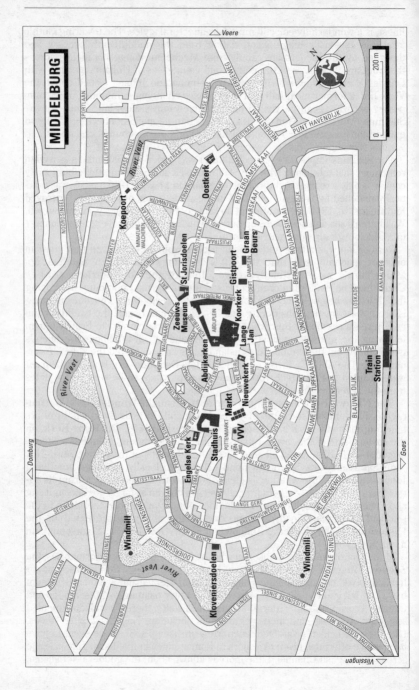

though it's possible she was also a goddess of flowers, akin to Flora. Elsewhere in the museum are some lively tapestries, commissioned by the local authorities between 1591 and 1604 to celebrate the naval battles against the Spanish, and a comprehensive display of local costumes.

East of the abbey, **Damplein** was recently restored to its original breadth by the demolition of a couple of rows of houses. It forms a quieter focus for bars than the Markt and is the site of the **Graanbeurs**, a grain exchange rebuilt in the nineteenth century and today containing some intriguing (and humorous) stone plaques by international artists – a project known as "Podio del Mondo per l'Arte". To the western side of the square, the **Blauwpoort** (also known as the **Gistpoort** or Ycast Gate) forms a decorative entrance to the abbey complex. Built at the beginning of the sixteenth century from blue limestone, it was virtually destroyed in the last war and what you see today is an indifferent renovation.

Directly north of Damplein on Molenwater, **Miniature Walcheren** (April–Oct daily 10am–5pm; ƒ11, children ƒ8) has scaled-down models of Walcheren island's best buildings. It's about as enjoyable as you'd imagine, but might entertain kids for an hour or so. Further east, the distinctive profile of the domed, octagonal **Oostkerk** (July–Aug Thurs 10am–4pm; free) stands high above the surrounding suburbs, near the main road to Veere: built in 1647 to designs by Pieter Post and others, it was one of the first churches in Holland to be built expressly for Protestant use.

While the streets around the Abdijkerken and Stadhuis are the most atmospheric, it's worth walking to the western edge of town to reach the landmark of the **Kloveniersdoelen** at the end of Langeviele. Built in 1607 in exuberant Flemish Renaissance style, this was the home of the city's civic guard, the Arquebusiers, until the end of the eighteenth century, later becoming the local headquarters of the East India Company, and later still a military hospital. Restored in 1969 (as you might have guessed if you had spotted the weather vane), it's now a recital hall for concerts and is particularly renowned for presenting new and experimental music (there's a festival every year in July; call ☎623 650 for details). A short walk north or south of the Kloveniersdoelen, by the edge of Middelburg's old encircling defensive canal, are a couple of eighteenth-century **windmills**: *De Hoop* mill to the south was once a barley peeling mill; *De Seismolen* to the north a cereal mill, though it's not possible to enter either today.

There are two further **minor museums** that might capture your attention if you have an hour or two to spare. The **Ramschip de Schorpioen**, moored off Loskade opposite the train station (March–Oct daily 10am–5pm; ƒ5), is one of only three iron ramming-ships left in the world. Built in France in 1867, it was designed to ram and sink wooden ships – slowly becoming obsolete with the development of "iron-clads" since the American Civil War. Ignominiously, the Schorpioen never rammed so much as a paddle-boat but was itself sunk on several occasions. Nowadays it serves as a floating maritime museum – worth a scramble around if only for the ornate, if cramped, interior. The **Roosevelt Study Centre**, Abdij 9 (Mon–Fri 10am–12.30pm & 1.30–4.30pm), centre for the study of twentieth-century American history (one of the largest in Europe), has a permanent exhibition on presidents Theodore and Franklin Delano Roosevelt and the latter's remarkable wife Eleanor.

Finally, open-top **boats** offer trips on the canals, leaving from the Lange Viele bridge on Achter de Houttuinen (mid-May to mid-Sept, Mon–Sat 10am–5pm, Sun noon–4pm; April & Oct Mon–Sat 11am–4pm, ƒ7.50).

Eating and drinking

Vlasmarkt, running northwest of Markt, has Middelburg's widest selection of **restaurants**. *La Lupa* at the bottom end of the street offers cheap pizzas; the café-bar *De Lachende Vis* at no. 20 serves average-priced *dagschotels*, while *De Mug*, Vlasmarkt 56, has good Dutch–French cooking at moderate prices, an excellent array of beers, and live jazz every last Tuesday of the month. A little pricier but still good value, *No 7*, east of Damplein at Rotterdamsekai 7, and *de Cameel*, by the canal at Kinderdijk 82, both have fabulous local food. If your budget is tight, there are a couple of decent shoarma joints in town: *Ramses*, at 45 St Janstraat and *Cleopatra* at Vlasmarkt 2. Most other restaurants are situated on or around Markt and many are tourist-geared and pricey for what you get: *De Ploeg*, Markt 55, offers best value. Elsewhere in town, *Surabaya*, Stationstraat 20, is an Indonesian restaurant with reasonably priced *rijsttafels*. On Thursdays the market stands supply limitless cheap and tasty snacks, especially fresh fishy things.

Bars and cafés are also concentrated on or near the Markt; *De Bommel* is the pick of the bars here, although *77* gets a huge crowd at the weekends. At the bottom of Vlasmarkt, *Rooie Oortjes* and the popular *Schuttershof* (down the tiny alley) are both excellent and the latter gets occasional live bands. Damplein is another good stretch for drinking: *Rockdesert* at no. 20 is young and raucous while *Café Solo* at no. 48, with a garden terrace in summer, is a more relaxed spot. *De Geer*, Lange Viele 55, has the cheapest beer in town.

Listings

Carillon concerts The carillon at Lange Jan plays every 15min and there are year-round concerts Thurs noon–1pm; May to mid-Sept additional concerts Sat 11am–noon; May also Thurs 7–7.30pm; July & Aug also Thurs 7.30–8.30pm.

Cycling Bike rental from the station or *L. Petiet*, Korte Noordstraat 53 (☎624 394). If you intend to cycle around, get hold of a copy of the yellow *Zuid-Holland Fietskaart* from the VVV (see p.280) or any bookshop/newsagent; the VVV also sells detailed maps of Walcheren and Zeeland and a book of twenty cycle routes in the region, *Fietsen in Zeeland*.

Markets General market on the Markt Thurs 8.30am–4pm; flower and produce market Sat 8.30am–4pm. Vismarkt has a flea market on the first Sat of the month 9am–4pm; and an antique and curio market from June to Aug Thurs 9am–4pm.

Police station Achter de Houttuinen 10 (☎688 000).

Post office Lange Noordstraat 48.

Ring tilting *Ringrijderij*, a horseback competition where riders try to pick off rings with lances, takes place at the Koepoort city gate near Molenwater on one day in July and one day in Aug, 9am–4pm. Check with the VVV (see p.280) for dates.

Taxis *Taxicentrale*, ☎612 600 or 613 200.

The Zeeland coast

The coastline west of Middleburg offers some of the country's finest beaches as well as good walking and cycling country, although on midsummer weekends parts of it virtually disappear beneath the crowds of Dutch and German holiday-makers. Bus #54 from Middleburg station (hourly) runs through **Oostkapelle**, notable for its striking church tower (July–Aug Tues & Fri 7–8pm; *f*1.50), before passing the thirteenth-century Castle Westhove, now a youth hostel. Next door, the *Zeeland Biological Museum* (June–Aug Mon–Fri & Sun 10am–6pm, Sat noon–6pm; April, May, Sept & Oct Mon & Sat noon–5pm, Tues–Fri & Sun 10am–5pm; Nov-March Tues–Sun noon–5pm) has an aquarium and displays on local flora and fauna.

A couple of kilometres further on, **Domburg**, 14km from Middleburg, is the area's principal resort, a favourite haunt for artists since early this century when Jan Toorop gathered together a group of like-minded painters (including, for a while, Piet Mondrian), inspired by the peaceful scenery and the fine quality of the light. Toorop built a pavilion to exhibit the paintings and the building has been recreated as the **Museum Domburg** (April–Nov Tues–Sun 1–5pm; *f*5) on Ooststraat 10a, near its original location, where revolving exhibitions continue to display works by members of the group. Parts of the Domburg church, including the tower, date from the thirteenth century, although it's off-limits to visitors at present. On the whole, though, you're here to walk on the dunes and through the woods or to cycle the coastpath. An easy seven-kilometre ride west of Domburg is **Westkapelle**, a quieter beach resort with a picturesque lighthouse and a critical spot where the dyke was breached during the 1953 flood.

Practicalities

Domburg's **VVV** is at Schuitvlotstraat 32 (Sept–June Mon–Sat 9am–noon & 1-4.30pm; July & Aug Mon–Sat 9am–6pm, Fri also until 8pm; ☎0118/581 342); ask the bus driver to drop you nearby. They'll help with accommodation and provide you with a map of the village. The cheapest **hotel** is *De Brouwerij*, Brouwerijweg 6 (☎0118/581 285; ②), and the place has dozens of **pensions** starting at around *f*25 per person – *Duinlist* is a safe bet at Badhuisweg 28 (☎0118/582 943; ②). The **youth hostel** is at Kasteel Westhove (☎0118/581 254; April–Oct), a couple of kilometres towards Middleburg on bus #54, and there are several **campsites**, the nearest being *Hof Domburg* at Schelpveg 7 (☎0118/583 210; April–Oct), a few minutes' walk west of town. There are plenty of **cafés** to choose from, though don't expect haute cuisine; for something a little different try the great pizzas at *Pizzeria Milano* on Ooststraat. For drinking, *Tramzicht* and *Pacha*, both on Stationstraat, are your best bet.

The other resorts also have plenty of pensions and campsites, although you may need to book rooms through one of the VVVs in busy times. The VVV in **Oostkapelle** is at Duinweg 2a (Sept–May Mon–Fri 9am–12.30pm & 1–4.30pm, Sat 9am–2pm; June–Aug Mon–Sat 9am–6pm, Fri also until 9pm; ☎0118/581 342), while in Westkapelle it is at Markt 69a (☎0118/571 281).

Veere

Eight kilometres northeast of Middleburg, **VEERE** is a resolutely picturesque little town by the banks of the Veerse Meer. Today it's a centre for all things maritime, its small harbour jammed with yachts and its cafés packed with weekend admirals: but a handful of buildings and a large church point to a time when Veere was rich and quite independent of other, similar towns in Zeeland.

Veere made its wealth from an odd Scottish connection: in 1444 Wolfert VI van Borssele, the lord of Veere, married Mary, daughter of James I of Scotland. As part of the dowry, van Borssele was granted a monopoly on trade with Scottish wool merchants; in return, Scottish merchants living in Veere were granted special privileges. A number of their houses still stand, best of which are those on the dock facing the harbour: *Het Lammetje* (The Lamb) and *De Struys* (The Ostrich), dating from the mid-sixteenth century, were combined offices, homes and warehouses for the merchants; they now house the **Museum Schotse Huizen** (April–Oct Mon–Sat 10am–5pm; *f*3), a rather lifeless collection of local costumes, old books, atlases and furniture, along with an exhibit devoted to fishing. Elsewhere there are plenty of Gothic buildings, whose rich decoration leaves you in no doubt that the Scottish wool trade earned a bundle for the sixteenth- and seventeenth-century burghers of Veere: many of the buildings (which are usually step-gabled with distinctive green and white shutters) are embellished with whimsical details that play on the owners' names or their particular line of business. The **Stadhuis** at Markt 5 (June–Sept Mon–Sat noon–5pm; *f*2) is similarly opulent, dating from the 1470s with an out-of-scale, boastful Renaissance tower added a century later. Its facade is decorated with statues of the lords of Veere and their wives (Wolfert VI is third from the left), and, inside, a small museum occupies what was formerly the courtroom, pride of place going to a goblet that once belonged to Maximilian of Burgundy.

Of all Veere's buildings the **Grote Kerk** (May–Oct Mon–Sat 10am–5pm, Sun 2–5pm; *f*3) seems to have suffered most: finished in 1560, it was badly damaged by fire a century later and restoration removed much of its decoration. In 1808 invading British troops used the church as a hospital and three years later Napoleon's army converted it into barracks and stables, destroying the stained glass, bricking up the windows and adding five floors in the nave; later, in the nineteenth century, it became a poorhouse. Despite all this damage, the church's blunt 42-metre **tower** (same opening hours and ticket as church; last entrance 4.30pm) adds a glowering presence to the landscape, especially when seen across the misty polder fields. According to the original design, the tower was to have been three times higher, but even as it stands there's a great view from the top, back to the pinnacled skyline of Middelburg and out across the breezy Veerse Meer.

Veere fell from importance with the decline of the wool trade. The opening of the Walcheren Canal in the nineteenth century, linking the town to Middelburg and Vlissingen, gave it a stay of execution, but the construction of the Veersegatdam and Zandkreekdam in the 1950s finally sealed the port to seagoing vessels and simultaneously created a freshwater lake ideal for watersports. The **VVV** office, Oudestraat 28 (Jan–March & Nov–Dec Mon–Sat 1.30–4.30pm; April–June & Sept–Oct Mon–Sat 11.30am–4.30pm; July & Aug Mon–Sat 10am–5pm; ☎0118/501 365), can advise on the rental of all types of watercraft and has details of **private rooms**. If you prefer to organize your own accommodation, the cheaper of Veere's two **hotels** is *'t Waepen van Veere* at Markt 23–27 (☎0118/501 231; ④). To reach Veere from Middelburg, catch a #31 bus (Mon–Sat hourly, Sun every 2hr), or rent a bike from Middelburg train station and take either the main road or the circuitous but picturesque routes from the north of the town.

The Delta Project – and the Delta Expo

On February 1, 1953, a combination of an exceptionally high spring tide and powerful northwesterly winds drove the North Sea over the dykes to flood much of Zeeland. The results were catastrophic: 1855 people drowned, 47,000 homes and 500km of dykes were destroyed and some of the country's most fertile agricultural land was ruined by salt water. Towns as far west as Bergen-op-Zoom and Dordrecht were flooded and Zeeland's road and rail network wrecked. The government's response was immediate and on a massive scale. After patching up the breached dykes, work was begun on the **Delta Project**, one of the largest engineering schemes the world has ever seen and one of phenomenal complexity and expense.

The plan was to ensure the safety of Zeeland by radically shortening and strengthening its coastline. The major estuaries and inlets would be dammed, thus preventing unusually high tides surging inland to breach the thousands of kilometres of small dykes. Where it was impractical to build a dam – such as across the Westerschelde or Nieuwe Waterweg, which would have closed the seaports of Antwerp and Rotterdam respectively – secondary dykes were to be greatly reinforced. New roads across the top of the dams would improve communications to Zeeland and South Holland and the freshwater lakes that formed behind the dams would enable precise control of the water table of the Zeeland islands.

It took thirty years for the full Delta Project to be completed. The smaller, secondary dams – the Veersegat, Haringvliet and Brouwershaven – were completed first, a plan designed to provide protection from high tides as quickly as possible and a process that enabled engineers to learn as they went along. In 1968, work began on the largest dam, intended to close the **Oosterschelde** estuary that forms the outlet of the Maas, Waal and Rijn rivers. It soon ran into intense opposition from environmental groups, who realized the importance of the flora and fauna in and around the Oosterschelde: at low tides, the mud flats and sandbanks were an important breeding ground for birds and the estuary itself formed a nursery for plaice, sole and other North Sea fish. Local fishermen saw their livelihoods in danger: if the Oosterschelde were closed the oyster, mussel and lobster beds would be destroyed and even without taking into account the social problems caused by the loss of jobs in an area dependent on fishing and related industries, the loss to the economy was estimated (then) at ƒ200 million.

The environmental and fishing lobbies argued that strengthening the estuary dykes would provide sufficient protection; the water board and agricultural groups raised the emotive spectre of the 1953 flood. In the end a compromise was reached, with the design of a supremely elegant and intelligent piece of engineering: in 1976 work began on the **Storm Surge Barrier**, a device that would stay open under normal tidal conditions, allowing water to flow in and out of the estuary, but close ahead of unusually high tides.

The Delta Expo

It's on this barrier, completed in 1986, that the fascinating **Delta Expo** (April–Oct daily 10am–5pm; ƒ14; Nov–March Wed–Sun 10am–5pm; ƒ10) is housed. In spring and summer admission includes a boat trip for a close look at the huge computer-controlled sluice gates. Only once you're inside the Expo itself, though, do you get an idea of the scale of the whole project. It's best to start with the film history of the barrier before taking in the exhibition, which is divided into three areas: the historical background of Holland's response to its water problems; the mechanical and scientific developments that enabled it to protect itself; the environmental problems caused by the project and the solutions that have minimized the damage. The Surge Barrier (and the Delta Project as a whole) have been completely successful. Computer simulations are used to predict high tides, though if an unpredicted rise occurs the sluice gates are programmed to close automatically in a matter of minutes. On average, a dangerously high tide occurs once every eighteen months.

Reaching the Delta Expo is easy: from Middelburg take the hourly #104 bus from Hof van Tange on the west side of town or allow ninety minutes to cycle; from Rotterdam, take the metro to Spijkenisse and then bus #104.

Brouwershaven and Zierikzee

The Storm Surge Barrier stretches across to the "island" of **Schouwen-Duiveland**. Most of the Dutch tourists who come here head directly west for the 800 hectares acres of beach and dune between **HAAMSTEDE** and **RENESSE**, themselves pretty villages but with only the **Slot Moermond** (tours of garden arranged by Renesse VVV mid-June to mid-Aug; ☎0111/462 120), a castle built for the local lords just north of Renesse, worth breaking your journey for. You can get to Renesse from Middelburg by bus #104 and from Renesse to **BROUWER-SHAVEN**, in the middle of Schouwen-Duiveland's northern coast, by bus #134, which runs hourly. Until the building of the Nieuwe Waterweg linked Rotterdam to the coast, Brouwershaven was a busy seaport, with boats able to sail right into the centre of town. Other than the pretty gabled houses flanking the harbour and a few narrow streets around the Markt, the **Stadhuis** is the single thing to see, an attractive Flemish Renaissance building of 1599.

Schouwen-Duiveland's most interesting town, though, lies to the south. **ZIERIKZEE**'s position at the intersection of shipping routes between England, Flanders and Holland led to it becoming an important port in the late Middle Ages. It was also famed for its salt and madder – a root that, when dried and ground, produces a brilliant red dye.

Encircled by a defensive canal and preferably entered by one of two sixteenth-century watergates, Zierikzee's centre is small and easily explored, easier still if you arm yourself with a map from the **VVV** at Havenpark 29 (Oct–April Mon–Fri 10am–5pm, Sat 9am–noon; May–Sept 9am–5pm, Sat 9am–3pm; ☎0111/412 450). A few minutes' walk from the office, the Gothic **'s Gravensteen** building at Mol 25 (April–Oct Mon–Sat 10am–5pm, Sun noon–5pm; *f*2) was once the jail and is today home to a maritime museum. However, the building is far more interesting than the exhibits: the old cells from the prison are pretty authentic and the removal of plaster walls in 1969 uncovered graffiti and drawings by the prisoners. The basements contain torture chambers and iron cage cells built to contain two prisoners.

Zierikzee's **Stadhuis** is easy enough to find – just head for the tall, fussy spire on Meelstraat 6. Inside, the **Gemeentemuseum** (May–Oct Mon–Fri 10am–5pm; *f*2) has collections of silver, costumes and a regional history exhibition. Also worth seeing is the **Monstertoren** (April to mid-Sept Mon–Sat 11am–4pm, Sun noon–4pm; *f*2), a tower designed by the Keldermans family on which work was stopped when it reached 97 of its planned 167 metres.

If you need to **stay over**, the VVV has details of **private rooms**; alternatives include the *Pension Beddegoed*, Meelstraat 53 (☎0111/415 935; ③); or, slightly more expensive, *Hotel Monique*, Driekoningenlaan 5 (☎0111/412 323; ③) and the *Hotel Van Oppen*, Verrenieuwstraat 11 (☎0111/412 288; ③). Heading to or from Goes from Zierikzee on bus #10 you'll pass over the **Zeelandbrug**, a graceful bridge across the Oosterschelde that, at 5022m, is the longest in Europe.

NORTH BRABANT

North Brabant, Holland's largest province, stretches from the North Sea to the German border. Originally, it was part of the independent Duchy of Brabant, which was taken over by the Spanish, and, eventually, split in two when its northern towns joined the revolt against Spain. This northern part was ceded to the United Provinces under the terms of the 1648 Treaty of Munster; the southern part formed what today are the Belgian provinces of Brabant and Antwerp.

The **Catholic influence** is still strong in North Brabant: it takes its religious festivals seriously and if you're here in March the boozy **carnivals** (especially in the province's capital, 's Hertogenbosch) are well worth catching – indeed, it's difficult to miss them. Geographically, woodland and heath form most of the natural scenery, the gently undulating arable land a welcome change in a country whose landscape is ruthlessly featureless.

Bergen-op-Zoom

BERGEN-OP-ZOOM is an untidy town, a jumble of buildings old and new that are the consequence of being the butt of various European powers from the sixteenth century onwards. In 1576 Bergen-op-Zoom sided with the United Provinces against the Spanish and as a result was under near-continuous siege until 1622. The French bombarded the city in 1747 and took it again in 1795, though it managed to withstand a British attack in 1814.

The town

Walk straight out of the train station and you'll soon find yourself on the **Grote Markt**, an insalubrious square-cum-car park, most cheerful during summer when it's decked out with open-air cafés and the like. The **Stadhuis**, on the north side of the square (Mon–Fri 9.30am–12.30pm & 1.30–5.30pm; free), is Bergen's most attractive building, spruced up following a recent renovation and comprising three separate houses: to the left of the gateway an alderman's house of 1397, to the right a merchant's house of 1480 and on the far right a building known as "De Olifant" whose facade dates from 1611. Ask inside the Stadhuis and someone will show you the council chamber and the *Trouwzaal*, the room where marriages take place. All of this is a lot more appealing than the blunt ugliness of the **Grote Kerk**, a uniquely unlucky building that's been destroyed by siege, fire and neglect innumerable times over the last four hundred years.

To the left of the Stadhuis, Fortuinstraat leads to the **Markiezenhof Museum**, Steenbergsestraat 8 (Sept–May Tues–Sun 2–5pm; June–Aug Tues–Fri

---

CARNAVAL IN BERGEN-OP-ZOOM

In February each year Bergen-op-Zoom hosts one of southern Holland's most vibrant **carnivals**, with virtually every inhabitant joining in its Sunday procession. It's a great time to be in the town if you can manage it, although you shouldn't expect to find any accommodation – the town gets packed; just do as the locals do and party all night.

11am–5pm, Sat & Sun 2–5pm; *f*5), a first-rate presentation of an above average collection that has a little of everything: domestic utensils and samplers from the sixteenth century onward, sumptuous period rooms, architectural drawings, pottery and galleries of modern art. All this is housed in a palace built by Anthonis Keldermans between 1485 and 1522 to a late Gothic style that gives it the feel of an Oxford college. Before reaching the Markiezenhof's main entrance on Steenbergsestraat, you pass the **Galerie Etcetera** (Tues–Sun 2–5pm), an exhibition space for twentieth-century artists, worth dropping in on if you're interested in what's on show.

Of the rest of old Bergen-op-Zoom little remains: at the end of Lievevrouwestraat, near the entrance to the Markiezenhof, the **Gevangenpoort** is practically all that's left of the old city defences, a solid-looking fourteenth-century gatehouse that was later converted to a prison.

Practicalities

Outside Carnaval, it's hard to imagine why you'd want to stay over in Bergen, but if you do, the **VVV**, at Beursplein 7 (Mon–Fri 9am–6pm, Sat & Sun 9am–5pm; ☎0164/266 000) has details of **private rooms**, along with a free map of the centre. The cheapest **hotel** is the *Old Dutch*, Stationstraat 31 (☎0164/235 780; ④) while the **youth hostel**, *Klavervelden* (mid-March to mid-Oct), is 4km out of town at Boslustweg 1; take bus #1 or #2 from the station. There is a variety of **restaurants** grouped around the Grote Markt and, while the town's **drinking scene** is not exactly buzzing, *Kunst-en Proeflokaal de Hemel* is a lively spot at Moeregrebstraat 35, just off Steenbergsestraat.

Breda

Though it doesn't boast an awful lot to see, **BREDA**, the prettiest town of North Brabant, is a pleasant, easy-going place. The centre is compact and eminently strollable, with a magnificent church, a reasonable art gallery and a brand new cultural centre; there's a range of well-priced accommodation, inexpensive restaurants and lively bars; and it's a good springboard for exploring central North Brabant. In short, it's a fine target, whether you're visiting for the day or looking for a base from which to branch out to Zeeland, Dordrecht, 's Hertogenbosch or even Antwerp.

Though there's little evidence of it today, Breda developed as a strategic fortress town and was badly damaged following its capture by the Spanish in 1581. The local counts were scions of the House of Nassau, which in the early sixteenth century married into the House of Orange. The first prince of the Orange-Nassau line was **William the Silent**, who spent much of his life in the town and would probably have been buried here – had Breda not been in the hands of the Spanish at the time of his assassination in Delft. In 1566 William was among the group of Netherlandish nobles who issued the **Compromise of Breda** – an early declaration against Spanish domination of the Low Countries. The town later fell to the Spanish, was retaken by Maurice, William's son, captured once more by the Spanish, but finally ceded to the United Provinces in 1648.

King Charles II of England lived in the town for a while (it was here that he issued his **Declaration of Breda** in 1660, the terms by which he was prepared to

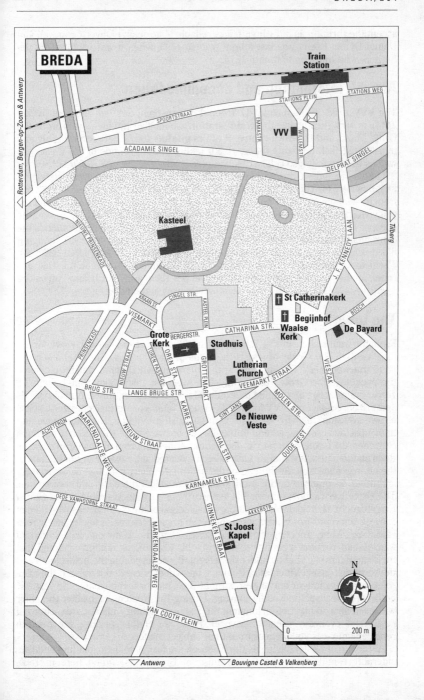

accept the throne), as did (though less reliable historically) Oliver Cromwell and Daniel Defoe. Breda was last fought over in 1793, when it was captured by the French, who hung on to it until 1813.

Arrival, information and accommodation

The **VVV** office, Willemstraat 17 (Mon–Fri 9am–6pm, Sat 9am–5pm; ☎076/522 2444) is straight outside the **train station**, about five minutes' walk from the Grote Markt and the town centre. It offers **guided tours** between mid-July and mid-August (ask for exact times; ƒ6.50) taking in the grounds of the Kasteel as well as the town; it also sells a detailed guide, *Strolling through Breda* (ƒ3.50).

Hotels include *Graumans* (☎076/521 6271; ③), near the train station at Delpratsingel 14. The others are all too far to reach on foot – take a yellow #130 bus from the station and ask to be dropped off at Duivelsbruglaan, where you'll find the somewhat overpriced *Aard Ster*, Duivelsbruglaan 92 (☎076/565 1666; ③) and the cheaper *Donkers*, Duivelsbruglaan 72 (☎076/565 4332; ③). Up a notch, there's the conveniently located *De Klok* at Grote Markt 26–28 (☎076/521 4082; ④), though it fills quickly in summer and the *Van Ham*, Van Coothplein 23 (☎076/521 5229; ③). The nearest **campsite**, *Liesbos* (March–Sept), is 8km out of town on the #111 bus route; further still, the nearest **youth hostel** lies 15km away at Chaam, Putvenweg 1 (☎0161/491323); bus #132 and a ten minute walk at the other end.

The town

From the train station and VVV, head down Willemstraat and cross the park for the town centre. The **Grote Markt** is the focus of life, site of a general and second-hand **market** every Tuesday and Friday morning, when stands push up against the pocket-Gothic **Grote Kerk** (May–Oct Mon–Sat 10am–5pm, Sun 1–5pm; ƒ2. Tower open as part of a guided tour only: May–Oct Sat 3pm, July & Aug also Weds 3pm; ƒ3.50; contact the VVV for details), whose intimate interior generates a sense of awe you don't usually associate with so small a building, the short nave and high, spacious crossing adding to the illusion of space. Like the majority of Dutch churches, the Grote Kerk had its decorations either removed or obscured after the Reformation, but a few murals have been uncovered and reveal just how colourful the church once was. At the end of the south aisle there's a huge *St Christopher* and other decorations in the south transept embellish the walls and roof bosses. The Grote Kerk's most remarkable feature, though, is the **Mausoleum of Count Engelbrecht II**, a Stadholder and Captain-General of the Netherlands who died in 1504 of tuberculosis – vividly apparent in the drawn features of his intensely realistic face. Four kneeling figures (Caesar, Regulus, Hannibal and Philip of Macedonia) support a canopy that carries his armour, so skilfully sculpted that their shoulders sag slightly under the weight. It's believed that the mausoleum was the work of Tomaso Vincidor of Bologna, but whoever created it imbued the mausoleum with grandeur and power without resorting to flamboyance: the result is both eerily realistic and oddly moving. During the French occupation the choir was used as a stable, but fortunately the sixteenth-century misericords, showing rustic and everyday scenes, survived. A couple of the carvings are modern replacements – as you'll guess from their subject matter.

At the top of Kasteelplein sits the **Kasteel**: too formal to be forbidding and considerably rebuilt since the Compromise of Breda was signed here in 1566.

Twenty-five years later the Spanish captured Breda, but it was regained in 1590 thanks to a neat trick by Maurice of Nassau's troops: the Spanish garrison was regularly supplied by barge with peat, so, using the Trojan Horse strategy, seventy troops under Maurice's command hid beneath the peat on the barge and were towed into the castle, jumping out to surprise the Spanish and regain the town. The Spanjaardsgat, an early sixteenth-century watergate with twin defensive bastions that's just west of the Kasteel, is usually (but inaccurately) identified as the spot where this happened. Today the Kasteel is a military academy and there's no admission to its grounds, unless you join one of the VVV tours.

To the east of Kasteelplein on Catherinastraat, the **Begijnhof**, built in 1531, was until quite recently the only *hofje* in Holland still occupied by Beguines. Today it has been given over to elderly women, some of whom look after the dainty nineteenth-century chapel at the rear, the St Catherinakerk, and tend the herb garden that was laid out several hundred years ago. To the right of the Begijnhof entrance, incidentally, is the **Walloon Church**, where Pieter Stuyvesant, governor of New York, was married.

Catherinastraat, which is lined with stately houses from the seventeenth century, twists around to **De Beyaard**, Boschstraat 22 (Tues–Fri & Sun 1–5pm, Sat 11am–5pm; *f*3), a gallery with changing exhibitions of contemporary art housed in what was once a lunatic asylum. Back in town, **de Nieuwe Veste** is a lively cultural centre at St Janstraat 18; the converted building dates from 1534 and offers regular theatre and concerts, as well as a chance to catch some local art-in-progress during the day. Finally, the **Breda Museum**, closed at the time of writing but due to reopen in late 1997 at a new location on Oude Vest, holds a forgettable collection of ecclesiastical art and oddments, along with exhibits concerning Breda's history.

Eating and drinking

Breda has a decent range of places to **eat**. For cheap, central food, *Da Attilio* is a pizzeria at Grote Markt 35, *Willy's Pizza* on Halstraat is handy for snacks, and *Cafe de Boulevard* at Grote Markt 10 has a variety of dishes. If you want to splash out, the *Auberge de Arent* at Schoolstraat 2, off Havermarkt, has excellent food or, less pricey, there's the popular *Beecker & Wetselaar* by the Grote Kerk. Elsewhere, the *Maharajah of India*, Havermarkt 25, has reasonably priced curries, while *Pols*, Halstraat 15, is a small and excellent *eetcafé*. For down-to-earth **drinking**, try *De Groene Sael*, Havermarkt 8, an unpretentious bar serving draft *Palm* beer and with a small dance floor at the back; *Nickelodeon*, Halstraat 2, is a more upmarket affair, with a swish interior. Connoisseurs of Low Countries beer generally make for *De Beyerd*, Boschstraat 26 while, back in the centre, *Café de Bommel* at Halstraat 3 is a large and lively café-bar with a good mix of customers. *De Graanbeurs*, Reigerstraat 20, is a late night disco and bar.

Tilburg

TILBURG is a faceless and unwelcoming industrial town, its streets a maze of nineteenth-century houses and anonymous modern shopping precincts. If you're passing through there are four decent museums within easy walking distance of the train station although, if that's as far as you get into town, you haven't missed much.

Tilburg developed as a textile town, though today most of its mills have closed in the face of cheap competition from India and southeast Asia. The **Nederlands Textielmuseum**, housed in an old mill at Goirkestraat 96 (out of the station, walk west along Spoorlaan, turn right along Gasthuisring and Goirkestraat is the fourth turn on the right; Tues–Fri 10am–5pm, Sat & Sun noon–5pm; *f*7.50), displays aspects of the industry relating to design and textile arts, with a collection of textile designs by Dutch artists and demonstrations of weaving and spinning, as well as a range of looms and weaving machines from around the world. The shiny new **Scryption**, Spoorlaan 434a (Tues–Fri 10am–5pm, Sat & Sun 1–5pm; *f*6), is a fancy name for a collection of writing implements – everything from lumps of chalk to word processors. Particularly interesting are the old, intricate typewriters, some of which you can operate yourself. Next door, the **Noordbrabants Natuurmuseum** (Tues–Fri 10am–5pm, Sat & Sun 1–5pm; *f*6) is basically a load of dead animals and (live) creepy crawlies. The **De Pont** modern art museum (Tues–Sun 11am–5pm; *f*5) is behind the station at Wilheminapark 1.

The **VVV** office is at Stadhuisplein 128 (Mon–Fri 9am–5.30pm, Sat 10am–4pm; ☎013/535 1135), ten minutes' walk from the station – cross the main road and keep straight ahead. You'll need their town map to have any chance of finding the **Poppenmuseum** at Telefoonstraat 13–15 (Sun & Wed 2–4pm; *f*5), a small private collection of dolls. There's little reason why you'd want to stay in Tilburg, but, for the record, the least expensive room in town is at the *Het Wapen van Tilburg* hotel, Spoorlaan 362 (☎013/542 2692; ③). There are several good cafés around the Stadhuis and the *Horse-Shoe* is a popular drinking spot by the Grote Markt.

Around Tilburg: De Eftelin

Hidden in the woods fifteen minutes' drive north of Tilburg, the **De Efteling** theme park (April–Oct daily 10am–6pm, July & Aug until 10pm; *f*32.50) is one of the country's principal attractions. Inevitably, the place can't quite match Disney, but it has some excellent rides and, if the weather is reasonable, makes for a great day out, although, particularly on summer weekends, the queues can get rather daunting.

The place is attractively landscaped and, especially in spring when the tulips are out, delightful to walk around. Of the rides, *Python* is the most hair-raising, a rollercoaster twister with great views of the park before plunging down the track; *De Bob*, a recreation bob-sleigh run, is almost as exhilarating although over far too quickly, especially if you've queued for ages. *Piranha* takes you through some gentle white-water rapids (expect to get wet). Of the quieter moments, *Villa Volta* is the latest attraction – a slightly unsettling room that revolves around you – and just about worth enduring the lengthy introduction in Dutch. For kids, the *Fairy-Tale Wood*, where the park began – a hop from Gingerbread House to Troll King to Cinderella Castle – is still popular. *Carnaval Festival* and *Droomvlucht* are the best of the rides, and there are afternoon shows in the Efteling Theatre. In addition, there are a number of fairground attractions, canoes and paddle-boats, and a great view over the whole shebang and the surrounding woods from the *Pagoda*. If you're not up to doing it all, skip the disappointing *Haunted Castle* and the *Fata Morgana*, with its faintly disturbing trawl through a bunch of Moroccan stereotypes.

Practicalities

If you are coming to De Efteling by **train** it is worth buying a *Rail Idee* ticket, which combines the price of the train ticket, the connecting bus service and entry to the park. Bus #137 runs to De Efteling every thirty minutes from Tilburg (15min), and from Den Bosch (40min); in summer, the direct services #182 from Tilburg and #181 from Den Bosch are slightly faster. If you are driving, the park is well-signposted just off the A261 between Tilburg and Waalwijk; parking costs *f*7.50. Though there's little need to **stay**, if you're eager for another day's fun, the *Efteling Hotel* is right by the park (☎0416/282 000, fax 281 515; ⑤). There are plenty of **maps** posted around the park, and snack-bars and refreshment stops at every turn.

's Hertogenbosch (Den Bosch)

Capital of North Brabant, **'s HERTOGENBOSCH** is officially known as Den Bosch, the name deriving from the words "the Count's Woods" after the hunting lodge established here by Henry I, Duke of Brabant, in the twelfth century. Hieronymous Bosch lived here all his life, but as the town has only two paintings doubtfully attributed to him, the main draws are its cathedral, a number of museums and, not least, an enjoyable nightlife. Consider staying over for a couple of days.

Arrival, information and accommodation

Den Bosch's centre is fifteen minutes' walk from the **train station**. Stop by the **VVV** office, Markt 77 (Mon 11am–5.30pm, Tues–Fri 9am–5.30pm, Sat 9am–4pm; ☎06/911 22 334, *f*0.50 per min) to pick up a copy of the useful *Wandering around Old Den Bosch* leaflet.

There are three budget **hotels**: most convenient is the *Terminus* at Stationsplein 19 (☎613 0666; ③); the *Bosch*, Boschdijkstraat 39a (☎613 8205; ③) is slightly cheaper; and there's the seedy but friendly *All In* (☎613 4057; ③), just down the street at Gasselstraat 1, on the corner of Hinthamerpromenade. A little pricier but more central, *Eurohotel* is at Hinthamerstraat 63 (☎613 7777, fax 612 8795; ④).

If you want to see a lot of the town, but want to save your legs, there are **boat trips** along the city moat. You've a choice between plying along in a traditional open boat (May–Sept Mon hourly 2–5pm, Tues–Sun hourly 11am–5pm; *f*6) from Van Molenstraat (next to *Café van Puffelen*); or a closed boat (May–Sept 11am, 12.30pm, 2pm & 3.30pm daily, *f*7.50) from St Janssingel near the Wilhelmina bridge, which also takes in the River Dommel and nearby Ertveld Lake.

The town

If you were to draw a picture of the archetypal Dutch Markt it would probably look like the one in Den Bosch. It's broad and cobbled, home to the province's largest market on Wednesday and Saturday and is lined with typical seventeenth-century houses. The sixteenth-century **Stadhuis** (Mon–Fri 9am–5pm) has a car-

The telephone code for Den Bosch is ☎073

illon that's played every Wednesday between 10 and 11am and that chimes the half-hour to the accompaniment of a group of mechanical horsemen.

From just about anywhere in the centre of town it's impossible to miss **St Jan's Cathedral** (daily 10am–5pm; restricted entrance during services). Generally regarded as the finest Gothic church in the country, it was built between 1330 and 1530 and has recently undergone a massive restoration. But if Breda's Grote Kerk is Gothic at its most intimate and exhilarating, then St Jan's is Gothic at its most gloomy, the garish stained glass – nineteenth-century or modern – only adding to the sense of dreariness that hangs over the nave. You enter beneath the oldest and least well-preserved part of the cathedral, the western **tower** (open, if you want to climb it, in July & Aug; ƒ2): blunt and brick-clad, it's oddly prominent amid the wild decoration of the rest of the exterior, which includes some nasty-looking creatures scaling the roof – symbols of the forces of evil that attack the church. Inside, there's much of interest. The **Lady Chapel** near the entrance contains a thirteenth-century figure of the Madonna known as *Zoete Lieve Vrouw* (Sweet Dear Lady), famed for its miraculous powers in the Middle Ages and still much venerated today. The brass **font** in the southwest corner was the work of Alard Duhamel, a master mason who worked on the cathedral in the late fifteenth century. It's thought that the stone pinnacle, a weird twisted piece of Gothicism at the eastern end of the nave, was the sample piece that earned him the title of master mason.

Almost filling the west wall of the cathedral is an extravagant **organ case**, assembled in 1602. It was described by a Victorian authority as "certainly the finest in Holland and probably the finest in Europe . . . it would be difficult to conceive a more stately or magnificent design". Equally elaborate, though on a much smaller scale, the south transept holds the **Altar of the Passion**, a retable (a piece placed behind and above the altar to act as a kind of screen) made in Antwerp in around 1500. In the centre is a carved Crucifixion scene, flanked by Christ bearing the Cross on one side and a Lamentation on the other. Though rather difficult to make out, a series of carved scenes of the life of Christ run across the retable, made all the more charming by their attention to period (medieval) costume detail.

Though a few painted sections of the cathedral remain to show how it would have been decorated before the Reformation, most works of art that it possessed were destroyed in the iconoclastic fury of 1566. These included several paintings by **Hieronymus Bosch**, who lived in the town all his life: only two works by Bosch remain (in the north transept) and even their authenticity is doubtful. What is more certain is that Bosch belonged to the town's Brotherhood of Our Lady, a society devoted to the veneration of the Virgin, and that as a working artist he would have been expected to help adorn the cathedral. Though none of his major works remain in Den Bosch today, there's a collection of his prints in the Noordbrabants Museum (see p.298) and reproductions of his major works are rather strangely housed in the **Orangerie**, St Josephstraat 15 (Mon–Sat 11am–5pm, Sun noon–5pm; free), a converted church that now holds a series of restaurants.

Opposite the cathedral at Hinthamerstraat 94, the **Zwanenbroedershuis** (Fri 11am–3pm; free) has an intriguing collection of artefacts, liturgical songbooks and music scores that belonged to the Brotherhood of which Bosch was a member. Founded in 1318, there's nothing sinister about the Brotherhood: membership is open to all and its aim is to promote and popularize religious art and music.

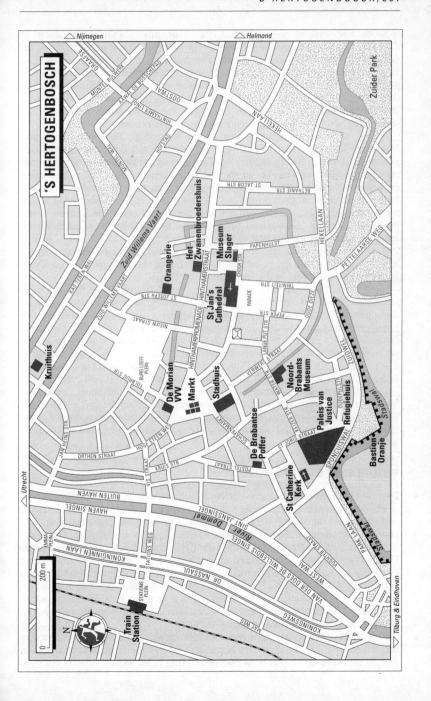

'S HERTOGENBOSCH

△ Nijmegen △ Helmond

Zuider Park

Kruithuis

Orangerie
Het Zwanenbroedershuis
Museum Slager

Zuid Willems Vaart

St Jan's Cathedral

De Morian
VVV
Markt
Stadhuis

Noord-Brabants Museum

De Brabantse Poffer

Paleis van Justice
Refugiehuis

St Catherine Kerk

Bastion Oranje

△ Utrecht

River Dommel

Emma Plein

Stations Plein

Train Station

N

200 m
0

△ Tilburg & Eindhoven

South and east of the cathedral, the **Museum Slager**, Choorstraat 16 (Tues–Fri & Sun 2–5pm; free), contains the works of three generations of the Slager family who lived in Den Bosch. The paintings of the family's doyen, P.M. Slager, such as *Veterans of Waterloo*, have the most authority, but some of the other works are competent, encompassing the major trends in European art as they came and went. Over the hundred and thirty years they have been active (the remaining Slager, Tom, lives in France) the Slager family seems to have spent most of its time painting Den Bosch – or their relatives.

A few minutes' walk southwest of the cathedral, the **Noordbrabants Museum**, Verwersstraat 41 (Tues–Fri 10am–5pm, Sat & Sun noon–5pm; ƒ7.50), is housed in an eighteenth-century building that was once the seat of the provincial commissioner and has been enlarged with two new wings. The good-looking collection of local art and artefacts here is uniformly excellent and interesting – unlike many regional museums – and the downstairs galleries often hold superb temporary exhibitions of modern art. The permanent collection includes drawings and prints by Hieronymus Bosch, works by other medieval painters and assorted early torture equipment. There's also a rare *Schandhuik* or "Cloak of Infamy", a wooden cloak carved with adders and toads, symbols of unchastity. In it, women who had been unfaithful to their husbands were paraded on a cart through the city streets in the seventeenth century.

Just down the road from the museum, the **Refugiehuis** at the end of St Jorisstraat (Mon–Fri 9am–5pm), originally a sixteenth-century safe house for those persecuted for their religious beliefs, is today a commercial crafts centre. St Jorisstraat leads down to the site of the old city walls, which still marks the southern limit of Den Bosch. The **Bastion Oranje** once defended the southern section of the city walls, but, like the walls themselves, it has long gone. Still remaining is a large cannon, **De Boze Griet** (The Devil's Woman), cast in 1511 in Cologne and bearing the German inscription "Brute force I am called, Den Bosch I watch over".

For the rest, the backstreets of Den Bosch are a mass of intriguing facades and buildings. To name just one, the **Kruithuis** at Citadellelaan 7 (Tues–Sat 11am–5pm, Sun 1–5pm; ƒ3), northwest of the centre, is an old gunpowder magazine that's been converted into an arts centre, with changing exhibitions of (mostly) contemporary art.

Eating and drinking

Den Bosch's **restaurants** can be pricey: many of those in the centre are geared to expense accounts and are poor value for money. *Da Peppone* at Kerkstraat 77 and *Taormina*, at Verwersstraat 46 are both inexpensive pizzerias. *Bagatelle*, Hinthamerpromenade 29, has well-priced Dutch food, as does *Hof van Holland* at Kolperstraat 12. *De Opera*, Hinthamerstraat 115–117, offers a range of wonderful Dutch–French cooking in a relaxed setting: well worth a splurge. *Dry Hamerkens*, Hinthamerstraat 57 (closed Tues), is similarly expensive, though this is hardly surprising, given that you dine in the neatly elegant ambience of a seventeenth-century house that looks as if it's fallen out of a Vermeer. A fairly short distance from the centre of town, *Van Puffelen* at Van Molenstraat 4, is an attractive *eetcafé* above a canal with affordable *dagschotels*.

For **drinking**, it's easy enough to wander up and down Hinthamerstraat or the streets that radiate from the Markt and find somewhere convivial. *Keulse Kar*, Hinthamerstraat 101, is as good a starting point as any, a fairly conservative bar near the cathedral; the nearby *Basilique* on the corner of Torenstraat is also a decent spot. At Hinthamerstaat 97, *'t Bonte Palet* is a tiny, popular and hence often crowded bar that's good for a swift one as you're working your way along the street. Up a few notches on the trendiness scale, *Café Cordes*, Parade 4 (just southwest of the cathedral), is a stylish, aluminium-clad café-bar that brings in Den Bosch's bright young things. *Café Pavlov*, Kerkstraat 38, is also a popular meeting place for the city's youth. *De Blauwe Druif*, at the corner of Markt and Kolperstraat, is a big, boozy pub that takes off on market days and the bar at 13 Kolperstraat is a friendly place to drink and smoke dope. *Duvelke*, Verwersstraat 55, is a deftly decorated drinking den near the Noordbrabants Museum.

Eindhoven

You might wonder why a town the size of **EINDHOVEN** only merits a page in a guidebook; half an hour there and a few statistics, will tell you why.

In 1890 Eindhoven's population was 4500. In 1990 it was around 197,000. What happened in between was **Philips**, the multinational electrical firm and the name of Eindhoven's benevolent dictator is everywhere – on bus stops, parks, even the stadium of the famous local football team. The town is basically an extended industrial and research plant for the company, and, save for one impressive art gallery, there's no need to come here unless business (or a football game – PSV Eindhoven, basically the Philips company team, are one of Holland's most consistently successful) forces you.

Eindhoven's only real attraction is **Van Abbe Museum**, Bilderdijklaan 10 (Tues–Sun 11am–5pm; *f*5), with its superb collection of modern paintings that includes works by Picasso, Klein, Chagall, Kandinsky and Bacon. To see this, you need to come between June and September; at other times most of the collection disappears and the place has rotating exhibitions of modern art.

Practicalities

Eindhoven's VVV is outside the train station (Mon–Fri 9am–5.30pm, Sat 9am–4pm; ☎040/244 9231). It can provide a handy brochure on the city and a list of pensions – only *De Swaan*, Wilhelminaplein 5 (☎040/244 8892; ③), is anywhere near the centre. The one central, affordable **hotel** is the *Corso* at Vestdijk 17 (☎040/244 9131; ③). There's a campsite, *Camping Witven* (open all year), 5km outside the city at Runstraat 40 in **VELDHOVEN**; buses #177 and #7 run from the station.

As for eating and drinking, Eindhoven's modern streets contain some stylish **bars** that have sprung up over the last few years to assuage the thirst of the town's affluent youth. Kleine Berg is the best place for food: *Le Connaisseur* at no. 12 serves cheap Italian food in its bookshelved interior; *Sorman's*, next door, offers reasonable Turkish food; and the *Grand Café Berlage* at no. 16, as slick as anything you'll find in Amsterdam, has a good menu and reasonable prices, while *Hoeden Cafe* at no. 34B, though simpler, is also pretty good. *Café Bommel*, a little further down, is a more old-fashioned traditional bar, good for a quiet drink.

Eindhoven's main strip for drinking is **Stratumseind**, which starts just south of Cuypers' gloomy neo-Gothic **St Catherinakerk**. The *Miller* bar at Stratumseind 51 is usually packed with teenagers; *De Krabbedans* at no. 32 is an arts complex with a pricey bar; Cafe Bonzo at no. 49 has a good variety of ales.

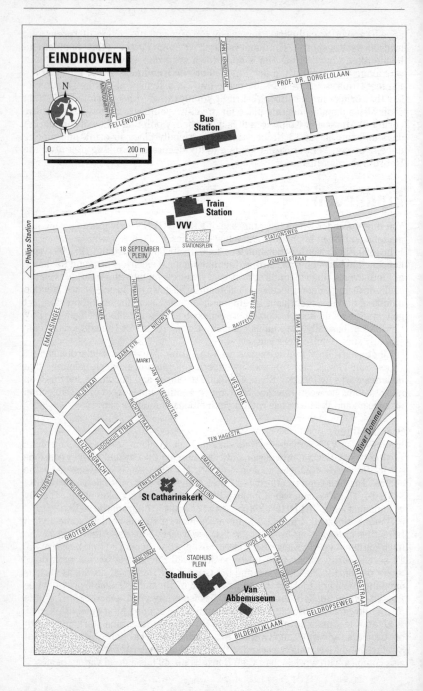

Along with *Ajax* of Amsterdam and *Feyenoord* of Rotterdam, Eindhoven's football team, **PSV Eindhoven**, is one of Holland's best. Catch games at the **Philips Stadion**, ten minutes' walk west from the train station.

East from Eindhoven: Helmond

HELMOND, on the main train line from Eindhoven to Venray, just about merits a stop for its moated late medieval **Kasteel** (Tues–Fri 10am–5pm, Sat & Sun 2–5pm; ƒ3.50) that contains a museum with a small historical collection and changing exhibitions of art (though wandering around the castle itself is most fun); and a collection of futuristic houses, the **Paalwoningen**, designed by Piet Blom and opened in 1977. Designed to look like Cubist tree-huts, the buildings most resemble a group of tumbling dice – try and get into the small theatre here (box office open Mon–Sat 10am–1pm) to have a look.

LIMBURG

Limburg is Holland's southernmost province, a finger of land that pushes down into Belgium. The north, around **Venlo**, is mostly farmland and woods; the centre, around **Roermond**, is dominated by the rivers and canals; and in the south, down to Maastricht, rise Holland's only hills. Like North Brabant it's a deeply Catholic area (if anything even more so) and has been influenced both architecturally and socially by the countries it neighbours.

Venlo

Just a few kilometres from the Dutch–German border, **VENLO** has been repeatedly destroyed and recaptured throughout its history, particularly during the last war, when most of its ancient buildings were knocked down during the Allied invasion of Europe. As a result the town is short of sights, and there is little reason to do anything but make a brief stop en route to the National War and Resistance Museum at Overloon.

The cramped streets of Venlo's centre wind medievally around the town's one architectural highlight, the fancily turreted and onion-domed **Stadhuis**, a much-amended building dating from the sixteenth century. Nearby, along Grote Kerkstraat, is the louring pile of **St Martinuskerk**, rebuilt after bombing in 1944, but still holding a brilliant golden seventeenth-century reredos. From the Stadhuis, signs direct you southeast to the **Limburgs Museum**, Goltziusstraat 21 (Tues–Fri 10am–4.30pm, Sat & Sun 2–5pm; ƒ4.50), the city's historical collection. Best exhibit is the nineteenth-century kitchenware, the largest assortment in western Europe. Venlo's other museum, the **Van Bommel-Van Dam**, Deken van Oppensingel 8 (Tues–Fri 10am–4.30pm, Sat & Sun 2–5pm; ƒ2.50), has changing exhibitions of the work of contemporary, mostly local artists. From the train station, take the second right off the roundabout and then turn first right.

Venlo's **VVV**, Koninginneplein 2 (Mon–Fri 9am–5.30pm, Sat 9am–4pm; ☎077/354 3800), opposite the train station, hands out glossy leaflets and can help find accommodation. Otherwise try the *Grolsche Quelle*, Eindhovenseweg 3–5 (☎077/351 3560; ③), or the convenient *Stationshotel*, Keulsepoort 16 (☎077/351 8230, fax 352 12 79; ④). For **eating and drinking**, try the *Labierint*, in the centre at Houtstraat 2, for snacks and a few samples of their huge range of beers. Otherwise, there are cheap light lunches at several cafés around the Stadhuis.

From beside the train station, bus #83 makes the ten-kilometre trip north up along the Maas to the village of Arcen, home to the **Huis Arcen** (April–late Oct daily 10am–6pm; ƒ16), a trim seventeenth-century moated castle surrounded by a fine series of formal gardens set beside narrow canals and a string of tiny lakes.

Venray and the National War and Resistance Museum

A few minutes by train from Venlo, **VENRAY** is a cosy residential town and a stepping stone to **OVERLOON**, site of the **National War and Resistance Museum**. To reach the museum from Venray, bus #97 leaves the station hourly but your best bet is to take the *treintaxi* (ƒ6 each way) or to rent a bike (ask at the station). A six-kilometre ride through fields of wheat brings you to Overloon (which is actually across the provincial border back in North Brabant), an affluent little town that was rebuilt following destruction in the last war during a fierce battle in October 1944 in which 2400 men died. The final stages took place in the woods to the east, where hand-to-hand fighting was needed to secure the area and it's on this site that the museum (Sept–May daily 10am–5pm; June–Aug daily 9.30am–6pm; ƒ10 plus ƒ3 for essential guidebook) now stands, founded with the military hardware that was left behind after the battle. Its purpose is openly didactic: "Not merely a monument for remembrance, it is intended as an admonition and warning, a denouncement of war and violence." This the museum powerfully achieves, with the macabre machinery of war (which includes tanks, rocket launchers, armoured cars, a Bailey bridge and a V1 flying bomb) forming a poignant prelude to the excellent collection of documents and posters. To tour the whole museum takes a couple of hours and it's a moving experience.

Roermond

ROERMOND, the chief town of central Limburg, is an oddity. Except for a few churches and a museum of fairly specialized interest, there's precious little to see here: its nightlife can't hold a candle to that of Maastricht to the south, cultural happenings are few, and, to be honest, it's not one of Holland's prettier towns either. Yet the town has great personality, caused in part by its long adherence to **Catholicism**. In 1579, seven years after William the Silent had captured Roermond from the Spanish, it fell back into their hands without a struggle and remained under the control of the Spanish (or Austrian) Hapsburgs, who actively encouraged Catholic worship, until the town was finally incorporated into the Netherlands in 1839. Reminders of the pre-eminence of the faith are everywhere, most visibly in the innumerable **shrines** to the Virgin built into the sides of houses. Usually high enough off the street to prevent damage, they contain small figures of the Virgin,

---

The telephone code for Roermond is ☎04753

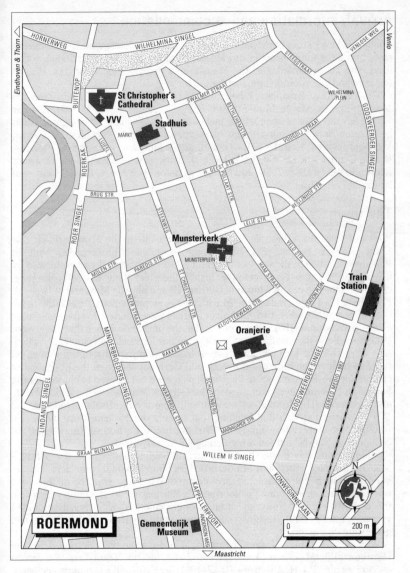

sometimes decorated with flowers. And it was in Roermond that P.J.H. Cuypers, the architect who crowded the country with Gothic-revival Catholic churches in the nineteenth century, lived and had his workshops. Roermond is also a handy stopover on the way to Maastricht and the south, Aachen, or Düsseldorf and Cologne in Germany and useful as a base for visiting nearby **THORN**.

Arrival, information and accommodation

Though it looks straightforward enough on the map, Roermond is a confusing place to walk around, its series of wide streets and broad squares irritatingly similar to the unacquainted. Use the Munsterkerk and river as landmarks, consult our map and you shouldn't get lost for too long.

The **VVV** office, Kraanport 1, behind Markt (April–Sept Mon–Fri 9am–6pm, Sat 10am–4pm; Oct–March Mon–Fri 9am–5pm, Sat 9am–4pm; ☎333 205), is a fair walk from the train station, which makes it worth deciding on accommodation before you arrive. A good range of inexpensive **hotels** includes *De Toerist*, Mariagardestraat 3 (☎318 831; ②); and, just a little more expensive, *Fuserhof*, Raadhuisstraat 1 (☎329 298, fax 340 669; ③). Other possibilities include *De Pauw*, Roerkade 1–2 (☎316 597; ④), and a single **pension**, *Van Eyden*, Burg. Moorenhof 22 (☎320 771; ②).

The town

Walk into town from the train station and you'll come to the **Munsterkerk** (Fri 10am–noon & 2–5pm, Sat 10am–4pm; free) on Munsterplein, built in Romanesque style in the thirteenth century, but much altered and gothicized by Cuypers in the nineteenth century. Inside, the chief thing to see is the polychrome thirteenth-century **tomb** of Gerhard III and his wife Margaret of Brabant. From here it's a short walk to the **Markt**, a large sloping square that hit the headlines in May 1990, when two Australian tourists were gunned down by members of the **provisional IRA**, who were under the mistaken belief that they were British soldiers. Its proximity to the German border made Roermond a particularly attractive site for such an action: soldiers often pass through the town en route to their Rhine bases; and fleeing into Germany lessened the likelihood of capture for the assassins, since the Dutch police are not allowed to chase over the border and the minutes taken to alert the German force allowed additional time for a getaway. The town's early eighteenth-century **Stadhuis** stands on the Markt's eastern side, a dull building that's easily overlooked. More noticeable (though not more interesting), **St Christopher's Cathedral** (April–Sept Sat 2–5pm; free) was rebuilt following damage in World War II.

Making your way down the larger streets leading south from the Markt – Marktstraat, Neerstraat and Minderbroeders Singel – you'll come across some later and much more attractive architecture. Wherever you are in town, it's worth keeping an eye open for Roermond's alluring twentieth-century **facades**: the majority are Art Nouveau, often strongly coloured with heavily moulded vegetal patterns and designs, sometimes with stylized animal heads and grotesque characters.

Roermond's principal architectural claim to fame is celebrated at the **Gemeentelijk Museum**, Andersonweg 2–8 (Tues–Fri 11am–5pm, Sat & Sun 2–5pm; ƒ2.50). **P.J.H. Cuypers** (1827–1921) was Holland's foremost ecclesiastical architect in the nineteenth century, his work paralleling that of the British Gothic revivalist, Augustus Pugin. Almost every large city in the country has a Catholic church by him – those in Eindhoven, Leeuwarden and Hilversum are notable – though his two most famous buildings aren't churches, but the Rijksmuseum and the Centraal Station in Amsterdam. The museum is the building in which Cuypers lived and worked for much of his life and preserves a small private chapel as well as a large extension in which masses of decorative panels, mouldings and fixtures were produced. Other exhibits show his plans and paintings, along with a collection of works by other local artists, chiefly Hendrik Luyten.

Eating and drinking

The three main areas to **eat and drink** are those around the Markt, the Munsterkerk and the train station, although *Il Corso*, an excellent and classily decorated Italian restaurant, is away from all these places at Willem II Singel 16a, the continuation of Godsweerder Singel. On Stationsplein, *Le Journal* and *De Tramhalte*, both at no. 17, are inexpensive café-bars, and although it's pricey for dinner, the restaurant of the *De La Station* hotel, Stationsplein 9, is worth checking out for its fixed-price lunches. *Le Chapeau* is a croissanterie ideal for breakfast and snacks, just down from Stationsplein at Hamstraat 54; *Tin San* is the best of several Chinese places, just south of the Markt at Varkensmarkt 1.

Roermond lacks first-rate **watering-holes**. The cafés at Stationsplein are often the liveliest nightspots; otherwise try *Herman's Beer Boetiek*, Schuitenberg 34, for a good range of beers. For a more artistic night out, check out the *Orangerie*, a multicultural centre at Kloosterwandplein 12–16.

Thorn

If you do end up staying in Roermond, the village of **THORN** makes for an enjoyable half-day outing. Regular buses link it to the town, but it's more fun to rent a bike from the train station and cycle the 14km through the almost rolling Limburg farmland. If you do cycle, take a map that shows cycle routes – the signs marking the route off the main road are none too good.

Once you get here, it's easy to see why Thorn is a favourite for travel agents' posters. Its houses and farms are all painted white, a tradition for which no one seems to have a credible explanation, but one that distinguishes what would, in any case, be a resolutely picturesque place. The farms intrude right into the village itself, giving Thorn a barnyard friendliness that's increased by its cobblestone streets, the closed-shuttered propriety of its houses and, at the centre, the **Abdijkerk** (March–Oct daily 10am–5pm; Nov–Feb Sat & Sun noon–5pm; ƒ2.50).

The abbey was founded at the end of the tenth century by a powerful count, Ansfried and his wife Hilsondis, as a sort of religious retirement home after Ansfried had finished his tenure as bishop of Utrecht. Under his control the abbey and the land around it was granted the status of an independent principality under the auspices of the Holy Roman Empire and it was in the environs of the abbey that the village developed. The abbey was unusual in having a double cloister that housed both men and women (usually from local noble families), a situation that carried on right up until the French invasion of 1797, after which the principality of Thorn was dissolved, the monks and nuns dispersed and all the abbey buildings save the church destroyed. Most of what can be seen of the church today dates from the fifteenth century, with some tidying up by P.J.H. Cuypers in the nineteenth. The interior decoration, though, is congenially restrained Baroque of the seventeenth century, with some good memorials and side chapels. If you're into the macabre, the crypt under the chancel has a couple of glass coffins containing conclusively dead members of the abbey from the eighteenth century: this and other highlights are described in the notes that you can pick up on entry (in English) for a self-guided walking tour.

Thorn has two small museums worth catching: the good-natured **Radio en Grammofoon Museum** at Wijngracht 13 (mid-April to mid-Oct daily 10am–4.30pm; *f*3), with ancient radios, record players, telephones and televisions; and the **Poppenmuseum**, opposite the Abdijkerk (April to mid-Oct daily 11am–6pm; *f*1.50), packed with dolls, glove puppets, marionettes and old porcelain dolls.

Practicalities

The **VVV**, Houtstraat 10 (daily 10.30am–4.30pm; ☎0475/562 761) can do little more than sell you postcards. Thorn makes a great place to stay if you want to get away from it all: the cheaper of two **hotels** is the *Crasborn*, Houtstraat 10 (☎0475/561 281, fax 562 233; ④), though the atmospheric *Hostellerie La Ville Blanche*, Hoogstraat 2 (☎0475/562 341, fax 562 828; ⑤) offers surprisingly affordable luxury. There's also a private **campsite**, reached by turning right halfway down Hofstraat.

Maastricht

MAASTRICHT was jettisoned into the headlines in the early 1990s. Up until then, few people had heard of this provincial Dutch town. Since the signing of the Masstricht treaty, however, in 1992, everyone at least knows its name, even if they couldn't place it on a map.

Don't, however, let Maastricht's Euro-connections put you off visiting. Far from being the bland, concrete Eurocity you might be expecting, it is on the contrary one of the most delightful cities in Holland, quite different in feel to the kitsch waterland centres of the north. Indeed it's obvious why the Eurocrats chose it as the place to sign their united Europe agreement. Outward-looking, vibrant and youthful, situated in the corner of the thin finger of land that reaches down between Belgium and Germany, where three languages and currencies happily coexist, it epitomizes the most positive aspects of European union.

Maastricht is a key industrial centre, with long-established manufacturing companies like Mosa (which produces domestic ceramic products from its plant on the east bank of the river) and Sphinx just north of the city centre, whose name graces toilets nationwide, spearheading Maastricht's prosperity. The town's position in the heart of Europe is also being traded on by the local authorities, keen to draw new money into the region – exemplified in projects like the newly completed MECC conference centre to the south of the city, where the treaty business was conducted.

Maastricht is also one of the oldest towns in the country. The first settlers here were Roman and Maastricht became an important stop on their trade route between Cologne and the coast – the town's name derives from the words *Mosae*

The Maastricht area telephone code is ☎043

Trajectum or "Maas Crossing". The Romans left relatively few obvious traces, but the later legacy of Charlemagne – whose capital was at nearby Aachen – is manifest in two churches that are among the best surviving examples of the Romanesque in the Low Countries.

Arrival and information

The centre of Maastricht is on the west bank of the river and most of the town spreads out from here toward the Belgian border. You're likely to arrive, however, on the east bank, in the district known as **Wijk**, a sort of extension to the centre that's home to the train and bus stations and many of the city's hotels. The train station itself is about ten minutes' walk from the St Servaas bridge, which takes you across the river into the centre. All local (ie non-yellow) buses connect with Markt from here, but really, if you have no heavy luggage, it's easy enough to walk. If you're flying direct to Maastricht, the **airport** is north of the city at Beek, a twenty-minute journey away by bus; take bus #61, which runs every thirty minutes to Markt and the train station, or a taxi – a *f*25 ride.

For local information, the main **VVV** (April–Oct Mon–Sat 9am–6pm; Nov–March Mon–Fri 9am–6pm, Sat 9am–5pm; ☎325 2121) is housed just across the river in the Dinghuis, a tall late fifteenth-century building at Kleine Straat 1, at the end of the main shopping street. As well as information on the city and on film, theatre and music events around town, they have decent maps (*f*1.50) and good walking guides. In July and August they organize **city tours** (in English) currently leaving from the VVV at 12.30pm (*f*5). There is also a small VVV office at the train station (Mon–Fri 9am–7pm & Sat 9am–5pm); they are less useful but can help with getting a room.

Getting around, you only really need to use buses to get from the station to the town centre at Markt, or out to St Pietersburg; otherwise it's easy to walk everywhere. Between mid-April and the end of Sept, *Stiphout Cruises* runs hourly **cruises** down the Maas Mon–Sat 10am–3pm, Sun 1–3pm; *f*8.75 per person. *Stiphout* also offers trips taking in the St Pietersberg caves or even as far as Liège (day-trip *f*28). Phone ☎325 4151 for details.

Accommodation

For **accommodation**, there's nothing super-cheap. The VVVs have a list of **private rooms** and will either book them for you at the usual fee or sell you the list. There are several good central **pensions** including *Zwets*, Bredestraat 39 (☎321 6482; ③) and *Tilly*, Coxstraat 42 (☎325 2305; ③), just off Klein Gracht. **Hotels** include the slightly seedy *Porte du Paradis*, Markt 76 (☎321 7324, fax 321 7325; ③), the more comfortable *de Ossekop*, Boschstraat 1 (☎325 0154, fax 325 8754; ④), and *de Hotelboot*, (☎321 9023; ③), moored on the river at Maasboulevard, not far from the Helpoort, and with an excellent breakfast. Up a notch in price are *La Colombe*, Markt 30 (☎321 5774, fax 325 8077; ⑤) and the very central *du Casque*, Helmstraat 14 (☎321 4343, fax 325 5155; ⑥). If you're **camping**, the *De Dousberg* site (☎343 2171), almost in Belgium on the far western side of town, is open all year, large and well equipped; take bus #8 from the train station and walk for about 1km. The same bus also takes you to the **youth hostel** at Dousbergweg 4 (☎346 6777).

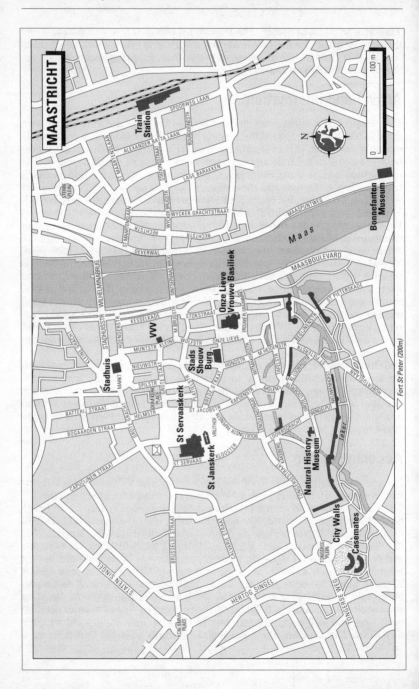

The town

The busiest of Maastricht's squares is the **Markt**, at its most crowded on Wednesday and Friday mornings, when people hop over the nearby borders for the town's cheap general market. At the centre of the square, which is a car park the rest of the time, the **Stadhuis** (Mon–Fri 8.30am–12.30pm & 2–5.30pm; free) of 1664 was designed by Pieter Post, a square, grey limestone building that is a fairly typical slice of mid-seventeenth-century Dutch civic grandeur. Its double staircase was designed so that the rival rulers of Brabant and nearby Liège didn't have to argue about who should go first on the way in. Inside, the building has an imposing main hall, which gives way to a rear octagonal dome supported by heavy arches.

The second of the town's main central squares, **Vrijthof**, is just west of the Markt, a larger, rather grander open space flanked by a couple of churches on one side and a line of cafés on the other, with tables smothering the wide pavement in summer. During the Middle Ages, Vrijthof was the scene of the so-called "Fair of the Holy Relics", a seven-yearly showing of the bones of Saint Servaas, the first bishop of Maastricht, which brought plenty of pilgrims and funds into the town but resulted in such civil disorder that it was eventually banned. The church which holds the relics now, the **St Servaaskerk** (April–Nov daily 10am–5pm; July & Aug until 6pm; Dec–March daily 10am–4pm; ƒ3.50), dominates the far side of the square. Dating from 950, it's the elaborate amalgamation of an earlier shrine dedicated to Saint Servaas and the site of his burial in 384. Only the crypt remains of the tenth-century church, containing the tomb of the saint himself, and the rest is mostly of medieval or later construction.. You enter on the north side of the church, where a fifteenth-century Gothic cloister leads into the **treasury**, which holds a large collection of reliquaries, goblets and liturgical accessories, including a bust reliquary of Saint Servaas, decorated with reliefs telling the saint's story, which is carried through the town in Easter processions. There's also a coffin-reliquary of the saint, the so-called "Noodkist", dating from 1160 and bristling with saints, stones and ornate copperwork, as well as a jewelled crucifix from 890 and a twelfth-century Crucifixion in ivory. Beyond the Treasury is the entrance to the rich and imposing interior, the round-arched nave supporting freshly painted Gothic vaulting. Don't miss the mid-thirteenth-century Bergportaal on the south side of the church, the usual entrance during services.

The second most prominent building on the square, next door, is Maastricht's main Protestant church, the fourteenth century **St Janskerk** (April–Oct daily except Sun, 11am–4pm), the baptistery of the church of St Servaas when it was a cathedral and nowadays competing for attention with its high and faded, delicate red fifteenth-century Gothic tower, which you can climb for ƒ2.50. The church has some medieval murals, but a climb up the tower is the church's main appeal. On the south side of the square, the sixteenth-century **Spanish Government House** (guided tours only; Wed–Fri & first Sat & Sun of the month every hour on the hour 2–5pm; ƒ4.50) has an attractive Renaissance arcade and a number of period rooms furnished in Dutch, French and the more local Liège–Maastricht style. Among various exhibits are statues and figurines, porcelain and applied arts and a handful of seventeenth-century paintings, though none is exactly essential viewing.

Maastricht's other main church, the **Onze Lieve Vrouwe Basiliek**, is a short walk south of Vrijthof, down Bredestraat, in a small, shady square crammed with café tables in summer. It's unusual for its fortified west front, with barely more than one or two slits for windows. First built around the year 1000, it's a solid, dark and eerily devotional place after the bright Protestant churches of the North – or even the relative sterility of the St Servaaskerk. The Gothic vaulting of the nave springs from a Romanesque base, while the galleried choir is a masterpiece of proportion, raised under a high half-dome, with a series of capitals exquisitely decorated with Old Testament scenes. Off the north aisle, the treasury (Easter to mid-Sept Mon–Sat 11am–5pm, Sun 1–5pm; *f*3.50) holds the usual array of reliquaries and ecclesiastical garments, most notably the dalmatic of Saint Lambert – the evangelical bishop of Maastricht who was murdered at Liège in 705, allegedly by a local noble whom he had rebuked for adultery. Entrance to the church is through a side chapel housing the statue of Stella Mare, an object of pilgrimage for centuries and which attracts as many devotees as the church itself.

Around the corner from the square, on Plankstraat, on the edge of a district of narrow streets known as the **Stokstraat Kwartier** after its main gallery- and boutique-lined spine, Stokstraat, is the **Museumkelder Derlon** (Sun noon–4pm; free), in the basement of the hotel of the same name. This contains one of the few remnants of Roman Maastricht – the remains of a temple to Jupiter, a well and several layers of pavement, discovered before the building of the present hotel in the mid-1980s. On the other side of Onze Lieve Vrouweplein lies another of Maastricht's most appealing quarters, narrow streets winding out to the remains of the town battlements alongside the fast-flowing River Jeker, which weaves in and out of the various houses and ancient mills. The best surviving part of the walls is the **Helpoort** of 1229, close to a stretch overlooking the river at the end of St Bernadusstraat; and from here you can walk along the top of the walls almost as far as the **Natural History Museum** at De Bosquetplein 6 (Mon–Fri 10am–12.30pm & 1.30–5pm, Sat & Sun 2–5pm; *f*3.50), where there's a small collection on the geology, flora and fauna of the surrounding area, along with a small, lush garden display. A little way south of here, the **Casemates** in the Waldeck Park (tours July & Aug daily, 12.30pm & 2pm; other months Sun 2pm only; f5.25) are further evidence of Maastricht's once impressive fortifications, a system of galleries created through mining between 1575 and 1825 that were used in times of siege for surprise attacks on the enemy. There used to be many more casemates around the town, but only these survive, making for a fairly draughty way to spend an hour, tours taking you through a small selection of the 10km or so of damp passages. Probably the most interesting thing about them is the fact that the fourth "musketeer", d'Artagnan, was killed here, struck down while engaged in an attack on the town as part of forces allied to Louis XIV in 1673.

Ten minutes' walk from the Saint Servaas bridge, the **Bonnefanten Museum** (Tues–Sun 11am–5pm; *f*10) is one of Maastricht's highlights. Named after the Bonnefanten monastery where it once was housed, the museum now inhabits an impressive modern building on the banks of the Maas. The first floor has a local archeological collection, with relics from pre-history through Roman times to the Middle Ages, much of it dredged up from the river bed, and a modest collection of medieval sculpture and early Italian and Dutch paintings. The rest of the museum is given over to temporary exhibitions of modern and contemporary art, superbly displayed if erratic in quality. Don't miss the lunar capsule-style cupola, usually given over to a single piece of art.

Outside the centre: St Pietersberg

There are more dank passageways to explore fifteen minutes' walk from the casemates on the southern outskirts of Maastricht, where the flat-topped hill of **St Pietersberg** rises up to a height of about 110m – a popular picnic spot on warm summer weekends. Again these aren't so much caves as galleries created by quarrying, hollowed out of the soft sandstone, or marl, which makes up the hill – an activity which has been going on here since Roman times. The marl hardens in exposure to the air, so is a much more useful material than might at first be imagined. Of the two cave systems, the **Zonneberg** is probably the better, situated on the far side of the St Pietersberg hill at Casino Slavante (guided tours in English: July & Aug daily 2.45pm; *f*5.25). The caves here were intended to be used as air-raid shelters during World War II and were equipped accordingly, though they were only in fact utilized during the last few days before Maastricht's liberation. There is some evidence of wartime occupation, plus what everyone claims is Napoleon's signature on a graffiti-ridden wall. Also on the walls are recent charcoal drawings, usually illustrating a local story and acting as visual aids for the guides, not to mention the ten varieties of bat that inhabit the dark (and cold) corridors.

The other, more northerly system of caves, the **Grotten Noord** (guided tours in English: daily at 2.15pm; *f*5.25) is easier to get to (a 15-min walk from the centre of town), but it has less of interest. The entrance is at Chalet Bergrust, on the near side of St Pietersberg close by **Fort St Pieter**, a low brick structure, pentagonal in shape and built in 1702, which nowadays houses a pricey restaurant. You can visit – guided tours (July & Aug 3.15pm; *f*5.25) leave from the restaurant – but (especially if you've had your fill of fortifications) you'd probably do just as well nursing a drink on the restaurant's terrace, which gives panoramic views over the town and surrounding countryside.

Eating, drinking and nightlife

Maastricht has some of the best cooking in the Netherlands and three or four major breweries, so options abound for good **eating** and **drinking**. There are a number of inexpensive **restaurants** around the Markt, including *Pizzeria Napoli* at no. 71, while elsewhere they include the snackbar *Stap-In*, Kesselkade 61 by the river, and the rather better *de Roeje Knien*, Rechtsraat 76 on the other side, which serves good Dutch food. *Charlemagne* in Onze Lieve Vrouweplein also has reasonably priced steaks, chicken and ribs. Up a notch in price, there are two good Dutch/French restaurants on Tongersestraat, a few minutes from the centre: *'t Orgelke*, at no. 40, and *de Cuyp* at no. 30. *Il Giardino della Mamma*, Onze Lieve Vrouweplein 15, has good pizzas and pasta from *f*15; *L'Hermitage*, St Bernardusstraat 13, around the corner and near the Helpoort, has Mexican food from *f*20; and *In 't Knijpe*, opposite, has a pleasant bar/restaurant and great onion soup.

For drinking, the **bars** on the east side of the Vrijthof have most of the pulling power, particularly in summer when the pavement cafés are packed; *In den Ouden Vogelstuys*, on the corner of Platielstraat, is one of the nicest. Away from the Vrijthof crowds, *de Bobbel*, on Wolfstraat just off Onze Lieve Vrouweplein, is a bare-boards place, lively in the early evening, while *In de Moriaan*, Stokstraat 12, is a delight – possibly the smallest bar in the country and with a cosy terrace in the summer. The no-frills *Cafe de Stadssleutel*, Kesselkade 60, has about the cheapest beer in town, and the student quarter around Tongesestraat has a couple of excellent bars in *Van Sloun* at no.3 and *Tribunal* opposite. On the other side of the river, *De Gijsbrecht*, toward the station on Wycker Brugstraat, is a very busy bar while *Take One*, Rechstraat 28, is a good bet for beer connoisseurs.

If you don't want to drink, bear in mind that the *Lumière Filmhuis*, Bogaardenstraat 40b (☎321 4080), regularly shows interesting **movies**, often English or American and always subtitled in Dutch.

Listings

Books There's a branch of *De Slegte* at Grote Straat 53, good for second-hand English-language paperbacks and much else besides. Try also *Bergmans* on Nieuwestraat, off Markt, which has a good selection of new English-language titles.

Bureau de change There's a GWK office at the train station, open every day.

Car rental *Europcar*, Spoorweglaan 18 (☎325 1081). The major companies also have desks at the airport.

Post office The main city post office is on Keizer Karelplein, just off the northwest corner of Vrijthof.

Around South Limburg

South Limburg boasts Holland's only true hills and as such is a popular holiday area for the Dutch, many of the villages crammed in summer with walkers from the north taking in the scenery. And this is certainly worth doing, the countryside green and rolling, studded with castles (many of which have been converted to hotels), seamed with river valleys and dotted with the timber-framed houses that are unique to the area. Everywhere is within easy reach of Maastricht and perfectly feasible on day-trips, though without a car you shouldn't try to cover too much in one day as public transport connections are patchy. **Valkenburg**, the main resort, is perhaps the easiest place to visit, on the main train line from Maastricht to Aachen, though it is packed throughout the summer. Further east down the train line, **Heerlen** and **Kerkrade** are also easily reached, though neither is any great shakes. To the south of the train line, toward the Belgian border, the countryside is wilder and more impressive, the roads snaking over hills and giving long, expansive views all around. It's not at all a Dutch scene and perhaps not what you came to Holland for. But after the grindingly flat landscapes of the northern provinces, it can be excellent therapy – as numerous hotels, at least one for every tiny village, testify.

Cadier-en-Keer, Margraten, Gulpen and Vaals

Five kilometres east of Maastricht, the first stop on the #54 bus route – which eventually goes to Vaals on the German border – **CADIER-EN-KEER** is a small suburb of the city best known for its **Africa Centre** (April–Oct Mon–Fri 1.30–5pm, Sun 2–5pm; otherwise Sun only 2–5pm; *f*5), ten minutes' walk off to the left of the main road (follow the signs). Housed in the headquarters of the African Missionaries Society, this contains a small museum of (mainly West) African artefacts, masks, jewellery and statuary arranged by tribe and dating back as far as the thirteenth century – as well as giving details on the contemporary way of life of African peoples. Nearby, the **Maastricht Wine Museum** (Mon–Fri 9am–5pm, Sat 10am–4pm; ƒ6) has displays on production and a free sampler or two.

Bus #54 continues on to **MARGRATEN**, where just before the town proper there's an **American War Cemetery** (daily sunrise–sunset), a peaceful and moving memorial to over eight thousand American servicemen who died in the Dutch and Belgian campaigns of late 1944 and 1945. Buses stop right outside. The centrepiece is a stone quadrangle recording the names of the soldiers, together with a small visitors' room and a pictorial representation and narrative describing the events in this area leading up to the German surrender – while beyond the quadrangle, the white marble crosses that mark the burial places of the soldiers cover a depressingly huge area.

There's not much else to Margraten, nor is there to **GULPEN**, a few kilometres beyond, a nondescript place though with good bus connections all over South Limburg. The town is known for its *Gulpener* beer, the name of which you see all over the province and indeed the rest of Holland, though that aside the only thing that distinguishes Gulpen is the 161-metre-high **Gulpenberg**, which rises roundly behind the town and is home to a **campsite**. If you continue to the end of the #54 route, the pretty village of **VAALS** is notable not only for being the highest point in the country, but also for "Drielandenpunt", where the borders of Belgium, Germany and the Netherlands meet. South of Gulpen, the countryside makes for a pretty route back to Maastricht, either driving yourself or via the # 57 bus route from Gulpen's bus station, taking in the scenically sited villages of **Mechelen**, **Epen** and **Slenaken**.

Valkenburg

Set in the gently wooded valley of the River Geul, **VALKENBURG**, ten minutes east of Maastricht by train, is southern Limburg's major tourist resort, the unloading point for buses full of tourists throughout the summer, with innumerable hotels, restaurants and even a casino. While you wouldn't want to stay here, it's a nice enough place to visit, about as far away from the clogs and canals of the rest of the country as it's possible to get, with a feel more of a Swiss or Austrian alpine resort, its small restaurant-ridden centre sloping up from its fake castle train station to the surrounding green hills, full of grottoes, castles and thermal centres.

Theo Dorrenplein, five minutes' walk from the train station, is the centre of town, fringed with cafés and home to the VVV, from where the main Grote Straat leads up through the pedestrianized old centre through the old **Grendelpoort** arch to **Grendelplein**, which provides a second focus, the streets which lead off going to Valkenburg's main attractions. A great many of these are directed at children – things like bob-sleigh runs, a fairytale wood, a hopeful reconstruction of Rome's catacombs – and even those that aren't are the kind of things kids enjoy.

It's worth a walk up to the **Castle** (April–Oct daily 10am–5pm; ƒ3.50 or combined ticket with Fluwelengrot ƒ7.50; entrance off Grendelplein), a ruined edifice which overlooks the town from a neatly placed peak above Grote Straat. It was blown up in 1672 on the orders of William III, after he had retrieved it from its French occupiers. Repair and restoration on the castle began in 1921 and continue still, uncovering a series of underground passages that served as an escape route in times of siege. These form part of the **Fluwelengrot** (guided tours only; April–Nov daily 10am–5pm; Dec–March Sat & Sun 11am–4pm; ƒ6 or combined

ticket with castle *f*7.50), further up the road on the left, a series of caves formed
– like those of St Pietersberg in Maastricht – by the quarrying of marl, which has
been used for much of the building in this area over the years. Tours leave every
ten minutes or so in high summer (much less frequently outside this period), but
on the whole they're a damp, cold way to spend an hour, the most interesting features the signatures and silhouettes of American soldiers who wintered here from
1944 to 1945 and a clandestine chapel that was used during the late eighteenth-
century French occupation.

If you particularly like caves, or can't be bothered to walk around the
Fluwelengrot, the **Gemeentegrot** (same times; *f*5.25), just off Grendelplein on
Cauberg, is similar, but has a train which whips you around its charcoal drawings,
memorials to local dignitaries, giant sculptures of dinosaurs and fish hewn out of
the rock, and, most engagingly, a weirdly, brightly lit underground lake. The
whole tour takes about thirty minutes and costs a guilder extra. Further up the
same road as the Fluwelengrot, on the left, the **Steenkolemijn** (guided tours only
April–Oct daily 10am–5pm; Nov–March Sat & Sun 2pm & 3pm; *f*8.50) is a reconstruction of a coal mine whose 75-minute tours include a short film on coal-
mining, some fake mine-workings and a small fossil museum. Again, good for the
kids but not exactly riveting viewing. If the idea of trudging around dank underground passages doesn't appeal to you, you can ascend to the top of the hill above
the castle by way of a **cable car** (July & Aug daily 10am–5pm; rest of the year
daily 1–5pm; *f*5 return), five minutes' walk down Berkelstraat from the top of
Grote Straat – or you can cut through the passage between the castle and the
Fluwelengrot. This, a fairly primitive structure of the kind used for ski lifts, with
two-person open cars, takes you up to the **Wilhemina Toren**, where you can
enjoy the view from the terrace of the inevitable bar-restaurant. Finally, if you
need a break from the sight-seeing, **Thermae 2000** on Cauberg (daily
9am–11pm; *f*28 for 2hr), the country's first official spa, has saunas, steam rooms
and indoor and outdoor pools.

Practicalities

The **VVV** at Theo Dorrenplein 5 (Easter–Nov Mon–Fri 9am–6pm, Sat 9am–5pm;
Dec–Easter Mon–Fri 9am–5pm, Sat 9am–1pm; ☎043/601 3364) has maps and
information on all Valkenburg's attractions, as well as lists of the dozens of **hotels**
and **private rooms**. Among the cheapest hotels are *de Grendel*, Grendelplein 17
(☎043/601 4868; ③), *'t Centrum*, Grendelplein 14 (☎043/601 5333; ③) and *Casa*,
Grotestraat 25–27 (☎043/601 2180; ③). Up a level in price there are: *De Toerist*,
Hovetstraat 3 (☎043/601 2484, fax 601 4320; ④), and *de Uitkijk*, Broekhem 68
(☎043/601 3589, fax 601 4744; ④). **Camping**, the nearest site is a short walk up
Dahlemerweg from Grendelplein on the left (☎043/601 2025). As virtually every
second building in Valkenburg is a restaurant, there's little point in listing specific places to **eat**. Suffice to say you can dine cheaply and fairly reasonably at most
of the places in the centre – though don't expect haute cuisine.

Heerlen and Kerkrade

HEERLEN, ten minutes further from Valkenburg by train, is quite different, an
ugly modern town that sprawls gracelessly over the rolling countryside. But it has
one definite attraction in the excellent **Thermen Museum** (Tues–Fri 10am–5pm,
Sat & Sun 2–5pm; *f*3), which incorporates the excavations of a bath complex from

the Roman city of Coriovallum here – a key settlement on the Cologne–Boulogne trade route. These have been enclosed in a gleaming hi-tech purpose-built structure, with walkways leading across the ruins and tapes (in English) explaining what's what. An adjacent room displays finds and artefacts from the site, including glasswork from Cologne, shards of pottery, tombstones and coins, all neatly labelled. To get to the museum, follow Saroleastraat from the station as far as Raadhuisplein and turn right.

Fifteen minutes on from Heerlen lies **KERKRADE**, again an unappealing place, but worthy of a visit for its **Abdij van Rolduc** complex (opening hours vary, call ☎045/546 6888), situated on the far side of town, about a twenty-minute walk from the station. Originally founded by one Ailbert, a young priest who came here in 1104, this is now almost entirely sixteenth-century, used as a seminary and conference centre, but it does preserve a fine twelfth-century church, a model of simplicity and elegance, with contemporary frescoes and a marvellous mosaic floor. The clover leaf-shaped crypt, dark and mysterious after the church and with pillar capitals carved by Italian craftsmen, contains the relics of Ailbert, brought here from Germany where he died. Beside the train station the **Industrion**, an industrial archeology museum incorporating the old local mining museum, is scheduled to open in early 1998.

travel details

Trains

Breda to: Dordrecht (every 20min; 20min); 's Hertogenbosch (every 30min; 40min); Middleburg (every 30 min; 1hr 15min); Maastricht (every 30 min; 1hr 45 min).

Eindhoven to: Roermond (every 30min; 30min); Venlo (every 30min; 45min).

's Hertogenbosch to: Eindhoven (every 30min; 22min).

Middelburg to: Bergen-op-Zoom (every 30min; 45min); Goes (every 30min; 15min); Roosendaal (every 30min; 55min).

Roermond to: Maastricht (hourly; 30min); Venlo (every 30min; 26min).

Roosendaal to: Breda (every 30min; 18min); Dordrecht (every 30min; 30min).

Tilburg to: Eindhoven (every 30min; 30min); 's Hertogenbosch (every 30min; 15 min).

Vlissingen to: Middelburg (every 30min; 7min).

Buses

Middelburg to: Delta Expo (hourly; 30min); Renesse (hourly; 45min); Veere (hourly; 10min).

Renesse to: Bouwershaven (hourly; 1hr 30min).

Zierikzee to: Goes (every 30min; 30min).

Ferries

Vlissingen to: Breskens (Mon–Fri every 30min, Sat & Sun hourly; 20min).

International trains

Maastricht to: Bruges (hourly; 2hr 50min); Brussels (hourly; 2hr); Gent (hourly; 2hr 30min); Leuven (hourly; 1hr 30min); Liège (hourly; 30min).

Roosendaal to: Antwerp (every 30min; 30min); Bruges (hourly; 1hr 50min); Brussels (hourly; 40min); Gent (hourly; 1hr 15min); Oostende (hourly; 2hr); Paris (4 daily; 4hr).

CONTEXTS

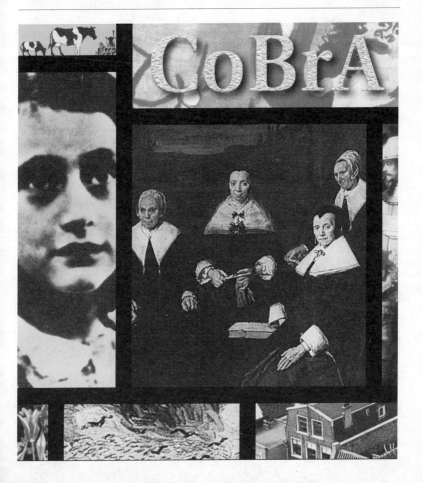

THE HISTORICAL FRAMEWORK

The country now known as The Netherlands didn't reach its present delimitations until 1830. Until then the borders of the entire region, including present-day Belgium and to some extent Luxembourg were continually being redrawn following battles, treaties and alliances. Inevitably, then, what follows is, in its early parts at least, an outline of the history of the whole region, rather than a straightforward history of The Netherlands. Please note, incidentally, that the term "Holland" refers to the province – not the country – throughout.

BEGINNINGS

Little is known of the prehistoric settlers of **The Netherlands**, and their visible remains are largely confined to the far north of the country, where mounds known as *terpen* were built to keep the sea at bay in Friesland and Groningen, and in Drenthe megalithic tombs, *hunebeds*, stretch scattered across a low ridge of hills, the *hondsrug*, north of Emmen.

Clearer details of the region begin to emerge at the time of Julius Caesar's conquest of Gaul in 57BC to 50 BC. He found three tribal groupings living in the region: the mainly Celtic **Belgae** (hence the nineteenth-century term

"Belgium") settled by the Rhine, Maas and Waal to the south; the Germanic **Frisians** living on the marshy coastal strip north of the Scheldt; and the **Batavi**, another Germanic people, inhabiting the swampy river banks of what is now the southern Netherlands. The Belgae were conquered and their lands incorporated into the imperial province of Gallia Belgica, but the territory of the Batavi and Frisians was not considered worthy of colonisation, and these tribes were granted the status of allies, a source of recruitment for the Roman legions and curiosity for imperial travellers. In 50 AD Pliny observed "Here a wretched race is found, inhabiting either the more elevated spots or artificial mounds . . . When the waves cover the surrounding area they are like so many mariners on board a ship, and when again the tide recedes their condition is that of so many shipwrecked men".

The **Roman occupation** of Gallia Belgica continued for 500 years and the Germanic **Franks** filled the power vacuum to the south. A great swathe of forest extending from the Scheldt to the Ardennes separated the Frankish kingdom from the more confused situation in the north and east, where other tribes of Franks settled along the Scheldt and Leie, Saxons occupied parts of Overijssel and Gelderland, and the Frisans clung to the shore. Towards the end of the fifth century, the Merovingian king, Clovis, was converted to Christianity and the faith slowly filtered north, spread by energetic missionaries like Saint Willibrord, first bishop of Utrecht from about 710, and Saint Boniface, who was killed by the Frisians in 754 in a final act of pagan resistance before they too were converted. United by faith, the whole region was soon to be united in a single kingdom under **Charlemagne**, son of Pepin III and king of the west Franks from 768. In a dazzling series of campaigns, Charlemagne extended his empire south into Italy, west to the Pyrenees, north to Denmark and east to the Oder, his secular authority bolstered by his coronation as the first Holy Roman Emperor in 800, a title bestowed on him by the Pope in order to legitimise his claim as the successor to the emperors of Imperial Rome.

The strength and stability of Charlemagne's court at Aachen spread to the Low Countries, bringing a flurry of building of superb Romanesque churches like Maastricht's St Servaas, and a trading boom, utilizing the region's principal rivers. However, unlike his Roman predecessors, Charlemagne was subject to the divisive inheritance laws of the Salian tribe of Franks, and after his death in 814, his kingdom was divided between his grandsons into three roughly parallel strips of territory, the precursors of France, the Low Countries and Germany.

THE GROWTH OF THE TOWNS

The tripartite division of Charlemagne's empire placed the Low Countries between the emergent French- and German-speaking nations, a dangerous location which was subsequently to decide much of its history, though this was not apparent in the cobweb of local alliances that made up early feudal western Europe in the ninth and tenth centuries. During this period, French kings and German emperors exercised a general authority over the region, but power was effectively in the hands of local lords who, remote from central control, brought a degree of local stability. From the twelfth century, feudalism slipped into a gradual decline, the intricate pattern of localized allegiances undermined by the increasing strength of certain lords, whose power and wealth often exceeded that of their nominal sovereign. Preoccupied by territorial squabbles, this streamlined nobility was usually willing to assist the growth of towns by granting charters which permitted a certain amount of autonomy in exchange for tax revenues, and military and labour services. The first major cities were the cloth towns of Flanders. Meanwhile, their smaller northern neighbours concentrated on trade, exploiting their strategic position at the junction of several of the major waterways and trade routes of the day.

BURGUNDIAN RULE

By the late fourteenth century the political situation in the Low Countries was fairly clear: five lords controlled most of the region, paying only nominal homage to their French or German overlords. In 1419 **Philip the Good** of Burgundy succeeded to the countship of Flanders and by a series of adroit political moves gained control over Holland, Zeeland, Brabant and Limburg to the north, and Antwerp, Namur and Luxembourg to the south. He consolidated his power by establishing a strong central administration in Bruges and restricting the privileges granted in the towns' charters. During his reign Bruges

became an emporium for the Hanseatic League, a mainly German association of towns who acted as a trading group and protected their interests by an exclusive system of trading tariffs. Philip died in 1467 to be succeeded by his son, Charles the Bold, who was killed in battle ten years later, plunging his carefully crafted domain into turmoil. The French seized the opportunity to take back Arras and Burgundy and before the people of Flanders would agree to fight the French they kidnapped Charles's daughter, Mary, and forced her to sign a charter that restored the civic privileges removed by her grandfather Philip.

THE HABSBURGS

After her release, Mary married the **Habsburg** Maximilian of Austria, who was forced to assume sole authority when Mary was killed in a riding accident in 1482. Maximilian continued to rule until 1494, when he became Holy Roman Emperor and transferred control of the Low Countries to his son, Philip the Handsome, and subsequently to his grandson **Charles V**, who in turn became King of Spain and Holy Roman Emperor in 1516 and 1519 respectively. Charles was suspicious of the turbulent burghers of Flanders and, following in Maximilian's footsteps, favoured Antwerp at their expense; it soon became the greatest port in the empire, part of a general movement of trade and prosperity away from Flanders to the cities to the north.

STIRRINGS OF THE REFORMATION

An alliance of church and state had dominated the medieval world: pope and bishops, kings and counts were supposedly the representatives of God on earth, and crushed religious dissent wherever it appeared. Much of their authority depended on the ignorance of the population, who were entirely dependent on their priests for the interpretation of the scriptures, their view of the world carefully controlled.

There were many complex reasons for the **Reformation**, the stirring of religious revolt that stood sixteenth-century Europe on its head, but certainly the **development of typography** was a key. For the first time, printers were able to produce relatively cheap Bibles in quantity, and the religious texts were no longer the exclusive property of the church. A welter of debate spread across much of western Europe, led initially by theologians who wished to cleanse the Catholic church of its corruptions, superstitions and extravagant ceremony; only later did many of these same thinkers decide to support a breakaway church. Humanists like **Erasmus of Rotterdam** (1465–1536) saw man as the crowning of creation rather than the sinful creature of the Fall; and, most importantly, in 1517 **Martin Luther** produced his 95 theses against indulgences, rejecting among other things Christ's presence in the sacrament of the Eucharist, and denying the Church's monopoly on the interpretation of the Bible. His works and Bible translations were printed in the Netherlands and his ideas gained a following in a group known as the Sacramentarians. They, and other reforming groups branded as **Lutheran** by the Church, were persecuted and escaped the towns to form fugitive communes where the doctrines of another reformer, **John Calvin** (1509–64), became popular. Luther stated that the Church's political power was subservient to that of the state; Calvin emphasised the importance of individual conscience and the need for redemption through the grace of Christ rather than the confessional. The seeds of Protestantism fell on fertile ground among the merchants of the cities of the Low Countries, whose wealth and independence could not easily be accommodated within a rigid caste society. Similarly, their employees, the guildsmen and their apprentices, had a long history of opposing royal authority, and many were soon convinced of the need to reform an autocratic, venal church. In 1555, Charles V abdicated, transferring his German lands to his brother Ferdinand, and his Italian, Spanish and Low Countries territories to his son, the fanatically Catholic **Philip II**. The scene was set for a massive confrontation.

THE REVOLT OF THE NETHERLANDS

On his father's abdication, Philip decided to teach his heretical subjects a lesson. He garrisoned the towns of the Low Countries with Spanish mercenaries, imported the Inquisition and passed a series of anti-Protestant edicts. The opposition to these measures was, however, so widespread that he was pushed into a tactical withdrawal, recalling his soldiers and transferring control to his sister Margaret in

1559, who implemented the policies of her brother with gusto. In 1561 she reorganized the church and created fourteen new bishoprics, a move that was construed as a wresting of power from civil authority, and an attempt to destroy the local aristocracy's powers of religious patronage. Protestantism and Protestant sympathies spread to the nobility, who petitioned Philip for moderation but were dismissed out of hand. In 1565 a harvest failure caused a winter famine among the workers, and in many towns they ran riot in the churches, sacking them of their wealth and destroying their rich decoration in the **Iconoclastic Fury**.

The ferocity of this outbreak shocked the higher classes into renewed support for Spain, and Margaret regained the allegiance of most nobles – with the principal exception of the country's greatest landowner, Prince William of Orange-Nassau, known as **William the Silent** (though William the Taciturn is a better translation). Of Germanic descent, he was raised a Catholic but the excesses and rigidity of Philip had caused him to side with the Protestant movement. A firm believer in individual freedom and religious tolerance, William became – and for the Dutch remains – a symbol of liberty; but after the Fury had revitalized the pro-Spanish party, he prudently slipped away to his estates in Germany.

Philip II saw himself as responsible to God for the salvation of his subjects and therefore obliged to protect them from heresy. In 1567, keen to take advantage of the opportunity provided by the increased support for Margaret, he appointed the **Duke of Alva**, with an army of 10,000 men, to enter the Netherlands and suppress his religious opponents absolutely. Alva's first act was to set up the **Council of Blood**, which tried and condemned 12,000 of those who had taken part in the rioting of the year before. The policy briefly worked: when William attempted an invasion from Germany in 1568 the towns, garrisoned by the Spanish, offered no support. William waited and conceived other means of defeating Alva. In April 1572 a band of privateers entered Brielle on the Maas and captured it from the Spanish. Known as *Waterguezen* or sea-beggars, these commando-style units initially operated from England, but it was soon possible for them to secure bases in the Netherlands, whose citizens had grown to loathe Alva and his Spaniards.

The revolt spread rapidly: by June the rebels controlled the province of Holland and William was able to take command of his troops from Delft. Alva and his son Frederick fought back, taking Gelder, Overijssel and the towns of Zutphen and Naarden, and in June 1573 Haarlem, massacring the Calvinist ministers and most of the garrison. But the Netherlanders retaliated: utilizing their superior naval power the dykes were cut and the Spanish forces, unpaid and threatened with destruction, were forced to withdraw. Frustrated, Philip replaced Alva with Luis de Resquesens, who initially had some success in the south, where the Catholic majority were more willing to compromise with Spanish rule than their northern neighbours.

William's triumphant relief of Leiden in 1574 increased the pride of the rebel forces, and when de Resquesens died in 1576, his unpaid garrison in Antwerp mutinied and attacked the town, slaughtering some 8000 of its people in what was known as the **Spanish Fury**. Though Spain still held several towns, the massacre alienated the south and pushed its peoples into the arms of William, whose troops now controlled most of the region. Momentarily, it seemed possible for the whole region to unite behind William, and the various provinces signed the **Pacification of Ghent** in 1576, an agreement that guaranteed freedom of religious belief. However, differences between Protestant north and Catholic south proved irreconcilable, with many Walloons and Flemings suspicious both of William's ambitions and his Calvinist cronies. Consequently, when another army arrived from Spain, under the command of Alexander Farnese, Duke of Parma, the south was reoccupied without much difficulty, beginning a separation that would lead, after many changes, to the creation of two modern countries.

In 1579 seven provinces (Holland, Zeeland, Utrecht, Groningen, Friesland, Overijssel and Gelderland) signed the **Union of Utrecht**, an alliance against Spain that was to be the first unification of the Netherlands as an identifiable country – the **United Provinces**. The agreement stipulated freedom of belief in the provinces, an important step since the struggle against Spain wasn't simply a religious one: many Catholics disliked the Spanish occupation and William did not wish to alienate this possible source of support. This liberalism did not, however, extend to freedom of worship, although a blind eye was turned to the celebration of Mass if it was done privately and inconspicuously, giving rise to the "hidden churches" found throughout the country.

THE UNITED PROVINCES (1579–1713)

In order to follow the developments of the sixteenth and seventeenth centuries in what is today The Netherlands, it's necessary to have an idea of the organization of the **United Provinces**. Holland, comprising North and South Holland, was by far the dominant province economically and politically. The provinces maintained a decentralized independence, but as far as the United Provinces as a whole were concerned, what Holland said, went.

The assembly of the provinces was known as the **States General**, and met at The Hague; it had no domestic legislative authority, and could only carry out foreign policy by unanimous decision. The role of **Stadholder** was the most important in each province, roughly equivalent to that of governor, though the same person could occupy this position in any number of provinces. The Council Pensionary was another major post and in both cases the man who held the title in Holland was a powerful statesman.

In 1584 a French Catholic tricked his way into William's court in Delft and shot him, his family receiving the reward Philip II had promised for such an assassination. As William's son **Maurice** was only 17, control of the United Provinces was handed to **Johan van Oldenbarneveldt**, later Council Pensionary of Holland. Things were going badly in the fight against the Spanish: Nijmegen had fallen and Henry III of France refused help even with the offer of sovereignty. In desperation the United Provinces turned to Elizabeth I of England, who offered the Earl of Leicester as governor general. He was accepted but completely mishandled the situation militarily, alienating the Dutch into the bargain. Oldenbarneveldt and Maurice took over and had great success in routing the Spanish from much of the country. By 1609 the English had defeated the Spanish Armada and Philip II was dead; the **Twelve Year Truce** was signed and the United Provinces were consolidated.

THE EARLY SEVENTEENTH CENTURY: INTERNAL DISCORD AND FURTHER FIGHTING

In the breathing space created by the truce, the long-standing differences between Maurice and Oldenbarneveldt polarized. An obscure argument within the Calvinist church on predestination proved the catalyst of Oldenbarneveldt's downfall.

The quarrel, between two Leiden theologians, began in 1612: Armenius argued that God gave man the choice of accepting or rejecting faith; Gomarus, his opponent, that predestination was absolute – to the degree that God chooses who will be saved and who damned with man powerless in the decision. This row between the two groups (known respectively as Remonstrants and counter-Remonstrants) became closely linked to the political divisions of the early seventeenth century. When a synod was arranged at Dordrecht to resolve the matter, the State of Holland, led by Oldenbarneveldt, refused to attend, insisting on Holland's right to decide its own religious orthodoxies. He and his fellow deputies supported the provincial independence favoured by Remonstrant sympathisers, whereas Maurice sided with the counter-Remonstrants who favoured a strong central authority. The counter-Remonstrants won at Dordrecht: Maurice, with his troops behind him, quickly overcame his opponents and had Oldenbarneveldt arrested. In May 1619 he was executed in The Hague "for having conspired to dismember the states of the Netherlands and greatly troubled God's church".

With the end of the Twelve Year Truce in 1621, fighting with Spain once more broke out, this time part of the more general **Thirty Years' War** (1618–48), a largely religious-based conflict between Catholic and Protestant countries that involved most of western Europe. In the Low Countries, the Spanish were initially successful, but they were weakened by war with France and by the fresh attacks of Maurice's successor, his brother Frederick Henry. From 1625, the Spaniards suffered a series of defeats on land and sea that forced them out of what is today the southern part of the Netherlands, and in 1648 they were compelled to accept the humiliating terms of the **Peace of Westphalia**. This was a general treaty that ended the Thirty Years' War, whose terms recognized the independence of the United

Provinces and closed the Scheldt estuary, an action designed to destroy the trade and prosperity of Antwerp. The commercial expansion and pre-eminence of Amsterdam was assured, and the Golden Age began.

THE GOLDEN AGE

The brilliance of **Amsterdam**'s explosion on the European scene is as difficult to underestimate as it is to detail. The size of its merchant fleet had long been considerable, bringing masses of Baltic grain into Europe. Even the determined Spaniards had been unable to undermine Dutch naval power, and following the effective removal of Antwerp as a competitor, Amsterdam became the emporium for the products of north and south Europe and the new colonies in the East and West Indies. Amsterdam didn't only prosper from its markets – her own ships carried the produce, a cargo trade that greatly increased the city's wealth. Dutch banking and investment brought further prosperity, and by the mid-seventeenth century Amsterdam's wealth was spectacular. The Calvinist bourgeoisie indulged themselves gently in fine canal houses and commissioned their reflections in group portraits. Civic pride burgeoned, and if some were hungry, few starved, with the poor cared for in municipal almshouses. The arts flourished and religious tolerance stretched even to the traditional scapegoats, the Jews, many of whom quickly became enterprising merchants. Huguenot refugees from France were drawn to the city, along with Protestants escaping persecution in the Catholic south.

One organization that kept the country's coffers brimming throughout the Golden Age was the **East India Company**. Formed by the newly powerful Dutch Republic in 1602, the Amsterdam-controlled enterprise sent ships to Asia, Indonesia, and as far as China to bring back spices, woods and other assorted plunder. Given a trading monopoly in all lands east of the Cape of Good Hope, it had unlimited military powers over the lands it controlled, and was effectively the occupying government in Malaya, Ceylon and Malacca. Twenty years later the **West Indies Company** was inaugurated to protect new Dutch interests in the Americas and Africa. Expending most of its energies in waging war on Spanish and Portuguese colonies from a base in Surinam, it never achieved the success of the East India Company, and was dismantled in 1674, ten years after its small colony of New Amsterdam had been captured by the British – and renamed New York. Elsewhere, the Netherlands held on to its colonies for as long as possible – **Java** and **Sumatra** were still under Dutch control after World War II.

A constant problem in the seventeenth century was the conflict between central authority and provincial autonomy. Although the **House of Orange** had established its royal credentials, many of Holland's leading citizens were reluctant to accept its right to power. On William II's death in 1650 the state of Holland used the fact that his heir was still an infant to force through measures abolishing the position of Stadholder, thereby reducing the powers of the Orangists and increasing those of the provinces, chiefly Holland itself.

Holland's foremost figure in these years was **Johan de Witt**, Council Pensionary to the States General. He guided the country through wars with England and Sweden, concluding a triple alliance between the two countries and the United Provinces in 1678. This didn't succeed, however, and when France and England marched on the Provinces two years later, the republic was in trouble. The previous victories had been at sea, and the army, weak and disorganized, could not withstand an attack. The country turned to **William III of Orange** for leadership and Johan de Witt was brutally murdered by a mob of Orangist sympathisers in The Hague. By 1678 William had defeated the French and made peace with the English – and was rewarded (along with his wife Mary) with the English crown ten years later.

THE UNITED PROVINCES IN THE EIGHTEENTH CENTURY

Though King William had defeated the French, Louis XIV retained designs on the United Provinces. When William's grandson inherited the Spanish throne and control of the Spanish Netherlands in 1700, Louis forced him to hand the latter over to French control. This threatened the balance of power in Europe, and the Provinces, England and Austria formed an alliance against the French and so began the **War of the Spanish Succession**, a haphazard series of campaigns distinguished by the spectacular victories of the Duke of Marlborough – Blenheim, Ramillies, Malplaquet – that dragged on till 1713 and the **Treaty of Utrecht**.

The fighting drained the United Provinces' riches and a slow economic and political decline began, accelerated by a mood of unadventurous conservatism that reflected the development of an increasingly socially static society, with power and wealth concentrated within a small elite.

Effectively freed from the threat of foreign conquest by the treaty of 1713, the next decades were marred by internal fighting between the Orangists and the pro-French ruling families (who called themselves "Patriots"). The situation deteriorated even further in the latter half of the century and the last few years of the United Provinces were dogged by interminable rivalry and conflict.

In 1795 the French, aided by the Patriots, invaded, setting up the **Batavian Republic** and dissolving the United Provinces and much of the control of the rich Dutch merchants. Effectively part of the Napoleonic empire, the Netherlands were obliged to wage unenthusiastic war with England, and in 1806 Napoleon appointed his brother Louis as their king in an attempt to create a commercial gulf between the country and England. Louis, however, wasn't willing to allow the Netherlands to become a simple satellite of France; he ignored Napoleon's directives and after just four years of rule was forced to abdicate. The country was then formally incorporated into the French Empire, and for three gloomy years suffered occupation and heavy taxation to finance French military adventures.

Following Napoleon's disastrous retreat from Moscow, the Orangist faction once more surfaced to exploit weakening French control. In 1813, Frederick William, son of the exiled William V, returned to the country and eight months later, under the terms of the **Congress of Vienna**, was crowned King William I of the United Kingdom of the Netherlands, incorporating both the old United Provinces and the Spanish (Austrian) Netherlands. A strong-willed man, he spent much of the later part of his life trying to control his disparate kingdom, but he failed primarily because of the north's attempt to dominate the south. The southern provinces revolted against his rule and in 1830 the Kingdom of Belgium was proclaimed.

1830 TO THE PRESENT DAY

A final invasion of Belgium in 1839 gave William most of Limburg, and all but ended centuries of changes to borders and territory. The Netherlands benefited from this new stability, the trade surplus picked up and canal building opened Rotterdam and Amsterdam to the North Sea. The outstanding political figure of the times, **J. R. Thorbecke**, formed three ruling cabinets (1849–53, 1862–66 and 1872, in the year of his death) and steered the Netherlands through a profound change. The political parties of the late eighteenth century had wished to resurrect the power and prestige of the seventeenth-century Netherlands; Thorbecke and his allies resigned themselves to the country's reduced status of a small power and eulogized its advantages. For the first time, from about 1850, liberty was seen as a luxury made possible by the country's very lack of power, and the malaise which had long disturbed public life gave way to a positive appreciation of the narrowness of its national existence. One of the results of Thorbecke's liberalism was a gradual extension of the franchise, culminating in the Act of Universal Suffrage in 1917.

At the outbreak of **World War I** the Netherlands remained neutral, but suffered privations as a result of the Allied blockade of ports through which Germany might be supplied. Similar attempts to remain neutral in **World War II** soon failed: the Germans invaded on May 10, 1940, destroying Rotterdam four days later. The Dutch were quickly overwhelmed, Queen Wilhelmina fled to London, and opposition to Nazi occupation was continued by the Resistance. Instrumental in destroying German supplies and munitions, they also helped many downed airmen escape back to England. A heavy price was paid for their contribution to the war effort: 23,000 resistance fighters were killed in the war years. In Amsterdam, the old Jewish community, swollen by those who had fled Germany to escape the persecution of the 1930s, was obliterated, leaving only the deserted Jodenhoek and the diary of **Anne Frank** as testament to the horrors.

Liberation began in autumn 1944 with **Operation Market Garden**. This was a British plan to finish the war quickly by creating a corridor stretching from Eindhoven to Arnhem, gaining control of the three main rivers en route, isolating the occupying forces to the west in the Netherlands and pushing straight into Germany. It was a gamble, but if successful would hasten the end of hostilities. On September 17 the 1st Airborne Division parachuted into the countryside around Oosterbeek, a small village near the most northerly target of the operation, the bridge at **Arnhem**. German opposition was much stronger than expected, and after heavy fighting the Allied forces could only take the northern end of the bridge. The advancing British army was unable to break through fast enough, and after four days the decimated battalion defending the bridge was forced to withdraw.

With the failure of Operation Market Garden, the Allies were obliged to resort to more orthodox military tactics to clear the south and east Netherlands of the Germans, a slow process that took all the winter and spring of 1945. As the assault was concentrated on Germany itself, the coastal provinces of the country were left alone, but they suffered terribly from lack of food and fuel. Finally, on April 5, 1945, the German army surrendered to the Canadians at Wageningen.

The postwar years were spent patching up the damage of occupation. Rotterdam was rapidly rebuilt, and the dykes blown in the war to slow the German advance repaired. Two events were to mar the late 1940s and early 1950s: the former Dutch colonies of Java and Sumatra, taken by the Japanese at the outbreak of the war, were now run by a nationalist Republican government in Java that refused to recognize Dutch sovereignty. Following the failure of talks on Dutch control the troops were sent in; world opposition to this was strong, and after much condemnation and pressure the Dutch reluctantly handed over their colonies.

Back at home, tragedy struck on February 1, 1953 when an unusually high tide was pushed over Zeeland's sea defences by a westerly wind, flooding 40,000 acres of land and drowning over 1800 people. The response was to secure the area with the **Delta Project**, closing off the western part of the Scheldt and Maas estuaries with massive sea dykes. A brilliant and graceful piece of engineering, the main storm surge barrier on the Oosterschelde was finally completed in 1986.

Elsewhere rebuilding continued; in Amsterdam all the land projected in 1947 for use by the year 2000 was in fact used up by the "garden cities" of the dormitory suburbs by 1970, and the polder towns on the reclaimed stretches of Flevoland also expanded. But growth wasn't only physical: the social consciousness and radicalism of the 1960s reached the country early, and the word of the psychedelic revolution was quick to catch on. It was quick to fade, too, replaced by the cynicism of the 1970s, but one manifestation of the spread of radical thinking that had some tangible positive results was the **squatting movement**, which precipitated major riots in Amsterdam and other cities throughout the late 1960s and early 1970s. The squatters and other activists won considerable success in attempting to prevent the wholesale destruction of low cost urban housing, a move that would have turned the country's city centres into places where only the rich could afford to live.

Today, the country's finely balanced system of proportional representation forces almost continuous political compromise and debate, but brings little rapid change, politics and politicking seeming a bland business conducted between the three main parties, the **Protestant-Catholic CDA coalition**, the **Liberal VVD** and the **Socialist PvdA**.

A governmental system that has so effectively incorporated the disparate elements of a modern and diverse state – Catholic and Protestant, management and union, city and country, socialist and conservative – has earned the Netherlands a well-deserved reputation for comfortable complacency, and outbreaks of opposition, when they do appear, on such items as eco-issues, housing and racism, provoke a mad rush to the bargaining table.

NETHERLANDISH ART: AN INTRODUCTION

The following piece is the very briefest of introductions to the subject, designed to serve only as a quick reference on your way round the major galleries; for the reasons already given in "History", above, it includes reference to the early art of the whole region, rather than just The Netherlands – hence the title. For more in-depth and academic studies, see the recommendations in the "Books" listings, p.352. For where to find the paintings themselves, turn to the hit list at the end.

THE EARLY FLEMISH MASTERS

Until the sixteenth century the area now known as the Low Countries was in effect one country, the most artistically productive part of which was Flanders in modern Belgium, and it was there that the solid realist base of later Dutch painting developed. Today the works of these early Flemish painters, known as the **Flemish Primitives**, are relatively sparse in the Low Countries, and even in Belgium few collections are as complete as they might be – indeed, many ended up as the property of the ruling Habsburgs and were removed to Spain. Most major galleries do, however, have a few examples.

Jan van Eyck (1385–1441) is generally regarded as the originator of Low Countries painting, and has even been credited with the invention of oil painting itself – though it seems more likely that he simply perfected a new tech-

nique by thinning his paint with the recently discovered turpentine, thus making it more flexible. His fame partially stems from the fact that he was one of the first artists to sign his work – an action that indicates how highly his talent was regarded in his own time. Van Eyck's most famous work is still in the Low Countries, the altarpiece of St Baaf's Cathedral in Ghent, known as the *Adoration of the Mystic Lamb*. It was debatably painted with the help of his lesser-known brother, Hubert, and was revolutionary in its realism, for the first time using elements of native landscape in depicting Biblical themes. His work was also rich in a complex symbolism, whereby everyday objects take on a disguised, usually religious meaning, the nature of which has generated analysis and discussion ever since. Van Eyck's style and technique were to influence several generations of Low Countries artists.

Firmly in this Eyckian tradition were the **Master of Flemalle** (1387–1444) and **Rogier van der Weyden** (1400–64). The Flemalle master is a shadowy figure: some believe he was the teacher of van der Weyden, others that the two artists were in fact the same person. There are differences between the two, however. The Flemalle master's paintings are close to van Eyck's, whereas van der Weyden shows a more emotional and religious intensity; few of his more important paintings remain in Belgium. Van der Weyden influenced such painters as **Dieric Bouts** (1415–75), who was born in Haarlem but was active in Leuven (where his *Altarpiece of the Sacrament* remains in the St Pieterskerk) and is recognizable by his stiff, rather elongated figures and horrific subject matter against carefully drawn landscapes. **Petrus Christus** (d.1472), a contemporary of Bouts, was also influenced by van der Weyden and van Eyck: he was the next painter of importance to work in Bruges after van Eyck, and may have been his pupil. His portraits have a directness and simple clarity, but with the exception of a *Lamentation* in the Musée d'Art Ancien, Brussels, most of his masterpieces are now outside the Low Countries. **Hugo van der Goes** (d.1482) was the next Ghent master after van Eyck, most famous for the *Portinari Altarpiece* in Florence's Uffizi. After a short painting career, he died insane, and his late works have strong hints of his impending madness in their subversive use of space and implicit acceptance of the viewer's presence. Few doubt that **Hans Memling** (1440–94) was a pupil of van der Weyden. Active in Bruges throughout his life, he is best remembered for the pastoral charm of his landscapes and the quality of his portraiture, much of which survives on the rescued side panels of triptychs. The museum named after him in Bruges has an excellent survey of his work. **Gerhard David** (d.1523) moved to Bruges in 1484, and was the last of the great painters to work in that city, before it was overtaken in prosperity by Antwerp – which itself became the focus of a more Italianate school of art in the sixteenth century.

Hieronymus Bosch (1450–1516) lived for most of his life in Holland, though his style is linked to that of the Flanders painters (see below). His frequently reprinted religious allegories are filled with macabre visions of tortured people and grotesque beasts, and appear at first faintly unhinged, though it's now thought that these are visual representations of contemporary sayings, idioms and parables. While their interpretation is far from resolved, Bosch's paintings draw strongly on subconscious fears and archetypes, giving them a lasting, haunting fascination.

THE SIXTEENTH CENTURY

Meanwhile, there were movements to the north of Flanders. **Geertgen tot Sint Jans** "Little Gerard of the Brotherhood of St John" (d.1490), a student of **Albert van Ouwater**, had been working in **Haarlem**, initiating – in a strangely naive style – an artistic tradition in the city that would prevail throughout the seventeenth century. **Jan Mostaert** (1475–1555) took over after Geertgen's death, and continued to develop a style that diverged more and more from that of the southern provinces. **Lucas van Leyden** (1489–1533) was the first painter to effect real changes in northern painting. Born in Leiden, his bright colours and narrative technique were refreshingly new at the time, and he introduced a novel dynamism into what had become a rigidly formal treatment of devotional subjects. There was rivalry, of course. Eager to publicize Haarlem as the artistic capital of the northern Netherlands, Carel van Mander (see p.330) claimed Haarlem native **Jan van Scorel** (1495–1562) as the better painter, complaining, too, of Lucas's dandyish ways.

Certainly van Scorel's influence should not be underestimated. At this time every painter was expected to travel to Italy to view the works of Renaissance artists. When the Bishop of Utrecht became Pope Hadrian VI, he took van Scorel with him as court painter, giving him the opportunity to introduce Italian styles into what had been a completely independent tradition. Hadrian died soon after, and van Scorel returned north, combining the ideas he had picked up in Italy with Haarlem realism and passing them on to **Maerten van Heemskerk** (1498–1574), who later went off to Italy himself in 1532, staying there five years before returning to Haarlem.

Bruges' pre-eminence in the medieval Low Countries gradually began to give way to Antwerp, and the artists who worked there at the beginning of the sixteenth century combined the influence of the Italian painters with the domestic Flemish tradition. **Quentin Matsys** (1464–1530) introduced florid classical architectural detail and intricate landscape backgrounds to his works, influenced perhaps by the work of Leonardo da Vinci. As well as religious works, he painted portraits and genre scenes, all of which have recognizably Italian facets, and paved the way for the Dutch genre painters of later years. His follower, **Joos van Cleve** (c.1485–1540/1), painted in a similarly refined and realistic manner. **Jan Gossaert** (d. c.1523) made the pilgrimage to Italy, and his dynamic works are packed with detail, especially finely drawn classical architectural backdrops. He was the first Low Countries artist to introduce the subjects of classical mythology into his works, part of a steady trend through the period towards secular subject matter, which can also be seen in the work of **Joachim Patenier** (d.c.1524), who painted small landscapes of fantastic scenery.

The latter part of the sixteenth century was dominated by the work of **Pieter Bruegel the Elder** (c.1525–69), whose gruesome allegories and innovative interpretations of religious subjects are firmly placed in Low Countries settings. Most famous are his paintings of peasant lowlife, though he himself was well connected in court circles in Antwerp and, later, Brussels. **Pieter Aertsen** (c.1508–75) also worked in the peasant genre, adding aspects of the still life: his paintings often show a detailed kitchen scene in the foreground, with a religious episode going on behind. Towards the latter half of the century the stylized Italianate portrait was much in vogue, its chief exponents being **Adrien Key**, **Anthonis Mor** and **Frans Pourbus**.

RUBENS AND HIS FOLLOWERS

Pieter Paul Rubens (1577–1640) was the most influential Low Countries artist of the early seventeenth century and the most important exponent of Baroque painting in northern Europe. Born in Siegen, Westphalia, his parents returned to their native Antwerp when Rubens was a child. He entered the Antwerp Guild in 1598, became court painter to the Duke of Mantua in 1600, and until 1608 travelled extensively in Italy, absorbing the art of the High Renaissance and classical architecture. By the time of his return to Antwerp in 1608 he had acquired an enormous artistic vocabulary: the paintings of Caravaggio in particular were to influence his work strongly. His first major success was *The Raising of the Cross*, painted in 1610 and kept today in Antwerp cathedral. A large, dynamic work, it caused a sensation at the time, establishing Rubens' reputation and leading to a string of commissions that enabled him to set up his own studio. The *Descent from the Cross*, his next major work (also in the cathedral), consolidated this success: equally Baroque, it is nevertheless quieter and more restrained.

The division of labour in Rubens' studio, and the talent of the artists working there (who included Antony van Dyck and Jacob Jordaens) ensured a high output of excellent work. The degree to which Rubens personally worked on a canvas would vary – and would determine its price. From the early 1620s onwards he turned his hand to a plethora of themes and subjects – religious works, portraits, tapestry designs, landscapes, mythological scenes, ceiling paintings (including that of the Banqueting Hall in Whitehall, London – a commission for Charles I, by whom he was knighted) – each of which was handled with supreme vitality and virtuosity. From his Flemish antecedents he inherited an acute sense of light, and used it not to dramatize his subjects (a technique favoured by Caravaggio and other Italian artists), but in organic association with colour and form. The drama in his works comes from the tremendous animation of his characters. His large-scale allegorical works, especially, are packed with heaving, writhing figures that appear to tumble out from the canvas.

The energy of Rubens' paintings was reflected in his private life. In addition to his career as an artist, he also undertook diplomatic missions to Spain and England on behalf of the governors of Holland, and used the opportunities to study the works of other artists and – as in the case of Velázquez – to meet them personally. In the 1630s, gout began to hamper his activities, and from this time his painting became more domestic and meditative. Hélène Fourment, his second wife, was the subject of many portraits and served as a model for characters in his allegorical paintings, her figure epitomizing the buxom, well-rounded women found throughout his work.

Rubens' influence on the artists of the period was enormous. The huge output of his studio meant that his works were universally seen, and widely disseminated by the engravers he employed to copy his work. Chief among his followers was the portraitist **Antony van Dyck** (1599–1641), who worked in Rubens' studio from 1618, often taking on the depiction of religious figures in his master's works that required particular sensitivity and pathos. Like Rubens, he was born in Antwerp and travelled widely in Italy, though his initial work was influenced less by the Italian artists than by Rubens himself. Eventually van Dyck developed his own distinct style and technique, establishing himself as court painter to Charles I in England, and creating portraits of a nervous elegance that would influence the genre there for the next hundred and fifty years. Most of his great portraiture remains in England, though his best religious works – such as the *Crucifixion* in Mechelen cathedral and a *Lamentation* in Antwerp's Museum voor Schone Kunsten – can be found in Belgium. **Jacob Jordaens** (1593–1678) was also an Antwerp native who studied under Rubens. Although he was commissioned to complete several works left unfinished by Rubens at the time of his death, his robustly naturalistic works have an earthy – and sensuous – realism that's quite distinct in style and technique.

Other artists working in this part of the Low Countries during the early seventeenth century were also, understandably, greatly influenced by the output of Rubens' studio. **Gerhard Seghers** (1591–1651) specialized in painting flowers, usually around portraits or devotional figures painted by other artists, including Rubens himself.

Theodor Rombouts (1579–1637) was strongly influenced by Caravaggio following a trip to Italy, but changed his style to fall in line with that of Rubens when he returned from Antwerp from Holland. **Jacob van Oost the Elder** chose to live and work in Bruges: his delicate work embraces Dutch and Italian elements. **Frans Snyders** (1579–1657) took up the genre of the still life where Aertsen left off, amplifying his subject – food and drink – to even larger, more sumptuous canvases. He too was part of the Rubens art machine, painting animals and still life sections for the master's works.

THE DUTCH GOLDEN AGE

Carel van Mander (1548–1606) had a tremendous impact in Holland at the beginning of the sixteenth century. A Haarlem painter, art impresario, and one of the few chroniclers of the art of the Low Countries, his *Schilderboek* of 1604 put Flemish and Dutch traditions into context for the first time and specified the rules of fine painting. Examples of his own work are rare, but his followers were many, among them **Cornelis Cornelisz van Haarlem** (1562–1638), who produced elegant renditions of Biblical and mythical themes; and **Hendrik Goltzius** (1558–1616), who was a skilled engraver and an integral member of van Mander's Haarlem academy. These painters' enthusiasm for Italian art, combined with the influence of a late revival of Gothicism, resulted in works that combined Mannerist and classical elements. An interest in realism was also felt, and, for them, the subject became less important than the way in which it was depicted. Biblical stories became merely a vehicle whereby artists could apply their skills in painting the human body, landscapes, or copious displays of food – all of which served to break religion's stranglehold on art, and make legitimate a whole range of everyday subjects for the painter.

In Holland (and this was where the north and the south finally diverged) this break with tradition was compounded by the **Reformation**: the austere Calvinism that had supplanted the Catholic faith in the northern provinces had no use for images or symbols of devotion in its churches. Instead, painters catered to the public, and no longer visited Italy to learn their craft; the real giants of the seventeenth century – Hals, Rembrandt, Vermeer – stayed in the Low Countries all their lives. Another departure was

that painting split into more distinct categories – genre, portrait, landscape, etc – and artists tended (with notable exceptions) to confine themselves to one field throughout their careers. So began the greatest age of Dutch art.

HISTORICAL AND RELIGIOUS PAINTING

If Italy continued to hold sway in the Low Countries it was not through the Renaissance painters but rather via the fashionable new realism of Caravaggio. Many artists – Rembrandt for one – continued to portray classic subjects, but in a way that was totally at odds with the Mannerists' stylish flights of imagination. Though a solid Mannerist throughout his career, the Utrecht artist **Abraham Bloemaert** (1564–1651) encouraged these new ideas, and his students – **Gerard van Honthorst** (1590–1656), **Hendrik Terbrugghen** (1588–1629), and **Dirk van Baburen** (1590–1624) – formed the nucleus of the influential **Utrecht School**, which followed Caravaggio almost to the point of slavishness. Honthorst was perhaps the leading figure, learning his craft from Bloemaert and travelling to Rome, where he was nicknamed "Gerardo delle Notti" for his ingenious handling of light and shade. This was, however, to become in his later paintings more routine technique than inspired invention, and though a supremely competent artist, Honthorst remains somewhat discredited among critics today. Terbrugghen's reputation seems to have aged rather better: he soon forgot Caravaggio and developed a more personal style, his lighter, later work having a great impact on the young Vermeer. After the obligatory jaunt to Rome, Baburen shared a studio with Terbrugghen and produced some fairly original work – work which also had some influence on Vermeer – but few of his paintings survive today, and he is the least studied member of the group.

But it's **Rembrandt** who was considered the most original historical artist of the seventeenth century, painting religious scenes throughout his life. In the 1630s, the poet and statesman Constantijn Huygens procured for him his greatest commission – a series of five paintings of the Passion, beautifully composed and uncompromisingly realistic. Later, however, Rembrandt received fewer and fewer commissions, since his treatment of Biblical and historical subjects was far less dramatic than that of his contemporaries. It's significant that while the more conventional Jordaens, Honthorst and van Everdingen were busy decorating the Huis ten Bosch near The Hague for patron Stadholder Frederick Henry, Rembrandt was having his monumental *Conspiracy of Claudius Civilis* (completed for the new Amsterdam town hall) rejected – probably because it was thought too pagan an interpretation of what was an important symbolic event in Dutch history. **Aert van Gelder** (1645–1727), Rembrandt's last pupil and probably the only one to concentrate on historical painting, followed the style of his master closely, producing shimmering Biblical scenes well into the eighteenth century.

GENRE PAINTING

The term **genre** refers to scenes from everyday life, a subject that, with the decline of the church as patron, became popular in Holland by the mid-seventeenth century. Many painters devoted themselves solely to such work. Some genre paintings were simply non-idealized portrayals of common scenes, while others, by means of symbols or carefully disguised details, made moral entreaties to the viewer.

Among early seventeenth-century painters, **Hendrik Terbrugghen** and **Gerard Honthorst** spent much of their time on religious subjects, but also adapted the realism and strong chiaroscuro learned from Caravaggio to a number of tableaux of everyday life. **Frans Hals**, too, is better known as a portraitist, but his early genre paintings no doubt influenced his pupil, **Adriaen Brouwer** (1605–38), whose riotous tavern scenes were well received in their day and collected by, among others, Rubens and Rembrandt. Brouwer spent only a couple of years in Haarlem under Hals before returning to his native Flanders to influence the younger **David Teniers** (1610–90), who worked in Antwerp, later in Brussels. His earlier paintings are Brouwer-like peasant scenes, his later work more delicate and diverse, including *Kortegaardje* – guardroom scenes that show soldiers carousing. Like Brouwer, **Adriaen van Ostade** (1610–85) studied under Hals but chose to remain in Haarlem, skilfully painting groups of peasants and tavern brawls – though his later acceptance by the establishment led him to water down the realism he had learnt from Brouwer. He was teacher to his brother **Isaak**

(1621–49), who produced a large number of open-air peasant scenes, subtle combinations of genre and landscape work.

The English critic E. V. Lucas dubbed Teniers, Brouwer and Ostade "coarse and boorish" compared with **Jan Steen** (1625–79), who, along with Vermeer, is probably the most admired Dutch genre painter. You can see what he had in mind: Steen's paintings offer the same Rabelaisian peasantry in full fling, but they go their debauched ways in broad daylight, and nowhere do you see the filthy rogues in shadowy hovels favoured by Brouwer and Ostade. Steen offers more humour, too, as well as more moralizing, identifying with the hedonistic mob and reproaching them at the same time. Indeed, many of his pictures are illustrations of well-known proverbs of the time – popular epithets on the evils of drink or the transience of human existence that were supposed to teach as well as entertain.

Gerrit Dou (1613–75) was Rembrandt's Leiden contemporary and one of his first pupils. It's difficult to detect any trace of the master's influence in his work, however, Dou instead initiating a style of his own – tiny, minutely realized, and beautifully finished views of a kind of ordinary life that was decidedly more genteel than Brouwer's, or even Steen's for that matter. He was esteemed, above all, for his painstaking attention to detail: he would, it was said, sit in his studio for hours waiting for the dust to settle before starting work. Among his students, **Frans van Mieris** (1635–81) continued to produce highly finished portrayals of the Dutch bourgeoisie, as did **Gabriel Metsu** (1629–67) – perhaps Dou's greatest pupil – whose pictures often convey an overtly moral message. Another pupil of Rembrandt's, though a much later one, was **Nicholaes Maes** (1629–93), whose early paintings were almost entirely genre paintings, sensitively executed and again with a moralizing message. His later work shows the influence of a more refined style of portrait, which he had picked up in France.

As a native of Zwolle, **Gerard ter Borch** (1619–81) found himself far from all these Leiden/Rembrandt connections, and despite trips abroad to most of the artistic capitals of Europe, he remained very much a provincial painter all his life, depicting Holland's merchant class at play and becoming renowned for his curious doll-like figures and his enormous ability to capture the textures of different cloths. His domestic scenes were not unlike those of **Pieter de Hooch** (1629–after 1684), whose simple depictions of everyday life are deliberately unsentimental, and, for the first time, have little or no moral commentary. De Hooch's favourite trick was to paint darkened rooms with an open door leading through to a sunlit courtyard, a practice that, along with his trademark rusty red colour, makes his work easy to identify – and, at its best, exquisite. That said, his later pictures reflect the encroaching decadence of the Dutch republic: the rooms are more richly decorated, the arrangements more contrived and the subjects far less homely.

It was, however, **Jan Vermeer** (1632–75) who brought the most sophisticated methods to painting interiors, depicting the play of natural light on indoor surfaces with superlative skill; it's for this and the curious peace and intimacy of his pictures that he is best known. Another recorder of the better-heeled Dutch households, and, like de Hooch, without any overt moral tone, he is regarded (with Hals and Rembrandt) as one of the big three Dutch painters – though, he was, it seems, a slow worker, and only about forty small paintings can be attributed to him with any certainty. Living all his life in Delft, Vermeer is perhaps the epitome of the seventeenth-century Dutch painter – rejecting the pomp and ostentation of the High Renaissance to quietly record his contemporaries at home, painting for a public that demanded no more than that.

PORTRAITURE

Naturally, the ruling bourgeoisie of Holland's flourishing mercantile society wanted to put their success on record, and it's little wonder that portraiture was the best way for a young painter to make a living. **Michiel Jansz Miereveld** (1567–1641), court painter to Frederick Henry in The Hague, was the first real portraitist of the Dutch Republic, but it wasn't long before his stiff and rather conservative figures were superseded by the more spontaneous renderings of **Frans Hals** (1585–1666). Hals is perhaps best known for his "corporation-pictures" – portraits of the members of the Dutch civil guard regiments that had been formed in most larger towns while the threat of invasion by the Spanish was still imminent. These large group pieces demanded superlative technique, since the painter had to create a collection of

individual portraits while retaining a sense of the group, and accord prominence based on the importance of the sitter and the size of the payment each had made. Hals was particularly good at this, using innovative lighting effects, arranging his sitters subtly, and putting all the elements together in a fluid and dynamic composition. He also painted many individual portraits, making the ability to capture fleeting and telling expressions his trademark; his pictures of children are particularly sensitive. Later in life, his work became darker and more akin to that of Rembrandt.

Jan Cornelisz Verspronck (1597–1662) and **Bartholomeus van der Helst** (1613–70) were the other great Haarlem portraitists after Frans Hals – Verspronck recognizable by the smooth, shiny glow he always gave to his sitters' faces, van der Helst by a competent but unadventurous style. Of the two, van der Helst was the more popular, influencing a number of later painters and leaving Haarlem while still young to begin a solidly successful career as portrait painter to Amsterdam's burghers.

The reputation of **Rembrandt van Rijn** (1606–69) is still relatively recent – nineteenth-century connoisseurs preferred Gerrit Dou – but he is now justly regarded as one of the greatest and most versatile painters of all time. Born in Leiden, the son of a miller, he was apprenticed at an early age to **Jacob van Swanenburgh** – a then quite important, though uninventive, local artist. He shared a studio with **Jan Lievens**, a promising painter and something of a rival for a while (now all but forgotten), before going up to Amsterdam to study under the fashionable **Pieter Lastman**. Soon he was painting commissions for the city elite and an accepted member of their circle. The poet and statesman Constantijn Huygens acted as his agent, pulling strings to obtain all of Rembrandt's more lucrative jobs, and in 1634 he married Saskia van Ulenborch, daughter of the burgomeister of Leeuwarden and quite a catch for the still relatively humble artist. His self-portraits at the time show the confident face of security – on top of things and quite sure of where he's going.

Rembrandt would not always be the darling of the Amsterdam smart set, but his fall from grace was still some way off when he painted the *Night Watch* – a group portrait often associated with the artist's decline in popularity. Although Rembrandt's fluent arrangement of his subjects was totally original, there's no evidence that the military company who commissioned the painting were anything but pleased with the result. More likely culprits are the artist's later pieces, whose obscure lighting and psychological insight took the conservative Amsterdam burghers by surprise. His patrons were certainly not sufficiently enthusiastic about his work to support his taste for art collecting and his expensive house on Jodenbreestraat, and in 1656 possibly the most brilliant artist the city would ever know was declared bankrupt, dying thirteen years later, as his last self-portraits show, a broken and embittered old man. Throughout his career Rembrandt maintained a large studio, and his influence pervaded the next generation of Dutch painters. Some – Dou, Maes – more famous for their genre work, have already been mentioned. Others turned to portraiture.

Govert Flinck (1615–60) was perhaps Rembrandt's most faithful follower, and he was, ironically, given the job of decorating Amsterdam's new town hall after his teacher had been passed over. He died before he could execute his designs, and Rembrandt was one of several artists commissioned to paint them – though his contribution was removed shortly afterwards. The work of **Ferdinand Bol** (1616–80) was so heavily influenced by Rembrandt that for a long time art historians couldn't tell the two apart. Most of the pitifully slim extant work of **Carel Fabritius** (1622–54) was portraiture, but he too died young, before he could properly realise his promise as perhaps the most gifted of all Rembrandt's students. Generally regarded as the teacher of Vermeer, he forms a link between the two masters, combining Rembrandt's technique with his own practice of painting figures against a dark background, prefiguring the lighting and colouring of the Delft painter.

LANDSCAPES

Aside from Bruegel, whose depictions of his native surroundings make him the first true Low Countries landscape painter, **Gillis van Coninxloo** (1544–1607) stands out as the earliest Dutch landscapist. He imbued the native scenery with elements of fantasy, painting the richly wooded views he had seen on his travels around Europe as backdrops to Biblical scenes. In the early seventeenth century, **Hercules Seghers** (1590–1638), apprenticed to Coninxloo, carried on his mentor's style of depicting forested and mountainous landscapes, some real, others not: his work is scarce but is believed to have had considerable impact on the landscape work of Rembrandt. **Esaias van der Velde**'s (1591–1632) quaint and unpretentious scenes show the first real affinity with the Dutch countryside, but – though his influence, too, was great – he was soon overtaken in stature by his pupil **Jan van Goyen** (1596–1656), a remarkable painter who belongs to the so-called "tonal phase" of Dutch landscape painting. Van Goyen's early pictures were highly coloured and close to those of his teacher, but it didn't take him long to develop a markedly personal touch, using tones of greens, browns and greys to lend everything a characteristic translucent haze. His paintings are, above all, of nature, and if he included figures it was merely for the sake of scale. Neglected until a little over a century ago, his fluid and rapid brushwork became more acceptable as the Impressionists rose in stature.

Another "tonal" painter and a native of Haarlem, **Salomon van Ruisdael** (1600–70) was also directly affected by van der Velde, and his simple, atmospheric, though not terribly adventurous, landscapes were for a long time consistently confused with those of van Goyen. More esteemed is his nephew, **Jacob van Ruisdael** (1628–82), generally considered the greatest of all Dutch landscapists, whose fastidiously observed views of quiet flatlands dominated by stormy skies were to influence European painters' impressions of nature right up to the nineteenth century. (Constable, certainly, acknowledged a debt to him.) Ruisdael's foremost pupil was **Meindert Hobbema** (1638–1709), who followed the master faithfully, sometimes even painting the same views (his *Avenue at Middelharnis* may be familiar).

Nicholas Berchem (1620–83) and **Jan Both** (1618–52) were the "Italianizers" of Dutch landscapes. They studied in Rome and were influenced by Claude, taking back to Holland rich, golden views of the world, full of steep gorges and hills, picturesque ruins and wandering shepherds. **Allart van Everdingen** (1621–75) had a similar approach, but his subject matter stemmed from travels in Scandinavia, which, after his return to Holland, he reproduced in all its mountainous glory.

Aelbert Cuyp (1620–91), on the other hand, stayed in Dordrecht all his life, painting what was probably the favourite city skyline of Dutch landscapists. He inherited the warm tones of the Italianizers, and his pictures are always suffused with a deep, golden glow.

Of a number of **specialist seventeenth-century painters** who can be included here, **Paulus Potter** (1625–54) is rated as the best painter of **domestic animals**. He produced a fair amount of work in a short lifetime, most reputed being his lovingly executed pictures of cows and horses. The accurate rendering of **architectural features** also became a specialized field, of which **Pieter Saenredam** (1597–1665), with his finely realized paintings of Dutch church interiors, is the most widely known exponent. **Emanuel de Witte** (1616–92) continued in the same vein, though his churches lack the spartan crispness of those of Saenredam. **Gerrit Berckheyde** (1638–98) worked in Haarlem soon after, but limited his views to the outside of buildings, producing variations on the same scenes around town.

In the seventeenth century another thriving category of painting was the **still life**, in which objects were gathered together to remind the viewer of the transience of human life and the meaninglessness of all worldly pursuits: often a skull would be joined by a book, a pipe or a goblet, and some half-eaten food. Again, two Haarlem painters dominated this field: **Pieter Claesz** (1598–1660) and **Willem Heda** (1594–1680), who confined themselves almost entirely to these carefully arranged groups of objects.

THE EIGHTEENTH CENTURY

With the demise of Holland's economic boom, the quality – and originality – of Dutch painting began to decline. The delicacy of some of the classical seventeenth-century painters was replaced by finicky still lifes and minute studies of flowers, or finely finished portraiture and religious scenes, as in the work of **Adrian van der Werff** (1659–1722). Of the era's big names, **Gerard de Lairesse** (1640–1711) spent most of his time decorating the splendid civic halls and palaces that were going up all over the place, and, like the buildings he worked on, his style and influences were French. **Jacob de Wit** (1695–1754) continued where Lairesse left off, receiving more church commissions as

Catholicism was allowed out of the closet. The period's only painter of any true renown was **Cornelis Troost** (1697–1750), who, although he didn't produce anything really new, painted competent portraits and some neat, faintly satirical pieces that have since earned him the title of "The Dutch Hogarth". Cosy interiors also continued to prove popular, and the Haarlem painter **Wybrand Hendriks** (1744–1831) satisfied demand with proficient examples.

French influence was dominant in the area that was to become Belgium. Artists such as **Jan Joseph Horemans I** and **Balthasar van den Bossche** took the Flemish genre painting of the previous century and made it palatable for Parisian tastes. Towards the end of the century neo-Classicism became the vogue, and the entire period was marked by the weakening of domestic tradition in favour of external influences. **Laurent Delvaux** (1696–1778) was also an important figure during this period, a Flemish sculptor who produced a large number of works for Belgian churches, including the pulpit of Ghent's cathedral and other pieces in Brussels.

THE NINETEENTH CENTURY

Johann Barthold Jongkind (1819–91) was the first great artist to emerge from nineteenth-century Holland, painting landscapes and seascapes that were to influence Monet and the early Impressionists. He spent most of his life in France and his work was exhibited in Paris with the Barbizon painters, though he owed less to them than to the landscapes of van Goyen and the seventeenth-century "tonal" artists.

Jongkind's work was a logical precursor to the art of the **Hague School**, a group of painters based in and around that city between 1870 and 1900 who tried to re-establish a characteristically Dutch national school of painting. They produced atmospheric studies of the dunes and polderlands around The Hague, pictures that are characterised by grey, rain-filled skies, windswept seas, and silvery, flat beaches – and that, for some, verge on the sentimental. **J. H. Weissenbruch** (1824–1903) was a founding member, a specialist in low, flat beach scenes dotted with stranded boats. The banker-turned-artist **H. W. Mesdag** (1831–1915) did the same but with more skill than imagination, while **Jacob Maris** (1837–99), one of three artist brothers, was perhaps the most typical Hague School painter, with his rural and sea scenes dominated by gloomy chasing skies. His brother, **Matthijs** (1839–1917), was less predictable, ultimately tiring of his colleagues' interest in straight observation and going to London to design windows, while **Willem** (1844–1910), the youngest, is best known for his small, unpretentious studies of nature.

Anton Mauve (1838–88) is a better known artist, an exponent of soft, pastel landscapes and an early teacher of van Gogh. Profoundly influenced by the French Barbizon painters – Corot, Millet *et al* – he went to Hilversum in 1885 to set up his own group, which became known as the "Dutch Barbizon". **Jozef Israëls** (1826–1911) has often been likened to Millet, though it's generally agreed that he had more in common with the Impressionists, and his best pictures are his melancholy portraits and interiors. Lastly, **Johan Bosboom**'s (1817–91) church interiors may be said to sum up the nostalgia of the Hague School – shadowy works, populated by figures in seventeenth-century dress, that seem to yearn for Holland's Golden Age.

Vincent van Gogh (1853–90) was one of the least "Dutch" of Dutch artists, and he lived out most of his relatively short painting career in Belgium and France. After countless studies of peasant life in his native North Brabant – studies which culminated in the sombre *Potato Eaters* – and a spell in the industrial Borinage area of southern Belgium, he went to live in Paris with his art-dealer brother, Theo. There, under the influence of the Impressionists, he lightened his palette, following the pointillist work of Seurat and "trying to render intense colour and not a grey harmony". Two years later he went south to Arles, the "land of blue tones and gay colours", and, struck by the harsh Mediterranean light, his characteristic style began to develop. A disastrous attempt to live with Gauguin, and the much-publicized episode when he cut off part of his ear and presented it to a woman in a nearby brothel, led eventually to committal to an asylum at St-Remy, where he produced some of his most famous, and most Expressionistic, canvases – strongly coloured and with the paint thickly, almost frantically, applied.

Like van Gogh, **Jan Toorop** (1858–1928) went through multiple artistic changes, though he didn't need to travel the world to do so; he radically adapted his technique from a fairly conventional pointillism through a tired Expressionism to Symbolism with an Art Nouveau feel. Roughly contemporary, **G. H. Breitner** (1857–1923) was a better painter, and one who refined his style rather than changed it. His snapshot-like impressions of his beloved Amsterdam figure among his best work and offered a promising start to the new century.

THE TWENTIETH CENTURY

Most of the trends in the visual arts of the early twentieth century found their way to Holland at one time or another: of many minor names, **Jan Sluyters** (1881–1957) was the Dutch pioneer of Cubism. But only one movement was specifically Dutch – **de Stijl** (literally "the Style").

Piet Mondrian (1872–1944) was de Stijl's leading figure, developing the realism he had learned from the Hague School painters – via Cubism, which he criticized for being too cowardly to depart totally from representation – into a complete abstraction of form which he called **neo-plasticism**. He was something of a mystic, and this was to some extent responsible for the direction that de Stijl – and his paintings – took: canvases painted with grids of lines and blocks made up of the three primary colours and white, black and grey. Mondrian believed this freed the work of art from the vagaries of personal perception, and made it possible to obtain what he called "a true vision of reality".

De Stijl took other forms, too: there was a magazine of the same name, and the movement introduced new concepts into every aspect of design, from painting to interior design to architecture. But in all these media lines were kept simple, colours bold and clear. **Theo van Doesburg** (1883–1931) was a de Stijl co-founder and major theorist: his work is similar to that of Mondrian except for the noticeable absence of thick, black borders and the diagonals that he introduced into his work, calling his paintings "contra-compositions" – which, he said, were both more dynamic and more in touch with twentieth-century life. **Bart van der Leck** (1876–1958) was the third member of the circle, identifiable by white canvases covered by seemingly randomly placed interlocking coloured triangles.

Mondrian split with de Stijl in 1925, going on to attain new artistic extremes of clarity and soberness before moving to New York in the 1940s and producing atypically exuberant works such as *Victory Boogie Woogie* – so named because of the artist's love of jazz.

During and after de Stijl, a number of other movements flourished, though their impact was not so great and their influence largely confined to the Low Countries. The Expressionist **Bergen School** was probably the most localized, its best-known exponent **Charley Toorop** (1891–1955), daughter of Jan, who developed a distinctively glaring but strangely sensitive realism. **De Ploeg** (The Plough), centred in Groningen, was headed by **Jan Wiegers** (1893–1959) and influenced by Kirchner and the German Expressionists; the group's artists set out to capture the uninviting landscapes around their native town, and produced violently coloured canvases that hark back to van Gogh. Another group, known as the **Magic Realists**, surfaced in the 1930s, painting quasi-surrealistic scenes that, according to their leading light, **Carel Willink** (b.1900), reveal "a world stranger and more dreadful in its haughty impenetrability than the most terrifying nightmare".

Postwar Dutch art began with CoBrA: a loose grouping of like-minded painters from Denmark, Belgium and Holland, whose name derives from the initial letters of their respective capital cities. Their first exhibition, at Amsterdam's Stedelijk Museum in 1949, provoked a huge uproar, at the centre of which was **Karel Appel** (b.1921), whose brutal Abstract Expressionist pieces, plastered with paint inches thick, were, he maintained, necessary for the era – indeed, inevitable reflections of it. "I paint like a barbarian in a barbarous age," he claimed. In the graphic arts the most famous twentieth-century figure is **M. C. Escher** (1898–1970).

As for **today**, there's as vibrant an art scene as there ever was, best exemplified in Amsterdam by the rotating exhibitions of the Stedelijk or the nearby Overholland Museum, and some of the numerous private Amsterdam galleries. Of contemporary Dutch artists, look out for the abstract work of **Edgar Fernhout** and **Ad Dekkers**; the reliefs of **Jan Schoonhoven**; the multi-media productions of **Jan Dibbets**; the glowering realism of **Marlene Dumas**; the imprecisely coloured geometric designs of **Rob van Koningsbruggen**; the smeary Expressionism of **Toon Verhoef**; and the exuberant figures of **Rene Daniels** – to name only the most important figures.

DUTCH GALLERIES: A HIT LIST

In **Amsterdam**, the *Rijksmuseum* gives a complete overview of Dutch art up to the end of the nineteenth century, in particular the work of Rembrandt, Hals, and the major artists of the Golden Age; the *Van Gogh Museum* is best for the Impressionists and, of course, van Gogh; and, for twentieth-century and contemporary Dutch art, there's the *Stedelijk*. Within easy reach of the city, the *Frans Hals Museum* in **Haarlem** holds some of the best work of Hals and the Haarlem School; also in Haarlem, the *Teyler's Museum* is strong on eighteenth- and nineteenth-century Dutch works. In **Leiden**, the *Lakenhal* has works by, among others, local artists Dou and Rembrandt, and the *Centraal* in **Utrecht** has paintings by van Scorel and the Utrecht School. Also in Utrecht, the *Catherine Convent Museum* boasts an excellent collection of works by Flemish artists and by Hals and Rembrandt.

Further afield, **The Hague**'s *Gemeente Museum* owns the country's largest set of Mondrians, and its *Mauritshuis* collection contains works by Rembrandt, Vermeer and others of the era. The *Boymans van Beuningen Museum* in **Rotterdam** has a weighty stock of Flemish primitives and surrealists, as well as works by Rembrandt and other seventeenth-century artists; and nearby **Dordrecht**'s *Municipal Museum* offers an assortment of seventeenth-century paintings that includes work by Aelbert Cuyp, and later canvases by the Hague School and Breitner.

The *Kroller-Muller Museum*, just outside **Arnhem**, is probably the country's finest modern art collection, and has a superb collection of van Goghs; a little further east, **Enschede**'s *Rijksmuseum Twenthe* has quality works from the Golden Age to the twentieth century.

HOLLAND IN FICTION

A fair amount of Dutch literature has been translated into English in recent years, notably the work of Cees Nooteboom, Marga Minco, Harry Mulisch and Simon Carmiggelt. There's also, of course, English-language fiction set in Amsterdam or the Netherlands, of which the detective writer Nicolas Freeling is perhaps the best-known exponent. And for variety – and a contemporay slant – we've also included a short piece by Maria Stahlie, first published in the Dutch English-language publication, *The Magazine*.

SIMON CARMIGGELT

Humour is a frequent theme of Dutch literature, and Simon Carmiggelt was one of the country's best-loved humorous writers – and a true poet of Amsterdam in his own way. He moved to the capital during the war, working as a production manager and journalist on the then illegal newspaper, *Het Parool*. In 1946, he started writing a daily column in the paper, entitled *Kronkel*, meaning "twist" or "kink". It was an almost immediate success, and he continued to write his *Kronkels* for several decades, in the end turning out almost 10,000. They're a unique genre – short, usually humorous anecdotes of everyday life, with a strong undercurrent of melancholy and a seriousness at their heart. They concern ordinary people, poignantly observed with razor-sharp – but never cruel – wit and intelligence. Some of the strongest have been bundled together in anthologies, two of which – *A Dutchman's Slight Adventures* (1966) and *I'm Just Kidding* (1972) – were translated into English. Simon Carmiggelt died in 1989.

CORNER

In a café in the Albert Cuypstraat, where the open-air market pulses with sounds and colour, I ran into my friend Ben.

"Did you know Joop Groenteman?" he asked.

"You mean the one who sold fruit?" I replied.

"Yes. You heard about his death?"

I nodded. A fishmonger had told me. "It's a shame," said Ben. "A real loss for the market. He had a nice stall – always polished his fruit. And he had that typical Amsterdam sense of humour that seems to be disappearing. He'd say "Hi" to big people and "Lo" to little ones. If somebody wanted to buy two apples, he'd ask where the party was. No one was allowed to pick and choose his fruit. Joop handed it out from behind the plank. Somebody asked him once if he had a plastic bag, and he said, 'I got false teeth. Ain't that bad enough?' He never lost his touch, not even in the hospital."

"Did you go see him there?" I enquired.

"Yes, several times," Ben said. "Once his bed was empty. On the pillow lay a note: 'Back in two hours. Put whatever you brought on the bed.' He had to go on a diet because he was too fat. They weighed him every day. One morning he tied a portable radio around his waist with a rope, put his bathrobe over it, and got on the scale. To the nurse's alarm he'd suddenly gained eight pounds. That was his idea of fun in the hospital. During one visit I asked him when he'd get out. He said, 'Oh, someday soon, either through the front door or the back.'"

Ben smiled sadly.

"He died rather unexpectedly," he resumed. "There was an enormous crowd at his funeral. I was touched by the sight of all his friends from the market standing round the grave with their hats on and each one of them shovelling three spadesful of earth on to his coffin. Oh well, he at least attained the goal of his life."

"What goal?" I asked.

"The same one every open-air merchant has," Ben answered, "a place on a corner. If you're on a corner, you sell more. But it's awfully hard to get a corner place."

"Joop managed it, though?"

"Yes – but not in the Albert Cuyp," said Ben. "That corner place was a sort of obsession to him. He knew his chance was practically nil. So then he decided that if he couldn't get one while he was alive, he'd make sure of it when he died. Every time the collector for the burial insurance came along, he'd say 'Remember, I want a corner grave.' But when he did die, there wasn't a single corner to be had. Well, that's not quite right. It just happened that there was one corner with a stone to the memory of someone who had died in the furnaces of a concentration camp. Nobody was really buried there. And the cemetery people gave permission to have the stone placed somewhere else and to let Joop have that plot. So he finally got what he wanted. A place on the corner."

HERRING-MAN

It was morning, and I paused to buy a herring at one of those curious legged vending carts that stand along Amsterdam's canals.

"Onions?" asked the white-jacketed herring-man. He was big and broad-shouldered, and his hair was turning grey – a football believer, by the looks of him, who never misses Sunday in the stadium.

"No onions," I answered.

Two other men were standing there eating. They wore overalls and were obviously fellow-workers.

"There's them that take onions, and them that don't," one of the men said tolerantly. The herring-man nodded.

"Take me, now, I never eat pickles with 'em," said the other in the coquettish tone of a girl revealing some little charm that she just happens to possess.

"Give me another, please," I said.

The herring-man cut the fish in three pieces and reached with his glistening hand into the dish of onions.

"No, no onions," I said.

He smiled his apology. "Excuse me. My mind was wandering," he said.

The men in overalls also ordered another round and then began to wrangle about some futility or other on which they disagreed. They were still at it after I had paid and proceeded to a café just across from the herring-cart, where I sat down at a table by the window. For Dutchmen they talked rather strenuously with their hands. A farmer once told me that when the first cock begins to crow early in the morning, all the other roosters in the neighbourhood immediately raise their voices, hoping to drown him out. Most males are cut from the same cloth.

"What'll it be?" asked the elderly waitress in the café.

"Coffee." As she was getting it a fat, slovenly creature came in. Months ago she had had her hair dyed straw yellow, but later had become so nostalgic for her own natural brown that her skull was now dappled with two colours.

"Have you heard?" she asked.

"What?"

"The herring-man's son ran into a streetcar on his motorbike yesterday," she said, "and now he's good and dead. The docs at the hospital couldn't save him. They came to tell his pa about a half an hour ago."

The elderly waitress served my coffee.

"How awful," she said.

I looked across the street. The overalled quarrellers were gone, and the broad, strong herring-man stood cleaning his fish with automatic expertness.

"The kid was just seventeen," said the fat woman. "He was learning to be a pastry cook. Won third prize at the food show with his chocolate castle."

"Those *motorbikes* are rotten things," the waitress said.

"People are mysterious," a friend of mine once wrote, and as I thought of those words I suddenly remembered the onions the herring-man nearly gave me with my second fish, his smiling apology: "My mind was wandering."

GENIUS

The little café lay on a broad, busy thoroughfare in one of the new sections of Amsterdam. The barkeeper-host had only one guest: an ancient man who sat amiably behind his empty genever glass. I placed my order and added, "Give grandfather something, too."

"You've got one coming," called the barkeeper. The old man smiled and tipped me a left-handed military salute, his fingers at his fragile temple. Then he got up, walked over to me, and asked, "Would you be interested in a chance on a first-class smoked sausage, guaranteed weight two pounds?"

"I certainly would be," I replied.

"It just costs a quarter, and the drawing will take place next Saturday," he said.

I fished out twenty-five cents and put it on the bar, and in return he gave me a piece of cardboard on which the number 79 was written in ink.

"A number with a tail," he said. "Lucky for you."

He picked up the quarter, put on his homburg hat, and left the café with a friendly "Good afternoon, gentlemen." Through the window I saw him unlocking an old bicycle. Then, wheeling his means of transport, he disappeared from view.

"How old is he?" I asked.

"Eighty-six."

"And he still rides a bicycle?"

The barkeeper shook his head.

"No," he replied, "but he has to cross over, and it's a busy street. He's got a theory that traffic can see someone with a bicycle in his hand better than someone without a bicycle. So that's the why and the wherefore. When he gets across, he parks the hike and locks it up, and then the next day he's got it all ready to walk across again."

I thought it over.

"Not a bad idea," I said.

"Oh, he's all there, that one," said the barkeeper. "Take that lottery, now. He made it up himself. I guess he sells about a hundred chances here every week. That's twenty-five guilders. And he only has to fork over one sausage on Saturday evening. Figure it out for yourself."

I did so, cursorily. He really got his money's worth out of that sausage, no doubt of it.

"And he runs the drawing all by himself," the barkeeper went on. "Clever as all get out. Because if a customer says, 'I've bought a lot of chances from you, but I never win,' you can bet your boots he *will* win the very next Saturday. The old man takes care that he does. Gets the customer off his neck for a good long time. Pretty smart, huh?"

I nodded and said, "He must have been a businessman?"

"Well no. He was in the navy. They've paid him a pension for ages and ages. He's costing them a pretty penny."

All of a sudden I saw the old man on the other side of the street. He locked his bicycle against a wall and wandered away.

"He can get home from there without crossing any more streets," said the barkeeper.

I let him fill my glass again.

"I gave him a drink, but I didn't see him take it," I remarked.

The barkeeper nodded.

"He's sharp as tacks about that, too," he said. "Here's what he does. He's old and spry, and nearly everybody buys him something. But he never drinks more than two a day. So I write all the free ones down for him." He glanced at a notepad that lay beside the cash register. "Let's

see. Counting the one from you, he's a hundred and sixty-seven to the good."

CEES NOOTEBOOM

Cees Nooteboom is one of Holland's best-known writers. He published his first novel in 1955, but only really came to public attention after the publication of his third novel, *Rituals*, in 1980. The central theme of all his work is the phenomenon of time: *Rituals* in particular is about the passing of time and the different ways of controlling the process. Inni Wintrop, the main character, is an outsider, a "dilettante" as he describes himself. The book is almost entirely set in Amsterdam, and although it describes the inner life of Inni himself, it also paints a vivid picture of the decaying city. Each section details a decade of Inni's life; the one reprinted below describes an encounter from his forties.

RITUALS

There were days, thought Inni Wintrop, when it seemed as if a recurrent, fairly absurd phenomenon were trying to prove that the world is an absurdity that can best be approached with nonchalance, because life would otherwise become unbearable.

There were days, for instance, when you kept meeting cripples, days with too many blind people, days when you saw three times in succession a left shoe lying by the roadside. It seemed as if all these things were trying to mean something but could not. They left only a vague sense of unease, as if somewhere there existed a dark plan for the world that allowed itself to be hinted at only in this clumsy way.

The day on which he was destined to meet Philip Taads, of whose existence he had hitherto been unaware, was the day of the three doves. The dead one, the live one, and the dazed one, which could not possibly have been one and the same, because he had seen the dead one first. These three, he thought later, had made an attempt at annunciation that had succeeded insofar as it had made the encounter with Taads the Younger more mysterious.

It was now 1973, and Inni had turned forty in a decade he did not approve of. One ought not, he felt, to live in the second half of any century, and this particular century was altogether bad.

There was something sad and at the same time ridiculous about all these fading years piling on top of one another until at last the millennium arrived. And they contained a contradiction, too: in order to reach the hundred, and in this case the thousand, that had to be completed, one had to add them up; but the feeling that went with the process seemed to have more to do with subtraction. It was as if no one, especially not Time, could wait for those ever dustier, ever higher figures finally to be declared void by a revolution of a row of glittering, perfectly shaped noughts, whereupon they would be relegated to the scrap heap of history. The only people apparently still sure of anything in these days of superstitious expectation were the Pope, the sixth of his name already, a white-robed Italian with an unusually tormented face that faintly resembled Eichmann's, and a number of terrorists of different persuasions, who tried in vain to anticipate the great witches' cauldron. The fact that he was now forty no longer in itself bothered Inni very much.

"Forty," he said, "is the age at which you have to do everything for the third time, or else you'll have to start training to be a cross-tempered old man," and he had decided to do the latter.

After Zita, he had had a long-lasting affair with an actress who had finally, in self-preservation, turned him out of the house like an old chair.

"What I miss most about her," he said to his friend the writer, "is her absence. These people are never at home. You get addicted to that."

He now lived alone and intended to keep it that way. The years passed, but even this was noticeable only in photographs. He bought and sold things, was not addicted to drugs, smoked less than one packet of Egyptian cigarettes a day, and drank neither more nor less than most of his friends.

This was the situation on the radiant June morning when, on the bridge between the Herenstraat and the Prinsenstraat, a dove flew straight at him as if to bore itself into his heart. Instead, it smashed against a car approaching from the Prinsengracht. The car drove on and the dove was left lying in the street, a gray and dusty, suddenly silly-looking little thing. A blonde-haired girl got off her bicycle and went up to the dove at the same time as Inni.

"Is it dead, do you think?" she asked.

He crouched down and turned the bird onto its back. The head did not turn with the rest of the body and continued to stare at the road surface.

"Finito," said Inni.

The girl put her bike away.

"I daren't pick it up," she said, "Will you?"

She used the familiar form of you. As long as they still do that, I am not yet old, thought Inni, picking up the dove. He did not like doves. They were not a bit like the image he used to have of the Holy Ghost, and the fact that all those promises of peace had never come to anything was probably their fault as well. Two white, softly cooing doves in the garden of a Tuscan villa, that was all right, but the gray hordes marching across the Dam Square with spurs on their boots (their heads making those idiotic mechanical pecking movements) could surely have nothing to do with a Spirit which had allegedly chosen that particular shape in which to descend upon Mary.

"What are you going to do with it?" asked the girl.

Inni looked around and saw on the bridge a wooden skip belonging to the Council. He went up to it. It was full of sand. Gently he laid the dove in it. The girl had followed him. An erotic moment. Man with dead dove, girl with bike and blue eyes. She was beautiful.

"Don't put it in there," she said. "The workmen will chuck it straight into the canal."

What does it matter whether it rots away in sand or in water, thought Inni, who often claimed he would prefer to be blown up after his death. But this was not the moment to hold a discourse on transience.

"Are you in a hurry?" he asked.

"No."

"Give me that bag then." From her handlebar hung a plastic bag, one from the Athenaeum Book Store.

"What's in there?"

"A book by Jan Wolkers."

"It can go in there then," said Inni. "There's no blood."

He put the dove in the bag.

"Jump on the back."

He took her bike without looking at her and rode off.

"Hey," she said. He heard her rapid footsteps and felt her jumping on the back of the bike. In the shop windows he caught brief glimpses of something that looked like happiness. Middle-aged gentleman on girl's bicycle, girl in jeans and white sneakers on the back.

He rode down the Prinsengracht to the Haarlemmerdijk and from a distance saw the barriers of the bridge going down. They got off, and as the bridge slowly rose, they saw the second dove. It was sitting inside one of the open metal supports under the bridge, totally unconcerned as it allowed itself to be lifted up like a child on the Ferris wheel.

For a moment Inni felt an impulse to take the dead dove out of the plastic bag and lift it up like a peace offering to its slowly ascending living colleague, but he did not think the girl would like it. And besides, what would be the meaning of such a gesture? He shuddered, as usual not knowing why. The dove came down again and vanished invulnerably under the asphalt. They cycled on, to the Westerpark. With her small, brown hands, the girl dug a grave in the damp, black earth, somewhere in a corner.

"Deep enough?"

"For a dove, yes."

He laid the bird, which was now wearing its head like a hood on its back, into the hole. Together they smoothed the loose earth on top of it.

"Shall we go and have a drink?" he asked.

"All right."

Something in this minimal death, either the death itself or the summary ritual surrounding it, had made them allies. Something now had to happen, and if this something had anything to do with death, it would not be obvious. He cycled along the Nassaukade. She was not heavy. This was what pleased him most about his strange life – that when he had gotten up that morning, he had not known that he would now be cycling here with a girl at his back, but that such a possibility was always there. It gave him, he thought, something invincible. He looked at the faces of the men in the oncoming cars, and he knew that his life, in its absurdity, was right. Emptiness, loneliness, anxiety – these were the drawbacks – but there were also compensations, and this was one of them. She was humming softly and then fell silent. She said suddenly, as if she had taken a decision, "This is where I live."

Translated by Adrienne Dixon;
© Louisiana State University Press, 1983.

RUDI VAN DANTZIG

Rudi van Dantzig is one of Holland's most famous choreographers, and was, until 1991, artistic director of the Dutch National Ballet. *For a Lost Soldier*, published in 1986, is his debut novel, an almost entirely autobiographical account of his experiences as a child during the war years. It's an extremely well-written novel, convincingly portraying the confusion and loneliness of the approximately 50,000 Dutch children evacuated to foster families during the hunger winter. The novel's leading character is Jeroen, an eleven-year-old boy from Amsterdam who is sent away to live with a family in Friesland. During the Liberation celebrations, he meets an American soldier, Walt, with whom he has a brief sexual encounter; Walt disappears a few days later. The extract below details Jeroen's desperate search for Walt shortly after his return to Amsterdam.

FOR A LOST SOLDIER

I set out on a series of reconnoitring expeditions through Amsterdam, tours of exploration that will take me to every corner. On a small map I look up the most important streets to see how I can best fan out to criss-cross the town, then make plans on pieces of paper showing exactly how the streets on each of my expeditions join up and what they are called. To make doubly sure I also use abbreviations: H.W. for Hoofdweg, H.S. for Haarlemmerstraat. The pieces of paper are carefully stored away inside the dust-jacket of a book, but I am satisfied that even if somebody found the notes, they wouldn't be able to make head or tail of them. It is a well-hidden secret.

For my first expedition I get up in good time. I yawn a great deal and act as cheerfully as I can to disguise the paralysing uncertainty that is governing my every move.

"We're going straight to the field, Mum, we're going to build a hut," but she is very busy and scarcely listens.

"Take care and don't be back too late."

The street smells fresh as if the air has been scrubbed with soap. I feel dizzy with excitement and as soon as I have rounded the corner I start to run towards the bridge. Now it's beginning, and everything is sure to be all right, all my waiting and searching is about to come to an end; the solution lies hidden over there, somewhere in the clear light filling the streets.

The bright air I inhale makes me feel that I am about to burst. I want to sing, shout, cheer myself hoarse.

I have marked my piece of paper, among a tangle of crossing and twisting lines, with H.W., O.T., W.S.: Hoofdweg, Overtoom, Weteringschans.

The Hoofdweg is close by, just over the bridge. It is the broad street we have to cross when we go to the swimming baths. I know the gloomy houses and the narrow, flowerless gardens from the many times I've walked by in other summers, towel and swimming trunks rolled under my arm. But beyond that, and past Mercatorplein, Amsterdam is unknown territory to me, ominous virgin land.

The unfamiliar streets make me hesitate, my excitement seeps away and suddenly I feel unsure and tired. The town bewilders me: shops with queues outside, people on bicycles carrying bags, beflagged streets in the early morning sun, squares where wooden platforms have been put up for neighbourhood celebrations, whole districts with music pouring out of loudspeakers all day. An unsolvable jigsaw puzzle. Now and then I stop in sheer desperation, study my hopelessly inadequate piece of paper, and wonder if it would not be much better to give up the attempt altogether.

But whenever I see an army vehicle, or catch a glimpse of a uniform, I revive and walk a little faster, sometimes trotting after a moving car in the hope that it will come to a stop and he will jump out.

Time after time I lose my way and have to walk back quite far, and sometimes, if I can summon up enough courage, I ask for directions.

"Please, Mevrouw, could you tell me how to get to the Overtoom?"

"Dear me, child, you're going the wrong way. Over there, right at the end, turn left, that'll take you straight there."

The Overtoom, when I finally reach it, seems to be a street without beginning or end. I walk, stop, cross the road, search: not a trace of W.S. Does my plan bear any resemblance to the real thing?

I take off my shoes and look at the dark impression of my sweaty foot on the pavement. Do I have to go on, search any more? What time is it, how long have I been walking the streets?

Off we sail to Overtoom,
We drink milk and cream at home,
Milk and cream with apple pie,
Little children must not lie.

Over and over again, automatically, the jingle runs through my mind, driving me mad.

As I walk back home, slowly, keeping to the shady side of the street as much as I can, I think of the other expeditions hidden away in the dust-jacket of my book. The routes I picked out and wrote down with so much eagerness and trust seem pointless and unworkable now. I scold myself: I must not give up, only a coward would do that. Walt is waiting for me, he has no one, and he'll be so happy to see me again.

At home I sit down in a chair by the window, too tired to talk, and when I do give an answer to my mother my voice sounds thin and weak, as if it were finding it difficult to escape from my chest. She sits down next to me on the arm of the chair, lifts my chin up and asks where we have been playing such tiring games, she hasn't seen me down in the street all morning, though the other boys were there.

"Were you really out in the field?"

"Ask them if you don't believe me!" I run onto the balcony, tear my first route map up into pieces and watch the shreds fluttering down into the garden like snowflakes.

When my father gets back home he says, "So, my boy, you and I had best go into town straightway, you still haven't seen the illuminations."

With me on the back, he cycles as far as the Concertgebouw, where he leans the bike against a wall and walks with me past a large green space with badly worn grass. Here, too, there are soldiers, tents, trucks. Why don't I look this time, why do I go and walk on the other side of my father and cling – "Don't hang on so tight!" – to his arm?

"Now you'll see something," he says, "something you've never even dreamed of, just you wait and see."

Walt moving his quivering leg to and fro, his warm, yielding skin, the smell of the thick hair in his armpits . . .

I trudge along beside my father, my soles burning, too tired to look at anything.

We walk through the gateway of a large building, a sluice that echoes to the sound of voices, and through which the people have to squeeze before fanning out again on the other side. There are hundreds of them now, all moving in the same direction towards a buzzing hive of activity, a surging mass of bodies.

There is a sweet smell of food coming from a small tent in the middle of the street in front of which people are crowding so thickly that I can't see what is being sold.

I stop in my tracks, suddenly dying for food, dying just to stay where I am and to yield myself up to that wonderful sweet smell. But my father has already walked on and I have to wriggle through the crowds to catch up with him.

Beside a bridge he pushes me forward between the packed bodies so that I can see the canal, a long stretch of softly shimmering water bordered by overhanging trees. At one end brilliantly twinkling arches of light have been suspended that blaze in the darkness and are reflected in the still water. Speechless and enchanted I stare at the crystal-clear world full of dotted lines, a vision of luminous radiation that traces a winking and sparkling route leading from bridge to bridge, from arch to arch, from me to my lost soldier.

I grip my father's hand. "Come on," I say, "let's have a look. Come on!"

Festoons of light bulbs are hanging wherever we go, like stars stretched across the water, and the people walk past them in silent, admiring rows. The banks of the canal feel as cosy as candle-lit sitting-rooms.

"Well?" my father breaks the spell. "It's quite something, isn't it? In Friesland, you'd never have dreamed that anything like that existed, would you now?"

We take a short cut through dark narrow streets. I can hear dull cracks, sounds that come as a surprise in the dark, as if a sniper were firing at us.

My father starts to run.

"Hurry, or we'll be too late."

An explosion of light spurts up against the black horizon and whirls apart, pink and pale green fountains of confetti that shower down over a brilliant sign standing etched in the sky.

And another shower of stars rains down to the sound of muffled explosions and cheers from the crowd, the sky trembling with the shattering of triumphal arches.

I look at the luminous sign in the sky as if it is a mirage.

"Daddy, that letter, what's it for? Why is it there? Why did I have to ask, why didn't I just add my own letters, fulfil my own wishful thinking?

"That W? You know what that's for. The W, the W's for Queen Wilhelmina . . ." I can hear a scornful note in his voice as if he is mocking me.

"Willy here, Willy there," he says, "but the whole crew took off to England and left us properly in the lurch."

I'm not listening, I don't want to hear what he has to say.

W isn't Wilhelmina: it stands for Walt! It's a sign specially for me . . .

Reprinted by permission of The Bodley Head.

MARGA MINCO

Marga Minco's *Empty House*, first published in 1966, is another wartime novel. During the German occupation her entire family, being Jewish, was deported and killed in concentration camps. Minco herself managed to escape this fate and spent much of the war in hiding in Amsterdam. In 1944 she moved to Kloveniersburgwal 49, which served as a safe house for various Dutch artists during the ensuing hunger winter; it's this house – or, rather, the house next door – that is the model for the various empty houses in the novel. In the following extract, the main character, Sepha, meets Yona, another Jewish survivor and later to become a great friend, when travelling back from Friesland to the safe house.

AN EMPTY HOUSE

As soon as we were in the centre Yona put on her rucksack and tapped on the window of the cab. We'd been delayed a lot because the lorry which had picked us up at our spot beyond Zwolle had to go to all kinds of small villages and made one detour after another. We sat in the back on crates. Yona had grazed her knee heaving herself up over the tail-gate. I'd not seen it because I'd been making a place for us to sit.

"What have you done?" I asked.

"Damn it," she cried, "I'm not as agile as you. I told you. I spent all my time holed up in a kind of loft." She tied a hanky round her knee. "One step from the door to the bed. Do you think I did keep-fit exercises or something?"

I thought of the fire-escape which I'd gone up and down practically every day. In the end I could do it one-handed.

"Have you somewhere to go to in Amsterdam?"

I expected her to say it was none of my business, but she seemed not to hear me. The lorry thundered along a road where they'd just cleared away barricades.

"Do you know," she said, "at first I didn't know where I was?" Suddenly her voice was much less sharp. "All I knew was that it was a low house with an attic window above the back door. "You don't live here," said the woman of the house. She always wore a blue striped apron. "But I am here though," I said. "No," she said, "you must remember that you're not here, you're nowhere." She didn't say it unpleasantly, she wished me no harm. But I couldn't get it out of my mind — you're nowhere. It's as if, by degrees, you start believing it yourself, as if you begin to doubt yourself. I sometimes sat staring at my hands for ages. There was no mirror and they'd whitewashed the attic window. It was only by looking at my hand that I recognized myself, proved to myself that I was there."

"Didn't anybody ever come to see you?"

"Yes. In the beginning. But I didn't feel like talking. They soon got the message. They let me come downstairs in the evenings occasionally, the windows were blacked out and the front and back doors bolted. It didn't impress me as being anything special. Later on, I even began to dislike it. I saw that they were scared stiff when I was sitting in the room. They listened to every noise from outside. I told them that I'd rather stay upstairs, that I didn't want to run any risks. You can even get used to a loft. At least it was mine, my loft."

While talking, she had turned round; she sat with her back half turned towards me. I had to bend forward to catch her last words. Her scarf had slipped off. Her hair kept brushing my face. Once we were near Amsterdam, she started talking about her father who went with her to the Concertgebouw every week, accompanied her on long walks and ate cakes with her in small tea-rooms. She talked about him as if he were a friend. And again I had to hear details of the house. She walked me through rooms and corridors, showed me the courtyard, the cellar with wine-racks, the attic with the old-fashioned pulley. I knew it as if I had lived there myself. Where would she sleep tonight?

"If you want to, you can come home with me," I said. "I shan't have any time. I've so much to do. There's a case of mine somewhere as well. I can't remember what I put in it."

We drove across Berlage Bridge. It was still light. She'd fallen silent during the last few kilometres and sat with her chin in her hands. "The south district," I heard her say. "Nothing has changed here, of course."

I wrote my address on a little piece of paper and gave it to her. She put it in the pocket of her khaki shirt without looking at it.

"You must come," I shouted after her when she had got out at Ceintuurbaan. She walked away without a backward glance, hands on the straps of her rucksack, hunched forward as if there were stones in it. I lost sight of her because I was looking at a tram coming from Ferdinand Bolstraat. The trams were running again. There were tiny flags on the front. Flags were hanging everywhere. And portraits of the Queen. And orange hangings. Everyone seemed to be in the streets. It was the last evening of the Liberation celebrations. The driver dropped me off at Rokin. I'd not far to go. If I walked quickly, I could be there in five minutes. The door was usually open, the lock was broken — less than half a minute for the three flights of stairs. I could leave my case downstairs.

People were walking in rows right across the full width of the street. The majority had orange buttonholes or red, white and blue ribbons. There were a lot of children with paper hats, flags and tooters. Two mouth-organ players and a saxophonist in a traditional *Volendammer* costume drifted with the mass, though far apart. I tried to get through as quickly as possible. I bumped into a child who dropped his flag, which was about to be trodden underfoot. I made room with my case, grabbed the flag from the ground and thrust it into his hand. Jazz music resounded from a bar in Damstraat. The door was open. Men and women were sitting at the bar with their arms around each other. Their bodies shook. All that was left in the baker's window were breadcrumbs. Here it was even busier. Groups of Canadians stood at the corners, besieged by whores, black-market traders and dog-end collectors.

I'd not seen much of the Liberation in the Frisian village. The woman I'd stayed with baked her own bread; she had done so throughout the war and she just went on doing it. When I was alone in the kitchen with her she asked with avid interest about my experiences in the hunger winter. She wanted to know everything about the church with corpses, the men with rattles, the people suffering from beriberi on the steps of the Palace, the emaciated children who went to the soup-kitchen with their pans. I spared her no details. About the recycled fat which gave us diarrhoea, the rotten fen potatoes, the wet, clay-like bread, about the ulcers and legs full of sores. I saw it as a way of giving something back.

At last I was at the bridge. I looked at the house with the large expanses of window and the grimy door. At the house next door, the raised pavement and the neck gable. The windows were bricked up. The debris was piled high behind. All that was left were bare walls. I put down my case to change hands. It was as if, only then, that I felt how hungry I was, how stiff my knees were from sitting for hours on the crate. There was something strange about the houses, as if I'd been away for years. But it could have been that I'd never stopped on the bridge before, never looked at them from that angle. The barge was still there. An oil-lamp was burning behind the portholes.

Our front door was closed. The lock had been mended in the meantime. I ought to have had a key somewhere. I didn't want to ring. I'd never realized that the staircase was so dark when the front door was shut. Without thinking, I groped for the banister and banged my hand against the rough wall. "It's nice, soft wood," Mark had said as he sawed the banister into logs. "You can cut it nicely into pieces with a sharp knife." The steps on the upper flight grated as if there were sand on them. I pushed the door open with my case.

There was a black lady's handbag on the bed. A leather bag with a brass clasp. Who had a bag like that? The leather was supple and smooth, except for some creases on the underside. I walked to the table which was full of bottles and glasses. I saw a long dog-end lying in one of the ashtrays. The cigarette must have been carefully put out. Afterwards the burnt tobacco had been nipped off. I found the empty packet on the floor, Sweet Caporal. The divan was strewn with newspapers. Eisenhower standing in a car. Montgomery standing in a car. A new Bailey bridge built in record time.

I had to look among the piled-up crockery in the kitchen for a cup. I rinsed it a long time before I drank from it. I felt the water sink into my stomach; it gurgled as if it was falling into a smooth, cold hollow. The tower clock sounded the half-hour. The house became even quieter. There appeared to be nobody home on the other floors either. Half nine? It got dark quickly now. It was already dark under the few trees left along the canal. I opened one of the windows and leant outside. A man and a woman tottered along the pavement on the other side. They held each other firmly under the arm. They would suddenly lurch forward a few metres, slowly right themselves and start up again. The nine o'clock man always walked there too. I'd not heard him since the Liberation.

Reprinted by permission of Peter Owen Publishers, London.

NICOLAS FREELING

Creator of the Dutch detective Van der Valk, Nicolas Freeling was born in England but has lived all his life in Europe, where most of his novels are set. He actually left Amsterdam over twenty years ago and nowadays rarely returns to the city. But in the Van der Valk novels he evokes Amsterdam (and Amsterdammers) as well as any writer ever has, subtly and unsentimentally using the city and its people as a vivid backdrop to his fast-moving action. The following extract is from A *Long Silence*, first published in 1972.

A LONG SILENCE

Arlette came out into the open air and saw that spring had come to Amsterdam. The pale, acid sun of late afternoon lay on the inner harbour beyond the Prins Hendrik Kade: the wind off the water was sharp. It gave her a shock. A succession of quick rhythmic taps, as at the start of a violin concerto of Beethoven. That she noticed this means, I think, that from that moment she was sane again. But it is possible that I am mistaken. Even if insane one can have, surely, the same perceptions as other people, and this "click" is a familiar thing. Exactly the same happens when one takes a night train down from Paris to the Coast, and one wakes somewhere between Saint Raphael and Cannes and looks out, and there is the Mediterranean. Or was.

The pungent salt smell, the northern, maritime keynotes of seagull and herring, the pointed brick buildings, tall and narrow like herons, with their mosaic of parti-coloured shutters, eaves, sills, that gives the landscapes their stiff, heraldic look (one is back beyond Brueghel, beyond Van Eyck, to the primitives whose artists we do not know, so that they have names like the Master of the Saint Ursula Legend). The lavish use of paint in flat bright primary colours which typifies these Baltic, Hanseatic quaysides is startling to the visitor from central Europe. Even the Dutch flags waving everywhere (there are no more determined flag-wavers) upset and worried Arlette: she had not realised how in a short time her eye had accustomed itself to the subtle and faded colourings of France, so that it was as though she had never left home. The sharp flat brightness of Holland! The painters' light which hurts the unaccustomed eye . . . Arlette never wore sunglasses in France, except on the sea, or on the snow, yet here, she remembered suddenly, she had practically gone to bed in them. It was all so familiar. She had lived here, she had to keep reminding herself, for twenty years.

She had no notion of where she wanted to go, but she knew that now she was here, a small pause would bring the spinning, whirling patterns of the kaleidoscope to rest. She crossed the road and down the steps to the little wooden terrace – a drink, and get her breath back! Everything was new – the pale heavy squatness of the Dutch café's cup-and-saucer, left on her table by the last occupant; the delightful rhythmic skyline across the harbour of the Saint Nicolaas church and the corner of the Zeedijk! Tourists were flocking into waterbuses, and now she was a tourist too. An old waiter was wiping the table while holding a tray full of empty bottles, which wavered in front of her eye.

"Mevrouw?"

"Give me a chocomilk, if at least you've got one that's good and cold."

Another click! She was talking Dutch, and as fluently as ever she had! He was back before she had got over it.

"Nou, mevrouwtje – cold as Finnegan's feet." His voice had the real Amsterdam caw to it. "You aren't Dutch though, are you now?"

"Only a tourist," smiling.

"Well now, by-your-leave: proper-sounding Dutch you talk there," chattily, bumping the glass down and pouring in the clawky chocomilk.

"Thank you very much."

"Tot Uw dienst. Ja ja ja, kom er aan" to a fussy man, waving and banging his saucer with a coin.

Neem mij niet kwa-a-lijk; een be-hoor-lijk Nederlands spreekt U daar. Like a flock of rooks. *Yah, yah ya-ah, kom er a-an.* And she was blinded by tears again, hearing her husband's exact intonation – when with her he spoke a Dutch whose accent sometimes unconsciously – ludicrously – copied hers, but when with the real thing, the *rasecht* like himself his accent would begin to caw too as though in self-parody.

Next door to her were sitting two American girls, earnest, quiet, dusty-haired, looking quite clean though their jeans were as darkly greasy as the mud the dredger over there was turning up off the harbour bottom. Scraps of conversation floated across.

"She's a lovely person, ever so quiet but really mature, you know what I mean, yes, from Toledo." Arlette knew that Van der Valk would have guffawed and her eyes cleared.

I see her there, at the start of her absurd and terrifying mission. She has the characteristic feminine memory for detail, the naively earnest certainty that she has to get everything right. Had I asked what those two girls were drinking she would have known for sure, and been delighted at my asking.

I have not seen Amsterdam for four or five years, and it might be as long again before I shall. This is just as well. I do not want my imagination to get in the way of Arlette's senses. Piet, whose imagination worked like mine, saw things in an entirely different way to her. We were sitting once together on that same terrace.

"Look at that dam building," pointing at the Central Station, a construction I am fond of, built with loving attention to every useless detail by an architect of the last century whose name I have forgotten (a Dutch equivalent of Sir Giles Gilbert Scott). "Isn't it lovely?" Lovely is not the word I would have chosen but it is oddly right.

"The Railway Age," he went on. "Make a wonderful museum – old wooden carriages, tuff-tuff locos with long funnels, Madame Tussaud figures of station-masters with beards, policemen wearing helmets, huge great soup-strainer moustaches, women with bustle and reticules . . ." Yes, indeed, and children in sailor suits. Arlette's mind does not behave like this.

I am changed, thought Arlette, and unchanged. I am the same housewife, familiar with these streets, these people. I am not pricked or tickled by anything here, like a tourist. I see all this with the coolness and objectivity of experience. I am not going to rush into anything stupid or imprudent. This is a town I know, and I am going to find myself perfectly able to cope with the problem. I am not alone or helpless; I have here many friends, and there are many more who were Piet's friends and who will help me for his sake. But I am no longer the thoughtless and innocent little wife of a little man in a little job, standing on the corner with shopping bag wondering whether to have a cabbage or a cauli. I am a liberated woman, and that is going to make a difference.

A tout was circling around the cluster of tables, sizing up likely suckers. A year or so ago he would have been handing out cards for a restaurant or hotel, looking for a quickie trip around the sights, with waterbus, Anne Frank and the Rembrandthuis all thrown in for only ten guilders. Now – he had closed in on the two American girls and she could hear his pidgin-German patois that is the international language of the European tout – selling live sex-shows. The two girls glanced up for a second with polite indifference, and went back to their earnest, careful, intense conversation, paying no further attention to him at all. He broke off the patter, circled backwards like a boxer and gave Arlette a careful glance: Frenchwomen, generally fascinated by the immoralities and debaucheries of these English and these Scandinavians – a likely buyer, as long as they have first done their duty with a really good orgy at Marks and Spencer's. Arlette met his eye with such a chill and knowing look that he shuffled back into the ropes and made off sideways: cow has been to the sex-show and has no money left. Amsterdam too has changed and not changed, she thought.

"Raffishness" was always the first cliché tourists used, the Amsterdammers were always intensely, idiotically proud of their red-light district and since time immemorial a stroll to look at "the ladies behind the windows" was proposed to every eager tourist the very first night.

They have taken now with such relish to the new role of exhibitionist shop-window that it is hard not to laugh – the visitor's first reaction generally is roars of laughter. The Dutch have a belief that sex has made them less provincial somehow – for few attitudes are more provincial than the anxious striving to be modern-and-progressive. Paris doesn't exist any more, and London is slipping, they will tell one with a boastful pathos, and Holland-is-where-it's-at. A bit immature, really, as the two nineteen-year-olds from Dubuque were probably at that moment saying. Arlette was a humble woman. She saw herself as snobbish, narrow, rigid, French provincial bourgeois. Piet, born and bred in Amsterdam, used to describe himself as a peasant. This humility gave them both an unusual breadth, stability, balance. I remember his telling me once how to his mind his career if not his life had been an abject failure.

"But there," drinking brandy reflectively, being indeed a real soak and loving it, "what else could I have done?"

Arlette, walking through the lazy, dirty sunshine of late afternoon in Amsterdam, was thinking too, "What else could I have done?" She had come to lay a ghost. Not that she – hardheaded woman – believed in ghosts, but she had lived long enough to know they were there. Piet was a believer in ghosts. "I have known malign influences outside the bathroom door," he used to say. He was delighted when I gave him to read the finely-made old thriller of Mr A.E.W. Mason which is called *The Prisoner in the Opal*: he saw the point at once, and when he brought it back he said that he too, with the most sordid, materialistic, bourgeois of enquiries, always made the effort "to pierce the opal crust". Poor old Piet.

Once we were having dinner together in a Japanese restaurant. We had had three pernods, big ones, the ones Piet with his horrible Dutch ideas of wit which he took for *esprit* described as "*Des Grand Pers*". We were watching the cook slicing raw fish into fine transparent slices.

"There is poetry," said Piet suddenly, "in those fingers." I turned around suspiciously, because this is a paraphrase from a good writer, whom Piet had certainly not read. I used the phrase as an epigraph to a book I once wrote about cooks – which Piet had not read either. "Poetry in the fat fingers of cooks" – I looked at Piet suspiciously.

"So," with tactful calm, "is that a quotation?"

"No," innocent, "Just a phrase. Thought it would please you, haw." That crude guffaw; completely Piet. The stinker; to this day I don't know whether he was kidding me. A skilful user of flattery, but damn it, a friend.

The Damrak, the Dam, the Rokin. Squalid remnants of food, flung upon the pavements. The young were unable or unwilling to spend much on food, she thought, and what they got for their money probably deserved to be flung: one could not blame them too much, just because one felt revolted. But one did blame them: beastly children.

The Utrechtsestraat. The Fredericksplein. And once out of the tourist stamping-ground, Arlette knew suddenly where she was going. She was heading unerringly and as though she had never been away straight towards the flat where she had lived for twenty years. It was a longish way to walk, all the way from the Central Station and carrying a suitcase too. Why had she done it? She would have said, "What else could I have done?" crossly, for when she got there she was very tired and slightly footsore, dishevelled, her hair full of dust, smelling of sweat and ready to cry.

"Arlette! My dear girl! What are you doing? – but come in! I'm so happy to see you – and at the same time, my poor child, I'm so sad! Not that we know anything – what one reads in the paper nowadays – Pah! And again Pah! come in, my dear girl, come in – you don't mean to say you walked . . . from the station? You didn't! You couldn't! Sit down child, do. The lavy? But of course you know where it is, that's not something you'll have forgotten. I'll make some coffee. My dear girl, marvellous to see you, and the dear boys? – no no, I must be patient, go and have a pee child, and a wash, do you good." The old biddy who had always had a ground floor flat, and still did . . . She taught the piano. It had been the most familiar background noise to Arlette's life throughout the boys' childhood; her voice carried tremendously.

"One, Two, not so hasty. Pedal there, you're not giving those notes their value, that's a sharp, can't you hear it?" And coming back from shopping an hour later another one was being put through its hoops. "Watch your tempo, not so much espressivo, you're sentimentalising, this is the Ruysdaelskade, not the Wiener Wald or something."

"Lumpenpack," she would mutter, coming out on the landing for a breather and finding Arlette emptying the dustbin.

Old Mother Counterpoint, Piet always called her, and sometimes in deference to Jane Austen "Bates" ("Mother hears perfectly well; you only

have to shout a little and say it two or at the most three times"). A wonderful person really. A mine of information on the quarter, possessor of efficient intelligence networks in every shop, an endless gabble on the telephone, forever fixing things for someone else. She could find anything for you; a furnished room, a second-hand pram scarcely used, a boy's bike, a shop where they were having a sale of materials ever so cheap – even if she didn't have her finger on it she knew a man who would let you have it wholesale. Warm-hearted old girl. Gushing, but wonderfully kind, and gentle, and sometimes even tactful.

"You take yours black, dear, oh yes, I hadn't forgotten – you think I'd forget a thing like that? Not gaga yet, thank God. Good heavens, it must be seven years. But you haven't aged dear, a few lines yes – badges of honour my pet, that's what I call them. Tell me – can you bear to talk about it? Where are you staying? By the look of you you could do with a square meal."

"I don't know, I was wondering . . ."

"But my poor pet of course, how can you ask, you know I'd be more than pleased and I've plenty of room, it's just can you bear all the little fussinesses of a frightened old maid – oh nonsense child, now don't be tiresome. Now I'll tell you what, no don't interrupt, I'm going to the butcher, yes still the same awful fellow, all those terrible people, how they'll be thrilled, just wait till he hears, I'll frighten him, he gave me an escalope last week and tough . . . my poor girl, since you left him thinks everything is permitted him. I'll get a couple of nice veal cutlets and we'll have dinner, just you wait and I'll get something to drink too, I love the excuse and what's more I'll make pancakes. I never bother by myself, you take your shoes off and put your feet up and read the paper, nonsense you'll do no such thing, I want to and anyway I'll enjoy it: would you perhaps love a bath, my pet?" The voice floated off into the hallway.

"Where's my goloshes, oh dear, oh here they are now how did they get that way, oh wait till I tell the wretch the cutlets are for you, he'll jump out of his skin . . ." The front door slammed. Arlette was home.

It was a nice evening. Bates brought Beaujolais – Beaujolais! "I remember you used to buy it, child, I hope you still like it. Cutlets."

"He practically went on his knees when he heard, with the tears in his eyes he swore on his mother's grave you'd be able to cut them with a fork and I just looked and said 'She'd better', that's all."

"Bananas – I've got some rum somewhere, hasn't been touched in five years I'd say, pah, all dusty, do you think it'll still be all right dear, not gone poisonous or anything, one never knows now, they put chemicals in to make things smell better, awful man in the supermarket and I swear he squirts the oranges with an aerosol thing to make them smell like oranges, forlorn hope is all I can say."

The rum was tasted, and pronounced fit for pancakes.

"And how's Amsterdam?" asked Arlette, laughing.

It wasn't what it was; it wasn't what it had been. Arlette had been prepared to be bored with old-maidish gush about how we don't sleep safe in our beds of nights, not like when we had a policeman in the house, which did give someone a sense of security somehow. She ought to have known better really, because old mother Counterpoint had the tough dryness, the voluble energy, the inconsequent loquacity she expected – and indeed remembered, but the warm-hearted kindness was illuminated by a shrewd observation she had never given the old biddy credit for.

"Well, my dear, it would ill become me to complain. I'll have this flat for as long as I live and they can't put my rent up, I have to spread my butter thinner but I'm getting old and I need less of it. I have the sunshine still and the plants and my birds and they'll all last my time. I think it comes much harder on a girl your age, who can remember what things used to be, and who still has to move with the changes and accept them, whereas people expect me to be eccentric and silly. And I'm sorrier still for the young ones. They don't have any patterns to move by: it must give a terrible sense of insecurity and I think that's what makes them so unhappy. Everyone kowtows to them and it must be horrid really. Look at the word young, I mean it used to mean what it said and no more, young cheese or a young woman and that was that – and now they talk about a young chair or a young frock and it's supposed to mean good, and when you keep ascribing virtue to people, and implying all the time that they should be admired and imitated, well dear, it makes their life very difficult and wearisome; I used to know a holy nun and

she said sometimes that everybody being convinced one was good made a heavy cross to carry. When the young do wicked things I can't help feeling that it's because they're dreadfully unhappy. Of course there's progress, lots and lots of progress, and it makes me very happy. I don't have many pupils now, but I'm always struck when they come, so tall and healthy and active, so unlike the pale little tots when I was a young woman, and I remember very hard times, my dear, all the men drunk always because their lives were so hard, but they don't seem to me any happier or more contented and they complain more because they expect much more. I can't really see what they mean talking about progress because that seems to me that people are good and get better and the fact is, my pet, as you and I know, people are born bad and tend to get worse and putting good before evil is always a dreadful struggle dear, whatever they say. One is so vain and so selfish."

And Arlette, who had had a good rest, a delicious bath, and a good supper, found herself pouring out her whole tale and most of her heart.

"Well," said Bates at the end with great commonsense, "that has done you a great deal of good my dear, and that's a fact, just like taking off one's stays, girls don't wear stays any more and they don't know what they miss."

Arlette felt inclined to argue that it was a good thing to be no longer obliged to wear stays.

"Of course dear, don't think I don't agree with you, healthy girls with good stomach muscles playing tennis, and no more of that fainting and vapouring. But I maintain that it was a good thing for a girl to know constraint. Sex education and women's lib, all dreadful cant. Girls who married without knowing the meaning of the word sex were sometimes very happy and sometimes very unhappy, and I don't believe they are any happier now. I married a sailor, dear, and learned how to go without."

"It doesn't make me any happier now," said Arlette dryly.

"No dear, and that's just what I felt in 1940 when my ship got torpedoed. So now let's be very sensible. You've come here very confused and embittered, and you don't want anything to do with the police, and you're probably quite right because really poor dears they've simply no notion, but at the present you've no notion either. You'd never of thought about asking my advice because I'm a silly old bag but I'll give it you, and it is that you probably can find out who killed your husband, because it's surprising what you can do when you try, but it's as well to have friends you can count on, and you can count on me for a start, and with that my dear we'll go to bed, your eyes are dropping out."

"Did you join the resistance, in 1940 I mean?" asked Arlette.

"Yes I did, and what's more once I threw a bomb at a bad man in the Euterpestraat, and that was a dreadful place, the Gestapo headquarters here in Amsterdam and it was very hard because I was horribly frightened of the bomb, and even more frightened of the bad man who had soldiers with him and most of all because I knew they would take hostages and execute them, but it had to be done, you see."

"I do see," said Arlette seriously, "it wasn't the moment to take off one's stays and feel comfortable."

"Right, my pet, right," said old mother Counterpoint.

© *Nicolas Freeling 1972.*
Reprinted with the kind permission of
Curtis Brown Ltd.

MARIE STAHLIE

The Dutch author Maria Stahlie (b. 1955) began her career as a literary translator. She wrote her first novel, *Unisono,* **in 1988. Since then, she has published, among other works,** *In the Spirit of the Monadinis* **and** *The Sin of Death.* **1994 saw the appearance of her sixth novel,** *The Beast with Two Backs,* **a title taken from Rabelais's description of a couple making love. Inspired by Nabokov's** *Lolita,* **the novel deals with a 38-year-old journalist who falls in love with an 18-year-old; conscience and the integrity of human action are major themes. Maria Stahlie lives in Amsterdam with her husband, the writer Dick Schouten.**

A DUTCH CROSS

A Dutch critic wrote that my last book but one, The Plague of Butterflies, breathes an un-Dutch atmosphere. I took this as a compliment. But did I try to write an un-Dutch book? I think I did, for who would like to have a typically Dutch book flow from their pen? A typically Dutch book is full of realism, it is written in an economic style; the author sets out not so much to surprise as to convince. A typically Dutch book is small-minded and boring. Little wonder, then, that many a Dutch writer wants to shake off their Dutchness and express themselves in a grand and compelling way.

Unfortunately, there is a world of difference between literary flamboyance and a natural, real-life flamboyance. Even if I sometimes overindulge myself in florid extravagance, even if I allow imagination to triumph, and reconcile the irreconcilable, in everyday life I am, I'm afraid, Dutch to the core. This was thrown into sharp relief during the periods I spent living in foreign countries.

Together with my husband, my love, I twice had the good fortune to be in un-Dutch surroundings. For about eighteen months we lived and worked in America, in Minneapolis, and not long after that we sought contentment on a Greek island in the Aegean Sea. We visited the New World and we visited the Old World, but we never really managed to leave the Middle of the Road. Face-to-face with the pleasure in which Americans, in their own inimitable fashion, indulge, and face-to-face with the overwhelming heartiness, and equally overwhelming melancholy, of the Greeks, we had to conclude with some dismay, that, in our greyness, we were very fond of our privacy, and our certainty. It was these oppressive moments of insight which led us to the understanding that, despite all our travels, we were probably weighed down most by what can only be decribed as a typically Dutch sense of proportion.

It did not come as a surprise that our sense of proportion did not match the excess held up to be the norm in America. True, we could laugh about it all at the beginning, those enormous helpings, those extravagant colours, that shameless kitsch, the unassailable cheerfulness with which everybody passes the time of day to everybody, the enthusiasm with which the TV audience shows their approval or approbation. But the laugh began to stick in our throats.

On one occasion, during a speech I was giving at the university in front of students, colleagues and new friends, I made a small digression eulogising the imagination. "Yee-haa!" shouted at least ten voices in approval. Halfway through the speech I threw in a joke about airbags, which were a new phenomenon for American cars at the time. Two-thirds of the audience noisily approved. A warm sense of solidarity, almost of love, spread over my whole body. I finished my address with the statement that Minneapolis was capable of holding its own with any other city; all those present rose in unison to indicate, with whoops and applause, that they were in complete accord. The sense of warmth rose into my cheeks; blushing deeply, I was ashamed. Looking through my emotion, on closer analysis I realized that the approval of my audience seemed over-done to me.

Two years later, our frugal Dutch character was brought home to us again. During a stay of ten months on the island of Paros, one of the Cyclades, we got acquainted with a peasant named Dimitri. Dimitri was eighty-four years old; he lived in accordance with age-old tradition, season by season. We first met him in the autumn, but it was winter when we saw him for a second time, Christmas Day to be exact. It was raining and the wind was nasty. I looked from the window, and in the distance I could see the silhouette of a donkey, loaded down and carrying a little man, coming closer. Only when they halted in front of our door did I recognize Dimitri. He had come more than four miles through the hills to bring us, the foreigners, some gifts – cheese and wine and bread and red-painted eggs. He knew that, for Westerners, Christmas was a more important celebration than Easter. Just before he left to plod through the wind and rain back to his farm in the middle of the island, Dimitri sang us a long and sad song, so that we could share in his wintry mood. He left us alone in confusion; our cosy sense of proportion finally dictated to us that Dimitri's unselfishness, his warm hearted-ness and understanding had been too much of a good thing.

This Dutch rationality, this thoroughly Dutch sense of proportion ... we experienced it in Greece even more than we had done in America, a heavy cross to bear. We would have given anything to be able to react in kind, stylized and with a sense of drama, to the people and the situations that surrounded us. For it had become crystal-clear to us that what we regarded as over-done, or too much of a good thing, in truth did a lot more justice to the world than our highly personal, critical sense which whittled everything down to nothing.

In the weeks that followed Dimitri's visit, we somehow succeeded in lightening our load. Being Dutch, we had an excuse for our heavy cross: apart from the Second World War, our country has not gone through one single drama in the last three-and-a-half centuries. Geographically speaking, no spot is better sheltered on the entire globe, and, compared to other countries, Sloughs of Despond and Heights of Majesty are rather thin on the ground in Holland. It was to be our fate that our sense of drama got bogged down in an excess of certainty and security. But not only did we have an excuse for our behaviour, we even had a secret passage to scamper down: whenever we wanted to, we could write un-Dutch books, and, by doing so, leave the cheese-paring of the Low Countries far behind.

Meanwhile, I am well and truly back in Amsterdam. But every day, fleeing from my typically Dutch sense of proportion, I try to go too far and write as many un-Dutch sentences as possible. I dread that my secret passage of escape might just be leading me back to where I started from.

BOOKS

Dedalo Carasso *A Short History of Amsterdam* (Amsterdam Historical Museum). Brief account written from a left-wing perspective, well illustrated with photos of artefacts from the Amsterdam Historical Museum.

Geoffrey Cotterell *Amsterdam* (Saxon House/Little, Brown o/p). Popularised, offbeat history giving a highly readable account of the city up to the late 1960s.

Pieter Geyl *The Revolt of The Netherlands 1555–1609*; *The Netherlands in the Seventeenth Century 1609–1648* (Cassell/Barnes & Noble). Geyl's two volumes of history present a concise account of the Netherlands during its formative years, chronicling the uprising against the Spanish and the formation of the United Provinces. Without doubt the definitive books on the period.

J. H. Huizinga *Dutch Civilisation in the Seventeenth Century* (Collins/Ungar o/p). Analysis of life and culture in the Dutch Republic by the late, widely respected historian.

E. H. Kossmann *The Low Countries 1780–1940* (OUP, UK). Gritty, technically detailed but ultimately rather turgid narrative of the Low Countries from the Austrian era to World War II. Concentrates on the narrow arena of party politics.

Geoffrey Parker *The Dutch Revolt* (Penguin). Compelling account of the struggle between the Netherlands and Spain. Perhaps the best work of its kind.

J. L. Price *Culture and Society in the Dutch Republic in the Seventeenth Century* (Batsford/Scribner o/p). An accurate, intelligent account of the Golden Age.

Simon Schama *The Embarrassment of Riches: An Interpretation of Dutch Culture in the Golden Age* (Collins/Univ. of California Press). The most recent – and one of the most accessible – works on the Golden Age, drawing on a huge variety of archive sources. Justifiably the biggest selling book on Dutch history ever written.

Sir William Temple *Observations upon the United Provinces of The Netherlands* (OUP/Gregg International). Written by a seventeenth-century English diplomat, and a good, evocative account of the country at the time.

Svetlana Alpers *Rembrandt's Enterprise* (Thames & Hudson/Univ. of Chicago Press). Intriguing study of Rembrandt, positing the theory – in line with the recent findings of the Leiden-based Rembrandt Research Project – that many previously accepted works are not by Rembrandt at all but merely the products of his studio.

Pierre Cabanne *Van Gogh* (Thames & Hudson). Standard mix of art criticism and biography, drawing heavily on the artist's own letters, which are published in the UK by Flamingo.

Kenneth Clark *Civilization* (Penguin). This includes a warm and scholarly rundown on the Dutch Golden Age, with illuminating insights on the way in which the art reflected the period.

Max J. Friedlander *From Van Eyck to Bruegel* (Phaidon/Cornell Univ. Press). Definitive and learned account of the early Flemish masters, though stylistically and factually (in the light of modern research) beginning to show its age.

Eugene Fromentin *The Masters of Past Time: Dutch and Flemish Painting from Van Eyck to Rembrandt* (Phaidon/Cornell Univ. Press). Entertaining essays on the major Dutch and Flemish painters.

R. H. Fuchs *Dutch Painting* (Thames & Hudson). As complete an introduction to the subject – from Flemish origins to the present day – as you could wish for in a couple of hundred pages.

H. L. C. Jaffe *De Stijl: Visions of Utopia* (Phaidon/Abbeville Press). A good, informed introduction to the movement and its philosophical and social influences.

Jacob Rosenberg et al. *Dutch Art and Architecture 1600–1800* (Penguin). Full and erudite anthology of essays on the art and buildings of the Golden Age and after. Strictly for dedicated Dutch art fans.

Alastair Smart *The Renaissance and Mannerism outside Italy* (Thames & Hudson/Harcourt Brace). A very readable survey that includes lengthy chapters on van Eyck and his contemporaries, their successors, Bosch and Bruegel, and the later, more Mannerist-inclined painters of the Low Countries. A fine introduction to a lengthy period.

Wolfgang Stechow *Dutch Landscape Painting of the Seventeenth Century* (Phaidon). All-encompassing rundown on the many and varied landscapists of the Dutch Golden Age.

Irving Stone *Lust for Life* (Methuen/NAL Dutton). Everything you ever wanted to know about Vincent van Gogh in a pop genius-is-pain biography.

Christopher White *Rembrandt* (Thames & Hudson). The most widely available – and wide-ranging – study of the painter and his work.

SPECIFIC GUIDES

Guus Kemme (ed.) *Amsterdam Architecture: A Guide* (Thoth). Illustrated guide to the architecture of Amsterdam, with potted accounts of the major buildings.

Christian Rheinwald *Amsterdam Art Guide* (Art Guide Pubs). Comprehensive guide to the city's galleries, shops and contact points for both artists and those wanting to tour the art scene.

Jan Stoutenbeek et al. *A Guide to Jewish Amsterdam* (De Haan). Fascinating, though perhaps over-detailed, guide to just about every Jewish monument in the city. Purchase a copy before you leave from the *Netherlands Board of Tourism*, or in better Amsterdam bookshops.

LITERATURE

Jerome Brouwers *Sunken Red* (Peter Owen). A best-selling novel in Holland that tells a bleak tale of a child's imprisonment in Japan during World War II.

Simon Carmiggelt *Kronkels* (De Arbeiderspers o/p). Simon Carmiggelt wrote these short pieces, usually concise, wry anecdotes concern-ing everyday Dutch life, for *Het Parool,* an Amsterdam daily newspaper he helped to found. This is the second collection of what he termed his "slight adventures".

Anne Frank *The Diary of a Young Girl* (Pan/Pocket Books). Lucid and moving, the most revealing thing you can read on the plight of Amsterdam's Jews during the war years.

Nicolas Freeling *A City Solitary; Love in Amsterdam; Cold Iron; Strike Out Where Not Applicable* (Penguin/Carroll & Graf). Freeling writes detective novels, and his most famous creation is the rebel cop, van der Valk, around whom a successful British TV series was made. These are light, carefully crafted tales, with just the right amount of twists to make them classic cops 'n' robbers reading – and they sport some good Dutch locations.

Etty Hillesum *Etty: An Interrupted Life* (Granada/Pocket Books). Diary of a young Jewish woman uprooted from her life in Amsterdam and taken to Auschwitz, where she died. As with Anne Frank's more famous journal, penetratingly written – though on the whole much less readable.

Richard Huijing (ed & trans.) *The Dedalus Book of Dutch Fantasy* (Dedalus). A fun and artfully selected collection of stories that contains contributions from some of the greats of Dutch literature, including a number whose work does not as yet appear in translation anywhere else.

Margo Minco *Bitter Herbs* (Penguin). A diary that traces Minco's experiences as a young Jewish girl in wartime Breda and Amsterdam. *The Glass Bridge* and *An Empty House* (Peter Own/Dufour), two novels, also concentrate on the plight of Dutch Jews during the last war. *The Glass Bridge* sold half a million copies in Holland, and *An Empty House*, its sequel follows the main character back to Amsterdam, where she tries to pick up the pieces of her life.

Harry Mulisch *The Assault* (Penguin/Pantheon). Set part in Haarlem, part in Amsterdam, *The Assault* traces the story of a young boy who loses his family in a Nazi reprisal-raid. A powerful tale, made into an excellent and effective film. Mulisch's later novel, *Last Call*, is a more introspective, less specifically Dutch work, more concerned with metaphysical questions concerning the nature of reality and fiction.

Multatuli *Max Havelaar: or the Coffee Auctions of the Dutch Trading Company* (Penguin/Univ. of Massachusetts Press). Classic nineteenth-century Dutch satire of colonial life in the East Indies. Eloquent and, at times, amusing.

Cees Noteboom *Rituals* (Penguin/Louisiana Univ. Press). An absorbing, sparsely written novel, by perhaps the most well-known name in current Dutch literature, that maps the empty existence of a rich Amsterdammer who dabbles in antiques. The later *In the Dutch Mountains* (Penguin) is similarly aloof in style, and not directly about Holland, but it is nonetheless compelling at times, casting up offbeat philosophical musings like pearls. Noteboom's latest novel, *The Following Story* (Harvill), is a typically adroit and economical exploration of the author's favourite themes of memory and the nature of reality. Its starting point is the startling image of a narrator who goes to sleep in one city and wakes up in a completely different place.

Jona Oberski *Childhood* (Hodder & Stoughton/NAL Dutton). First published in 1978, this is a Jewish child's eye-witness account of the war years, the camps and executions. Written with feeling and precision.

Janwillem van de Wetering *Hard Rain* (Gollancz/Ballantine). An offbeat detective tale set in Amsterdam and provincial Holland. Like van de Wetering's other stories (sadly only available in the US), it's a humane, quirky and humorous story, worth reading for characters and locations as much as for inventive narrative.

Jan Wolkers *Turkish Delight* (Marion Boyars). Wolkers is one of the Netherlands' best-known artists and writers, and this is one of his early novels, examining closely a relationship between a bitter, working-class sculptor and his young, middle-class wife. It's not one of his best books by any means, but at times shows flashes of Wolkers' typically sardonic wit.

LANGUAGE

In Holland the principal language is **Dutch. Most Dutch-speakers, however, particularly in the main towns of Holland and in the tourist industry, speak English to varying degrees of excellence. The Dutch have a seemingly natural talent for languages, and your attempts at speaking theirs may be met with bewilderment.**

Dutch is a Germanic language – the word "Dutch" itself is a corruption of *Deutsche*, a label inaccurately given by English sailors in the seventeenth century. Though the Dutch are at pains to stress the differences between the two languages, if you know any German you'll spot many similarities. As noted above, English is very widely spoken, but in smaller towns and in the countryside, where things aren't quite as cosmopolitan, the notes that follow will prove handy; they can be supplemented with the detailed "Food Glossary" on pp.34–35.

Of the **phrase books and dictionaries** available, *Dutch at your Fingertips* (Routledge) is the most up-to-date and useful companion. To continue your studies, take a look at *Colloquial Dutch* (Routledge).

PRONUNCIATION

Dutch is pronounced much the same as English. However, there are a few Dutch sounds that don't exist in English, which can be difficult to pronounce without practice.

Consonants

v is like the English f in **f**ar
w like the v in **v**at
j like the initial sound of **y**ellow
ch and *g* are considerably harder than in English, enunciated much further back in the throat; in Amsterdam at least, where the pronunciation is particularly coarse, there's no real English equivalent. They become softer the further south you go, where they're more like the Scottish lo**ch.**
ng is as in bri**ng**
nj as in o**ni**on
Otherwise double consonants keep their separate sounds – *kn*, for example, is never like the English "knight".

Vowels and Dipthongs

Doubling the letter lengthens the vowel sound:
a is like the English **a**pple
aa like c**a**rt
e like l**e**t
ee like l**a**te
o as in p**o**p
oo in p**o**pe
u is like the French t**u** if preceded but not followed by a consonant (eg *nu*); it's like w**oo**d if followed by a consonant (eg *bus*).
uu the French t**u**
au and *ou* like h**o**w
ei and *ij* as in f**i**ne, though this varies strongly from region to region; sometimes it can sound more like l**a**ne.
oe as in s**oo**n
eu is like the dipthong in the French l**eu**r
ui is the hardest Dutch dipthong of all, pronounced like h**ow** but much further forward in the mouth, with lips pursed (as if to say "oo").

DUTCH WORDS AND PHRASES

Basics and greetings

yes	*ja*	do you speak English?	*spreekt u Engels?*
no	*nee*	I don't understand	*Ik begrijp het niet*
please	*alstublieft*	women/men	*vrouwen/mannen*
(no) thank you	*[nee] dank u* or *bedankt*	children	*kinderen*
hello	*hallo* or *dag*	when?	*wanneer?*
good morning	*goede morgen*	I want	*ik wil*
good afternoon	*goedemiddag*	I don't want	*Ik wil niet. . .(+verb)*
good evening	*goedenavond*		*ik wil geen. . .(+noun)*
goodbye	*tot ziens*	how much is. . .?	*wat kost. . .?*
see you later	*tot straks*		

Finding the way

how do I get to. . .?	*hoe kom ik in. . .?*	left/right	*links/rechts*
where is. . .?	*waar is. . .?*	straight ahead	*recht uit gaan*
how far is it to. . .?	*hoe ver is het rnaar. . .?*	platform	*spoor* or *perron*
far/near	*ver/dichtbij*		

Money

post office	*postkantoor*	cashier	*kassa*
stamp(s)	*postzegel(s)*	ticket office	*loket*
money exchange	*wisselkantoor*		

Useful words

good/bad	*goed/slecht*	cheap/expensive	*goedkoop/duur*
big/small	*groot/klein*	hot/cold	*heet/koud*
open/shut	*open/gesloten*	with/without	*met/zonder*
push/pull	*duwen/trekken*	here/there	*hier/daar*
new/old	*nieuw/oud*	men's/women's toilets	*heren/damen(s)*

Days and times

Sunday	*Zondag*	Saturday	*Zaterdag*	minute	*minuut*
Monday	*Maandag*	yesterday	*gisteren*	hour	*uur*
Tuesday	*Dinsdag*	today	*vandaag*	day	*dag*
Wednesday	*Woensdag*	tomorrow	*morgen*	week	*week*
Thursday	*Donderdag*	tomorrow morn-	*morgenochtend*	month	*maand*
Friday	*Vrijdag*	ing		year	*jaar*

Numbers

When saying a number, the Dutch generally transpose
the last two digits: eg, *drie gulden vijf en twintig* is ƒ3.25.

0	*nul*	9	*negen*	18	*achttien*	80	*tachtig*
1	*een*	10	*tien*	19	*negentien*	90	*negentig*
2	*twee*	11	*elf*	20	*twintig*	100	*honderd*
3	*drie*	12	*twaalf*	21	*een en twintig*	101	*honderd een*
4	*vier*	13	*dertien*	30	*dertig*	200	*twee honderd*
5	*vijf*	14	*veertien*	40	*veertig*	201	*twee honderd een*
6	*zes*	15	*vijftien*	50	*vijftig*	500	*vijf honderd*
7	*zeven*	16	*zestien*	60	*zestig*	1000	*duizend*
8	*acht*	17	*zeventien*	70	*zeventig*		

GLOSSARIES

ABDIJ Abbey or group of monastic buildings.

AMSTERDAMMERTJE Phallic-shaped objects placed alongside Amsterdam streets to keep drivers off pavements and out of canals.

BEIAARD Carillon chimes.

BEGIJNHOF Similar to a *hofje* but occupied by Catholic women (*Begijns*) who led semi-religious lives without taking full vows.

BELFORT Belfry.

BURGHER Member of the upper or mercantile classes of a town in the fifteenth to eighteenth centuries, usually with certain civic powers.

FIETSPAD Bicycle path.

GASTHUIS Hospice for the sick or infirm.

GEMEENTE Municipal: eg *Gemeentehuis* – town hall.

GEVEL Gable. The only decoration practical on the narrow-fronted canal house was on its gables. Initially fairly simple, they developed into an ostentatious riot of individualism in the late seventeenth century before turning to a more restrained classicism in the eighteenth and nineteenth centuries.

GILD Guild.

GERECHTSHOF Law Courts.

GRACHT Canal.

HALLE Hall.

HIJSBALK Pulley beam, often decorated, fixed to the top of a gable to lift goods, furniture etc. Essential in canal houses whose staircases were narrow and steep, *hijsbalken* are still very much in use today.

HOF Courtyard.

HOFJE Almshouse, usually for elderly women who could look after themselves but needed small charities such as food and fuel; usually a number of buildings centred around a small, peaceful courtyard.

HUIS House.

JEUGDHERBERG Youth hostel.

KERK Church; eg *Grote Kerk* – the principal church of the town; *Onze Lieve Vrouwe kerk* – church dedicated to the Virgin Mary.

KONINKLIJK Royal.

LAKENHAL Cloth hall. The building in medieval weaving towns where cloth would be weighed, graded and sold.

LUCHTHAVEN Airport.

MARKT Central town square and the heart of most Dutch communities, normally still the site of weekly markets.

OMMEGANG Procession.

POLDER An area of land reclaimed from the sea.

POSTBUS Post office box.

PLEIN A square or open space.

RAADHUIS Town hall.

RANDSTAD Literally "rim-town", this refers to the urban conurbation that makes up much of North and South Holland, stretching from Amsterdam in the north down to Rotterdam and Dordrecht in the south.

RIJKS State.

SCHEPENZAAL Alderman's Hall.

SCHOUWBURG Theatre.

SIERKUNST Decorative arts.

SCHONE KUNSTEN Fine arts.

SPIONNETJE Small mirror on canal house enabling occupant to see who is at the door without descending stairs.

SPOOR Platform (on a train station).

STADHUIS The most common word for a town hall.

STICHTING Institute or foundation.

STEDELIJK Civic, municipal.

STEEN Fortress.

VOLKSKUNDE Folklore.

VVV Dutch tourist information office

WAAG Old public weighing-house, a common feature of most towns – usually found on the Markt.

ARCHITECTURAL TERMS

AMBULATORY Covered passage around the outer edge of the choir of a church.

APSE Semicircular protrusion at (usually) the east end of a church.

ART DECO Geometrical style of art and architecture popular in the 1930s.

ART NOUVEAU Style of art, architecture and design based on highly stylized vegetal forms. Popular in the early part of the twentieth century.

BAROQUE High Renaissance period of art and architecture, distinguished by extreme ornateness, exuberance and complex spatial arrangement of interiors.

CABINET-PIECE Small, finely detailed painting of a domestic scene.

CARILLON A set of tuned church bells, either operated by an automatic mechanism or played by a keyboard.

CARYATID A sculptured female figure used as a column.

CAROLINGIAN Dynasty founded by Charlemagne; late eighth to early tenth century. Also refers to art, etc, of the time.

CLASSICAL Architectural style incorporating Greek and Roman elements – pillars, domes, colonnades etc – at its height in the seventeenth century and revived, as **Neoclassical**, in the nineteenth century.

CLERESTORY Upper story of a church, incorporating the windows.

FLAMBOYANT Florid form of Gothic (see below).

FRESCO Wall painting – durable through application to wet plaster.

GABLE The triangular upper portion of a wall – decorative or supporting a roof. See *Gevel*, above.

GOTHIC Architectural style of the thirteenth to sixteenth centuries, characterized by pointed arches, rib vaulting, flying buttresses and a general emphasis on verticality.

MEROVINGIAN Dynasty ruling France and parts of Germany from sixth to mid-eighth centuries. Refers also to art, etc, of the period.

MISERICORD Ledge on choir stall on which occupant can be supported while standing; often carved with secular subjects (bottoms were not thought worthy of religious ones).

NAVE Main body of a church.

NEOCLASSICAL Architectural style derived from Greek and Roman elements – pillars, domes, colonnades, etc – popular in the Low Countries during French rule in the early nineteenth century.

ROCOCO Highly florid, light and graceful eighteenth-century style of architecture, painting and interior design, forming the last phase of Baroque.

RENAISSANCE Movement in art and architecture developed in fifteenth-century Italy.

RETABLE Altarpiece.

ROMANESQUE Early medieval architecture distinguished by squat forms, rounded arches and naive sculpture.

STUCCO Marble-based plaster used to embellish ceilings, etc.

TRANSEPT Arms of a cross-shaped church, placed at ninety degrees to nave and chancel.

TRIPTYCH Carved or painted work on three panels. Often used as an altarpiece.

TYMPANUM Sculpted panel above a church door.

VAUBAN Seventeenth-century military architect – his fortresses still stand all over Europe and the Low Countries.

VAULT An arched ceiling or roof.

INDEX

direct orders from

		UK£8.99	US$14.95	CAN$19.99
Amsterdam	1-85828-218-7	UK£8.99	US$14.95	CAN$19.99
Andalucia	1-85828-219-5	9.99	16.95	22.99
Australia	1-85828-220-9	13.99	21.95	29.99
Bali	1-85828-134-2	8.99	14.95	19.99
Barcelona	1-85828-221-7	8.99	14.95	19.99
Berlin	1-85828-129-6	8.99	14.95	19.99
Belgium & Luxembourg	1-85828-222-5	10.99	17.95	23.99
Brazil	1-85828-223-3	13.99	21.95	29.99
Britain	1-85828-208-X	12.99	19.95	25.99
Brittany & Normandy	1-85828-224-1	9.99	16.95	22.99
Bulgaria	1-85828-183-0	9.99	16.95	22.99
California	1-85828-181-4	10.99	16.95	22.99
Canada	1-85828-130-X	10.99	14.95	19.99
China	1-85828-225-X	15.99	24.95	32.99
Corfu	1-85828-226-8	8.99	14.95	19.99
Corsica	1-85828-227-6	9.99	16.95	22.99
Costa Rica	1-85828-136-9	9.99	15.95	21.99
Crete	1-85828-132-6	8.99	14.95	18.99
Cyprus	1-85828-182-2	9.99	16.95	22.99
Czech & Slovak Republics	1-85828-121-0	9.99	16.95	22.99
Dublin Mini Guide	1-85828-294-2	5.99	9.95	12.99
Edinburgh Mini Guide	1-85828-295-0	5.99	9.95	12.99
Egypt	1-85828-188-1	10.99	17.95	23.99
Europe	1-85828-289-6	14.99	19.95	25.99
England	1-85828-160-1	10.99	17.95	23.99
First Time Europe	1-85828-270-5	7.99	9.95	12.99
Florida	1-85828-184-4	10.99	16.95	22.99
France	1-85828-228-4	12.99	19.95	25.99
Germany	1-85828-309-4	14.99	23.95	31.99
Goa	1-85828-275-6	8.99	14.95	19.99
Greece	1-85828-300-0	12.99	19.95	25.99
Greek Islands	1-85828-310-8	10.99	17.95	23.99
Guatemala	1-85828-189-X	10.99	16.95	22.99
Hawaii: Big Island	1-85828-158-X	8.99	12.95	16.99
Hawaii	1-85828-206-3	10.99	16.95	22.99
Holland	1-85828-229-2	10.99	17.95	23.99
Hong Kong	1-85828-187-3	8.99	14.95	19.99
Hungary	1-85828-123-7	8.99	14.95	19.99
India	1-85828-200-4	14.99	23.95	31.99
Ireland	1-85828-179-2	10.99	17.95	23.99
Italy	1-85828-167-9	12.99	19.95	25.99
Jamaica	1-85828-230-6	9.99	16.95	22.99
Kenya	1-85828-192-X	11.99	18.95	24.99
Lisbon Mini Guide	1-85828-297-7	5.99	9.95	12.99
London	1-85828-231-4	9.99	15.95	21.99
Madrid Mini Guide	1-85828-353-1	5.99	9.95	12.99
Mallorca & Menorca	1-85828-165-2	8.99	14.95	19.99
Malaysia, Singapore & Brunei	1-85828-232-2	11.99	18.95	24.99
Mexico	1-85828-044-3	10.99	16.95	22.99
Morocco	1-85828-040-0	9.99	16.95	21.99
Moscow	1-85828-118-0	8.99	14.95	19.99
Nepal	1-85828-190-3	10.99	17.95	23.99
New York	1-85828-296-9	9.99	15.95	21.99
Norway	1-85828-234-9	10.99	17.95	23.99

In the UK, Rough Guides are available from all good bookstores, but can be obtained from Penguin by contacting: Penguin Direct, Penguin Books Ltd, Bath Road, Harmondsworth, West Drayton, Middlesex UB7 0DA; or telephone the credit line on 0181-899 4036 (9am–5pm) and ask for Penguin Direct. Visa and Access accepted. Delivery will normally be within 14 working days. Penguin Direct ordering facilities are only available in the UK and the USA. The availability and published prices quoted are correct at the time of going to press but are subject to alteration without prior notice.

around the world

Pacific Northwest	1-85828-092-3	9.99	14.95	19.99
Paris	1-85828-235-7	8.99	14.95	19.99
Poland	1-85828-168-7	10.99	17.95	23.99
Portugal	1-85828-180-6	9.99	16.95	22.99
Prague	1-85828-122-9	8.99	14.95	19.99
Provence	1-85828-127-X	9.99	16.95	22.99
Pyrenees	1-85828-308-6	10.99	17.95	23.99
Rhodes & the Dodecanese	1-85828-120-2	8.99	14.95	19.99
Romania	1-85828-305-1	10.99	17.95	23.99
San Francisco	1-85828-299-3	8.99	14.95	19.99
Scandinavia	1-85828-236-5	12.99	20.95	27.99
Scotland	1-85828-302-7	9.99	16.95	22.99
Sicily	1-85828-178-4	9.99	16.95	22.99
Singapore	1-85828-237-3	8.99	14.95	19.99
South Africa	1-85828-238-1	12.99	19.95	25.99
Soutwest USA	1-85828-239-X	10.99	16.95	22.99
Spain	1-85828-240-3	11.99	18.95	24.99
St Petersburg	1-85828-298-5	9.99	16.95	22.99
Sweden	1-85828-241-1	10.99	17.95	23.99
Thailand	1-85828-140-7	10.99	17.95	24.99
Tunisia	1-85828-139-3	10.99	17.95	24.99
Turkey	1-85828-242-X	12.99	19.95	25.99
Tuscany & Umbria	1-85828-243-8	10.99	17.95	23.99
USA	1-85828-307-8	14.99	19.95	25.99
Venice	1-85828-170-9	8.99	14.95	19.99
Vietnam	1-85828-191-1	9.99	15.95	21.99
Wales	1-85828-245-4	10.99	17.95	23.99
Washington DC	1-85828-246-2	8.99	14.95	19.99
West Africa	1-85828-101-6	15.99	24.95	34.99
More Women Travel	1-85828-098-2	10.99	16.95	22.99
Zimbabwe & Botswana	1-85828-186-5	11.99	18.95	24.99
Phrasebooks				
Czech	1-85828-148-2	3.50	5.00	7.00
French	1-85828-144-X	3.50	5.00	7.00
German	1-85828-146-6	3.50	5.00	7.00
Greek	1-85828-145-8	3.50	5.00	7.00
Hungarian	1-85828-304-3	4.00	6.00	8.00
Italian	1-85828-143-1	3.50	5.00	7.00
Japanese	1-85828-303-5	4.00	6.00	8.00
Mexican	1-85828-176-8	3.50	5.00	7.00
Portuguese	1-85828-175-X	3.50	5.00	7.00
Polish	1-85828-174-1	3.50	5.00	7.00
Spanish	1-85828-147-4	3.50	5.00	7.00
Thai	1-85828-177-6	3.50	5.00	7.00
Turkish	1-85828-173-3	3.50	5.00	7.00
Vietnamese	1-85828-172-5	3.50	5.00	7.00
Reference				
Classical Music	1-85828-113-X	12.99	19.95	25.99
European Football	1-85828-256-X	14.99	23.95	31.99
Internet	1-85828-288-8	5.00	8.00	10.00
Jazz	1-85828-137-7	16.99	24.95	34.99
Opera	1-85828-138-5	16.99	24.95	34.99
Reggae	1-85828-247-0	12.99	19.95	25.99
Rock	1-85828-201-2	17.99	26.95	35.00
World Music	1-85828-017-6	16.99	22.95	29.99

the perfect getaway vehicle

low-price holiday car rental.

rent a car from holiday autos and you'll give yourself real freedom to explore your holiday destination. with great-value, fully-inclusive rates in over 4,000 locations worldwide, wherever you're escaping to, we're there to make sure you get excellent prices and superb service.

what's more, you can book now with complete confidence. our £5 undercut* ensures that you are guaranteed the best value for money in holiday destinations right around the globe.

drive away with a great deal, call holiday autos now on **0990 300 400** and quote ref RG.

holiday autos miles ahead

Trans*HIRE*

the

A *uckland*

to

Z *urich*

of Leisure Car Rental!

Booking car rental <u>before</u> you travel can save you money and problems locally, so take advantage of our fast, friendly service, providing car rental in over 2,000 locations in 30 countries throughout Europe, South Africa, U.S.A., Canada, New Zealand and Australia.

Tel: 00 44 + (0)171 - 978 1922
Fax: 00 44 + (0)171-978 1797

Unit 16, 88 Clapham Park Rd, LONDON SW4 7BX

TRANSHIRE is a member of the ABTA Travel Industry Partners scheme.